BANKRUPTCY
(INCLUDING BAPCPA):
21st CENTURY DEBTOR–CREDITOR LAW

Second Edition

By

David G. Epstein
Professor of Law
Dedman School of Law
Southern Methodist University

Bruce A. Markell
United States Bankruptcy Judge
District of Nevada
Senior Fellow, Bankruptcy and Commercial Law
William S. Boyd School of Law
University of Nevada, Las Vegas

Steve H. Nickles
C.C. Hope Chair in Law and Management
Wake Forest University

Elizabeth L. Perris
United States Bankruptcy Judge
District of Oregon

AMERICAN CASEBOOK SERIES®

Mat #40447226

610 Opperman Drive
P.O. Box 64526
St. Paul, MN 55164–0526
1–800–328–9352

Printed in the United States of America

ISBN-13: 978–0–314–16741–5
ISBN-10: 0–314–16741–2

Dedications

To Kate, my daughter in law.

DGE

To Richard F. Broude, Richard W. Havel, Marc A. Levinson, Sally S. Neely, Richard T. Peters, and especially Robert H. Shutan and J. Ronald Trost, each of whom is at least partially responsible for this book. One time, long ago, they took a chance on a confused attorney who knew nothing about bankruptcy.

BAM

To our other children, Brittany and Justin Hopkins.

SHN

To the law students whose questions and observations have provided me with valuable insight about teaching and about bankruptcy.

ELP

Preface

1. *Who We Are*

David G. Epstein

Bruce A. Markell

Elizabeth L. Perris

Steve H. Nickles

Obviously, all of us are prime candidates for one of the reality-television "makeover" shows. Two of us — David and Steve — are now law professors; two of us — Liz and Bruce — are now bankruptcy judges. Among the four of us, we have taught bankruptcy courses at more than 20 different law schools.

2. *Why We Wrote this Book*

While we have had different professional experiences, we have a common understanding about how to learn and how to "do" bankruptcy law. There are a handful of basic bankruptcy building blocks. Learn the building blocks; see the relationship among the building blocks; find how these building blocks affect the legal issues that arise in consumer bankruptcy cases and in business bankruptcy cases.

3. *How the Book Works (And How You Will Work with this Book)*

In a sense, this book starts in the middle of a story. It is a story that had a happy beginning. C thought well enough of D to extend credit to D. Now there are problems with D and C's debtor-creditor relationship: D is not paying C, or C is concerned about whether D will be able to continue paying it. This book is about what lawyers can do to fix the problems.

In the "real world." these problems are typically fixed without litigation or other formal recourse to the legal process, and without lawyers. D pays C or D and C work out some sort of alternative payment plan. Sometimes, however, lawyers' help is needed. But lawyers can be helpful in resolving debtor-creditor problems, with or without recourse to bankruptcy and other legal process, only if they know the legal rights and remedies of debtors and creditors.

And, except for the "lawyers" on *Boston Legal* (or whatever lawyers show is currently popular) or a John Grisham novel, most lawyers spend most of their time in the office working on problems. So, you will spend most of your time in this book working on problems.

All of the problems in the book can be understood and discussed from materials already considered in the book.

We have made a special effort to design problems that could be discussed on the basis of the materials surrounding them.

Bankruptcy impacts so many aspects of what lawyers do, from business transactions to consumer protection to litigation of domestic relations matters. Understanding bankruptcy is thus critically important for almost every lawyer. To meet this challenge, we want you to learn the basics of debtor-creditor law, to become familiar with the issues of debtor-creditor law that you are likely to encounter in practice, and to think about the policy questions that underlie those issues. While policy questions are consistently and constantly raised, the book does not espouse any particular theory or philosophy of debtor-creditor law. You are left to develop your own opinions on these policy issues. The only 'message' that we are trying to convey is that this stuff is important, interesting and intellectually challenging.

A couple of notes before we get to the "fun stuff." Bankruptcy law is largely statutory law; to be more precise, it is largely federal statutory law. The main text of statutes is the "Bankruptcy Code," found in title 11 of the United States Code. When we refer to the "Code" in this book, it is to the Bankruptcy Code as found in title 11. In addition, there are rules that govern the day-to-day practice and procedure in bankruptcy courts. They are the Federal Rules of Bankruptcy Procedure, which should be in your statutory supplement. We refer to them as the "Rules" or cite to them as "Bankr. R. XXX."

We do think bankruptcy law is "fun." Fun because it can be intellectually challenging; fun because it can be helpful in solving problems that really matter to the people involved. We had fun working together on this book. We hope you'll have fun working through it.

October 2005

DGE
Dallas, Texas

BAM
Las Vegas, Nevada

SHN
Winston-Salem, North Carolina

ELP
Portland, Oregon

Summary of Contents

Detailed Table of Contents

Unit 2

Unit 3

Unit 6

Table of Authorities

*Principal Cases appear in **bold** type*
Cases cited or discussed in text or notes appear in roman *type*

Cases

Statutes

Bankruptcy Rules

Other Authorities

BANKRUPTCY

(INCLUDING BAPCPA):

21st CENTURY DEBTOR–CREDITOR LAW

Second Edition

Part I

What You Need to Know and Think About Before You Start Studying the Bankruptcy Code

Unit 1

How Should Bankruptcy Cases End?

A. *HOW SHOULD THE ENRON BANKRUPTCY, CASE NUMBER 01-22621 AND MILLIONS OF OTHER BANKRUPTCIES END?*

On December 2, 2001, a Sunday, Enron Corporation and a number of its affiliates ("Enron")[1] filed a Chapter 11 bankruptcy petition in New York. Bankruptcy courts are not usually open on Sunday, but the Enron bankruptcy was not a usual bankruptcy.[2]

The next day, Monday, December 3, 2001, thousands of other bankruptcy petitions were filed on that day in New York and other states. And on most days.[3]

One of those thousands of bankruptcy petitions filed on December 3, 2001, was Case Number 01-22621, a

---

[1]Lawyers have a habit, which we continue in this book, of using "short definitions." That is, they carefully define something using a lot of words, and then place a descriptive word in quotation marks inside parentheticals at the end. In the above example, we intend you to think "Enron and its affiliates" every time you read Enron. Saves ink and wear and tear on the eyes.

[2]If you're wondering about the mechanics of the filing, the lawyers went to the judge's house and gave him a copy of the bankruptcy petition. That started the case. If you're wondering about the legality of such an action, see Bankruptcy Rule 5001(a) which says "[t]he courts shall be deemed always open for the purpose of filing any pleading . . . . ," and Bankruptcy Rule 5005(a)(1) which says that "[t]he judge of that court may permit the papers to be filed with the judge, . . . "

[3]I understand that "And on most days" is a sentence fragment. My tenth grade Language Arts teacher, Miss Lindemann, told me that I could use sentence fragments after I had a book published. DGE

And the other authors are OK with sentence fragments. And split infinitives. And dangling participles. And . . . . ELP, BAM & SHN.

Chapter 7 bankruptcy petition, filed in Las Vegas by a man who had owned and operated a tuxedo business in Las Vegas and Reno. We will refer to him as "CN226" for short.

Enron was once the world's largest energy trader, involved in one out of every four electricity and natural gas deals. At the time of the bankruptcy filing, Enron had more than 21,000 employees. The schedules filed with the bankruptcy court showed total assets of almost $50 billion and debts of more than $31 billion.[4]

On July 15, 2004, a United States bankruptcy court in New York entered a 49-page order "confirming" a 117-page plan for restructuring Enron and paying its creditors.[5] According to Enron's press release, Enron's creditors whose "allowable" claims are approximately $63 billion dollars will receive a combination of cash and equity in Prisma International, Enron's international energy asset business, valued at "around $12 billion."[6]

That Enron press release did not mention the thousands of former Enron employees who are now looking for work. Nor did the Enron press release mention the thousands of lawyers, accountants and other professionals who were paid for working on the Enron bankruptcy.[7]

---

[4]At the time of the bankruptcy filing, Enron stock was selling for less than $1 a share; a year earlier, investors were paying more than $85 a share for Enron stock. WorldCom's stock was also selling for less than $1 a share at the time of its filing; a year earlier, investors were paying more than $14 a share, and two years before the filing they were paying over $46 a share.

[5]http://www.enron.com/corp/por/pdfs/ConfirmationOrder.pdf

[6]http://www.enron.com/corp/pressroom/releases/2004/ene/071504Release.html

[7]Current estimates are that Enron will have paid more than a billion dollars to lawyers, accountants and other professionals for their Enron bankruptcy work, Houston Chronicle, September 4, 2004, 2004 WL 55626100. In other words, Enron estimates that its bankruptcy will result in its creditors being paid, at best, 18% of what they were owed and that Enron will have spent more than 8% of what it pays its creditors to pay attorneys and other professionals 100% of what they are owed.

As best we can tell, neither CN226 nor any of the other businesses or individuals that filed bankruptcy petitions on December 3, 2001 issued a press release explaining how his or her or its bankruptcy case ended. CN226's bankruptcy schedules showed debts of more than $147,000 – primarily CN226's personal debts related to his tuxedo business that he had run as a sole proprietor. And, according to the schedules, CN226's most valuable asset (and his only asset besides a few bucks in the bank and some clothes) was a 2000 Toyota Camry, and CN226 still owed $20,000 on the Camry car loan.

For all practical purposes, CN226's bankruptcy case ended on June 24, 2002, when he received a court order proclaiming that he was "released from all dischargeable debts." CN226's unsecured creditors received nothing. CN226's bankruptcy attorney was paid $750 for his services.

Since Enron's and CN226's bankruptcy filings, more than 6,000,000 other individuals and businesses have filed for bankruptcy relief. Why?

This question, like most questions, that law professors or judges ask, leads to still other questions: What can an individual or business accomplish by filing for bankruptcy? And, what should an individual or business be able to accomplish by filing for bankruptcy?

Historically, the purposes of bankruptcy were to force debtors into a court proceeding in which their assets were divided up among claimants in some form of collective setting in which all creditors participated, or to criminalize insolvency, or both. Beyond those general purposes, however, outcomes varied. If a debtor's assets were insufficient to pay all creditors, for example, ancient Romans gave themselves the power to dismember and distribute a debtor's body to creditors in proportion to the amount of debts owed each.[8] Mediaeval Italians, who gave us the term "bankruptcy,"[9] remitted criminal penalties for those who could not pay all their debts if that they exposed their naked bodies in public, and then banged their backsides on a public post while loudly proclaiming "I am bankrupt" three times.[10] In France, those who could not pay their debts were made to wear a "Green Cap" at all times so that others would know that they had stiffed their creditors.[11]

Even if you didn't know [and really don't care about] this history, you should be able to answer the question of "In the 21st Century, what should an individual or business be able to accomplish by filing for bankruptcy" without reading this book. [Although if this book is as good as West told your professor it is, you should be able to provide a more "nuanced"[12] answer after reading this book.]

---

[8]*See* 2 WILLIAM BLACKSTONE, COMMENTARIES 472 (1766) ("[Under Roman law], creditors might cut the debtor's body into pieces, and each of them take his proportionate share...."). *See also* Vern Countryman, *Bankruptcy and the Individual Debtor – and a Modest Proposal to Return to the Seventeenth Century*, 32 CATH. U.L. REV. 809, 810 (1983).

[9]From the concatenation of "banca" – bench or table – and "rotta," – broken or ruptured. Medieval merchants traded from benches or tables in a common area, and the breaking of such a bench signaled the revocation of the merchant's trading privileges or his banishment from the city. ["Concatenation"? This is Markell's footnote. DGE, SHN, ELP]

[10]*See* James Q. Whitman, *The Moral Menace of Roman Law and the Making of Commerce: Some Dutch Evidence*, 105 YALE L.J. 1841, 1872-73 (1996).

[11]*Id.* at 1874.

[12]I have always wanted to use the word "nuanced." Since 1981, the word has appeared in the YALE LAW JOURNAL 123 times. I have yet to appear in the YALE LAW JOURNAL. DGE

B. Problems: How Bankruptcy Cases Should End

Problem 1-1: Business Bankruptcy Case

Your client, Perris Printing Co (P) is considering bankruptcy and wants to know how its bankruptcy case would end. P's major customer was Enron, which owes P $1,500,000. Because of Enron's failure to pay P, P owes:

- $800,000 to vendors
- $400,000 to the IRS
- $30,000 to employees (salaries and benefits)
- $60,000 to its landlord
- $100,000 to other creditors

P is also in default on a $2,000,000 loan from Security Bank (S). S has a lien on all of P's assets. P's assets are primarily: (i) printing equipment, (ii) printing supplies and (iii) accounts receivable. P has 16 employees. The Perris family owns 90% of the stock of the company; employees own the other 10%.

How should P's bankruptcy end?

Problem 1-2: Young Individual's Bankruptcy Case

B.A. "Buzz" Markell is also considering bankruptcy. He is a comparatively young attorney. He was employed at Enron at a salary of $140,000. After being unemployed for four months, he now has a job with a small law firm at $85,000 a year. His debts include:

- school loans of $60,000
- car loan (BMW, of course) of $25,000
- credit card bills of $30,000
- back condo rent of $7,000 ($3,500 a month rent)
- other miscellaneous debts of $10,000

Buzz's only assets are: (i) the BMW, (ii) Enron stock, (iii) a 1931 Ford fire truck and (iv) his wine collection. How should Buzz's bankruptcy end?

PROBLEM 1-3: SENIOR CITIZEN'S BANKRUPTCY CASE

Gus Epstein, a 61 year old former employee of Enron, is also considering bankruptcy. He was employed as an accountant at a salary of $75,000. He is now "self-employed, playing his accordion and singing at bar mitzvahs, birthdays and weddings. His wife has returned to school to get a teaching certificate and is looking for a teaching job for next year. Debts include:

- hospital bills of $19,000 (his mother-in-law has serious health problems and no insurance)
- back payments of $700 on a car lease ($350 a month for 24 more months)
- back payments of $6,000 on a home mortgage ($2,000 a month; $80,000 unpaid balance)
- credit card bills of $8,000
- other miscellaneous debts of $4,000

Epstein's only assets are: (i) the house, (ii) an IRA account with a $40,000 balance and (iii) household furnishings. How should Epstein's bankruptcy end?

C. What Did the National Bankruptcy Review Commission Think About How Bankruptcy Cases End?

In 1994, Congress enacted legislation establishing a commission to review business and consumer bankruptcy. In 1997, the Commission submitted a report (that looks a lot like the Greater Dallas Smart Yellow Pages) with 170 individual recommendations.

Congress has ignored this big yellow book. You shouldn't. As law students, you get it free and "un-yellow" on Westlaw: NBRCR database. Hundreds of pages of helpful explanations of bankruptcy concepts and discussions of bankruptcy problems. For now, just these "teasers" from the Commission's Report:

> 1. Business Bankruptcy
>
> Business bankruptcies are only a small fraction of all filings - about 4% overall - but the bankruptcy system is a critical part of the cycle of business life and death in the American economy. Principally through Chapter 11, business bankruptcy creates the opportunity to restructure failing businesses, to preserve jobs, to prevent the spread of economic failure to smaller suppliers and other dependent businesses, and to permit communities to retain their tax base. Liquidation is also an important part of the business bankruptcy system, providing an efficient and orderly way to dissolve a business and to distribute its assets equitably among parties who might otherwise see no recovery at all.

NAT'L BANKRUPTCY REV. COMM'N, BANKRUPTCY: THE NEXT TWENTY YEARS, THE NATIONAL BANKRUPTCY REVIEW COMMISSION FINAL REPORT 303 (1997).

> 2. Consumer Bankruptcy
>
> Consumer bankruptcy has become part of America's economic landscape. Once regarded as an unlikely legal alternative chosen by only a few desperate families, bankruptcy had become a refuge for one in every 96 American

> families by the time the National Bankruptcy Review Commission filed its report. . . .
>
> As bankruptcy filings increase, creditors justifiably worry whether a promise to repay has any meaning, while consumer advocates express concern that the financial distress of more than a million American families each year foreshadows a larger economic problem. The inherent conflict between the twin goals of bankruptcy - appropriate relief for those in trouble and equitable treatment for their creditors - ensures that it always will be an area of contention. To deal with financial loss, the bankruptcy system necessarily embraces competing interests. Recommendations fully endorsed by either debtors or by creditors would not maintain the balance essential to any consumer bankruptcy system. Bankruptcy is a system born of conflict and competing values. To function well, it must remain unpopular and controversial. . . . No area of bankruptcy law is more complex than consumer bankruptcy

NAT'L BANKRUPTCY REV. COMM'N, BANKRUPTCY: THE NEXT TWENTY YEARS, THE NATIONAL BANKRUPTCY REVIEW COMMISSION FINAL REPORT 77-78 (1997).

D. WHAT SHOULD YOU KNOW AT THIS POINT IN THE COURSE ABOUT HOW BANKRUPTCY CASES END?

Later in the course we will learn about bankruptcy cases ending in a discharge, bankruptcy cases ending because the court grants relief from the automatic stay, bankruptcy cases ending because the court is unwilling to "cram down" a plan, bankruptcy cases ending because the debtor is not able to make the payments mandated by the plan approved by the bankruptcy court, bankruptcy cases ending with a section 363 sale, . . .

For now, we simply need to know that there are not always (or even often) "happy endings" in bankruptcy stories. More specifically,

- bankruptcy can't fix all problems — can't even fix all debt problems;
- in bankruptcy, most creditors do ***not*** get paid most of what they are owed;
- the ending of a bankruptcy case depends in the main on:
    - the liquidation and going concern values of the debtor's assets;
    - the debtor's cash flow;
    - creditors' interests and needs; and
    - the attorneys' and bankruptcy judge's ability to work creatively and effectively with the bankruptcy concepts covered in this book

The end of a bankruptcy case also depends on constitutional law concepts not covered in your constitutional law course, and contract law concepts not covered in your contracts course, and property concepts not covered in your property course. First, constitutional law.[13] The United States Constitution delegates to Congress the exclusive power to establish "uniform laws on the subject of Bankruptcies" in Article 1, section 8, clause 4.

Now, con law and contracts. Article I, section 10 of the Constitution bars states (not the federal government) from impairing contract obligations. When read

---

[13]Your authors refer to this course as "con law," since that is a more apt description of what it promises and what it covers.

together, this means that Congress may enact "uniform laws on the subject of Bankruptcies" which impair the obligation of contracts. As the Seventh Circuit explained: "All parties to a contract are, of necessity, aware of the existence of, and subject to, the power of Congress to legislate on the subject of bankruptcies. They were and are chargeable with knowledge that their rights and remedies . . . are affected by existing bankruptcy laws and all future bankruptcy legislation which might be enacted." *In re* Prima Co., 88 F.2d 785, 788 (7th Cir. 1937).

Now property law and con law. A lien is a property interest. A creditor who has a lien on the debtor's property has a property interest. The Fifth Amendment prohibits taking private property without just compensation. And, the Article 1 Congressional power to enact bankruptcy laws is "subject to the Fifth Amendment's prohibition against taking private property without compensation." United States v. Security Indus. Bank, 459 U.S. 70, 75 (1982). Accordingly, the Bankruptcy Code [and this book] regularly distinguishes between what bankruptcy can do to a creditor's right to payment (which is the nature of a contract right) and what bankruptcy can do to a creditor's lien (which is the nature of a property right).

Unit 2

Why Are There So Many Bankruptcy Cases?

The following represents the number of annual bankruptcy filings from 2000 through the second quarter of 2004:

Business and Non-Business Filings Years Ended June 30, 2000-2004[14]

	Total	*Non-Business*	*Business*
2004	1,635,725	1,599,986	35,739
2003	1,650,279	1,613,097	37,182
2002	1,505,306	1,466,105	39,201
2001	1,386,606	1,349,471	37,135
2000	1,276,922	1,240,012	36,910

A legitimate question is why there are so many filings. An equally legitimate question is why there are so few. The point of these two questions is that you should approach the investigation of bankruptcy with an open mind; to label the numbers above too many (or too few) means that you have already made some assumptions about bankruptcy relief. Before those assumptions

[14]You can look up the official bankruptcy statistics on line. *See* http://www.uscourts.gov/bnkrpctystats/bankruptcystats.htm.

harden, let us first explore some of the causes of bankruptcy.

A. What Can Creditors Do Outside of Bankruptcy?

Creditors are generally happy to do nothing. More specifically, creditors are happy to do nothing so long as their debtors are paying them.

When debtors default in paying an obligation, creditors will first attempt through "persuasion" to get the debtor to pay "voluntarily." The creditor may even hire a collection agency or attorney to help persuade the debtor.[15] If these nonjudicial collection efforts are unsuccessful, the creditor will resort to the debt collection remedies provided by either (i) law or (ii) contract to seize and sell the debtor's assets to satisfy the debt.

At the broadest level, the law of creditors' remedies involves only two issues: (1) when and how a creditor gets a lien on property of the debtor (or the property itself), and (2) the lien's priority in relation to third parties' rights to the property, including other creditors' liens and the claims of transferees. These two issues are common to every kind of creditors' remedy.

Why the focus on "liens"? A creditor cannot seize and sell its debtor's property unless it has some property interest in the debtor's property, and the principal way to obtain such an interest is to obtain a "lien" on that property.

Understanding this involves understanding a little bit of the law of sales, and a little bit of the law of secured

---

[15]When the debt is a consumer debt, these nonjudicial persuasion efforts are controlled by the federal Fair Debt Collection Practices Act and various state consumer protection statutes.

transactions. When I sell something to you, you "own" it, which for our purposes typically means that you obtain the right to exclude all others from the use or possession of that property. If I sell you my car, you can exclude the world from driving it.

You obtain this right regardless of whether you have paid the full purchase price. Say for example that I sell you my car for the promise that you will pay me next Tuesday for it. Come next Tuesday you default; you don't pay. On Wednesday, I can't take the car back. It is yours. By selling on credit, I took the risk that you would not pay and, without more, parting with all property interests in the car, typically upon your taking possession of it. Indeed, if I ignore this learning, and forcibly take your car, you can sue me for civil conversion; *i.e.*, civil theft.

This example illustrates the most general rule of the law of creditors' remedies: generally a creditor does not acquire or retain a lien or other property interest in the debtor's property until the creditor reduces her claim to judgment and enforces this judgment through appropriate postjudgment process, namely execution.[16]

You may wonder why action beyond a judgment is necessary. The answer is that a judgment is no more than another form of debt; it is a new form of the obligation that the debtor owes the creditor. A judgment does, however, differ from the original obligation in that a judgment is the State's recognition of the legitimacy of the creditor's claim against the debtor. Along with this recognition comes (1) a judgment lien, which attaches by force of law to the debtor's real property once the

---

[16]There is a small exception to the rule that a creditor cannot seize property of the debtor except through postjudgment execution. In a narrow class of cases, property sufficient to satisfy a creditor's claim can be impounded by judicial lien at the time suit is filed. The means is a provisional remedy known as *prejudgment attachment* or, when the property is held by a third person, *prejudgment garnishment*.

judgment is appropriately recorded, and also (2) a willingness by the state to use its coercive power to enforce this lien and otherwise collect the amount of the judgment forcibly from the debtor's property (both real and personal) if the judgment debtor does not pay "voluntarily."

This power is brought to bear through the process of execution which is triggered simply by a judgment creditor requesting it. A creditor with a judgment initiates the execution process by applying to the court for a *writ of execution*. The writ of execution is ordinarily issued from the court that rendered the judgment and is directed to a sheriff. The writ orders the sheriff to seize property of the debtor, sell it, and apply the proceeds in satisfaction of the judgment.

To reach tangible property of a debtor held by third persons, and to collect debts owed to the debtor, there is a special proceeding at law in the nature of an adversary suit against the person who holds the debtor's property or owes it money: *garnishment*. Garnishment is in essence a special form of execution – designed for reaching property of the debtor held by a third party. For example, when a creditor wishes to levy or execute upon a bank account, it seeks to obtain property of the debtor's held by a third person. In this context, the proper nomenclature regarding what occurs when, for example, the IRS tries to go against a bank account of delinquent taxpayer, is that the IRS is garnishing the bank account.

Most lawyers do not like to do this kind of legal work; most creditors do not like to pay for this kind of legal work. Obtaining a judgment and getting a sheriff to seize and sell property of a debtor (read "voter", read "neighbor" . . .) can be difficult and time consuming and stressful and unsuccessful.

Why? One of the initial largest roadblocks to collection of debts is that there is no guarantee that the debtor will have property that can be seized and sold, or that the property will be in the same place as the creditor told the sheriff to go look.

Second, even if the debtor has property, that property may be encumbered by other creditors' liens that have priority. These other liens may have been created because of (i) a prior judicial collection effort, or (ii) statute, or (iii) agreement.

Tax liens, mechanics' liens and landlords' liens are examples of common statutory liens. These are liens that arise by operation of law; the debtor need not consent to the imposition of the lien. It only has to fail to pay a debt protected by the statute.

While important, statutory liens do not comprise the majority of creditors' property interests in a debtor's property. Instead, consensual liens are the most common form of liens. So common are these consensual interests is that most debt deals which are large enough to involve lawyers also involve consensual liens.

Federal bankruptcy law does not govern the creation of these liens. Instead, state law controls here, and state law tends to categorize the types of consensual liens by the type of property involved, and the two basic divisions in this regard are real property (that is, dirt and things built on and attached to the dirt) and personal property (that is, things that are not real property).

There are various devices for creating consensual liens on real property - the mortgage, the deed of trust, and the land-sale contract. The differences in these devices largely concern the procedures for (a) applying the collateral in satisfaction of the secured obligation, and (b) safeguarding the debtor's rights and interests.

When the creditor and debtor create a consensual lien on personal property or fixtures, the governing law is Uniform Commercial Code Article 9, the subject of another course in law school sometimes called "Secured Transactions" or "Commercial Law." Article 9 provides only one device for creating a lien: the Article 9 security interest. "Security interest" is Article 9's name for a lien. A "secured party" is a creditor in whose favor a security interest exists. The obligation owed the secured party is the secured debt. The property subject to the lien/security interest is the "collateral."

B. PROBLEMS: DEBT COLLECTION ISSUES

PROBLEM 2-1: WHAT CAN YOU DO?

Your firm's client, C, has a $1,000,000 Title VII judgment against D Corp. D's assets include:

(i) a building,
(ii) equipment,
(iii) supplies,
(iv) accounts receivable, and
(v) various bank accounts in S Bank

D's other creditors include:

(i) S Bank,
(ii) IRS,
(iii) trade creditors,
(iv) employees who are to be paid $70,000 in wages, benefits, etc. at the end of the week

What can C do to collect its judgment?

PROBLEM 2-2: HOW MUCH CAN YOU "BILL?"

How much should your firm charge C for collecting the $1,000,000 judgment? How much should your firm charge if C's judgment is only a $100,000 judgment? How much should you charge if, at the end of the day, you collect nothing for C despite good faith and reasonable attempts to do so?

C. WHAT CAN A DEBTOR DO OUTSIDE OF BANKRUPTCY?

There is not much a debtor can do outside of bankruptcy to fix its debt problems. At least not much that a debtor can do without the help and support of its creditors.

Recall that when a debtor does not pay a debt despite the requests (and then demands) of a creditor, the creditor can go to court – sue on the debt. Such a suit usually results in a default judgment; that is, in most cases the debtor will not defend or show up, and the creditor will get everything it asked for in its complaint "by default." A creditor with a judgment can then obtain an "execution lien" from the court that issued the judgment. And, with an execution lien, the creditor can get the sheriff to "levy on," or take physical possession of, the debtor's property. The sheriff will then sell the property at an execution sale, the terms of which will be set by state statute.

A debtor can try to work out some sort of debt repayment agreement with its creditors. Professors who teach first year contracts courses call these agreements "compositions" and "extensions." Real lawyers call these agreements "workout agreements."

Whatever you call them, they are "agreements" and only bind the creditors who agree. If even one creditor refuses to participate in the workout agreement, that dissenting creditor, can in essence, "blow up" any deal by suing on its debt and using the execution process to levy on and sell assets of the debtor that are essential to the debtor's performing its workout obligations to the assenting creditors.

Assume, for example, that Perris Printing Company has reached an agreement with nine out of ten of its largest creditors to pay 90% of their debts over three years at a new, higher interest rate. That tenth, non-assenting creditor is not bound. And, that creditor can sue on its debt, obtain a judgment, and levy on and cause the sale of equipment essential to Perris Printing's continued business operations.

If the debtor is an individual, state and federal laws exempt certain property of the debtor from the collection efforts of certain creditors. At most, these exemption statutes enable a debtor to keep some of his or her property from some of his or her creditors; exemption statutes do not enable a person with debt problems to "fix" the problems.

State exemption laws vary significantly from state to state. In most states, the amount of property that a debtor can designate as exempt is very limited. And, in all states, creditors with a mortgage or security interest in property that is designated as exempt can still seize and sell that property. If, for example, First Bank has a mortgage on Gus Epstein's house and Epstein defaults, First Bank can seize and sell Epstein's house even if Epstein has designated the house as his exempt homestead.

D. BUT WHY BANKRUPTCY?

More than 1,500,000 bankruptcy petitions are filed each year. More than 99% of these petitions are filed by debtors, less than 1% are filed by creditors against debtors.

Why? "Inquiring minds want to know." These guys must know something we don't. But not for long.

Unit 3

What Happens In A Bankruptcy Case?

A great bankruptcy teacher, Stefan Riesenfeld, accurately (and repeatedly) observed, "Bankruptcy is not mashed potatoes. You need to study it a lump at a time."

If this book is anything, it is very "lumpy" [big on lumps]. We have tried to isolate bankruptcy concepts and introduce you to one concept at a time.

Nonetheless, it is important that you understand what happens in a bankruptcy case, that you "see the big picture". [This book is also big on trite expressions.] Accordingly, in the Appendix we have reproduced the overview of bankruptcy from the senior author's incredibly helpful and inexpensive student text, *Bankruptcy and Related Law in a Nutshell* 7th edition. We recommend that you read this soon. And often. But for now . . . .

A. Basic Structure of the Bankruptcy Code

The Bankruptcy Code may initially seem daunting, but a little knowledge of how it is put together can dispel that unease.

1. The Bankruptcy Code as a "Code"

The first thing to realize is that the Bankruptcy Code is, well, a code. What does that mean? That means that it is an integrated and comprehensive approach to a particular statutory problem. It is not supposed to have outright conflicts, and it is supposed to contain a balance of interests reached through legislative compromise.

The fact that your instructor will no doubt point out repeatedly throughout the course that this ideal is not attained often or with consistency does not diminish this starting point. There is a logic and a structure. It may not be readily apparent, but it is there.

2. *The Underlying Structure*

The underlying structure of the Bankruptcy Code is fairly simple. It consists of one title of the United States Code (title 11), and within title 11 are nine chapters. Each of these chapters has a different function, outlined as follows:

Chapter 1—Definitions
Chapter 3—Administration
Chapter 5—Claims and Creditors
Chapter 7—Liquidation
Chapter 9—Municipal Bankruptcy
Chapter 11—Reorganization
Chapter 12—Family Farmer Rehabilitation
Chapter 13—Rehabilitation of Individuals with Income
Chapter 15—Ancillary and Other Cross-Border Cases

Of these, Chapters 1, 3 and 5 apply in all chapters. That is to say, all general defined terms are found in Chapter 1.[17] There are a lot of them. So many, in fact that Congress has lost the ability to consecutively

[17]Some specific sections have their own internal definitions, applicable only within that section. *See* 11 U.S.C. § 547(a), which contains definitions that are applicable only to preference actions governed by Section 547.

number them correctly.[18] The general structure of bankruptcy administration – what happens between the time the bankruptcy case is filed and the time that it is over – is found in Chapter 3. The way in which the Code collects and distributes assets to creditors is found in Chapter 5.

Chapters 7, 9, 11, 12, 13, and 15 each deal with a different type of debtor or a different type of relief. Chapter 7 is the baseline relief. It provides for the independent liquidation of assets held at filing – that is, their sale – and distribution of the sale proceeds pro rata to creditors in accordance with statutory guidelines and priorities. Chapter 11 can be used by most debtors who would qualify under Chapter 7 (including flesh and blood humans), and it allows variation in Chapter 7's statutory scheme according to a general level of creditor control. It also has the fairly unique quality of allowing a debtor to remain in possession of assets and become a "debtor in possession," or "DIP." Chapter 13 allows for special reorganization for individuals; instead of liquidation of assets held at filing and distribution to creditors, under Chapter 13 a debtor agrees to give 3-5 years of disposable income to creditors in return for broader relief in the form of a more expansive discharge. Chapter 13 also allows, as Chapter 7 does not, the debtor to modify and cure secured claims. For example, a Chapter 13 debtor has a right to cure missed payments on a home mortgage even if such cure is not anticipated or permitted by state law. Chapter 12 allows Chapter 13 type relief, without limitations on plan life, for "family farmers" – which is one of the many definitions you'll find in Chapter 1.

The advantages of Chapter 13 to a debtor have been "tempered" by the 2005 legislation. While a Chapter 13 debtor's discharge is still more expansive

---

[18]Check out 11 U.S.C. § 101(53), which is followed by Section 101(53A), 101(53B), 101(53C), 101(53D), and then 101(54). Which would be fine, except that 101(55) is followed by 101(56A); there is no 101(56).

than a Chapter 7 discharge, not as much more. And, while a Chapter 13 debtor can still, to some extent, modify and cure secured claims, not as much as before.

Chapter 15 provides an alternative to a debtor who has a bankruptcy case pending in some other country. Instead of commencing a full bankruptcy case in the United States, a "foreign representative" of the debtor may file a petition under Chapter 15. Upon the issuance of an order for recognition under section 1517, certain provisions of the Bankruptcy Code become effective. Most basic bankruptcy courses do not cover Chapter 15, we cover it later in the book.

3. *The Role of Non-Bankruptcy Law*

We cannot stress enough that bankruptcy law is federal law. Under the Constitution's Supremacy Clause found in Article VI, federal law preempts contrary state law. So a state that passes a law that says "Debts owed to the health care providers shall not be subject to a bankruptcy discharge" has passed a nullity; it will simply not be enforced. At the same time, if Congress passed such a law, it would be given effect, since the Constitution allocates to Congress the ability to craft bankruptcy law.

But there are times – actually many, many times – when bankruptcy law is not enough. A truly complete bankruptcy code would contain all sorts of definitions of property and regulate priorities with respect to the property interests so defined. The United States Bankruptcy Code does not do this. Rather, in most cases, it tries not to tamper with the result under non-bankruptcy law, so as to minimize litigants' strategic reasons to seek bankruptcy relief. As one consequence, the Code has many provisions for property schemes that are not uniform across the fifty states. Instead of a uniform federal rule on marital property, for example, the Code permits schemes of community property and tenancy by the entireties to control distributions to creditors for debtors in states which have adopted those schemes.

The interface between federal bankruptcy law and non-bankruptcy law consists of a zone that is well-defined in the main, but fuzzy and contentious at the edges. Many of the issues and points in this book will draw on non-bankruptcy law for their resolution. Some of the issues will draw on federal law to override state law. The basic point, however, is that one thrust of the Code is to try and provide a procedural system of bankruptcy that disturbs as few non-bankruptcy law entitlements as possible, but that does disturb such entitlements when necessary.

4. *Tips for Reading the Bankruptcy Code*

One of the early mentors for one of the junior authors of this book once took that author aside and pointed to the Code. He then said the following magic words: "There are two rules for reading this or any other Code. Number 1: Read carefully. Number 2: Read on." Truer words were never spoken.

With respect to Rule #1, there is, of course, no substitute for careful textual reading of any statute. In the case of a code such as the Bankruptcy Code, such an admonition is especially important because the Bankruptcy Code was drafted, at least initially, as an integrated whole, with care toward the consequences in one part of the Code if changes were made in another part. The Bankruptcy Code of 1978 started in 1968 with the formation of the Bankruptcy Review Commission, which rendered its report in 1973. Five years, and many, many bills after that, Congress passed the Code. During those ten years, countless individuals labored long and hard to ensure that the Code was as good as it could be. Many times clarity prevailed, but often political compromises left untidy text. Although interesting as history, the practical effect of these events is that the Code cannot be approached with the view that obvious alternatives were not considered. To the contrary, if anything, too many approaches were considered, and then melded into one pot.

With respect to Rule #2, the integrated nature of the Bankruptcy Code's text, and the style of its drafting, require you to read more than just the text you may initially focus upon. A general rule is often stated at the beginning of a section of the Code, only to be gutted by the exceptions that follow. In any contest in bankruptcy court, one side will often champion the general rule; the other the exception. The victor will often be the one who understands how the two are supposed to fit together.

B. Typical Players in a Bankruptcy Case

1. *Bankruptcy as Litigation, and as Public Litigation*

Bankruptcy takes place in a court. There are rules of procedure, and a person in a black robe presides. There are usually two tables. But although one of us likes to think of bankruptcy as a class action by the debtor against all of its creditors, the true parallels to typical civil litigation are few. Part of this comes from the fact that a debtor may have many different types of creditors – secured, unsecured, friendly, unfriendly – and part comes from the public interest in debt relief. In every bankruptcy the federal government may, and usually does, take some interest. Thus, unlike typical civil litigation, there is always the possibility that someone other than a creditor may appear in the case and make a request. Keep in mind these many possible roles when going over the different players listed next.

2. *Players and Roles in Bankruptcy Cases*

Here is a short listing of the major players that we will encounter in this book:

- ***Debtor.*** Most simply, the person, individual or business entity that is the subject of the bankruptcy case. Put another way, it is the person who owes money and is seeking some form of relief. *See* 11 U.S.C. § 101(13).

- ***Debtor in Possession.*** A special type of debtor that only appears in Chapter 11 cases. A debtor in possession (or "DIP") is the debtor, but with expanded duties as a representative of the bankruptcy estate. Indeed, a DIP has fiduciary duties to the estate that the debtor does not. *See* 11 U.S.C. § 1101(1).

- ***Creditor.*** Again, most simply, a person to whom the debtor owes a monetary obligation. "Creditor" is defined at 11 U.S.C. § 101(10) in a way that may be more expansive than a lay or common definition. We'll explore this more when we talk about "claims" in Unit 4.

- ***Creditors' Committee.*** Most generally, this refers to a committee of unsecured creditors in a Chapter 11 case. Such committees are recognized by statute, 11 U.S.C. § 1102, and are given statutory duties, 11 U.S.C. § 1103(c). They may hire their own professionals, who will be paid from the estate and not by the individual members of the committee (a mixed blessing, because it also means that the professionals for any committee serve the estate and not the individual interests of the committee members). Although creditors' committees can be formed in Chapter 7 cases, see 11 U.S.C. § 705, they rarely are.

- ***"Professionals."*** This is more a term of art, and refers to the lawyers, accountants and sometimes the investment bankers hired to assist the bankruptcy estate or an official committee. In many cases, in order to be paid from the estate, these professionals have to seek permission to be employed, must not have any conflicts or adverse interests with respect to the estate, and must apply publicly for payment of their fees (which means that their time sheets become a matter of public record).

- ***Trustee.*** This term can mean a number of different things in a bankruptcy case. Most often it refers to the representative of the estate charged with administering the case. But there are different flavors of this office.

  - *Chapter 7 Trustee* (also of "panel" trustees). A person who represents the estate in a Chapter 7 case, collects and liquidates the debtor's assets, and distributes the proceeds to creditors. An interim trustee is appointed upon the filing of the bankruptcy case, 11 U.S.C. § 701, and creditors can then vote for a permanent trustee at the first meeting of creditors. *See* 11 U.S.C. § 702. Most of the time, the interim trustee becomes the "trustee" for the case.

    Trustees more often than not are drawn from a "panel" of individuals qualified under 28 U.S.C. § 586(a)(1) maintained by the Office of the United States Trustee (see below).

    The things to remember are that in Chapter 7, trustees are required by the Code in all Chapter 7 cases, and that they "work for" the debtor's unsecured creditors.

- *Chapter 11 Trustee.* A person who represents the estate in a Chapter 11 case. Unlike Chapter 7, Chapter 11 does not provide for the automatic appointment of a trustee; instead, the debtor in possession is the norm. Only when the debtor is unwilling to serve as the debtor in possession, or when the court is convinced that a Chapter 11 trustee should be appointed, will a Chapter 11 case be administered by a trustee. When appointed, however, the duties of a Chapter 11 trustee are similar, although not identical, to those of a Chapter 7 trustee. *See* 11 U.S.C. § 1106.

- *Chapter 12 and 13 Trustees* (also of "standing" trustees). Trustees in Chapter 12 and 13 cases perform administrative functions; they monitor the debtor's development and performance of his or her plan, they collect and disburse plan payments and occasionally object to plan confirmation if they believe that the debtor has not complied with the requirements of confirming a plan. *See* 11 U.S.C. §§ 1202; 1302. They are called "standing" trustees because there are one or more individuals who usually undertake the duties of the office as a full-time job.

- ***United States Trustee*** (or sometimes, the Office of the United States Trustee, or just "OUST"). The Attorney General appoints a "United States Trustee" for various regions (consisting of one or more judicial districts) across the country; at present there are twenty-one regions nationwide. The OUST is a representative of the executive branch of government. He or she employs counsel, financial analysts and case administrators. He or she also appoints trustees under the various chapters (such as Chapter 7 and Chapter 13 trustees), and monitors all cases for debtor compliance (for such things as whether the debtor has filed schedules, operating reports and similar required information). The OUST also monitors the retention of, and fee requests by, professionals.

- ***Examiner.*** In Chapter 11 cases only, an examiner may be appointed to investigate the pre-petition activities of the debtor. In both Enron and in WorldCom, examiners were appointed and authored lengthy reports.

- ***Bankruptcy Judge.*** The judicial officer that presides over a bankruptcy case. Although a federal judge, bankruptcy judges are judges appointed under Article I of the Constitution. They thus do not have life tenure, and serve 14-year terms, for pay that equals 92% of what an Article III federal judge makes. 28 U.S.C. § 153(a). Congress has determined that Circuit Judges shall select the bankruptcy judges for the circuits in which they sit. 28 U.S.C. § 152. Appeals from decisions of bankruptcy judges are to Article III district judges, or in some circuits, to Bankruptcy Appellate Panels (also know as "BAPs") which consist of three bankruptcy judges. *See* 28 U.S.C. § 158(b). Appeals from district court decision or BAPs are to the Circuit Courts of Appeal. 28 U.S.C. § 158(d).

- ***Clerk of the Court.*** In most districts, the bankruptcy court is a separate court, with separate records maintained by a separate person known as the clerk of the court. 28 U.S.C. § 156.

C. Procedure and Procedural Terms in a Bankruptcy Litigation

Bankruptcy procedure is somewhat like Russian *matryoshka*, the nesting dolls that fit one within the other. All litigation revolves in some way around the debtor, and we start with the basic unit of bankruptcy procedure involving the debtor, the bankruptcy case.

1. The Basic Rules of the Game (herein of the Federal Rules of Bankruptcy Procedure)

As we have indicated before, bankruptcy litigation is federal litigation. It happens in a federal courthouse. As such, you might initially suspect that procedure within bankruptcy is governed by the Federal Rules of Civil Procedure that you studied in your Civil Procedure class. That suspicion, however, would prove (mostly) wrong. Bankruptcy has its own rules of procedure, known as the Federal Rules of Bankruptcy Procedure. They are likely reprinted in your statutory supplement (if your supplement was designed for a bankruptcy course instead of a commercial law course). We refer to them in this book as "Bankr. R. XXX."[19]

To complicate matters, it is often the case that the Federal Rules of Bankruptcy Procedure incorporate parts of (or even whole rules found in) the Federal Rules of Civil Procedure. Bankr. R. 9016, for example, simply states that "Rule 45 F.R.Civ.P. applies in cases under the Code." F.R.Civ.P. 45, in turn, refers to subpoenas, and so Bankr. R. 9016 means that the general federal rule on subpoenas applies in bankruptcy "cases." But what is a "case"?

[19]Although not particularly important for this course, but very important for the practitioner, are the *local* bankruptcy rules in each separate bankruptcy court. These rules are authorized by Bankr. R. 9029, and often govern things such as number of copies of documents to file, and the amount of time a party has to respond to a motion.

2. *The Case (herein of "**In re** Debtor")*

The debtor files a petition with the clerk of the bankruptcy court and commences a bankruptcy *case*.[20] The case is a unified piece of litigation, in which all other actions, motions and the like relate. To use the metaphor of the Russian *matryoshka* again, it is the main outside nesting doll.

The general way bankruptcy practitioners refer to litigation is that they have filed it "in" the debtor's case. The caption of the case on the pleading filed which initiated the case, and hence the way most case reporting services such as West's *Bankruptcy Reporter* pick up and index the case, is usually just "*In re* Debtor," where "Debtor" is the name of the person about whom the case is filed.[21] Since many different types of litigation and issues can be resolved within a debtor's case, the simple designation "*In re* Debtor" does not tell you much.

3. *The Adversary Proceeding (herein of "X v. Y (In re Debtor)")*

The Federal Rules of Bankruptcy Practice acknowledge that some types of litigation which occur in bankruptcy court are more like typical civil litigation. The rules specify what types of litigation are in this "special" class, and label them "adversary proceedings." That is, some litigation has to proceed by "adversary proceeding," which means that Part VII of the Bankruptcy Rules will apply, and that the litigation will have to be commenced by summons and complaint, just like an ordinary piece of civil litigation.

---

[20]In an involuntary case, the petition is filed by creditors, but it does not change the naming conventions except that until the involuntary case is decided, the debtor is referred to as the "alleged debtor."

[21]There is no distinction made in citation form between the debtor and the debtor in possession. On the caption, the convention is to state the debtor's name, and then follow it with "debtor and debtor in possession."

The rules for adversary proceedings for the most part incorporate the Federal Rules of Civil Procedure. The types of litigation that are to be prosecuted by adversary proceeding are found in Bankr. R. 7001, which states that adversary proceedings include: "a proceeding (1) to recover money or property, . . . (2) to determine the validity, priority, or extent of a lien or other interest in property, . . . (3) to obtain approval pursuant to § 363(h) for the sale of both the interest of the state and of a co-owner in property, (4) to object to or revoke a discharge, (5) to revoke an order of confirmation of a Chapter 11, Chapter 12, or Chapter 13 plan, (6) to determine the dischargeability of a debt, (7) to obtain an injunction or other equitable relief, (8) to subordinate any allowed claim or interest, . . . (9) to obtain a declaratory judgment relating to any of the foregoing, or (10) to determine a claim or cause of action removed pursuant to 28 U.S.C. § 1452."

Again, the traditional caption of an adversary proceeding determines how the case is cited. When an adversary proceeding is filed, the pleading notes the case to which it refers – it has "In re Debtor" at the beginning. But then, since the relief requested typically involves less than all of the debtor's creditors, the pleading will also have a traditional caption indicating a plaintiff and a defendant, along the lines of "X v. Y." The convention that has evolved is to combine these two designations when referring to an adversary proceeding. As a consequence, the citation form for an adversary proceeding is usually "X v. Y (*In re* Debtor)," where X is the plaintiff, Y the defendant and "Debtor" is the debtor.[22]

---

[22]Note that often the debtor is also one of the litigants, so that you will often see "X v. Y (*In re* X)."

4. *The Contested Matter*

Some disputes are very important to a bankruptcy case, yet are not resolved in full-blown adversary proceedings. For example, the confirmation of a Chapter 11 plan is not among the actions or proceedings listed in Bankr. R. 7001. These proceedings have a name nonetheless. They are called "contested matters." They differ from adversary proceedings in that they may be initiated by motion, and are heard on a much faster time schedule.

Bankr. R. 9014 governs the conduct of contested matters, although the rule leaves much to local rules of procedure, including the minimum time upon which a motion may be heard. It also permits, in appropriate cases, the bankruptcy judge to incorporate some of the adversary proceeding rules (such as discovery rules). The general convention in citation form is to cite to a contested matter the same way that you would cite to a case, *i.e.*, "*In re* Debtor."

5. *The Concept of "Notice and a Hearing"*

Notice has a key role in bankruptcy. Because of the power of the bankruptcy court to regulate debtor-creditor relations, finding out about what is happening is critical. At the start of the case, for example, all creditors receive notice of the case based on a list filed initially by the debtor.

After a case commences, the Code conditions many actions taken in bankruptcy court on giving "notice and a hearing." The plain reading of that phrase would seem to require both notice *and* a hearing. But the Code is subtle. Read the definition of "after notice and a hearing."

---

11 U.S.C. § 102(1)

"after notice and a hearing", or a similar phrase -

(A) means after such notice as is appropriate in the particular circumstances, and such opportunity for a hearing as is appropriate in the particular circumstances; but

(B) authorizes an act without an actual hearing if such notice is given properly and if -

(i) such a hearing is not requested timely by a party in interest; or

(ii) there is insufficient time for a hearing to be commenced before such act must be done, and the court authorizes such act . . . .

Read this statute carefully. It actually authorizes action *without* a hearing if no one objects, or if "there is insufficient time for a hearing to be commenced" and the court approves. Bankruptcy is no place for the slothful or non-diligent. And the bankruptcy rules take advantage of this concept, especially with the sale of assets. *See* Bankr. R. 6004.

---

6. The Role of Electronic Case Filing

Bankruptcy courts are very quickly moving to filing everything electronically. Indeed, as of January 1, 2005, all filings with the bankruptcy court are supposed to be made by electronic means. This conversion means that lawyers, by pre-arrangement with the court, file and "sign" things essentially by email or through web access. This results in wonderful access to all court filings, but has raised concerns about privacy.

To gain access to the electronic filing system, you'll need to register and be prepared to pay $.08 per page for each page you view. The web site for access is called PACER, and can be found at: http://pacer.psc.uscourts.gov/.

Part II

Core Concepts of Bankruptcy

Unit 4

What Are the Basic Bankruptcy Building Blocks?

A. "EQUALITY OF DISTRIBUTION"

Equality of distribution is consistently described as an important, even the most important, purpose of bankruptcy. The Supreme Court in *Bailey v. Glover*, 88 U.S. 342, 346 (1874), stated: "It is obviously one of the purposes of the Bankruptcy law that there should be a speedy disposition of the bankrupt's assets. **This is second only in importance to securing equality of distribution."** (emphasis added).

Similar statements can be found in more recent Supreme Court opinions and in reported cases from other courts. No such statement, however, can be found in the Code. No Code section mentions or directly requires equality of distribution. *But cf.* 11 U.S.C. § 726(b)(distribution should be "pro rata among claims of the kind specified in each such particular paragraph").

As we will see, most provisions in the Code and most court orders in bankruptcy cases are consistent with a policy of equality of distribution. However, we will also see provisions in the Code and court orders in bankruptcy cases that are consistent with the policy of equality of distribution only in the "Animal Farm" sense of that phrase. *Cf.* GEORGE ORWELL, ANIMAL FARM 133 (Signet 1996) (1946) ("*All Animals Are Equal but Some Animals Are More Equal than Others*").

B. "FRESH START" AND THE DISCHARGE

The Supreme Court has also stated, "The federal system of bankruptcy is designed not only to distribute the property of the debtor, not by law exempted, fairly and equally among his creditors, but as a main purpose of the act, intends to aid the unfortunate debtor by giving him a fresh start in life, free from debts, except of a certain character, after the property which he owned at the time of bankruptcy has been administered for the benefit of creditors. Our decisions lay great stress upon this feature of the law--as one not only of private but of great public interest in that it secures to the unfortunate debtor, who surrenders his property for distribution, a new opportunity in life." Stellwagen v. Clum, 245 U.S. 605, 616 (1918).

And, the phrase "fresh start" nowhere appears in the Code. Courts and commentators however consistently connect the bankruptcy "fresh start" policy with the bankruptcy discharge. The term "discharge" does appear in the Code. A lot.

A debtor who receives a bankruptcy discharge is relieved from any further personal, legal liability on her dischargeable debts. Reread this sentence and notice the limitations on the concept of discharge.

First, not every person who is a debtor in a bankruptcy case receives a discharge. The tests for whether a debtor receives a discharge vary from chapter to chapter.

In Chapter 7 cases, corporations and business entities other than humans cannot receive a discharge. With respect to humans, Section 727(a) lists twelve bases for withholding a discharge from an individual debtor in a Chapter 7 case. Most of these "objections" to discharge are based on a debtor's misdeeds before or during the bankruptcy case.

In Chapter 11 cases involving debtors who are business entities such as corporations or limited liability companies or partnerships, the biggest hurdle for obtaining a discharge is court approval of the plan of reorganization. Under section 1141(d), a business entity in Chapter 11 generally receives a discharge on the "confirmation of a plan." The business debtor's completion of payments under the plan is not a condition precedent to a Chapter 11 discharge.

By contrast, in Chapter 13 cases, individual debtors receive discharges only if there has been both (1) confirmation of the plan and (2) payments under the plan have been made or judicially excused and (3) a course on personal financial management has been completed. Similarly, in Chapter 11 cases involving individual debtors, there will generally be no discharge until payments under the plan have been made.

Second, a discharge does not make a debt disappear; it does not vaporize or obliterate it. The discharge only relieves the debtor from *personal* liability on the debt. Accordingly, if D's debt is guaranteed by X, D's discharge does not affect X's guarantee. The creditor can sue X on the guaranty and not worry about D's discharge. And, if D's debt to M is secured by a mortgage on Blackacre, then D's discharge does not affect M's rights as a mortgage holder with respect to Blackacre. This means that, if done correctly, M may foreclose and evict D regardless of D's discharge. Section 524 of the Code governs the effect of a discharge. Please read 11 U.S.C. § 524(a)(1), (2) and (e).

Third, a discharge does not relieve the debtor from personal liability on *all* debts. A discharge only affects "dischargeable" debts. Whether a debt is dischargeable depends on:

- whether the case is a 7, 11 or 13 case;

- when the debt arose; and
- whether the debt is excepted from discharge. *See* 11 U.S.C. § 523.

We consider dischargeability of debts elsewhere in Unit 9.

---

11 U.S.C. § 524(a)

(a) A discharge in a case under this title--

(1) voids any judgment at any time obtained, to the extent that such judgment is a determination of the personal liability of the debtor with respect to any debt discharged under section 727, 944, 1141, 1228, or 1328 of this title, whether or not discharge of such debt is waived;

(2) operates as an injunction against the commencement or continuation of an action, the employment of process, or an act, to collect, recover or offset any such debt as a personal liability of the debtor, whether or not discharge of such debt is waived; . . .

Form 18
(10/05)

United States Bankruptcy Court

_______________ District Of _______________

In re ____,)
[Set forth here all names including married,)
maiden, and trade names used by debtor within)
last 8 years.])
Debtor) Case No. _______________
)
)
Address _____________________________________)
)
_____________________________________) Chapter 7
)
Last four digits of Social Security No(s).: ____________________)
____)
Employer's Tax Identification No(s). *[if any]:*________________)
____)

DISCHARGE OF DEBTOR

It appearing that the debtor is entitled to a discharge, **IT IS ORDERED:** The debtor is granted a discharge under section 727 of title 11, United States Code, (the Bankruptcy Code).

Dated: ____________________

BY THE COURT

____

United States Bankruptcy Judge

SEE THE BACK OF THIS ORDER FOR IMPORTANT INFORMATION.

Official Form 18 - Contd.
(10/05)

EXPLANATION OF BANKRUPTCY DISCHARGE
IN A CHAPTER 7 CASE

This court order grants a discharge to the person named as the debtor. It is not a dismissal of the case and it does not determine how much money, if any, the trustee will pay to creditors.

Collection of Discharged Debts Prohibited

The discharge prohibits any attempt to collect from the debtor a debt that has been discharged. For example, a creditor is not permitted to contact a debtor by mail, phone, or otherwise, to file or continue a lawsuit, to attach wages or other property, or to take any other action to collect a discharged debt from the debtor. *[In a case involving community property:* There are also special rules that protect certain community property owned by the debtor's spouse, even if that spouse did not file a bankruptcy case.] A creditor who violates this order can be required to pay damages and attorney's fees to the debtor.

However, a creditor may have the right to enforce a valid lien, such as a mortgage or security interest, against the debtor's property after the bankruptcy, if that lien was not avoided or eliminated in the bankruptcy case. Also, a debtor may voluntarily pay any debt that has been discharged.

Debts That are Discharged

The chapter 7 discharge order eliminates a debtor's legal obligation to pay a debt that is discharged. Most, but not all, types of debts are discharged if the debt existed on the date the bankruptcy case was filed. (If this case was begun under a different chapter of the Bankruptcy Code and converted to chapter 7, the discharge applies to debts owed when the bankruptcy case was converted.)

Debts that are Not Discharged.

Some of the common types of debts which are not discharged in a chapter 7 bankruptcy case are:

a. Debts for most taxes;

b. Debts incurred to pay nondischargeable taxes;

c. Debts that are domestic support obligations;

d. Debts for most student loans;

e. Debts for most fines, penalties, forfeitures, or criminal restitution obligations;

f. Debts for personal injuries or death caused by the debtor's operation of a motor vehicle, vessel, or aircraft while intoxicated;

g. Some debts which were not properly listed by the debtor;

h. Debts that the bankruptcy court specifically has decided or will decide in this bankruptcy case are not discharged;

i. Debts for which the debtor has given up the discharge protections by signing a reaffirmation agreement in compliance with the Bankruptcy Code requirements for reaffirmation of debts.

j. Debts owed to certain pension, profit sharing, stock bonus, other retirement plans, or to the Thrift Savings Plan for federal employees for certain types of loans from these plans.

This information is only a general summary of the bankruptcy discharge. There are exceptions to these general rules. Because the law is complicated, you may want to consult an attorney to determine the exact effect of the discharge in this case.

PROBLEM 4-1: DISCHARGE AND WHAT CREDITORS CAN DO TO THE DEBTOR

1. D owes C $10,000. D files a Chapter 7 petition. C receives $500 from D's Chapter 7 trustee. D receives a discharge. Can C sue D for the other $9,500?

2. Same facts. Can C call D and politely ask D to pay the other $9,500?

3. D Corp. owes C $100,000. D Corp. files a Chapter 11 petition. D Corp.'s Chapter 11 plan is confirmed and D Corp. obtains a discharge, 11 U.S.C. § 1141(d). The plan provides for 10 monthly payments of $5,000 to C. D Corp. makes two of the monthly payments and then fails to make the other 8 monthly payments of $5,000. Can C sue D Corp. for $40,000? For $90,000?

4. D owes his dentist Dr. Szell $4,000. D files for bankruptcy. Dr. Szell receives $200 from D's bankruptcy. D receives a discharge. Can Dr. Szell refuse to treat D and his children?

PROBLEM 4-2: DISCHARGE AND WHAT A SECURED CREDITOR CAN DO

D owes S $20,000. The debt is secured by a lien on D's truck. D files a Chapter 7 petition, claims the truck as exempt, receives a discharge, and retains the truck. Can S still repossess the truck?

PROBLEM 4-3: DISCHARGE AND WHAT A CREDITOR CAN DO TO THIRD PARTIES

1. D owes C $30,000. The debt is guaranteed by G. D files a Chapter 7 petition. C receives $3,000 from D's Chapter 7 trustee. D receives a discharge. Can C sue G for the other $27,000?

2. C has a $1,000,000 malpractice judgment against Dr. D. Dr D files a Chapter 7 petition and receives a discharge. Can C recover from Dr. D's malpractice insurer?

PROBLEM 4-4: DISCHARGE AND WHAT THE DEBTOR CAN DO

1. D owes various credit card issuers $40,000. D files a Chapter 7 petition. D gets a discharge. Her creditors get nothing – a no asset case. Can D still voluntarily pay the card credit debts?

2. D borrows $4,000 from C. In the loan agreement, D agrees to pay the debt even if she later files for bankruptcy and gets a discharge. D later files for bankruptcy and gets a discharge. Is the waiver enforceable? *Cf.* 11 U.S.C. § 727(a)(10); 11 U.S.C. § 524(c); 11 U.S.C. § 524(d).

3. Same facts except that D agrees to pay C the $4,000, after she files for bankruptcy but before she receives a discharge? Why would a debtor make such an agreement? Should such an agreement be enforceable? *Cf.* 11 U.S.C. § 524(c).

See the title of section 525: protection against discriminatory treatment. When you see and apply the language of section 525, you will see that section 525 "promises" more than it "delivers."

---

11 U.S.C. § 525

§ 525. Protection against discriminatory treatment

(a) . . .[A] governmental unit may not deny, revoke, suspend, or refuse to renew a license, permit, charter, franchise, or other similar grant to, condition such a grant to, discriminate with respect to such a grant against, deny employment to, terminate the employment of, or discriminate with respect to employment against, a person that is or has been a debtor under this title. . . or another person with whom such . . . debtor has been associated, solely because such. . . debtor is or has been a debtor under this title . . . has been insolvent before the commencement of the case under this title, or during the case but before the debtor is granted or denied a discharge, or has not paid a debt that is dischargeable in the case under this title . . .

(b) No private employer may terminate the employment of, or discriminate with respect to employment against, an individual who is or has been a debtor under this title. . . ,or an individual associated with such debtor. . ., solely because such debtor—

(1) is or has been a debtor under this title . . . ;

(2) has been insolvent before the commencement of a case under this title or during the case but before the grant or denial of a discharge; or

(3) has not paid a debt that is dischargeable in a case under this title . . .

PROBLEM 4-5: DISCHARGE AND WHAT GOVERNMENTAL ENTITIES CAN DO

D lives in a public housing project, Highland Park Homes ("HPH"). D has missed his last three rent payments. D files for bankruptcy and obtains a discharge. D is paying current rent to HPH but has not made the three rent payments he missed before bankruptcy. Can HPH evict D because of D's having missed the three rent payments? *See* section 525(a).

PROBLEM 4-6: DISCHARGE AND WHAT AN EMPLOYER CAN DO

D files for bankruptcy and receives a discharge. D applies for a job with your client, T Trust Co. ("T") as a cashier. T wants to know if it can tell D that T has decided to hire someone other than D because of D's bankruptcy. *See* section 525(b).

PROBLEM 4-7: "FRESH START" OR "HEAD START"

X Airline and Y Airline both have the same unfavorable labor contracts; both have the same unfavorable airplane leases. X files for bankruptcy and eliminates the unfavorable labor contracts and leases. Did X receive a "fresh start" or the unfair advantage of a "head start"?

C. CLAIMS

In a Chapter 7 case, property of the estate is liquidated and the proceeds are used to pay "claims." 11 U.S.C. § 726. In a case under Chapter 11 or Chapter 13, the plan provides for distributions to "claims." 11 U.S.C. § 1123; 11 U.S.C. § 1322. Similarly section 362 stays actions to recover a "claim." 11 U.S.C. § 362. (The discharge provisions of the Code generally use the word "debt" rather than the word "claim." Section 101(12) defines "debt" as "liability on a claim.").

The term "claim" is defined in section 101(5). Please read 11 U.S.C. § 101(5). Note that a claim can be "unliquidated", "contingent", "unmatured", and "disputed."

---

11 U.S.C. § 101(5)

(5) "claim" means–

(A) right to payment, whether or not such right is reduced to judgment, liquidated, unliquidated, fixed, contingent, matured, unmatured, disputed, undisputed, legal, equitable, secured, or unsecured; or

(B) right to an equitable remedy for breach of performance if such breach gives rise to a right to payment, whether or not such right to an equitable remedy is reduced to judgment, fixed, contingent, matured, unmatured, disputed, undisputed, secured, or unsecured; . . . .

---

1. Types of Claims

PROBLEM 4-8: DISPUTED CLAIMS

P sues D for $100,000. D files an answer denying liability. D later files a bankruptcy petition. Does P have a claim?

PROBLEM 4-9: CONTINGENT CLAIMS

1. C loans D $200,000. G guarantees payment. D files for bankruptcy. Does C have a claim against D? Does G?

2. C gets her car painted by D, Inc. The paint job has a five-year, no crack, no peel warranty. Two years after the paint job, D, Inc. files for bankruptcy.

Does C have a claim? Does it matter if the paint shows no sign of cracking or peeling?

PROBLEM 4-10: UNMATURED CLAIMS

L leases a building to D on a 25-year lease. Two years later, D files a bankruptcy petition. At the time of the bankruptcy filing, D is current on its rent obligations to L. Does L have a claim?

Please re-read section 101(5). Note that a claim must be a "right to payment." Obviously, if D is arrested for driving while intoxicated and ordered by the court to attend drunk driving school, then D's later bankruptcy will not affect D's obligation to attend drunk driving school. While drunk driving school is a legal obligation, there is no "claim" - there is no "right to payment." Similar issues arise with respect to certain types of government regulation – such as antitrust injunctions.

Some of the questions of as to whether there is a "right to payment," and thus a claim that can be affected by the bankruptcy, are much less obvious. The question in the *Kovacs* case, which follows, was sufficiently "non-obvious" that deciding it divided the Supreme Court.

---

2. Right to payment and clean-up obligation

OHIO V. KOVACS
469 U.S. 274 (1985)

JUSTICE WHITE delivered the opinion of the Court.

Petitioner, State of Ohio, obtained an injunction ordering respondent William Kovacs to clean up a hazardous waste site. A receiver was subsequently appointed. Still later, Kovacs filed a petition for bankruptcy. The question before us is whether, in the circumstances present here, Kovacs' obligation under the injunction is a "debt" or "liability on a claim" subject to discharge under the Bankruptcy Code. . . .

Kovacs was the chief executive officer and stockholder of Chem-Dyne Corp., which with other business entities operated an industrial and hazardous waste disposal site in Hamilton, Ohio. In 1976, the State sued Kovacs and the business entities in state court for polluting public waters, maintaining a nuisance, and causing fish kills, all in violation of state environmental laws. In 1979, both in his individual capacity and on behalf of Chem-Dyne, Kovacs signed a stipulation and judgment entry settling the lawsuit. Among other things, the stipulation enjoined the defendants from causing further pollution of the air or public waters, forbade bringing additional industrial wastes onto the site, required the defendants to remove specified wastes from the property, and ordered the payment of $75,000 to compensate the State for injury to wildlife.

Kovacs and the other defendants failed to comply with their obligations under the injunction. The State then obtained the appointment in state court of a receiver, who was directed to take possession of all property and other assets of Kovacs and the corporate defendants and to implement the judgment entry by cleaning up the Chem-Dyne site. The receiver took possession of the site but had not completed his tasks when Kovacs filed a personal bankruptcy petition.

Seeking to develop a basis for requiring part of Kovacs' postbankruptcy income to be applied to the unfinished task of the receivership, the State then filed a motion in state court to discover Kovacs' current income and assets. Kovacs requested that the Bankruptcy Court stay those proceedings, which it did. The State also filed a complaint in the Bankruptcy Court seeking a declaration that Kovacs' obligation under the stipulation and judgment order to clean up the Chem-Dyne site was not dischargeable in bankruptcy because it was not a "debt," a liability on a "claim," within the meaning of the Bankruptcy Code. In addition, the complaint sought an injunction against the bankruptcy trustee to restrain him from pursuing any action to recover assets of Kovacs in the hands of the receiver. The Bankruptcy Court ruled against Ohio, as did the District Court. The Court of Appeals for the sixth circuit affirmed, holding that Ohio essentially sought from Kovacs only a monetary payment and that such a required payment was a liability on a claim that was dischargeable under the bankruptcy statute. We granted certiorari to determine the dischargeability of Kovacs' obligation under the affirmative injunction entered against him.

III

Except for the nine kinds of debts saved from discharge by § 523(a)[23] for re-expenses, a discharge in bankruptcy discharges the debtor from all debts that arose before bankruptcy. § 727(b). It is not claimed here that Kovacs' obligation under the injunction fell within any of the categories of debts excepted from discharge by § 523. Rather, the State submits that the obligation to clean up the Chem-Dyne site is not a debt at all within the meaning of the bankruptcy law.

For bankruptcy purposes, a debt is a liability on a claim. § 101(11).[24] A claim is defined by § 101(4) as follows:

> "(4) 'claim' means-
> "(A) right to payment, whether or not such right is reduced to judgment, liquidated, unliquidated, fixed, contingent, matured, unmatured, disputed, undisputed, legal, equitable, secured, or unsecured; or
> "(B) right to an equitable remedy for breach of performance if such breach gives rise to a right to payment, whether or not such right to an equitable remedy is reduced to judgment, fixed, contingent, matured, unmatured, disputed, undisputed, secured, or unsecured."

The provision at issue here is § 101(4)(B). For the purposes of that section, there is little doubt that the State had the right to an equitable remedy under state law and that the right has been reduced to judgment in the form of an injunction ordering the cleanup. The State argues, however, that the injunction it has secured is not a claim against Kovacs for bankruptcy purposes because (1) Kovacs' default was a breach of the statute, not a breach of an ordinary commercial contract which concededly would give rise to a claim; and (2) Kovacs' breach of his obligation under the injunction did not give rise to a right to payment within the meaning of § 101(4)(B). We are not persuaded by either submission.

There is no indication in the language of the statute that the right to performance cannot be a claim unless it arises from a contractual arrangement. The State resorted to the

[23] [As originally enacted, there were only nine exceptions; present law has expanded the list to nineteen. Eds.]

[24][Editor's note: Section 101(5) was denominated as Section 101(4) at the time of the *Kovacs* decision.]

courts to enforce its environmental laws against Kovacs and secured a negative order to cease polluting, an affirmative order to clean up the site, and an order to pay a sum of money to recompense the State for damage done to the fish population. Each order was one to remedy an alleged breach of Ohio law; and if Kovacs' obligation to pay $75,000 to the State is a debt dischargeable in bankruptcy, which the State freely concedes, it makes little sense to assert that because the cleanup order was entered to remedy a statutory violation, it cannot likewise constitute a claim for bankruptcy purposes. Furthermore, it is apparent that Congress desired a broad definition of a "claim" and knew how to limit the application of a provision to contracts when it desired to do so.

The injunction surely obliged Kovacs to clean up the site. But when he failed to do so, rather than prosecute Kovacs under the environmental laws or bring civil or criminal contempt proceedings, the State secured the appointment of a receiver, who was ordered to take possession of all of Kovacs' nonexempt assets as well as the assets of the corporate defendants and to comply with the injunction entered against Kovacs. As wise as this course may have been, it dispossessed Kovacs, removed his authority over the site, and divested him of assets that might have been used by him to clean up the property. Furthermore, when the bankruptcy trustee sought to recover Kovacs' assets from the receiver, the latter sought an injunction against such action. Although Kovacs had been ordered to "cooperate" with the receiver, he was disabled by the receivership from personally taking charge of and carrying out the removal of wastes from the property. What the receiver wanted from Kovacs after bankruptcy was the money to defray cleanup costs. At oral argument in this Court, the State's counsel conceded that after the receiver was appointed, the only performance sought from Kovacs was the payment of money. Had Kovacs furnished the necessary funds, either before or after bankruptcy, there seems little doubt that the receiver and the State would have been satisfied. On the facts before it, and with the receiver in control of the site, we cannot fault the Court of Appeals for concluding that the cleanup order had been converted into an obligation to pay money, an obligation that was dischargeable in bankruptcy.

IV

It is well to emphasize what we have not decided. First, we do not suggest that Kovacs' discharge will shield him from prosecution for having violated the environmental laws of Ohio or for criminal contempt for not performing his obligations under the injunction prior to bankruptcy. Second, had a fine or monetary penalty for violation of state law been imposed on Kovacs prior to bankruptcy, § 523(a)(7) forecloses any suggestion that his obligation to pay the fine or penalty would be discharged in bankruptcy. Third, we do not address what the legal consequences would have been had Kovacs taken bankruptcy before a receiver had been appointed and a trustee had been designated with the usual duties of a bankruptcy trustee. Fourth, we do not hold that the injunction against bringing further toxic wastes on the premises or against any conduct that will contribute to the pollution of the site or the State's waters is dischargeable in bankruptcy; we here address, as did the Court of Appeals, only the affirmative duty to clean up the site and the duty to pay money to that end. Finally, we do not question that anyone in possession of the site-whether it is Kovacs or another in the event the receivership is liquidated and the trustee abandons the property, or a vendee from the receiver or the bankruptcy trustee-must comply with the environmental laws of the State of Ohio. Plainly, that person or firm may not maintain a nuisance, pollute the waters of the State, or refuse to remove the source of such conditions. As the case comes to us, however, Kovacs has been dispossessed and the State seeks to enforce his cleanup obligation by a money judgment.

The judgment of the Court of Appeals is

Affirmed.

JUSTICE O'CONNOR, concurring.

I join the Court's opinion and agree with its holding that the cleanup order has been reduced to a monetary obligation dischargeable as a "claim" under § 727 of the Bankruptcy Code. I write separately to address the petitioner's concern that the Court's action will impede States in enforcing their environmental laws.

To say that Kovacs' obligation in these circumstances is a claim dischargeable in bankruptcy does not wholly excuse the obligation or leave the State without any recourse against Kovacs' assets to enforce the order. Because "Congress has generally left the determination of property rights in the assets of a bankrupt's estate to state law," the classification of Ohio's interest as either a lien on the property itself, a perfected security interest, or merely an unsecured claim depends on Ohio law. That classification-a question not before us-generally determines the priority of the State's claim to the assets of the estate relative to other creditors. *Cf.* § 545 (trustee may avoid statutory liens only in specified circumstances). Thus, a State may protect its interest in the enforcement of its environmental laws by giving cleanup judgments the status of statutory liens or secured claims.

The Court's holding that the cleanup order was a "claim" within the meaning of § 101(4) also avoids potentially adverse consequences for a State's enforcement of its order when the debtor is a corporation, rather than an individual. In a Chapter 7 proceeding [*sic*] under the Bankruptcy Code, a corporate debtor transfers its property to a trustee for distribution among the creditors who hold cognizable claims, and then generally dissolves under state law. Because the corporation usually ceases to exist, it has no postbankruptcy earnings that could be utilized by the State to fulfill the cleanup order. The State's only recourse in such a situation may well be its "claim" to the prebankruptcy assets.

For both these reasons, the Court's holding today cannot be viewed as hostile to state enforcement of environmental laws.

QUESTIONS ABOUT *KOVACS*

1. *Facts*

1.1 Who is the "debtor" in this case? Is that fact important in this case?

1.2 Are there any other facts that were important to the Court's concluding that Kovacs' obligation to remove wastes from the property is a "claim?

1.3 Who is arguing that Kovacs' obligation to remove wastes from the property is not a "claim" under section 101?

2. *Law*

2.1 What language in section 101 did the majority rely on in concluding that Kovacs' obligation to remove wastes from the property is a "claim"?

2.2 What is the point of Justice O'Connor's point about a State protecting its interest by giving cleanup judgments the status of statutory liens?

D. PROPERTY OF THE ESTATE

1. *Why Is "Property of the Estate" an Important Concept?*

The filing of a bankruptcy petition automatically creates an estate. *See* 11 U.S.C. § 541(a).

In a Chapter 7 case, the bankruptcy trustee is charged with collecting and selling "property of the estate"; the proceeds from the sale of the property of the estate are then distributed to creditors. 11 U.S.C. § 704; 11 U.S.C. § 726. In other words, the loss of property of the estate to the bankruptcy trustee is the primary cost of Chapter 7 bankruptcy to the debtor; the receipt of the proceeds from the sale of property of the estate is the primary benefit creditors derive from a Chapter 7 bankruptcy.

In most Chapter 11 and 12 cases, the debtor will remain in possession of "property of the estate" as "debtor-in-possession." However, the Chapter 11 or Chapter 12 debtor-in-possession's use of the property of the estate will be subject to bankruptcy court supervision. Consider the example of Chapter 11 cases involving business debtors. Successful rehabilitation of a business generally requires continued operation of the business. Continued operation of the business generally requires continued possession of the business property. A debtor will continue to operate its business in Chapter 11 as debtor-in-possession unless a request is made by a "party in interest" for the appointment of a trustee, and the bankruptcy court, after notice and hearing, grants the request. (When a trustee is appointed in a Chapter 11 case, she takes possession of property of the estate.) Even if a trustee is not appointed in a Chapter 11 case, the debtor-in-possession's use and sale of the property of the estate is subject to the supervision of the bankruptcy judge as provided in section 363, which is considered later. 11 U.S.C. § 363.

Similarly, in Chapter 12 cases, the debtor will generally retain possession of the property and continue to operate the farm. As in Chapter 11, a "party in interest" can request that the debtor-in-possession be dispossessed and a trustee takeover. And, again as in Chapter 11, if a trustee is not so installed, the Chapter 12 debtor in possession's use and sale of the property of the estate is subject to the supervision of the bankruptcy court as provided in sections 363 and 1206. *See* 11 U.S.C. § 363; 11 U.S.C. § 1206.

While Chapter 13 contemplates that there will be a trustee in every case, a Chapter 13 trustee does not take possession of property of the estate. A debtor who files for Chapter 13 relief retains possession of his property. *See* 11 U.S.C. § 1306(b). Again, however, the use and sale of "property of the estate" is subject to the supervision of the bankruptcy court as section 363 provides. 11 U.S.C. § 363.

In both Chapter 12 and Chapter 13 cases, the value of the property of the estate determines the minimum amount that must be offered to holders of unsecured claims in the debtor's plan of repayment. 11 U.S.C. § 1225(a)(4); 11 U.S.C. § 1325(a)(4). Chapter 11 imposes a similar requirement as to nonassenting holders of unsecured claims. 11 U.S.C. § 1129(a)(7)(A)(ii).

Finally, a number of general provisions in Chapters 3 and 5 that are applicable in all bankruptcy cases use the phrase "property of the estate." For example, the automatic stay bars a creditor from collecting a claim from property of the estate. 11 U.S.C. § 362(a)(3),(4).

In short, in all bankruptcy cases and in all bankruptcy classes, it is necessary to be able to answer the question what does property of the estate include?

---

2. *What Does "Property of the Estate" Include?*

With only minor exceptions, property of the estate includes all property of the debtor as of the time of the filing of the bankruptcy petition.

The seven numbered paragraphs of section 541 specify what property becomes property of the estate. Paragraph one is by far the most comprehensive and significant. Section 541(a)(1) provides that property of the estate includes "all legal or equitable interests of the debtor in property as of the commencement of the case." 11 U.S.C. § 541(a)(1). This is a very broad statement. Property of the estate thus includes both real property and personal property, both tangible and intangible property, both property in the debtor's possession and property that is held by others in which the debtor has an interest.

The application of section 541(a)(1) requires answering these three questions:

#1. Is the item in question "property" for purposes of section 541(a)(1)?

#2. If so, what is the debtor's interest in that property? [Note that section 541(a)(1) reaches merely the debtor's interest in property rather than simply the debtor's property.]

#3. If so, did the debtor have this interest in the property as of the time of the commencement of the bankruptcy case?

---

11 U.S.C. § 541. Property of the Estate

(a) The commencement of a case under section 301, 302, or 303 of this title creates an estate. Such estate is comprised of all the following property, wherever located and by whomever held:

(1) Except as provided in subsections (b) and (c)(2) of this section, all legal or equitable interests of the debtor in property as of the commencement of the case. . . .

(6) Proceeds, product, offspring, rents, or profits of or from property of the estate, except such as are earnings from services performed by an individual debtor after the commencement of the case.

---

11 U.S.C. § 1306. Property of the Estate

(a) Property of the estate includes, in addition to the property specified in section 541 of this title,

(1) all property of the kind specified in such section that the debtor acquires after the commencement of the case but before the case is closed, dismissed, or converted to a case under Chapter 7, 11, or 12 of this title, whichever occurs first; and

(2) earnings from services performed by the debtor after the commencement of the case but before the case is closed, dismissed, or converted to a case under Chapter 7, 11, or 12 of this title, whichever occurs first.

(b) Except as provided in a confirmed plan or order confirming a plan, the debtor shall remain in possession of all property of the estate.

After reading section 1306, please look at section 1115, which adopts a "section 1306" approach to property of the estate for Chapter 11 individual debtor cases.

PROBLEM 4-11: "AS OF THE COMMENCEMENT OF THE CASE"

1. D is paid every Friday. D files a bankruptcy petition on Friday, April 1. Is the paycheck that she receives on April 8th property of the estate?

2. D owns a rental house. She files a Chapter 7 petition on September 30. Is the October rent on D's house property of the estate?

3. ANC Rental Corp, files a Chapter 11 petition on November 13 and continues to rent cars and operate its business. Are rentals received after November 13 property of the estate?

4. Delta Airlines, Inc. filed its Chapter 11 petition on September 14, 2005. Are its post-September 14, 2005 earnings "property of the estate"? Is "as of the commencement of the case" a significant limitation on property of the estate in a business Chapter 11 case?

5. How do you know what the debtor's interests in property are? *See* 11 U.S.C. § 521.

PROBLEM 4-12: "ALL LEGAL OR EQUITABLE INTERESTS"

T tortuously injures P. P sues T for damages for her personal injuries. While the law suit is pending, P files for bankruptcy. Is the pending law suit "property of the estate"? If so, so what? Would T care? P? P's creditors? P's personal injury attorney?

PROBLEM 4-13: "INTERESTS OF THE DEBTOR IN PROPERTY"

1. D and T each own an undivided 50% interest in Blackacre. D files for bankruptcy. Is Blackacre property of the estate?

2. D is leasing Blackacre for ten years. D files for bankruptcy. Is Blackacre property of the estate?

3. F loaned D $100,000 to buy Blackacre and retained a mortgage on Blackacre as security. D later files for bankruptcy. Is Blackacre property of the estate?

E. SECURED CLAIMS

Under nonbankruptcy law, certain creditors have greater rights than other creditors because they have liens. These liens are property interests in the debtor's property. Perhaps the most familiar example of a lien is a real estate mortgage. Students who have taken a secured credit course are familiar with consensual liens on personal property called security interests. Law professors who teach civil procedure regularly assure us that their students are also familiar with execution liens, garnishment liens, judgment liens, *i.e.*, liens created by judicial proceedings. And, some creditors are granted liens by statute: federal tax liens and mechanics' liens are examples.

When the debtor defaults, these creditors with liens (also known as secured creditors) have all of the rights of other creditors (also known as unsecured creditors). Lien creditors also have additional rights because of their property interests.

Under non-bankruptcy law, a secured creditor has greater rights than unsecured creditors have in both the property subject to its lien and the proceeds from any disposition thereof. More specifically, under nonbankruptcy law, a secured creditor can seize and sell the property subject to its lien and use the proceeds to satisfy its claim.

Somewhat similar rights exist under the Code. First, bankruptcy law does not eliminate the right of a holder of a secured claim to seize and to sell the property subject to its lien. However, bankruptcy law makes such seizure and sale subject to the automatic stay: the creditor with a lien must obtain relief from the automatic stay before seizing its collateral, before selling its collateral.

Second, bankruptcy law, in its own way, recognizes that the holder of a lien enjoys special rights in the property subject to its lien and in the proceeds from any disposition thereof. (Remember the definition of "property of the estate" in section 541: the phrase "interest of the debtor")

---

11 U.S.C. § 506(a)(1)

(a)(1) An allowed claim of a creditor secured by a lien on property in which the estate has an interest, or that is subject to setoff under section 553 of this title, is a secured claim to the extent of the value of such creditor's interest in the estate's interest in such property, or to the extent of the amount subject to setoff, as the case may be, and is an unsecured claim to the extent that the value of such creditor's interest or the amount so subject to setoff is less than the amount of such allowed claim. Such value shall be determined in light of the purpose of the valuation and of the proposed disposition or use of such property, and in conjunction with any hearing on such disposition or use or on a plan affecting such creditor's interest.

---

11 U.S.C. § 506(a)(2)

(a)(2) If the debtor is an individual in a case under Chapter 7 or 13, such value with respect to personal property securing an allowed claim shall be determined

> based on the replacement value of such property as of the date of the filing of the petition without deduction for costs of sale or marketing. With respect to property acquired for personal, family, or household purposes, replacement value shall mean the price a retail merchant would charge for property of that kind considering the age and condition of the property at the time value is determined.

PROBLEM 4-14: FIRST SENTENCE OF SECTION 506(a)(1)

[Note the phrase in the first sentence of section 506(a)(1): "to the extent of the value of such creditor's interest in the estate's interest in such property." Apply that phrase to the following simple (we hope) problems.]

1. D owes M $100,000. D owns Blackacre. M has a first mortgage on Blackacre. Blackacre has a value of $60,000. What is the amount of M's secured claim?

2. D owes M $100,000. D only has a 50% ownership interest in Blackacre. M has a first mortgage on Blackacre. Blackacre has a value of $60,000. What is the amount of M's secured claim?

3. D owes M $100,000. D owns Blackacre. M has a second mortgage on Blackacre. F has a first mortgage for $20,000. Blackacre has a value of $60,000. What is the amount of M's secured claim?

4. D owes M $100,000. M has a mortgage on Blackacre. D files for bankruptcy. M obtains relief from the stay and forecloses on Blackacre. M sells Blackacre for $40,000. Does M still have a secured claim? Does M still have a claim?

5. Review question: In the above problems, is Blackacre "property of the estate"? Yes

---

1. Determination of "value of such creditor's interest" and Rash

The problems above were unrealistic. Too simple. In the problems, we simply "made up" the value of Blackacre. In the "real world", the difficult problem presented by the language of section 506 is determining the value of Blackacre. This is such a hard problem that a divided Supreme Court addressed the question of how to value collateral for purposes of determining the amount of the secured claim in the recent *Rash* decision.

ASSOCIATES COMMERCIAL CORP. V. RASH
520 U.S. 953 (1997)

JUSTICE GINSBURG delivered the opinion of the Court.

We resolve in this case a dispute concerning the proper application of 11 U.S.C. § 506(a) of the Bankruptcy Code when a bankrupt debtor has exercised the "cram down" option for which 11 U.S.C. § 1325(a)(5)(B) provides. Specifically, when a debtor, over a secured creditor's objection, seeks to retain and use the creditor's collateral in a Chapter 13 plan, is the value of the collateral to be determined by (1) what the secured creditor could obtain through foreclosure sale of the property (the "foreclosure-value" standard); (2) what the debtor would have to pay for comparable property (the "replacement-value" standard); or (3) the midpoint between these two measurements? We hold that 506(a) directs application of the replacement-value standard. greater

In 1989, respondent Elray Rash purchased for $73,700 a Kenworth tractor truck for use in his freight-hauling business. Rash made a downpayment on the truck, agreed to pay the seller the remainder in 60 monthly installments, and pledged the truck as collateral on the unpaid balance. The seller assigned the loan, and its lien on the truck, to petitioner Associates Commercial Corporation (ACC).

In March 1992, Elray and Jean Rash filed a joint petition and a repayment plan under Chapter 13 of the Bankruptcy Code (Code), 11 U.S.C.§§1301-1330. At the time of the bankruptcy filing, the balance owed to ACC on the truck loan was $41,171. Because it held a valid lien on the truck, ACC was listed in the bankruptcy petition as a creditor holding a secured claim. Under the Code, ACC's claim for the balance owed on the truck was secured only to the extent of the value of the collateral; its claim over and above the value of the truck was unsecured. See 11 U.S.C. § 506(a).

To qualify for confirmation under Chapter 13, the Rashes' plan had to satisfy the requirements set forth in 11 U.S.C. § 1325(a) of the Code. The Rashes' treatment of ACC's secured claim, in particular, is governed by subsection (a)(5).Under this provision, a plan's proposed treatment of secured claims can be confirmed if one of three conditions is satisfied: The secured creditor accepts the plan, see 11 U.S.C. § 1325(a)(5)(A) ; the debtor surrenders the property securing the claim to the creditor, see 1325(a)(5)(C); or the debtor invokes the so-called "cram down" power, see 1325(a)(5)(B). Under the cram down option, the debtor is permitted to keep the property over the objection of the creditor; the creditor retains the lien securing the claim, see 1325(a)(5)(B)(i), and the debtor is required to provide the creditor with payments, over the life of the plan, that will total the present value of the allowed secured claim, i.e., the present value of the collateral, see 1325(a)(5)(B)(ii). The value of the allowed secured claim is governed by § 506(a) of the Code.

The Rashes' Chapter 13 plan invoked the cram down power. It proposed that the Rashes retain the truck for use in the freight-hauling business and pay ACC, over 58 months, an amount equal to the present value of the truck. That value, the Rashes' petition alleged, was $28,500. ACC objected to the plan and asked the Bankruptcy Court to lift the automatic stay so ACC could repossess the truck. ACC also filed a proof of claim alleging that its claim was fully secured in the amount of $41,171. The Rashes filed an objection to ACC's claim. The Bankruptcy Court held an evidentiary hearing to resolve the dispute over the truck's value. At the hearing, ACC and the Rashes urged different valuation benchmarks. ACC maintained that the proper valuation was the price the Rashes would have to pay to purchase a like vehicle, an amount ACC's expert estimated to be $41,000. The Rashes, however, maintained that the proper valuation was the net amount ACC would realize upon foreclosure and sale of the collateral, an amount their expert estimated to be $31,875. The Bankruptcy Court agreed with the Rashes and fixed the amount of ACC's secured claim at $31,875; that sum, the court found, was the net amount ACC would realize if it exercised its right to repossess and sell the truck. The Bankruptcy Court thereafter approved the plan, and the United States District Court for the Eastern District of Texas affirmed. A panel of the Court of Appeals for the Fifth Circuit reversed.

On rehearing en banc, however, the Fifth Circuit affirmed the District Court, holding that ACC's allowed secured claim was limited to $31,875, the net foreclosure value of the truck. . . .

The Code provision central to the resolution of this case is 506(a), which states:

> "An allowed claim of a creditor secured by a lien on property in which the estate has an interest ... is a secured claim to the extent of the value of such creditor's interest in the estate's interest in such property, ... and is an unsecured claim to the extent that the value of such creditor's interest ... is less than the amount of such allowed claim. Such value shall be determined in light of the purpose of the valuation and of the proposed disposition or use of such property...." 11 U.S.C. § 506(a).

Over ACC's objection, the Rashes' repayment plan proposed, pursuant to 1325(a)(5)(B), continued use of the property in question, i.e., the truck, in the debtor's trade or business. In such a "cram down" case, we hold, the value of the property (and thus the amount of the secured claim under 506(a)) is the price a willing buyer in the debtor's trade, business, or situation would pay to obtain like property from a willing seller. Rejecting this replacement-value standard, and selecting instead the typically lower foreclosure-value standard, the Fifth Circuit trained its attention on the first sentence of 506(a). In particular, the Fifth Circuit relied on these first sentence words: A claim is secured "to the extent of the value of such creditor's interest in the estate's interest in such property." The Fifth Circuit read this phrase to instruct that the "starting point for the valuation [is] what the creditor could realize if it sold the estate's interest in the property according to the security agreement," namely, through "repossess[ing] and sell [ing] the collateral."

We do not find in the 506(a) first sentence words--"the creditor's interest in the estate's interest in such property"--the foreclosure-value meaning advanced by the Fifth Circuit. Even read in isolation, the phrase imparts no valuation standard: A direction simply to consider the "value of such creditor's interest" does not expressly reveal how that interest is to be valued.

Reading the first sentence of 506(a) as a whole, we are satisfied that the phrase the Fifth Circuit considered key is not an instruction to equate a "creditor's interest" with the net value a creditor could realize through a foreclosure sale. The first sentence, in its entirety, tells us that a secured creditor's claim is to be divided into secured and unsecured portions, with the secured portion of the claim limited to the value of the collateral. To separate the secured from the unsecured portion of a claim, a court must compare the creditor's claim to the value of "such property," i.e., the collateral. That comparison is sometimes complicated. A debtor may own only a part interest in the property pledged as collateral, in which case the court will be required to ascertain the "estate's interest" in the collateral. Or, a creditor may hold a junior or subordinate lien, which would require the court to ascertain the creditor's interest in the collateral. The 506(a) phrase referring to the "creditor's interest in the estate's interest in such property" thus recognizes that a court may encounter, and in such instances must evaluate, limited or partial interests in collateral. The full first sentence of 506(a), in short, tells a court what it must evaluate, but it does not say more; it is not enlightening on how to value collateral.

The second sentence of 506(a) does speak to the how question. "Such value," that sentence provides, "shall be determined in light of the purpose of the valuation and of the proposed disposition or use of such property." 11 U.S.C. § 506(a) . By deriving a foreclosure-value standard from 506(a)'s first sentence, the Fifth Circuit rendered inconsequential the sentence that expressly addresses how "value shall be determined." As we comprehend 506(a), the "proposed disposition or use" of the collateral is of paramount importance to the valuation question. If a secured creditor does not accept a debtor's Chapter 13 plan, the debtor has two options for handling allowed secured claims: surrender the collateral to the creditor, see § 1325(a)(5)(C); or, under the cram down option, keep the collateral over the creditor's objection and provide the creditor, over the life of the plan, with the equivalent of the present value of the collateral, see 1325(a)(5)(B). The "disposition or use" of the collateral thus turns on the alternative the debtor chooses--in one case the collateral will be surrendered to the creditor, and in the other, the collateral will be retained and used by the debtor. Applying a foreclosure-value standard when the cram down option is invoked attributes no significance to the different consequences of the debtor's choice to surrender the property or retain it. A replacement-value standard, on the other hand, distinguishes retention from surrender and renders meaningful the key words "disposition or use."

Tying valuation to the actual "disposition or use" of the property points away from a foreclosure-value standard when a Chapter 13 debtor, invoking cram down power, retains and uses the property. Under that option, foreclosure is averted by the debtor's choice and over the creditor's objection. From the creditor's perspective as well as the debtor's, surrender and retention are not equivalent acts. When a debtor surrenders the property, a creditor obtains it immediately, and is free to sell it and reinvest the proceeds. We recall here that ACC sought that very advantage.

If a debtor keeps the property and continues to use it, the creditor obtains at once neither the property nor its value and is exposed to double risks: The debtor may again default and the property may deteriorate from extended use. Adjustments in the interest rate and secured creditor demands for more "adequate protection," 11 U.S.C. § 361 , do not fully offset these risks.

Of prime significance, the replacement-value standard accurately gauges the debtor's "use" of the property. It values "the creditor's interest in the collateral in light of the proposed [repayment plan] reality: no foreclosure sale and economic benefit for the debtor derived from the collateral equal to ... its [replacement] value." The debtor in this case elected to use the collateral to generate an income stream. That actual use, rather than a foreclosure sale that will not take place, is the proper guide under a prescription hinged to the property's "disposition or use."

In sum, under § 506(a), the value of property retained because the debtor has exercised the § 1325(a)(5)(B) "cram down" option is the cost the debtor would incur to obtain a like asset for the same "proposed ... use."[6]

---

[6]Our recognition that the replacement-value standard, not the foreclosure-value standard, governs in cram down cases leaves to bankruptcy courts, as triers of fact, identification of the best way of ascertaining replacement value on the basis of the evidence presented. Whether replacement value is the equivalent of retail value, wholesale value, or some other value will depend on the type of debtor and the nature of the property. We note, however, that replacement value, in this context, should not include certain items. For example, where the proper measure of the replacement value of a vehicle is its retail value, an adjustment to that value may be necessary: A creditor should not receive portions

For the foregoing reasons, the judgment of the Court of Appeals is reversed, and the case is remanded for further proceedings consistent with this opinion. It is so ordered.

---

2. *Questions about Rash*

1. What fact was most important to the Court's decision to look to the replacement value standard?

2. Did the Court base its decision on language in the Code? If so, what words?

3. Do you think that *Rash* affected lenders' making car loans? Debtors' filing for Chapter 13 relief? Courts' approving Chapter 13 plans? Bankruptcy courts' approving Chapter 11 plans?

4. Section 506(a)(2) was added by the 2005 amendments. Why did your professor ask you to read both section 506(a)(2) and *Rash*? Is *Rash* of any practical significance after October 17, 2005?

PROBLEM 4-15: *RASH* AND ISSUES IN A BUSINESS CASE

D Furniture Stores, Inc. (D) is in Chapter 11. S Bank (S) has a first mortgage on D's building. D owes S $3,200,000. D's Chapter 11 plan provides for D to continue operating as a furniture store in the same building. How should the court determine the amount of S's secured claim?

---

of the retail price, if any, that reflect the value of items the debtor does not receive when he retains his vehicle, items such as warranties, inventory storage, and reconditioning. Nor should the creditor gain from modifications to the property--e.g., the addition of accessories to a vehicle--to which a creditor's lien would not extend under state law.

F. AUTOMATIC STAY

1. *Overview*

After the filing of a bankruptcy petition, a debtor usually needs immediate protection from the collection efforts of creditors. If the petition is a voluntary Chapter 7, the bankruptcy trustee needs time to collect the "property of the estate" and make pro rata distributions to creditors. If the petition is a voluntary Chapter 11 or Chapter 12, the debtor needs time to prepare a plan. And, if the petition is an involuntary Chapter 7 or Chapter 11, the debtor needs time to controvert the petition.

Accordingly, the filing of a voluntary petition under Chapter 7, Chapter 11, Chapter 12 or Chapter 13, or the filing of an involuntary petition under Chapter 7 or Chapter 11 automatically "stays," *i.e.*, restrains, creditors from taking further action against the debtor, the property of the debtor, or the property of the estate to collect their claims or enforce their liens. 11 U.S.C. § 362.

---

11 U.S.C. § 362(a)

(a) Except as provided in subsection (b) of this section, a petition filed under section 301, 302, or 303 of this title, . . . operates as a stay, applicable to all entities, of—

(1) the commencement or continuation, including the issuance or employment of process, of a judicial, administrative, or other action or proceeding against the debtor that was or could have been commenced before the commencement of the case under this title, or to recover a claim against the debtor that arose before the commencement of the case under this title;

(2) the enforcement, against the debtor or against property of the estate, of a judgment obtained before the commencement of the case under this title;

> (3) any act to obtain possession of property of the estate or of property from the estate or to exercise control over property of the estate;
>
> (4) any act to create, perfect, or enforce any lien against property of the estate;
>
> (5) any act to create, perfect, or enforce against property of the debtor any lien to the extent that such lien secures a claim that arose before the commencement of the case under this title;
>
> (6) any act to collect, assess, or recover a claim against the debtor that arose before the commencement of the case under this title;
>
> (7) the setoff of any debt owing to the debtor that arose before the commencement of the case under this title against any claim against the debtor; and

---

With respect to Section 362, there are five questions that lawyers (and law students) are asked:

(1) When does the automatic stay become effective?

(2) What is covered by the automatic stay?

(3) When does the automatic stay end?

(4) How can a creditor obtain relief from the stay?

(5) What are the consequences of violating the stay?

2. *Time Stay Arises*

The automatic stay is triggered by the filing of a bankruptcy petition. No court action at all is needed for the stay to be created. The filing itself "operates as a stay."

Note that the stay dates from the time of the filing, not from the time that a creditor receives notice of or learns of the bankruptcy. If D files a voluntary bankruptcy petition on April 5, the stay becomes effective April 5. If D's creditors file an involuntary bankruptcy petition on April 5, the stay becomes effective on April 5. The stay dates from April 5 even if creditors do not learn of the bankruptcy until much later.

---

3. *Scope of the Stay: A First View*

Paragraph (a) of section 362 defines the scope of the automatic stay by listing all of the acts and actions that are stayed by the commencement of a bankruptcy case. It is comprehensive and includes virtually all creditor collection activity. Creditors commonly summarize the scope of section 362(a) in terms similar to the following: "If something is worth doing, you can't do it because it will be stayed by section 362(a)."

While paragraph (a) of section 362 indicates what is stayed, paragraph (b) lists actions that are not stayed, i.e., exceptions to the automatic stay. For example, section 362(b)(2) (a)(iv) provides a limited exception for "domestic support obligations.[7] Notwithstanding bankruptcy and the automatic stay, such claims can be collected from property that is not property of the estate.

Most of the section 362(b) exceptions to stay are narrowly drawn. In other words, most of the automatic stay exceptions in section 362(b) apply in relatively few bankruptcy cases.

There is an important limitation on the scope of section 362 that is not dealt with in paragraph (b) of section 362. The automatic stay of section 362(a) only covers the debtor, property of the debtor, and property of the estate. It does not protect third parties. Assume, for

---

[7]The definition of "domestic support obligations" in section 101 is almost a full page long.

example, that D borrows $30,000 from C and G guarantees repayment. If D files for bankruptcy, section 362(a) will stay C from attempting to collect from D. Section 362(a) will not, however, protect G.

While section 362 does not protect third parties such as guarantor G, section 1301 might. When a debtor files for relief under Chapter 13, section 1301 expands the protection of the automatic stay to certain third parties such as Momma who guarantees payment of the note on Bubba's pickup truck.

---

4. *Termination of the Stay*

Remember that the automatic stay begins when the bankruptcy petition is filed and generally bars a creditor from taking any action to collect its debt from the debtor or the debtor's property.

Section 362(c) describes situations in which the automatic stay ends automatically. Section 362(c)(1) provides that the automatic stay ends as to particular property when the property ceases to be property of the estate. Assume, for example, that M has a mortgage on D Corp.'s office building. D Corp. Files a bankruptcy petition. M is stayed from foreclosing on its mortgage. The bankruptcy trustee then sells the building to X. M is no longer stayed from foreclosing its lien.

Under section 362(c)(2), the automatic stay ends when the bankruptcy case is closed or dismissed or the debtor who is an individual receives a discharge. Remember that the typical Chapter 7 is completed in a matter of months, but Chapter 11 cases can take years to complete.

The 2005 legislation added grounds for automatic termination of the automatic stay based on the debtor's recent bankruptcy history. Section 362(c)(3) is set out below in "understandable" part:

11 U.S.C. § 362(c)(3)

> (c) Except as provided in subsections (d),(e), (f) and (h) of this section—
>
> . . .
>
> (3) if a single or joint case is filed by or against debtor who is an individual in a case under chapter 7, 11, or 13, and if a single or joint case of the debtor was pending within the preceding 1-year period but was dismissed, other than a case refiled under a chapter other than chapter 7 after dismissal under section 707(b)—
>
> (A) the stay under subsection (a) with respect to any action taken with respect to a debt or property securing such debt or with respect to any lease shall terminate with respect to the debtor on the 30th day after the filing of the later case;

The remainder of new section 362(c)(3) establishes a "good faith" exception to this automatic termination of the bankruptcy stay.

PROBLEM 4-16: A END OF STAY FOR INDIVIDUAL WHO DID NOT STAY IN BANKRUPTCY

D files a Chapter 13 petition on November 25, 2005, the day before M is scheduled to foreclose on D's property. A month later, D files a motion to dismiss her Chapter 13 petition which the court grants.

Shortly thereafter, the requisite number of D's creditors file an involuntary bankruptcy petition against her pursuant to section 303. Advise M. See also sections 362(d)(4)(B), 109(g) and 362(b)(21).

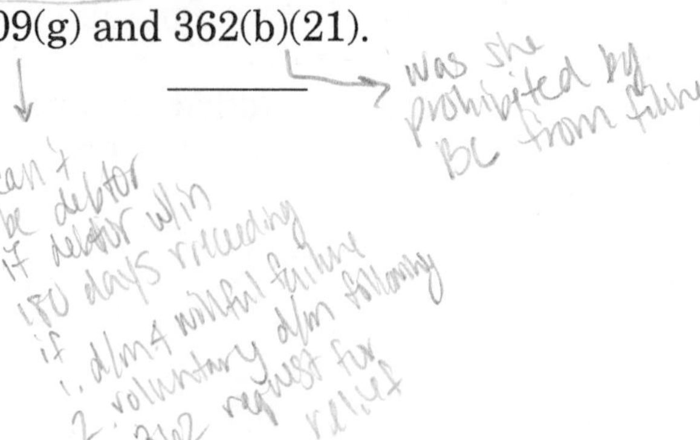

5. *Relief from the Stay*

Creditors in a Chapter 11 case or a Chapter 12 case often would have to wait several years for an automatic stay to terminate automatically. Is there any affirmative action that a creditor can take to obtain earlier relief from the stay?

A creditor can file a motion requesting relief from the automatic stay, Bankruptcy Rule 4001. The bankruptcy court can order the end of the automatic stay or place conditions on continuation of the stay. Paragraphs (d) through (g) of section 362 deal with requests for relief from the automatic stay. We look at relief from stay in more detail later.

---

6. *Consequences of Violating the Stay*

There are two major consequences of violating the stay. First, the conduct has no legal effect as against the debtor and bankruptcy estate. Courts disagree as to whether actions in violation of the stay are "void", or merely "voidable." Second, "[a]n individual injured by any willful violation of a stay provided by this section shall recover actual damages, including costs and attorneys' fees, and, in appropriate circumstances, may recover punitive damages." 11 U.S.C. § 362(h). Courts disagree as to whether debtors who are not individuals can also recover actual or punitive damages because of a stay violation.

---

7. *Scope of the Stay: A Closer View*

PROBLEM 4-17: COLLECTION OF PREPETITION JUDGMENT

On January 15, D borrows $10,000 from C. On February 22, D defaults. On June 6, C files a collection action. On August 8, C obtains a default judgment. On September 9, D files a bankruptcy petition. What is the effect of the automatic stay on the pending collection action?

PROBLEM 4-18: PENDING LITIGATION

P brings a civil antitrust action against D Corp. After the second week of what is projected to be a seven week trial, D Corp. files for bankruptcy. What is the effect of the automatic stay?

PROBLEM 4-19: LITIGATION OF POSTPETITION DEBT

On April 5, D files a bankruptcy petition. On June 1, D negligently injures X. Does the automatic stay prevent X from commencing an action in state court against D? Does the automatic stay prevent X from enforcing a judgment entered in such a state court action?

PROBLEM 4-20: LIEN ENFORCEMENT

When D defaulted on her debt, C foreclosed its mortgage on D's building. C's foreclosure sale is scheduled for Thursday afternoon. If D files for bankruptcy on Thursday morning, will the foreclosure sale be stayed?

PROBLEM 4-21: INFORMAL COLLECTION EFFORTS

On April 10, 2000, D filed a voluntary petition for protection under Chapter 7 of the Code. D attended a meeting of creditors on May 8, 2000. Following the meeting, American General Finance's representative stopped her in the courthouse's hallway, repeatedly asking her why she was not going to pay the debt she owed American General Finance. Any violation of the automatic stay?

Problem 4-22: Stay and Third Parties

C makes a loan to D. G guarantees D's payment. D later files for bankruptcy. Does the automatic say bar C from suing G?

---

8. Protection of Third Parties and Section 105

11 U.S.C. § 105. Power of court

(a) The court may issue any order, process, or judgment that is necessary or appropriate to carry out the provisions of this title. . . .

SAS Overseas Consultants and Asia Contracting, Ltd. v. Benoit

2000 Westlaw 140611 (E.D. La., Feb. 7, 2000)

ORDER AND REASONS

VANCE, J.

Before the Court is the motion of defendant, Michael M. Benoit, to stay this matter pending the resolution of bankruptcy proceedings filed by Offshore Consultants U.S.A., Ltd. . . .

I. BACKGROUND

On November 4, 1997, plaintiffs, SAS Overseas Consultants and Asia Trading & Contracting, Ltd., filed suit in this Court against Offshore Consultants U.S.A., Ltd. SAS-ATAC sought to recover damages for the purported breach of an Agreement executed on September 12, 1996 between Offshore and SAS-ATAC. Pursuant to the Agreement, SAS-ATAC was to recruit foreign-national workers and arrange for their transportation to the United States.

Offshore was then to employ the foreign-national workers and provide their services to third-party customers in return for compensation. SAS-ATAC and Offshore pledged to divide equally the net profits from the third- party customers. The Agreement also required Offshore to render to SAS-ATAC a contemporaneous accounting for its receipts with respect to each payroll for the foreign workers. In their suit against Offshore, SAS-ATAC argued that Offshore failed to pay after employing these workers. When Offshore filed for relief under Chapter 11 of the Bankruptcy Code after nearly two years of litigation, this Court stayed that action on May 17, 1999.

Two weeks after Offshore filed under Chapter 11, SAS-ATAC filed this suit against Michael M. Benoit, Offshore's president and majority stockholder. The complaint asserts the following theories of liability against Benoit: tortious interference with contract; breach of personal duties owed to SAS-ATAC under LA C.C. article 2315 ; and fraud. SAS-ATAC also claims that Benoit is Offshore's alter ego, which justifies piercing the corporate veil to impose liability on Offshore's shareholders, including Benoit, for Offshore's breach of contract.

II. DISCUSSION

A. Motion to Stay

Benoit requested a stay of this matter pending the outcome of Offshore's bankruptcy proceedings under either the automatic stay provided in Bankruptcy Code section 362 or under Bankruptcy Code section 105. . . . The Court does not reach the applicability of the automatic stay, however, because it finds that the facts here clearly warrant a discretionary stay under section 105(a).

This Court has the inherent power to stay any matter pending before it in the interests of justice and "economy of time and effort for itself, for counsel and for litigants.". To determine whether to grant a discretionary stay of this matter pending the outcome of Offshore's bankruptcy proceedings, the Court will look to the standard used by the bankruptcy courts to resolve this issue.

A bankruptcy court has broader authority under section 105 of the Bankruptcy Code to grant a stay than it does under the automatic stay provisions of section 362, and may use its equitable powers to ensure the orderly resolution of reorganization proceedings. In pertinent part, section 105 allows a bankruptcy court to "issue any order, process, or judgment that is necessary or appropriate to carry out the provisions of this title." 11 U.S.C. § §105(a) .

The Fifth Circuit has held that a court may temporarily enjoin actions against a nondebtor under "unusual circumstances." See In re Zale Corp., 62 F.3d 746 , 761 (5th Cir.1995). Stays under section 105(a) are also subject to the usual rules for the issuance of an injunction under Federal Rule of Civil Procedure 65. Accordingly, the Court must examine whether both "unusual circumstances" and the prerequisites to issuance of an injunction exist so as to stay this litigation against Benoit.

1. "Unusual Circumstances"

As referenced above, this Court may issue a temporary stay of the action against Benoit, a nondebtor, if "unusual circumstances" exist. These circumstances include 1) when the nondebtor and the debtor enjoy such an identity of interests that the suit against the nondebtor is essentially a suit against the debtor, and 2) when the third-party action will have an adverse impact on the debtor's ability to accomplish reorganization. In re Zale Corp., 62 F.3d 761 .

The test is disjunctive and an injunction may be warranted under either set of circumstances. Here, the suit against Benoit is clearly a suit against Offshore for breach of the Agreement. SAS-ATAC filed this action against Offshore's president and controlling shareholder less than two weeks after this Court stayed the action against Offshore as a result of its bankruptcy filing. Although SAS-ATAC has recast their allegations against Benoit personally, they ultimately seek to pierce the corporate veil and to hold Benoit liable for breach of a contract by Offshore. Additionally, the rights and liabilities of SAS-ATAC under the Agreement with Offshore will necessarily have to be determined before SAS-ATAC can prevail on their claims against Benoit.

Furthermore, permitting this action to continue will have an adverse impact on Offshore's ability to accomplish reorganization. Offshore has the right to have the bankruptcy court adjudicate claims to its corporate assets, including the Agreement in this case. Nothing in the record indicates that Offshore misused the bankruptcy process or that it is not entitled to the normal considerations of a debtor in bankruptcy.

Proceeding with this action would divert Offshore's president and controlling shareholder from assisting in his company's reorganization efforts. Moreover, the suit against Benoit, if successful, might prejudice Offshore's future defense against identical claims based upon identical facts. For the foregoing reasons, the Court finds that this case meets the "unusual circumstances" identified by In re Zale Corp., and the Court may therefore temporarily stay the proceedings against the nondebtor, Benoit, provided the prerequisites for issuance of a preliminary injunction are met.

2. Merits of Injunctive Relief

The four prerequisites to issuance of a preliminary injunction are: (1) a substantial likelihood of success on the merits; (2) a substantial threat of irreparable injury if the injunction is not granted; (3) that the threatened injury to the movant outweighs the threatened harm an injunction may cause the party opposing the motion; and (4) that the granting of the injunction will not disserve the public interest. The Fifth Circuit employs a sliding scale when analyzing the degree of "success on the merits" a movant must demonstrate to justify injunctive relief. This involves "balancing the hardships associated with the issuance or denial of a preliminary injunction with the degree of likelihood of success on the merits." Moreover, when the other factors weigh in favor of an injunction, a showing of some likelihood of success on the merits will justify temporary injunctive relief. Bankruptcy courts have defined success on the merits as "the probability of a successful plan or reorganization."

At the outset, the Court finds it more likely that Offshore will successfully reorganize if this action is stayed and Benoit is permitted to give his full attention to developing and implementing a viable plan of reorganization. The Court now examines the potential harms to the debtor, creditor and the public to determine if this showing of success on the merits is sufficient.

When assessing the nature of irreparable harm in a proceeding against a nondebtor, as is the case here, the Court focuses on whether the debtor will suffer irreparable harm if the proceedings against the nondebtor go forward. Bankruptcy courts have repeatedly found irreparable harm warranting a stay under section 105(a) when actions brought against nondebtor officers and principals would distract them from the debtor's daily business affairs and divert resources from the debtor's reorganization efforts. As discussed above, the Court finds that Offshore's reorganization efforts would be seriously impaired if its president and controlling shareholder were forced to defend himself in ancillary proceedings in this Court. Additionally, because the rights and liabilities of Offshore and SAS-ATAC under the Agreement will also be addressed by the bankruptcy court, proceeding with the Benoit case could produce inconsistent results on the same issues. SAS-ATAC have also directed discovery at Benoit, much of which involves records of Offshore. The privileges applicable to these materials are Offshore's, and such discovery may force Offshore to intercede to protect its interests. Based on all of these facts, the Court concludes that the reorganization efforts of the debtor, Offshore, will suffer irreparable harm if this action is not stayed.

Furthermore, there is no evidence that SAS-ATAC will suffer any harm if this litigation is stayed. SAS-ATAC is a creditor in the bankruptcy proceeding by virtue of the Agreement with Offshore. The bankruptcy court will determine the rights and liabilities of the parties under that Agreement. The resolution of those issues are central to this case. The Court also notes that no discovery has been conducted to date. A temporary stay will not prejudice SAS- ATAC's ability to proceed against Benoit in this Court but merely delays the litigation temporarily.

Finally, it is clear that the public interest will be served by promoting Offshore's successful reorganization.

After reviewing all of the foregoing considerations, the Court finds that Benoit has satisfied all of the elements necessary for the Court to issue a stay of SAS-ATAC's action against him. The facts of this case demonstrate that continuation of this litigation would adversely effect the debtor's estate and interfere with the debtor's ability to formulate and implement a plan of reorganization. The Court notes that granting a stay here also comports with the general policies underlying the Bankruptcy Code. In particular, a stay of this litigation will give the debtor and its control persons the breathing room necessary to reorganize its finances. For the foregoing reasons, the Court hereby grants Benoit's motion to stay this litigation pending the outcome of the bankruptcy proceedings involving Offshore Consultants U.S.A., Ltd.

The Court finds that Benoit has satisfied all of the elements necessary for the Court to issue a stay of SAS-ATAC's action against him. The facts of this case demonstrate that continuation of this litigation would adversely effect the debtor's estate and interfere with the debtor's ability to formulate and implement a plan of reorganization. The Court

> notes that granting a stay here also comports with the general policies underlying the Bankruptcy Code. In particular, a stay of this litigation will give the debtor and its control persons the breathing room necessary to reorganize its finances. For the foregoing reasons, the Court hereby grants Benoit's motion to stay this litigation pending the outcome of the bankruptcy proceedings involving Offshore Consultants U.S.A., Ltd.

QUESTIONS ABOUT *BENOIT*

1. In which court did SAS file its law suits? In which court did Benoit file his motion for relief?

2. What did Judge Vance mean by her statement "this Court stayed that action . . ."?

3. Did Judge Vance rely on section 105 in deciding to "issue a stay"? What is the statutory basis for the "unusual circumstances" test?

PROBLEM 4-23: ARGUING FOR BANKRUPTCY COURT'S PROTECTION OF PERSON WHO IS NOT A PARTY IN THE BANKRUPTCY CASE

Your client, D, Inc. has filed a Chapter 11 petition. D, Inc.'s debt to C is guaranteed by G, who is the CEO and principal stockholder of D, Inc. C has sued G in state court on the guarantee. G has "asked" you to do something about this. What, if anything, can you do? Can you represent G? Can D, Inc's attorney ask the bankruptcy court to protect G? What are the reasons that a bankruptcy court might protect a person who is not a party in the bankruptcy case?

---

9. *Protection of Third Parties in Chapter 13 and Section 1301*

11 U.S.C. § 1301. STAY OF ACTION AGAINST CODEBTOR

(a) Except as provided in subsections (b) and (c) of this section, after the order for relief under this chapter, a creditor may not act, or commence or continue any civil action, to collect all or any part of a consumer debt of the debtor from any individual that is liable on such debt with the debtor, or that secured such debt, unless--

. . .

(c) On request of a party in interest and after notice and a hearing, the court shall grant relief from the stay provided by subsection (a) of this section with respect to a creditor, to the extent that--

. . .

(2) the plan filed by the debtor proposes not to pay such claim; . . .

PROBLEM 4-24: CODEBTOR STAY IN CHAPTER 13

Doug Deen (D) owes Southeastern Bank (B) $3,000 on an unsecured loan when he files a Chapter 13 petition. His father, Robert Deen (R), had guaranteed payment. D's Chapter 13 plan proposes to pay B $50 a month for 60 months. Advise S as to its rights, if any, against R.

---

10. *Relief From Stay*

11 U.S.C. § 362(d)(1) AND (2)

(d) On request of a party in interest and after notice and a hearing, the court shall grant relief from the stay provided under subsection (a) of this section, such as by terminating, annulling, modifying, or conditioning such stay--

(1) for cause, including the lack of adequate protection of an interest in property of such party in interest'

(2) with respect to a stay of an act against property under subsection (a) of this section, if - -

(A) the debtor does not have an equity in such property; and

(B) such property is not necessary to an effective reorganization; . . . .

BANKR. R. 4001. RELIEF FROM AUTOMATIC STAY

(a) Relief from stay; . . .

(1) Motion

A motion for relief from an automatic stay provided by the Code . . . shall be made in accordance with Rule 9014 . . .

PROBLEM 4-25: CAUSE FOR RELIEF FROM STAY

P files a civil suit against D and D's insurer for injuries from an automobile accident. D files a bankruptcy petition the day that closing arguments are scheduled in that civil suit. Is P's civil suit subject to the automatic stay? Can P obtain relief from the automatic stay? If so, what relief?

PROBLEM 4-26: PRE-BANKRUPTCY LOAN RESTRUCTURING AGREEMENTS AS CAUSE FOR RELIEF FROM STAY

D owns and operates a tavern. S has a mortgage on the tavern building. When D defaults on the mortgage payments, D and S change, the mortgage loan terms, reducing the amount of monthly payments and the interest rate. Their new mortgage agreement provides that if D files for bankruptcy, S's concessions in the loan restructuring are "cause" for relief from stay so that S can foreclose on its mortgage.

D files for bankruptcy. S files a motion for relief from stay under section 362(d)(1) so that it can foreclose. Should the court grant S such relief from the stay? Will other holders of claims in D's bankruptcy be adversely affected by the court's grant of relief from stay to S? Should that be relevant?

PROBLEM 4-27: "EFFECTIVE REORGANIZATION"

Your client, C, has a mortgage on the buildings of Community Hospital, Inc. (D) to secure a $19,000,000 debt. D has just filed a Chapter 11 petition. What do you have to prove in order to obtain relief from stay under section 362(d)(2) and how do you prove it?

G. ADEQUATE PROTECTION OF AN INTEREST IN PROPERTY

The lack of "adequate protection" of an interest in property is an important section 362 concept, a ground for relief from stay under section 362(d)(1). "Adequate protection" is a basic bankruptcy concept, an important part of several Code provisions.

Section 361 describes adequate protection. 11 U.S.C. § 361. Understanding "adequate protection" is critical to understanding what happens to holders of secured claims during the course of a bankruptcy case. And the course of many Chapter 11 and 13 cases is longer than this course in bankruptcy.

Recalling the nature of a lien and recalling some of the stuff that you learned in constitutional law is critical to understanding "adequate protection." A creditor with a lien or a right of setoff has not only a right to payment but also an interest in property of the debtor securing that right to payment.

The Fifth Amendment protects interests in property: Federal law cannot deprive a person of her interest in property without due process or without just compensation. Congress's exercise of its bankruptcy powers under Article I, section 8, clause 4 of the Constitution is subject to this Fifth Amendment prohibition on taking property. In general, the Fifth Amendment requires that the value of the creditor's collateral be maintained during the course of the bankruptcy case or that the creditor be compensated for any decline in the value of its collateral.

---

11 U.S.C. § 361. ADEQUATE PROTECTION

When adequate protection is required under section 362, 363, or 364 of this title of an interest of an entity in property, such adequate protection may be provided by--

(1) requiring the trustee to make a cash payment or periodic cash payments to such entity, to the extent that the stay under section 362 of this title, use, sale, or lease under section 363 of this title, or any grant of a lien under section 364 of this title results in a decrease in the value of such entity's interest in such property;

(2) providing to such entity an additional or replacement lien to the extent that such stay, use, sale, lease, or grant results in a decrease in the value of such entity's interest in such property; or

(3) granting such other relief, other than entitling such entity to compensation allowable under section 503(b)(1) of this title as an administrative expense, as will result in the realization by such entity of the indubitable equivalent of such entity's interest in such property.

PROBLEM 4-28: WHAT IS ADEQUATELY PROTECTED?

D owes C $100,000. C has a lien on D's equipment worth $40,000. What right of C qualifies for adequate protection: C's contract right to be paid $100,000 or C's property rights in equipment worth $40,000? Who cares?

PROBLEM 4-29: DEPRECIATION PAYMENTS AS ADEQUATE PROTECTION

D owes C $200,000. C has a lien on equipment worth $180,000. If the value of this equipment is declining by $5,000 a month, can D provide adequate protection by paying C $5,000 a month? Should any such "adequate protection" payments reduce the amount of C's claim?

PROBLEM 4-30: EQUITY CUSHION AS ADEQUATE PROTECTION

D owes C $200,000. C has a lien on equipment worth $250,000. The value of the equipment is declining by $5,000 a month. Under these facts, can C's "equity cushion" be the adequate protection? What if D's debt to C is based on a note which provides for interest of 10% per year? Reconsider your answer after considering section 506(b) in *Timbers* below.

UNITED SAVINGS ASSOCIATION OF TEXAS V. TIMBERS OF INWOOD FOREST ASSOCIATES, LTD.

484 U.S. 365 (1988)

Justice SCALIA delivered the opinion of the Court.

Petitioner United Savings Association of Texas seeks review of an en banc decision of the United States Court of Appeals for the Fifth Circuit, holding that petitioner was not entitled to receive from respondent debtor, which is undergoing reorganization in bankruptcy, monthly payments for the use value of the loan collateral which the bankruptcy stay prevented it from possessing.

. . .

On June 29, 1982, respondent Timbers of Inwood Forest Associates, Ltd., executed a note in the principal amount of $4,100,000. Petitioner is the holder of the note as well as of a security interest created the same day in an apartment project owned by respondent in Houston, Texas. The security interest included an assignment of rents from the project. On March 4, 1985, respondent filed a voluntary petition in the United States Bankruptcy Court for the Southern District of Texas.

On March 18, 1985, petitioner moved for relief from the automatic stay of enforcement of liens triggered by the petition, see 11 U.S.C. §§ 362(a), on the ground that there was lack of "adequate protection" of its interest within the meaning of 11 U.S.C.§§ 362(d)(1) . At a hearing before the Bankruptcy Court, it was established that respondent owed petitioner $4,366,388.77, and evidence was presented that the value of the collateral was somewhere between $2,650,000 and $4,250,000. The collateral was appreciating in value, but only very slightly. It was therefore undisputed that petitioner was an undersecured creditor.

Respondent had agreed to pay petitioner the postpetition rents from the apartment project (covered by the after-acquired property clause in the security agreement), minus operating expenses. Petitioner contended, however, that it was entitled to additional compensation. The Bankruptcy Court agreed and on April 19, 1985, it conditioned continuance of the stay on monthly payments by respondent, at the market rate of 12% per annum, on the estimated amount realizable on foreclosure, $4,250,000--commencing six months after the filing of the bankruptcy petition, to reflect the normal foreclosure delays.. The court held that the postpetition rents could be applied to these payments. . . . The District Court affirmed but the Fifth Circuit en banc reversed.

We granted certiorari to determine whether undersecured creditors are entitled to compensation under 11 U.S.C. §§ 362(d)(1) for the delay caused by the automatic stay in foreclosing on their collateral.

II

When a bankruptcy petition is filed, § 362(a) of the Bankruptcy Code provides an automatic stay of, among other things, actions taken to realize the value of collateral given by the debtor. The provision of the Code central to the decision of this case is § 362(d), which reads as follows:

> "On request of a party in interest and after notice and a hearing, the court shall grant relief from the stay provided under subsection (a) of this section, such as by terminating, annulling, modifying, or conditioning such stay--
>
> "(1) for cause, including the lack of adequate protection of an interest in property of such party in interest; or
>
> "(2) with respect to a stay of an act against property under subsection (a) of this section, if--
>
> > "(A) the debtor does not have an equity in such property; and
> >
> > "(B) such property is not necessary to an effective reorganization."

The phrase "adequate protection" in paragraph (1) of the foregoing provision is given further content by § 361 of the Code, which reads in relevant part as follows:

> "When adequate protection is required under section 362 ... of this title of an interest of an entity in property, such adequate protection may be provided by--
>
> "(1) requiring the trustee to make a cash payment or periodic cash payments to such entity, to the extent that the stay under section 362 of this title ... results in a decrease in the value of such entity's interest in such property;
>
> "(2) providing to such entity an additional or replacement lien to the extent that such stay ... results in a decrease in the value of such entity's interest in such property; or
>
> "(3) granting such other relief ... as will result in the realization by such entity of the indubitable equivalent of such entity's interest in such property."

It is common ground that the "interest in property" referred to by §362(d)(1) includes the right of a secured creditor to have the security applied in payment of the debt upon completion of the reorganization; and that that interest is not adequately protected if the security is depreciating during the term of the stay. Thus, it is agreed that if the apartment project in this case had been declining in value petitioner would have been entitled, under § 362(d)(1), to cash payments or additional security in the amount of the decline, as § 361 describes. The crux of the present dispute is that petitioner asserts, and respondent denies, that the phrase "interest in property" also includes the secured party's right (suspended by the stay) to take immediate possession of the defaulted security, and apply it in payment of the debt. If that right is embraced by the term, it is obviously not adequately protected unless the secured party is reimbursed for the use of the proceeds he is deprived of during the term of the stay.

. . .

Section 506 of the Code defines the amount of the secured creditor's allowed secured claim and the conditions of his receiving postpetition interest. In relevant part it reads as follows:

> "(a) An allowed claim of a creditor secured by a lien on property in which the estate has an interest ... is a secured claim to the extent of the value of such creditor's interest in the estate's interest in such property, ... and is an unsecured claim to the extent that the value of such creditor's interest ... is less than the amount of such allowed claim....
>
> "(b) To the extent that an allowed secured claim is secured by property the value of which ... is greater than the amount of such claim, there shall be allowed to the holder of such claim, interest on such claim, and any reasonable fees, costs, or charges provided for under the agreement under which such claim arose."

In subsection (a) of this provision the creditor's "interest in property" obviously means his security interest without taking account of his right to immediate possession of the collateral on default. If the latter were included, the "value of such creditor's interest" would increase, and the proportions of the claim that are secured and unsecured would alter, as the stay continues--since the value of the entitlement to use the collateral from the date of bankruptcy would rise with the passage of time. No one suggests this was intended. The phrase "value of such creditor's interest" in § 506(a) means "the value of the collateral." We think the phrase "value of such entity's interest" in § 361(1) and (2), when applied to secured creditors, means the same.

Even more important for our purposes than § 506's use of terminology is its substantive effect of denying undersecured creditors postpetition interest on their claims--just as it denies over secured creditors postpetition interest to the extent that such interest, when added to the principal amount of the claim, will exceed the value of the collateral. Section 506(b) provides that "[t]o the extent that an allowed secured claim is secured by property the value of which ... is greater than the amount of such claim, there shall be allowed to the holder of such claim, interest on such claim." (Emphasis added.) Since this provision permits postpetition interest to be paid only out of the "security cushion," the undersecured creditor, who has no such cushion, falls within the general rule disallowing postpetition interest. See 11 U.S.C. §§ 502(b)(2) . If the Code had meant to give the undersecured creditor, who is thus denied interest on his claim, interest on the value of his collateral, surely this is where that disposition would have been set forth, and not obscured within the "adequate protection" provision of § 362(d)(1). Instead of the intricate phraseology set forth above, § 506(b) would simply have said that the secured creditor is entitled to interest "on his allowed claim, or on the value of the property securing his allowed claim, whichever is lesser." Petitioner's interpretation of § 362(d)(1) must be regarded as contradicting the carefully drawn disposition of § 506(b).

. . .

The Fifth Circuit correctly held that the undersecured petitioner is not entitled to interest on its collateral during the stay to assure adequate protection under 11 U.S.C. §§ 362(d)(1). . . . Accordingly, the judgment of the Fifth Circuit is

Affirmed.

QUESTIONS AFTER *TIMBERS*

1. What facts are important in *Timbers*? Is it important that the value of the collateral is less than the amount of the debt? Is it important that the note secured by the mortgage provided for interest? Is it important that "the collateral was appreciating in value"?

2. What provision of the Code was important in *Timbers*? Do you agree with Justice Scalia's statement that "the provision of the Code central to the decision of this case is section 362(d)"? With his statement "Even more important for our

purposes than section 506's use of terminology is its substantive effect of denying undersecured creditors postpetition interest on their claims? Is the Petitioner asking for interest on its $4,366,338.77 claim?

PROBLEM 4-31: RELIEF FROM STAY AFTER *TIMBERS*

D owes your client C $3,000,000. The debt is secured by a first mortgage on Blackacre. D files a Chapter 11 petition. You have credible appraisals of Blackacre ranging from $2,500,000 to $3,500,000. What, if any action, do you recommend to C? What, if any, additional facts would be helpful to you in deciding what to recommend to C?

PROBLEM 4-32: RELIEF FROM STAY UNDER SECTION 362(d)(2) REVIEW

D, a Chapter 11 debtor owns a ski resort – Colorado Outdoor Lodge (COL). D owes F $4,000,000; F has a first mortgage on COL that provides for 5% interest. D also owes S $2,000,000; S has a second mortgage on COL that provides for 10% interest. The value of COL is no more than $5,500,000 and not less than $5,000,000.

1 If S moved for relief from stay under section 362(d)(2), could S satisfy the burden of proof under section 362(d)(2)(A)?

2. If F moved for relief from stay under section 362(d)(2), could F satisfy the burden of proof under section 362(d)(2)(A)?

3. Would F be allowed interest on its secured claim under section 506(b)?

4. Would S be allowed interest on its secured claim under section 506(b)?

5. To the extent that either F or S would be allowed interest on its claim under section 506(b), does section 506(b) require that the interest be paid monthly? Quarterly? Annually?

6. If F was allowed interest on its secured claim and that interest accrued, what is S's strongest argument for relief from stay under section 362(d)(1)?

Section 362(d)(3) which is applicable only in "single asset real estate" cases is considered infra in new materials of one single asset real estate cases. And, new section 362(d)(4), added in 2005, is excerpted below. Please compare section 362(d)(4), excerpted below, with section 362(c)(3), considered earlier.

---

11 U.S.C. § 362(d)(4)

(4) with respect to a stay of an act against real property under subsection (a), by a creditor whose claim is secured by an interest in such real property, if the court finds that the filing of the petition was part of a scheme to delay, hinder, and defraud creditors that involved either—

(A) transfer of all or part ownership of, or other interest in, such real property without the consent of the secured creditor or court approval; or

(B) multiple bankruptcy filings affecting such real property.

. . .

PROBLEM 4-33: A RELIEF FROM REAL PROPERTY FORECLOSURE DELAY

M has a mortgage on the building in which D operates a restaurant. D defaults and M proceeds to foreclose under state law. A day before the foreclosure sale, D files a Chapter 11 petition. Advise M.

Part III

Issues That Regularly Arise in Bankruptcy Cases Under Every Chapter of the Code

Unit 5

Issues That Regularly Occur in Bankruptcy Cases Under Any Chapter: Eligibility And Dismissal

Recall that a bankruptcy case begins with the filing of a bankruptcy petition, and that more than 99% of the bankruptcy petitions are filed by the person seeking bankruptcy relief, by the "debtor." These bankruptcy cases are called "voluntary cases" by both section 301 and the lawyers and judges who work with section 301. Less than one per cent of the bankruptcy petitions are filed by creditors against a debtor. These bankruptcy cases are called "involuntary cases" by both section 303 and the lawyers and judges who work with section 303. Both sections 301 and 303 provide that the case is "commenced" when a petition is filed by or against an eligible debtor.

A. Overview of Eligibility

Eligibility issues can involve challenges to (1) the person who is the debtor, (2) the petition that commences the case, and (3) the particulars that triggered the filing.

1. Person

First, the person. Section 109 focuses on the person who is the debtor and provides the statutory basis for answering the questions:

(i) is this person eligible to be a debtor in a case under the Code?

(ii) is this person eligible to be a debtor in a bankruptcy case under this particular chapter of the Code?

---

11 U.S.C. § 109. WHO MAY BE A DEBTOR?

(a) Notwithstanding any other provision of this section, only a person that resides or has a domicile, a place of business, or property in the United States, or a municipality, may be a debtor under this title.

(b) A person may be a debtor under chapter 7 of this title only if such person is not--

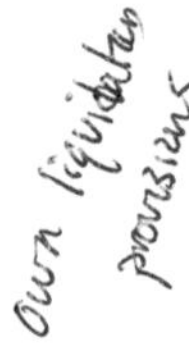

(1) a railroad;

(2) a domestic insurance company, bank, savings bank, cooperative bank, savings and loan association, building and loan association, . . .

(d) Only a person that may be a debtor under chapter 7 . . . may be a debtor under chapter 11 of this title.

(e) Only an individual with regular income that owes, on the date of the filing of the petition, noncontingent, liquidated, unsecured debts of less than $[307,675] and noncontingent, liquidated, secured debts of less than $[922,975],[8] may be a debtor under chapter 13 of this title.

(g) Notwithstanding any other provision of this section, no individual or family farmer may be a debtor under this title who has been a debtor in a case pending under this title at any time in the preceding 180 days if--

(1) the case was dismissed by the court for willful failure of the debtor to abide by orders of the court, or to appear before the court in proper prosecution of the case; or

---

[8]We've put these numbers in brackets because Congress, through Section 104 of the Code, had indicated that they should be adjusted every three years to match inflations. These numbers are the numbers current as of April 1, 2004.

(2) the debtor requested and obtained the voluntary dismissal of the case following the filing of a request for relief from the automatic stay provided by section 362 of this title.

(h)(1) Subject to paragraphs (2) and (3), and notwithstanding any other provision of this section, an individual may not be a debtor under this title unless such individual has, during the 180-day period preceding the date of filing of the petition by such individual, received from an approved nonprofit budget and credit counseling agency described in section 111(a) an individual or group briefing (including a briefing conducted by telephone or on the Internet) that outlined the opportunities for available credit counseling and assisted such individual in performing a related budget analysis. . . .

(3)(A) Subject to subparagraph (B), the requirements of paragraph (1) shall not apply with respect to a debtor who submits to the court a certification that—

(i) describes exigent circumstances that merit a waiver of the requirements of paragraph (1);
(ii) states that the debtor requested credit counseling services from an approved nonprofit budget and credit counseling agency, but was unable to obtain the services referred to in paragraph (1) during the 5-day period beginning on the date on which the debtor made that request; and
(iii) is satisfactory to the court.

PROBLEM 5-1: AN INDIVIDUAL

D, a self-employed long distance trucker, tells you that the finance company is "fixing to" repossess his tractor and trailer and that he is "maxed out" on his credit cards, and has doctor bills, and... If D files for bankruptcy, the automatic stay will provide at least short-term protection. What, if anything, do you have to do **before** filing a bankruptcy petition for D? See section 109(h); see also sections 342(b); 521(a), 526, 527, 528.

[We will reconsider what you have to do **before** filing a bankruptcy petition for an individual when we consider Chapter 7 eligibility and dismissal. We will also later consider what an attorney has to do **after** filing a bankruptcy petition for an individual.]

PROBLEM 5-2: PARTNERSHIP, AND OTHER ENTITIES

Can King & Spalding, a law partnership with hundreds of partners, file for bankruptcy? If so, who at King & Spalding makes the decision to file for bankruptcy? *Cf.* 11 U.S.C. § 302(b)(3).

PROBLEM 5-3: SOLE PROPRIETORSHIP

Epstein owns a bar (Eppie's Bar), a barbershop (Eppie's Barbershop) and a barbecue stand (Eppie's Barbecue). Epstein is the only owner; he keeps a separate set of books for each business. Eppie's Bar and Eppie's Barbecue are profitable. Epstein is losing money on the barbershop. Can Epstein file a bankruptcy petition for Eppie's Barbershop?

PROBLEM 5-4: RECIDIVISM

Epstein filed for bankruptcy in 2004. Can Epstein file for bankruptcy again in 2006? *Cf.* section 727(a)(8). Can his creditors file a bankruptcy petition against him in 2006? *Cf.* section 303.

PROBLEM 5-5: INSOLVENCY

EMNP, Inc. has "liquidity" problems. While the market value of its assets exceeds its debt, its current earnings are not sufficient to satisfy its current payment obligations. Is EMNP, Inc. eligible for bankruptcy? *Cf.* section 101(32).

PROBLEM 5-6: PREBANKRUPTCY AGREEMENT

In 2003, C makes a real estate loan to L Limited Partnership (L). In 2004, L is in default. C and L agree to restructure the loan. The workout agreement reduces the interest rate, extends the payment period, forgives default interest that had accrued, eliminates some of the financial covenants and operational restrictions, and provides that L will not file a bankruptcy petition for three years. L files a bankruptcy petition in 2005. What result?

PROBLEM 5-7: BANKRUPTCY-PROOF ENTITY

In 2003, C makes a secured loan to L Limited Partnership (L). The loan agreement provides inter alia that:

(i) GP, Inc., shall be the sole general partner of L,

(ii) GP, Inc., shall at all times have an "independent director", acceptable to C;

(iii) L cannot file a bankruptcy petition without the affirmative vote of all of the directors of GP, Inc;

(iv) L cannot incur more than $10,000 of debt other than its debt to C without the affirmative vote of all of the directors of GP, Inc.

In 2005, L is in default, and C commences foreclosure procedures. What can L do?

---

2. *Petition*

Second, the petition. Section 301 requires that a "petition" be used by a debtor to commence a "voluntary" case, and section 303 requires that a "petition" be used by creditors to file an involuntary case. Form 1 (titled "Voluntary Petition") contains the information required by section 301 for a "voluntary" case, and Form 5 (titled "Involuntary Petition") contains the allegations required by section 303 for an involuntary case.

Section 301 provides that the filing of the petition both commences the bankruptcy case and operates as "an order for relief", i.e., no formal adjudication of bankruptcy is necessary. While section 303 provides that the filing of the creditors' petition commences the case, a bankruptcy petition filed by creditors does not operate as an order for relief. Adjudication of bankruptcy is necessary. The debtor has a right to file an answer. If the debtor does not timely answer the petition or if the debtor answers the petition and the creditors are able to establish one of the grounds for relief in section 303(h) - generally 'the debtor is generally not paying his debts as such debts become due", then the bankruptcy court shall enter an order for relief.

PROBLEM 5-8: INVOLUNTARY PETITIONS

On January 15, Markell, Nickles and Perris file a bankruptcy petition against Epstein. Epstein files a pro se answer: "I don't know anything about bankruptcy, but I don't belong here." What are the litigable issues?

---

3. *Particulars*

Third, the particulars that triggered the filing. The facts and other particulars that triggered the filing can become important in motions to dismiss a voluntary or involuntary petition. While section 305 is entitled "Abstention," it empowers the bankruptcy judge to dismiss a petition "if the interests of creditors and the debtor would be better served by such dismissal." More important, each chapter has its own dismissal section, setting out the standards for the dismissal of a case under that chapter.

B. CHAPTER 7 ELIGIBILITY AND DISMISSAL

11 U.S.C. § 109(b)– [CHAPTER 7 ELIGIBILITY]

(b) A person may be a debtor under Chapter 7 of this title only if such person is not - -

(1) a railroad;

(2) a domestic insurance company, bank, savings bank, cooperative bank, savings and loan association, building and loan association, homestead association . . .

DISMISSAL OF CHAPTER 7 CASE

11 U.S.C. § 707(a)

(a) The court may dismiss a case under this chapter only after notice and a hearing and only for cause, including - -

(1) unreasonable delay by the debtor that is prejudicial to creditors;

(2) nonpayment of any fees or charges required under Chapter 123 of Title 28; and

(3) failure of the debtor in a voluntary case to file, within fifteen days or such additional time as the court may allow after the filing of the petition commencing such case, the information required by paragraph (1) of section 521, but only on a motion by the United States trustee.

PROBLEM 5-9: CHAPTER 7 DEBTOR'S MOTION TO DISMISS

On September 28, Jessica McCullough files a Chapter 7 bankruptcy petition. On October 11, her minor son, while driving an automobile titled and owned by her, was involved in an accident post-petition (the "Accident"), and, because of her interest in the vehicle involved in the Accident, she may have potential liability as a result of the Accident. On November 17, McCullough files a motion to dismiss her present Chapter 7 case without prejudice to her ability to file another Chapter 7 proceeding within 180 days of the dismissal of the present Chapter 7.

On December 8, responses objecting to the motion to dismiss were filed by the Assistant United States Trustee and by the Chapter 7 Trustee in the case. Both objections essentially state that dismissal of the case may serve as a prejudice to the creditors in the case as the value of any assets which may be recovered and distributed to creditors in this case will be depleted by the amount of the additional claims of creditors which the Debtor wishes to add in a subsequent Chapter 7 case. On December 14, McCullough filed responses to both of the above mentioned objections, stating that "dismissal will not prejudice any creditors because the Chapter 7 case is a no asset case." How should the court rule?

One of the most noted 2005 changes in bankruptcy law is the section 707(b) grounds for "involuntary" dismissal (or, with the debtor's consent, conversion to Chapter 13) of a Chapter 7 case filed by an individual debtor with primarily consumer debts. Previously, the section 707(b) standard for such involuntary dismissal was "substantial abuse." Now the section 707(b) standard is merely "abuse."

"Abuse" for purposes of section 707(b) can be established in one of two ways:

1. A rebuttable presumption of "abuse" that arises under a means test is set out in great detail in section 707(b)(2); or

2. Whatever else the bankruptcy judge finds to be "abuse" under section 707(b)(1), including "bad faith" in filing the petition, section 707(b)(3)(A) and the "totality of the circumstances" of the debtor's financial situation, section 707(b)(3)(B).

The second alternative is easy to learn in law school, harder to do in practice. The first alternative is hard to do anywhere and will probably be done more in law schools than in law offices.

The first alternative, the means test presumption of section 707(b)(2), will not be applicable in most Chapter 7 cases. Section 707(b)(7) provides that the means test presumption is totally inapplicable to debtors whose income is below the state median, and the income of the overwhelming majority of Chapter 7 debtors is below the state median.

Nonetheless, the following is a "short guide" to the new means test prepared by Judge Markell.

In concept, the means test is simple. The theory is that if debtors can afford to pay their creditors something between $6,000 and $10,000 over five years, they should. But as with the rest of life, the devil is in the details, and Congress has packed a lot of details into the means test.

Before delving into the details, however, you must understand that the means test calculation is a blend of actual facts and presumed (or dictated) facts. Approach the means test by first telling yourself that important terms such as income and expenses will likely be determined not by reference to what debtors actually earn and spend, but by an artificial construct designed to remove discretion.

With a high level of generality, the means test means:

- First, take the debtor's "current monthly income," a new defined term.

- Second, subtract from that monthly income the following:

  - Living expenses, as calculated under certain IRS collection standards; and

  - Projected payments on actual secured debt; and

  - Projected payments on actual priority debt, such as tax debt or domestic support obligations;

  - Other and sundry administrative and special interest expenses, such as up to 10% of all projected payments under a chapter 13 plan, and most charitable contributions.

- Third, multiply the difference by 60. There is presumed to be abuse (and the debtor "flunks" the means test) if the product so obtained is greater than:

  - the greater of $6,000, or 25% of the debtor's nonpriority unsecured debt; or

  - $10,000

While the above "means" test may have to be calculated in every case,[9] it doesn't directly apply if the debtor's annualized "current monthly income" is below

[9] 11 U.S.C. § 707(b)(2)(C). Section 1232 of the 2005 Act amends 28 U.S.C. § 2075 to add the following: "The bankruptcy rules promulgated under this section shall prescribe a form for the statement required under section 707(b)(2)(C) of Title 11 and may provide general rules on the content of such statement."

the median for households of the same size as the debtor's in the state in which the debtor lives.

C. GETTING STARTED ON THE MEANS TEST — THE DEFINITIONS

The calculations above use two key definitions in the Bankruptcy Code and one concept borrowed from the IRS that you must master before attempting to calculate whether any particular debtor "passes" the means test:

(1) current monthly income, 11 U.S.C. § 101(10A),

(2) median family income, 11 U.S.C. § 101(39A), and

(3) the IRS's financial collection standards.

---

11 U.S.C. § 101(10A) — "CURRENT MONTHLY INCOME"

The new definition of "current monthly income" states:

(10A) The term "current monthly income" —

(A) means the average monthly income from all sources that the debtor receives (or in a joint case the debtor and the debtor's spouse receive) without regard to whether such income is taxable income, derived during the 6-month period ending on —

(i) the last day of the calendar month immediately preceding the date of the commencement of the case if the debtor files the schedule of current income required by section 521(a)(1)(B)(ii); or

(ii) the date on which current income is determined by the court for purposes of this title if the debtor does not file the schedule of current income required by section 52a(a)(1)(B)(ii); and

(B) includes any amount paid by any entity other than the debtor (or in a joint case the debtor and the debtor's spouse), on a regular basis for the household expenses of the debtor or the debtor's dependents (and in a joint case the debtor's spouse if not otherwise a dependent), but excludes benefits received under the Social Security Act, payments to victims of war crimes or crimes against humanity on account of their status as victims of such crimes, and payments to victims of international terrorism (as defined in section 2331 of title 18) or domestic terrorism (as defined in section 2331 of title 18) on account of their status as victims of such terrorism.

Note that this is a highly artificial definition. It calls for the average income during the six month's preceding bankruptcy, with no room for adjustment due to a cessation of income (layoff) or an increase (raise). There is much room for counseling the debtor here; for some debtors, calculation of "current monthly income" can be affected by the time of filing.

And, note that the income does not have to be taxable (the most benign example might be income from municipal bonds). Also note that social security benefits do not count.

---

11 U.S.C. § 101(39A) — "MEDIAN FAMILY INCOME"

(39A) The term "median family income" means for any year —

(A) the median family income both calculated and reported by the Bureau of the Census in the then most recent year; and

(B) if not so calculated and reported in the then current year, adjusted annually after such most recent year until the next year in which median family income is both calculated and reported by the Bureau of the Census, to reflect the percentage change in the Consumer Price Index for All Urban Consumers during the period of years occurring after such most recent year and before such current year;

The applicable "median family income" is critical. If twelve times the debtor's "current monthly income" is less than the applicable "median family income," no party can file a presumptive abuse motion under new Section 707(b)(2), and only the judge or the United States Trustee's Office can file a motion for dismissal under the general "abuse" standard of Section 707(b)(1).

Where do you find information about "median family income?" You could go to the Census Bureau's website and try to work through the numbers (and the adjustments for inflation), but the Office of the United States Trustee has posted what it believes the relevant number are at its website, www.usdoj.gov/ust. What does that mean? Here are the tables for three states, Connecticut, Nevada and West Virginia:

State	1 Earner	2 People	3 People	4 People
Connecticut	$52,530	$61,374	$76,506	$88,276
Nevada	$37,243	$50,387	$51,645	$52,750
West Virginia	$32,599	$35,183	$45,629	$51,795

If the household is larger than four people, the chart says to add $6,300 for each person above four.

So if the annualized current monthly income for a family of three in Connecticut is below $76,506, the presumptive means test of Section 707(b)(2) will not apply. The same numbers for Nevada and West Virginia would be $51,645 and $45,629, respectively.

D. IRS' FINANCIAL COLLECTION STANDARDS

Recall that the third critical component of the section 707(b)(2) means test is the IRS' Financial Collection Standards.[10] These are estimated living expenses for various categories of items, originally developed by the IRS to determine whether they would take an offer in compromise from a taxpayer. One needs to know their origins in part to understand that they are designed to be frugal.

These guidelines provide for national standards for five necessary expenses: food, housekeeping supplies, apparel and services, personal care products and services, and miscellaneous.[11] There are then local standards for two additional categories: housing and utilities, and transportation. The housing and utilities standards are derived fro Census and BLS data, and are provided by state down to the county level. The transportation standards consist of nationwide figures for monthly loan or lease payments referred to as ownership costs, and additional amounts for monthly operating costs broken down by Census Region and Metropolitan Statistical Area (MSA).[12]

---

[10] This information comes from http://www.irs.gov/individuals/article/0,,id=96543,00.html, which is the IRS' website at which they publish and update these numbers. This information can also be obtained from the United States Trustee's website. http://www.usdoj.gov/ust.

[11] All standards except miscellaneous are derived from the Bureau of Labor Statistics (BLS) Consumer Expenditure Survey (CES). The miscellaneous standard has been established by the IRS.

[12] Under these standards, if a taxpayer has a car payment, the allowable ownership cost added to the allowable operating cost equals the allowable transportation expense. If a taxpayer has no car payment, or no car, only the operating costs portion of the transportation standard is used to come up with the allowable transportation expense.

Here are comparisons for three cities for a family of three with a monthly gross income of $4,150 who rent an apartment, and who have one car: Las Vegas, Nevada, Wheeling, West Virginia, and New Haven, Connecticut:

Expenses	Las Vegas	Wheeling	New Haven
Food	$546	$546	$546
Housekeeping	$55	$55	$55
Apparel and Services	$188	$188	$188
Personal Care	$52	$52	$52
Miscellaneous	$161	$161	$161
Housing/Utilities	$1,433	$892	$1,647
Transportation	$880	$717	$773
Totals:	$3,315	$2,611	$3,422

E. Additional Adjustments For The Means Test

To review, a determination of whether a consumer debtor is subject to the means test presumption of section 707(b)(2) depends primarily on whether the "current monthly income" exceeds the expenses as provided by the IRS standards. There are, however, other adjustments that need to be made. For example:

> *Additional Approved Food and Clothing Expenses.* The statute allows, upon a demonstrated showing that it is reasonable and necessary to do so, an upward adjustment of 5% on the food and clothing standards. It also allows

expenses to maintain safety as necessary to protect against "family violence."[13] 11 U.S.C. § 707(b)(2)(A)(ii)(I).

Medical Expenses. The statute also explicitly states that the "deemed" expenses "shall include reasonably necessary health insurance, disability insurance, and health savings account expenses for the debtor, the spouse of the debtor, or the dependents of the debtor." 11 U.S.C. § 707(b)(2)(A)(ii)(I).

Expenses for Care of Family Member. The statute allows additional expenses for the reasonable and necessary costs of taking care of an elderly, chronically ill or disabled household member, but those expenses must have been ongoing before the debtor files. 11 U.S.C. § 707(b)(2)(A)(ii)(II).

Chapter 13 Trustee Expenses. The debtor can also add up to 10% of his or her proposed plan payments under chapter 13 for the chapter 13 trustee's actual administrative expenses. 11 U.S.C. § 707(b)(2)(A)(ii)(III). (These amounts will be determined by schedules published by the Office of the United States Trustee).

Certain Educational Expenses. The debtor may also add up to $1,500 annually for each child under the age of eighteen for reasonable and necessary educational expenses so long as the debtor can justify why such expenses are not already

---

[13] The Code borrows the definition from title 42, "As used in this chapter: (1) The term "family violence" means any act or threatened act of violence, including any forceful detention of an individual, which— (A) results or threatens to result in physical injury; and (B) is committed by a person against another individual (including an elderly person) to whom such person is or was related by blood or marriage or otherwise legally related or with whom such person is or was lawfully residing." 42 U.S.C. § 10408(1).

accounted for in the IRS Standards. 11 U.S.C. § 707(b)(2)(A)(ii)(IV).

Additional Costs Related to Home Energy Consumption. The debtor may also add such reasonable and necessary additional energy costs if actually incurred (think Las Vegas in the summer, or Maine in the winter). 11 U.S.C. § 707(b)(2)(A)(ii)(V).

Secured Debt. The debtor may also add the amount of all secured debt scheduled to be paid during the five years following the filing, and any amounts necessary to keep a car and house, presumably such as any late fees, arrearages and the like. 11 U.S.C. § 707(b)(2)(A)(iii).

Priority Debt. The debtor may also add the amount of all priority debts. 11 U.S.C. § 707(b)(2)(A)(iv).

Charitable Contributions. The 2005 Act did not amend the provisions that allow debtors to continue to make charitable contributions of up to 15% of their gross income.

Other Exceptions. The statute permits variance only in the case of "special circumstances" such as a "serious medical condition" or active duty in the military. Perhaps even a natural disaster, such as the devastation caused in 2005 by Hurricane Katrina. There must be "no reasonable alternative" to the extra expenses, and such expenses must be documented and accompanied by "a detailed explanation of the special circumstances." 11 U.S.C. § 702(b)(2)(B).

There is also, to the extent of actual expenditures, permissible additions for "Other Necessary Expenses" as scheduled by the IRS.[14]

F. Application Of The Means Test

Let's see how the means test would apply to the three families mentioned above. Our assumptions would be that each family has a gross monthly income of $4,150, and has had that level of income for the last six months. Assume also that they each have a rental payment equal to $1,200, a $475 monthly car payment (which is already included in the IRS calculations), and pay $730 in payroll and other taxes a month.

Here's how their various calculations would work out:

	Las Vegas	Wheeling	New Haven
Income	$4,150	$4,150	$4,150
IRS Expenses	$3,315	$2,611	$3,422
Taxes	$730	$730	$730
Means Test—Disposable Income[15]	$105	$809	($2)

Note that the Wheeling, West Virginia debtor's income ($49,800) is above the applicable median income for West

---

[14] The closest match to this would seem to be Section 5.15.1.10 of the Internal Revenue Manual. See http://www.irs.gov/irm/part5/ch14s01.html#d0e121441.

[15] Under the new Code, "disposable income" in a chapter 13 will be actual expenses, unless the debtor's "current monthly income" exceeds the applicable state median income. In the later case, the figure produced by applicable of the factors listed in Section 707(b) will control. *See* 11 U.S.C. § 1325(b)(3).

Virginia three-person households ($45,629), so if that debtor elects to file under chapter 7, he is subject to claim of abuse bought by any creditor, the Office of the United States Trustee or the bankruptcy judge. 11 U.S.C. § 707(b)(1); U.S.C. § 707(b)(2)(A). Moreover, if the debtor elects to file under chapter 13, the disposable income he or she will have to contribute to the plan will be the presumed number of $809. 11 U.S.C. § 1325(b)(3).

Neither the Las Vegas or the New Haven debtor will be subject to an abuse test under the *presumptive* abuse standards since their imputed annual income in each case ($49,800) is less than the respective medians for each state for a three-person family ($51,645 and $76,506, respectively). 11 U.S.C. § 707(b)(7); 11 U.S.C. § 707(b)(2)(A). The Office of the United States Trustee or the judge, however, may still bring a motion that the filing is an abuse. 11 U.S.C. § 707(b)(6). That might succeed, at least in the Las Vegas debtor's case, depending on the debtor's other expenses. Note that as currently presented, the debtor would be able under the IRS standards to fund the minimum $100 per month that constitutes the floor for presumptive abuse under Section 707(b)(2).

Moreover, for both the Las Vegas and the New Haven debtor, any chapter 13 plan will be based upon actual expenses, rather than the IRS standards. 11 U.S.C. § 1325(b)(2).

Finally, note that the Wheeling debtor could have avoided application of the means test by buying a house (secured debt) and transforming rent payments into house payments. Or by simply not working for one month prior to filing, and thus having the imputed "currently monthly income" be $4,150 times 5 ($20,750), divided by 6 or $3,458.33, multiplied by 12, that would make the annual income $41,500, which would be below the median income level ($45,629). That would leave open the possibility of filing for chapter 7, and would allow any chapter 13 plan to use actual, as opposed to IRS, expenses.

PROBLEM 5-10: MEANS TEST QUESTIONS

1. Recall Buzz Markell in Problem 1-2 on page 7. Does section 707(b)(2) affect his bankruptcy options?

2. Recall Gus Epstein in Problem 1-3 on page 8. Does section 707(b)(2) affect his bankruptcy options?

3. X and Y are a gay couple that live together in a state that bans gay marriage. If only X files for bankruptcy, is Y's earnings relevant to determining X's current monthly income? Are the after school and summer earnings of C, X's 16 year old adopted son, relevant in determining X's current monthly income?

4. H is divorced from W. While H lives in a different house from W, H pays W's living expenses and shares custody of their two children with her. If H files for bankruptcy, should his attorney look at the median family income for a 4-person family? Would your answer be different if H and W were separated but not divorced?

5. If the IRS Financial Standards guideline for housing/utilities in the debtor's city is $1,433 a month, but the debtor only spends $1,000 a month, which amount— $1,433 or $1,000— is relevant in section 707(b)(2) calculations? Assume instead that the debtor is spending $2,000 a month on mortgage payments. Now, which amount— $1,433 or $2,000— is relevant in section 707(b)(2) calculations?

6. D is paying $1,000 a month on her educational loans from college and law school. Is that relevant in section 707(b)(2) calculations?

These section 707(b)(2) questions are especially relevant to attorneys who file Chapter 7 bankruptcy petitions for individual debtors because of section 707(b)(4) set out below.

---

11 U.S.C. § 707(b)(4)(A)

The court, on its own initiative or on the motion of a party in interest, in accordance with the procedures described in rule 9011 of the Federal Rules of Bankruptcy Procedure, may order the attorney for the debtor to reimburse the trustee for all reasonable costs in prosecuting a motion filed under section 707(b), including reasonable attorneys' fees, if—

(i) a trustee files a motion for dismissal or conversion under this subsection; and

(ii) the court—

(I) grants such motion; and

(II) finds that the action of the attorney for the debtor in filing a case under this chapter violated rule 9011 of the Federal Rules of Bankruptcy Procedure.

G. CHAPTER 13 ELIGIBILITY AND DISMISSAL

IN RE VAUGHN
276 B.R. 323 (Bankr. N.H. 2002)

MARK W. VAUGHN, Chief Judge.

The Court has before it the Chapter 13 Trustee's ("Trustee's") motion to dismiss or convert to Chapter 7 Russell P. Vaughn's ("Debtor's") bankruptcy case. Based upon the record before the Court and for the reasons set out below, the Court grants Trustee's motion and dismisses the Debtor's case because he does not meet the Chapter 13 eligibility requirements set forth in section 109(e) of the United States Bankruptcy Code (the "Code"). . . .

FACTS

On December 6, 2001, the Debtor filed for bankruptcy under Chapter 13. The Debtor listed unsecured claims totaling $615,313.22, plus two claims with "unknown" value, on Schedule F of his petition. A majority of these claims stem from lawsuits pending in the federal courts of Ohio and Michigan against the Debtor, Numismatic Investments of America, Inc. ("NIA"), the entity to which the Debtor served as a director and officer, and NIA's president (collectively "defendants"). The lawsuit filed by the Heminger Group alleges two counts of RICO and Fraud against the Debtor individually and seeks recovery of non-refunded deposits for rare coins that were never delivered in the amount of $485,780, plus treble damages and costs. The Palenshus lawsuit alleges three counts against the Debtor individually, RICO, Fraud and Conspiracy, and seeks recovery of non-refunded deposits in the amount of $120,000, plus tremble damages and costs. The Hoeschele lawsuit seeks to "pierce the corporate veil" to charge Debtor with fraud and to recover of the purchase price of the coins, plus costs and fees. Unlike the Heminger Group and Palenshus claims against him, the Debtor assigns an unknown value to the Hoeschele claim in Schedule F of his petition. The Debtor contends that all of the unsecured claims against him are contingent, unliquidated, and disputed.

DISCUSSION

Section 109 provides that:

(e) Only an individual with regular income that owes, on the date of the filing of the petition, noncontingent, liquidated, unsecured debts of less than $290,525 and noncontingent, liquidated, secured debts of less than $871,550, or an individual with regular income and such individual's spouse, except a stockbroker or a commodity broker, that owe, on the date of the filing of the petition, noncontingent, liquidated, unsecured debts that aggregate less than $290,525 and noncontingent, liquidated, secured debts of less than $871,550 may be a debtor under chapter 13 of this title.

11 U.S.C. § 109(e). Relevant to the Court's present inquiry, the § 109(e) dollar limits apply to unsecured debts that are noncontingent and liquidated as of the filing date. Id. In his

motion, the Trustee argues that the Debtor's unsecured debt exceeds the $290,525 limit based on the debt amounts listed in the Debtor's schedules. In response, the Debtor filed an objection, arguing that the Trustee erroneously included unliquidated amounts in his § 109(e) Chapter 13 eligibility calculation.

A debt is noncontingent "if all events giving rise to liability occurred prior to the filing of the bankruptcy petition." The Debtor does not dispute that all events giving rise to liability occurred pre-petition and are therefore noncontingent for purposes of § 109(e).

Whether debt is liquidated depends on "'whether it is subject to ready determination and precision in computation of the amount due.' " A debt is subject to a ready determination when only a simple hearing is required, as compared to an extensive, contested evidentiary hearing. Further, if the debt amount is dependent upon a future exercise of discretion by a court and is not restricted by specific criteria, the debt is unliquidated. .

In the present case, the Court does not need any further proceedings to determine the value of a majority of the Debtor's unsecured claims. The Debtor was able to value the claims against him and, since the underlying matter involves a contract dispute, there is a readily determinable figure relating to the value of what was delivered to the plaintiffs in the pending litigation and what they should have received as a result of the bargain struck with the defendants. In other words, the plaintiffs agreed to purchase coins and those plaintiffs did not receive all of their coins and are now collectively alleging violations of RICO, fraud and conspiracy. The difference between the bargain and what was received on that bargain are the amounts listed in the Debtor's schedules.

. . .

Additionally, this Court concludes that " 'the concept of a liquidated debt relates to the amount of liability, not the existence of liability.' " . . . Although the Debtor disputes whether he is liable on his unsecured debts stemming from the Michigan and Ohio law suits, the issue of whether a debtor is liable for a particular debt is separate from whether that debt is liquidated as of the filing date for purposes of § 109(e). See Slack v. Wilshire Ins. Co. (In re Slack), 187 F.3d 1070, 1074-75 (9th Cir.1999) ("Even if a debtor disputes the existence of liability, if the amount of the debt is calculable with certainty, then it is liquidated for the purposes of § 109(e)."); .

> . . . Undisputed is not one of the terms used in the statute and to suggest that it is relevant to the determination of Chapter 13 eligibility would render the distinctions made in § 109(e) meaningless, as almost all Debtors would introduce evidence of the disputed nature of claims against them in order to ensure that their debt amounts remain below the § 109(e) limitations. . . . Accordingly, since the debt amounts listed in the Debtor's schedules are otherwise noncontingent and liquidated, the fact that they are disputed will not alter their applicability to the computation of the Debtor's unsecured debt for § 109(e) eligibility purposes.

The Court finds that the Debtor is ineligible to file under Chapter 13 of the Code because the amount of his unsecured debts exceeds the statutory limits set forth in § 109(e). Accordingly, the Court hereby grants the Trustee's motion and dismisses Debtor's case without prejudice.

PROBLEM 5-11: INCOME

Denny Crane is a partner in the law firm of Crane, Poole & Schmidt. Some years his partnership earnings are as high as $2,000,000. Some years as low as $500,000. Is Denny Crane eligible for Chapter 13?

What do they owe

PROBLEM 5-12: DEBTS

Denny Crane is being sued for malpractice. The complaint seeks damages of $1,000,000. Is Denny Crane eligible for Chapter 13 relief? No

---

PROBLEM 5-13: "CHAPTER 20" CASES

Johnson (Debtor) owed Home State Bank (Bank) $470,000. The debt was secured by mortgages on Debtor's farm. When Debtor defaulted on these notes, the Bank initiated foreclosure proceedings in state court. During the pendency of these proceedings, Debtor filed a petition under Chapter 7 of the Code. Pursuant to 11 U.S.C. § 727, the Bankruptcy Court discharged petitioner from personal liability on his promissory notes to the Bank. Notwithstanding the discharge, the Bank's right to proceed against petitioner in rem survived the Chapter 7 liquidation. [Remember the limited effect of discharge on the rights of a holder of a secured claim, *supra* at 63.]

After the close of the Chapter 7 case, the Bank reinitiated the foreclosure proceedings. Before the foreclosure sale was scheduled to take place, Debtor filed a Chapter 13 petition. Why did Debtor file a Chapter 13 petition instead of another Chapter 7 case petition? Was Debtor eligible to file another bankruptcy petition? Should the court dismiss the petition?

Should the court grant the Bank relief from stay? Reconsider section 362(d)(4)(B) ("filing of the petition was part of a scheme to delay, hinder and defraud creditors that involved. . . multiple bankruptcy filings affecting such real property") [We will later read section 1328(f)(1) on discharge in 13 and learn that Johnson could not get a discharge in his Chapter 13 case. And we will later read section 1328(b)(2) on curing default in 13 and learn that discharge was probably not the reason for Johnson's Chapter filing.]

H. ELIGIBILITY TO BE A CHAPTER 11 DEBTOR

11 U.S.C. § 109(d)

Only a person that may be a debtor under Chapter 7 of this title may be a debtor under Chapter 11 of this title.

PROBLEM 5-14: INDIVIDUAL

Can Epstein, an individual who is not in business (or "bidness") and has only consumer debts, file for Chapter 11 relief?

PROBLEM 5-15: LIQUIDATION, NOT REORGANIZATION

S has a lien on most but not all of D's, Inc.'s assets. D, Inc. is in default on its loan from S. D, Inc. has stopped its business operations and is trying to sell its assets. S commences foreclosure proceedings. Can D, Inc. file a Chapter 11 petition and sell its assets in Chapter 11?

Unit 6

Issues Can Arise In Cases Under Any Chapter: Claims

We have already looked at "claims" in Unit 4 and learned that claims are what get (1) paid by in bankruptcy distributions, (2) discharged after a bankruptcy discharge and (3) stayed during a bankruptcy case. And, we saw the broad definition of "claim" in section 101.

Lawyers generally see issues relating to claims more than once in a bankruptcy case. So, here is our second, closer look at claims.

A. Avoiding or Reducing Claims

1. Disallowance under 11 U.S.C. § 502(b)

In a sense, bankruptcy is a "zero-sum" game. In Chapter 7 cases, creditors are limited to the proceeds from the liquidation of the property of the estate. In Chapter 12 and 13 cases, creditors' recoveries are limited to the debtor's disposable income. In Chapter 11, the creditors are limited to payments as provided in the proposed plan.

The larger the claims that are made against the Chapter 7 liquidation proceeds or the Chapter 11, 12 or 13 plan payments, the smaller the distribution to a particular claim. To mix metaphors, the size of the pie is finite – a claimant gets a bigger share of the pie by reducing the other claims on that pie. And a claimant can reduce the other claims to the bankruptcy pie – win the zero sum game – by successfully objecting to the allowance of other claims.

An unsecured claim must go through the allowance process in order to participate in the bankruptcy distribution. Section 502 governs allowance.

The first step in the allowance process is the filing of a proof of claim. And the first step to understanding the allowance process is to recall how creditors learn about a bankruptcy.

Section 521 requires the debtor to file a "list of creditors." Creditors on the list receive a notice of the bankruptcy pursuant to Rule 2002. The form of notice Form 9, varies with the "form" of the bankruptcy case.

The Bankruptcy Rules and Official Forms prescribe the time for and contents of the filing. In Chapter 11 cases, certain claims listed on the debtor's schedules are deemed filed, section 1111(a).

Once a claim is filed or deemed filed it is automatically deemed allowed unless a "party in interest" objects. We are not making this up– *see* 11 U.S.C. § 502(a); Bankr. R. 3001(f). Grounds for objection to the allowance of a claim are set out in section 502(b), (d), (e), and (k).

The most frequently invoked ground for disallowance of a claim is section 502(b)(1): "The claim is unenforceable . . . under any agreement or applicable law for a reason other than because such claim is contingent or unmatured." In other words, a defense that the debtor would have had to the enforceability of the claim outside of bankruptcy is a defense to the allowance of the claim in bankruptcy. Statute of limitations, statute of frauds, and failure of consideration are examples of such defenses.

Read the last part of section 502(b)("other than because such claim is contingent or unmatured) together with section 502(c). Notice: the fact that a claim is speculative or contingent or that its amount is difficult to ascertain is not a basis for disallowance. In these circumstances, the court can either estimate the amount of the claim or delay distribution and closing of the bankruptcy case until the amount of the claim has been determined.

---

11 U.S.C. § 502(a), (b)

(a) A claim or interest, proof of which is filed under section 501 of this title, is deemed allowed, unless a party in interest, . . ., objects.

(b) [I]f such objection to a claim is made, the court, after notice and a hearing, shall determine the amount of such claim in lawful currency of the United States as of the date of the filing of the petition, and shall allow such claim in such amount, except to the extent that--

(1) such claim is unenforceable against the debtor and property of the debtor, under any agreement or applicable law for a reason other than because such claim is contingent or unmatured;

(2) such claim is for unmatured interest;[16]

(6) if such claim is the claim of a lessor for damages resulting from the termination of a lease of real property, such claim exceeds--

(A) the rent reserved by such lease, without acceleration, for the greater of one year, or 15 percent, not to exceed three years, of the remaining term of such lease, following the earlier of--

---

[16] *But cf.* 11 U.S.C. § 506(b).

(i) the date of the filing of the petition; and

(ii) the date on which such lessor repossessed, or the lessee surrendered, the leased property; plus

(B) any unpaid rent due under such lease, without acceleration, on the earlier of such dates;

(9) proof of such claim is not timely filed, except to the extent tardily filed as permitted . . . under the Federal Rules of Bankruptcy Procedures.

BANKR. R. 3007

An objection to the allowance of a claim shall be in writing and filed. A copy of the objection with notice of the hearing thereon shall be mailed or otherwise delivered to the claimant, the debtor or debtor in possession and the trustee at least 30 days prior to the hearing.

PROBLEM 6-1: UNMATURED INTEREST

D owes C $200,000 on an unsecured basis. The D-C contract provides for interest-only payments of $1,100 a month. D files a Chapter 11 petition on January 15. D's Chapter 11 plan is confirmed later that year, on December 7. Does C have an allowable claim for the interest that accrued between January 15 and December 7?

PROBLEM 6-2: LEASE CLAIM

D rents a building from L in April 2000. The term of the lease is 32 years; the lease terms call for monthly rental payments of $20,000 a month. In April 2003, D files a Chapter 7 bankruptcy petition. At the time of D's bankruptcy filing, D owes L $60,000 in back rent.

What is the amount of L's maximum allowable claim?

What additional information is needed to determine the amount of L's actual allowable claim?

What additional information is needed to determine the amount of the actual payment on L's allowable claim?

What are the consequences of determining that only part of L's claim is allowable?

PROBLEM 6-3: TRADING CLAIMS

D Co. files a Chapter 11 petition. V, one of D Co.'s vendor's has an unsecured claim against D Co. for $600,000 and has filed its proof of claim for $600,000. T has offered to buy V's claim for $50,000. Can V sell its claim? If V sells the claim to T, can other creditors move to disallow all but $50,000 of T's assigned claim?

---

2. *Disallowance of Contingent, Reimbursement, or Contribution Claims Under 11 U.S.C. § 502(e)(1)(B)*

11 U.S.C. § 502(e)(1)(B)

(e)(1) Notwithstanding subsections (a), (b), and (c) of this section and paragraph (2) of this subsection, the court shall disallow any claim for reimbursement or contribution of an entity that is liable with the debtor on or has secured, the claim of a creditor, to the extent that--

. . .

(B) such claim for reimbursement or contribution is contingent as of the time of allowance or disallowance of such claim for reimbursement or contribution.

PROBLEM 6-4: CONTINGENT CONTRIBUTION CLAIM

D has filed a Chapter 11 petition. Your client, Chemical Solvent Corp. (CS) is solvent. CS and D were jointly responsible for chemical releases. CS's experts estimate that it will cost more than $2,500,000 to address the environmental problems caused by these releases. Under the relevant federal environmental laws, CS and D are jointly and severally liable, and each has a right of contribution against the other. Thus far, the Environmental Protection Agency (EPA) has not taken any action against either CS or D. What, if anything, can CS do? What, if anything, should CS do?

Get EPA to declare so not contingent

B. DENIAL OF "CLAIM" STATUS

1. *Review: Comparison of Determination That Obligation Is Not a Claim With Determination That Obligation Is a Claim That Is Not Allowable*

You have just learned about disallowance of a claim under section 502. Disallowance affects bankruptcy distributions. A claim that is disallowed will not receive a distribution from the liquidation of the property of the estate in a Chapter 7 case or from the confirmed plan in a Chapter 11 or Chapter 13 case. Disallowance does not however affect discharge. Even though a claim is disallowed in whole or in part, it will still be subject to any discharge resulting from a Chapter 7 case, Chapter 11 case, Chapter 13 case.

In sum, to a creditor, the disallowance of a claim is a "lose-lose" proposition. The creditor loses in bankruptcy – no distribution on its *disallowed* claim. The creditor loses after bankruptcy – discharge of its disallowed *claim*. A creditor will never make the argument that its own claim should be disallowed.

Earlier, in the *Kovacs* case, the State of Ohio argued (unsuccessfully) that the debtor's obligation under an injunction was not a "claim" as that term is defined in section 101 and so was not discharged. A creditor can "win" by establishing that it does not hold a "claim" as defined in the Code. No claim, no discharge.

In the next case, the senior bankruptcy author (but not his clients) lost by arguing that the people who had not yet fallen out of the sky because the Piper aircraft that they were flying in was negligently designed or manufactured prior to July 1, 1991, had section 101(5) claims in the Piper Aircraft Corporation Chapter 11 bankruptcy case. Shortly after losing this case, he returned to full-time teaching.

---

2. *"Future Claims" And Denial Of "Claim" Status*

IN RE PIPER AIRCRAFT CORPORATE

58 F.3d 1573 (11th Cir. 1995)

BLACK, Circuit Judge:

This is an appeal by David G. Epstein, as the Legal Representative for the Piper future claimants (Future Claimants), from the district court's order of June 6, 1994, affirming the order of the bankruptcy court entered on December 6, 1993. The sole issue on appeal is whether the class of Future Claimants, as defined by the bankruptcy court, holds claims against the estate of Piper Aircraft Corporation (Piper), within the meaning of §101(5) of the Bankruptcy Code. After review of the relevant provisions, policies and goals of the Bankruptcy Code and the applicable case law, we hold that the Future Claimants do not have claims as defined by §101(5) and thus affirm the opinion of the district court.

I. FACTUAL AND PROCEDURAL BACKGROUND

For purposes of this appeal, the relevant facts are as follows. Piper has been manufacturing and distributing general aviation aircraft and spare parts throughout the United States and abroad since 1937. Approximately 50,000 to 60,000 Piper aircraft still are operational in the United States. Although

Piper has been a named defendant in several lawsuits based on its manufacture, design, sale, distribution and support of its aircraft and parts, it has never acknowledged that its products are harmful or defective.[1]

On July 1, 1991, Piper filed a voluntary petition under Chapter 11 of Bankruptcy Code in the United States Bankruptcy Court for the Southern District of Florida. Piper's plan of reorganization contemplated finding a purchaser of substantially all of its assets or obtaining investments from outside sources, with the proceeds of such transactions serving to fund distributions to creditors. On April 8, 1993, Piper and Pilatus Aircraft Limited signed a letter of intent pursuant to which Pilatus would purchase Piper's assets. The letter of intent required Piper to seek the appointment of a legal representative to represent the interests of future claimants by arranging a set-aside of monies generated by the sale to pay off future product liability claims.

On May 19, 1993, the bankruptcy court appointed Appellant Epstein as the legal representative for the Future Claimants. The Court defined the class of Future Claimants to include:

> All persons, whether known or unknown, born or unborn, who may, after the date of confirmation of Piper's Chapter 11 plan of reorganization, assert a claim or claims for personal injury, property damages, wrongful death, damages, contribution and/or indemnification, based in whole or in part upon events occurring or arising after the Confirmation Date, including claims based on the law of product liability, against Piper or its successor arising out of or relating to aircraft or parts manufactured and sold, designed, distributed or supported by Piper prior to the Confirmation Date.

This Order expressly stated that the court was making no finding on whether the Future Claimants could hold claims against Piper under §101(5) of the Code.

On July 12, 1993, Epstein filed a proof of claim on behalf of the Future Claimants in the approximate amount of

---

[1]Piper made a decision in 1987 to self-insure and therefore does not have any product liability insurance covering events or occurrences taking place after that year.

$100,000,000. The claim was based on statistical assumptions regarding the number of persons likely to suffer, after the confirmation of a reorganization plan, personal injury or property damage caused by Piper's pre-confirmation manufacture, sale, design, distribution or support of aircraft and spare parts. The Official Committee of Unsecured Creditors (Official Committee), and later Piper, objected to the claim on the ground that the Future Claimants do not hold §101(5) claims against Piper. After a hearing on the objection, the bankruptcy court agreed that the Future Claimants did not hold §101(5) claims, and, on December 6, 1993, entered an Order Sustaining the Committee's Objection and Disallowing the Legal Representative's Proof of Claim. In a Memorandum Opinion dated January 14, 1994, that court entered final findings of fact and conclusions of law to support its December Order. Epstein, as Legal Representative, then appealed from the bankruptcy court's order. On June 6, 1994, the district court affirmed and accepted the decision of the bankruptcy court. Epstein now appeals from the district court's order, challenging in particular its use of the prepetition relationship test to define the scope of a claim under §101(5).

II. DISCUSSION

The sole issue on appeal, whether any of the Future Claimants hold claims against Piper as defined in §101(5) of the Bankruptcy Code, is one of first impression in this Circuit.

A. Statute

Under the Bankruptcy Code, only parties that hold preconfirmation claims have a legal right to participate in a Chapter 11 bankruptcy case and share in payments pursuant to a Chapter 11 plan. 11 U.S.C.A. §§ 101(10), 501, 502 In order to determine if the Future Claimants have such a right to participate, we first must address the statutory definition of the term "claim." The Bankruptcy Code defines claim as:

(A) right to payment, whether or not such right is reduced to judgment, liquidated, unliquidated, fixed, contingent, matured, unmatured, disputed, undisputed, legal, equitable, secured, or unsecured; or

(B) right to an equitable remedy for breach of performance if such breach gives rise to a right to payment, whether or not such right to an equitable remedy is reduced to judgment, fixed, contingent, matured, unmatured, disputed, undisputed, secured, or unsecured.

11 U.S.C.A. §101(5). The legislative history of the Code suggests that Congress intended to define the term claim very broadly under §101(5), so that "all legal obligations of the debtor, no matter how remote or contingent, will be able to be dealt with in the bankruptcy case."

B. Case Law

Since the enactment of §101(5), courts have developed several tests to determine whether certain parties hold claims pursuant to that section: the accrued state law claim test,[2] the conduct test, and the prepetition relationship test. The bankruptcy court and district court adopted the prepetition relationship test in determining that the Future Claimants did not hold claims pursuant to §101(5).

Epstein primarily challenges the district court's application of the prepetition relationship test. He argues that the conduct test, which some courts have adopted in mass tort cases, is more consistent with the text, history, and policies of the Code.[4] Under the conduct test, a right to payment arises when the conduct giving rise to the alleged liability occurred. Epstein's position is that any right to payment arising out of the prepetition conduct of Piper, no matter how remote, should be deemed a claim and provided for, pursuant to §101(5), in this case. He argues that the relevant conduct giving rise to the alleged liability was Piper's prepetition manufacture, design, sale and distribution of allegedly defective aircraft. Specifically, he contends that, because Piper performed these acts prepetition, the potential victims, although not yet identifiable, hold claims under §101(5) of the Code.

The Official Committee and Piper dispute the breadth of the definition of claim asserted by Epstein, arguing that the scope of claim cannot extend so far as to include unidentified, and presently unidentifiable, individuals with no discernible

---

[2]The accrued state law claim theory states that there is no claim for bankruptcy purposes until a claim has accrued under state law.

[4]Epstein claims that the prepetition relationship test, by requiring identifiability of claimants, eliminates the words "contingent," "unmatured," "unliquidated," and "disputed" from the statute. He further argues that requiring a prepetition relationship is contrary to the Congressional objective that bankruptcy permit a complete settlement of the affairs of the debtor and a complete discharge and fresh start, as the claims of those persons whose injuries become manifest after the petition is filed could prove a drain on the reorganized debtor's assets for years to come.

prepetition relationship to Piper. Recognizing, as Appellees do, that the conduct test may define claim too broadly in certain circumstances, several courts have recognized "claims" only for those individuals with some type of prepetition relationship with the debtor. The prepetition relationship test, as adopted by the bankruptcy court and district court, requires "some prepetition relationship, such as contact, exposure, impact, or privity, between the debtor's prepetition conduct and the claimant" in order for the claimant to hold a §101(5) claim.

Upon examination of the various theories, we agree with Appellees that the district court utilized the proper test in deciding that the Future Claimants did not hold a claim under §101(5). Epstein's interpretation of "claim" and application of the conduct test would enable anyone to hold a claim against Piper by virtue of their potential future exposure to any aircraft in the existing fleet. Even the conduct test cases, on which Epstein relies, do not compel the result he seeks. In fact, the conduct test cases recognize that focusing solely on prepetition conduct, as Epstein espouses, would stretch the scope of §101(5). Accordingly, the courts applying the conduct test also presume some prepetition relationship between the debtor's conduct and the claimant.

While acknowledging that the district court's test is more consistent with the purposes of the Bankruptcy Code than is the conduct test supported by Epstein, we find that the test as set forth by the district court unnecessarily restricts the class of claimants to those who could be identified prior to the filing of the petition. Those claimants having contact with the debtor's product post-petition but prior to confirmation also could be identified, during the course of the bankruptcy proceeding, as potential victims, who might have claims arising out of debtor's prepetition conduct.

We therefore modify the test used by the district court and adopt what we will call the "Piper test" in determining the scope of the term claim under §101(5): an individual has a §101(5) claim against a debtor manufacturer if (i) events occurring before confirmation create a relationship, such as contact, exposure, impact, or privity, between the claimant and the debtor's product; and (ii) the basis for liability is the debtor's prepetition conduct in designing, manufacturing and selling the allegedly defective or dangerous product. The debtor's prepetition conduct gives rise to a claim to be administered in a case only if there is a relationship established before confirmation between an identifiable claimant or group of claimants and that prepetition conduct.[5]

In the instant case, it is clear that the Future Claimants fail the minimum requirements of the Piper test. There is no preconfirmation exposure to a specific identifiable defective product or any other preconfirmation relationship between Piper and the broadly defined class of Future Claimants. As there is no preconfirmation connection established between Piper and the Future Claimants, the Future Claimants do not hold a §101(5) claim arising out of Piper's prepetition design, manufacture, sale, and distribution of allegedly defective aircraft.

III. CONCLUSION

For the foregoing reasons, we hold that the Future Claimants do not meet the threshold requirements of the Piper test and, as a result, do not hold claims as defined in §101(5) of the Bankruptcy Code.

QUESTIONS ABOUT *PIPER*

1. Why did the Official Committee of Unsecured Creditors take the position that the future claims were not section 101(5) claims?

2. Why did Epstein take the position that the future claims were section 101(5) claims? If Piper sold all of its assets to Pilatus, would Pilatus be liable for damages from planes that Piper manufactured before the bankruptcy sale to Pilatus that crashed after the bankruptcy sale to Pilatus? yes

---

[5]This modified test was set forth by the bankruptcy court in a related case, In re: Piper Aircraft Corp., 169 B.R. 766 (Bankr.S.D.Fla.1994). By changing the focal point of the relationship from the petition date to the confirmation date, the test now encompasses those with injuries occurring post-petition but pre-confirmation, consistent with the policies underlying the Bankruptcy Code.

3. "The Piper test" for the existence of a claim requires that "there is a relationship established before confirmation between an identifiable claimant or group of claimants and that prepetition conduct." What does that mean? What is the statutory basis for any such requirement?

4. If the bankruptcy court had concluded that the future claimants had claims under section 101(5), would their claims have been allowable under section 502? See section 502(c) below.

C. Estimation and Reconsideration of Claims

11 U.S.C. §§ 502(c)(1), (j)

(c) There shall be estimated for purpose of allowance under this section–

(1) any contingent or unliquidated claim, the fixing or liquidation of which, as the case may be, would unduly delay the administration of the case;

. . .

(j) A claim that has been allowed or disallowed may be reconsidered for cause. A reconsidered claim may be allowed or disallowed according to the equities of the case. Reconsideration of a claim under this subsection does not affect the validity of any payment or transfer from the estate made to a holder of an allowed claim on account of such allowed claim that is not reconsidered, but if a reconsidered claim is allowed and is of the same class as such holder's claim, such holder may not receive any additional payment or transfer from the estate on account of such holder's allowed claim until the holder of such reconsidered and allowed claim receives payment on account of such claim proportionate in value to that already received by such other holder. . . .

PROBLEM 6-5: 502(c) AND A PENDING PERSONAL INJURY CLAIM

Perris Pupik Piercing LLP, "P", files a Chapter 7 bankruptcy. The major unsecured claims against P include a $6,000 claim for pre-petition rent, $70,000 on an unsecured loan, $8,000 to jewelry suppliers and $100,000 tort claim by C, a customer who claims that her belly button was damaged by P's negligent piercing. C's law suit was pending at the time of P's Chapter 7 filing. Should the bankruptcy court estimate C's claim, and, if so, how?

PROBLEM 6-6: A MORE COMPLICATED 502(c) PROBLEM

Nickles Naches Nachos, Inc. "N", the nation's largest kosher Nachos fast food chain with 250 restaurants, files for Chapter 11 relief. Major unsecured claims against N include $600,000 for unpaid rent, $700,000 in unsecured loans, $800,000 to suppliers and a not yet verified, not yet quantified, claim that N required hourly employees to work "off the clock" (i.e., required employees to clock out after 8 hours and then work overtime without pay) in violation of the Fair Labor Standards Act. Should the bankruptcy court estimate this FLSA claim by employees, and if so, how?

D. INCREASING PAYMENT ON A CLAIM BY REASON OF PRIORITIES

1. *Overview of Priorities*

In virtually all bankruptcy cases, the amount of claims exceeds the amount available to be distributed to claims. It is kind of like that first Phish concert after the "hiatus" in Madison Square Garden on December 31, 2002. More people wanting seats than seats.

Some people got seats for the Madison Square Garden Phish concert because of a past relationship with Trey or some other Phish members. *Cf.* 11 U.S.C. § 507(a)(1). Other people got seats (albeit less desirable seats because they worked on making the concert happen.) *Cf.* 11 U.S.C. § 507(a)(2). In "bankruptcy talk," these were people with priorities.

There are a number of statements in reported cases, books, and articles about equality of distribution to creditors in bankruptcy cases. Such statements must be using the term "equality" in the Phish concert or perhaps *Animal Farm* sense.

In bankruptcy cases, some claims are more equal than others. Secured claims are more equal than unsecured claims. And, some unsecured claims are more equal than other unsecured claims.

In a bankruptcy case, certain allowed unsecured claims are entitled to priority in distribution over other unsecured claims. Section 507(a) sets out the levels of priorities.

Chapter 7 requires that the various priority classes are paid in the order in which they are listed in section 507, section 726(a)(1). In other words, each first priority claim is to be paid in full before any second priority claim is paid at all. If there are not sufficient funds to pay all claims within a particular class, then generally all claims entitled to that priority are paid pro rata.

Chapter 11, Chapter 12, and Chapter 13, require the plan to provide for payment in full of all priority claims, although the payments of claims within certain priority classes may be stretched over a period of time, sections 1129(a)(9); 1222(a)(2), 1322(a)(2).

In its proof of claim form, a creditor can assert a priority and state the amount and basis therefore. Most of the litigation over whether a "claim" is entitled to a priority involve assertions of administrative "expense" status, under section 507(a)(1) [and also section 503(b) and often also sections 327 and 330].

---

11 U.S.C. § 507. PRIORITIES

(a) The following expenses and claims have priority in the following order:

(1) First,

(A) Allowed unsecured claims for domestic support obligations that, as of the date of the filing of the petition in a case under this title, are owed to or recoverable by a spouse, former spouse, or child of the debtor, or such child's parent, legal guardian, or responsible relative, without regard to whether the claim is filed by such person or is filed by a governmental unit on behalf of such person, on the condition that funds received under this paragraph by a governmental unit under this title after the date of the filing of the petition shall be applied and distributed in accordance with applicable nonbankruptcy law.

. . .

(2) Second, administrative expenses allowed under section 503(b) of this title, and any fees and charges assessed against the estate under chapter 123 of title 28.

(3) Third, unsecured claims allowed under section 502(f) of this title.

(4) Fourth, allowed unsecured claims, but only to the extent of $10,000 for each individual or corporation, as the case may be, earned within 180 days before the date of the filing of the petition or the date of the cessation of the debtor's business, whichever occurs first, for —

(A) wages, salaries, or commissions, including vacation, severance, and sick leave pay earned by an individual; or

. . .

(5) Fifth, allowed unsecured claims for contributions to an employee benefit plan—

(A) arising from services rendered within 180 days before the date of the filing of the petition or the date of the cessation of the debtor's business, whichever occurs first; but only

(B) for each such plan, to the extent of—

(i) the number of employees covered by each such plan multiplied by $10,000; less

(ii) the aggregate amount paid to such employees under paragraph (4) of this subsection, plus the aggregate amount paid by the estate on behalf of such employees to any other employee benefit plan.

. . .

(8) Eighth, allowed unsecured claims of governmental units, only to the extent that such claims are for—

(A) a tax on or measured by income or gross receipts for a taxable year ending on or before the date of the filing of the petition—

. . .

---

2. Administrative Expenses

a. Professional Fees as Administrative Expenses

11 U.S.C. § 503(b)

(b) After notice and a hearing, there shall be allowed, administrative expenses, including–

. . .

(2) compensation and reimbursement awarded under section 330(a) of this title;

---

11 U.S.C. § 327(a)

(a) Except as otherwise provided in this section, the trustee[6] with the court's approval, may employ one or more attorneys, accountants, appraisers, auctioneers, or other professional persons, that do not hold or represent an interest adverse to the estate, and that are disinterested persons, to represent or assist the trustee in carrying out the trustee's duties under this title.

---

11 U.S.C. § 330(a)(1)

(a)(1) After notice to the parties in interest and the United States Trustee and a hearing, and subject to sections 326, 328, and 329, the court may award to a trustee, an examiner, a professional person employed under section 327 or 1103 - -

(A) reasonable compensation for actual, necessary services rendered by the trustee, examiner, professional person, or attorney and by any paraprofessional person employed by any such person; and

(B) reimbursement for actual, necessary expenses.

---

11 U.S.C. § 330(a)(4)

(4)(A) Except as provided in subparagraph (B), the court shall not allow compensation for—

. . .

(ii) services that were not—
(I) reasonably likely to benefit the debtor's estate; or
(II) necessary to the administration of the case.

(B) In a chapter 12 or chapter 13 case in which the debtor is an individual, the court may allow reasonable compensation to the debtor's attorney for representing the interests of the

---

[6]Under section 1107, a Chapter 11 debtor in possession shall have "all the rights . . . and powers . . . of a trustee"

debtor in connection with the bankruptcy case based on a consideration of the benefit and necessity of such services to the debtor and the other factors set forth in this section.

PROBLEM 6-7: ATTORNEYS FOR CHAPTER 11 DEBTORS IN POSSESSION AND CREDITORS' COMMITTEES

In the *Piper Aircraft* case, the attorneys for the debtor-in-possession and the attorneys for the creditors' committee spent hundreds of hours on the future claims litigation. Who paid for their work? Who paid for the hundreds of hours of time billed by the attorneys for Pilatus and other prospective purchasers?

PROBLEM 6-8: CHAPTER 7 DEBTOR'S ATTORNEY'S DISCHARGE WORK AND SECTIONS 503, 327(a) AND 330(a)

Waxman is a Chapter 7 debtor. He retained and paid Isaac Blachor, Esq. $1,500.00 prepetition for the preparation and filing of the bankruptcy petition and schedules and representing him at the meeting of creditors in the bankruptcy case.

Shortly after the petition was filed, Waxman's principal creditor retained bankruptcy counsel who commenced an adversary proceeding against Waxman to have his debt deemed non-dischargeable pursuant to Section 523 of the Code, and to deny Waxman a discharge pursuant to Section 727 of the Code." What should Isaac Blachor, Esq. do? Who will pay Mr. Blachor?

---

b. Other Administrative Expenses

11 U.S.C. § 503(b)(1)(A)(i)

(b) After notice and a hearing, there shall be allowed, administrative expenses, other than claims allowed under section 502(f) of this title, including –

(1)(A) the actual, necessary costs and expenses of preserving the estate, including—

(i) wages, salaries, and commissions for services rendered after the commencement of the case; and

. . .

PROBLEM 6-9: ADMINISTRATIVE EXPENSES IN A LIQUIDATION CASE

Davidoff of Tuscaloosa, Inc. (D), a cigar store, files for Chapter 7. Are the costs that the Chapter 7 trustee incurs in advertising the sale of D's assets an administrative expense? Are the costs that the Chapter 7 trustee incurs in storing the cigars an administrative expense?

PROBLEM 6-10: ADMINISTRATIVE EXPENSES IN AN OPERATING CASE

D cigar store files for Chapter 11 on June 30.

1. Is the July salary for its store manager an administrative expense?

2. The store manager's June salary?

3. The tort claim of a customer who slipped, fell, and hurt herself in D's store in July, after D had filed its Chapter 11 petition?

---

11 U.S.C. § 503(c)

(c) Notwithstanding subsection (b), there shall neither be allowed, nor paid—

(1) a transfer made to, or an obligation incurred for the benefit of, an insider of the debtor for the purpose of inducing such person to remain with the debtor's business, absent a finding by the court based on evidence in the record that—

(A) the transfer or obligation is essential to retention of the person because the individual has a bona fide job offer from another business at the same or greater rate of compensation;

(B) the services provided by the person are essential to the survival of the business; and

(C) either—

(i) the amount of the transfer made to, or obligation incurred for the benefit of, the person is not greater than an amount equal to 10 times the amount of the mean transfer or obligation of a similar kind given to non-management employees for any purpose during the calendar year in which the transfer is made or the obligation is incurred; or

(ii) if no such similar transfers were made to, or obligations were incurred for the benefit of, such non-management employees during such calendar year, the amount of the transfer or obligation is not greater than an amount equal to 25 percent of the amount of any similar transfer or obligation made to or incurred for the benefit of such insider for any purpose during the calendar year before the year in which such transfer is made or obligation is incurred.

(2) a severance payment to an insider fo the debtor, unless—

(A) the payment is part of a program that is generally applicable to all full-time employees; and

> (B) the amount of the payment is not greater than 10 times the amount of the mean severance pay given to nonmanagement employees during the calendar year in which the payment is made; or
>
> . . .

PROBLEM 6-11: RETAINING KEY EXECUTIVES

D Corp. is planning to file a Chapter 11 petition. Your law firm is one of several firms that P and G, president and general counsel, consider retaining. In the interviews, P and G ask whether your firm would be able to obtain bankruptcy court approval of a key employee retention plan (KERP). Under the KERP, selected top executives would receive a substantial bonus for remaining with D Corp. during the course of the bankruptcy. How do you respond?

11 U.S.C. § 503(b)(9)

> After notice and a hearing, there shall be allowed administrative expenses,. . . including
>
> (9) the value of any goods received by the debtor within 20 days before the date of commencement of a case under this title in which the goods have been sold to the debtor in the ordinary course of such debtor's business.

PROBLEM 6-12: RECOVERING FOR GOODS DELIVERED WITHIN 20 DAYS BEFORE BANKRUPTCY

D, a chain of convenience stores, files a Chapter 11 petition. In the 20 days before D's bankruptcy filing, D obtained the following:

A. New software from A,

B. Inventory from B,

C. Equipment from C.

Before its bankruptcy filing, D did not make any payments to A or B but D made a 50% down payment to C. Are the amounts owed to A, B, and C administrative expenses under section 503(b)(9)?

---

3. *Other Priorities*

PROBLEM 6-13: PRIORITY FOR DOMESTIC SUPPORT OBLIGATION

W comes to you for advice. Her husband, H, who just graduated from medical school, has filed for divorce. H and W have no children. They were married during H's first year of medical school, and W worked two jobs to pay H's medical school tuition and their living costs. H has offered to make monthly payments to W for four years measured by 75% of W's earnings during the four years he was in medical school. What is the relevance, if any, of section 507 to this problem? *See also* 11 U.S.C. §§ 523(a)(5), (15).

PROBLEM 6-14: PRIORITY FOR EMPLOYEES

E is an employee of D Co. She wants to know what the effect of D Co.'s bankruptcy will be on her pension and other benefits. What is the relevance, if any, of section 507 to this problem?

PROBLEM 6-15: PRIORITY FOR PRE-BANKRUPTCY TAXES

On April 15, 2003. T filed her 2000 Form 1040 U.S. Individual Income Tax Return. T's tax return showed that she owed $165,000 in taxes for 2000. T made a $2,000 payment with her return and made a $2,000 payment each month until March 1, 2006, when she hired your firm to file a bankruptcy petition for her. Does the date of the bankruptcy filing matter to the IRS? See section 507(a)(8)(a)(i). To T? See also section 523(a)(1)(A). What if prior to T's bankruptcy filing, the IRS had obtained a federal tax lien?

---

4. *Review: Priorities, and Lien Priority*

The Code uses the term "priorities" to identify those **UNSECURED** allowable claims that are to be satisfied before other **UNSECURED** allowable claims. One more time, **UNSECURED** allowable claims. In bankruptcy, priorities are unsecured allowable claims and allowable expenses.

Outside of bankruptcy, laws and lawyers use the term "priority" to identify those liens that are to be satisfied over other liens. A first mortgage has priority over a second mortgage, a purchase money security interest in equipment that complied with UCC § 9-324(a) has priority over other security interests in the same equipment.

In general, the Code does not change the priority of liens outside of bankruptcy. If, outside of bankruptcy, P's purchase money security in D's equipment has priority over S's security interest in D's equipment, then, in bankruptcy, P's security interest will still have priority over S's. If the value of the equipment is more than the amount owed to P but less than the total amount owed to both P and S, then P's secured claim will be satisfied first.

And, in general,[7] in bankruptcy, even the lowest priority secured claim will be satisfied for collateral proceeds before unsecured claims with section 507 priorities will be paid for any collateral proceeds. In the hypothetical in the previous paragraph, S's secured claim will be satisfied before proceeds from S's collateral will be used to pay section 507 priorities.

PROBLEM 6-16: PRIORITIES, LIENS AND PRIORITY

D, a Chapter 7 debtor, owes $400,000 to various employees with section 507(a)(3) and (4) claims and $80,000 for federal withholding taxes for the past year, section 507(a)(8). If the Chapter 7 trustee only has $100,000 to distribute, how should she distribute it? What additional information do you need? What if the IRS has obtained a federal tax lien?

PROBLEM 6-17: LIENS, LIEN PRIORITY AND SECTION 507 PRIORITIES

D Corporation is in Chapter 11 bankruptcy. D Corporation owns Blackacre. D Corporation's creditors include F, S, T, U, V, W, X, Y and Z. F has a $700,000 first mortgage on Blackacre; S has a $500,000 second mortgage on Blackacre. Blackacre has a value of $1,000,000. X, Y and Z are asserting section 507 priorities. Is that important to F? To S?

---

[7]Section 506(c) codifies an exception to this rule. Administrative expenses that benefit a holder of a secured claim can be recovered first from that claimant's collateral. Assume, for example, that (i) D owes S $1000, (ii) the debt is secured by D's Eppielator, (iii) after D's bankruptcy filing, the trustee spends $20 in storing the Eppielator, and (iv) the Eppielator is later sold for $600. Under section 506, the trustee could recover the $20 from S. *See generally* Hartford Underwriters Insurance Company v. Union Planters Bank N.A., 530 U.S. 1 (2000).

PROBLEM 6-18: IMPACT OF SECTION 507 PRIORITIES ON LIEN CREDITOR

D Corporation is in Chapter 11 bankruptcy. D Corporation owns Blackacre. D Corporation's creditors include F, S, T, U, V, W, X, Y and Z. F has a $700,000 first mortgage on Blackacre; S has a $500,000 second mortgage on Blackacre. Blackacre has a value of $1,000,000. X, Y and Z are asserting section 507 priorities. Is that important to F? To S?

E. DECREASING PAYMENT ON A CLAIM BECAUSE OF SUBORDINATION

Think again about that Phish Madison Square Garden concert. If you are a Phish fan, you don't want to be at the end of the line – even if you have a ticket (think allowable claim). If you are at the end of the line, there probably will not be any seats left. Even if there are still seats, it is highly unlikely that the seats available to the guy at the end of the line will be as good as the seats that the guys at the beginning of the line have.

How can a person wind up at the end of the line at a Phish concert? It might be because of an agreement. Epstein agrees to buy the tickets if Nickles will get in line a day earlier and then yield that spot in line to Epstein 15 minutes before the doors open. *Cf.* 11 U.S.C. § 510(a). Or, it might be because of bad behavior. Markell and Perris get in line earlier but because of their bad behavior, the New York security guards move them to the end of the line. *Cf.* 11 U.S.C. § section 510(c).

---

1. Contractual Subordination and Section 510(a)

As a part of a financing deal, creditors sometimes agree that some creditors will be paid before other creditors. The business reasons creditors enter into such agreements can be complicated. Perhaps, the junior (subordinated creditors) receive a higher interest rate in return for their risk. Perhaps, the junior creditors preceded the senior creditors and agree to the subordination to induce new creditors to fund their borrower who needs the additional funding to continue business operations.

The legal effect of such a pre-bankruptcy subordination agreement in bankruptcy is not complicated. Section 510(a) provides "A subordination agreement is enforceable in a case under this title to the same extent that such an agreement is enforceable under applicable nonbankruptcy law." The legislative history of Section 510(a), H.R. NO. 595, 95TH CONG., 1ST SESS. 359 (1977); S. REP. NO. 959, 95TH CONG., 2D SESS. 74 (1978), "explains": "Subsection (a) requires the court to enforce subordination agreements."

The next problem provides a more straight-forward look at subordination.

PROBLEM 6-19: THE "WHYS" AND "WHAT IFS" OF CONTRACTUAL SUBORDINATION

In January of 2005, D Co. meets with its major creditors to try to work out its financial problems without having to file bankruptcy. D Co. proposes three alternatives for creditors to choose among:

(1) get paid 10% of what is owed now and agree to defer the payment of the remaining 90% of what is owed now until all other creditors are paid in full;

(2) get collateral valued at 20% of what is owed now and agree to defer payment of the balance of the claim until creditors who receive neither part payment nor collateral get paid;

(3) get neither part payment nor collateral but get paid principal and 8% interest before creditors who received either part payment or collateral are paid anything.

Your client C is one of the major creditors of D Co. Do you have any helpful advice for C?

---

2. *Equitable Subordination*

11 U.S.C. § 510(c)

(c) Notwithstanding subsections (a) and (b) of this section, after notice and a hearing, the court may--

(1) under principles of equitable subordination, subordinate for purposes of distribution all or part of an allowed claim to all or part of another allowed claim or all or part of an allowed interest to all or part of another allowed interest; . . .

SOUTHERN DISTRICT OF NEW YORK BANKRUPTCY JUDGE EXPLAINS "EQUITABLE SUBORDINATION" (WITH SOME "HELP" FROM ONE OF YOUR FAVORITE AUTHORS)

The doctrine of equitable subordination is codified in Section 510(c) of the Code. It empowers the Bankruptcy Court, under "principles of equitable subordination," to subordinate, for purposes of distribution, claims to other claims, and interests to other interests, and to transfer the lien securing the subordinated claim to the estate.

The power to subordinate a claim derives from the Bankruptcy Court's general equitable power to adjust equities among creditors in relation to the liquidation results. It involves viewing claims "through the eyes of equity and dealing with them on the basis of equitable considerations to prevent injustice or unfairness in the bankruptcy situation."

The doctrine is limited to reordering priorities, and does not permit disallowance of claims. It requires the court to consider whether, notwithstanding the apparent legal validity of a particular claim, the conduct of the claimant in relation to other creditors is or was such that it would be unjust or unfair to permit the claimant to share pro rata with the other claimants of equal status.

In considering the applicability of the doctrine, courts have uniformally[sic] applied the three-pronged test:

a) The claimant engaged in some type of inequitable conduct;
b) The misconduct caused injury to the creditors or conferred an unfair advantage on the claimant;

c) Equitable subordination of the claim is consistent with bankruptcy law.

Equitable subordination requires proof of "inequitable conduct" which, one commentator has noted, is a "very slippery concept with little predictive value." 2 David G. Epstein et al., Bankruptcy, § 6-93, at 256 (1992) ("Epstein"). . . .

In re 80 Nassau Associates, 169 B.R. 832, 836 (Bankr. S.D.N.Y. 1992).

PROBLEM 6-20: SIMPLE EQUITABLE SUBORDINATION STORY

Epstein is the principal shareholder in and creditor of Eppie's, Inc. Epstein invested $1,000 and loaned $700,000 to Eppie's Inc.

Eppie's, Inc. is in financial trouble. Epstein tells all of Eppie's, Inc vendors that he intends to loan Eppie's, Inc. another $500,000. Relying on this, the vendors continue to sell on credit to Eppie's, Inc. Epstein does not make the new loan. Eppie's, Inc. files for bankruptcy. Epstein files a proof of claim for the $700,000 he loaned Eppie's, Inc. Should Epstein's claim be disallowed under section 502(b)? Should Epstein's claim be subordinated under section 510(c) to the claims of the vendors who relied on his representation? From Epstein's perspective, what is the practical difference between disallowance and subordination?

Unit 7

Issues That Can Arise In Cases Under Any Chapter: Avoiding Powers

A. INCREASING PROPERTY OF THE ESTATE OR DECREASING THE PAYMENT TO A CLAIM THROUGH THE AVOIDING POWERS: AN OVERVIEW

In the absence of bankruptcy, some transfers of a debtor's property can be invalidated under state laws, such as state fraudulent conveyance laws. The Code incorporates these state laws in section 544(b) so that a transfer of a debtor's property that can be invalidated under state law in the absence of bankruptcy can be invalidated under section 544(b) in the event of bankruptcy.

Chapter 5 of the Code also contains several other "avoidance" provisions that are unique to bankruptcy. Accordingly, some payments, sales, exchanges, judicial liens, security interests and other transfers that are valid under state law can be avoided in bankruptcy.

The Code's avoidance provisions reach both "voluntary" transfers such as a debtor's making a gift to a relative or granting a mortgage to a creditor and "involuntary" transfers such as a creditor's garnishing the debtor's bank account or subjecting the debtor's real property to a judgment lien. See 101 (54) (definition of "transfer"). Note also that the Code's avoidance provisions reach both "absolute" transfers such as gifts, payments and sales, and "security transfers" such as mortgages and judgment liens.

In working with these avoidance provisions, law students and lawyers are called on to answer three basic questions:

(1) what are the consequences of avoiding a transfer, and

(2) which transfers can be avoided, and

(3) how does avoidance of a transfer happen.

Law students are called on to answer these questions both in class and on exams. Lawyers are called upon to answer these questions not only in negotiating and litigating in bankruptcy cases but also in structuring transactions outside of bankruptcy.

The last of these three questions is the easiest – at least for a law student. Avoidance does not occur by operation of law. Avoidance requires litigation and involves all of the usual litigation questions such as who can sue, whom can be sued, when the suit has to be brought, where the suit can be brought and what can be recovered.

The avoidance statutes generally use the phrase "the trustee may avoid." Recall that in Chapter 11 cases without a trustee, the debtor in possession has the rights of a trustee, section 1107(a). This means that any transfer that can be avoided by a trustee can be avoided by a debtor in possession in a Chapter 11 case. For example, D pays C $666,000. D then files for Chapter 11. If D's $666,000 payment to C is covered by one of the Code's avoiding powers, then D as the Chapter 11 debtor in possession can recover the $666,000 she earlier transferred to C.

Section 546 deals with the question of when an avoidance action must be brought. It is in essence a statute of limitations which requires that legal action be initiated within two years after the order for relief except that if a trustee is first appointed more than one year after the order for relief but within two years after the order for relief, she shall have one year.

Sections 541(a)(3), 502(d) and 550 deal with the first of the three questions - (1) what are the consequences of avoiding a transfer.

1. Increase in Property of the Estate

In the main, the consequence of avoiding a transfer is an increase in property of the estate. The avoiding powers are a part of a subchapter of the Code entitled "The Estate."

When the bankruptcy trustee avoids an absolute transfer of property, that property then becomes property of the estate. Assume that D owes C $25,000. D repays C $12,000 of that debt. D later files for bankruptcy. At the time of D's bankruptcy filing, the $12,000 paid to C is not property of D's estate. If the bankruptcy trustee is able to invoke one of the Code's avoidance provisions to avoid the payment and recover the $12,000, the $12,000 will then become property of D's estate, sections 541(a)(3), 550.

The avoidance of an absolute transfer can also affect the amount of a creditor's claim. In the above hypothetical, C had a $13,000 claim at the time of D's bankruptcy filing. Again, if the bankruptcy trustee is able to avoid the payment and recover the $12,000 D paid C, then C will have a $25,000 claim against D, section 502(h). If the bankruptcy trustee is able to establish a legal basis for avoiding the transfer but is unable to recover the payment, then C's claim for $13,000 will be disallowed under section 502(d).

The consequences of avoiding a security transfer are similar. Assume, for example, that D borrows $77,000 from C and grants C a mortgage on Blackacre which is worth $120,000. D later files for bankruptcy. Absent the trustee's use of one of the avoidance powers, C has a $77,000 secured claim. Recall that under section 541, Blackacre itself is not property of the estate; rather the estate's interest in Blackacre is only D's limited equity and other rights in Blackacre. If, however, the bankruptcy trustee is able to avoid the grant of the mortgage on Blackacre, then C will have a $77,000 unsecured claim, and Blackacre without any encumbrance will be property of the estate.

In the two examples, the consequences of avoidance were the recovery of the property interest transferred from the party to whom it had been transferred. Under section 550, the consequences of avoidance are not limited to recovery of the property transferred, or to the person to whom the transfer was made.

Under section 550(a), the court can order the recovery of the "value of the property" transferred, rather than the property. And, section 550 permits recovery not only from (i) the initial transferee but also (ii) from the later transferees or (iii) from a person who was not a transferee but benefitted from the transfer. And, section 550 provides protection for certain transferees.

---

11 U.S.C. § 550. Liability of Transferee of Avoided Transfer

(a) . . . [T]he trustee may recover, for the benefit of the estate, the property transferred, or, if the court so orders, the value of such property, from--

(1) the initial transferee of such transfer or the entity for whose benefit such transfer was made; or

(2) any immediate or mediate transferee of such initial transferee.

(b) The trustee may not recover under section (a)(2) of this section from–

(1) a transferee that takes for value, including satisfaction or securing of a present or antecedent debt, in good faith, and without knowledge of the voidability of the transfer avoided; or

(2) any immediate or mediate good faith transferee of such transferee.

Problem 7-1: Recovery of What, From Whom

D transfers real property to X. At the time of the transfer, the property was worth $400,000. X later sells the property to Y for $330,000. D later files for bankruptcy. Y still owns the real property. Because of declining property values, the property is now worth only $220,000. If the trustee is able to avoid the transfer, what can she recover under section 550? From whom?

---

2. *Decrease in Allowable Claims*

11 U.S.C. § 502(d) – Disallowance

(d) Notwithstanding subsections (a) and (b) of this section, the court shall disallow any claim of any entity from which property is recoverable under section 542, 543, 550, or 553 of this title or that is a transferee of a transfer avoidable under section 522(f), 522(h), 544, 545, 547, 548, 549, or 724(a) of this title, unless such entity or transferee has paid the amount, or turned over any such property, for which such entity or transferee is liable under section 522(i), 542, 543, 550, or 553 of this title.

Problem 7-2: Allowance of Claim and Avoidance Powers

In January, 2001, appellees received payment from the debtor on certain antecedent debts after commencement of the case. The statute controlling whether those transfers were avoidable is 11 U.S.C. § 549, but no actions under that section were ever commenced. Appellees thereafter filed claims against debtor's estate concerning other unpaid debts.

In March, 2002, the Committee of Unsecured Creditors (hereafter "Committee"), objected to those claims on the grounds set forth in section 502(d), which provides, in relevant part, that "the court shall disallow any claim of any entity . . . that is a transferee of a transfer avoidable under section . . . 549 of this title . . ." Appellees responded, asserting the time bar of section 549(d): "An action or proceeding under this section may not be commenced after the earlier of (1) two years after the date of the transfer sought to be avoided; or (2) the time the case is closed or dismissed."

Appellees submit that section 502(d) is inapplicable because a transfer is not "avoidable under section . . . 549" if an avoidance action cannot be maintained on account of the time bar.

B. Increasing Property of the Estate or Decreasing the Payment to a Claim Through Avoidance of Fraudulent Transfers and Fraudulent Obligations

For more than four hundred years, there have been statutes that empower creditors to avoid transfers that "hinder, delay or defraud creditors." Every state has such a fraudulent conveyance law. A bankruptcy trustee can use these state laws by invoking section 544(b) as discussed above.

Additionally, the bankruptcy trustee can avoid fraudulent transfers by invoking section 548 set out below. For the most part, the requirements of section

548 are the same as the requirements of most state fraudulent conveyance laws.

Section 548(a)(1)(A) empowers the bankruptcy trustee to avoid transfers made and obligations incurred with actual intent to hinder, delay or defraud creditors. There is rarely direct evidence of actual intent. Instead, there are certain facts recognized are strong indicia of actual fraudulent intent. Some of these "badges of fraud" are (i) the existence of a family or other close relationship between the transferor and the transferee, (ii) the absence or inadequacy of consideration, and (iii) secrecy of the transfer.

The classic illustration of "badges of fraud", Twyne's Case, involves sheep. Assume for example that Epstein and Perris are suing Markell, and Markell is concerned that Epstein and Perris will get a judgment against him and collect that judgment by having the sheriff seize and sell his prized sheep. Accordingly, Markell enters into a contract with Nickles, selling the sheep to Nickles.

Notwithstanding the sale, Markell keeps possession of the sheep. And, Markell continues to shear the sheep and whatever. When, however, Epstein and Perris get their judgment against Markell and get the sheriff out to levy on the sheep to satisfy what Markell owes them, Markell tells the sheriff that "The sheep are Nickles', not mine, and so sheriff, you can't take these sheep - Nickles sheep - to satisfy Epstein and Perris' judgment against me, Markell."

Under the rule of Twyne's Case, Epstein and Perris get the sheep. More precisely, Epstein and Perris can avoid Markell's sale of the sheep to Nickles because of the "badges of fraud" that indicate Markell's actual fraudulent intent.

We have not included Twyne's Case or even a citation to Twyne's Case in this book because most lawyers don't have a sheep case over the course of their career. More important, most cases under section 544(b) or section 548 do not involve actual fraudulent intent.

Instead, most cases under section 544(b) or 548 involve what is called "constructive fraud." That word "constructive" is used throughout the law: "constructive" adverse possession, "constructive" eviction, "constructive" trespass. According to Bryan Garner's Black's Law Dictionary, constructive is an adjective meaning "legally imputed, having an effect in law though not necessarily in fact."

In short, "constructive" means "let's pretend." And when a transfer is "constructive fraudulent", section 544 or section 548 pretends it is a fraudulent transfer and treats it as a fraudulent transfer even though there is nothing fraudulent about it.

Section 548(a)(1(B) provides for avoidance of transfers and obligations that are constructively fraudulent. Please read section 548(a)(1)(B) carefully. Note the two big "litigable" issues:

1. Adequacy of what the debtor got in return for what the debtor gave;

2. Financial condition of the debtor at the time of the transfer.

---

1. Section 548: Bankruptcy's Fraudulent Conveyance Law

11 U.S.C. § 548. Fraudulent Transfers and Obligations

(a)

(1) The trustee may avoid any transfer of an interest of the debtor in property, or any obligation incurred by the debtor, that was made or incurred on or within two years before the

date of the filing of the petition, if the debtor voluntarily or involuntarily--

(A) made such transfer or incurred such obligation with actual intent to hinder, delay, or defraud any entity to which the debtor was or became, on or after the date that such transfer was made or such obligation was incurred, indebted; ***or*** [emphasis added]

(B)

(i) received less than a reasonably equivalent value in exchange for such transfer or obligation; **and** [emphasis added]

(ii)(I) was insolvent on the date that such transfer was made or such obligation was incurred, or became insolvent as a result of such transfer or obligation;

(II) was engaged in business or a transaction, or was about to engage in business or a transaction, for which any property remaining with the debtor was an unreasonably small capital; or

(III) intended to incur, or believed that the debtor would incur, debts that would be beyond the debtor's ability to pay as such debts matured.

(c) Except to the extent that a transfer or obligation voidable under this section is voidable under section 544, 545, or 547 of this title, a transferee or obligee of such a transfer or obligation that takes for value and in good faith has a lien on or may retain any interest transferred or may enforce any obligation incurred, as the case may be, to the extent that such transferee or obligee gave value to the debtor in exchange for such transfer or obligation.

---

11 U.S.C. § 101(32)(A)– INSOLVENT

(32) "insolvent" means - -

(A) with reference to an entity other than a partnership and a municipality, financial condition such that the sum of such entity's debts is greater than all of such entity's property, at a fair valuation, exclusive of - -

(i) property transferred, concealed, or removed with intent to hinder, delay, or defraud such entity's creditors; and

(ii) property that may be exempted from property of the estate under section 522 of this title;

PROBLEM 7-3: INSOLVENCY AND CASH FLOW

D Ltd is a limited partnership that owns and develops real estate. Most of D Ltd land is still undeveloped. The market value of D Ltd's land is $4,000,000. Its debts are $3,000,000. D Ltd's monthly payment obligations to creditors - $200,000 - is much greater than D Ltd's monthly earnings - $100,000. In other words, D Ltd is not able to pay its debts as they mature. Is D Ltd "insolvent" as that term is used in the Code? Is the answer to that question important in the "real world"?

PROBLEM 7-4: GIFT TO RELATIVE

D's creditors are threatening to repossess his boat. D, who is insolvent, gives the boat to his father, F. Within a year, D files for bankruptcy. Can the trustee avoid the gift of the boat as a fraudulent transfer?

PROBLEM 7-5: GIFT TO CHARITY

Epstein's creditors are threatening to garnish his bank account. Epstein, who is insolvent, makes a gift of $20,000 to the United Jewish Appeal. Within a year, Epstein files for bankruptcy. Can the trustee avoid the gift as a fraudulent transfer? In considering this section 548(a)(2).

PROBLEM 7-6: SALE FOR LESS THAN REASONABLY EQUIVALENT VALUE

D's creditors are threatening to repossess his boat. D, who is insolvent, sells the boat to his friend F for $3,000. Within a year, D files for bankruptcy. Can the bankruptcy trustee avoid the sale if she can establish that the value of the boat at the time of the sale was $7,000? If so, what are F's rights?

PROBLEM 7-7: JUDICIAL SALE AND REASONABLE EQUIVALENT VALUE

One of D's creditor's with a judgment against D, who is insolvent, obtains an execution lien, and has the sheriff seize and sell D's boat. The judicial sale of the boat for $3,000 completely complies with state law. Within a year, D files for bankruptcy. Can the bankruptcy trustee avoid the sale by establishing that the value of the boat at the time of the sale was $7,000? *Cf.* BFP v. Resolution Trust Co., 511 U.S. 531, 545 (1994)("We deem, as the law has always deemed, that a fair and proper price, or a "reasonably equivalent value", for foreclosed property is the price in fact received at the foreclosure sale, so long as all of the requirements of the State's foreclosure law have been complied with.")

PROBLEM 7-8: GUARANTEE AND REASONABLE EQUIVALENT VALUE TO WHOM

National, TWO, Propper, USN and UMO are separate but related business entities. MHT loans $6,660,000 to National, TWO and Propper. USN and UMO, which are insolvent, guarantee the payment of this loan to National, TWO and Propper and mortgage their assets to MHT to secure payment of the loan. Within a year, USN and UMO file for bankruptcy. Can USN and UMO avoid the mortgage on their assets as a fraudulent transfer and the guarantee as a fraudulent obligation?

Rubin v. Manufacturers Hanover Trust Co., 661 F.2d 979 (2d Cir 1981), set out below, dealt with a similar question under the Bankruptcy Act of 1898.

RUBIN V. MANUFACTURERS HANOVER TRUST CO.

661 F.2d 979 (2d Cir. 1981)

KEARSE, Circuit Judge.

. . .

On appeal, the trustees renew their contentions that the obligations to repay the debts of National, TWO, and Propper assumed by USN and UMO under the system of guarantees were not supported by fair consideration, that these obligations were incurred at a time when USN and UMO were insolvent, and that MHT must therefore return to the trustees, pursuant to §67(d) [section 548 of the Bankruptcy Code] of the Bankruptcy Act, the value of the collateral given by the bankrupts that was applied to the debts of National, TWO, and Propper. For the reasons below we conclude that the district court's rulings as to fair consideration and insolvency were based on erroneous legal principles, and that the judgment must be vacated and the matter remanded for further proceedings.

III. DISCUSSION

When an overburdened debtor perceives that he will soon become insolvent, he will often engage in a flurry of transactions in which he transfers his remaining property, either outright or as security, in exchange for consideration that is significantly less valuable than what he has transferred. Although such uneconomical transactions are sometimes merely final acts of recklessness, the calculating debtor may employ them as a means of preferring certain creditors or of placing his assets in friendly hands where he can reach them but his creditors cannot. Whatever the motivation, the fraudulent conveyance provisions of §67(d) [section 548] of the Bankruptcy Act recognize that such transactions may operate as a constructive fraud upon the debtor's innocent creditors, for they deplete the debtor's estate of valuable assets without bringing in property of similar value from which creditors' claims might be satisfied. In addition, §67(d) recognizes that the incurring of an obligation chargeable against the debtor's property, as distinguished from the actual grant of an interest in that property, may unfairly deplete the debtor's estate if the debtor does not receive in exchange a consideration roughly equal in value to the obligation incurred. Thus, §67(d)(2) provides in relevant part as follows:

> Every transfer made and every obligation incurred by a debtor within one year prior to the filing of a petition initiating a proceeding under this title by or against him is fraudulent (a) as to creditors existing at the time of such transfer or obligation, if made or incurred without fair consideration by a debtor who is or will be thereby rendered insolvent, without regard to his actual intent; or (b) as to then existing creditors and as to other persons who become creditors during the continuance of a business or transaction, if made or incurred without fair consideration by a debtor who is engaged or is about to engage in such business or transaction, for which the property remaining in his hands is an unreasonably small capital, without regard to his actual intent. . . .

Section 67(d)(6) of the Act empowers the bankruptcy trustee to set aside transfers made or obligations incurred on uneconomical terms, and to recover for the benefit of creditors the value of the property removed from the debtor's estate through such transactions.

In the present case, in order to prove their claims that UMO's and USN's guarantees of the obligations of National, TWO, and Propper were constructively fraudulent, and therefore voidable under criteria set forth in §67(d)(2)(a) and (b), the trustees were required to show: (1) that USN and UMO made transfers or incurred obligations to MHT within one year of the January 1977 filings of their bankruptcy petitions, (2) that these transactions were entered into without "fair" consideration to USN and UMO, and (3) that the bankrupts were, or were rendered, insolvent or insufficiently capitalized as a result. We discuss these issues in turn.

A. The Timing of the Transactions

Subsections 67(d)(2)(a) and (b) apply only to transfers and obligations made or incurred "within one year prior to the filing" of bankruptcy petition. . . .

USN and UMO "incurred" "obligation(s)" within the meaning of the Act when MHT loaned money to National, TWO, and Propper in December 1976. This event of course occurred within the one-year period dealt with by the statute.

B. "Fair" Consideration

Even if the debtor has transferred property or incurred an obligation within one year of filing a bankruptcy petition, the trustee cannot set aside the transaction under §67(d)(2), (a), (b) if the debtor received "fair" consideration for his property or obligation. "Fair" consideration under the Bankruptcy Act, which is defined in §67(d)(1)(e), means more than just the "good and valuable" consideration needed to support a simple contract:

> (C)onsideration given for the property or obligation of a debtor is "fair" (1) when, in good faith, in exchange and as a fair equivalent therefor, property is transferred or an antecedent debt is satisfied, or (2) when such property or obligation is received in good faith to secure a present advance or antecedent debt in an amount not disproportionately small as compared with the value of the property or obligation obtained.

The reason for this requirement is obvious: if the debtor receives property or discharges or secures an antecedent debt that is substantially equivalent in value to the property given or obligation incurred by him in exchange, then the transaction has not significantly affected his estate and his creditors have no cause to complain. By the same token, however, if the benefit of the transaction to the debtor does not substantially offset its cost to him, then his creditors have suffered, and, in the language of §67(d), the transaction was not supported by "fair" consideration.

Three-sided transactions such as those at issue here present special difficulties under the §67(d)(1)(e) definition of fair consideration. On its face, the statute appears to sanction, as supported by "fair" consideration, a transaction in which the debtor transfers property or incurs an obligation as security for the debt of a third person, provided that the debt is "not disproportionately small" in comparison to that property or obligation. Nonetheless, if the debt secured by the transaction is not the debtor's own, then his giving of security will deplete his estate without bringing in a corresponding value from which his creditors can benefit, and his creditors will suffer just as they would if the debtor had simply made a gift of his property or obligation. Accordingly, courts have long recognized that "(t)ransfers made to benefit third parties are clearly not made for a 'fair' consideration," and, similarly, that "a conveyance by a corporation for the benefit of an affiliate (should not) be regarded as given for fair consideration as to the creditors of the conveying corporations."

The cases recognize, however, that a debtor may sometimes receive "fair" consideration even though the consideration given for his property or obligation goes initially to a third person. As we have recently stated, although "transfers solely for the benefit of third parties do not furnish fair consideration" under §67(d)(1)(e), the transaction's benefit to the debtor "need not be direct; it may come indirectly through benefit to a third person." If the consideration given to the third person has ultimately landed in the debtor's hands, or if the giving of the consideration to the third person otherwise confers an economic benefit upon the debtor, then the debtor's net worth has been preserved, and §67(d) has been satisfied-provided, of course, that the value of the benefit received by the debtor approximates the value of the property or obligation he has given up. For example, fair consideration has been found for an individual debtor's repayment of loans made to a corporation, where the corporation had served merely as a conduit for transferring the loan proceeds to him.

Thus the simple fact that National, TWO, and Propper, rather than USN and UMO, received the loan line advances need not compel a ruling in favor of the trustees on this point. The relationships among the Trent/Skowron firms and Propper were such that the advances to National, TWO, and Propper very likely did facilitate transfers of funds from those firms to the bank account shared by USN and UMO, benefitting each of those firms to some degree. Accordingly, the district court did not err in rejecting the trustees' argument that the corporate separateness of the loan recipients from their guarantors necessarily precluded a finding of fair consideration.

On the other hand, the district court did err in accepting MHT's argument that the existence of any indirect benefit whatever to USN and UMO from the advances to National, TWO, and Propper meant that the issuers' obligations as guarantors were necessarily supported by fair consideration. In a transfer for security, §67(d)(1)(e) requires that the present advance or antecedent debt be "not disproportionately small as compared with the value of the property or obligation" given by the bankrupt to secure it. In a three- sided transaction such as that presented here, it is not enough merely to compare the absolute amount of the third person's debt with the amount of security given by the bankrupt. The trustee, who has the burden of proving that the transaction was "without fair consideration," could establish lack of fair consideration under §67(d) by proving that the value of what the bankrupt actually received was disproportionately small compared to the value of what it gave. Accordingly, the court must attempt to measure the economic benefit, if any, that accrued to each bankrupt as a result of the third person's indebtedness, and it must then determine whether that benefit was "disproportionately small" when compared to the size of the security that that bankrupt gave and the obligations that it incurred.

The district court did not undertake such an analysis. The court observed that both USN and UMO "had a vital interest in inducing MHT to make . . . loans to (National, TWO, and Propper)," and it stated that the issuers' "receipt of indirect benefits because of (their) affiliation and identity of interest with the direct recipients of the loans was receipt of fair consideration"; but it did not attempt to quantify the indirect benefits to either issuer or to compare those benefits with the obligations assumed by the issuers under the guarantees. Without such an analysis, it was impossible for the court to determine whether the estate of either issuer had been conserved in accordance with the principles of §67(d), and it was therefore error for the court to conclude that those purposes had been satisfied.

Given the complexity of the transactions and relationships at issue here, we think it advisable to detail the inquiry to be pursued on remand. First, the court must attempt to determine the extent to which the December 1976 loans to National and TWO increased remittances from those firms to USN, their principal in the money order business. Next, it must attempt to determine the extent to which UMO shared in the increased remittances to USN by virtue of the pooling of the issuers' funds. Similarly, it must attempt to determine the extent to which the December 1976 loans to Propper increased remittances from Propper to UMO, and the extent to which USN shared in any such increases by virtue of the pooling arrangement. The court must then compare its estimate of the value thus received by each issuer with the magnitude of the obligation charged against that issuer under its guarantee. If the value received by either issuer is found to be disproportionately small as compared with its obligation, then, to that extent, the trustee for that issuer will have proved lack of fair consideration, and the court must proceed to consider the insolvency issue, discussed below.[14] However, if either trustee fails to establish that the value is disproportionately small, the court must rule for MHT against that trustee.

In making the determinations and comparisons called for above, the court need not strive for mathematical precision. Section 67(d) requires only "fair" consideration, not a penny-for-penny exchange. At the same time, however, the court must keep the equitable purposes of the statute firmly in mind, recognizing that any significant disparity between the value received and the obligation assumed by either issuer will have significantly harmed the innocent creditors of that firm. Given the financial weakness of National and TWO revealed by the present record, it may well be that the trustees will be able to show that those firms absorbed much of the money provided them under the loan lines, remitting little or nothing to their principal, USN. Or it may be that USN received the lion's share of any remittances, perhaps even an amount properly proportionate to its obligations as guarantor, but that UMO's benefit from the loans was "disproportionately small." Of course, we leave these factual questions to the district court.

C. Insolvency or Insufficiency of Capital

As the third principal element of their causes of action under §67(d)(2)(a), (b), the trustees were required to show that USN and UMO were, or were rendered, insolvent or insufficiently capitalized when they incurred obligations under their guarantees in September or December 1976. Under § 67(d)(1)(d), a person is insolvent "when the present fair salable value of his property is less than the amount required to pay his debts." The statute does not define insufficiency of capital, and the amount of capital deemed sufficient under §67(d)(2)(b) for the carrying on of a particular business will of course depend on its nature and size. [Discussion of financial status of UMO and USN omitted.]

. . .

We vacate the judgment of the district court and remand the matter for further consideration of the issues of fair consideration and insolvency in accordance with this opinion.

---

[14]Section 67(d)(1)(e) also requires that the consideration be given in good faith. The district court found that MHT acted in good faith. On the present record, we see no reason to disturb this finding.

QUESTIONS ABOUT *RUBIN*

1. *Questions about the facts:*

    1.1 Who was indebted to MHT?
    1.2 Who received funding from MHT?
    1.3 Who made a transfer to MHT?
    1.4 Who filed for bankruptcy?

2. *Questions about the law*:

    2.1 As the term "debtor" is used in the Code, who is the debtor?
    2.2 Would this case be decided differently under section 548 of the Code?

3. Do you agree with Professor Tabb's observation: "The real problem then, in cases such as intercorporate guaranties, where the value flows directly to a third party and only indirectly to the debtor, is to make the mathematical comparison between the value given and received. Often neither is readily measurable."? CHARLES JORDAN TABB, THE LAW OF BANKRUPTCY 445 (1997). Do you understand his observation?

PROBLEM 7-9: DISTRIBUTION TO OWNERS OF BUSINESS

In January 15, D Corp., which is insolvent, pays a dividend to its shareholders. On April 5, D Corp. files for bankruptcy. Can the debtor in possession recover the dividend from the shareholders under sections 548 and 550?

PROBLEM 7-10: PROOF OF INSOLVENCY

In all of the preceding problems, the insolvency of the debtor/transferor has been assumed. In the "real world," a party invoking section 548(a)(1)(B) has to prove that the debtor transferor was "insolvent on the date that such transfer was made." What sort of evidence would a trustee introduce to establish "insolvency"? *Cf.* 11 U.S.C. § 101(32).

PROBLEM 7-11: LBO "LITE"

O owns 100% of the stock of D, Inc. E, a long-time employee, wants to buy D, Inc. from O for $700,000. E does not have $700,000. E wants to borrow $700,000 from your client C. E will then use the $700,000 to pay O. As owner of D, Inc., E will then cause D, Inc. to borrow $700,000 from C and grant C a mortgage on D, Inc.'s real property and a security interest on D, Inc.'s personal property to secure repayment of the loan. D, Inc. will then loan the $700,000 to E who will repay his loan from C with the $700,000. D, Inc. files for bankruptcy eleven months later. Is there a section 548 fraudulent transfer? What can the bankruptcy trustee recover from whom?

MOODY V. SECURITY PACIFIC BUSINESS CREDIT, INC.

971 F.2d 1056 (3d Cir. 1992)

SCIRICA, Circuit Judge.

This bankruptcy case requires us to address, once again, the application of the fraudulent conveyance laws to a failed leveraged buyout. This case raises several questions about the application of this Act to the failed leveraged buyout of Jeannette Corporation.

On July 31, 1981, a group of investors acquired Jeannette in a leveraged buyout. Less than a year and a half later, Jeannette, which had been profitable for many years, was forced into bankruptcy. The bankruptcy trustee brought this action to set aside the advances made and obligations incurred in connection with the acquisition. The trustee alleges that the leveraged buyout constitutes a fraudulent conveyance under the UFCA and is voidable under the Bankruptcy Code. After a bench trial, the district court entered judgment for defendants. We will affirm.

Founded in 1898, Jeannette Corporation manufactured and sold glass, ceramic, china, plastic, and candle houseware products in the United States and Canada. For many years, Jeannette was a profitable enterprise.

In 1978, the Coca-Cola Bottling Company of New York, Inc. acquired Jeannette for $39.6 million.

In late 1979, Coca-Cola decided to sell Jeannette and focus attention on its core bottling business. In June 1981, John P. Brogan expressed an interest in acquiring Jeannette. Brogan was affiliated with a small group of investors in the business of acquiring companies through leveraged buyouts, the hallmark feature of which is the exchange of equity for debt.[2] On July 22, 1981, Coca-Cola agreed to sell Jeannette for $12.1 million on condition that Brogan complete the transaction by the end of the month. Brogan contacted Security Pacific Business Credit Inc., a lending group that had financed one of his prior acquisitions, about obtaining financing. He submitted one year of monthly projections, based in large part on Jeannette's 80-page business plan for 1981, which showed that Jeannette would have sufficient working capital under the proposed financing arrangement in the year following the acquisition. Before agreeing to finance the transaction, however, Security Pacific undertook its own investigation of Jeannette. Security Pacific assigned this task to credit analyst Stephen Ngan. Based on his discussions with Jeannette personnel and a review of the company's financial records, Ngan made his own set of projections. He concluded that Jeannette would earn a pre-tax profit of $800,000 after interest expenses in its first year of operation, and recommended that Security Pacific finance the acquisition. He thought Jeannette was a "well-established" company with "a good track record for growth and earnings."

---

[2]As this court recently explained: A leveraged buyout refers to the acquisition of a company ("target corporation") in which a substantial portion of the purchase price paid for the stock of the target corporation is borrowed and where the loan is secured by the target corporation's assets. Commonly, the acquirer invests little or no equity. Thus, a fundamental feature of leveraged buyouts is that equity is exchanged for debt.

After reviewing Ngan's recommendation, together with an inventory report, the 1978 appraisal of Jeannette's PP & E, Brogan's projections, and a 55-page report on Jeannette prepared by another bank, Security Pacific decided to finance the acquisition. At that point, Coca-Cola formally approved the sale of Jeannette to J. Corp., which had been incorporated for the purpose of acquiring Jeannette.

The acquisition of Jeannette was consummated on July 31, 1981. J. Corp. purchased Jeannette with funds from a $15.5 million line of credit Security Pacific extended Jeannette secured by first lien security interests on all Jeannette's assets. J. Corp. never repaid Jeannette any portion of, or executed a promissory note for, the amount ($11.7 million) Security Pacific initially forwarded to J. Corp. on behalf of Jeannette to finance the acquisition. Other than new management, the only benefit Jeannette received was access to credit from Security Pacific.[3]

As with most leveraged buyouts, the acquisition left Jeannette's assets fully encumbered by the security interests held by Security Pacific. Jeannette could not dispose of its assets, except in the ordinary course of business, without the consent of Security Pacific, and was prohibited from granting security interests to anyone else. As a result, Jeannette's sole source of working capital after the transaction was its line of credit with Security Pacific.

Although Jeannette's performance initially tracked expectations, its financial condition deteriorated steadily in 1982. Jeannette experienced a shrinking domestic glassware market, a marked increase in foreign competition, dramatic

---

[3]The transaction comprised the following steps, which were deemed by the parties to have taken place at once: (1) J. Corp. entered into an agreement with Coca-Cola and KNY Development Corporation, a wholly owned subsidiary of Coca-Cola, to purchase all outstanding stock of Jeannette; (2) J. Corp. obtained a $12.1 million unsecured loan from Security Pacific and executed a demand note therefor; (3) these funds were transferred from Security Pacific to Coca-Cola to fund the purchase of Jeannette stock, which was transferred from KNY Development to J. Corp.; (4) upon acquisition of the stock, J. Corp. appointed a new board of directors for Jeannette and named Brogan chairman; (5) Jeannette entered into a $15.5 million revolving credit arrangement with Security Pacific, in exchange for which it granted Security Pacific first lien security interests in all its assets; (5) on behalf of Jeannette, Brogan directed Security Pacific to remit $11.7 million from the revolving credit facility to J. Corp., which was used to repay all but $400,000 of the demand note to Security Pacific; and (6) Jeannette and Security Pacific entered into a "lock box" agreement, whereby Jeannette's accounts receivable would be forwarded to the Mellon Bank and credited against the outstanding balance on Jeannette's line of credit.

price slashing and inventory dumping by its domestic competitors, and a continued nationwide recession. In January 1982, orders for Jeannette products fell to 86% of projected levels and in February orders fell to 70%.

On October 4, 1982, an involuntary bankruptcy petition was filed under Chapter 7 of the Bankruptcy Code.

On September 22, 1983, plaintiff James Moody, the trustee of the bankruptcy estate of Jeannette, filed this action in federal district court against defendants Security Pacific, Coca-Cola, KNY Development, J. Corp., M-K Candle, Brogan, and other individuals. He alleges that the leveraged buyout constitutes a fraudulent conveyance under the UFCA, 39 Pa.Cons.Stat.Ann. SS 354-57, and is voidable under §544(b) of the Bankruptcy Code, 11 U.S.C. §544(b).[5] After a bench trial, the district court made findings of fact and conclusions of law and entered judgment for defendants.

According to the district court, the leveraged buyout was not intentionally fraudulent because it was "abundantly clear" that defendants expected the transaction to succeed and hoped to profit from it. Likewise, although the leveraged buyout was made for less than fair consideration to Jeannette, the district court held that it was not constructively fraudulent.

Because the leveraged buyout was made for less than fair consideration, the district court placed on defendants the burden of proving solvency by clear and convincing evidence. The court, however, concluded that defendants met this burden. Jeannette was not rendered insolvent in the "bankruptcy sense" because the "present fair salable value" of Jeannette's assets immediately after the leveraged buyout exceeded total liabilities by at least $1-2 million.. In making

---

[5]Section 544(b) of the Bankruptcy Code provides that "[t]he trustee may avoid any transfer of an interest of the debtor in property or any obligation incurred by the debtor that is voidable under applicable law by a creditor holding an unsecured claim . . ." 11 U.S.C. §544(b) (emphasis added). The "applicable law" here is the UFCA, and it is clear that there is an unsecured creditor into whose shoes plaintiff trustee may step. Plaintiff also alleges that the leveraged buyout is voidable under the fraudulent conveyance provisions of the Bankruptcy Code, 11 U.S.C. SS 548. After concluding that the transaction did not constitute a fraudulent conveyance under the UFCA, however, the district court summarily rejected these claims. It reasoned that, because the fraudulent conveyance provisions of the Bankruptcy Code are modeled after and typically interpreted in conjunction with those of the UFCA, it follows that if the leveraged buyout is not fraudulent under the UFCA, it is not fraudulent under §548 of the Bankruptcy Code.

this determination, the district court valued assets on a going concern basis.

Nor was Jeannette rendered insolvent in the "equity sense" or left with an unreasonably small capital. Based on the parties' projections, which it found "reasonable and prudent when made," and the availability on Jeannette's line of credit with Security Pacific, the district court found that Jeannette was not left with an unreasonably small capital after the acquisition. Rather than a lack of capital, the district court attributed Jeannette's demise to intense foreign and domestic competition, a continued recession, and, to a lesser degree, mismanagement, which led to a drastic decline in sales beginning in early 1982.

The UFCA proscribes both intentional and constructive fraud. Under the Act's intentional fraud provisions, any conveyance made or obligation incurred either without fair consideration by one who "intends or believes that he will incur debts beyond his ability to pay as they mature," or with an "actual intent . . . to hinder, delay, or defraud . . . creditors" is fraudulent. Actual intent to defraud may be inferred from the circumstances surrounding a transfer.

The UFCA's constructive fraud provisions operate without regard to intent. Under §4, any conveyance made or obligation incurred "by a person who is or will be thereby rendered insolvent" is fraudulent if it is made or incurred for less than fair consideration. Insolvency has two components under Pennsylvania law: insolvency in the "bankruptcy sense" (a deficit net worth immediately after the conveyance), and insolvency in the "equity sense" (an inability to pay debts as they mature). Fair consideration requires a "good faith" exchange of "a fair equivalent."

Under §5, any conveyance made or obligation incurred by a person engaged in "a business or transaction" is fraudulent if it is made or incurred without fair consideration and leaves that person with an "unreasonably small capital." The relationship between "insolvency" under §4 of the UFCA and "unreasonably small capital" under §5 is not clear. However, as we discuss below, the better view would seem to be that "unreasonably small capital" denotes a financial condition short of equitable insolvency. The UFCA's constructive fraud provisions furnish a standard of causation that attempts to link the challenged conveyance with the debtor's bankruptcy.

At first, the applicability of the UFCA's fraudulent conveyance provisions to leveraged buyouts was a matter of some dispute. However, we think it settled, as a general matter at least, that the fraudulent conveyance provisions of the UFCA extend to leveraged buyouts, and defendants do not contest their applicability here.

Because of the difficulty in proving intentional fraud, challenges to leveraged buyouts tend to be predicated on the constructive fraud provisions of the UFCA.

With these general principles in mind, we turn now to an analysis of the leveraged buyout of Jeannette under the constructive and then intentional fraud provisions of the UFCA.

According to the district court, the leveraged buyout was without fair consideration to Jeannette because, in exchange for granting Security Pacific security interests in all its assets and undertaking an $11.7 million demand obligation at 3 1/4 % above prime, all Jeannette received was new management and access to credit. Defendants do not challenge this finding, and we accept it for purposes of our analysis here.

We turn now to the thrust of plaintiff's attack, the district court's solvency and adequacy of capital analyses. As we have discussed, under §4 of the UFCA a conveyance is fraudulent if it is made without fair consideration and renders the transferor insolvent. "A person is insolvent when the present, fair, salable value of his assets is less than the amount that will be required to pay his probable liability on his existing debts as they become absolute and matured." The Pennsylvania Supreme Court has interpreted this provision as requiring solvency in both the "bankruptcy" and "equity" sense. Insolvency is determined "as of the time of the conveyance."

The district court valued Jeannette's assets on a going concern basis and found that immediately after the leveraged buyout the present fair salable value of Jeannette's total assets was at least $26.2-$27.2 million. It then found that the company's total liabilities were $25.2 million. Thus, the district court concluded that Jeannette was solvent in the bankruptcy sense "by at least $1-2 million and most probably by more.

At trial, plaintiff argued that Jeannette was rendered insolvent in the bankruptcy sense because the present fair salable value of Jeannette's total assets could not have exceeded the $12.1 million J. Corp. paid for Jeannette's stock. The district court rejected this argument and undertook its own valuation of Jeannette's assets. We find no error here. Although purchase price may be highly probative of a company's value immediately after a leveraged buyout, it is not the only evidence. The parties here viewed the $12.1 million purchase price as a "significant bargain," made possible by Coca-Cola's decision to focus attention on its bottling business and Brogan's ability to close the deal quickly.

Plaintiff argues that valuation on a going concern basis fails to give effect to "present" in the UFCA's "present fair salable value" language, and the district court should have calculated the amount the company would have received had it attempted to liquidate its PP & E on the date of the acquisition or immediately thereafter. We disagree. Where bankruptcy is not "clearly imminent" on the date of the challenged conveyance, the weight of authority holds that assets should be valued on a going concern basis.

Accordingly, we conclude that the district court did not err in finding that Jeannette was solvent in the bankruptcy sense after the leveraged buyout.

Next, we look at whether the leveraged buyout either rendered Jeannette insolvent in the equity sense or left it with an unreasonably small capital. Although it recognized that these issues were "conceptually distinct," the district court considered them together. Plaintiff contends this was improper because "unreasonably small capital" denotes a financial condition short of equitable insolvency.

As we have discussed, under §5 of the UFCA any conveyance made or obligation incurred by a person engaged in "a business or transaction" is fraudulent if it is made or incurred without fair consideration and leaves that person with an "unreasonably small capital." Unlike "insolvency," "unreasonably small capital" is not defined by the UFCA. This has engendered confusion over the relationship between these concepts: some courts have equated a finding of equitable insolvency with that of unreasonably small capital, whereas others have said that unreasonably small capital encompasses financial difficulties short of equitable insolvency.

We believe the better view is that unreasonably small capital denotes a financial condition short of equitable insolvency.

We think it telling that having adopted §4 of the UFCA, which proscribes conveyances made without fair consideration that render the debtor "insolvent," the drafters saw fit to add §5, which proscribes conveyances made without fair consideration that leave the debtor with an "unreasonably small capital." If the drafters viewed these concepts interchangeably, one would expect them to have employed the same language.

In undertaking its adequacy of capital analysis, the district court focused on the reasonableness of the parties' projections, but also considered the availability on Jeannette's line of credit with Security Pacific. It found the parties' projections reasonable and, based on the availability of credit as well as the company's historical cash flow needs, determined that Jeannette was not left with an unreasonably small capital under the circumstances. Rather than a lack of capital, the district court attributed Jeannette's demise to the "substantial drop in orders and sales that began in 1982," which it attributed in turn to increased foreign and domestic competition and the continued recession.

Because projections tend to be optimistic, their reasonableness must be tested by an objective standard anchored in the company's actual performance. Among the relevant data are cash flow, net sales, gross profit margins, and net profits and losses. However, reliance on historical data alone is not enough. To a degree, parties must also account for difficulties that are likely to arise, including interest rate fluctuations and general economic downturns, and otherwise incorporate some margin for error.

Defendants here relied on two sets of one-year projections, one prepared by Brogan and the other by Ngan. Brogan's projections were based on a month-by-month analysis of Jeannette's balance sheet, income statement, and resulting credit availability. Ngan's projections were grounded in his interviews with Jeannette personnel and examination of the company's financial records for the year and a half preceding the acquisition. The district court found these projections reasonable and prudent when made. We agree.

The district court properly found that Jeannette's failure was caused by a dramatic drop in sales due to increased foreign and domestic competition, rather than a lack of capital. Plaintiff plausibly contends that defendants should have anticipated some of these problems and incorporated a margin for error. But we cannot say the district court erred in finding that the drastic decline in sales was unforeseeable as of the date of the leveraged buyout. Therefore, we conclude that the district court properly determined that the leveraged buyout did not leave Jeannette with an unreasonably small capital.

Because we assume the notion of unreasonably small capital denotes a financial condition short of equitable insolvency, it follows that the transaction did not render Jeannette equitably insolvent either. And because the leveraged buyout neither left Jeannette with an unreasonably small capital nor rendered it equitably insolvent, we agree with the district court that the acquisition does not constitute a fraudulent conveyance under either §§ 4 or 5 of the UFCA.

All that remains to be decided is whether the district court properly determined that the leveraged buyout did not violate the UFCA's intentional fraud provisions. As we have discussed, a conveyance is intentionally fraudulent if it is made either without fair consideration by one who "intends or believes that he will incur debts beyond his ability to pay as they mature," or with an "actual intent . . . to hinder, delay, or defraud either present or future creditors."

The district court found that "defendants did not know or believe that Jeannette's creditors could not be paid, and did not intend to hinder, defraud, or delay creditors." This conclusion followed from the absence of any direct evidence of fraud, as well as defendants' profit motives, the parties' awareness of the transaction's leveraged nature, and Jeannette's operation as a going concern for at least five months following the acquisition.

We conclude, then, that the district court properly held that the leveraged buyout was not intentionally fraudulent.

In sum, we will affirm the district court's conclusions that the leveraged buyout does not constitute a fraudulent conveyance under either the constructive or intentional fraud provisions of the UFCA.

QUESTIONS ABOUT *MOODY*

1. Why does *Moody* focus on section 544(b) instead of section 548? Why does *Moody* discuss provisions of the UFCA?

2. Footnote 3 provides a helpful summary of the various transactions. Both section 548 and section 544(b) refer to a "transfer." What is the transfer that the trustee alleges is voidable under section 544(b)?

3. What is the basis for the court's statement "the leveraged buyout was made for less than fair consideration"? Did Coca-Cola get fair consideration? Is that relevant? Did Jeannette get fair consideration when it entered into a $15.5 million revolving credit arrangement with Security Pacific?

4. What is the difference between insolvency in the bankruptcy sense and insolvency in the equity sense? How would the trustee prove that Jeannette was insolvent in the bankruptcy sense? Insolvent in the equity sense? What does the court mean by the statement "unreasonably small capital denotes a financial condition short of equitable insolvency"?

5. In a more recent reported Delaware decision regarding LBOs as fraudulent conveyances, Judge McKelvie states: "Thus, leveraged buyouts will not be deemed fraudulent when the parties entering the transactions reasonably believed that the acquired company would be solvent when it emerged or that it would have a 'fair chance to survive financially. In such cases, value is exchanged for value." Hechinger Investment Company of Delaware v. Fleet Retail Financial Group, 274 B.R. 71 (Del. 2002). Is he just "shucking us"?

---

11 U.S.C. § 544(b) – State Fraudulent Conveyance Law in Bankruptcy

(b)(1) Except as provided in paragraph (2), the trustee may avoid any transfer of an interest of the debtor in property or any obligation incurred by the debtor that is voidable under applicable law by a creditor holding an unsecured claim that is allowable under section 502 of this title or that is not allowable only under section 502(e) of this title.

(2) Paragraph (1) shall not apply to a transfer of a charitable contribution (as that term is defined in section 548(d)(3)) that is not covered under section 548(a)(1)(B), by reason of section 548(a)(2).

Problem 7-12: Transfers More Than Two Years Before Bankruptcy

D, while insolvent, transfers Greenacre to T for less than reasonably equivalent value. Three years later, D files for bankruptcy. Can the trustee avoid the transfer of Greenacre? What additional facts do you need?

Problem 7-13: Payment of a Debt and Fraudulent Transfer Law

D is insolvent and unable to pay all of its creditors which include A, B and C. C obtains a judgment against D. Before C is able to levy on and sell D's assets, D sells its assets to X at a reasonable price and uses the proceeds from this sale to pay A and B, but not C. What, if anything, can C do? If D files for bankruptcy six months later, what, if anything, can the bankruptcy trustee do? *Cf.* 11 U.S.C. §§ 548, 547, 548(d).

Looking back at the material on fraudulent transfers, the essence of an argument that a transfer is a fraudulent transfer avoidable under section 548 or section 544(b) is that stuff that but for the transfer would be property of the estate was transferred before bankruptcy (1) to someone who was to a creditor (2) for less than reasonably equivalent value so that ALL creditors got less.

Looking ahead to the material on preferential transfers, the essence of an argument that a transfer is avoidable under section 547 is that stuff that but for the transfer would be property of the estate was transferred before bankruptcy (1) to someone who was a creditor (2) for a prior debt so that all OTHER creditors got less.

C. Increasing Property of the Estate by Avoiding Preferential Transfers

1. Elements of a preference

a. Overview of Elements of a Preference under 11 U.S.C. § 547(b)

As we have just seen, the Code provisions relating to fraudulent transfers are very similar to state statutes. As we will now see, the Code provisions relating to preferential transfers are different from both (i) the Code fraudulent conveyance provision and (ii) state statutes.

In looking for a fraudulent transfer, we looked for what the debtor/transferor received – we were concerned that a transferee who was not a creditor benefitted from the transfer to the disadvantage of creditors generally. In looking for a preference, we will look at to whom the transfer was made rather than what the debtor/transferor received for the transfer, and we will be concerned about whether one creditor transferee benefitted from a transfer to the disadvantage of other similar creditors.

There is no state law counterpart to the Code's preference provisions. State creditor's rights law does not "condemn" a preference.[6] Outside of bankruptcy, a debtor, even an insolvent debtor, can treat some creditors more favorably than other similar creditors. Although D owes X, Y, and Z $1,000 each, D can pay X in full before paying Y or Z anything.

Bankruptcy law *does* "condemn" *certain* preferences. A House report that accompanied a draft of the Code explained the rationale for such a bankruptcy policy as follows:

> The purpose of the preference section is two-fold. First, by permitting the trustee to avoid pre-bankruptcy transfers that occur within a short period before bankruptcy, creditors are discouraged from racing to the courthouse to dismember the debtor during his slide into bankruptcy. The protection thus afforded the debtor often enables him to work his way out of a difficult financial situation through cooperation with all of his creditors. Second, and more important, the preference provisions facilitate the prime bankruptcy policy of equality of distribution among creditors of the debtor. Any creditor that received a greater payment than others of his class is required to disgorge so that all may share equally.

H. REP. NO. 595, 95TH CONG., 1ST SESS. 117-18 (1977).

Section 547(b) sets out an initial unnumbered requirement of a transfer of an interest in property of the debtor and then five additional numbered requirements.

---

[6]Some state statutes void certain transfers because of their preferential character. The trustee may take advantage of such statutes by virtue of his powers under section 544(b): if the state anti-preference provision protects any actual creditor with an allowable claim, it protects the bankruptcy trustee. *See In re* Wilson, 106 B.R. 125 (Bankr. W.D. Ky. 1989).

The bankruptcy trustee may void a transfer of property of the debtor if she can establish:

- the transfer was "to or for the benefit of a creditor"; *and*

- the transfer was made for or on account of an "antecedent debt", i.e., a debt owed prior to the time of the transfer; *and*

- the debtor was insolvent at the time of the transfer; *and*

- the transfer was made within 90 days before the date of the filing of the bankruptcy petition, *or*, was made between 90 days and 1 year before the date of the filing of the petition to an "insider"; *and*

- the transfer has the effect of increasing the amount that the transferee would receive in a Chapter 7 case.

The first two numbered requirements of section 547(b) will usually be easy to apply. To illustrate, a true gift is not a preference—not to or for the benefit of a creditor. A pledge of stock to secure a new loan is not a preferential transfer—not for or on account of antecedent debt.

The third numbered element—insolvency of the debtor at the time of the transfer—requires a showing that debts exceed assets at fair valuation, 11 U.S.C. § 101(32). At first blush, this would seem to present significant problems of proof. Proving insolvency requires establishing the value[7] of the assets and the debts.[8] Proof of insolvency has been made much easier under the Code by section 547(f) which creates a rebuttable presumption[9] of insolvency for the 90 days immediately preceding the filing of the bankruptcy petition.

Section 547(b)(4) establishes the preference period as 90 days or one year for an insider. In determining whether the transfer was made within 90 days of the filing of the petition, look to Federal Rule of Civil Procedure 6(a) which provides that the day on which the transfer occurred is not included.[10] In determining whether the transfer was made to an "insider" so that the relevant time period is 1 year, not merely 90 days, look to Code section 101(31)'s definition of insider. Remember that the presumption of insolvency is limited to the 90 days immediately preceding the bankruptcy petition. Accordingly, in order to invalidate a transfer that occurred more than 90 days before the filing of the bankruptcy petition the trustee must establish that the transferee was an "insider" and the debtor was insolvent at the time of the transfer.

---

[7]Courts generally have valued assets at so-called "fair value" or "intrinsic value"—what a willing buyer would pay a willing seller within a reasonable time.

[8]Note that under Section 101(32) exempt property is not considered as an asset in determining solvency. The result is that many consumers are insolvent in the bankruptcy sense.

[9]The Federal Rules of Evidence are incorporated by sections 251 and 252 of Title II of the Bankruptcy Reform Act of 1978. Rule 301 of the Federal Rules of Evidence provides:

> A presumption imposes on the party against whom it is directed the burden of going forward with the evidence to rebut or meet the presumption, but does not shift to such party the burden of proof in the sense of the risk of nonpersuasion, which remains throughout the trial upon the party on whom it was originally cast."

[10]If under state law, a transfer is not fully effective against third parties until public notice of the transfer has been given and such public notice is not timely given, then section 547(e) deems the transfer to have occurred at the time public notice was given. The use of section 547 to invalidate transfers not recorded in a timely fashion is considered infra.

The fifth numbered element, which essentially tests whether the transfer improved the creditor's position, will be satisfied unless the creditor was fully secured before the transfer or the property of the estate is sufficiently large to permit 100 payment to all general claims. Assume, for example, that D makes a $1,000 payment to C, a creditor with a $10,000 general claim, on January 10. On February 20, D files a bankruptcy petition. The property of the estate is sufficient to pay each general creditor 50% of its claim. A general creditor with a $10,000 claim will thus receive $5,000. C, however, will receive a total of $5,500 from D and D's bankruptcy unless the January 10th transfer is avoided. ($1,000 + 50% X (10,000 - 1,000)). Accordingly, the bankruptcy trustee may avoid the January 10th transfer under section 547(b) to "facilitate the prime bankruptcy policy of equality of distribution among creditors."

---

b. Elements of a Preference and Section 547(b), (f), (g)

(b) Except as provided in subsection (c) of this section, the trustee may avoid any transfer of an interest of the debtor in property--

(1) to or for the benefit of a creditor;
(2) for or on account of an antecedent debt owed by the debtor before such transfer was made;
(3) made while the debtor was insolvent;
(4) made--
(A) on or within 90 days before the date of the filing of the petition; or

(B) between ninety days and one year before the date of the filing of the petition, if such creditor at the time of such transfer was an insider; and

(5) that enables such creditor to receive more than such creditor would receive if--
(A) the case were a case under chapter 7 of this title;
(B) the transfer had not been made; and
(C) such creditor received payment of such debt to the extent provided by the provisions of this title. . . .

(f) For the purposes of this section, the debtor is presumed to have been insolvent on and during the 90 days immediately preceding the date of the filing of the petition.

(g) For the purposes of this section, the trustee has the burden of proving the avoidability of a transfer under subsection (b) of this section, and the creditor or party in interest against whom recovery or avoidance is sought has the burden of proving the nonavoidability of a transfer under subsection (c) of this section.

PROBLEM 7-14: "INTEREST OF THE DEBTOR IN PROPERTY"

Bubba is in default on his payment obligations to 27 different creditors: A to Z. On January 15, Bubba's, mother, Momma, pays $3,300 to C, one of Bubba's creditors. Neither Momma nor Bubba pays any of the other creditors. On April 5, Bubba files a bankruptcy petition. Is the January 15 payment a section 547(b) preference?

PROBLEM 7-15: AN "EARMARKED LOAN"

Same facts as 7-14 above except Momma was unable to find C, and so she gave the $3,300 to Bubba with the specific direction to and for the sole purpose of paying C, and Bubba did indeed pay the $3,300 to C. Is the payment to C a section 547(b) preference?

PROBLEM 7-16: ANOTHER "EARMARKED LOAN"

D Corp. is in debt to 27 different creditors, from A Bank to Z Supplies. A Bank, D's largest creditor, makes an additional $330,000 loan to D Corp. to be used to pay Z Supplies so that Z Supplies will continue to supply D Corp. The D Corp./A Bank loan agreement expressly provides that D Corp. will use the loan proceeds only to pay Z Supplies. D Corp. does indeed use the $330,000 loaned by A Bank to pay Z Supplies. Eighty days later, D Corp. files for bankruptcy. Is the $330,000 payment to Z Supplies a preference?

PROBLEM 7-17: "ENABLE SUCH CREDITOR TO RECEIVE MORE" AND UNSECURED CREDITORS

D owes $100,000 to X, $200,000 to Y, and $300,000 to Z. On January 15, D makes a $150,000 payment to Z; D does not make a payment to either X or Y. On April 5, D files for Chapter 7 bankruptcy. If "the case were a case under Chapter 7 "and" the transfer had not been made" holders of unsecured claims would be paid 50% from D's bankruptcy. Why was the $150,000 payment to Z a section 547(b) preference?

PROBLEM 7-18: "ENABLE SUCH CREDITOR TO RECEIVE MORE: AND FULLY SECURED CLAIMS"

D owes S $6,000. The debt to S is secured by a first mortgage on Greenacre, real property owned by D that is valued at $8,000. On January 15, D pays S $3,000. On April 5, D files a bankruptcy petition. Was the $3,000 payment to S a section 547(b) preferential transfer? What, if any, additional information do you need to answer this question?

PROBLEM 7-19: "ENABLE SUCH CREDITOR TO RECEIVE MORE: AND A PARTLY SECURED CLAIM"

1. D owes C $100. C has a first lien on collateral worth $60. D surrenders the collateral to C and C reduces the debt from $100 to $40. Two months later, D files for bankruptcy. Was the transfer of the collateral to C a preference?

2. D owes C $100. C has a first lien on collateral worth $60. D pays C $60 in exchange for C's release of its lien. Two months later, D files for bankruptcy. Was the payment of $60 to C a preference?

3. D owes C $100. C has a first lien on collateral worth $60. D pays C $40. Two months later, D files for bankruptcy. If "the case were a case under Chapter 7" and "the transfer had not been made", holders of unsecured claims would receive 10% of their claims. Was the payment of $40 to C a preference?

---

2. *Avoiding Third Party Preferences and the Deprizio Problem*

OVERVIEW

Most of the above preference problems involve two parties: the debtor transferor and the creditor transferee. The phrase "to or for the benefit of a creditor" in section 547(b)(1) contemplates three party transactions in which D makes a transfer to C that is preferential as to S. *See also* 11 U.S.C. § 550(a)(1) ("or the entity for whose benefit the transfer was made.")

Assume, for example, Firm borrows money from Lender, with payment guaranteed by Firm's officer (Guarantor). It is obvious from reading the hypothetical that Lender is a creditor of Firm, and, while it is not obvious from reading the hypothetical or the Code's definition of creditor,[11] Guarantor is also a "creditor" of Firm—at least for purposes of section 547. As the Seventh Circuit explained,

---

[11]Section 101(10) of the Code defines a creditor as an "entity that has a claim against the debtor . . . ." Section 101(5) of the Code defines claim as a "right to payment, whether or not such right is . . . contingent, matured . . .."

> "Suppose Firm borrows money from Lender, with payment guaranteed by Firm's officer (Guarantor). . . . Guarantor is not Firm's creditor in the colloquial sense, but under § 101[10]of the Code any person with a 'claim' against Firm is a 'creditor,' and anyone with a contingent right to payment holds a 'claim' under § 101[5]. A guarantor has a contingent right to payment from the debtor: if Lender collects from Guarantor, Guarantor succeeds to Lender's entitlements and can collect from Firm. So Guarantor is a 'creditor' in Firm's bankruptcy. A payment (transfer) by Firm to Lender is 'for the benefit of' Guarantor under § 547(b)(1) because every reduction in the debt to Lender reduces Guarantor's exposure. Because the payment to Lender assists Guarantor, it is avoidable under § 547(b)(4)(B) unless one of the exemptions in § 547(c) applies."

Levit v. Ingersoll Rand Fin. Corp., (*In re* V.N. Deprizio Constr. Co.), 874 F.2d 1186, 1190 (7th Cir. 1989)("*Deprizio*").

Finding such an "indirect" preference can be important to Firm's bankruptcy trustee where the transferee, Lender, is insolvent. The transfer is also a preference as to Guarantor under section 547(b), and the trustee can recover from Guarantor under section 550(a)(1).

Finding such an indirect preference can also be important where the transfer is not avoidable as to the actual transferee. Assume that Firm does not file for bankruptcy until six months after it paid Lender. If Lender is not an "insider," the payment is not a preference as to Lender. If Guarantor, like virtually all guarantors, is an "insider," the payment to Lender would still seem to be a preference as to Guarantor. Under these facts, courts have consistently held that Firm's bankruptcy trustee can recover from Guarantor. Until *Deprizio* courts generally held that the bankruptcy trustee could not recover from Lender under these facts.

Deprizio held that a payment to a noninsider creditor where there is an insider guarantor could be recovered from that noninsider creditor even though it occurred more than ninety days before the bankruptcy filing. The methodology of *Deprizio* can be outlined as follows:

- First, look at section 547(b) and determine if there has been a preference to anybody.

- Second, if there has been a preference as to anybody, look at section 550(a)(1) and determine the possible responsible parties.

In essence, *Deprizio* views sections 547 and 550 as independent provisions to be applied independently. The party responsible under section 550 does not have to be the same party as to whom the transfer was preferential.

After *Deprizio*, law professors spent thousands of hours working on articles explaining, attacking or defending *Deprizio*. Practitioners spent even more hours trying to solve possible *Deprizio* problems in transactions involving an insider guarantee and finding possible *Deprizio* problems in very different transactions such as transactions involving a fully secured first mortgage and a partly secured second mortgage. Lenders spent even more time and dollars lobbying Congress. And, Congress added section 550(c) to fix the *Deprizio* problem.

And then in 2005, Congress added section 547(i) to insure that the problem was fully fixed. Please read sections 547(i), 550(a), and section 550(c). Are all indirect preference problems now fixed?

---

11 U.S.C. §§ 550(a)(1), (c)

(a) . . . [T]he trustee may recover . . . from

(1) the initial transferee of such transfer or the entity for whose benefit such transfer was made . . .

(c) If a transfer made between 90 days and one year before the filing of the petition–

(1) is avoided under section 547(b) of this title; and

(2) was made for the benefit of a creditor that at the time of such transfer was an insider; the trustee may not recover under subsection (a) from a transferee that is not an insider.

PROBLEM 7-20: INDIRECT PREFERENCES

1. D borrows $100,000 from C. G, an "insider" of D, guarantees D's payment to C and secures its guarantee by granting C a security interest in equipment worth more than $100,000. D later pays C the $100,000. One hundred days after paying C, D files for bankruptcy. Can D's bankruptcy trustee recover anything from anybody?

2. D owes F $300,000. D owes S $400,000. Both F and S have security interest in all of D's equipment. The equipment has a value of $500,000. D pays F in full. Thirty days after paying F in full, D files for bankruptcy. Can D's bankruptcy trustee recover anything from anybody?

3. D owed C $2,000,000 – an unsecured loan. On January 15, D gets B Bank to issue a $2,000,000 standby letter of credit, naming C as beneficiary. Under this letter of credit, C can draw on the letter of credit on March 1 and receive $2,000,000 from B by establishing unpaid obligations of D. B is willing to issue this letter of credit because D grants S a security interest in collateral worth more than $2,000,000. On March 1, C draws on the letter of credit and receives $2,000,000 from B. On April 5, D files for bankruptcy. What can the trustee recover from whom?

---

3. Exceptions

OVERVIEW OF PREFERENCES EXCEPTED FROM AVOIDANCE

Recall that section 547(b) sets out the elements of a preference. In order to avoid a transfer as a preference, the trustee must allege and establish each of the elements of section 547(b).

Even if the trustee proves her entire case under section 547(b), she may not be able to avoid the transfer. Section 547(c) contains seven exceptions from section 547(b): a creditor/transferee can prevent avoidance of the transfer by proving that the transfer is covered by section 547(c).

Remember the relationship between paragraphs (b) and (c) of section 547(b). "B" not only comes before "C" in the alphabet but also in section 547 of the Code. And, there is a reason that the elements of a preference are set out in section 547(b) before the exceptions are set out in section 547(c). Do section 547(b) first.

Section 547(c) protects transfers that would otherwise be avoidable by the trustee under section 547(b). Section 547(c) applies only in concert with section 547(b). If the trustee fails to establish a preference under section 547(b), it is not necessary to look to section 547(c). It is only after the trustee has proved her entire case under section 547(b) that it becomes necessary to determine whether section 547(c) protects all or part of the transfer from avoidance.

Section 547(c)(2) was amended, making it easier to establish the section 547(c)(2) ordinary course exception. More specifically, the creditor/transferee now has to prove only what was (A) and either what was (B) or (C), not both old (B) and (C).

---

11 U.S.C. §§ 547(c)(2), (4)

(c) The trustee may not avoid under this section a transfer–

(2) to the extent that such transfer was in payment of a debt incurred by the debtor in the ordinary course of business or financial affairs of the debtor and the transferee, and such transfer was—

(A) made in the ordinary course of business or financial affairs of the debtor and the transferee; or

(B) made according to ordinary business terms;

(4) to or for the benefit of a creditor, to the extent that, after such transfer, such creditor gave new value to or for the benefit of the debtor--

(A) not secured by an otherwise unavoidable security interest; and

(B) on account of which new value the debtor did not make an otherwise unavoidable transfer to or for the benefit of such creditor;

PROBLEM 7-21: LATE PAYMENT AS "ORDINARY COURSE"

Tolona, a maker of pizza, issued eight checks to Rose, its sausage supplier [and your client], within 90 days before being thrown into bankruptcy by its creditors. The checks, which totaled a shade under $46,000, cleared and as a result Tolona's debts to Rose were paid in full. Tolona's other major trade creditors stand to receive only 13 cents on the dollar under the plan approved by the bankruptcy court, if the preferential treatment of Rose is allowed to stand. Tolona, as debtor in possession, brought an adversary proceeding against Rose to recover the eight payments as voidable preferences.

Rose's invoices recited "net 7 days," meaning that payment was due within seven days. For years preceding the preference period, however, Tolona rarely paid within seven days; nor did Rose's other customers. Most paid within 21 days.

The eight payments at issue were made between 12 and 32 days after Rose had invoiced Tolona, for an average of 22 days. In the 34 months before the preference period, the average time for which Rose's invoices to Tolona were outstanding was 26 days and the longest time was 46 days. The trustee offers to settle her claim against Rose for $25,000. Do you settle?

PROBLEM 7-22: SUBSEQUENT ADVANCES

D Community Hospital, Inc., (D) filed for bankruptcy. D has approximately $300,000 to pay administrative and unsecured claims exceeding $4,500,000.

Before bankruptcy, C shipped drugs to D on credit. At the beginning of the 90 day preference period, D owed C $42,791. At the date of bankruptcy, D owed C $44,541.96.

During that 90 day period, C shipped D $76,459.04 of drugs on credit, and D made payments to C totaling $76,944.93. A comparison of the amounts invoiced by C with the amounts paid by D shows that each of the payments was on account of an invoice at least two months old.

A chart setting out the timing of the payments and shipments is set out below: The first column shows the dates that C received payments from D; the third column shows the net value of shipments by C to D between checks:

Check Date	Check Amount	Goods Shipped
11/15/89	$12,318.81	
		$21,416.10
11/30/89	$21,813.79	
		$9,752.18
12/15/89	$11,644.11	
		$12,190.38
12/29/89	$21,416.10	
		$14,821.70
1/15/90	$9,752.12	
		$17,529.88
		$748.80
Total:	$76,944.93	$76,459.04

You represent the trustee. Do you accept C's offer to withdraw its proof of claim for $44,541.96 to settle preference claims? *Cf.* 11 U.S.C. § 547(c)(4)

D. Increasing Property of the Estate by Avoiding or Preventing Setoffs

1. *What Is a Right of Setoff?*

Under nonbankruptcy law, certain creditors have a right of setoff. The Supreme Court in Citizens Bank of Maryland v. Strumpf, 516 U.S. 16 (1995) described the right of setoff as follows. "The right of setoff (also called 'offset') allows entities that owe each other money to apply their mutual debts against each other, thereby avoiding 'the absurdity of making A pay B when B owes A.'"

The most common setoff situation involves a person who has borrowed money from the same bank in which she deposits funds. For example, D owes S Bank $666,000 and is in default. D has an account at S Bank with a $400,000 balance. D and S Bank thus owe each other money. Obviously, D owes S Bank $666,000 because of the loan. And, it should be equally obvious that S Bank owes D $400,000 because of D's deposits to her account. Under these facts, S Bank has the right to setoff the $400,000 balance in D's account against the delinquent loan so that the balance owed on the loan is reduced by $400,000 to $266,000 and that the balance in the account is reduced by $400,000 to 0.

The use of setoffs is not limited to banks. The following hypothetical illustrates a setoff by a creditor other than a bank. D regularly buys goods from S. D files for bankruptcy in December. D has not paid S's $400,000 invoice for goods delivered in November because $600,000 of the goods delivered on the October and September orders were defective. D owes S $400,000 and S owes D $600,000. Why should D have to pay $400,000 to S and then S pay $600,000 to D? Setoff, as described by the *Strumpf* case, allows them to "apply their mutual debts against each other."

The Code does not create any new right of setoff. Instead, the Code generally recognizes whatever rights of setoff a creditor would have had outside of bankruptcy. As the introductory language of section 553 states, "this title [title 11, i.e., the Bankruptcy Code] does not affect any right of a creditor to offset."

---

11 U.S.C. § 553 – Setoff

(a) Except as otherwise provided in this section and in sections 362 and 363 of this title, this title does not affect any right of a creditor to offset a mutual debt owing by such creditor to the debtor that arose before the commencement of the case under this title against a claim of such creditor against the debtor that arose before the commencement of the case, except to the extent that–

(1) the claim of such creditor against the debtor is disallowed;

(2) such claim was transferred, by an entity other than the debtor, to such creditor–

(A) after the commencement of the case; or

(B) (i) after 90 days before the date of the filing of the petition; and

(ii) while the debtor was insolvent; or

(3) the debt owed to the debtor by such creditor was incurred by such creditor--

(A) after 90 days before the date of the filing of the petition;

(B) while the debtor was insolvent; and

(C) for the purpose of obtaining a right of setoff against the debtor.

(b) (1), if a creditor offsets a mutual debt owing to the debtor against a claim against the debtor on or within 90 days before the date of the filing of the petition, then the trustee may recover from such creditor the amount so offset to the extent that any insufficiency on the date of such setoff is less than the insufficiency on the later of–

(A) 90 days before the date of the filing of the petition; and

(B) the first date during the 90 days immediately preceding the date of the filing of the petition on which there is an insufficiency.

(2) In this subsection, "insufficiency" means amount, if any, by which a claim against the debtor exceeds a mutual debt owing to the debtor by the holder of such claim.

(c) For the purposes of this section, the debtor is presumed to have been insolvent on and during the 90 days immediately preceding the date of the filing of the petition.

---

2. *Overview of Bankruptcy Law on Setoff*

The bankruptcy law of setoff is primarily sections 506(a), 362(a)(7) and 553.

First, the secured claim status of section 506. As section 506(a) states, bankruptcy law equates the right of setoff with a lien. S Bank, the creditor with a $200,000 right of setoff gets the same recovery in bankruptcy as Z, the creditor with a $200,000 lien.

Second, the stay of setoff under section 362(a)(7). A creditor who did not do its setoff prior to the debtor's filing for bankruptcy cannot exercise the right of setoff after the bankruptcy filing without first obtaining relief from the stay from the bankruptcy court.

Third, the recognition of and limitations on a nonbankruptcy right of setoff in section 553. Again, neither section 553 nor any other provision of the Code creates a right of setoff. Instead, section 553 does three things:

- it generally recognizes a nonbankruptcy right of setoff;
- it protects any prebankruptcy setoff from avoidance under sections 545-548 and any

postbankruptcy setoff from avoidance under section 549;

- it provides a basis in section 553(b) for avoiding a prebankruptcy setoff in which the creditor improved its position within 90 days of bankruptcy and provides bases in section 553(a) for limiting the amount that can be setoff prepetition or postpetition.

PROBLEM 7-23: WHY A RIGHT TO SETOFF IS IMPORTANT IN BANKRUPTCY

D is in bankruptcy. D owes $200 to S, and S owes $100 to D. D owes $200 to A. B owes $100 to D. Compare the treatment in bankruptcy of S, A, and B.

PROBLEM 7-24: APPLYING SECTION 553(b) TO A PREBANKRUPTCY SETOFF

1. D files for bankruptcy. 90 days before bankruptcy, D owes C Bank $100,000 and has $20,000 on deposit in C Bank. 10 days before bankruptcy, C exercised its right of setoff. At that time, D owed C Bank $90,000 and its account in C Bank had a $50,000 balance. Can the trustee recover any part of the $50,000 under section 553(b)? If so, what are C Bank's rights? See 11 U.S.C. 502(h)

2. D files for bankruptcy. 90 days before bankruptcy, D owes C Bank $200,000 and has $220,000 on deposit in C Bank. Eighty-nine days before bankruptcy, D withdraws $180,000 from the account and a check for $22,000, drawn on D's account, is paid by C Bank. Twenty days before D's bankruptcy, C Bank exercises its right of setoff. At that time, D owes C $200,000 and D's account balance is $130,000. Can the bankruptcy trustee

recover any part of the $130,000 setoff under section 553(b)?

3. Note that section 553(b) only applies to prebankruptcy setoffs. Should the bank in problems 1 and 2 wait until after the bankruptcy petition is filed to setoff? *Cf.* 11 U.S.C. §§ 362(a)(7), 553(a). SEE COMMON SENSE.

PROBLEM 7-25: APPLYING SECTION 553(a) TO A PREBANKRUPTCY SETOFF

Acme and Baker are related corporations. D owes Acme $100,000 for goods bought on open account. Baker owes D $120,000 services rendered. Acme assigns its $100,000 account receivable to Baker. Ten days later, D files for bankruptcy. When the trustee demands Baker pay the estate the $120,000 for services rendered, Baker asserts a right of setoff and pays only $20,000. Advise the bankruptcy trustee as to her rights, if any, under section 553.

PROBLEM 7-26: THE "AROSE BEFORE" REQUIREMENTS OF SECTION 553(a)

TLC Hospitals, Inc. ("TLC") was the operator of skilled nursing facilities that provided many of their services subject to reimbursement by Medicare, a health insurance program administered by the United States Department of Health and Human Services ("HHS"). In June 1994, TLC filed a petition to reorganize its business under Chapter 11 of the Code. TLC thereafter continued to operate the skilled nursing facilities and participate in the Medicare program until it later converted its petition to a Chapter 7 liquidation case. Audits then revealed that HHS had overpaid TLC for services rendered prepetition and underpaid TLC for services rendered postpetition. Can HHS exercise its right of setoff to deduct prepetition overpayments HHS made to TLC from the sums it owes to TLC for postpetition services?

---

3. Distinguishing Setoff from Recoupment

a. Overview of Recoupment

Much like setoff, the doctrine of recoupment is a common law concept which dates to legal antiquity. Unlike a setoff, however, recoupment requires that the defense asserted arise out of the same transaction upon which plaintiff bases his claim.

The value of recoupment is grounded in the Code's treatment, or more accurately, nontreatment, of recoupment rights. Specifically, the Code fails to provide mention of, much less a system for dealing with, common law recoupment rights. Nonetheless, courts have virtually uniformly agreed that the Code preserves the right of a creditor to claim, and unilaterally exercise, any common law recoupment rights available against the debtor. As such, the 'same transaction' requirement within the context of bankruptcy provides the foundation for the equitable right of recoupment against the debtor: '[A]llowing the creditor to recoup damages simply allows the debtor precisely what is due when viewing the transaction 'as a whole.'

Recall that sections 362(a)(7), 506 and 553 expressly deal with setoffs. Recoupment is not mentioned in any of these three sections of the Bankruptcy Code; recoupment is not mentioned in any section of the Bankruptcy Code.

Gary E. Sullivan, *In Defense of Recoupment*, 15 BANKR. DEV. J. 63 (1998).

---

b. A Healthcare Financing View of Recoupment

IN RE HOLYOKE NURSING HOME, INC.
372 F.3d 1(1st Cir. 2004)

CYR, Senior Circuit Judge:

Chapter 11 debtor Holyoke Nursing Home, Inc. ("Holyoke") and its official unsecured creditors' committee challenge a bankruptcy court ruling which awarded summary judgment to the Health Care Financing Administration ("HCFA") on Holyoke's adversary proceeding complaint that HCFA;s postpetition efforts to collect prepetition Medicaid overpayments to Holyoke either constituted preferential transfers or violated the automatic stay. We affirm the judgment.

BACKGROUND

In 1990, Holyoke became a participant in the Medicare Reimbursement Program pursuant to a Provider Agreement whereby HCFA periodically reimburses health care providers like Holyoke for the estimated costs of services they have provided to Medicare patients subject to an annual audit aimed at determining the reasonableness of the costs of those services. In the event HCFA determines that the costs of a provider's past reimbursement requests were either overstated or understated, HCFA is authorized by statute to make "necessary adjustments [to the provider's current reimbursement requests] on account of previously made overpayments or underpayments."

In 2000, HCFA determined that it had overpaid Holyoke $373,639 for cost years 1997 and 1998, and proceeded to deduct a portion of the overpayment and interest–viz., $177.656.25–from Holyoke's pending reimbursement requests for cost-year 2000. In late 2000, Holyoke filed a voluntary chapter 11 petition, and thereupon commenced the instant adversary proceeding against HCFA, contending that HCFA's prepetition deductions ($99,965.97) constituted voidable preferential transfers, see 11 U.S.C. § 547(b), and that its postpetition deductions ($77,690.28) were effected in violation of the automatic stay, see id. § 362(a)(7).

In due course, the bankruptcy court entered summary judgment for HCFA, holding that the HCFA deductions from current reimbursement requests were in the nature of recoupment, and constituted neither voidable preferences nor violations of the automatic stay. The district court denied Holyoke's intermediate appeal in an unpublished opinion.

DISCUSSION

The lone issue on appeal–one of first impression in this circuit–is whether the HCFA deductions for a portion of the 1997-98 overpayments it made to Holyoke are more akin to a setoff, whose collection normally is barred by the automatic stay, see 11 U.S.C. § 362(a)(7) (staying "the setoff of any debt owing to the debtor that arose before the commencement of the [bankruptcy] case"), or to a recoupment, which normally is not barred.

The pertinent distinction between a setoff and a recoupment is whether the debt owed the creditor (viz., HCFA) arose out of the "same transaction" as the debt the creditor owes the debtor. For example, if A were to buy a truck worth $1,000 from B, but A finds that he must expend $100 to put the truck back into working condition, A might send B a check for only $900, rather than pay B $1,000 and await a $100 refund from B. The $100 A recovers by deducting it from the amount he owes B constitutes a recoupment because the reciprocal obligations arose out of the same transaction, viz., the purchase-sale of the truck. Had B filed for bankruptcy protection, A could recoup the $100 prepetition debt from B without violating the automatic stay because "it would be inequitable for [B] to enjoy the benefits of that transaction without also meeting its obligations." Univ. Med. Ctr. v. Sullivan (In re Univ. Med. Ctr.), 973 F.2d 1065, 1081 (3d Cir.1992) (emphasis added). Thus, in essence the recoupment doctrine constitutes an equitable exception to the Bankruptcy Code § 362(a)(7) prohibition against offsetting reciprocal debts.

However, were A to buy the same truck from B, but instead of sending a $1,000 check to B, sends a $900 check (deducting the $100 B still owes him for a bicycle A sold B earlier), the $100 which A has deducted constitutes a setoff because the mutual obligations did not arise out of the same transaction, but from different transactions, viz., the sale of the bicycle and the sale of the truck. Upon the intervention of B's bankruptcy proceeding, Bankruptcy Code § 362(a)(7) would prohibit A from effecting such a deduction, and A's claim for $100 would be collectible (if at all) through the normal distributive mechanisms prescribed by the Bankruptcy Code.

Neither the Medicare statute, the Bankruptcy Code, nor their respective legislative histories expressly treats the issue before us, and other courts of appeals have split on the issue.

We accept the majority view, and hold that the HCFA recovery of the $177,656.25 in overpayments previously made to Holyoke constituted a transaction in the nature of a recoupment, rather than a setoff. As such, it was neither a voidable preferential transfer nor a violation of the automatic stay. Both the Medicare statute and the provider agreement–by contemplating HCFA's payment of estimated costs, corrective audits, and retroactive adjustments or partial adjustments for overpayments and underpayments in determining HCFA's net liability for current cost-year services–strongly indicate that the contractual relationship between HCFA and Holyoke constitutes one, ongoing, integrated transaction.

Holyoke further contends that, even if HCFA's overpayment adjustments constitute recoupments, recoupment is an equitable doctrine, and therefore the case should be remanded to the bankruptcy court to determine the appropriate equitable balance to be struck as between itself and HCFA. Holyoke notes, for instance, that such recoupments for prepetition overpayments may either cut off or drastically reduce a bankruptcy provider's most prominent cash flow, thereby diminishing the prospects for a successful chapter 11 reorganization, and jeopardizing the availability of healthcare to Medicare recipients. Holyoke argues, on the other hand, that HCFA will not be deprived of all recovery, but likely will be able to recover (albeit partially) on its overpayment claims under Holyoke's chapter 11 Plan.

We perceive no need for equitable balancing. First, the recoupment doctrine is equitable for the very reason that "it would be inequitable for [Holyoke] to enjoy the benefits of [the same] transaction without also meeting its obligations." Thus, HCFA was *overcharged* for the services provided by Holyoke in 1997 and 1998, and in equity, Holyoke should not be allowed to retain the windfall. Moreover, to allow these overpayments to become property of the Holyoke bankrupt estate would mean that its estate might apply a portion of those government-provided funds to satisfy Holyoke's other debts, thus violating the manifest congressional intent that HCFA expend such funds only to defray the costs of services provided to Medicare beneficiaries.

Second, even assuming *arguendo* that further equitable balancing is permissible, the equitable powers of the bankruptcy court do not accord it "a roving commission to do equity," nor "authorize courts to create substantive rights that are otherwise, unavailable under the Code, or to expand the contractual obligations of parties." As we conclude that Congress contemplated that the Medicare provider agreements would constitute a single, ongoing, and integrated transaction, the equitable powers of the bankruptcy court do not entitle it to second-guess Congress's implicit policy choices. Both by statute and by contract, the HCFA has the unqualified right to recoup these overpayments *in full*, and to return the funds to the public fisc, where they can be used to fund other facilities providing care to Medicare beneficiaries. In our view, public policy would be ill-served by permitting insolvent providers–like Holyoke–a windfall at the expense of other Medicare providers which have managed their facilities prudently to avoid chapter 11. Accordingly, we conclude that a remand to the bankruptcy court for a balancing of the equities is not warranted.

AFFIRMED.

QUESTIONS ABOUT *HOLYOKE NURSING*

1. Is there a statutory basis for HCFA's right of recoupment?

2. Is there a statutory basis in the Code for the First Circuit's decision?

3. Is a creditor's exercise of its right of recoupment subject to the automatic stay? Should *Holyoke* have based its argument on section 362(a)(3)?

4. Review recoupment: According to *In re* Lincoln-Gerard USA, Inc., 2002 WL 1676564 (Bankr. M.D.N.C. 2002):

   Because it is based upon the same transaction, recoupment is essentially a defense to the debtor's claim against the creditor. See Epstein, Nickles & White, BANKRUPTCY § 6-45 (1992). Although recoupment is not expressly recognized in the

> Bankruptcy Code, recoupment nonetheless is allowed in bankruptcy cases when the requisite circumstances are present. Because recoupment works a preference not provided for in the Bankruptcy Code, the bankruptcy courts have been careful to limit the application of recoupment to situations in which the subject matter of the creditor's claim arises from the same transaction or contract as the debtor's claim against the creditor. . . . In determining whether conflicting claims arose from the same transaction or contract for purposes of recoupment, the courts generally have focused on the facts and the equities of each case, rather than resorting to a precisely defined test or standard."

Did you agree with the statement that "recoupment works a preference"?

E. INCREASING PROPERTY OF THE ESTATE BY AVOIDING UNRECORDED TRANSFERS

OVERVIEW

State law and federal law requires recordation or other public notice of many kinds of liens. For example,

- Real estate recording statutes require the recording of real property transfers (including mortgages).
- Article 9 of the Uniform Commercial Code provides for similar public notice, i.e., perfection, of liens on personal - property.
- The Federal Tax Lien Act provides for public filing of federal tax liens.

The Code does not have not its own public notice requirements. The Code does not impose any new, additional recordation requirements. Rather, the Code through provisions such as section 544(a) and 545 incorporates these non-bankruptcy recordation requirements.

A bankruptcy trustee [or Chapter 11 debtor in possession] can avoid certain pre-petition liens that are not recorded or otherwise perfected. A creditor's failure to give the required public notice of its lien can adversely affect other creditors. If creditor X does not record its lien on D's property, other creditors might not know that D's property is encumbered. Relying on the mistaken belief that D holds property free from liens, other creditors might extend credit, refrain from obtaining a lien, or forbear from instituting collection proceedings.

Section 544(a) empowers the bankruptcy trustee to invalidate any transfer that under non-bankruptcy law is voidable as to a creditor who extended credit and obtained a lien on the date of the filing of the bankruptcy petition, or is voidable as to a bona fide purchaser of real property, whether or not such a creditor or purchaser actually exists. In applying section 544(a), it is thus necessary to determine whether:

- non-bankruptcy law public notice requirements have been timely satisfied; and

- a creditor who extended credit and obtained a lien on the date that the petition was filed or a bona fide purchaser of real property on the date of the bankruptcy petition comes within the class of persons protected by such state law.

In applying section 544(a), it is not necessary to determine "whether or not such a creditor actually exists." Section 544(a) gives the trustee the status and rights of a hypothetical creditor who extends credit as of the date of the bankruptcy petition.

And, in applying section 544(a), it generally will not be necessary to "bill your time." Section 544(a) problems of unrecorded mortgages and unperfected security interests generally arise in law professors' problems, not in clients' deals.

---

11 U.S.C. § 544(a). Trustee as Lien Creditor and as Successor to Certain Creditors and Purchasers

(a) The trustee shall have, as of the commencement of the case, and without regard to any knowledge of the trustee or of any creditor, the rights and powers of, or may avoid any transfer of property of the debtor or any obligation incurred by the debtor that is voidable by–

(1) a creditor that extends credit to the debtor at the time of the commencement of the case, and that obtains, at such time and with respect to such credit, a judicial lien on all property on which a creditor on a simple contract could have obtained such a judicial lien, whether or not such a creditor exists;

(2) a creditor that extends credit to the debtor at the time of the commencement of the case, and obtains, at such time and with respect to such credit, an execution against the debtor that is returned unsatisfied at such time, whether or not such a creditor exists; or

(3) a bona fide purchaser of real property, other than fixtures, from the debtor, against whom applicable law permits such transfer to be perfected, that obtains the status of a bona fide purchaser and has perfected such transfer at the time of the commencement of the case, whether or not such a purchaser exists.

Problem 7-27: Unrecorded Mortgage

On January 15, D borrows $666,000 from M. M obtains a mortgage. M improperly records the mortgage. On April 5, D files for bankruptcy. Will the trustee be available to avoid M's mortgage under section 544(a)? If so, what are M's rights?

PROBLEM 7-28: UNPERFECTED SECURITY INTEREST

On January 15, D borrows $666,000 from S. S obtains a security interest on D's inventory. S fails to perfect its security interest. *Cf.* UCC § 9-317(a)(1). On April 5, D files for bankruptcy. Will the trustee be able to avoid S's security interest under section 544(a)?

PROBLEM 7-29: SNIDELY WHIPLASH'S DELAYED RECORDATION

On January 10, Dudley Doright, D, borrows $10,000 from Snidely Whiplash, S, and gives S a security interest in his horse, Horse. On December 29 later that year, S properly files the financing statement. On December 30, D files a bankruptcy petition. Will D's bankruptcy trustee be able to invalidate S's security interest UNDER SECTION 544?

F. INCREASING PROPERTY OF THE ESTATE BY AVOIDING TRANSFERS THAT ARE RECORDED, BUT NOT "TIMELY" RECORDED

OVERVIEW

In the Doright/Snidely Whiplash problem above, Doright's bankruptcy trustee cannot invalidate Snidely's security interest under section 544(a): Section 544(a)(1) gives the bankruptcy trustee the rights and powers of a creditor that obtained a lien on the date of bankruptcy. The security interest was perfected on the date of bankruptcy. A perfected security interest is effective as against a lien creditor. *SHOULD* Doright's bankruptcy trustee be able to invalidate Snidely's lien?

Remember the reasons for invalidating such "secret liens." Creditors of Doright may have been misled by Snidely Whiplash's failure to record or a delay in recording. Unaware of this "secret," unrecorded lien, a creditor might extend credit to Doright that it would not extend if aware of the lien. Unaware of a "secret," unrecorded lien, a creditor might delay in collecting a delinquent debt from Doright that it would try to collect if aware of the lien. Accordingly, the Code should invalidate transfers that are not timely recorded. And it does. In section 547.

Although it is easy to see the reason for invalidating liens that are not timely perfected, it is difficult to understand why section 547 should be the mechanism for invalidating such liens. The easy way to invalidate such secret liens would be to add a section to the Code to the effect that any lien required to be recorded by state law must be recorded within 10 (21? 30?) days after it is obtained in order to be valid in bankruptcy. While that is the "easy way," it is not the way of the Code.

Basically, the Code's method is to "deem" that, for purposes of applying the requirements of section 547(b), the date of transfer is the date of recordation or perfection, not the actual date of transfer. Thus, a transfer for new consideration that is not timely recorded or perfected will be treated as a transfer for antecedent debt.

The Doright/Snidely Whiplash hypothetical illustrates the practical significance of treating the recordation date as the transfer date. Remember, Doright borrowed $10,000 from Snidely Whiplash on January 10 and gave Snidely a security interest in equipment which Snidely perfected on December 29. Doright filed a bankruptcy petition on December 30. At first, it might seem that section 547 is not applicable—that the January 10 security "transfer" from Doright to Snidely Whiplash was not for an antecedent indebtedness and did not occur within 90 days of the bankruptcy petition. For purposes of section 547, however, the transfer will be deemed made on December 29, not January 10. [Under section

9-301, Snidely Whiplash's security interest would not be effective as against subsequent judicial lien creditors until that date. Accordingly, by reason of section 547(e), the transfer will not be deemed made until that date.] Thus, the "December 29 transfer" would be within 90 days of the bankruptcy petition. Thus, the "December 29 transfer" would be for an antecedent indebtedness, i.e., the $100,000 loaned on January 10. Thus, the trustee would be able to invalidate S's security interest under section 547.

The above hypothetical illustrates that a delay in perfection can result in a security interest actually given for present consideration being deemed made for an antecedent indebtedness and thus a section 547 preference. The Snidely Whiplash problem is an easy one – delay of more than 11 months in filing and then filing just before the debtor's bankruptcy. What if the creditor's delay in recording is a matter of days, instead of months? Section 547(e) does not require immediate perfection – it instead provides a "grace period."

---

11 U.S.C. § 547(e)

(e)(1) For the purposes of this section–

(A) a transfer of real property other than fixtures, but including the interest of a seller or purchaser under a contract for the sale of real property, is perfected when a bona fide purchaser of such property form the debtor against whom applicable law permits such transfer to be perfected cannot acquire an interest that is superior to the interest of the transferee; and

(B) a transfer of a fixture or property other than real property is perfected when a creditor on a simple contract cannot acquire a judicial lien that is superior to the interest of the transferee.

(2) For the purposes of this section, except as provided in paragraph (3) of this subsection, a transfer is made –

(A) at the time such transfer takes effect between the transferor and the transferee, if such transfer is perfected at, or within 30 days after, such time, except as provided in subsection (c)(3)(B);

(B) at the time such transfer is perfected, if such transfer is perfected after such 30 days; or

(C) immediately before the date of the filing of the petition, if such transfer is not perfected at the later of–

(i) the commencement of the case; or

(ii) 30 days after such transfer takes effect between the transferor and the transferee.

PROBLEM 7-30: SNIDELY WHIPLASH AND 547(e)(2)(B)

One more time: On January 10, Dudley Doright, D, borrows $10,000 from Snidely Whiplash, S. And, on January 10, at the very same time D signs a note promising to repay the $10,000, D signs a security agreement, granting S a security interest in his horse. Horse. On December 29, S properly files the financing statement. On December 30, D files a bankruptcy petition. Will D's bankruptcy trustee be able to avoid S's security interest under section 547?

PROBLEM 7-31: SNIDELY WHIPLASH AND 547(e)(2)(A)

Same facts as above except that (i) Snidely filed his financing statement on January 19, and (ii) Dudley filed his bankruptcy petition on April 15.

G. INCREASING PROPERTY OF THE ESTATE BY TURNOVER

Usually property of the estate will be in the possession of the debtor at the time of the bankruptcy. Property of the estate, however, is not limited to property in the possession of the debtor. "Interests of the debtor in property" "wherever located and by whomever held" are "property of the estate." Sections 542 and 543 govern the turnover of property of the estate in possession of a third party at the time of bankruptcy.

---

11 U.S.C. § 543(a), (b)(1) – TURNOVER OF PROPERTY BY A CUSTODIAN

(a) A custodian with knowledge of the commencement of a case under this title concerning the debtor may not make any disbursement from, or take any action in the administration of, property of the debtor, proceeds, product, offspring, rents, or profits of such property, or property of the estate, in the possession, custody, or control of such custodian, except such action as is necessary to preserve such property.

(b) A custodian shall--

(1) deliver to the trustee any property of the debtor held by or transferred to such custodian, or proceeds, product, offspring, rents, or profits of such property, that is in such custodian's possession, custody, or control on the date that such custodian acquires knowledge of the commencement of the case; . . .

PROBLEM 7-32: EFFECT OF BANKRUPTCY ON RECEIVERSHIP

Debtor owns and operates the New Society Court Apartments (the "Apartments") upon which WRH Mortgage, Inc. ("WRH") holds a Note and Mortgage. Upon Debtor's' default under the Mortgage, WRH instituted foreclosure proceedings. The state court enters its order appointing you receiver to take possession of and operate the Apartments. A day after your taking possession of the Apartments, Debtor files a Chapter 11 petition. What do you do?

---

11 U.S.C. § 542(a) – TURNOVER OF PROPERTY TO THE ESTATE

> [A]n entity, other than a custodian, in possession, custody, or control, during the case, of property that the trustee may use, sell, or lease under section 363 of this title, or that the debtor may exempt under section 522 of this title, shall deliver to the trustee, and account for, such property or the value of such property, unless such property is of inconsequential value or benefit to the estate.

UNITED STATES V. WHITING POOLS, INC.

462 U.S. 198 (1983)

JUSTICE BLACKMUN delivered the opinion of the Court.

Promptly after the Internal Revenue Service (IRS or Service) seized respondent's property to satisfy a tax lien, respondent filed a petition for reorganization under the Bankruptcy Reform Act of 1978, hereinafter referred to as the "Bankruptcy Code." The issue before us is whether § 542(a) of that Code authorized the Bankruptcy Court to subject the IRS to a turnover order with respect to the seized property.

Respondent Whiting Pools, Inc., a corporation, sells, installs, and services swimming pools and related equipment and supplies. As of January 1981, Whiting owed approximately $92,000 in Federal Insurance Contribution Act taxes and federal taxes withheld from its employees, but had failed to respond to assessments and demands for payment by the IRS. As a consequence, a tax lien in that amount attached to all of Whiting's property.[1]

On January 14, 1981, the Service seized Whiting's tangible personal property-- equipment, vehicles, inventory, and office supplies--pursuant to the levy and distraint provision of the Internal Revenue Code of 1954. According to uncontroverted findings, the estimated liquidation value of the property seized was, at most, $35,000, but its estimated going-concern value

---

[1]Section 6321 of the Internal Revenue Code of 1954, 26 U.S.C. § 6321, provides: "If any person liable to pay any tax neglects or refuses to pay the same after demand, the amount . . . shall be a lien in favor of the United States upon all property and rights to property, whether real or personal, belonging to such person."

in Whiting's hands was $162,876. The very next day, January 15, Whiting filed a petition for reorganization, under the Bankruptcy Code's Chapter 11, in the United States Bankruptcy Court for the Western District of New York. Whiting was continued as debtor- in-possession.

The United States, intending to proceed with a tax sale of the property,[4] moved in the Bankruptcy Court for a declaration that the automatic stay provision of the Bankruptcy Code, § 362(a), is inapplicable to the IRS or, in the alternative, for relief from the stay. Whiting counterclaimed for an order requiring the Service to turn the seized property over to the bankruptcy estate pursuant to § 542(a) of the Bankruptcy Code.[5] Whiting intended to use the property in its reorganized business.

The Bankruptcy Court determined that the IRS was bound by the automatic stay provision. Because it found that the seized property was essential to Whiting's reorganization effort, it refused to lift the stay. Acting under § 543(b)(1) of the Bankruptcy Code, rather than under § 542(a), the court directed the IRS to turn the property over to Whiting on the condition that Whiting provide the Service with specified protection for its interests.[7]

The United States District Court reversed, holding that a turnover order against the Service was not authorized by either § 542(a) or § 543(b)(1). The United States Court of Appeals for the Second Circuit, in turn, reversed the District Court. It

---

[4]Section 6335, as amended, of the 1954 Code, 26 U.S.C. § 6335, provides for the sale of seized property after notice. The taxpayer is entitled to any surplus of the proceeds of the sale. § 6342(b).

[5]Section 542(a) provides in relevant part: "[A]n entity, other than a custodian, in possession, custody, or control, during the case, of property that the trustee may use, sell, or lease under section 363 of this title, or that the debtor may exempt under section 522 of this title, shall deliver to the trustee, and account for, such property or the value of such property, unless such property is of inconsequential value or benefit to the estate."

[7]Section 363(e) of the Bankruptcy Code provides: "Notwithstanding any other provision of this section, at any time, on request of an entity that has an interest in property used, sold, or leased, or proposed to be used, sold, or leased by the trustee, the court shall prohibit or condition such use, sale, or lease as is necessary to provide adequate protection of such interest. In any hearing under this section, the trustee has the burden of proof on the issue of adequate protection." Pursuant to this section, the Bankruptcy Court set the following conditions to protect the tax lien: Whiting was to pay the Service $20,000 before the turnover occurred; Whiting also was to pay $1,000 a month until the taxes were satisfied; the IRS was to retain its lien during this period; and if Whiting failed to make the payments, the stay was to be lifted.

held that a turnover order could issue against the Service under § 542(a), and it remanded the case for reconsideration of the adequacy of the Bankruptcy Court's protection conditions. The Court of Appeals acknowledged that its ruling was contrary to that reached by the United States Court of Appeals for the Fourth Circuit. We granted certiorari to resolve this conflict in an important area of the law under the new Bankruptcy Code.

By virtue of its tax lien, the Service holds a secured interest in Whiting's property. We first examine whether §542(a) of the Bankruptcy Code generally authorizes the turnover of a debtor's property seized by a secured creditor prior to the commencement of reorganization proceedings. Section 542(a) requires an entity in possession of "property that the trustee may use, sell, or lease under § 363" to deliver that property to the trustee. Subsections (b) and (c) of § 363 authorize the trustee to use, sell, or lease any "property of the estate," subject to certain conditions for the protection of creditors with an interest in the property. Section 541(a)(1) defines the "estate" as "comprised of all the following property, wherever located: (1) . . . all legal or equitable interests of the debtor in property as of the commencement of the case." Although these statutes could be read to limit the estate to those "interests of the debtor in property" at the time of the filing of the petition, we view them as a definition of what is included in the estate, rather than as a limitation.

In proceedings under the reorganization provisions of the Bankruptcy Code, a troubled enterprise may be restructured to enable it to operate successfully in the future. Until the business can be reorganized pursuant to a plan under 11 U.S.C. §§ 1121- 1129, the trustee or debtor-in- possession is authorized to manage the property of the estate and to continue the operation of the business. By permitting reorganization, Congress anticipated that the business would continue to provide jobs, to satisfy creditors' claims, and to produce a return for its owners. Congress presumed that the assets of the debtor would be more valuable if used in a rehabilitated business than if "sold for scrap." The reorganization effort would have small chance of success, however, if property essential to running the business were excluded from the estate. Thus, to facilitate the rehabilitation of the debtor's business, all the debtor's property must be included in the reorganization estate.

This authorization extends even to property of the estate in which a creditor has a secured interest. § 363(b) and (c).

Although Congress might have safeguarded the interests of secured creditors outright by excluding from the estate any property subject to a secured interest, it chose instead to include such property in the estate and to provide secured creditors with "adequate protection" for their interests. § 363(e). At the secured creditor's insistence, the bankruptcy court must place such limits or conditions on the trustee's power to sell, use, or lease property as are necessary to protect the creditor. The creditor with a secured interest in property included in the estate must look to this provision for protection, rather than to the nonbankruptcy remedy of possession.

Both the congressional goal of encouraging reorganizations and Congress' choice of methods to protect secured creditors suggest that Congress intended a broad range of property to be included in the estate.

The statutory language reflects this view of the scope of the estate. As noted above, § 541(a) provides that the "estate is comprised of all the following property, wherever located: . . . all legal or equitable interests of the debtor in property as of the commencement of the case."[8] The House and Senate Reports on the Bankruptcy Code indicate that § 541(a)(1)'s scope is broad. Most important, in the context of this case, § 541(a)(1) is intended to include in the estate any property made available to the estate by other provisions of the Bankruptcy Code. Several of these provisions bring into the estate property in which the debtor did not have a possessory interest at the time the bankruptcy proceedings commenced.[10]

Section 542(a) is such a provision. It requires an entity (other than a custodian) holding any property of the debtor that the trustee can use under § 363 to turn that property over to the trustee. Given the broad scope of the reorganization

---

[8]Section 541(a)(1) speaks in terms of the debtor's "interests . . . in property," rather than property in which the debtor has an interest, but this choice of language was not meant to limit the expansive scope of the section. The legislative history indicates that Congress intended to exclude from the estate property of others in which the debtor had some minor interest such as a lien or bare legal title.

[10]See, e.g., §§ 543, 547, and 548. These sections permit the trustee to demand the turnover of property that is in the possession of others if that possession is due to a custodial arrangement, § 543, to a preferential transfer, § 547, or to a fraudulent transfer, § 548. We do not now decide the outer boundaries of the bankruptcy estate. We note only that Congress plainly excluded property of others held by the debtor in trust at the time of the filing of the petition.

estate, property of the debtor repossessed by a secured creditor falls within this rule, and therefore may be drawn into the estate. While there are explicit limitations on the reach of § 542(a), none requires that the debtor hold a possessory interest in the property at the commencement of the reorganization proceedings.

As does all bankruptcy law, § 542(a) modifies the procedural rights available to creditors to protect and satisfy their liens.[14] In effect, § 542(a) grants to the estate a possessory interest in certain property of the debtor that was not held by the debtor at the commencement of reorganization proceedings. The Bankruptcy Code provides secured creditors various rights, including the right to adequate protection, and these rights replace the protection afforded by possession.

This interpretation of § 542(a) is supported by the section's legislative history.

Moreover, this interpretation of § 542 in the reorganization context is consistent with judicial precedent predating the Bankruptcy . Under Chapter X, the reorganization chapter of the Bankruptcy Act of 1878, the bankruptcy court could order the turnover of collateral in the hands of a secured creditor. Nothing in the legislative history evinces a congressional intent to depart from that practice. Any other interpretation of § 542(a) would deprive the bankruptcy estate of the assets and property essential to its rehabilitation effort and thereby would frustrate the congressional purpose behind the reorganization provisions.

We conclude that the reorganization estate includes property of the debtor that has been seized by a creditor prior to the filing of a petition for reorganization.

We see no reason why a different result should obtain when the IRS is the creditor. The Service is bound by §

---

[14]One of the procedural rights the law of secured transactions grants a secured creditor to enforce its lien is the right to take possession of the secured property upon the debtor's default. A creditor's possessory interest resulting from the exercise of this right is subject to certain restrictions on the creditor's use of the property. Here, we address the abrogation of the Service's possessory interest obtained pursuant to its tax lien, a secured interest. We do not decide whether any property of the debtor in which a third party holds a possessory interest independent of a creditor's remedies is subject to turnover under § 542(a). For example, if property is pledged to the secured creditor so that the creditor has possession prior to any default, 542(a) may not require turnover.

542(a) to the same extent as any other secured creditor. The Bankruptcy Code expressly states that the term "entity," used in § 542(a), includes a governmental unit. § 101(14).

When property seized prior to the filing of a petition is drawn into the Chapter 11 reorganization estate, the Service's tax lien is not dissolved; nor is its status as a secured creditor destroyed. The IRS, under § 363(e), remains entitled to adequate protection for its interests, to other rights enjoyed by secured creditors, and to the specific privileges accorded tax collectors. Section 542(a) simply requires the Service to seek protection of its interest according to the congressionally established bankruptcy procedures, rather than by withholding the seized property from the debtor's efforts to reorganize. The judgment of the Court of Appeals is affirmed.
It is so ordered.

QUESTIONS ABOUT *WHITING POOLS*

1. What facts were important in this case? Was it important that the creditor was the IRS instead of a private secured creditor? Was it important that Whiting Pools filed for Chapter 11, instead of Chapter 7? Was it important the IRS had not yet sold the property it had taken from Whiting Pools?

2. What Code provisions were important to the Court's decision in this case? Why does the Court quote from section 541? What does this quotation from the Court mean:

   > Although these statutes could be read to limit the estate [property of the estate] to those interests of the debtor in property" at the time of the filing of the petition, we view them as a definition of what is included in the estate, rather than as a limitation.

3. At the time of the filing of the petition, did Whiting Pools have "interests" in the property that the IRS had seized? What if the IRS sale of the property is conducted by a dedicated

agent such as Jim Prufrock and nets an amount greater than the amount of the tax liability?

PROBLEM 7-34: PREPETITION REPOSSESSION OF MOTOR VEHICLE

In January, 2005, D purchased a 2005 Volvo for $35,700. The major part of the purchase price was financed by Southern Financial Corporation ("S"). The finance contract between D and S sets out the terms of repayment and grants S a security interest in D's Volvo. By December 2005, D has missed three monthly payments to S. On December 7, S exercised its rights under its contract and under the Uniform Commercial Code and (i) repossessed the Volvo and (ii) sent D a notice of a pending private sale. D's response was to file (i) a Chapter 13 petition and (ii) an adversary proceeding seeking the turnover of the Volvo under section 542 and a determination that S was violating the automatic stay of section 362 by its continued possession of the Volvo. Advise S. What, if any, additional information do you need to advise S?

Unit 8

Issues That Can Arise In Cases Under Any Chapter: Leases and Executory Contracts

Section 365 of the Code treats prebankruptcy unexpired leases and "executory contracts" different from other prebankruptcy transactions. Since there is a general understanding of how section 365 works and a general confusion over what a section 365 "executory contract" is, this book deals first with how section 365 works and then with the scope of section 365.

Recall that bankruptcy involves both the assets and the obligations of the debtor. Bankruptcy deals with these assets and obligations through the creation of a fictional estate. The assets of the debtor become property of the estate. The estate is administered by a trustee or debtor in possession to satisfy the secured and unsecured payment obligations of the debtor, i.e., the "claims." In the course of administration, the estate will incur its own obligations; these administrative expenses are given priority over the debtor's unsecured obligations.

Generally, the Code's provisions dealing with the debtor's assets are separate from the Code's provisions dealing with the debtor's obligations and the estate's obligations: property of the estate in section 541, allowable claims and administrative expenses in sections 502 and 503. A lease or executory contract involves potentially both property of the estate and a claim against the debtor or the estate.

This hybrid nature of a lease or executory contract is most apparent in lease situations in which the debtor is the lessee. Assume, for example, that D Store, Inc. (D) leases its store in the mall from L. D later files for bankruptcy. By reason of the lease, D has section 541 "interests . . . in property." D's rights to the use of the space in the mall is property of the estate. D's lease, however, involves burdens as well as benefits. D has performance obligations under the lease such as paying rent. Accordingly, by reason of the lease, L has a "right to payment," i.e., a section 101(5) claim.

For over sixty years, the American bankruptcy statutes have had special sections for leases and executory contracts. In 1938, the Chandler Act Amendments added section 70b and 63c. In 1978, the Code replaced these provisions with section 365 and 1110. And, later, section 1113. And, still later, section 1114. While there are now a few pages of bankruptcy statutes on leases and executory contracts instead of a couple of paragraphs, the core concepts from the Chandler Act have been retained.

A. What Are The Choices, Consequences Of Choices, And Time To Choose ?

1. *Choices In the Code*

In section 365, the bankruptcy treatment of a lease or executory contract can take one of three possible forms:

1. Rejection
2. Assumption
3. Assignment

Assumption and rejection are both mentioned in section 365(a) and throughout section 365. Assignment is not mentioned in section 365(a); assignment is, however, provided for in section 365(f).

In comparing rejection, assumption, and assignment, it is important to keep in mind that the lease or contract involves potentially both property of the estate and a claim against the estate. The following chart provides a general view of the effect of rejection, assumption, and assignment on property of the estate and claims against the estate.

	REJECTION	ASSUMPTION	ASSIGNMENT
Property of the estate	No property of the estate	Debtor's rights under contract or lease	Proceeds, if any, from assignment of debtor's rights under contract or lease
Claims	Unsecured claim for (1) pre-petition defaults and (2) breach resulting from rejection; administrative expense priority claim for post-petition obligations, if any.	Administrative expense priority claim for all obligations under contract or lease, post-petition or pre-petition.	No claim against the estate. Nondebtor party to an assigned contract or lease looks solely to the assignee.

Rejection, assumption, and assignment are the only three elections available to the debtor under the Code. A debtor does not have a statutory right to modify or change the terms of an unexpired lease or an executory contract.

To illustrate, assume that D Stores, Inc., (D) leases a space in a mall from L for $20,000 a year. D owes $600,000 to unsecured trade creditors and $3,000,000 to secured lenders. D files a Chapter 11 petition. D wants to continue operating in the mall and wants to retain the leasehold. D will have to assume the lease payment as is: $20,000 a year, no change. In its Chapter 11 plan, D will be able to alter its payment obligation to lenders and trade creditors, secured and unsecured. D cannot, however, use bankruptcy to effect a modification in its obligations under its leases or executory contracts. Rejection, assumption, or assignment. *No modification*.

The italicized statement in the text is both correct and misleading. A debtor does not have a right under the Code to change the terms of an unexpired lease or executory contract. Nonetheless, a debtor is often able to use its bargaining power and other legal rights under the Code to "persuade" the other party to the lease or contract to "agree" to modifications in the lease or contract. For example, D is leasing a building from L. D files for bankruptcy. D wants L to reduce her rent. D presents L with the choice that either D will reject the lease which will leave L with an empty building and a general claim in D's bankruptcy case or L will agree to modifications in the lease. L will often choose to modify the lease.

---

2. *Choices in Kmart*

6/24/02 Crain's Det. Bus. 3
2002 WL 10365602
Monday, June 24, 2002
Vol: 18 Num: 25

Slow auction leads Kmart to give up on sale of most leases: Less than 25% of closed stores are claimed

Brent Snavely & Jennette Smith

. . . Kmart, which filed for Chapter 11 bankruptcy protection Jan. 22, sold 59 leases and raised at least $46.6 million at the auction.

Some say the auction results were fairly good for a company that was selling the rights to occupy buildings that it does not own and no longer wants to occupy. But Kmart got rid of less than 25 percent of the 278 it tried to sell, leaving the retailer with more than 200 leases to deal with. . . .

"We are going to move forward on rejecting a number of these leases," said Michael Freitag, a partner with the New York City public-relations firm Kekst and Co. and a spokesman for Kmart. "But we have some where we might see if there is still some value to be maintained." . . .

Kmart needed to act swiftly to save money. Earlier this year it told the court that it was costing more than $11 million a month in rent and other fees to hold on to the leases, said Fred Ringel, an attorney who represents several landlords and a partner at New York City-based Robinson Brog Leinwand Green Genovese & Gluck P.C.

When Kmart announced plans to close 283 stores, the theory was that the unexpired leases would be desirable to other retailers because many offered low rent with multiyear terms. But a depressed economy, an excess supply of empty sites left over from other recent retail bankruptcies and the undesirable characteristics of the Kmart sites caused many potential buyers to turn away, retail experts say.

Plus, much of the interest in Kmart's leases ended before the auction began. That's because a motion submitted by Cleveland-based Developers Diversified Realty Corp. to change the bidding process was defeated at a hearing just before the auction. Developers Diversified argued that a bid on 53 stores submitted by a joint venture led by New Hyde Park, N.Y.-based Kimco Realty Group unfairly chilled the bidding. The bid was structured so that anyone bidding on any of the leases Kimco wanted had to bid on all 53 sites.

Developers Diversified said Kmart could get more money if it auctioned the stores individually. About a dozen other landlords made that argument, Ringel said.

But Kimco guaranteed Kmart $43 million and might pay more in the future, because Kimco agreed to share profits. And both of Kmart's creditors committees told the judge that they supported Kmart's argument that a store-by-store auction wasn't worth the risk of ending up with less money. The judge ruled against Developers Diversified. . . .

Kimco Vice President Ray Edwards said he wasn't surprised at the lack of interest shown in the majority of Kmart's leases. "This was the bottom group on a performance level. It was 300 stores, but it was the 300 bottom stores in a 2,100-store chain," Edwards said.

Many of the landlords are hoping Kmart terminates more leases.

Scott Campbell, vice president of equity research at Raymond James Financial Inc. in St. Petersburg, Fla., said having a center anchored by a closed Kmart store makes neighboring tenants and landlords anxious. In fact, Ringel said, some landlords are better off if Kmart terminates its leases. "They have stores that are empty, and rather than have continued uncertainty, they'd like to be able to move forward," he said.

In other Kmart news last week: Lead law firm Skadden, Arps, Slate Meagher & Flom asked the U.S. Bankruptcy Court in Chicago for $9.48 million in fees for work done in the first three months of the retailer's bankruptcy . . . The firm also sought reimbursement of $1.17 million for expenses incurred while working on Kmart's Chapter 11 case from Jan. 25 to April 30.

---

3. *Questions about Kmart's Leases*

1. Why was the Kimco joint venture willing to pay $43 million for the 54 leases? Who gets the $43 million? What do the landlords get? *See* section 365(f), (b). If Kimco defaults on a lease, can the landlord still recover from Kmart? *See* section 365(k).

2. The business journal article refers to Kmart's selling leases. Section 363 governs sales of property of the estate. Is a section 365 assignment the same as a sale? If so, which section controls– section 363 or section 365?

The article also refers to Kmart's terminating leases? Is a section 365 rejection the same as a termination? *Cf.* sections 365(g)("constitutes a breach"), 365(h)("may treat such lease as terminated by the rejection").

3. The article also suggests that some landlords are "better off if Kmart terminates [sic] its leases." What will a landlord get if its lease is rejected? *Cf.* sections 365(g), 502(g), 502(b)(6) and . . . What additional information do you need to be able to tell a landlord how much it will receive from Kmart if its lease is rejected in the Kmart bankruptcy?

   The excerpt from the article notes that Kmart has 1,800 other stores. Reading this in the article should raise the question how soon does a debtor like Kmart have to decide whether to assume or reject more than 2,000 leases.

4. Time to "Choose"

Prior to the 2005 legislation, the Bankruptcy Code provided that (1) a Chapter 11 debtor had to decide whether to assume or reject leases of commercial real estate within 60 days after filing for bankruptcy, but (2) the bankruptcy court could extend the time period "for cause." While there was no limit on the number of extensions or the duration of the extension, the common bankruptcy court practice was to extend the debtor's decision period until plan confirmation.

This bankruptcy court practice was prompted in substantial part by an opinion written by Judge Calabresi in *In re* Klein Sleep Prods., Inc., 78 F.3d 18 (2d Cir. 1996). There Klein Sleep Products, Inc. (Klein) assumed a commercial lease early in its Chapter 11 case. When the Chapter 11 reorganization efforts were unsuccessful, Klein surrendered the leasehold and moved to reject the lease. The landlord successfully sued the bankruptcy estate for the payment of all rent over the life of the lease. According to Judge Calabresi, "we hold that claims for future rent arising out of assumed leases are administrative expenses, regardless of whether they are subsequently rejected, and that they are not capped at a year's worth of unpaid rent under section 502(b)(6). We reach this conclusion in light of the prior practice under the Bankruptcy Act, the timing provisions of the Code, and an understanding that debtors generally benefit from court-approved assumption of executory contracts and unexpired leases."

The 2005 legislation changes the initial 60-day decision period to 120 days but allows the court to grant only a single 90-day extension "for cause." Any additional extension beyond 210 days (120 + 90) requires consent of the landlord. The new law also limits administrative expense priority claims arising from the later rejection of previously assumed leases to monetary obligations due in the two years following rejection.

A memo with the intriguing title, *"New Bankruptcy Law Amendments: A Creeping Repeal of Chapter 11"*, posted on a major law firm's website, http://www.skadden.com/Index.cfm?contentID=51&itemID=1017 concludes "the overall effect of these amendments is to force large retail debtors to make early decisions that could well prove disastrous for their overall business plans and creditor recoveries."

Note that the article refers to the bankruptcy court's approval of Kmart's assignment of leases and Judge Calabresi refers to the bankruptcy court's approval of Klein Sleep's assumption of lease. This raises the question . . .

B. WHO MAKES THE CHOICE OF REJECTION, ASSUMPTION OR ASSIGNMENT?

11 U.S.C. § 365(a) refers to the "trustee." "The trustee . . . may assume or reject." And section 1107 gives a Chapter 11 debtor in possession a trustee's powers.

Section 365(a) also requires court approval of assumption or rejection of leases or executory contracts. Section 365(a) does not indicate what standard the bankruptcy court should apply in determining whether to approve the assumption or rejection of a lease or executory contract. Bankruptcy judges generally apply a business judgment test and give great weight to the business judgment of the debtor. Should the Tampa bankruptcy judge grant Sabal Hotel's motion to reject its franchise contract with Holiday Inn set out below?

---

11 U.S.C. § 365(a) – EXECUTORY CONTRACTS AND UNEXPIRED LEASES

(a) Except as provided in section 765 and 766 of this title and in subsections (b), (c), and (d) of this section, the trustee, subject to the court's approval, may assume or reject any executory contract or unexpired lease of the debtor.

SABAL HOTEL MOTION TO REJECT EXECUTORY CONTRACT

IN THE UNITED STATES BANKRUPTCY COURT
FOR THE MIDDLE DISTRICT OF FLORIDA
TAMPA DIVISION

IN RE:	)	
	)	CASE NO. 91-91-35998131
SABAL HOTEL, LTD.,	)	
	)	CHAPTER 11
Debtor.	)	
________________________	)	

MOTION TO REJECT EXECUTORY CONTRACT

SABAL HOTEL, LTD., as Debtor and Debtor-in-Possession, by its undersigned attorneys, moves, pursuant to 11 U.S.C. 365, to reject its executory contract with Holiday Inns Inc. on the following grounds:

1. The Debtor has filed a voluntary Petition under Chapter 11 of the Bankruptcy Code and has been retained in possession of its assets as Debtor-in-Possession. No committee of creditors has been appointed in this case.

2. The Debtor owns and operates a hotel facility located in the Sabal Park industrial-business area in the eastern suburbs of Tampa, Florida. The Debtor's facility is a multi-story hotel comprising of 265 guest rooms and suites as well as various public areas, function rooms, restaurants, and the like. The Debtor's hotel facility is four years old, and can be described a "first rate" hotel facility.

3. On March 6, 1987, Debtor entered into a Holiday Inn License Agreement ("Contract") with Holiday Inns, Inc. The Contract expires on March 5, 2007. The Contract is an "executory contract" for purposes of section 365.

4. The Contract provides for termination by the Debtor on twelve months notice. Because it was the Debtor's business judgment that its Contract costs exceeded its Contract benefits, Debtor sent a termination notice to Holiday Inns, Inc. on or about March 7, 1991.

5. Similarly, it is the business judgment of the Debtor as Debtor-in-Possession that the costs of the Contract to the estate exceed the benefits to the estate from the Contract and that the Contract inhibits rather than enhances the prospects of an effective reorganization.

WHEREFORE, SABAL HOTEL, LTD. prays this Court to enter an order authorizing it to reject its executory contract with Holiday Inns Inc.

JOHNSON, BLAKELY, POPE, BOKOR, RUPPEL & BURNS, P.A.

PROBLEM 8-1: OBJECTION TO REJECTION BY NON-DEBTOR PARTY

Should the bankruptcy court approve the rejection if Holiday Inn objects? What if the License Agreement provides for liquidated damages of $100,000.00 if the License Agreement is rejected in a bankruptcy case?

PROBLEM 8-2: OBJECTION TO REJECTION BY OTHER CREDITORS IN THE CASE

Should the bankruptcy court approve the rejection if the bank that has a mortgage on the hotel objects?

PROBLEM 8-3: OBJECTION TO ASSUMPTION

Assume that the debtor Sabal Hotel was moving for court approval of an assumption of its contract with

Holiday Inn. As attorney for the creditors' committee, would you object?

C. CAN A CLAUSE IN A PRE-BANKRUPTCY LEASE OR CONTRACT CONTROL THE CHOICE IN BANKRUPTCY?

1. Bankruptcy Termination Clauses

11 U.S.C. § 365(e)(1)

(e)(1) Notwithstanding a provision in an executory contract or unexpired lease, or in applicable law, an executory contract or unexpired lease of the debtor may not be terminated or modified, and any right or obligation under such contract or lease may not be terminated or modified, at any time after the commencement of the case solely because of a provision in such contract or lease that is conditioned on--

(A) the insolvency or financial condition of the debtor at any time before the closing of the case;

(B) the commencement of a case under this title; or

(C) the appointment of or taking possession by a trustee in a case under this title or a custodian before such commencement.

PROBLEM 8-4: EFFECTIVENESS OF *AM JUR* BANKRUPTCY TERMINATION CLAUSE

Would you use the following clause in a real estate lease?

11B AM. JUR. LEGAL FORMS 2D LEASES OF REAL PROPERTY § 161:924 (Rev 1998).

Termination for Bankruptcy of Lessee – Lessor May Reenter and Terminate Lease or Relet Premises

It shall be a breach of this lease agreement if lessee shall (1) become insolvent, or (2) be declared a bankrupt, or (3) appoint a receiver to take possession of lessee's assets, or (4) make a general assignment for the benefit of creditors of lessee. In addition to the other legal rights and remedies, lessor shall have the following remedies on breach of this lease agreement:

(1) Lessor may reenter the demised premises immediately, and remove all personnel and property of lessee;

> (2) After reentry, lessor may terminate this lease agreement by giving ________ days' written notice of termination to lessee, or lessor may, without terminating this lease agreement, relet the demised premises or any part of the demised premises, for any term, at a rent and terms that lessor may choose . . .

---

2. *Section 365(f) and Contractual Prohibitions on Assignment*

11 U.S.C. § 365(f)

(f)

(1) Except as provided in subsections (b) and (c) of this section, notwithstanding a provision in an executory contract or unexpired lease of the debtor, or in applicable law, that prohibits, restricts, or conditions the assignment of such contract or lease, the trustee may assign such contract or lease under paragraph (2) of this subsection.

. . .

(3) Notwithstanding a provision in an executory contract or unexpired lease of the debtor, or in applicable law that terminates or modifies, or permits a party other than the debtor to terminate or modify, such contract or lease or a right or obligation under such contract or lease on account of an assignment of such contract or lease, such contract, lease, right, or obligation may not be terminated or modified under such provision because of the assumption or assignment of such contract or lease by the trustee.

PROBLEM 8-5: EFFECTIVENESS OF LEASE CLAUSES REQUIRING LESSOR'S CONSENT TO ASSIGNMENT

L leases a building to T. The lease contains the following provision: "The lessee shall not sell or assign this lease or sublet said premises or any part thereof without first obtaining the written consent of the lessor." T files for bankruptcy. What is the effect of this lease provision?

D. WHEN? WHAT HAPPENS DURING THE "GAP" BETWEEN THE FILING OF THE PETITION AND THE CHOICE?

11 U.S.C. § 365(d)(1)-(4)

(d)

(1) In a case under chapter 7 of this title, if the trustee does not assume or reject an executory contract or unexpired lease of residential real property or of personal property of the debtor within 60 days after the order for relief, or within such additional time as the court, for cause, within such 60- day period, fixes, then such contract or lease is deemed rejected.

(2) In a case under chapter 9, 11, 12, or 13 of this title, the trustee may assume or reject an executory contract or unexpired lease of residential real property or of personal property of the debtor at any time before the confirmation of a plan but the court, on the request of any party to such contract or lease, may order the trustee to determine within a specified period of time whether to assume or reject such contract or lease.

(3) The trustee shall timely perform all the obligations of the debtor, except those specified in section 365(b)(2), arising from and after the order for relief under any unexpired lease of nonresidential real property, until such lease is assumed or rejected, notwithstanding section 503(b)(1) of this title. The court may extend, for cause, the time for performance of any such obligation that arises within 60 days after the date of the order for relief, but the time for performance shall not be extended beyond such 60-day period. This subsection shall not be deemed to affect the trustee's obligations under the

provisions of subsection (b) or (f) of this section. Acceptance of any such performance does not constitute waiver or relinquishment of the lessor's rights under such lease or under this title.

(4)

(A) Subject to subparagraph (B), in any case under any chapter of this title, an unexpired lease of nonresidential real property under which the debtor is the lessee shall be deemed rejected, and the trustee shall immediately surrender that nonresidential real property to the lessor, if the trustee does not assume or reject the unexpired lease by the earlier of

(i) the date that is 120 days after the date of the order for relief; or

(ii) the date of the entry of an order confirming a plan.

(B)

(i) The court may extend the period determined under subparagraph (A), prior to the expiration of the 120-day period, for 90 days upon motion of the trustee or lessor for cause.

(ii) If the court grants an extension under clause (i), the court may grant a subsequent extension only upon prior written consent of the lessor in each instance.

PROBLEM 8-6: DECIDING ON COMMERCIAL REAL ESTATE LEASES

Gap, Inc. (GAP, Banana Republic, and Old Navy) has more than 3,000 stores in the United States, UK, France, and Japan. If Gap, Inc. files for bankruptcy, how long will Gap, Inc., have to decide whether to assume or reject its U.S. leases? *See* (again, we hope) section 365(d)(4). Is

Gap, Inc. required to continue making monthly rent payments until it decides whether to assume or reject these U.S. leases? *See* section 365(d)(3).

PROBLEM 8-7: DECIDING ON EQUIPMENT LEASES

Gap, Inc. also leases equipment from L. Gap, Inc. is uncertain how much of the leased equipment it will need in its "reorganized" business. How long can Gap, Inc. delay the decision to assume or reject equipment leases? What if any action can L take? *See* section 365(d)(2). Is Gap, Inc. required to continue making monthly rent payments until it decides whether to assume or reject? *See* section 365(d)(5) (formerly section 365(d)(10) as set out below.

> (5) The trustee shall timely perform all of the obligations of the debtor, except those specified in section 365(b)(2), first arising from or after 60 days after the order for relief in a case under chapter 11 of this title under an unexpired lease of personal property (other than personal property leased to an individual primarily for personal, family, or household purposes), until such lease is assumed or rejected notwithstanding section 503(b)(1) of this title, unless the court, after notice and a hearing and based on the equities of the case, orders otherwise with respect to the obligations or timely performance thereof. This subsection shall not be deemed to affect the trustee's obligations under the provisions of subsection (b) or (f). Acceptance of any such performance does not constitute waiver or relinquishment of the lessor's rights under such lease or under this title.

E. WHAT ARE THE REQUIREMENTS FOR ASSUMING A LEASE OR EXECUTORY CONTRACT?

11 U.S.C. § 365(b)

> (b)
>
> (1) If there has been a default in an executory contract or unexpired lease of the debtor, the trustee may not assume such contract or lease unless, at the time of assumption of such contract or lease, the trustee–

(A) cures, or provides adequate assurance that the trustee will promptly cure, such default other than a default that is a breach of a provision relating to the satisfaction of any provision (other than a penalty rate or penalty provision) relating to a default arising from any failure to perform nonmonetary obligations under an unexpired lease of real property, if it is impossible for the trustee to cure such default by performing nonmonetary acts at and after the time of assumption, except that if such default arises from a failure to operate in accordance with a nonresidential real property lease, then such default shall be cured by performance at and after the time of assumption in accordance with such lease, and pecuniary losses resulting from such default shall be compensated in accordance with the provisions of this paragraph;

(B) compensates, or provides adequate assurance that the trustee will promptly compensate, a party other than the debtor to such contract or lease, for any actual pecuniary loss to such party resulting from such default; and

(C) provides adequate assurance of future performance under such contract or lease

(2) Paragraph (1) of this subsection does not apply to a default that is a breach of a provision relating to--

(A) the insolvency or financial condition of the debtor at any time before the closing of the case;

(B) the commencement of a case under this title;

(C) the appointment of or taking possession by a trustee in a case under this title or a custodian before such commencement; or

(D) the satisfaction of any penalty rate or penalty provision relating to a default arising from any failure by the debtor to perform nonmonetary obligations under the executory contract or unexpired lease.

---

1. Requirements For Assumption If Default

PROBLEM 8-8: PAST PAYMENT DEFAULTS

Your client D has filed for Chapter 11 bankruptcy and has decided to assume all of its leases. One of the landlords, L, sends you a letter claiming that the amount necessary to cure the defaults under its lease is $52,000. The letter itemized the amount claimed as follows: (1) past rent due for the months of June, July, and September of 2001, $40,000 (2) late charges and interest, $7,800 and (3) attorney's fees, $4,200. Advise D as to what it has to pay in order to assume the lease. See section 365(b)(1)(A), (B), (2)(D).

---

2. Requirements For Assumption If No Default

PROBLEM 8-9: ASSUMPTION AND NO DEFAULT

L leases a building to D. D files for bankruptcy. If D is not in default under the lease, would D have to provide adequate assurance of future performance in order to obtain a court order approving its assumption of the lease?

F. WHAT ARE ADDITIONAL ISSUES WHEN THE CHOICE IS ASSIGNMENT?

1. Change In Use

MATTER OF U.L. RADIO CORP.

19 B.R. 537 (Bankr. S.D.N.Y. 1982)

JOHN J. GALGAY, Bankruptcy Judge.

Debtor, U.L. Radio Corp., has moved for an order, pursuant to Bankruptcy Code section 365(f), authorizing it to assume its lease ("Lease") with Jemrock Realty Company ("Jemrock"), the landlord, and authorizing U.L. Radio to assign the Lease to Just Heaven Restaurant, Ltd. ("Just Heaven").

U.L. Radio operates the leasehold as a television sales and service store. Just Heaven, the prospective assignee, will operate the premises as a small bistro. Jemrock opposes such an assignment, citing a use clause in the Lease which provides that the lessee shall use the premises only for television service and sale of electrical appliances. Jemrock asserts that the assignment of the Lease to Just Heaven would unlawfully modify the Lease by violating the use clause. Such modification, Jemrock avers, is not permitted under section 365 without the landlord's consent, which consent Jemrock withholds.

Use Clause

After a hearing, the Court ordered the parties to submit proposed findings of fact and conclusions of law (hereinafter "Findings and Conclusions"). The Court has considered all the papers submitted by the parties, the oral arguments and the applicable law and legislative history. The Court grants debtor's motion to assume and assign the Lease to Just Heaven.

I. Background

On September 17, 1979, the debtor entered into the Lease with Jemrock for a store located at 2656 Broadway, New York, New York. The store is located in a building which is also occupied by a grocery store, a Chinese restaurant, a liquor store, and 170 apartments. The term of the Lease is for ten years. . . . Paragraph 43 of the Rider to the Lease provides that the tenant may assign the Lease with the written consent of the Landlord, which consent is not to be unreasonably withheld.

On May 20, 1981, the debtor filed an original petition under Chapter 11 of the Bankruptcy Code and continues to operate its business as debtor in possession. No creditors' committee has been formed. The debtor intends to propose a liquidation plan of reorganization. The debtor is current in the payment of rent and related charges required by the terms of the Lease and is not in default of any of the Lease terms.

In furtherance of its intention to liquidate all of its assets and to propose a plan of reorganization, the debtor, subject to the approval of this Court, entered into an assignment of the Lease to Just Heaven. The proposed assignment provides, inter alia, that Just Heaven will pay to the Debtor as consideration for the assignment as follows: for the period commencing three months after this Court's approval of the assignment to October 31, 1988, the sum of $2000 per month. Such payments will fund a plan paying unsecured creditors

100 percent of their claims. Rockwell International, the largest creditor, recommends the assignment.

The president of Just Heaven has executed a personal guarantee for the payment of rent in favor of the landlord for the first two years of the assignment, together with a statement that her net worth exceeds $50,000.

The Lease provides in paragraph 45 of the rider to the Lease that "any noise emanating from said premises shall be deemed a breach of the terms and conditions of this Lease." Just Heaven has allocated $20,000 for construction, including soundproofing. David Humpal St. James, Vice President and Secretary as well as a director and a shareholder of Just Heaven, is a noted interior designer including the design of commercial restaurants. His design work has involved soundproofing.

II. Issues

Two issues confront this Court: (1) Have the provisions of section 365, regarding assumption and assignment of leases, been satisfied? (2) Can deviation from a use clause prevent the assignment of a lease, when the assumption and assignment otherwise comport with the requirements of section 365?

III. Assumption and Assignment Under Section 365

Code section 365 governs the assumption and assignment of executory contracts, providing broad authority to a trustee or debtor in possession[15] to assume and assign an unexpired lease. 11 U.S.C. §365(a). The aim of this statutory authority to assume a lease is to "assist in the debtor's rehabilitation or liquidation."

Assignment of a lease, which is at issue here, must comply with section 365(f), which states:

> (f)(1) Except as provided in subsection (c) of this section, notwithstanding a provision in an executory contract or unexpired lease of the debtor, or in applicable law, that prohibits, restricts, or conditions the assignment of such contract or lease, the trustee may

[15]Code section 1107 vests the rights, powers, and duties of a trustee in a debtor in possession.

assign such contract or lease under paragraph (2) of this subsection.

(2) The trustee may assign an executory contract or unexpired lease of the debtor only if-

(A) the trustee assumes such contract or lease in accordance with the provisions of this section; and

(B) adequate assurance of future performance by the assignee of such contract or lease is provided, whether or not there has been a default in such contract or lease.

(3) Notwithstanding a provision in an executory contract or unexpired lease of the debtor, or in applicable law that terminates or modifies, or permits a party other than the debtor to terminate or modify, such contract or lease or a right or obligation under such contract or lease on account of an assignment of such contract or lease, such contract, lease right, or obligation may not be terminated or modified under such provision because of the assumption or assignment of such contract or lease by the trustee.

. . .

A. Requirements of Assumption

The first requirement of assignment under section 365(f)(2) is proper assumption under section 365. The broad authority of a trustee or debtor in possession to assume is limited in Code section 365 by subsections (b), (c), and (d).

Section 365(b)(1) and (2) prescribe conditions to assumption of a lease if a default has occurred. "Subsection (b) requires the (debtor) to cure any default in the . . . lease and to provide adequate assurance of future performance . . . before he may assume." No default exists under the Lease before this Court; therefore, the subsection (b) requirements for assignment are not applicable.

Section 365(c) prohibits a debtor from assuming a lease if applicable nonbankruptcy law "independent of any language in the contract or Lease itself" excuses the other party from giving performance to or receiving performance from someone other than the debtor. Such "nondelegable" and, therefore, non-assumable contracts and leases include those for unique personal services, as well as those to extend credit, to make loans, and to issue securities. The Lease before this Court does not fall under the prohibition of section 365(c).

Section 365(d) sets time limits on the assumption of unexpired leases. The time requirements of subsection (d) have been met and are not at issue.

B. Adequate Assurance of Future Performance

The second requirement of assignment under section 365(f)(2) is adequate assurance of future performance ("adequate assurance"). Adequate assurance also appears in section 365(b) as a requirement of assumption if an executory contract is in default. The phrase "adequate assurance of future performance" is not found in the Bankruptcy Act.

Adequate assurance is not defined in section 365(f) nor in the legislative history of section 365(f), but "(t)he definition should generally be the same as in section 365(b)." In the legislative history of section 365(b), Congress while discussing assumption under section 365(b) and the bankruptcy clause under section 365(f), provided this explanation of adequate assurance: "If a trustee is to assume a contract or lease, the courts will have to insure that the trustee's performance under the contract or lease gives the other contracting party the full benefit of the bargain."

Beyond equating adequate assurance with the full benefit of the bargain, Congress offers no definition of adequate assurance except in the case of real property leases in shopping centers. The Lease at issue here is not located in a shopping center. Congress [House Report] described a shopping center as "often a carefully planned enterprise, and though it consists of numerous individual tenants, the center is planned as a single unit, often subject to a master lease or financing agreement." The building in which U.L. Radio is located is primarily a residential apartment building, with a liquor store, a grocery store, a restaurant, and U.L. Radio on the first floor. Thus the specific provisions of adequate assurance in the shopping center case do not apply to the assignment at issue here.

Apart from shopping center leases, Congress "entrusted the courts with the definition of adequate assurance of the performance of contracts and other leases." Adequate assurance of future performance are not words of art, but are to be given practical, pragmatic construction. What constitutes "adequate assurance" is to be determined by factual conditions. The broad authorization of the trustee or debtor to assume or assign unexpired leases, notwithstanding anti-assignment or bankruptcy clauses, prompted the admonition from Congress that the courts must "be sensitive to the rights of the nondebtor party to . . . unexpired leases."

The phrase "adequate assurance of future performance" was adopted from Uniform Commercial Code section 2-609. U.C.C. section 2-609 . . . indicates that "adequate assurance" focuses on the financial condition of a contracting party and his ability to meet his financial obligations. Regarding adequate assurance under an assignment pursuant to section 365(f)(2), the Court in In re Lafayette Radio Electronics stated, "(T)he Court's primary focus will be on the ability of (the assignee) to comply with the financial obligations under the agreement."

. . .

Thus, the primary focus of adequate assurance is the assignee's ability to satisfy financial obligations under the lease. In this case, the president of the assignee has executed a personal guarantee of the payment of rent in favor of the landlord for the first two years of the assignment, together with a statement that her net worth exceeds $50,000. The assignee has budgeted $20,000 for construction, enhancing the chances of success of the assignee's enterprise. The assignee will have operating capital of an additional $30,000. Upon these facts, the Court rules that adequate assurance of future financial performance has been provided by the assignee.

IV. Use Clause

However, adequate assurance of future financial performance is not the complete statutory requirement; adequate assurance of future performance is. The financial capability of an assignee may be sufficient for a finding of adequate assurance under an executory sales contract or a similar commercial transaction. In a landlord-tenant relationship, more than an assignee's ability to comply with the financial provisions of a lease may be required. More particularly, will compliance with a use clause be required in order to provide adequate assurance?

Congress indicates that adequate assurance will give the landlord the full benefit of his bargain. In its case-by-case determination of those factors, beyond financial assurance, which constitute the landlord's bargain, the Court will generally consider the provisions of the lease to be assigned.

However, it is equally clear that, by requiring provision of adequate assurance under section 365, i.e., "the lessor's receipt of the 'full benefit of his bargain'," Congress did not require the Court to assure "literal fulfillment by the lessee of each and every term of the bargain." Section 365, by its own terms, empowers the court to render unenforceable bankruptcy clauses and anti-assignment clauses which permit modification or termination of a lease for filing in bankruptcy or assignment of the lease. 11 U.S.C. § 365(e), (f)(3). Section 365(k) relieves the estate of liability for future breaches of a lease after assignment, notwithstanding lease provisions to the contrary.

. . .

Section 365 expresses a clear Congressional policy favoring assumption and assignment. Such a policy will insure that potential valuable assets will not be lost by a debtor who is reorganizing his affairs or liquidating assets for distribution to creditors. This policy parallels case law which disfavors forfeiture. To prevent an assignment of an unexpired lease by demanding strict enforcement of a use clause, and thereby contradict clear Congressional policy, a landlord or lessor must show that actual and substantial detriment would be incurred by him if the deviation in use was permitted.

In this case, the contemplated deviation in use is from an appliance store to a small bistro. The building in which the unexpired leasehold is located already contains a restaurant, a laundry, and a liquor store. The landlord has failed to demonstrate any actual and substantial detriment which he would incur if the proposed deviation in use is permitted. The Court also notes that the contemplated use, along with the planned soundproofing, will have no adverse effect on other tenants in the building. Thus, this Court rules that the use clause may not be enforced so as to block assignment of this lease to Just Heaven.

Congress, in section 365, has stated a general policy favoring assignment. Balanced against this general policy is the requirement that the non-debtor contracting party receive the full benefit of his bargain. Jemrock Realty will receive the full benefit of its bargain under the proposed assignment of the leasehold from U.L. Radio to Just Heaven. No defaults exist under the lease. The lease has properly been assumed and Just Heaven has provided adequate assurance of future performance. The landlord has shown no actual or substantial detriment to him from the proposed assignment. The statutory requirements have been satisfied. The assignment is authorized.

It is so ordered.

QUESTIONS RELATING TO *U.L. RADIO* CASE

1. The opinion states that the debtor was "not in default on any of the Lease terms." Note the prefatory language in section 365(b) -- "If there has been a default . . ." Since there was no default, why did the court require adequate assurance of future performance?

2. Note that in the last paragraph, the court finds that "the landlord has shown no actual or substantial detriment to him from the proposed assignment." How could the landlord show such detriment? Compare section 365(k) with section 365(f)(2)(B). If the landlord has shown that other tenants were moving out because of a bistro in the building, would Judge Galgay have reached a different decision?

3. The court mentions that "the lease at issue here is not located in a shopping center." Why is that relevant? *Cf.* section 365(b)(3).

---

2. *Special Requirements for Assigning Shopping Center Leases*

PROBLEM 8-10: SHOPPING CENTER LEASE ASSIGNMENT

Your client L owns and operates shopping centers. The "tenant mix" at its shopping center is important. More specifically, L wants one home improvement center at each of its shopping malls. L has agreed to lease space in 11 malls to Rickel Home Centers, Inc. and has employed your firm to prepare the leases. A senior lawyer seeks your advice as to whether the following language will effectively ensure that the leased space can only be used for a home improvement center:

> 2.08(b): Tenant's business operation in the Store shall be limited to a home improvement center. ["Home improvement center" is defined in paragraph 1 of the lease.]
>
> 10. The Store shall not be used by Tenant or its successors or assigns for any purpose other than a home improvement center."

---

3. *"Applicable Law" Prohibitions on Assignments and Delegation:*

11 U.S.C. § 365(c) AND "APPLICABLE LAW"

(c) The trustee may not assume or assign any executory contract or unexpired lease of the debtor, whether or not such contract or lease prohibits or restricts assignment of rights or delegation of duties, if--

(1)(A) applicable law excuses a party, other than the debtor, to such contract or lease from accepting performance from or rendering performance to an entity other than the debtor or the debtor in possession, whether or not such contract or lease prohibits or restricts assignment of rights or delegation of duties; and

(B) such party does not consent to such assumption or assignment; or

(2) such contract is a contract to make a loan, or extend other debt financing or financial accommodations, to or for the benefit of the debtor, or to issue a security of the debtor;

PROBLEM 8-11: ASSIGNMENT AND CONTRACT LAW

According to Professor Perillo, "if A agreed to paint B's portrait for a fee, B could not, by assignment of the right to C, obligate A to paint C's portrait. A's duty would be materially changed." JOSEPH M. PERILLO, CONTRACTS 705 (5th ed. 2003). Would the answer be different if A filed for Chapter 7 bankruptcy and her bankruptcy trustee assigned the executory contract right to C? Where does the Code answer this question?

IN RE PIONEER FORD SALES

729 F.2d 27 (1st Cir. 1984)

BREYER, Circuit Judge.

The Ford Motor Company appeals a federal district court decision, allowing a bankrupt Ford dealer (Pioneer Ford Sales, Inc.) to assign its Ford franchise over Ford's objection to a Toyota dealer (Toyota Village, Inc.). The district court decided the case on the basis of a record developed in the bankruptcy court. The bankruptcy court had approved the transfer, which ran from Pioneer to Fleet National Bank (Pioneer's principal secured creditor) and then to Toyota Village. Fleet sought authorization for the assignment because Toyota Village will pay $10,000 for the franchise and buy all parts and accessories in Pioneer's inventory at fair market value (about $75,000); if the franchise is not assigned, Ford will buy only some of the parts for between $45,000 and $55,000. Thus, the assignment will increase the value of the estate. Fleet is the appellee here.

The issue that the case raises is the proper application of § 365(c)(1)(A), an exception to a more general provision, § 365(f)(1), that allows a trustee in bankruptcy (or a debtor in possession) to assign many of the debtor's executory contracts even if the contract itself says that it forbids assignment.

The words "applicable law" in this section mean "applicable non-bankruptcy law." Evidently, the theory of this section is to prevent the trustee from assigning (over objection) contracts of the sort that contract law ordinarily makes nonassignable, *i.e.* contracts that cannot be assigned when the contract itself is silent about assignment. At the same time, by using the words in (1)(A) 'whether *or not* the contract prohibits assignment,' the section prevents parties from using contractual language to prevent the trustee from assigning contracts that (when the contract is silent) contract law typically makes assignable. *Id.* Thus, we must look to see whether relevant nonbankruptcy law would allow Ford to veto the assignment of its basic franchise contract "whether or not" that basic franchise contract itself specifically "prohibits assignment."

The nonbankruptcy law to which both sides point us is contained in Rhode Island's "Regulation of Business Practices Among Motor Vehicle Manufacturers, Distributors and Dealers" Act, R.I.Gen.Laws §31-5.1-4(C)(7). It states that

> [N]o dealer . . . shall have the right to . . . assign the franchise . . . without the consent of the manufacturer, except that such consent shall not be unreasonably withheld.

The statute by its terms, allows a manufacturer to veto an assignment where the veto is reasonable but not otherwise. The statute's language also indicates that it applies "whether or not" the franchise contract itself restricts assignment. Thus, the basic question that the case presents is whether Ford's veto was reasonable in terms of the Rhode Island law.

Neither the district court nor the bankruptcy court specifically addressed this question. Their failure apparently arose out of their belief that § 365(c)(1)(A) refers only to traditional personal service contracts. But in our view they were mistaken. The language of the section does not limit its effect to personal service contracts. It refers *generally* to contracts that are not assignable under nonbankruptcy law. State laws typically make contracts for personal services nonassignable (where the contract itself is silent); but they make other sorts of contracts nonassignable as well. The legislative history of § 365(c) says nothing about "personal services." To the contrary, it speaks of letters of credit, personal loans, and leases—instances in which assigning a contract may place the other party at a significant disadvantage. The history thereby suggests that (c)(1)(A) has a broader reach.

The source of the "personal services" limitation apparently is a bankruptcy court case, *In re Taylor Manufacturing, Inc.*, 6 B.R. 370 (Bkrtcy.N.D.Ga.1980), which other bankruptcy courts have followed. The *Taylor* court wrote that (c)(1)(A) should be interpreted narrowly, in part because it believed that (c)(1)(A) conflicted with another section, (f)(1), which states in relevant part:

> Except as provided in subsection (c) . . ., notwithstanding a provision . . . in applicable law that prohibits... the assignment of [an executory] contract . . . the trustee may assign [it] . . .

As a matter of logic, however, we see no conflict, for (c)(1)(A) refers to state laws that prohibit assignment "whether or not" the contract is silent, while (f)(1) contains no such limitation. Apparently (f)(1) includes state laws that prohibit assignment only when the contract is *not* silent about assignment; that is to say, state laws that enforce contract provisions prohibiting assignment. The section specifically excepts (c)(1)(A)'s state laws that forbid assignment even when the contract *is* silent; they are to be heeded. Regardless, we fail to see why a "conflict" suggests that (c)(1)(A) is limited to "personal services."

Indeed, since it often is difficult to decide whether or not a particular duty can be characterized by the label "personal service," it makes sense to avoid this question and simply look to see whether state law would, or would not, make the duty assignable where the contract is silent. We therefore reject the district court's conclusion in this respect.

Although the district court did not explicitly decide whether Ford's veto was reasonable, it decided a closely related question. Under other provisions of § 365 a bankruptcy court cannot authorize assignment of an executory contract if 1) the debtor is in default, unless 2) there is "adequate assurance of future performance." § 365(b)(1)(C). Pioneer is in default, but the bankruptcy and district courts found "adequate assurance." For the sake of argument, we shall assume that this finding is equivalent to a finding that Ford's veto of the assignment was unreasonable. On these assumptions, favorable to Fleet, we nonetheless must reverse the district court, for, in our view, any finding of unreasonableness, based on this record, is clearly erroneous.

Our review of the record reveals the following critical facts. First, in accordance with its ordinary business practice and dealer guidelines incorporated into the franchise agreement, Ford would have required Toyota Village, as a dealer, to have a working capital of at least $172,000, of which no more than half could be debt. Toyota Village, however, had a working capital at the end of 1981 of $37,610; and its net worth was $31,747. . . .

Second, at a time when Japanese cars have sold well throughout the United States, Toyota Village has consistently lost money. . . .

. . . In these circumstances, Ford would seem perfectly reasonable in withholding its consent to the transfer. Thus, Rhode Island law would make the franchise unassignable . . .

Therefore, neither the bankruptcy court nor the district court had the power to authorize the transfer.

QUESTIONS ABOUT *PIONEER FORD*

1. Who would benefit from Pioneer Ford's assignment of its franchise to Toyota Village?

2. Did the Ford contract with Pioneer Ford prohibit assignments? Is that relevant?

3. Do you agree with Professor Bussel's observation "Pioneer Ford invites state legislatures to override bankruptcy's pro-assignment policy to protect favored constituencies thereby undermining the uniformity and coherence of federal bankruptcy law on an ad hoc and state-by-state basis." Daniel J. Bussel & Edward A. Friedler, *The Limits on Assuming and Assigning Executory Contracts* 74 AM. BANKR. L.J. 321, 328 (2002).[16]

4. Reconsider Pioneer Ford when we consider section 365(b)'s requirements for assignment. Could Toyota Village provide "adequate assurance of future performance"?

---

[16]The article refers to a three volume treatise co-authored by two of your authors as a "leading treatise." 74 AM. BANKR. L.J. at 329

4. *"Applicable law" Prohibitions on Assignments and Assumption*

IN RE CATAPULT ENTERTAINMENT, INC.
165 F.3d 747 (9th Cir. 1999)

FLETCHER, Circuit Judge:

Appellant Stephen Perlman ("Perlman") licensed certain patents to appellee Catapult Entertainment, Inc. ("Catapult"). He now seeks to bar Catapult, which has since become a Chapter 11 debtor in possession, from assuming the patent licenses as part of its reorganization plan. Notwithstanding Perlman's objections, the bankruptcy court approved the assumption of the licenses and confirmed the reorganization plan. The district court affirmed the bankruptcy court on intermediate appeal. Perlman appeals that decision. We are called upon to determine whether, in light of § 365(c)(1) of the Bankruptcy Code, a Chapter 11 debtor in possession may assume certain nonexclusive patent licenses over a licensor's objection. We conclude that the bankruptcy court erred in permitting the debtor in possession to assume the patent licenses in question.

I.

Catapult, a California corporation, was formed in 1994 to create an online gaming network for 16-bit console videogames. That same year, Catapult entered into two license agreements with Perlman, wherein Perlman granted to Catapult the right to exploit certain relevant technologies, including patents and patent applications.

In October 1996, Catapult filed for reorganization under Chapter 11 of the Bankruptcy Code. . . .

On October 24, 1996, as part of the reorganization plan, Catapult filed a motion with the bankruptcy court seeking to assume some 140 executory contracts and leases, including the Perlman licenses. Over Perlman's objection, the bankruptcy court granted Catapult's motion and approved the reorganization plan. The district court subsequently affirmed the bankruptcy court. This appeal followed. . . .

II.

Section 365 of the Bankruptcy Code gives a trustee in bankruptcy (or, in a Chapter 11 case, the debtor in possession) the authority to assume, assign, or reject the executory contracts and unexpired leases of the debtor, notwithstanding any contrary provisions appearing in such contracts or leases. See 11 U.S.C. § 365(a) & (f). This extraordinary authority, however, is not absolute. Section 365(c)(1) provides that, notwithstanding the general policy set out in § 365(a):

> (c) The trustee may not assume or assign any executory contract or unexpired lease of the debtor, whether or not such contract or lease prohibits or restricts assignment of rights or delegation of duties, if
>
> (1)(A) applicable law excuses a party, other than the debtor, to such contract or lease from accepting performance from or rendering performance to an entity other than the debtor or the debtor in possession, whether or not such contract or lease prohibits or restricts assignment of rights or delegation of duties; and (B) such party does not consent to such assumption or assignment . . .

11 U.S.C. § 365(c). Our task, simply put, is to apply this statutory language to the facts at hand and determine whether it prohibits Catapult, as the debtor in possession, from assuming the Perlman licenses without Perlman's consent.

While simply put, our task is not so easily resolved; the proper interpretation of § 365(c)(1) has been the subject of considerable disagreement among courts and commentators. On one side are those who adhere to the plain statutory language, which establishes a so-called "hypothetical test" to govern the assumption of executory contracts. On the other side are those that forsake the statutory language in favor of an "actual test" that, in their view, better accomplishes the intent of Congress. We hold that we are bound by the plain terms of the statute and join the Third and Eleventh Circuits in adopting the "hypothetical test."

We begin, as we must, with the statutory language. The plain language of § 365(c)(1) "link[s] nonassignability under 'applicable law' together with a prohibition on assumption in bankruptcy." 1 *David G. Epstein, Steve H. Nickles & James J. White, Bankruptcy* § 5-15 at 474 (1992). In other words, the statute by its terms bars a debtor in possession from assuming an executory contract without the nondebtor's consent where applicable law precludes assignment of the contract to a third party. The literal language of § 365(c)(1) is thus said to establish a "hypothetical test": a debtor in possession may not assume an executory contract over the nondebtor's objection if applicable law would bar assignment to a hypothetical third party, even where the debtor in possession has no intention of assigning the contract in question to any such third party.

Before applying the statutory language to the case at hand, we first resolve a number of preliminary issues that are either not disputed by the parties, or are so clearly established as to deserve no more than passing reference. First, we follow the lead of the parties in assuming that the Perlman licenses are executory agreements within the meaning of § 365. Second, it is well-established that § 365(c)'s use of the term "trustee" includes Chapter 11 debtors in possession. Third, our precedents make it clear that federal patent law constitutes "applicable law" within the meaning of § 365(c), and that nonexclusive[17] patent licenses are "personal and assignable only with the consent of the licensor."

When we have cleared away these preliminary matters, application of the statute to the facts of this case becomes relatively straightforward:

> (c) Catapult may not assume . . . the Perlman licenses, . . . if (1)(A) federal patent law excuses Perlman from accepting performance from or rendering performance to an entity other than Catapult . . .; and (B) Perlman does not consent to such assumption. . . .

11 U.S.C. § 365(c) (substitutions in italics). Since federal patent law makes nonexclusive patent licenses personal and nondelegable, § 365(c)(1)(A) is satisfied. Perlman has withheld his consent, thus satisfying § 365(c)(1)(B). Accordingly, the plain language of § 365(c)(1) bars Catapult from assuming the Perlman licenses.

IV.

---

[17]One of the two Perlman licenses began its life as an exclusive license. Perlman in a sworn declaration stated that, pursuant to its terms, the license has since become nonexclusive. Because Catapult has not offered any rebuttal evidence, and because neither party raised the issue in connection with the issues raised in this appeal, we will assume that the Perlman licenses are nonexclusive. Accordingly, we express no opinion regarding the assignability of exclusive patent licenses under federal law, and note that we expressed no opinion on this subject in Everex. See Everex, 89 F.3d at 679 ("Federal law holds a nonexclusive patent license to be personal and nonassignable. . . .") (emphasis added).

Catapult urges us to abandon the literal language of § 365(c)(1) in favor of an alternative approach, reasoning that Congress did not intend to bar debtors in possession from assuming their own contracts where no assignment is contemplated. In Catapult's view, § 365(c)(1) should be interpreted as embodying an "actual test": the statute bars assumption by the debtor in possession only where the reorganization in question results in the nondebtor actually having to accept performance from a third party. Under this reading of § 365(c), the debtor in possession would be permitted to assume any executory contract, so long as no assignment was contemplated. Put another way, Catapult suggests that, as to a debtor in possession, § 365(c)(1) should be read to prohibit assumption and assignment, rather than assumption or assignment.

Catapult has marshalled considerable authority to support this reading. The arguments supporting Catapult's position can be divided into three categories: (1) the literal reading creates inconsistencies within § 365; (2) the literal reading is incompatible with the legislative history; and (3) the literal reading flies in the face of sound bankruptcy policy. Nonetheless, we find that none of these considerations justifies departing from the plain language of § 365(c)(1).

. . .

Policy arguments cannot displace the plain language of the statute; that the plain language of § 365(c)(1) may be bad policy does not justify a judicial rewrite. . . .

V.

Because the statute speaks clearly, and its plain language does not produce a patently absurd result or contravene any clear legislative history, we must "hold Congress to its words." Accordingly, we hold that, where applicable nonbankruptcy law makes an executory contract nonassignable because the identity of the nondebtor party is material, a debtor in possession may not assume the contract absent consent of the nondebtor party. A straightforward application of § 365(c)(1) to the circumstances of this case precludes Catapult from assuming the Perlman licenses over Perlman's objection. Consequently, the bankruptcy court erred when it approved Catapult's motion to assume the Perlman licenses, and the district court erred in affirming the bankruptcy court.

QUESTIONS ABOUT *CATAPULT ENTERTAINMENT*

1. In *Pioneer Ford,* the debtor wanted to assign the lease. In *Catapult,* the debtor wanted to assume the lease. What are the practical differences between assumption and assignment? The "policy differences"? According to Professor Bussel, "Section 365 gets off on the wrong foot by equating assumption and assignment notwithstanding sharp policy distinctions between the two." Daniel J. Bussel & Edward Friedler, *The Limits on Assuming and Assigning Executory Contracts,* 74 AM. BANKR. L.J. 321, 323 (2000).[18]

2. Why did Catapult want to assume the Perlman licenses? Do we know why Perlman opposed the assumption? Is that relevant?

3. What was the "applicable law"?

4. In the *Catapult* opinion, the Ninth Circuit states that it is joining the Third Circuit and Eleventh Circuit in applying the "hypothetical" test. What is the "hypothetical" test and how is it different from the "actual test"?

---

[18]Remember, this article refers to a treatise co-authored by two of your authors as a "leading treatise", 74 AM. BANKR. L.J.329 [The co-author of this casebook who is editing this footnote [BAM] wonders which way the other authors (that is, those who authored the treatise) think this should cut.]

G. What Are The Bankruptcy Possibilities If The Debtor Is A Landlord?

11 U.S.C. § 365(h) and Landlord Bankruptcy

(h)(1)(A) If the trustee rejects an unexpired lease of real property under which the debtor is the lessor and–

(i) if the rejection by the trustee amounts to such a breach as would entitle the lessee to treat such lease as terminated by virtue of its terms, applicable nonbankruptcy law, or any agreement made by the lessee, then the lessee under such lease may treat such lease as terminated by the rejection; or

(ii) if the term of such lease has commenced, the lessee may retain its rights under such lease (including rights such as those relating to the amount and timing of payment of rent and other amounts payable by the lessee and any right of use, possession, quiet enjoyment, subletting, assignment, or hypothecation) that are in or appurtenant to the real property for the balance of the term of such lease and for any renewal or extension of such rights to the extent that such rights are enforceable under applicable nonbankruptcy law.

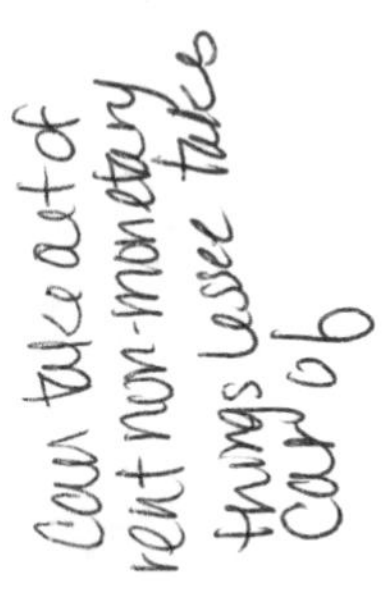

(B) If the lessee retains its rights under subparagraph (A)(ii), the lessee may offset against the rent reserved under such lease for the balance of the term after the date of the rejection of such lease and for the term of any renewal or extension of such lease, the value of any damage caused by the nonperformance after the date of such rejection, of any obligation of the debtor under such lease, but the lessee shall not have any other right against the estate or the debtor on account of any damage occurring after such date caused by such nonperformance. . . .

Problem 8-12: Rejection By Debtor Landlord

D owns the office building in which your law firm, Y, has its office. The lease agreement between D and Y provides for:

- payment of rental of $100,000 a month by Y;
- exclusive use of floors 7-13 by Y;

- option to rent the 6th floor;
- maintenance and security service by D;
- concierge service by D.

Can D reject the lease with Y? If so, can

- D evict Y?
- change the amount of rent that Y pays?

If not, why would D reject the lease?

H. What Are The Bankruptcy Possibilities If The Debtor Is A Licensor of Intellectual Property?

11 U.S.C. § 365(n)

(n)

(1) If the trustee rejects an executory contract under which the debtor is a licensor of a right to intellectual property[19], the licensee under such contract may elect--

(A) to treat such contract as terminated by such rejection if such rejection by the trustee amounts to such a breach as would entitle the licensee to treat such contract as terminated by virtue of its own terms, applicable nonbankruptcy law, or an agreement made by the licensee with another entity; or

(B) to retain its rights (including a right to enforce any exclusivity provision of such contract, but excluding any other right under applicable nonbankruptcy law to specific performance of such contract) under such contract and under any agreement supplementary to such contract, to such intellectual property (including any embodiment of such intellectual property to the extent protected by applicable nonbankruptcy law), as such rights existed immediately before the case commenced, for--

(i) the duration of such contract; and

---

[19]"Intellectual property" is defined in section 101(35A).

(ii) any period for which such contract may be extended by the licensee as of right under applicable nonbankruptcy law.

(2) If the licensee elects to retain its rights, as described in paragraph (1)(B) of this subsection, under such contract--

(A) the trustee shall allow the licensee to exercise such rights;

(B) the licensee shall make all royalty payments due under such contract for the duration of such contract and for any period described in paragraph (1)(B) of this subsection for which the licensee extends such contract; and

(C) the licensee shall be deemed to waive--

(i) any right of setoff it may have with respect to such contract under this title or applicable nonbankruptcy law; and

(ii) any claim allowable under section 503(b) of this title arising from the performance of such contract.

(3) If the licensee elects to retain its rights, as described in paragraph (1)(B) of this subsection, then on the written request of the licensee the trustee shall--

(A) to the extent provided in such contract, or any agreement supplementary to such contract, provide to the licensee any intellectual property (including such embodiment) held by the trustee; and

(B) not interfere with the rights of the licensee as provided in such contract, or any agreement supplementary to such contract, to such intellectual property (including such embodiment) including any right to obtain such intellectual property (or such embodiment) from another entity.

(4) Unless and until the trustee rejects such contract, on the written request of the licensee the trustee shall--

(A) to the extent provided in such contract or any agreement supplementary to such contract–

(i) perform such contract; or

(ii) provide to the licensee such intellectual property (including any embodiment of such intellectual property to the extent protected by applicable nonbankruptcy law) held by the trustee; and

(B) not interfere with the rights of the licensee as provided in such contract, or any agreement supplementary to such contract, to such intellectual property (including such embodiment), including any right to obtain such intellectual property (or such embodiment) from another entity.

COMPARISONS OF SECTION 365(h) (BANKRUPTCY OF LANDLORD) WITH SECTION 365(n) (BANKRUPTCY OF LICENSOR)

First, the similarity. That is easy. We will do that part. Under section 365(h), the tenant can continue to occupy the leased building or land, notwithstanding the landlord's bankruptcy and rejection of the lease. Under section 365(n), the licensee can continue to use the intellectual property, notwithstanding the licensor's bankruptcy and rejection of the lease.

Now, the differences. That is harder. You can do that part. Compare what the tenant gets under section 365(h)(1)(A)(ii) with what the licensee gets under 365(n)(1)(B). Compare what the tenant pays under section 365(h)(1)(B) with the licensee pays under 365(n)(2)(B).

PROBLEM 8-13: REJECTION OF PATENT LICENSE

In 2000, Debtor invented and obtained a patent on a tire shredding machine. Debtor filed a Chapter 13 petition in 2006.

On December 8, 2000, Debtor and Controlled Shredders entered into a twenty-year license agreement which licensed Controlled Shredders to manufacture and sell the tire shredding machine invented by Debtor and covered by his patent. The license to Controlled Shredders was exclusive. The License Agreement gave Controlled Shredders the right to incorporate into its manufacture any improvements or modifications developed by Debtor during the term of the patent. This license was subject to payment of royalties to Debtor on all tire shredders made or sold by Controlled Shredders.

The License Agreement also imposed other rights and obligations on the parties. The agreement required both parties to provide each other with any "assistance, cooperation, know-how, expertise, and information as may be reasonably required or beneficial to facilitating or improving the manufacture, operation, or use of the shredder. Each party was required to share "any improvements, developments, know-how, or information . . . which in any way affects the manufacture, operation, or use of the shredder."

Can the Debtor reject the License? If he does, can Controlled Shredders continue to use the patent? If so, will the Debtor have to provide postpetition modifications and improvements in the intellectual property to Controlled Shredders?

PROBLEM 8-14: REJECTION OF TRADEMARK LICENSE

D grants an exclusive license to use a trademark to S. D files for bankruptcy and rejects the trademark license agreement. Can S still use the trademark? *Cf.* section 101(35A).

I. WHAT IS AN "EXECUTORY CONTRACT"?

NATIONAL BANKRUPTCY REVIEW COMMISSION REPORT

As the previous discussions have explored, section 365 of the Bankruptcy Code governs the "assumption" (performance), "rejection" (breach), and "assignment" (transfer) of contracts and leases in bankruptcy. Because section 365 currently refers to executory contracts and not to all contracts, commencing the inquiry on the appropriate disposition of a contract depends on whether the parties believe and the court determines that the contract is "executory."

Development of the Bankruptcy Term "Executory." Under nonbankruptcy law, the term "executory" is a broad modifier, referring to all contracts not fully performed.. Bankruptcy law has developed a different interpretation of the term starting well before the enactment of the Bankruptcy Code of 1978. Section 365 is derived from section 70b of the Bankruptcy Act of 1898, a provision that codified judicially created rules allowing a trustee to reject the debtor's economically burdensome contracts and assume and perform economically beneficial leases or executory contracts. The Bankruptcy Act offered very little additional guidance for dealing with executory contracts. If courts did not supervise contract dealings, an estate improvidently could become obligated to perform contracts to the detriment of other creditors. For example, a debtor in possession could prefer one unsecured creditor over all others by assuming a debt obligation that then would be entitled to full repayment. To avoid this result, courts developed a more restrictive interpretation of the term "executory" for bankruptcy purposes to ensure contracts would be assumed only if economically beneficial for the estate. However, by many accounts, those approaches were not always consistent. To ameliorate some of this confusion, Professor Vern Countryman articulated the following "material breach" analysis to identify an "executory" contract that could be assumed or rejected:

> A contract under which the obligation of both the bankrupt and the other party to the contract are so far unperformed that the failure of either to complete performance would constitute a material breach excusing the performance of the other.

Using the material breach test, courts gauged remaining future performance of both the debtor and the nondebtor to determine whether the estate would benefit by becoming administratively obligated to perform. The 1973 Report of the Commission on the Bankruptcy Laws of the United States indicated that "executory" referred to incompletely performed agreements but did not endorse a succinct statutory definition. Congress declined to define "executory contract" when it enacted section 365 of the Bankruptcy Code. According to the legislative history, executory contracts were those in which "performance remains due on both sides."

It seems clear that the requirement of executoriness was developed in large part to prevent unwise or inadvertent assumptions or rejections by trustees, because under the Bankruptcy Act of 1898 there was no requirement of court approval and notice to creditors for those actions. The Bankruptcy Reform Act of 1978 closed that gap by requiring court approval for assumption or rejection, largely eliminating the underlying reason for the constraining concept. Even using a deferential business judgment standard commonly employed by courts in reviewing motions to assume or reject, a trustee cannot assume a contract if the benefits to the estate clearly were outweighed by the burdens. The goal to be served by the executoriness test is now met directly by court review.

A growing case law trend de-emphasizes a strict analysis of the term "executory" in favor of a "functional" analysis, an approach articulated by Professor Jay Westbrook, Michael Andrew, and others. Using a functional analysis, a court does not consider remaining mutual material performance but instead considers the goals that assumption or rejection were expected to accomplish: enhancement of the estate. Under this approach, the term "executory" ultimately serves no purpose, for the executory or nonexecutory label is an after-the-fact description designed to fit the court's conclusions about the value of the contract to the estate. Recognizing this fact, a few courts taking the functional approach have declined to make the threshold finding of executoriness at all and simply have focused on whether the estate would be benefitted by performance or breach. Likewise, some courts have taken circuitous analytical routes to avoid lost value that would result from a rigid application of the executory requirement.

The term "executory" is not merely harmless surplusage. First, even though courts decide that a functional analysis of contracts is analytically superior and yields results more consistent with bankruptcy policy objectives, such analysis would appear to depart from the statutory guidelines. To use an arguably more efficient approach, a statutory amendment is advisable to assure that shift and to cause all courts to follow the same route. Second, few would dispute the persistent inconsistencies and difficulties in identifying an executory contract for bankruptcy purposes, a condition that is exacerbated as courts use different tests to identify an executory contract. Finally, the traditional strict interpretation of the executory requirement leads some courts to results that contravene the initial purpose of the restriction because it does not isolate valuable contracts and does not preclude improvident elections to perform or breach. Some very valuable contracts may be unassumable on account of a strict executory test.] An executoriness analysis therefore can hamper the process of permitting the bankruptcy estate to elect to perform contracts that will be highly beneficial.

So long as the term "executory" remains in the statute, this issue will continue to incite debate and to increase litigation costs without an evident corresponding advantage. Therefore, the Commission recommends the elimination of all references to the term "executory." This change would not alter the other substantive parameters of section 365 such as the statutory exclusion of loan and financial accommodation contracts. Rather, the Proposal would streamline the analysis of the debtor's contracts and provide a directive to courts to analyze the relevant considerations guiding one's decision to perform, breach, or transfer a contract, just as a contracting party would do outside of bankruptcy. By putting all contracts on the same track for analysis rather than creating distinctive groups of creditors with uncertain rights (e.g., the limbo state of the undefined class of contracts found to be nonexecutory), the Proposal would promote the goal of equality of treatment among creditors. Moreover, this Proposal bypasses the nonuniformity created by the threshold question of executoriness and thus is fairer to all parties.

Competing Considerations. Notwithstanding recent case law developments that de-emphasize the executory requirement, some might be concerned that eliminating any term already in use, including "executory," could have an unsettling effect on case law and thereby encourage new litigation. However, this Proposal would not introduce a foreign concept, but rather would streamline the analysis so that courts can focus on the critical issue of the benefit to the estate, which originally was the intended goal of the executoriness requirement.

No proposal in this area of the law can eliminate all litigation because court approval is a crucial component and the review of the perform-or- breach-election is an assessment based on the facts and circumstances of each case and each contract. The removal of the threshold executory requirement would permit courts to focus on pertinent case- and estate-related factors and would curtail litigation on tangential issues relating to the term "executory." By eliminating this source of confusion, costs and unnecessary delays should be minimized.

NAT'L BANKRUPTCY REV. COMM'N, BANKRUPTCY: THE NEXT TWENTY YEARS, THE NATIONAL BANKRUPTCY REVIEW COMMISSION FINAL REPORT 303 (1997).

IN RE SUNTERRA CORP.

361 F.3d 257 (4th Cir. 2004)

KING, Circuit Judge

RCI Technology Corporation appeals from an order entered in the District of Maryland affirming the bankruptcy court's ruling in favor of Sunterra Corporation. RCI contends that the district court erred in ruling that Sunterra, as the Chapter 11 debtor in possession, was entitled to assume a nonexclusive license of copyrighted software. On appeal, we are called upon to decide whether, pursuant to 11 U.S.C. § 365(c), such a debtor in possession may assume, over the licensor's objection, a nonexclusive software license. . . .

At all times material to this appeal, RCI conducted business as a software development company for the resort and hospitality industry. RCI's software products were used by entities in this industry, such as Sunterra, for functions such as recording reservations, managing resort properties, and marketing and financing timeshares. Sunterra owns or controls more than 150 subsidiaries and related entities, constituting one of the world's largest resort management businesses.

In 1997, RCI and Sunterra entered into a software license agreement (the "Agreement"), pursuant to which RCI granted Sunterra a nonexclusive license to use Premier Software (the "Software"). Under the Agreement, effective December 31, 1997, RCI was required to provide Sunterra a "non-exclusive, worldwide, perpetual, irrevocable, royalty-free license to . . . use, copy, modify, and distribute" the Software (the "License"). Agreement § 3.1. Sunterra paid RCI $3.5 million for the License. Because the Software, as marketed, did not meet

Sunterra's requirements, the Agreement authorized Sunterra to utilize the Software to develop its own software system. Under the Agreement, Sunterra owned any enhancements it made to the Software (the "Sunterra Enhancements"). Id. §§ 2.15, 3.6.3. Sunterra, in turn, granted RCI a license to use the Sunterra Enhancements. Id. § 3.2.2. Sunterra thereafter invested approximately $38 million in developing the SWORD System.

B.

On May 31, 2000, Sunterra filed a Chapter 11 bankruptcy petition in the District of Maryland. Two years later, on June 21, 2002, the bankruptcy court confirmed Sunterra's Plan of Reorganization, effective July 29, 2002. Prior to the Plan's confirmation, on March 28, 2002, RCI filed a motion to have the court deem the Agreement rejected (the "Motion"). RCI claimed that the Agreement was an executory contract and that Sunterra, as debtor in possession, was precluded by 11 U.S.C. § 365(c) (hereinafter "§ 365(c)" or the "Statute") from assuming the Agreement without RCI's consent.

(1)(A) applicable law excuses a party, other than the debtor, to such contract . . . from accepting performance from or rendering performance to an entity other than the debtor or the debtor in possession, whether or not such contract . . . prohibits or restricts assignment of rights or delegation of duties; and

(B) such party does not consent to such assumption or assignment . . .

11 U.S.C. § 365(c) (emphasis added). The term "trustee," as used in the Statute, includes a Chapter 11 debtor in possession. See, e.g., In re Catapult Entm't, Inc., 165 F.3d 747, 750 (9th Cir. 1999). And the term "applicable law" means "applicable non-bankruptcy law." In re Pioneer Ford Sales, Inc., 729 F.2d 27, 28 (1st Cir. 1984).

Sunterra opposed the Motion, asserting that the Statute was inapplicable because the Agreement was not an executory contract. . . .

On June 6, 2002, the bankruptcy court . . . held, in a bench ruling, that the Statute did not prohibit Sunterra, as debtor in possession, from assuming the Agreement. It decided that the Agreement was not an executory contract . . . The district court disagreed with the bankruptcy court's finding that the Agreement was not executory, but concluded that the Statute did not preclude Sunterra, as debtor in possession, from assuming it. . . .

Sunterra contends that the Statute does not prohibit assumption of the Agreement because the Statute applies only to executory contracts and the Agreement was not executory. . . .. Under the Countryman Test, a contract is executory if the "'obligations of both the bankrupt and the other party to the contract are so far unperformed that the failure of either to complete the performance would constitute a material breach excusing the performance of the other.'" Gloria Mfg. Corp. v. Int'l Ladies' Garment Workers' Union, 734 F.2d 1020, 1022 (4th Cir. 1984) (quoting Countryman, Executory Contracts in Bankruptcy: Part I, 57 Minn. L.Rev. 439, 460 (1973)). Applying the Countryman Test, the Agreement was not executory unless it was executory as to both Sunterra and RCI when Sunterra petitioned for bankruptcy.[12] We must therefore asess whether, at the time of the Chapter 11 filing, the obligations of both Sunterra and RCI were so unperformed that the failure of either to complete performance would constitute a material breach of the Agreement.

On this point, we agree with the district court that the Agreement was executory when Sunterra petitioned for bankruptcy. When the bankruptcy petition was filed, each party owed at least one continuing material duty to the other under the Agreement–they each possessed an ongoing obligation to maintain the confidentiality of the source code of the software developed by the other, i.e., the Software and the Sunterra Enhancements.

[The court then looked to nonbankruptcy law prohibiting the assignment of patent licenses, section 365(c) and cases such as Catapult, supra at page 255 to hold that Sunterra could not assume the License and thus could not continue to use the Software.]

QUESTIONS ABOUT *SUNTERRA*

1. Who is arguing the license is not an "executory contract"? Why?

---

[12]The date a bankruptcy petition is filed is the critical time for determining whether a contract is executory.

2. Will the nondebtor party to a contract ever argue that its contract is not an executory contract? Why?

Part IV

Issues That Regularly Arise in Bankruptcy Cases Under Specific Chapters of the Code

Unit 9

Legal and Other Issues To Watch For In Chapter 7 Cases

A. OVERVIEW OF CHAPTER 7

This would be a good time to look at Chapter 7 in your copy of the Code. Chapter 7 is divided into four subchapters, of which we will study only the first two in any detail.[13]

Remember there is an overview of Chapter 7 bankruptcy (and other forms of bankruptcy) in the Appendix. This would also be a good time to "re-read" that. A really good time.

1. Chapter 7 People

In particular, notice who works on a Chapter 7 case. The attorney for the debtor (or that attorney's paralegal staff) does most of the pre-bankruptcy work, preparing the petition and accompanying schedules. *See* Official Forms 1, 6, 7, and 8. After a Chapter 7 petition has been filed, most of the work is done by the bankruptcy trustee. She collects and sells "property of the estate." *See* 11 U.S.C. § 704. Then she distributes the proceeds

[13]We will not be looking at Subchapter III which applies only if the debtor is a "stockbroker" as defined in section 101 or Subchapter IV which applies only if the debtor is a "commodity broker" as defined in section 101.

from the sale of property of the estate to creditors in the manner set out in section 726– if there are any such proceeds. In more than 90% of Chapter 7, there are no distributions to holders of unsecured claims.

---

2. *Chapter 7 End Game*

Think again about how Chapter 7 cases end. Costs and benefits. In every Chapter 7 case, the costs to the debtor include (i) attorney's fees, and (ii) loss of "property of the estate." In every Chapter 7 case, the benefit to creditors is the trustee's distribution of the money received from the sale of property of the estate in the manner set out in section 726.

---

3. *Chapter 7 Distributions and 11 U.S.C. § 726*

11 U.S.C. § 726(a)

(a) Except as provided in section 510 of this title, property of the estate shall be distributed--

(1) first, in payment of claims of the kind specified in, and in the order specified in, section 507 of this title . . . ;

(2) second, in payment of any allowed unsecured claim, other than a claim of a kind specified in paragraph (1), (3), or (4) of this subsection . . . ;

(5) fifth, in payment of interest at the legal rate from the date of the filing of the petition, on any claim paid under paragraph (1), (2) . . .;

PROBLEM 9-1: CHAPTER 7 DISTRIBUTION

The Chapter 7 trustee sells the property of the estate for $220,000. The costs of administering and selling the property of the estate are $20,000. There are the following "allowed unsecured claims":

- A, $30,000
- B, $40,000
- C, $50,000
- D, $60,000
- E, $70,000
- F, $150,000

(Total equals $400,000)

How should the trustee distribute the $220,000?

Section 726 distribution is a part of the end game in every Chapter 7 case: Chapter 7 cases involving debtors who are individuals, Chapter 7 cases involving debtors who are corporations or other business entities.

Most of the rest of the legal issues to watch for in Chapter 7 cases and most of the legal issues in this unit of the book arise only in Chapter 7 cases involving individual debtors.

---

4. Preview of Legal Issues That Can Arise in Chapter 7 Cases Involving Individual Debtors

Most of the "legal issues" that arise in the Chapter 7 case involve either disputes with respect to an individual debtor's exemptions or her discharge. Section 522 governs exemptions. Note that section 522(b) begins: "an ***individual*** debtor may exempt."

Corporations and partnerships and other business entities cannot claim their property as "exempt."

Exemptions are limited to individuals. Exemptions are not limited to individuals who are in Chapter 7 bankruptcy. While section 522 issues on exemptions can arise in a Chapter 13 case or a Chapter 11 case in which the debtor is an individual[14], these issues arise most frequently in Chapter 7 cases.

Similarly discharge issues can arise in a Chapter 11 or a Chapter 13 case. Again, however, most discharge issues arise in Chapter 7 cases, and, in Chapter 7 cases, only a individual debtor can receive a discharge. Section 727(a)(1) denies a discharge if "the debtor is not an individual."

Section 727(a) lists twelve grounds for withholding a discharge in a Chapter 7 case. These section 727(a)(1)-(12) grounds are generally referred to as "objections to discharge."

There are relatively few reported cases applying section 727. A careful review of section 727 is an important part of the pre-bankruptcy work of the debtor's attorney. If the debtor's attorney determines that there is a section 727 basis for objecting to discharge, she will generally recommend that the debtor not use Chapter 7.

B. EXEMPTIONS

1. *What Is Exempt?*

Every state has exemption statutes – statutes which identify property that an individual is able to retain even if she is unable to pay her creditors. Section 522 provides that an individual debtor in a bankruptcy case— 7, 11, or 13, can assert the exemptions to which she is entitled

---

[14]Only an individual can claim exempt property under section 522. In Chapter 11, only an individual debtor is subject to the section 523 exceptions to discharge, *see* 11 U.S.C. § 1141. And, of course, only an individual debtor can use Chapter 13.

under the laws of the state of her domicile [as determined by section 522(b)(3)] and under federal laws other than Title 11.

In less than 1/4 of the states, individual debtors have the choice of asserting either these nonbankruptcy exemptions or the exemptions in section 522(d). The exemptions in section 522(d) are available only to individual debtors in states that have not enacted "opt out" legislation under section 522(b). Under section 522(b), a state legislature can preclude its residents from electing to utilize section 522(d). And, more than 3/4 of the states have enacted this "opt-out" legislation. Accordingly, we have "opted out" of coverage of section 522(d).

To the extent that a Chapter 7debtor is able to win a battle of whether property is exempt, he will be able to keep more and his creditors get less. While creditors are directly affected by the result of a legal battle over what property of the Chapter 7 debtor is exempt, individual creditors are generally not directly involved in the legal battles. Rather, exemption litigation in Chapter 7 cases typically involves the attorney for the debtor and the attorney for the Chapter 7 trustee who acts as representative of the creditors.[15]

---

11 U.S.C. § 522(b)(1) THROUGH 522(b)(3)(C)

(b)(1) Notwithstanding section 541 of this title, an individual debtor may exempt from property of the estate the property listed in either paragraph (2) or, in the alternative, paragraph (3) of this subsection. . . .

---

[15]Judge Conrad Cyr, a distinguished bankruptcy judge before appointment to the United States Court of Appeals for the First Circuit, described a Chapter 7 trustee as 'the representative of all unsecured creditors." *In re* Thompson, 965 F.2d 1136, 1145 (1st Cir. 1992); *see also In re* Fordu, 201 F.3d 693, 705 (6th Cir. 1999)("A bankruptcy trustee is the representative of all creditors of the bankruptcy estate. As such, the Trustee is not simply the successor-in-interest to the Debtor – he represents all of the creditors of the Debtor's bankruptcy estate.")

(2) Property listed in this paragraph is property that is specified under subsection (d), unless the State law that is applicable to the debtor under paragraph (3)(A) specifically does not so authorize;

(3) Property listed in this paragraph is—

(A) subject to subsections (o) and (p) any property that is exempt under Federal law, other than subsection (d) of this section, or State or local law that is applicable on the date of the filing of the petition at the place in which the debtor's domicile has been located for the 730 days immediately preceding the date of the filing of the petition, or if the debtor's domicile has not been located at a single State for such 730-day period, the place in which the debtor's domicile was located for 180 days immediately preceding the 730-day period or for a longer portion of such 180-day period than in any other place;

(B) any interest in property in which the debtor had, immediately before the commencement of the case, an interest as a tenant by the entirety or joint tenant to the extent that such interest as a tenant by the entirety or joint tenant is exempt from process under applicable nonbankruptcy law; and

(C) retirement funds to the extent that those funds are in a fund or account that is exempt from taxation under section 401, 403, 408, 408A, 414, 457, or 501(a) of the Internal Revenue Code of 1986.

If the effect of the domiciliary requirement under subparagraph (A) is to render the debtor ineligible for any exemption, the debtor may elect to exempt property that is specified under subsection (d).

---

11 U.S.C. § 522(p)(1)(D)

(p)(1). . .[A] debtor may not exempt any amount of interest that was acquired by the debtor during the 1215-day period preceding the date of the filing of the petition that exceeds in the aggregate $125,000 in value in—. . .

(D) real or personal property that the debtor or dependent of the debtor claims as a homestead.

PROBLEM 9-2: DETERMINING STATE OF DOMICILE

D lived for more than 50 years in Alabama, a state with very limited exemptions. D then moved to Florida, a state with very generous exemptions, and lived in Florida for a year. D then moved back to Alabama. 727 days after returning to Alabama, D filed a bankruptcy petition. Under section 522(b)(3) which state is the "debtor's domicile? Alabama? Florida?

PROBLEM 9-3: DETERMINING AMOUNT OF EXEMPT HOMESTEAD

D has lived all of his life in Texas, a state with a virtually unlimited homestead. D is retired, living off his investments, in a $1,500,000 home, encumbered by a $700,000 mortgage. Because of some bad investment decisions, D is considering filing for bankruptcy. D has $250,000 in his bank account. If D used that $250,000 to reduce his $700,000 mortgage, would that be another bad investment decision?

BANKR. R. 4003. EXEMPTIONS

(a) **Claim of exemptions**

A debtor shall list the property claimed as exempt under § 522 of the Code on the schedule of assets required to be filed by Rule 1007. If the debtor fails to claim exemptions or file the schedule within the time specified in Rule 1007, a dependent of the debtor may file the list within 30 days thereafter.

(b) **Objecting to a claim of exemptions**

(1) . . . A party in interest may file an objection to the list of property claimed as exempt within 30 days after the meeting of creditors held under § 341(a) is concluded or within 30 days after any amendment to

the list or supplemental schedules is filed, whichever is later. The court may, for cause, extend the time for filing objections if, before the time to object expires, a party in interest files a request for an extension. . . .

(c) **Burden of proof**

In any hearing under this rule, the objecting party has the burden of proving that the exemptions are not properly claimed. After hearing on notice, the court shall determine the issues presented by the objections.

---

2. *Form 6, Schedule C*

FORM B6C
(6/90)

In re ______________________________, Debtor

Case No. ____________________ (If known)

SCHEDULE C - PROPERTY CLAIMED AS EXEMPT

Debtor elects the exemptions to which debtor is entitled under:
(Check one box)

☐ 11 U.S.C. § 522(b)(1): Exemptions provided in 11 U.S.C. § 522(d). **Note: These exemptions are available only in certain states.**

☐ 11 U.S.C. § 522(b)(2): Exemptions available under applicable nonbankruptcy federal laws, state or local law where the debtor's domicile has been located for the 180 days immediately preceding the filing of the petition, or for a longer portion of the 180-day period than in any other place, and the debtor's interest as a tenant by the entirety or joint tenant to the extent the interest is exempt from process under applicable nonbankruptcy law.

DESCRIPTION OF PROPERTY	SPECIFY LAW PROVIDING EACH EXEMPTION	VALUE OF CLAIMED EXEMPTION	CURRENT MARKET VALUE OF PROPERTY WITHOUT DEDUCTING EXEMPTION

PROBLEM 9-4: TIMELY OBJECTION TO CLAIMED EXEMPTIONS

Emily Davis declared bankruptcy while she was pursuing an employment discrimination claim in the state courts. Davis filed a Chapter 7 bankruptcy petition. Robert J. Taylor, became the trustee of Davis' bankruptcy estate. Wendell G. Freeland, Richard F. Kronz, and their law firm, represented Davis in the discrimination suit. On a schedule filed with the Bankruptcy Court, Davis claimed as exempt property the money that she expected to win in her discrimination suit against TWA. She described this property as "Proceeds from lawsuit--[Davis] v. TWA" and "Claim for lost wages" and listed its value as "unknown."

Performing his duty as a trustee, Taylor held the required initial meeting of creditors in January 2002. *See* 11 U.S.C. § 341; Bankr. R. 2003(a). At this meeting, Freeland and Kronz told Taylor that they estimated that Davis might win $90,000 in her suit against TWA. Several days after the meeting, Taylor wrote a letter to Freeland and Kronz telling them that he considered the potential proceeds of the lawsuit to be property of Davis' bankruptcy estate.

Taylor decided not to object to the claimed exemption. Taylor doubted that the lawsuit had any value.

Taylor proved mistaken. TWA agreed to pay Davis a total of $110,000. TWA paid part of this amount by issuing a check to Davis for $71,000. Davis apparently signed this check over to respondents in payment of their fees. TWA paid the remainder of the $110,000 by other means. Upon learning of the settlement, Taylor filed a complaint against Freeland and Kronz in the Bankruptcy Court. He demanded that they turn over the money that they had received from Davis because he considered it property of Davis' bankruptcy estate.

30 days to object

What result? *See* 11 U.S.C. § 522(*l*).

———

3. *Exemption Planning*

THE NATIONAL BANKRUPTCY REVIEW COMMISSION ON EXEMPTION PLANNING

Although different intrastate values and historical artifact may be perfectly appropriate factors to determine exemptions in the context of state collection laws, they create difficulties when integrated with a national statute that contains a delicate balance between all parties in a collective proceeding. . . .

In deferring to state law exemptions, the current system also multiplies the opportunities for forum shopping and prebankruptcy asset conversion. It does not, however, establish whether state or federal laws should control questions concerning the propriety of prebankruptcy planning, yielding tremendous litigation for debtors and creditors. According to most commentators, Congress intended that the system permit debtors to maximize the use of exemptions, but the case law has not yielded coherent rules on what constitutes appropriate pre-bankruptcy planning. This sometimes leads to decisions holding that debtors have overreached in their efforts to maximize the value of their exemptions. As a consequence, some debtors unwittingly risk losing their entitlement to exemptions, seeing transactions unwound, or losing their discharges altogether, while others engage in similar behavior and successfully protect substantial sums of property.

The opportunities for prebankruptcy planning created by the exemption opt-out have called the integrity of the bankruptcy system into question, particularly in the context of a small handful of high-visibility debtors. People with no other familiarity with the bankruptcy system can cite celebrities who have shielded millions on dollars in an expensive homestead in certain states, a behavior that erroneously is attributed to federal law, even though the federal exemptions would not have allowed this shielding to occur.

The Commission recommends the elimination of the provision in section 522 that permits states to opt out of bankruptcy exemptions. State exemption law would be fully applicable to individuals who deal with their creditors under state law and for the creditors who pursue their rights through state law. Yet, for debtors who seek the protection and unique attributes of federal law, such as the automatic stay and the discharge, the implicit bargain is different. To receive federal protection, a debtor should be willing to give up all property in excess of a federally-determined amount.

NAT'L BANKRUPTCY REV. COMM'N, BANKRUPTCY: THE NEXT TWENTY YEARS, THE NATIONAL BANKRUPTCY REVIEW COMMISSION FINAL REPORT 124-25 (1997).

IN RE TVETEN

848 F.2d 871 (8th Cir. 1988)

TIMBERS, Circuit Judge.

Appellant Omar A. Tveten, a physician who owed creditors almost $19,000,000, mostly in the form of personal guaranties on a number of investments whose value had deteriorated greatly, petitioned for Chapter 11 bankruptcy. He had converted almost all of his non-exempt property, with a value of about $700,000, into exempt property that could not be reached by his creditors. The bankruptcy court, on the basis of its findings of fact and conclusions of law, entered an order on February 27, 1987, denying a discharge in view of its finding that Tveten intended to defraud, delay, and hinder his creditors. The district court affirmed the bankruptcy court's order. On appeal, Tveten asserts that his transfers merely constituted astute pre-bankruptcy planning. We hold that the bankruptcy court was not clearly erroneous in inferring fraudulent intent on the part of Tveten.

We affirm.

I.

We shall summarize only those facts and prior proceedings believed necessary to an understanding of the issues raised on appeal.

Tveten is a 59 year old physician in general practice. He is the sole shareholder of Omar A. Tveten, P.A., a professional corporation. He has no dependents. He began investing in various real estate developments. These investments initially were quite successful. Various physician friends of Tveten joined him in organizing a corporation to invest in these ventures. These investments were highly leveraged.

The physicians, including Tveten, personally had guaranteed the debt arising out of these investments. In mid-1985, Tveten's investments began to sour. He became personally liable for an amount close to $19,000,000--well beyond his ability to pay. Appellees became creditors of Tveten as a result of his various investment ventures.

Tveten filed a Chapter 11 petition on January 7, 1986. . . . On the date the Chapter 11 petition was filed, Tveten owed his creditors close to $19,000,000. Before filing for bankruptcy, Tveten consulted counsel. As part of his pre- bankruptcy planning, he liquidated almost all of his non-exempt property, converting it into exempt property worth approximately $700,000. All of the liquidated property was converted into life insurance or annuity contracts with the Lutheran Brotherhood, a fraternal benefit association, which, under Minnesota law, cannot be attached by creditors. Tveten concedes that the purpose of these transfers was to shield his assets from creditors. Minnesota law provides that creditors cannot attach any money or other benefits payable by a fraternal benefit association. Unlike most exemption provisions in other states, the Minnesota exemption has no monetary limit. Indeed, under this exemption, Tveten attempted to place $700,000 worth of his property out of his creditors' reach.

Tveten sought a discharge with respect to $18,920,000 of his debts. Appellees objected to Tveten's discharge. In its order of February 27, 1987, the bankruptcy court concluded that, although Tveten's conversion of non-exempt property to exempt property just before petitioning for bankruptcy, standing alone, would not justify denial of a discharge, his inferred intent to defraud would.[1] The bankruptcy court held that, even if the exemptions were permissible, Tveten had abused the protections permitted a debtor under the Bankruptcy Code (the "Code"). His awareness of a judgment against him and of several pending lawsuits, his rapidly deteriorating business investments, and his exposure to extensive liability well beyond his ability to pay, all were cited by the court in its description of the circumstances under which Tveten converted his property. Moreover, the court concluded that Tveten intended to hinder and delay his creditors. Accordingly, the bankruptcy court denied Tveten a discharge.

---

[1]Several creditors also objected to Tveten's claimed exemptions. In response, the bankruptcy court, by order entered September 16, 1986, certified the question to the Minnesota Supreme Court. The bankruptcy court decided that it need not wait for the Supreme Court's decision, since the determinative factor on the issue of discharge was Tveten's intent.

Tveten appealed from the bankruptcy court order to the federal district court. In a memorandum opinion and order entered July 10, 1987, the district court affirmed the denial of a discharge, concluding that the bankruptcy court's finding as to Tveten's intent was not clearly erroneous.[2]

The instant appeal followed. Basically, Tveten asserts on appeal that as a matter of law we should reject the factors relied on by the bankruptcy court to infer that Tveten intended to delay, hinder and defraud creditors. We disagree. We affirm.

II.

The sole issue on appeal is whether Tveten properly was denied a discharge in view of the transfers alleged to have been in fraud of creditors.

At the outset, it is necessary to distinguish between (1) a debtor's right to exempt certain property from the claims of his creditors and (2) his right to a discharge of his debts. The Code permits a debtor to exempt property either pursuant to the provisions of the Code if not forbidden by state law, 11 U.S.C. §522(b) & (d) , or pursuant to the provisions of state law and federal law other than the minimum allowances in the Code. 11 U.S.C. § 522(b)(2). When the debtor claims a state-created exemption, the scope of the claim is determined by state law. . .

A debtor's right to a discharge, however, unlike his right to an exemption, is determined by federal, not state, law. The Code provides that a debtor may be denied a discharge under Chapter 7 if, among other things, he has transferred property "with intent to hinder, delay, or defraud a creditor" within one year before the date of the filing of the petition. 11 U.S.C. § 727(a)(2) Although Tveten filed for bankruptcy under Chapter 11, the proscription against discharging a debtor with fraudulent intent in a Chapter 7 proceeding is equally

---

[2]Before the district court entered its order, the Supreme Court of Minnesota held in a decision entered March 27, 1987, that annuities and life insurance contracts issued by a fraternal benefit society were exempt under Minnesota law, but that these statutory provisions violated the Minnesota Constitution. In re Tveten, 402 N.W.2d 551 (Minn.1987). Accordingly, Tveten no longer will be able to claim these exemptions. Following the opinion of the Supreme Court of Minnesota, Tveten claimed an exemption for his pension in the amount of approximately $200,000. He and his creditors settled this issue before the bankruptcy court. He will retain this property as exempt.

applicable against a debtor applying for a Chapter 11 discharge. The reason for this is that the Code provides that confirmation of a plan does not discharge a Chapter 11 debtor if "the debtor would be denied a discharge under section 727(a) of this title if the case were a case under chapter 7 of this title." 11 U.S.C. § 1141(d)(3)(C)

Although the determination as to whether a discharge should be granted or denied is governed by federal law, the standard applied consistently by the courts is the same as that used to determine whether an exemption is permissible, i.e. absent extrinsic evidence of fraud, mere conversion of non-exempt property to exempt property is not fraudulent as to creditors even if the motivation behind the conversion is to place those assets beyond the reach of creditors.

As the bankruptcy court correctly found here, therefore, the issue in the instant case revolves around whether there was extrinsic evidence to demonstrate that Tveten transferred his property on the eve of bankruptcy with intent to defraud his creditors. The bankruptcy court's finding that there was such intent to defraud may be reversed by us only if clearly erroneous. . . .

[T]his case presents a situation in which the debtor liquidated almost his entire net worth of $700,000 and converted it to non-exempt property in seventeen transfers on the eve of bankruptcy while his creditors, to whom he owed close to $19,000,000, would be left to divide the little that remained in his estate. Borrowing the phrase used by another court, Tveten "did not want a mere fresh start, he wanted a head start." His attempt to shield property worth approximately $700,000 goes well beyond the purpose for which exemptions are permitted. Tveten's reliance on his attorney's advice does not protect him here, since that protection applies only to the extent that the reliance was reasonable. The bankruptcy court, as affirmed by the district court, examined Tveten's entire pattern of conduct and found that he had demonstrated fraudulent intent. We agree. While state law governs the legitimacy of Tveten's exemptions, it is federal law that governs his discharge. Tveten still is entitled to retain, free from creditors' claims, property rightfully exempt under relevant state law. . . .

To summarize:

We hold that the bankruptcy court was not clearly erroneous in inferring fraudulent intent on the part of the debtor, rather than astute pre- bankruptcy planning, with respect to his transfers on the eve of bankruptcy which were intended to defraud, delay and hinder his creditors.

Affirmed.

ARNOLD, Circuit Judge, dissenting.

The Court reaches a result that appeals to one's general sense of righteousness. I believe, however, that it is contrary to clearly established law, and I therefore respectfully dissent.

Dr. Tveten has never made any bones about what he is doing, or trying to do, in this case. He deliberately set out to convert as much property as possible into a form exempt from attachment by creditors under Minnesota law. Such a design necessarily involves an attempt to delay or hinder creditors, in the ordinary, non-legal sense of those words, but, under long-standing principles embodied both in judicial decisions and in statute, such a purpose is not unlawful. . . .

A debtor's right to make full use of statutory exemptions is fundamental to bankruptcy law. To unsecured creditors, a debtor's conversion of his assets into exempt categories of property will always appear unfair, but this apparent unfairness is simply a consequence of the existence of exemptions under the jurisdiction's bankruptcy law. . . .

The same principle was confirmed by Congress when it enacted the Bankruptcy Code of 1978. The report of the House Judiciary Committee states as follows:

As under current law, the debtor will be permitted to convert nonexempt property into exempt property before filing a bankruptcy petition. See Hearings, Pt. III, at 1355-58. The practice is not fraudulent as to creditors, and permits the debtor to make full use of the exemptions to which he is entitled under the law.

. . . The House Report's language plainly says that debtors may convert nonexempt property into exempt property, that doing so is not fraudulent, and that debtors may make "full use" of any applicable exemption.

To be sure, if there is extrinsic evidence of fraud, or of a purpose to hinder or delay creditors, discharge may and should be denied, but "extrinsic," in this context, must mean something beyond the mere conversion of assets into exempt form for the purpose of putting them out of the reach of one's creditors. If Tveten had lied to his creditors or misled them in some way, or transferred property for less than fair value to a third party, we would have a very different case. There is absolutely no evidence of that sort of misconduct in this record, and the Court's opinion filed today cites none.

One is tempted to speculate what the result would have been in this case if the amount of assets converted had been $7,000, instead of $700,000. Where courts punish debtors simply for claiming exemptions within statutory limits, troubling problems arise in separating judicial from legislative power. As Judge Kishel explained in his excellent opinion in In re Johnson, 80 B.R. 953 (Bankr.D.Minn.1987):

> The legislative branch alone determines what is necessary ... to meet a debtor's needs, by establishing the nature and value of the property subject to claims exemption.... To deny discharge for a debtor's non-fraudulent invocation of these protections is, overtly or covertly, to make a political and/or value judgment on these legislative determinations. To equate a non-fraudulent intent to 'place assets beyond the reach of creditors' with an invidious intent to 'hinder or delay creditors' is ultimately to frustrate statutory exemption rights by causing a chilling effect on the full exercise of those rights. A court which causes such a chilling effect is, in a very real sense, invading legislative prerogatives by substituting its own judgment for that of the legislature.

If there ought to be a dollar limit, and I am inclined to think that there should be, and if practices such as those engaged in by the debtor here can become abusive, and I admit that they can, the problem is simply not one susceptible of a judicial solution according to manageable objective standards. A good statement of the kind of judicial reasoning that must underlie the result the Court reaches today appears in In re Zouhar, 10 B.R. 154 (Bankr.D.N.M.1981), where the amount of assets converted was $130,000. The Bankruptcy Court denied discharge, stating, among other things, that " 'there is a principle of too much; phrased colloquially, when a pig becomes a hog it is slaughtered.' " Id. at 157. If I were a member of the Minnesota Legislature, I might well vote in favor of a bill to place an over- all dollar maximum on any exemption.[3] But sitting as a judge, by what criteria do I

---

[3]There is some irony in the fact that the exemption sought by the debtor in this case, that for benefits under annuities or life-insurance policies issued by fraternal associations, has been held unconstitutional under two provisions of the Minnesota Constitution. One such provision, Article 1, Section 12, provides that "[a] reasonable amount of property shall be exempt...." The Supreme Court of

determine when this pig becomes a hog? If $700,000 is too much, what about $70,000? Would it matter if the debtor were a farmer, as in Forsberg, rather than a physician? (I ask the question because the appellee creditor's brief mentions the debtor's profession, which ought to be legally irrelevant, several times.)

Debtors deserve more definite answers to these questions than the Court's opinion provides. In effect, the Court today leaves the distinction between permissible and impermissible claims of exemption to each bankruptcy judge's own sense of proportion. As a result, debtors will be unable to know in advance how far the federal courts will allow them to exercise their rights under state law.

Where state law creates an unlimited exemption, the result may be that wealthy debtors like Tveten enjoy a windfall that appears unconscionable, and contrary to the policy of the bankruptcy law. I fully agree with Judge Kishel, however, that [this] result ... cannot be laid at [the] Debtor's feet; it must be laid at the feet of the state legislature. Debtor did nothing more than exercise a prerogative that was fully his under law. It cannot be said that his actions have so tainted him or his bankruptcy petition as to merit denial of discharge.

I submit that Tveten did nothing more fraudulent than seek to take advantage of a state law of which the federal courts disapprove.

I would reverse this judgment and hold that the debtor's actions in converting property into exempt form do not bar a discharge in bankruptcy.

PROBLEM 9-5: EXEMPTION PLANNING

On March 3, 2004, Curtis Wadley purchased a 2004 Heritage Harley Davidson Motorcycle. By June of 2005, Curtis Wadley realized he could no longer ride the

---

Minnesota has held that the exemption statute involved in the present case is unconstitutional precisely because it contains no dollar limit. *In re* Tveten, 402 N.W.2d 551, 556-58 (Minn.1987). So the principle of limitation has been upheld, the debtor has in any event lost the exemption he sought, but he also loses his discharge under today's decision.

motorcycle due to surgery that limited the use of his hands.

In early August of 2005, Curtis Wadley and his wife, Vickie Wadley, met with attorney Harry Zornow regarding the filing of a bankruptcy petition. After the meeting and with the knowledge that he and his wife were insolvent and would file a petition in the near future, Curtis Wadley sold his motorcycle for $12,000.00 on August 23, 2005. Curtis Wadley made the following payments with the proceeds from the sale:

1.	PERS (Curtis Wadley's retirement)	$3,800
2.	Harry Zornow (bankruptcy attorney)	$600
3.	Doctor's Bills	$200
4.	Glasses Eye Exam	$300
5.	Groceries, etc.	$100
6.	Purchase of Whole Life Insurance Policy (Beneficiary Vickie Wadley)	$7,000

Following the disbursal of the proceeds in the above manner, the Wadleys filed a joint Chapter 7 bankruptcy petition on October 21, 2005. In their schedules, they declared as exempt that portion of the proceeds from the sale of the motorcycle used to purchase the whole life insurance policy and to augment Curtis Wadley's retirement account. What, if any action, should the Chapter 7 trustee take?

———

4. Claims That Are "Exempt" from the Exemptions and 11 U.S.C. § 522(c)

11 U.S.C. § 522(c)

(c) Unless the case is dismissed, property exempted under this section is not liable during or after the case for any debt of the debtor that arose, or that is determined under section 502 of this title as if such debt had arisen, before the commencement of the case, except —

(1) a debt or a kind specified in paragraph (1) or (5) of section 523(a) . . .

(2) a debt secured by a lien that is —

(A)(i) not avoided under subsection (f) or (g) of this section or . . .

(4) a debt in connection with fraud in the obtaining or providing of any scholarship, grant, loan, tuition, discount, award, or other financial assistance for purposes of financing an education at an institution of higher education (as that term is defined in section 101 of the Higher Education Act).

---

5. Liens on Exempt Property

If you have bought a house or a car then you can probably recognize liens on exempt property. And, section 522(c) generally recognizes the validity of such liens in bankruptcy.

There are some liens on exempt property that can be eliminated because of bankruptcy. *Cf.* 11 U.S.C. § 522(c)(2). The general avoidance provisions discussed in Unit 8 generally apply to exempt property. Additionally, section 522(f) empowers the debtor to avoid (1) judicial liens on exempt property and (2) security interests that are nonpossessory, nonpurchase money and encumber property of a type identified in section 522(f)(2).

---

6. *Avoidance of Liens on Exempt Property*

11 U.S.C. § 522(f)

(f)(1) Notwithstanding any waiver of exemptions . . . , the debtor may avoid the fixing of a lien on an interest of the debtor in property to the extent that such lien impairs an exemption to which the debtor would have been entitled under subsection (b) of this section, if such lien is—

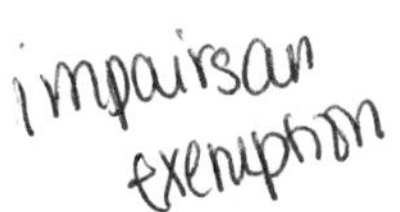

(A) a judicial lien . . .

(B) a nonpossessory, nonpurchase-money security interest in any—

(i) household furnishings, household goods [defined in section 522(f)(4)], wearing apparel, appliances, books, animals, crops, musical instruments, or jewelry that are held primarily for the personal, family, or household use of the debtor or a dependent of the debtor;

(ii) implements, professional books, or tools, of the trade of the debtor or the trade of a dependent of the debtor; or

(iii) professionally prescribed health aids for the debtor or a dependent of the debtor.

(2)(A) For the purposes of this subsection, a lien shall be considered to impair an exemption to the extent that the sum of--

(i) the lien;

(ii) all other liens on the property; and

> (iii) the amount of the exemption that the debtor could claim if there were no liens on the property; exceeds the value that the debtor's interest in the property would have in the absence of any liens.

PROBLEM 9-6: WHEN DO YOU APPLY SECTION 522(f)?

Can debtors use section 522(f) to avoid:

1. GMAC's security interest in their car?
2. A second mortgage on their home?
3. Sears' security interest in all furniture that the debtors have purchased from Sears?

PROBLEM 9-7: HOW DO YOU APPLY SECTION 522(f)?

Snyder and his spouse own their residence as tenants by the entirety. Snyder is three years older than his spouse. On September 16, 1997, Snyder and his spouse filed a declaration of homestead with the Norfolk Registry of Deeds. On March 2, 1998, Snyder filed for relief in the Bankruptcy Court pursuant to Chapter 7 of the Code. Snyder elected the federal exemptions, which limited the homestead to $15,750.

The parties have stipulated that the fair market value of the residential property is $240,750. The property is subject to a mortgage to Randolph Savings Bank in the amount of $170,000 and a judgment lien in favor of Rockland Trust Company ("Rockland") in the amount of $65,000.

On May 8, 1998, he filed a Motion to Avoid Lien pursuant to 11 U.S.C. § 522(f)(1)(A), in which he asserted that the Rockland judgment lien impaired his exemption in his residence. What result?

C. Objections to Discharge

Overview of Objections to Discharge

Recall that in some bankruptcy cases such as *Tveten*, the debtor does not receive a discharge. In Chapter 7 bankruptcy cases, the availability of a discharge is controlled by11 U.S.C. § 727 and Bankr. R. 4004.

Section 727 sets out the twelve grounds for withholding a discharge from a Chapter 7 debtor. These twelve "objections" to discharge are the only statutory grounds for withholding a discharge in a Chapter 7 case.

Dean Ponoroff of the Tulane Law School provides the following overview of the conceptual basis for and the consequences of these objections to discharge:

> The fresh start is neither a formal legal status nor a cognizable right in the usual sense of the terms. Instead, it represents an aspiration of the bankruptcy system. . . . [T]he defining aspect of the fresh start, and perhaps in the public mind the defining characteristic of the modern bankruptcy system generally, is the discharge from debts. . . .
>
> In what was even then already a time-worn aphorism, the Supreme Court in 1934 described the primary purpose of the discharge as relieving "the honest debtor from the weight of oppressive indebtedness." One clear implication of this "honest-but- unfortunate debtor" maxim is that the fresh start objectives of the consumer bankruptcy system are not without limits. There is no constitutional right to a discharge in bankruptcy. In fact, most of the grounds on which global denial of an individual's discharge may be ordered are premised upon some type of opprobricus conduct by the debtor. Ultimately, however, the phrase, "honest-but-unfortunate debtor," is itself wholly indeterminate. While it offers the normative ideal of an individual debtor facing dire financial peril through no fault of his own, few debtors actually fit the prototype. Therefore, the phrase only takes on meaning as a practical matter where it finds concrete instantiation in the Bankruptcy Code. The statutory grounds for

> objection to discharge represent several examples of what is meant by an honest-but-unfortunate debtor because they usually relate to the quality of the debtor's pre-bankruptcy conduct or circumstances.
>
> Outright denial of discharge will ordinarily have ruinous consequences for the debtor, which go considerably beyond the loss of the fresh start. This is due to the fact that the bankruptcy court's refusal to grant a discharge does not trigger automatic dismissal of the case. Rather, subject to the debtor's right to convert the case, the liquidation of the debtor's nonexempt property usually will proceed as in any Chapter 7 case with the notable exception that, after the close of the case, creditors whose claims were not fully satisfied by their dividend in bankruptcy are free to pursue the debtor personally for the unpaid deficiency on their original claims.

Lawrence Ponoroff, *Vicarious Thrills: the Case for Application of Agency Rules in Bankruptcy Dischargeability Litigation*, 70 TULANE L. REV. 2515 (1996).

---

11 U.S.C. § 727

(a) The court shall grant the debtor a discharge, unless—

(1) the debtor is not an individual;

(2) the debtor, with intent to hinder, delay, or defraud a creditor or an officer of the estate charged with custody of property under this title, has transferred, removed, destroyed, mutilated, or concealed, or has permitted to be, transferred, removed, destroyed, mutilated, or concealed—

(A) property of the debtor, within one year before the date of the filing of the petition; or . . .

(3) the debtor has concealed, destroyed, mutilated, falsified, or failed to keep or preserve any recorded information, including books, documents, records, and papers, from which the debtor's financial condition or business transactions might be ascertained, unless such act or failure to act was justified under all of the circumstances of the case;

(4) the debtor knowingly and fraudulently, in or in connection with the case—

(A) made a false oath or account;

(B) presented or used a false claim;

(C) gave, offered, received, or attempted to obtain money, property, or advantage, or a promise of money, property, or advantage, for acting or forbearing to act; or

(D) withheld from an officer of the estate entitled to possession under this title, any recorded information, including books, documents, records, and papers, relating to the debtor's property or financial affairs;

(5) the debtor has failed to explain satisfactorily, before determination of denial of discharge under this paragraph, any loss of assets or deficiency of assets to meet the debtor's liabilities; . . .

(8) the debtor has been granted a discharge under this section, . . . in a case commenced within eight years before the date of the filing of the petition;

(10) the court approves a written waiver of discharge executed by the debtor after the order for relief under this chapter. . . .

(11) after filing the petition, the debtor failed to complete an instructional course concerning personal financial management described in section 111 . . ."

(c) (1) The trustee, a creditor, or the United States trustee may object to the granting of a discharge under subsection (a) of this section. . . .

BANKR. R. 4004(a)

(a) **Time for filing complaint objecting to discharge; notice of time fixed**

In a chapter 7 liquidation case a complaint objecting to the debtor's discharge under § 727(a) of the Code shall be filed no later than 60 days after the first date set for the meeting of creditors under § 341(a).

PROBLEM 9-8: OBJECTIONS TO DISCHARGE BASED ON WHAT DEBTOR HAS DONE BEFORE BANKRUPTCY

1. Brewer filed for Chapter 7 bankruptcy on October 18, 2004. He received a discharge on January 25, 2005. Brewer is again in financial difficulty and comes to you for advice in February 2007. Can Brewer file a second Chapter 7 bankruptcy petition? If so, can Brewer obtain a second Chapter 7 discharge?

2. Richard shows up to your office for an initial interview. After discovering that his house is scheduled to be foreclosed upon tomorrow morning at 10:00 a.m., you ask him for his creditors and his debts. Richard then dumps a shoe box full of receipts and other documents on your desk. Rummaging through them, you find payroll stubs, receipts from Goodwill and several oily receipts from the local drive-through burger joint. There is no order to the mess. You ask Richard if he has any more papers, and he just shrugs. Before filing the case, what should you discuss with Richard? *See* 11 U.S.C. § 727(a)(3). *See* also 11 U.S.C. § 521.

PROBLEM 9-9: OBJECTION TO DISCHARGE BASED ON WHAT THE DEBTOR DOES IN THE BANKRUPTCY CASE

Dr. Sholdra ("Sholdra") filed a voluntary Chapter 7 petition on January 3. On March 23, Chilmark Financial LLC ("Chilmark") who holds an unsatisfied judgment against Sholdra for more than $1,470,000 filed an adversary proceeding in the bankruptcy court objecting to Sholdra's bankruptcy discharge, alleging that discharge should be denied under 11 U.S.C. § 727(a)(2) for concealing assets, and/or under 11 U.S.C. § 727(a)(4)(A) for making a false oath or account in filing schedules and a statement of financial affairs. Sholdra testified in his deposition that some information in his schedules and statement was false.

One week after the deposition, Sholdra filed amended schedules and statement of financial affairs purporting to correct such false statements. Thereafter, Chilmark filed a motion for summary judgment on June 30 seeking summary judgment for Sholdra's violation of 11 U.S.C. § 727(a)(4)(A), and for a judgment denying discharge. Sholdra argued that there are genuine issues of material fact precluding summary judgment – that the amended schedules and statement of financial affairs create genuine issues of material fact as to his intent to defraud. He also argues that he is merely a medical doctor who is inexperienced with financial affairs and relied on incorrect information from a paralegal employed by his bankruptcy counsel, Mr. Clifford F. McMaster, and on his wife's role as business manager handling his financial affairs. How should the bankruptcy judge rule? *See* also Rule 1008, 18 U.S.C. § 152(a). Likely rule against debtor as he likely knew he was lying

PROBLEM 9-10: SETTLEMENT OF AN OBJECTION TO DISCHARGE

Your firm represents Chillmark. Your client and Dr. Sholdra have negotiated a settlement under which Dr.

Sholdra agrees to execute a $500,000 note in favor of Chillmark. The settlement requires Chillmark to dismiss its objection to Dr. Sholdra's discharge. The senior lawyer on the matter tells you to "take care of this." How do you "take care of" the settlement and dismissal of the discharge complaint?

PROBLEM 9-11: WAIVER OF DISCHARGE

Seven banks – Bank 1, Bank 2, Bank 3, Bank 4, etc. – have loaned more than $270,000,000 to various real estate development firms controlled by Charlie Croker who has personally guaranteed payment of all of the loans. All of the loans are in default. You represent the banks who are willing to restructure all of the loans, extending the time of repayment and reducing the amount of the monthly payments. The banks are insisting that Croker waive his "right" to a discharge in any bankruptcy case that might be filed before the loans are repaid. Can a person waive a discharge? *Cf.* 11 U.S.C. § 727(a)(10), 11 U.S.C. § 524(d).

D. DISCHARGEABILITY OF SPECIFIC DEBTS

1. *Overview of Dischargeability*

Even if a Chapter 7 debtor obtains a discharge, that discharge does not always cover all of the Chapter 7 debtor's legal obligations. Certain legal obligations are not affected by a discharge. Issues as to whether a debt is affected by a discharge are commonly referred to as "dischargeability issues."

2. *What Debts Are Discharged?*

11 U.S.C. § 727(b)

Except as provided in section 523 of this title, a discharge under subsection (a) of this section discharges the debtor from all debts that arose before the date of the order for relief under this chapter . . . "

PROBLEM 9-12: DISCHARGE AND POST-PETITION DEBTS

D files for Chapter 7 bankruptcy on September 9. On October 10, she borrows $1,000 from C. On November 11, D obtains a discharge in her Chapter 7 bankruptcy case. Is the October 10th debt covered by the November 11th discharge?

---

3. *What Debts Are Excepted from Discharge and 11 U.S.C. § 523*

Section 523, entitled "Exceptions to discharge" lists the kinds of debt that are not covered by a bankruptcy discharge. The phrase "exceptions to discharge" is unfortunately similar to the phrase "objections to discharge."

It is important to understand the difference between an "objection to discharge" under section 727 and an "exception to discharge" under section 523. Proof of an objection to discharge benefits all of that debtor's creditors. Proof of an exception to discharge benefits only the very creditor that established that its debt was excepted from discharge.[4]

---

[4]There is a second basic difference between sections 727 and 523. Section 727 only applies in Chapter 7 cases and some Chapter 11 cases. Section 523 applies in all cases under Chapters 7 and 12 and all Chapter 11 cases in which the debtor is an individual and some Chapter 13 cases.

Assume, for example, that Epstein files for bankruptcy and his creditors included Nickles, Markell and Perris. If Perris or any other creditor or, more likely, the Chapter 7 trustee is able to establish a section 727 objection to Epstein's bankruptcy discharge, then Epstein will not receive a discharge. Markell and Nickles as well as Perris will be able to proceed against Epstein personally to collect the remainder of their claims.

If, on the other hand, Perris establishes a section 523 exception to discharge, then Epstein will still receive a discharge. Neither Markell nor Nickles will be able to proceed against Epstein personally to collect the remainder of their claims. Only Perris, whose debt was excepted from the discharge, will be able to proceed against Epstein personally after the bankruptcy discharge.

The previous topic - objections to discharge - like the topic before it, exemptions, affect the Chapter 7 debtor and all holders of unsecured claims. This topic - exceptions to discharge - like the topic after it, reaffirmation—affects only the debtor and a particular creditor.

---

11 U.S.C. § 523

(a) A discharge under section 727, 1141, 1228(a), 1228(b), or 1328(b) of this title does not discharge an individual debtor from any debt--

(1) for a tax or a customs duty--

(A) of the kind and for the periods specified in section 507(a)(3) or 507(a)(8) of this title, whether or not a claim for such tax was filed or allowed;

(B) with respect to which a return . . . , if required--

(i) was not filed . . . ; or

(ii) was filed after the date on which such return was last due, under applicable law or under any extension, and after two years before the date of the filing of the petition; or

(C) with respect to which the debtor made a fraudulent return or willfully attempted in any manner to evade or defeat such tax;

(2) for money, property, services, or an extension, renewal, or refinancing of credit, to the extent obtained by--

(A) false pretenses, a false representation, or actual fraud, other than a statement respecting the debtor's or an insider's financial condition;

(B) use of a statement in writing--

(i) that is materially false;

(ii) respecting the debtor's or an insider's financial condition;

(iii) on which the creditor to whom the debtor is liable for such money, property, services, or credit reasonably relied; and

(iv) that the debtor caused to be made or published with intent to deceive . . .

(C)

(i) for purposes of subparagraph (A)–

(I) consumer debts owed to a single creditor and aggregating more than $500 for luxury goods or services incurred by an individual debtor on or within 90 days before the order for relief under this title are presumed to be nondischargeable; and

(II) cash advances aggregating more than $750 that are extensions of consumer credit under an open end credit plan obtained by an individual debtor on or within

70 days before the order for relief under this title, are presumed to be nondischargeable; and

(ii) for purposes of this subparagraph–

. . .

(II) the term 'luxury goods or services' does not include goods or services reasonably necessary for the support or maintenance of the debtor or a dependent of the debtor.

(4) for fraud or defalcation while acting in a fiduciary capacity, embezzlement, or larceny;

(5) for a domestic support obligation;

(8) unless excepting such debt from discharge under this paragraph would impose an undue hardship on the debtor and the debtor's dependents, for—

(A)(i) an educational benefit overpayment or loan made, insured or guaranteed by a governmental unit, or made under any program funded in whole or in part by a governmental unit or nonprofit institution, or

(ii) an obligation to repay funds received as an educational benefit, scholarship or stipend, or . . .

(B) any other educational loan that is a qualified education loan, as defined in section 221(d)(1) of the Internal Revenue Code of 1986, . . .

(15) to a spouse, former spouse, or child of the debtor and not of the kind described in paragraph (5) that is incurred by the debtor in the course of a divorce or separation or in connection with a separation agreement, divorce decree or other order of a court of record, a determination made in accordance with State or territorial law by a governmental unit--

(c)(1) the debtor shall be discharged from a debt of a kind specified in paragraph (2), (4), or (6) of subsection (a) of this section, unless, on request of the creditor to whom such debt is owed, and after notice and a hearing, the court determines such debt to be excepted from discharge under paragraph (2),

(4), or (6), as the case may be, of subsection (a) of this section.

---

4. *Rule 4007 and Debt Exception Procedures*

BANKR. R. 4007

(a) **Persons entitled to file complaint**

A debtor or any creditor may file a complaint to obtain a determination of the dischargeability of any debt.

(b) **Time for commencing proceeding other than under § 523(c) of the Code**

A complaint other than under § 523(c) may be filed at any time. A case may be reopened without payment of an additional filing fee for the purpose of filing a complaint to obtain a determination under this rule.

(c) **Time for filing complaint under § 523(c) in a chapter 7 liquidation, . . . notice of time fixed.**

[A] complaint to determine the dischargeability of a debt under § 523(c) shall be filed no later than 60 days after the first date set for the meeting of creditors under § 341(a). The court shall give all creditors no less than 30 days' notice of the time so fixed in the manner provided in Rule 2002. On motion of a party in interest, after hearing on notice, the court may for cause extend the time fixed under this subdivision. The motion shall be filed before the time has expired.

---

5. *Exceptions to Discharge Based on Nature of Debt*

PROBLEM 9-13: OVERVIEW OF EXCEPTIONS TO DISCHARGE BASED ON WHAT THE DEBT IS

D is considering filing a Chapter 7 bankruptcy petition because he owes $100,000 on his educational loans, $20,000 on federal taxes, and $6,000 on his credit card for a new HDTV Flat-Screen Plasma lap top computer. Will Chapter 7 help D?

Problem 9-14: Exception To Discharge Of Family Obligations

In January 2003, Linda Louise Parnham and Wayne Lee Parnham were divorced. Their final decree of divorce incorporated a negotiated marital dissolution agreement. This agreement disposed of the parties' marital property and debts and made provisions for the custody and support of their sixteen year old child Bubba Sue.

Ms. Parnham received custody of Bubba Sue, and Mr. Parnham agreed to pay $437 monthly child support until Bubba Sue reached eighteen years of age. The agreement also provided that Mr. Parnham would pay Bubba Sue's tuition for college and graduate school and professional school until Bubba Sue was married. In addition, the decree provided that Mr. Parnham would be required to pay Ms. Parnham's attorney's fees, related expenses, and court costs if she was required to return to court to enforce the provisions in the marital dissolution agreement.

In November 2005, Mr. Parnham filed a Chapter 7 bankruptcy petition. On March 21, 2006, he received a Chapter 7 discharge.

In June 2006, Ms. Parnham filed a petition in state court to enforce the support provisions in the parties' marital dissolution agreement. She asserted that:

(i) Bubba Sue decided to transfer from Volunteer State Community College, and

(ii) Bubba Sue had been admitted to the sophomore class at Washington & Lee [#2 party school in America, according to the 2004 Princeton Review], and

(iii) Mr. Parnham refused to pay Bubba Sue's $30,000 tuition.

Mr. Parnham's answer alleges (i) his obligation to pay college tuition has been discharged and (ii) the state court lacks subject matter jurisdiction to determine whether his obligation to pay college tuition has been discharged.

What can and should Ms. Parnham's attorney do?

---

6. *Exceptions to Discharge Based on How Debt Was Incurred*

PROBLEM 9-15: EXCEPTION TO DISCHARGE BASED ON PARTNER'S FRAUD

Bill Morgan and Patsy McCreight formed the accounting partnership M.M. Associates ("Partnership"). Your client, Deodati, became a client of the Partnership. Only McCreight worked on Deodati's file. Deodati authorized the Partnership to buy and sell certificates of deposit on his behalf. McCreight used the authorization to place Deodati's money in her personal bank account. She generated fictitious income statements to conceal the fraud. Morgan was unaware of the fraud and did not receive any of the stolen money individually or through the Partnership. The Partnership did receive roughly $3,500 from Deodati for "accounting services rendered." These services were related to certificate of deposit transactions and inflated tax returns that McCreight filed for Deodati.

Morgan discovered the fraud and reported it to Deodati. Deodati filed suit against the Partnership in state court. Deodati filed an unopposed motion for summary judgment. The court granted the motion and imposed joint and several liability against the Partnership and the individual partners Morgan and McCreight (under vicarious liability) for over $290,000.

Morgan filed for bankruptcy under Chapter 7. As attorney for Deodati, what should you do? *See* 11 U.S.C. § 523(a)(2)(A) 523(a)(4); 523(c).

---

7. *Credit Card Debt and Dischargeability*

According to Travis Plunkett, lobbyist for the nonprofit Consumer Federation of America, "The big winner under the new law (2005 bankruptcy law) will be the credit card issuers whose reckless and abusive lending practices have driven many American to the brink of bankruptcy." Kathleen Day, *House Passes Bankruptcy Bill*, WASHINGTON POST, April 15, 2005, 2005 WLNR 5853110. Similarly, according to Jonathan Alter of *Newsweek*, "The law was literally written by the credit-card industry, the same folks whose siren-song targeting of high-risk borrowers caused much of the bankruptcy problem in the first place. . . . History should remember the 109th as the Credit Card Congress." Jonathan Alter, *They're The Credit Card Congress*, NEWSWEEK, April 25, 2005, 2005 WLNR 6098149.

The only 2005 changes affecting the dischargeability of credit card debt were numerical changes to section 523(a)(2)(c). The amount that the debtor must charge for "luxury goods" was reduced from $1,250 to $500 and the time period increased from 60 to 90 days. The amount that the debtor must withdraw in cash advances was reduced from $1,225 to $750 and the time period increased from 60 days to 70 days. Are these significant changes? Reconsider your answer after considering the following credit card problem and reported case.

PROBLEM 9-16: CREDIT CARD DEBT AND SECTION 523(a)(2)

D is a 50 year old paralegal with a junior college degree and a gross annual income of approximately $25,000. In September 2005, C sent D an unsolicited, pre-approved credit card with a $3,000 limit. D used the credit card to obtain 14 separate cash advances totaling more than $3,200 from automatic teller machines in casinos. In January 2006, D filed for Chapter 7 bankruptcy relief. She had lost more than $25,000 gambling in 2005 and owed C more than $3,500 including interest. If D obtains a Chapter 7 discharge, will C's $3,500 claim be excepted from the discharge? Is section 523(a)(2) helpful? Is the *Bungert* case below helpful?

IN RE BUNGERT, 315 B.R. 735 (BANKR. E.D. WISC. 2004)

SUSAN V. KELLEY, Bankruptcy Judge:

The issue is whether the Debtors' credit card debt to Capital One Bank ("Capital One") is discharged in bankruptcy. Capital One properly filed and served a nondischargeability complaint on the Debtors and their attorney, but the Debtors did not answer. Capital One then moved for default judgment.

Facts

According to the complaint and affirmation of Heath S. Berger, one of Capital One's lawyers, between May 9, 2003 and September 19, 2003, the Debtors used their Capital One credit card for twenty-three purchases totaling $1,771.41 and received twenty cash advances in the amount of $8,035.00, for a total of $9,806.41. The exhibit attached to the Complaint shows that many of the purchases were made at grocery stores and pharmacies. The cash advances within 60 days of the bankruptcy petition totaled $2,385, including a check purchased on August 15, 2003 for $1,000. There is no evidence in the record of how the Debtors used the cash advances. The Debtors made payments of $100 each on June 4, 2003, July 4, 2003, and July 25, 2003, and filed a chapter 7 bankruptcy petition on October 10, 2003.

Capital One alleged that each time they used the credit card, the Debtors made an implied representation of an intent to repay the amounts they charged. Further, Capital One stated "upon information and belief" that the Debtors knew that the alleged representations were false and were made to induce Capital One to continue to extend credit fo the Debtors. Capital one also alleged "upon information and belief" that the Debtors purchased "luxury good(s) and/or service(s), including but not limited to jewelry, gifts, furniture and home furnishings," and used cash advances to pay other debts and expenses.

The complaint alleged that Capital One justifiably relief on the representations, continued to extend credit to the Debtors, and sustained damages in the amount of $12,336.70. Finally, the complaint stated that the Debtors were insolvent at the time they incurred the charges, and incurred the charges with a reckless disregard of whether they could repay the debt to the Capital One. This is the extent of the record; there are no transcripts of the § 341 meeting of creditors, evidence of when the Debtors first met with their bankruptcy attorney, nor any other details supporting Capital One's allegations.

Discussion

I. Plaintiff must prove a prima facie case for nondischargeability in order to succeed on a Motion for Default Judgment.

A default by a defendant does not automatically entitle a plaintiff to entry of a default judgment. *See* FED. R. BANKR.P. 7055 (making Rule 55 applicable to bankruptcy adversary proceedings). . . .

II. Various approaches have been used to analyze nondischargeability actions involving credit cards. These include the "assumption of the risk," "totality of the circumstances" and "implied representation" tests.

The "assumption of the risk" view evaluates the reasonableness of the issuer's decision to allow the debtor to use the credit card in the face of circumstances that suggest abuse of the privilege or imminent default. Courts adopting this test are reluctant to deny dischargeability of credit card obligations incurred before the issuer revoked the card. Briese, These courts often are critical of the credit assessment and card issuance policies of the issuer, and hold the issuer equally, if not more, responsible than the debtor for the debtor's predicament.

The 'misrepresentation/reliance" test is now the most common view. The test, depending on the circuit, incorporates the elements of common law fraud: 1) the debtor made a representation; 2) the debtor knew the representation was false; 3) the representation was made with the intent to deceive; 4) the creditor relied on the representation; and 5) the creditor suffered an injury or loss.

One difficulty with application of the misrepresentation/reliance test is that in a credit card situation, a debtor makes no express representation to the issuer of the card at the time of the card's use. The debtor is usually dealing with a third party (salesperson), or no person at all (cash machine); rarely, if ever, the issuer.

In order to circumvent the problem of the lack of face-to-face contact and any actual representation being made, courts have developed the legal fiction of an "implied representation" for credit card transactions. Early decisions held that the use of a credit card carried implied representations of both the ability and intent to repay the issuer. However, the implied representation of the ability to repay was eliminated in light of the language of Bankruptcy Code § 523(a)(2)(A) making debts nondischargeable "other than a statement respecting the debtor's or an insider's financial condition." Currently, the "implied representation" analysis applies the fiction that with each use of the credit card, the debtor represents an intent to repay.

Some courts are critical of the "implied representation" theory. AT&T Universal Card Services v. Alvi (*In re* Alvi), 191 B.R. 724, 731-32 (Bankr. N.D.Ill. 1996); Three arguments are made against application of the legal fiction employed in the theory. First, using a credit card, like issuing a check, is not a representation at all. According to the Supreme Court, checks are not factual assertions, and therefore cannot be categorized as "true" or "false." Williams v. U.S., 458 U.S. 279, 284, 102 S.Ct. 3088, 73 L.Ed.2d 767 (1982). From this, the Alvi court determined that the similarities between credit card use and the issuance of a check "make it illogical to conclude that the use of a credit card in an ordinary credit transaction necessarily involves a representation."

Second, no representation was made at the time of the transaction, because the entire agreement between the debtor and the credit card issuer was made when the card was issued. According to this argument, the credit card agreement delineates the terms and conditions of card use, and therefore embodies the debtor's intent to repay the credit extended.

Lastly, from a policy standpoint, to infer an "implied representation" in a credit card transaction runs counter to the fundamental principle of bankruptcy law that exceptions to discharge must be strictly construed in favor of the debtor. By inferring a representation is made when a credit card is used, the creditor is effectively "relieved of the obligation of proving that a false representation was made."

Avoiding the fray surrounding the appropriateness of the "misrepresentation/reliance" and "implied representation" theories for § 523(a)(2)(A) nondischargeability actions, the Seventh Circuit offered an analysis of "actual fraud" that circumvents the shortcomings of the other approaches. McClellan v. Cantrell, 217 F.3d 890, 892-93 (7th Cir. 2000). In McClellan, the court noted that many courts and commentators assume that fraud requires proof of a misrepresentation. However, the language of § 523(a)(2)(A) is not limited to "fraudulent misrepresentations," but also includes "actual fraud." In McClellan, the court defined "actual fraud" as "any deceit, artifice, trick, or design involving direct and active operation of the mind, used to circumvent and cheat another." One commentator noted that McClellan's "actual fraud" analysis "may prompt a new and more realistic analysis of credit card abuse under § 523(a)(2)(A)." David F. Snow, *Cheers for the Common Law? A Response*, 74 AM. BANKR.L.J. 161, 171 (2000).

Applying the McClellan test In Citibank (South Dakota), N.A. v Brobsten (*In re* Brobsten), 2001 WL 34076352, at 3-4 (Bankr. C.D. Ill. Nov. 20, 2001), Bankruptcy Judge Perkins stated: "This Court is of the opinion that a credit card issuer may establish actual fraud for purposes of

Section 523(a)(2)(A) by proving that the debtor's use of the card was made with an actual, subjective intent not to repay the issuer by discharging the debt in bankruptcy or otherwise." 2001 WL 34076352, at 4. Since debtors rarely admit to an intent not to repay, the plaintiff must resort to circumstantial evidence to prove the debtor's state of mind. Judge Perkins adopted the reasoning of *In re* Alvi, in which the Bankruptcy Court for the Northern District of Illinois listed the twelve factors used in determining whether a debtor intended to repay the credit card obligations:

1. The length of time between charges made and bankruptcy filing.
2. Whether an attorney was consulted regarding bankruptcy before the charges were made.
3. The number of charges made.
4. The amount of the charges.
5. The debtor's financial condition when the charges were made.
6. Whether the charges exceeded the credit limit of the card.
7. Whether multiple charges were made on the same day.
8. Whether the debtor was employed.
9. The debtor's prospects for employment.
10. The debtor's financial sophistication.
11. Sudden changes in the debtor's buying habits.
12. Whether the purchases were for luxuries or necessities.

III. Applying the approaches to the case at bar.

Capital One has relied upon the implied representation/reliance theory in its complaint and affirmation in support of its Motion for Default Judgment. However, even if Capital One had employed the less strenuous test suggested by McClellan, Capital One has not met its burden of proof by presenting evidence of the Debtors' fraudulent intent not to repay the credit card debt. Capital One has relied on the unsupported allegations in its complaint and a declaration of its counsel, drawing sweeping legal conclusions, but offering no evidence other than a list of the credit card charges and cash advances on the card.

Moreover, Capital One has pled certain allegations, including that the debtors purchased luxury goods with the credit card and knew that their representations were false, "upon information and belief." Such statements are totally insufficient to sustain a prima facie case of fraud. Judge Posner called such allegations, clearly improper locution under the current federal rules, which impose (in the amended Rule 11) a duty of reasonable precomplaint inquiry not satisfied by rumor or hunch. . . [T]he duty to plead the circumstances constituting fraud with particularity could not be fulfilled by pleading those circumstances on "information and belief" unless they were facts inaccessible to the plaintiff in which event he had to plead the grounds for his suspicions. Bankers Trust Co. v. Old Republic Ins. Co., 959 F.2d 677, 683-84 (7th Cor. 1992)

Although Capital One's unsupported allegations of fraud have gone unchallenged by the Debtors, due to the conclusory nature of the claims, this Court declines to accept them as admissions of the Debtors. In this respect, the Court heartily agrees with FDS Nat'l Bank v. Alam (*In re* Alam), 314 B.R. 834, 841 (Bankr. N.D.Ga. 2004), in which the court stated:

> The Court in the exercise of its discretion will not, however, enter default judgment in a nondischargeability proceeding alleging actual fraud based on technical compliance with notice pleading rules. Unless there are specific factual allegations from which actual, subjective fraudulent intent may be inferred or Plaintiff produces evidence at a hearing that proves such intent, entry of default judgment based on actual fraud is not appropriate.

Since, in this case, Capital One has not provided specific factual allegations about the Debtors' conduct, and has provided no evidence of fraud, other than a list of the charges and cash advances, which do not alone establish the requisite fraudulent intent on the Debtors' part, Capital One has not satisfied its prima facie case of nondischargeability under Bankruptcy Code § 523(a)(2)(A).

Conclusion

Capital One's Motion for Default Judgment is denied, and its Complaint is dismissed for failure to state a cause of action.

QUESTIONS

1. Why didn't the debtor file an answer? Does the debtor care whether his credit card debt to Capital One is discharged?

2. The court concludes that "Capital One has not met its burden of proof by presenting evidence of the Debtor's fraudulent intent not to repay the credit card debt." What is the statutory basis for requiring "fraudulent intent?" How can Capital One produce evidence of Debtor's fraudulent intent?

3. And, what is the statutory basis for the court's placing the "burden of proof" on Capital One on producing such evidence on Capital One? What is the relevance of section 523(a)(2)(C)?

4. Again, the only 2005 changes affecting the dischargeability of credit card debt were numerical changes to section 523(a)(2)(C). The amount that the debtor must charge for "luxury goods" was reduced from $1,250 to $500, and the time period increased from 60 to 90 days. The amounts that the debtor must withdraw in cash advances was reduced from $1,225 to $750 and the time period increased from 60 days to 70 days. Are these significant changes?

5. Should the *Bungert* decision also have discussed section 523(d)?

PROBLEM 9-17: SETTLEMENT AND NON-DISCHARGEABLE DEBTS

You represent UCS. After the Fifth Circuit's *en banc* decision, you receive a settlement offer from Ms. Mercer's attorney for $1,000. Do you recommend that your client accept the offer? If so, do you need to obtain bankruptcy court approval of the settlement? *Cf.* § 523(d).

---

8. *Reaffirmation Agreements*

Remember what a discharge is and what a discharge is not. We have just seen that a discharge does not cover all debts – certain debts are excepted from the discharge.

And, earlier, we saw that a discharge does not extinguish the debts that it covers. The discharge merely protects the debtor from any further personal liability on the discharged debts. Again, a discharged debt does not disappear. A discharged debt can still be enforced against any third party obligors and against any property that secures its payment. And, the debtor can of course voluntarily pay a debt even though it has been discharged although she is not legally obligated to.

There is a procedure by which a debtor can incur a legal obligation during her bankruptcy case to pay dischargeable debts. This procedure, generally known as "reaffirmation", is described in section 524(c) and (d).

REAFFIRMATION PROCEDURE

11 U.S.C. §§ 524(c) AND (d)

(c) An agreement between a holder of a claim and the debtor, the consideration for which, in whole or in part, is based on a debt that is dischargeable in a case under this title is enforceable only to any extent enforceable under applicable nonbankruptcy law, whether or not discharge of such debt is waived, only if--

(1) such agreement was made before the granting of the discharge under section 727, 1141, 1228, or 1328 of this title;

(2) the debtor received the disclosures described in subsection (k) at or before the time at which the debtor signed the agreement;

(3) such agreement has been filed with the court and, if applicable, accompanied by a declaration or an affidavit of the attorney that represented the debtor during the course of negotiating an agreement under this subsection, which states that–

(A) such agreement represents a fully informed and voluntary agreement by the debtor;

(B) such agreement does not impose an undue hardship on the debtor or a dependent of the debtor; and

(C) the attorney fully advised the debtor of the legal effect and consequences of--

(i) an agreement of the kind specified in this subsection; and

(ii) any default under such an agreement;

(4) the debtor has not rescinded such agreement at any time prior to discharge or within sixty days after such agreement is filed with the court, whichever occurs later, by giving notice of rescission to the holder of such claim;

(5) the provisions of subsection (d) of this section have been complied with; and

(6) (A) in a case concerning an individual who was not represented by an attorney during the course of negotiating an agreement under this subsection, the court approves such agreement as--

(i) not imposing an undue hardship on the debtor or a dependent of the debtor; and

(ii) in the best interest of the debtor.

(B) Subparagraph (A) shall not apply to the extent that such debt is a consumer debt secured by real property.

(d) In a case concerning an individual, when the court has determined whether to grant or not to grant a discharge under sections 727, 1141, 1228, or 1328 of this title, the court may hold a hearing at which the debtor shall appear in person. At any such hearing, the court shall inform the debtor that a discharge has been granted or the reason why a discharge has not been granted. If a discharge has been granted and if the debtor desires to make an agreement of the kind specified in subsection (c) of this section and was not represented by an attorney during the course of negotiating such agreement, then the court shall hold a hearing at which the debtor shall appear in person and at such hearing the court shall--

(1) inform the debtor--

(A) that such an agreement is not required under this title, under nonbankruptcy law, or under any agreement not made in accordance with the provisions of subsection (c) of this section; and

(B) of the legal effect and consequences of--

(i) an agreement of the kind specified in subsection (c) of this section; and

(ii) a default under such an agreement; and

(2) determine whether the agreement that the debtor desires to make complies with the requirements of subsection (c)(6) of this section, if the consideration for such agreement is based in whole or in part on a consumer debt that is not secured by real property of the debtor.

PROBLEM 9-18: REASONS FOR REAFFIRMATION

D files for Chapter 7 bankruptcy. Which of the following debts should he consider reaffirming?

a. $2,200 to the family orthodontist.

b. $3,300 debt co-signed by his sister.

c. $4,444 debt to the credit union at D's employer arising from a loan in which D's credit application was inaccurate and incomplete.

d. $5,500 debt secured by a security interest in D's car.

PROBLEM 9-19: PROCEDURES FOR REAFFIRMATION

The new credit manager of a client asks the following questions about reaffirmation procedure:

1. *Timing*: Can a reaffirmation agreement be entered into before bankruptcy? After the bankruptcy discharge?

2. *Role of the Bankruptcy Judge*: Does the reaffirmation agreement have to be filed with the bankruptcy judge? Approved by the bankruptcy judge? What happens if reaffirmation agreements are not filed with the bankruptcy judge?

3. *Debtor's Attorney*: Can I deal with the debtor directly or do you have to deal with the debtor's attorney? Will the debtor's attorney care whether his client enters into a reaffirmation agreement? Would you, as debtor's counsel, write/sign such an agreement?

PROBLEM 9-20: REAFFIRMATION AND THE AUTOMATIC STAY

You file a Chapter 7 petition for Steve and Lynn Jamo ("Debtors"). Kentucky Fried Credit Union ("KFCU") had a first mortgage ("Mortgage") on the Debtors' home. Debtors had missed three Mortgage payments before filing their bankruptcy petition. Debtors also were indebted to KFCU on several unrelated unsecured loans.

You advise Debtors to contact KFCU about reaffirming the mortgage. KFCU tells the Debtors that it is unwilling to agree to reaffirmance of the home mortgage unless the Debtors also agree to reaffirm the unsecured loans. KFCU's attorney tells you that unless the Debtors agree to reaffirm all of their KFCU loans, KFCU will foreclose on the house as soon as the Chapter 7 case ends. WHAT DO YOU DO NEXT?

E. CHAPTER 7 SECURED DEBT ISSUES

As the above examples (and common sense) suggest, secured debt is the most common reaffirmation fact pattern. However, reaffirmation is not the most common secured debt issue in Chapter 7 cases.

1. *Recovery of the Collateral During the Bankruptcy Case – Review of the Automatic Stay*

Recall that the automatic stay bars the holder of a secured claim from seizing and selling its collateral during the bankruptcy case, section 362(a). Recall also that section 362(c) governs when the automatic stay ends automatically and section 362(d) sets out the grounds for earlier relief from the stay.

2. *Payment by the Trustee – Review of Property of the Estate*

Chapter 7 contemplates liquidation: the trustee sells the property of the estate and the proceeds from the sale of property of the estate are distributed to creditors. *Cf.* 11 U.S.C. § 726. Recall that property of the estate is limited to the interest of the debtor in property. If D owns Blackacre and M has a mortgage on Blackacre, both

D and M have interests in the property and, in the event of D's bankruptcy, only D's interest in the property is property of the estate. Accordingly, if D owed M $100,000 secured by Blackacre and D's bankruptcy trustee's sale of Blackacre netted $125,000, then the trustee would pay M $100,000. *Cf.* 11 U.S.C. §§ 363(f)(3), 506(c), 506(d).

---

3. *Abandonment of Encumbered Property by the Trustee*

11 U.S.C. § 554(a)

(a) After notice and a hearing, the trustee may abandon any property of the estate that is burdensome to the estate or that is of inconsequential value and benefit to the estate.

BANKR. R. 6007(a)

(a) **Notice of proposed abandonment or disposition; objections; hearing**

Unless otherwise directed by the court, the trustee or debtor in possession shall give notice of a proposed abandonment or disposition of property to the United States trustee, all creditors, indenture trustees, and committees elected pursuant to § 705 or appointed pursuant to § 1102 of the Code. A party in interest may file and serve an objection within 15 days of the mailing of the notice, or within the time fixed by the court. If a timely objection is made, the court shall set a hearing on notice to the United States trustee and to other entities as the court may direct.

---

4. *Recovery of the Collateral after the Bankruptcy Case: Review of Discharge and Exemptions*

Recall that a discharge only affects the personal liability of the debtor. A discharge does not affect the interests in property of a secured creditor. Assume, for example, that S makes a home loan to D and obtains a mortgage on D's home. D files for bankruptcy, claims his home as exempt, and receives a discharge. Neither the exemption nor discharge would not affect S's right to foreclose on D's home if D was in default.

PROBLEM 9-21: CHAPTER 7 TRUSTEE AND OVER-ENCUMBERED PROPERTY

You are the bankruptcy trustee in the Chapter 7 case of Eppie's Cleansing Tide Laundro-Mat, Inc., (E). E's two principal assets are commercial laundry equipment and a laundromat building. Maytag Finance (MF) has a security interest on the equipment to secure its $12,000 claim and Security Bank (SB) has a mortgage on the building to secure its $34,000 claim. MF and SB want you to sell the building and equipment together. They believe that such a package may sell for as much as $40,000, and that the equipment alone would sell for no more than $7,000 and the building alone would sell for no more than $30,000. What should you do? *Cf.* 11 U.S.C. §§ 362(c), 704(1)-(2), 554.

---

5. Redemption

11 U.S.C. § 722

An individual debtor may, whether or not the debtor has waived the right to redeem under this section, redeem tangible personal property intended primarily for personal, family, or household use, from a lien securing a dischargeable consumer debt, if such property is exempted under section 522 of this title or has been abandoned under section 554 of this title, by paying the holder of such lien the amount of the allowed secured claim of such holder that is secured by such lien- in full at the time of redemption.

PROBLEM 9-22: AMOUNT AND FORM OF SECTION 722 PAYMENT

Ballard, a Chapter 7 debtor, owns a 1999 Chevrolet Cavalier. She owes GMAC $16,000 on her car loan. Interest rate on the loan is 5%. GMAC has a security interest on the car. A standard price guide shows that a used car dealer would pay $9,000 for a 1999 Chevrolet Cavalier and that a used car dealer would sell such a car for $10,500.

Ballard wants to keep her car.

1. If Ballard decides to redeem, what does she have to do?

2. As Ballard's attorney, what do you tell her about the advantages or disadvantages of redemption as compared with reaffirmation?

3. As Ballard's attorney, what do you tell her about the possible advantages and disadvantages of doing nothing during the bankruptcy and making the usual car payments to GMAC? Reconsider your answer after considering section 521 below.

---

6. *Section 521 Election: Reaffirmation, Redemption, Surrender*

11 U.S.C. § 521

The debtor shall--

(2) if an individual debtor's schedule of assets and liabilities includes debts which are secured by property of the estate--

(A) within thirty days after the date of the filing of a petition under chapter 7 of this title or on or before the date of the meeting of creditors, whichever is earlier, or within such additional time as the court, for cause, within such period fixes, the debtor shall file with the clerk a statement of his intention with respect to the retention or surrender of such property and, if applicable, specifying that such property is claimed as exempt, that the debtor intends to redeem such property, or that the debtor intends to reaffirm debts secured by such property;

(B) within thirty days after the first date set for the meeting of creditors under section 341(a), or within such additional time as the court, for cause, within such thirty day period fixes, the debtor shall perform his intention with respect to such property, as specified by subparagraph (A) of this paragraph; and

(C) nothing in subparagraphs (A) and (B) of this paragraph shall alter the debtor's or the trustee's rights with regard to such property under this title, except as provided in section 362(h); . . .

(6) in a case under chapter 7 of this title in which the debtor is an individual, not retain possession of personal property as to which a creditor has an allowed claim for the purchase price secured in whole or in part by an interest in such personal property unless the debtor, not later than 45 days after the first meeting of creditors under section 341(a), either—

(A) enters into an agreement with the creditor pursuant to section 524(c) with respect to the claim secured by such property; or

(B) redeems such property from the security interest pursuant to section 722.

If the debtor fails to so act within the 45-day period referred to in paragraph (6), the stay under section 362(a) is terminated with respect to the personal property of the estate or of the debtor which is affected, such property shall no longer be property of the estate, and the creditor may take whatever action as to such property as is permitted by applicable nonbankruptcy law,...

FORM 8

Form B8 (Official Form 8)
(9/97)

Form 8. INDIVIDUAL DEBTOR'S STATEMENT OF INTENTION

[*Caption as in Form 16B*]

CHAPTER 7 INDIVIDUAL DEBTOR'S STATEMENT OF INTENTION

1. I have filed a schedule of assets and liabilities which includes consumer debts secured by property of the estate.

2. I intend to do the following with respect to the property of the estate which secures those consumer debts:

a. *Property to Be Surrendered.*

Description of Property	**Creditor's name**

b. *Property to Be Retained* *[Check any applicable statement.]*

Description of Property	Creditor's Name	Property is claimed as exempt	Property will be redeemed pursuant to 11 U.S.C. § 722	Debt will be reaffirmed pursuant to 11 U.S.C. § 524(c)

Date: ________________

____
Signature of Debtor

CERTIFICATION OF NON-ATTORNEY BANKRUPTCY PETITION PREPARER (See 11 U.S.C. § 110)

I certify that I am a bankruptcy petition preparer as defined in 11 U.S.C. § 110, that I prepared this document for compensation, and that I have provided the debtor with a copy of this document.

________________________________ ________________
Printed or Typed Name of Bankruptcy Petition Preparer Social Security No.

____

____
Address

Names and Social Security Numbers of all other individuals who prepared or assisted in preparing this document.

If more than one person prepared this document, attach additional signed sheets conforming to the appropriate Official Form for each person.

X________________________________ ________________
Signature of Bankruptcy Petition Preparer Date

A bankruptcy petition preparer's failure to comply with the provisions of title 11 and the Federal Rules of Bankruptcy Procedure may result in fines or imprisonment or both. 11 U.S.C. § 110; 18 U.S.C. § 156.

PROBLEM 9-23: AND "RIDE THROUGH"

Your client D has far more debt than he can manage. D wants to file for Chapter 7 relief.

When mortgage rates were at a historic low, D refinanced his house with M and now has a 5% mortgage on his home. D has made all mortgage payments to M and is not in "payment default" on the mortgage. The mortgage agreement has a paragraph that lists "events of default," and D's filing for bankruptcy is included in that list of "events of default."

D wants to keep his house; D wants to keep his 5% mortgage. M is willing to enter into a reaffirmation agreement that increases the mortgage rate to 8%. What can D do?

Unit 10

Legal and Other Issues to Watch for in Chapter 13

A. OVERVIEW OF CHAPTER 13 (WHAT IS IN CHAPTER 13 OF THE BANKRUPTCY CODE?)

In Chapter 13, an individual debtor with a regular source of income proposes and performs a payment plan. During the year ending September 30, 2003, 29% of all bankruptcy debtors chose to file under Chapter 13 (approximately 473,000 total). Chapter 13 trustees disbursed approximately $4 billion to creditors that same year.

As will be discussed in greater detail later in this unit, Chapter 7 and Chapter 13 are quite different. For now,

- **What the debtor gives up.** In Chapter 7, the debtor surrenders his nonexempt assets, which are liquidated for the benefit of the debtor's creditors. In Chapter 13, the debtor commits part of her future income which, along with any other assets the debtor has committed to the plan, is distributed to creditors.

- **What the debtor gets.** The ability of a Chapter 7 debtor to deal with a secured creditor whose debt is in default and who does not want to make a deal with the debtor is limited. In Chapter 13, the debtor has the right to cure defaults over a period of time, even if the secured creditor does not agree, and, in the case of some undersecured creditors, to reduce the debt that has to be paid to the value of the collateral. In addition, the Chapter 13 debtor will be able to discharge a few debts that are nondischargeable in Chapter 7 and, with respect to those debts not dischargeable in Chapter 13, will be able to impose payment terms on those creditors.

- **How long it takes.** Obtaining a discharge in Chapter 7 is relatively quick; it usually takes four to six months. In Chapter 13, obtaining a discharge takes much longer, usually three to five years.

- **Who gets what.** In Chapter 7, the Code determines what is distributed and to whom. Central to Chapter 13 is a plan that establishes how much and when creditors will be paid. The following Model Chapter 13 Plan developed by practitioners at Advanced Consumer Bankruptcy Practice Institutes sponsored by the National Association of Chapter 13 Trustees shows you what a typical plan may cover. Many courts prescribe the form of the plan.

MODEL CHAPTER 13 PLAN

(Revised 7/03)

UNITED STATES BANKRUPTCY COURT
__________________ DISTRICT OF __________________

IN RE: CASE NO.:
CHAPTER 13

SSN: XXX XX ____

CHAPTER 13 PLAN AND MOTIONS ☐ Original ☐ Amended

Date__________________

YOUR RIGHTS WILL BE AFFECTED. You should read these papers carefully and discuss them with your attorney. Anyone who wishes to oppose any provision of this plan or any motion included below must file a timely written objection. This plan may be confirmed and the motions included below may be granted without further notice or hearing unless written objection is filed before the deadline stated on the separate Notice you should have received from the bankruptcy court. If you have a secured claim, this is notice that your lien may be voided or modified if you do not object to this plan.

THIS PLAN DOES NOT ALLOW CLAIMS. You must file a proof of claim to be paid under any plan that may be confirmed.

1. PAYMENT AND LENGTH OF PLAN

(a) Debtor shall pay $_________ per _________ to the Chapter 13 Trustee starting ________________for approximately _______ months.

☐ A payroll deduction order will issue to the Debtor's employer:____________________________________

☐ Debtor will pay directly to the trustee.

____

(Name & address of employer)

(b) Joint Debtor shall pay $________ per ______________ to the Chapter 13 Trustee starting _____________ for approximately __________ months.

☐ A payroll deduction order will issue to the Joint Debtor's employer:____

☐ Joint Debtor will pay directly to the trustee.________________________

(Name & address of employer)

(c) Other payments to trustee: ____

(d) Total amount to be paid to Trustee shall be not less than $________________.

2. PRIORITY CLAIMS (INCLUDING ADMINISTRATIVE EXPENSES AND SUPPORT)

All allowed priority claims will be paid in full unless creditor agrees otherwise:

Creditor	Type of Priority	Scheduled Amount
<Filing Fees>		
<Debtor's Attorney>		

3. SECURED CLAIMS; MOTIONS TO VALUE COLLATERAL AND VOID LIENS UNDER 11 U.S.C. § 506

(a) Debtor moves to value collateral as indicated in the "value" column immediately below. Trustee shall pay allowed secured claims the value indicated or the amount of the claim, whichever is less. The portion of any allowed claim that exceeds the value indicated shall be treated as an unsecured claim. Debtor moves to void the lien of any creditor with "NO VALUE" specified below.

Creditor	Collateral	Scheduled Debt	Value	Interest Rate	Monthly Pmt.

(b) Debtor surrenders or abandons the following collateral. Upon confirmation, the stay is lifted as to surrendered or abandoned collateral.

Creditor	Collateral to be Surrendered or Abandoned

4. UNSECURED CLAIMS

(a) **Not Separately Classified.** Allowed non-priority unsecured claims shall be paid:

☐ Not less than $_____________ to be distributed pro rata.

☐ Not less than _____________ percent.

☐ Other: ___________________________________

(b) **Separately Classified Unsecured Claims**

Creditor	Basis for Classification	Treatment	Amount

5. CURING DEFAULT AND MAINTAINING PAYMENTS

(a) Trustee shall pay allowed claims for arrearages, and Trustee shall pay regular postpetition contract payments to these creditors:

Creditor	Collateral or Type of Debt	Estimated Arrearage	Interest Rate (Arrearage)	Monthly Arrearage Payment	Regular Monthly Payment

(b) Trustee shall pay allowed claims for arrearages, and Debtor shall pay regular postpetition contract payments directly to these creditors:

Creditor	Collateral or Type of Debt	Estimated Arrearage	Interest Rate (Arrearage)	Monthly Arrearage Payment	Regular Monthly Payment

6. EXECUTORY CONTRACTS AND UNEXPIRED LEASES

Executory contracts and unexpired leases are assumed or rejected as follows:

Creditor/Lessor	Property Description	Assume	Reject
		☐	☐

7. OTHER PLAN PROVISIONS AND MOTIONS

(a) **Motion to Avoid Liens under 11 U.S.C. § 522(f).** Debtor moves to avoid the following liens that impair exemptions:

Creditor	Collateral	Amount of Lien to be Avoided

(b) **Lien Retention.** Except as provided above in Section 5, allowed secured claim holders retain liens until:

☐ Liens are released at discharge.

☐ Liens are released upon payment of allowed secured claim as provided above in Section 3.

☐ Liens are released upon completion of all payments under the plan.

(c) **Vesting of Property of the Estate.** Property of the estate shall revest in Debtor:

☐ Upon confirmation. ☐ Upon discharge. ☐ Other: _________

(d) **Payment Notices.** Creditors and lessors provided for above in Sections 5 or 6 may continue to mail customary notices or coupons to the Debtor or Trustee notwithstanding the automatic stay.

(e) **Order of Distribution.** Trustee shall pay allowed claims in the following order:
(1) ____________________
(2) ____________________
(3) ____________________
(4) ____________________
(5) ____________________

Signed: ________________________
Attorney for Debtor (or Debtor(s) if not represented by an attorney)

- **The Chapter 13 participants.** Several "players" have a role in administering the Chapter 13 plan.

---

1. Role of the Trustee in Chapter 13.

Each judicial district has one or more standing Chapter 13 trustees whose job is to administer the Chapter 13 cases in the district. Unlike the Chapter 7 trustee, the Chapter 13 trustee does not take possession of or liquidate the nonexempt property of the estate. Rather, the trustee acts as a disbursing agent, collecting and distributing the plan payments to creditors. Before confirmation Chapter 13 trustees review the plans proposed by debtors to determine both whether they are feasible and whether they comply with the legal requirements of Chapter 13. If there are any questions in that regard, the trustee asks the debtor the pertinent questions during the § 341(a) meeting of creditors, which the trustee conducts. At the confirmation hearing, the trustee advises the court whether the plan should be confirmed. When a debtor fails to make plan payments as required, the trustee takes appropriate remedial action. You can find out more about the Chapter 13 trustees in your area by using the web site http://www.bestcase.com/trustees13.htm, which provides links to the web sites of Chapter 13 trustees throughout the United States.

2. *Role of the Bankruptcy Judge in Chapter 13.*

Bankruptcy judges have a more active role in most Chapter 13 cases than they do in Chapter 7 cases. To obtain a discharge, the Chapter 13 debtor must have a plan specifically confirmed by a bankruptcy judge.

There are more disputes requiring judicial resolution in Chapter 13 cases than there are in Chapter 7 cases.

The judge presides at the confirmation hearing and resolves any disputes. After confirmation, if the debtor gets behind in plan payments, the judge will often hear motions for relief from stay filed by lessors or creditors with secured claims, motions to dismiss or convert the case to Chapter 7, and requests for a hardship (early) discharge by debtors who are unable to fully perform their plan. The judge will also consider confirmation of any modified plan proposed by the debtor, the trustee or an unsecured creditor.

3. *Role of the Debtor's Attorney in Chapter 13.*

Initially the debtor's attorney helps the debtor decide which chapter of the Code will best provide the relief the debtor needs. After the debtor decides to file Chapter 13, the lawyer has a lot of work to do. In addition to completing the bankruptcy schedules and statement of financial affairs, in most districts the lawyer has to help the debtor to develop and draft the payment plan, such as the one included above.

In order to draft a feasible and confirmable plan, the lawyer has to analyze the following questions, which are discussed in greater detail later in this unit: (1) what is the debtor's disposable income that is available for plan payments; (2) how much must be paid into the plan (this is usually an amount not less than the amount necessary to satisfy priority and secured claims being paid through the plan, amounts necessary to cure defaults on secured debt and leases being cured through the plan, amounts necessary to pay the costs of administering the Chapter 13 plan, and amounts necessary to pay the nonpriority unsecured claims being paid under the plan); and (3) how much would creditors receive if the debtor filed a Chapter 7 case.

Once the plan is drafted and filed, the lawyer attends the § 341(a) meeting of creditors with the debtor and responds to any concerns or objections that the trustee and/or creditors raise with respect to the plan, which sometimes entails preparing a modified plan. Before confirmation, the lawyer may have to help the debtor respond to a motion for relief from stay or adequate protection filed by a creditor that holds a secured claim or by a lessor whose postpetition payments the debtor has failed to pay. The lawyer may need to attend the confirmation hearing to respond to objections and possibly put on evidence. Even though § 1324 says that there shall be a confirmation hearing in every Chapter 13 case, the actual practice varies widely among the bankruptcy courts; some courts have a confirmation hearing only if an objection to confirmation is filed, while other courts have a confirmation hearing in every case.

After confirmation, the lawyer may have to provide further services if the debtor is unable to complete the plan as proposed. Such services may include responding to motions to convert or dismiss, assisting the debtor in modifying the plan to deal with unanticipated changes in income or expenses, responding to a trustee's or unsecured creditor's proposed modified plan increasing the plan payments if the debtor's income increases, and responding to creditor motions for relief from stay.

How much the debtor's attorney gets paid for a Chapter 13 case varies substantially depending on geographic location, the amount of work required, and the views of the judge(s) on the court regarding a reasonable fee. Sometimes lawyers are paid a flat fee for the entire case (usually in the range of $750 - $3,000), or are paid a flat fee for all work through confirmation of the initial plan and hourly rates for work thereafter, or are paid their customary hourly rate for all services. The fee is often double or triple the amount of the average Chapter 7 legal fee in the community because of the greater complexity and duration of Chapter 13 cases.

Although the fees in Chapter 13 are usually higher than in Chapter 7, the payment terms are more attractive to the debtor. In Chapter 7, many attorneys require that the debtor pay the attorney fee in full before the case is filed, because they do not want to deal with the legal question of whether all or part of their fee would be discharged if not paid in advance and they do not want to face the practical problem of collecting from a debtor who was unable to pay many of her creditors. The same attorneys may be willing to accept payment of their fees over time through the Chapter 13 plan, because they know the Chapter 13 trustee will collect the money for their fees and their claim for fees will be a priority claim that must be paid in full before the debtor gets a bankruptcy discharge. The lawyer has to have his or her fees approved by the court as reasonable. Some courts establish a fee amount that will be approved without time records, because the court deems the amount inherently reasonable.

PROBLEM 10-1: WHAT HAPPENS IN CHAPTER 13 TO THE DEBTOR'S ATTORNEY'S CLAIM FOR FEES?

You and your client have decided that Chapter 13 is her best alternative. Your client is short on cash and would like to pay your $1,500 fee over time. How will Chapter 13 treat your claim for fees? Consider §§

330(a)(4)(B), 503(b)(2), 507(a)(1), 1322(a)(2), 1325(a)(1), and 1328(a)(1).[5]

---

[5]Section 330(a)(4)(B) provides:

In a Chapter 12 or Chapter 13 case in which the debtor is an individual, the court may allow reasonable compensation to the debtor's attorney for representing the interests of the debtor in connection with the bankruptcy case based on a consideration of the benefit and necessity of such services to the debtor and the other factors set forth in this section.

Section 503(b)(2) provides:

(b) After notice and a hearing, there shall be allowed administrative expenses, other than claims allowed under section 502(f) of this title, including– . . . .

(2) compensation and reimbursement awarded under section 330(a) of this title;

Section 507(a)(1) provides:

(A) Allowed unsecured claims for domestic support obligations that, as of the date of the filing of the petition in a case under this title, are owed to or recoverable by a spouse, former spouse, or child of the debtor, or such child's parent, legal guardian, or responsible relative, without regard to whether the claim is filed by such person or is filed by a governmental unit on behalf of such person, on the condition that funds received under this paragraph by a governmental unit under this title after the date of the filing of the petition shall be applied and distributed in accordance with applicable nonbankruptcy law.

(B) Subject to claims under subparagraph (A), allowed unsecured claims for domestic support obligations that, as of the date of the filing of the petition are assigned by a spouse, former spouse, child of the debtor, or such child's parent, legal guardian, or responsible relative to a governmental unit (unless such obligation is assigned voluntarily by the spouse, former spouse, child, parent, legal guardian, or responsible relative of the child for the purpose of collecting the debt) or are owed directly to or recoverable by a governmental unit under applicable nonbankruptcy law, on the condition that funds received under this paragraph by a governmental unit under this title after the date of the filing of the petition be applied and distributed in accordance with applicable nonbankruptcy law.

(C) If a trustee is appointed or elected under section 701, 702, 703, 1104, 1202, or 1302, the administrative expenses of the trustee allowed under paragraphs (1)(A), (2), and (6) of section 503(b) shall be paid before payment of claims under subparagraphs (A) and (B), to the extent that the trustee administers assets that are otherwise available for the payment of such claims.

Section 1322(a)(2) is quoted on page 400.

Section 1325(a)(1) provides:

(a) Except as provided in subsection (b), the court shall confirm a plan if--

(1) the plan complies with the provisions of this chapter and with the other applicable provisions of this title;

4. *Understanding the Statutory Structure of Chapter 13.*

Chapter 13 of the Code consists of 18 statutory sections that control what an individual debtor with a regular income can do, and must do, in order to adjust her debts through the Chapter 13 process. In working through Chapter 13 legal issues, you should keep the following principles in mind. First, answering many problems will require consideration of more than one Code section. For instance, in order to begin to understand what the debtor must do to obtain relief under Chapter 13, one must consider both § 1322, which delineates what provisions a Chapter 13 plan can and must contain, and § 1325, which establishes the requirements for confirmation (court approval) of the plan. Second, remember that the provisions of Chapters 1, 3, and 5 of the Code are applicable in Chapter 13 cases.

Section 1328(a) provides:

(a) Subject to subsection (d), as soon as practicable after completion by the debtor of all payments under the plan, and in the case of a debtor who is required by a judicial or administrative order, or by statute, to pay a domestic support obligation, after such debtor certifies that all amounts payable under such order or such statute that are due on or before the date of the certification (including amounts due before the petition was filed, but only to the extent provided for by the plan) have been paid, unless the court approves a written waiver of discharge executed by the debtor after the order for relief under this chapter, the court shall grant the debtor a discharge of all debts provided for by the plan or disallowed under section 502 of this title, except any debt—

(1) provided for under section 1322(b)(5) of this title;

(2) of the kind specified in section 507(a)(8)(C) or in paragraph (1)(B), (1)(C), (2), (3), (4), (5), (8), or (9) of section 523(a) of this title; or

(3) for restitution, or a criminal fine, included in a sentence on the debtor's conviction of a crime; or

(4) for restitution, or damages, awarded in a civil action against the debtor as a result of willful or malicious injury by the debtor that caused personal injury to an individual or the death of an individual.

Therefore, in working through Chapter 13 problems, do not limit yourself to the statutory provisions you find in Chapter 13. Third, language identical to that used in a number of the Chapter 13 statutory provisions is found in other bankruptcy chapters. For instance, when trying to understand the requirements for confirmation imposed by § 1325, you may find similar language, and cases interpreting that language, in Chapters 11 and 12 (*e.g.*, compare §§ 1129(b)(2)(A)(i) and 1325(a)(5)(B)(ii)).

The following statutory overview will help you work through Chapter 13.

- **Eligibility for Chapter 13 Relief.** Chapter 13 permits an individual debtor with a regular source of income whose debts do not exceed certain limits to get bankruptcy relief by proposing and performing a plan. We learned about the debt limits in Unit 5.C, *supra* at page 119.

- **Property of the Chapter 13 Estate.** While generally all the property described in § 541 becomes property of the estate in Chapter 13, property that the debtor acquires during the pendency of the Chapter 13, including earnings, is also property of the estate. § 1306. That section also tells us that the debtor retains possession of the property of the estate unless the plan or the confirmation order provides otherwise. *See* Unit 4.

- **Role of the Chapter 13 Trustee and Debtor.** Section 1302 establishes that the United States Trustee appoints a person who acts as the trustee and establishes the duties of the trustee. Sections 1303 and 1304 define the rights and powers of the debtor and tell us what happens to the business of a Chapter 13 debtor who is self-employed.

- **Administrative Provisions**. There is a co-debtor stay in Chapter 13 that, under certain circumstances, prevents creditors from pursuing collection from those who have co-signed consumer obligations for the debtor. § 1301. Section 1305 describes under what circumstances claims arising after the Chapter 13 case is filed can be treated as allowed claims in Chapter 13. Conversion of the Chapter 13 case to a different type of bankruptcy case or dismissal of the case are controlled by § 1307.

- **The Plan and Plan Payments**. The plan is the heart of the Chapter 13 case. It determines how much the debtor pays to the Chapter 13 trustee for disbursement to creditors and which creditors receive the money. The Chapter 13 debtor must file a plan. § 1321. Section 1322 delineates what a plan must contain, and what it can contain. That section must be read in conjunction with § 1325, which sets forth the confirmation requirements, because a plan that meets the requirements of § 1322 but cannot be confirmed accomplishes nothing. The circumstances under which the plan can be modified are controlled by § 1323 (pre-confirmation modification) and § 1329 (post-confirmation modification). Section 1326 establishes certain requirements regarding the plan payments and disbursement of those payments.

- **Confirmation of the Plan.** Section 1324 tells us that a confirmation hearing is held and any interested party can object to confirmation. The court confirms the plan if it meets the requirements of § 1325. Those requirements include that the debtor filed the case and proposed the plan in good faith, unsecured creditors receive at least as much as they would have if debtor had filed Chapter 7, the plan is feasible, the debtor has paid all her domestic support obligations that became due postpetition, the debtor has filed all required tax returns, and creditors with secured claims have their claims satisfied in one of the manners specified in the statute. Creditors do not get to vote whether to accept the plan. The effect of confirmation is controlled by § 1327. Section 1330 defines when an order of confirmation may be revoked.

- **Discharge**. Section 1328 controls the Chapter 13 bankruptcy discharge. It incorporates most, but not all, of the frequently applicable exceptions to discharge that apply in Chapter 7 cases.

B. DEADLINES AND TIMELINES (WHAT HAPPENS WHEN?)

Chapter 13 is designed to move expeditiously and to keep costs to a minimum. The case starts when the debtor voluntarily files a Chapter 13 petition. Within 15 days after the petition is filed, the debtor is required to file her plan and schedules. Bankr. R. 1007(c) and 3015(b).[6] The debtor must start making the plan payments to the Chapter 13 trustee within 30 days after the earlier of the filing of the case or the plan. § 1326(a)(1).[7] A meeting of creditors is held in the Chapter

---

[6]Bankr. R. 3015 (b) provides:

The debtor may file a Chapter 13 plan with the petition. If a plan is not filed with the petition, it shall be filed within 15 days thereafter, and such time may not be further extended except for cause shown and on notice as the court may direct. If a case is converted to Chapter 13, a plan shall be filed within 15 days thereafter, and such time may not be further extended except for cause shown and on notice as the court may direct.

[7]Section 1326(a)(1) provides:

Unless the court orders otherwise, the debtor shall commence making payments not later than 30 days after the date of the filing of the plan or the order for relief, whichever is earlier.

13 case between 20 and 50 days after the case is filed. Bankr. R. 2003(a).[8]

Courts must hold the hearing on confirmation of the plan within 45 days after the § 341(a) meeting of creditors. § 1324(b).[9] Thus, the hearing at which the court considers whether to confirm the debtor's initial plan generally occurs between one month and three months after the case is filed.

Once the plan is confirmed, the trustee may begin disbursing to creditors the payments the debtor has made under the plan. § 1326(a)(2).[10] Before making such disbursements, the trustee will examine the proofs of claim the creditors have filed to make sure that the creditor has filed a claim and to determine that the claim is allowable. The deadline to file claims is 90 days after

---

[8]Bankr. R. 2003(a) provides:

Meeting of Creditors. .... In a Chapter 13 individual's debt adjustment case, the United States trustee shall call a meeting of creditors to be held no fewer than 20 and no more than 50 days after the order for relief. If there is an appeal from or a motion to vacate the order for relief, or if there is a motion to dismiss the case, the United States trustee may set a later date for the meeting. The meeting may be held at a regular place for holding court or at any other place designated by the United States trustee within the district convenient for the parties in interest. If the United States trustee designates a place for the meeting which is not regularly staffed by the United States trustee or an assistant who may preside at the meeting, the meeting may be held not more than 60 days after the order for relief.

[9]Section 1324(b) provides:

The hearing on confirmation of the plan may be held not earlier than 20 days and not later than 45 days after the date of the meeting of creditors under section 341(a), unless the court determines that it would be in the best interests of the creditors and the estate to hold such hearing at an earlier date and there is no objection to such earlier date.

[10]Section 1326(a)(2) provides:

A payment made [made by the debtor to the trustee] shall be retained by the trustee until confirmation or denial of confirmation of a plan. If a plan is confirmed, the trustee shall distribute any such payment in accordance with the plan as soon as is practicable. If a plan is not confirmed, the trustee shall return any such payment to the debtor [unless the payment has previously been paid to or is due to a personal property lessor or a creditor whose claim is secured by personal property], after deducting any unpaid claim allowed under section 503(b) of this title.

the meeting of creditors for all creditors except governmental units, which are given 180 days from the date the debtor files the petition to file their claims. Bankr. R. 3002(c). Either the trustee or the debtor may object to any of the claims. Objections to claims in a Chapter 13 case are resolved by the same process used in all bankruptcy cases. If a creditor fails to file a claim before the meeting of creditors, the debtor may file a claim on behalf of the creditor, provided the debtor does so no later than 30 days after the deadline for the creditor to file the claim. Bankr. R. 3004. Debtors will want to file a claim on behalf of a creditor who does not file a claim if the debt will not be discharged by the Chapter 13 case, § 1328(a), or the debt is secured by collateral that the debtor wants to keep.

Although the court may alter some of these deadlines, most Chapter 13 cases follow the timeline established by the Code and Bankruptcy Rules. Thus, in most Chapter 13 cases, the creditor payment plan is proposed, approved and the Chapter 13 trustee begins disbursing payments to creditors within four to six months after the debtor files her case.

The debtor does not receive a discharge until either the debtor makes all the payments required by her plan or the debtor qualifies for a hardship discharge. § 1328.[11] Depending on whether the debtor's income is above or below the median income, the debtor will have to make payments for either a three year or five year commitment period. (§ 1325(b)(1) & (4)). In some instances when the commitment period is three years, the plan may last as long as five years so that the debtor can meet the requirements discussed below and the debtor's objectives.

---

[11]Section 1328(a) is quoted on page 388.

PROBLEM 10-2: WHAT IS THE TYPICAL CHAPTER 13 TIMELINE?

Using the information from the preceding section, draw a timeline for a Chapter 13 case. Include the following on your timeline:

1. Deadline to file Chapter 13 plan.

2. Time when Chapter 13 plan payments begin.

3. Time frame when it is likely that the court will confirm the Chapter 13 plan.

4. Time when the Chapter 13 trustee begins to disburse the Chapter 13 plan payments to creditors.

5. Time when Chapter 13 plan payments are likely to end.

6. Time when the Chapter 13 debtor can expect to receive her discharge.

C. PLAN PAYMENTS (WHAT IS THE MINIMUM THAT THE DEBTOR HAS TO PAY?)

Section 1325, which sets forth the requirements for confirmation of a plan, sets a floor below which the debtor's total Chapter 13 plan payments cannot drop. There are two components to the floor. First, unless the debtor's plan pays the creditors in full, the debtor is often required to devote all of her projected "disposable income" to the plan for a three to five-year commitment period. § 1325(b). This is commonly referred to as the "best efforts test" or the "disposable income requirement." Second, creditors must receive at least as much as they would receive in a Chapter 7 case. § 1325(a)(4). This is commonly referred to as the "best interests test."

Sometimes a debtor will be required to pay more than the floor amount in order to confirm a plan, because Chapter 13 may impose requirements that can be met only if the debtor pays more. For instance, the debtor must pay priority claims in full, except support obligations owed to a government unit under certain circumstances, in order to confirm a plan. §§ 1322(a)(2) and (4). The most common types of priority claims that Chapter 13 debtors have are the costs of the Chapter 13 case (trustee charges and debtor's attorney fees paid through the plan), support obligations and certain tax obligations. If the amount of the priority claims exceeds the amount that the debtor must pay to meet the best interests test and the disposable income requirement, effectively the minimum amount that the debtor must pay is the amount necessary to pay the priority claims.

Sometimes a debtor will have to pay more than the floor amount to confirm a plan that accomplishes what the debtor wants to accomplish. If the debtor is behind on her house or car payments and she wants to keep the house or recently purchased car, she will either need to cure the default though the plan payments (bring the house or car loan current) or will have to pay the entire debt through the plan. §§ 1322(b)(2) - (5) and 1325(a)(5). Some debts, such as most student loans, are excepted from discharge in Chapter 13 even though they are not entitled to priority. The debtor will often want to pay the nondischargeable debt in full through the Chapter 13 plan in order to avoid facing debt collection actions by creditors after getting to the end of the Chapter 13 case.

---

1. *Disposable Income and its Impact on Chapter 13.*

How much disposable income a debtor has affects use of Chapter 13 in three distinct ways. First, it forces some debtors to proceed in Chapter 13 rather than Chapter 7. The bankruptcy court may dismiss as an abuse the case of a Chapter 7 debtor whose debts are primarily consumer debts. Abuse is presumed for debtors whose income equals or exceeds the applicable median income and who have the ability to pay a certain amount to unsecured creditors. § 707(b); *see* Unit 5.B. A consumer debtor who can afford to pay thus will likely be forced to use Chapter 13 if the debtor needs or wants a bankruptcy discharge.

Second, disposable income may affect the total amount the Chapter 13 debtor has to pay. If either the Chapter 13 trustee or a creditor with an allowed unsecured claim objects to confirmation of the debtor's payment plan, the court cannot approve the plan unless the debtor's proposed plan payments are not less than the debtor's projected disposable income and the payments continue for three years after the first plan payment is due if the debtor's income is below the median income or for five years if the debtor's income equals or exceeds the median income. §§ 1325(b)(1)(B)[12] & 1325(b)(4).[13] The minimum length of the plan is called the "commitment period." § 1325(b)(4).

---

[12]Section 1325(b)(1)(B) provides:

(b)(1) If the trustee or the holder of an allowed unsecured claim objects to the confirmation of the plan, then the court may not approve the plan unless, as of the effective date of the plan—

. . .

(B) the plan provides that all of the debtor's projected disposable income to be received in the applicable commitment period beginning on the date that the first payment is due under the plan will be applied to make payments to unsecured creditors under the plan.

[13]Section 1325(b)(4) provides:

(4) For purposes of this subsection, the "applicable commitment period"—

(A) subject to subparagraph (B), shall be —
(i) 3 years; or
(ii) not less than 5 years, if the current monthly income of the debtor and the debtor's spouse combined [is not less than the applicable median income] . . . [.]

(B) may be less than 3 or 5 years, whichever is applicable under subparagraph (A), but only if the plan provides for payment in full of all allowed unsecured claims over a shorter period.

Third, disposable income affects how much the debtor must pay to the unsecured creditors in particular. The court cannot approve a plan unless:

> the plan provides that all of the debtor's projected disposable income to be received in the applicable commitment period beginning on the date that the first payment is due under the plan will be applied to make payments **to unsecured creditors** under the plan.

§ 1325(b)(1)(B) (emphasis added).

---

2. *What Is Disposable Income?*

Disposable income is income less allowable expenses. Determining the amount of the debtor's disposable income thus requires analysis of two distinct aspects of the debtor's finances: (a) **income** and (b) **expenses**.

For all Chapter 13 debtors, income is the debtor's "current monthly income," a term defined by the Bankruptcy Code and discussed in the material on the means test that is inserted on page 107. Remember that the term focuses on money the debtor received in the six months before the bankruptcy filing, regardless of whether the debtor's finances have improved or taken a turn for the worse.

What expenses the debtor may deduct from her monthly income in calculating "disposable income" depends on whether the debtor's income is above the median income for a household the size of debtor's household.

a. Allowable expenses for debtors whose incomes do not exceed the median income.

If the debtor's monthly income does is below or equals the applicable median income, reasonably necessary expenses are deducted in calculating disposable income.

---

11 U.S.C. § 1325(b)(2)

For purposes of this subsection, the term "disposable income" means current monthly income received by the debtor (other than child support payments, foster care payments, or disability payments for a dependent child made in accordance with applicable nonbankruptcy law to the extent reasonably necessary to be expended for such child) less amounts reasonably necessary to be expended–

(A) (i) for the maintenance or support of the debtor or a dependent of the debtor, or for a domestic support obligation, that first becomes payable after the date the petition is filed; and

(ii) for charitable contributions (that meet the definition of "charitable contribution" under section 548(d)(3)) to a qualified religious or charitable entity or organization (as that term is defined in section 548(d)(4)) in an amount not to exceed 15 percent of the gross income of the debtor for the year in which the contributions are made; and

(B) if the debtor is engaged in business, for the payment of expenditures necessary for the continuation, preservation, and operation of such business.

Notice that section 1325(b)(2) does not define the term "dependent" and does not provide courts with any guidance as to what standard of living to use in determining whether an expense is "reasonably necessary." This lack of statutory guidance, coupled with the inherently factual nature of the inquiry, has resulted in numerous interpretation problems with respect to what are reasonably necessary expenses.

In order to allow the trustee, creditors, the court and the United States Trustee to analyze a debtor's disposable income, every individual debtor is required to file as part of her bankruptcy schedules a Schedule I, which details the amounts and sources of the debtor's and the debtor's spouse's income, describes tax withholdings and lists dependents, and a Schedule J, which provides information about the debtor's household expenses. The following two pages contain an example of the budget information provided by joint debtors in an actual Chapter 13 case.

Case No. ____________________

In re Stephen W. Sutton Erin K. Sutton

SCHEDULE I - CURRENT INCOME OF INDIVIDUAL DEBTOR(S)

The column labeled "Spouse" must be completed in all cases filed by joint debtors and by a married debtor in a chapter 12 or 13 case whether or not a joint petition is filed, unless the spouses are separated and a joint petition is not filed.

Debtor's Marital Status: **Married**	DEPENDENTS OF DEBTOR AND SPOUSE		
Debtor's Age: 34 Spouse's Age: 28	NAMES	AGE	RELATIONSHIP
	Alaura Sutton	**10**	**daughter**
	Andrew Sutton	**8**	**son**
	Austin Sutton	**4**	**son**

EMPLOYMENT:	DEBTOR	SPOUSE
Occupation	**Police officer**	**housewife/mother**
Name of Employer	**Milton-Freewater**	
How long employed	**3 years**	
Address of Employer	**P.O. Box 6 Milton-Freewater, OR 97862**	

Income: (Estimate of average monthly income)	DEBTOR	SPOUSE
Current monthly gross wages, salary, and commissions (pro rate if not paid monthly.)	$ **2,900.00**	$ **0.00**
Estimated monthly overtime	$ **0.00**	$ **0.00**
SUBTOTAL	$ **2,900.00**	$ **0.00**
LESS PAYROLL DEDUCTIONS		
a. Payroll taxes and social security	$ **259.00**	$ **0.00**
b. Insurance	$ **0.00**	$ **0.00**
c. Union dues	$ **43.00**	$ **0.00**
d. Other (Specify) **Vision**	$ **18.15**	$ **0.00**
SUBTOTAL OF PAYROLL DEDUCTIONS	$ **320.15**	$ **0.00**
TOTAL NET MONTHLY TAKE HOME PAY	$ **2,579.85**	$ **0.00**
Regular income from operation of business or profession or farm (attach detailed statement)	$ **0.00**	$ **0.00**
Income from real property	$ **0.00**	$ **0.00**
Interest and dividends	$ **0.00**	$ **0.00**
Alimony, maintenance or support payments payable to the debtor for the debtor's use or that of dependents listed above.	$ **0.00**	$ **0.00**
Social security or other government assistance (Specify)	$ **0.00**	$ **0.00**
Pension or retirement income	$ **0.00**	$ **0.00**
Other monthly income (Specify)	$ 0.00	$ 0.00
TOTAL MONTHLY INCOME	$ **2,579.85**	$ **0.00**

TOTAL COMBINED MONTHLY INCOME **$ 2,579.85** (Report also on Summary of Schedules)

Describe any increase or decrease of more than 10% in any of the above categories anticipated to occur within the year following the filing of this document: **NONE**

Case No.

In re Stephen W. Sutton Erin K. Sutton

SCHEDULE J - CURRENT EXPENDITURES OF INDIVIDUAL DEBTOR(S)

Complete this schedule by estimating the average monthly expenses of the debtor and the debtor's family. Prorate any payments made bi-weekly, quarterly, semi-annually, or annually to show monthly rate.

☐ Check this box if a joint petition is filed and debtor's spouse maintains a separate household. Complete a separate schedule of expenditures labeled "Spouse".

Rent or home mortgage payment (include lot rented for mobile home) WA Mutual & US Bank	$	543.00
Are real estate taxes included? Yes ✓ No ____		
Is property insurance included? Yes ✓ No ____		
Utilities Electricity and heating fuel	$	100.00
Water and sewer	$	0.00
Telephone	$	60.00
Other Cable	$	50.00
Home maintenance (repairs and upkeep)	$	25.00
Food	$	570.00
Clothing	$	50.00
Laundry and dry cleaning	$	50.00
Medical and dental expenses	$	127.00
Transportation (not including car payments)	$	50.00
Recreation, clubs and entertainment, newspapers, magazines, etc.	$	20.00
Charitable contributions	$	290.00
Insurance (not deducted from wages or included in home mortgage payments)		
Homeowner's or renter's	$	0.00
Life	$	0.00
Health	$	0.00
Auto	$	56.00
Other	$	0.00
Taxes (not deducted from wages or included in home mortgage payments) (Specify)	$	0.00
Installment payments: (In chapter 12 and 13 cases, do not list payments to be included in the plan)		
Auto	$	412.74
Other Les Schwab Tire Center	$	50.00
Alimony, maintenance or support paid to others	$	0.00
Payments for support of additional dependents not living at your home	$	0.00
Regular expenses from operation of business, profession, or farm (attach detailed statement)	$	0.00
Other	$	0.00
TOTAL MONTHLY EXPENSES (Report also on Summary of Schedules)	$	2,453.74

[FOR CHAPTER 12 AND 13 DEBTORS ONLY]

Provide the information requested below, including whether plan payments are to be made bi-weekly, monthly, annually, or at some other regular interval.

A. Total projected monthly income	$	2,579.85
B. Total projected monthly expenses	$	2,453.74
C. Excess income (A minus B)	$	126.11
D. Total amount to be paid into plan each Monthly (interval)	$	126.11

IN RE NICOLA

244 B.R. 795 (Bankr. N.D. Ill. 2000)

LEFKOW, Bankruptcy Judge.

Debtors Henry and Lori Nicola (the "Debtors") seek relief under Chapter 13 of the United States Bankruptcy Code (the "Code") and have submitted a First Amended Chapter 13 Plan (the "Plan") for confirmation. Glenn Stearns, the Standing Chapter 13 Trustee (the "Trustee"), objects to confirmation alleging that the debtors are not committing all of their disposable income to the plan. Additionally, the Trustee prays that the debtors' case be dismissed for cause under 11 U.S.C. § 1307(c). . . .

FACTS

On January 21, 2000, the debtors filed the First Amended Plan. It proposes that the debtors will pay $686 per month to the Trustee for a period of 40 months, from which the creditors with secured and § 507 . . . priority claims "shall be paid 100%." The Plan estimates that any general unsecured creditors will receive ten percent of the amount of their claims during the life of the Plan, or, if this does not occur, the Plan provides that the debtors will continue their monthly Plan payments for the shorter of 24 additional months or until the Trustee has received sufficient funds to pay the unsecured creditors ten percent of their claims.

The debtors' Schedule J indicates that they are expending $260 per month for private school tuition to send debtor Lori Nicola's daughter to St. Jude's School. In support of this expenditure, the debtors submitted to this court the Affidavit of Lori Nicola (the "Affidavit"). The Affidavit contains allegations that students at the public school in the debtors' area, Dirksen Junior High School ("Dirksen"), perform below state levels in all grades and in all subjects and that students at St. Jude's score substantially higher. Additionally, the Affidavit contains allegations that, based upon information and belief, there are substantial disciplinary problems at Dirksen. Debtor Lori Nicola testified that both she and the child's natural father, who is not a debtor in this case, are practicing Catholics and desire that their child attend a Catholic school and that she herself attended Catholic schools for 12 years. The child has attended Catholic school her entire life and wishes to continue doing so.

DISCUSSION

The Trustee contends that the debtors' payment of private school tuition is not a reasonably necessary expense and constitutes disposable income, and that, therefore, the debtors are not committing all of their disposable income to the Plan.

The court disagrees with the Trustee and concludes that his objection must be overruled in this instance because the private school tuition payments are reasonably necessary expenses. § 1325 of the Bankruptcy Code provides:

> (b)(1) If the trustee or the holder of an allowed unsecured claim objects to the confirmation of the plan, then the court may not approve the plan unless, as of the effective date of the plan-
>
> ....
>
> (B) the plan provides that all of the debtor's projected disposable income to be received in the three-year period beginning on the date that the first payment is due under the plan will be applied to make payments under the plan.

Disposable income is defined in § 1325:

> (b)(2) For the purposes of this subsection, "disposable income" means income which is received by the debtor and which is not reasonably necessary to be expended-
> (A) for the maintenance or support of the debtor or a dependent of the debtor....

Consequently, the disposable income requirement turns on whether the debtor's budgeted expenses are reasonably necessary. . . .

What is "reasonably necessary" is a question of fact for which the outcome can vary from judge to judge and jurisdiction to jurisdiction. . . . There is no bright line rule for determining what is "reasonably necessary." Because there is no precise standard, some courts have strictly scrutinized expenses, some have been more deferential to the debtor, and most have settled at a some median between these two extremes.

It is clear that food, clothing and other essentials are considered "reasonably necessary" for the debtor's maintenance and support. Some courts also allow expenditures for recreation, clubs, magazines, newspapers and the like. In any event, "reasonably necessary" probably means adequate, but not first class, and luxury items are excluded. . . . While judges should not allow debtors to continue in a lifestyle that drove them into bankruptcy, courts should not require debtors to alter their lifestyle where there is no obvious indulgence in luxuries. Expenses may amount to an obvious indulgence in luxuries when a debtor is enjoying luxuries that are not enjoyed by an average American family. . . . For example, a Chevrolet Blazer sport utility vehicle is an "obvious overindulgence" for a debtor who lives three miles from work and presumably near paved roads.

There is a split of authority on the issue of whether payment of school tuition is a reasonably necessary expense for a debtor in a Chapter 13 case. One line of cases holds that tuition payments are not a reasonably necessary expense. . . . The other line holds that tuition payments are a reasonably necessary expense. . . .

The holdings that the tuition payments were not reasonably necessary were based upon specific facts presented in the cases.

Here, the debtors are spending $260 per month to send the child to Catholic school. This is not an excessive amount; it is far less than the $2,000 in Ehret or the $1,000 total monthly expenditure in Jones, a case which was decided in 1985. The debtors here do not send the child away to boarding school; she attends a local Catholic school in Joliet, where the debtors reside. Additionally, the debtors have alleged that the local public school is inadequate and have provided a "School Report Card" indicating that, in fact, average standardized test scores at the public school are below those of the state as a whole. Additionally, the child has attended Catholic school her entire life, and therefore this is not a new expense for the debtors. The court is also mindful that there would likely be significant emotional cost to the child to change placement in her final year of elementary school. Finally, Lori Nicola stated in her deposition that she and the child's father are practicing Catholics and desire their daughter to attend Catholic school as Lori did. Any of the above facts alone may not be enough to warrant a finding that the tuition expense is reasonably necessary. However, taken as a whole, the facts in this case indicate that the debtors' monthly payment of $260 for Catholic school tuition is reasonably necessary.

Because the monthly payments for Catholic school tuition are a reasonably necessary expenditure for the debtors, the Trustee's objection to confirmation is overruled. . . .

---

b. Allowable expenses for debtors whose income exceed the median income.

If the debtor's household monthly income exceeds the median income, reasonable expenses are determined by applying the means test formula discussed in the material on the means test that starts on page 107. § 1325(b)(3).[14] Recall that the formula permits the deduction of four distinct types of expenses:

1. Living expenses, as determined by the Internal Revenue Service guidelines;

2. Monthly secured debt payments;

3. Amount required to pay priority debts in full;

4. Other administrative and special purpose expenses, including up to 10% of the projected Chapter 13 plan payments for administrative expenses, and most charitable contributions.

PROBLEM 10-3: HOW IS THE DEBTOR'S DISPOSABLE INCOME CALCULATED?

Joe lives in Las Vegas, Nevada and currently works as a warehouseman. He is divorced and lives alone. Until nine months ago, when his employer ceased doing business, he was a union truck driver earning $5 per hour more than he currently earns. After he lost his job, he spent six months looking for employment. While

---

[14]Section 1325(b)(3) provides:

> Amounts reasonably necessary to be expended under paragraph (2) shall be determined in accordance with subparagraphs (A) and (B) of section 707(b)(2), if the debtor has current monthly income, when multiplied by 12, greater than [the applicable median income].

unemployed, Joe's only income was $1,600 per month in severance pay. Joe explains that as a result of his unemployment, he fell behind in paying his bills.

Joe's gross income since he returned to work three months ago has been $3,400 per month and his net income after taxes is $2,500 per month. His monthly expenses (excluding amounts past due) are:

Home Mortgage	$	600.00
Utilities and Phone		150.00
Real Estate Taxes on Home		100.00
Home Maintenance		50.00
Current Child Support		400.00
Food		200.00
Recreation and Entertainment		100.00
Truck Payments		300.00[15]
Other truck expenses		100.00
Truck insurance		100.00
Health Insurance		100.00
Total Expenses	$	2,200.00

(a) What is Joe's current monthly income?

(b) Is Joe's current monthly income less than the median income in Nevada for one earner? As explained in the chart on page 111, the median income for a household with one earner in Nevada is $37,243.

---

[15] At $300.00 per month, Joe's truck will be paid off in 36 months.

(c) Itemize what expenses will be considered reasonably necessary expenses in determining Joe's disposable income.

(d) How much is Joe's disposable income?

(e) If you have concluded that Joe's income is below the applicable median income, is there anything that you might suggest that Joe consider that would result in his being an above-median income debtor?

(f) Would Joe's disposable income be more or less if he were an above-median income debtor? In answering the question, you should assume that Joe's secured debt payments for the next 60 months will total $835/month, he makes no charitable contributions, 10% of his projected Chapter 13 plan payments are $1,875 ($31/month if paid over 60 months) and his priority debt totals $4,600 ($77/month if paid over 60 months).

PROBLEM 10-4: WHAT IS A REASONABLE VEHICLE EXPENSE?

Debtor is driving a two-year-old Lexus RX 330, which is a small luxury sport utility vehicle. Debtor does not drive the vehicle off the road, but feels safer in an all-wheel-drive vehicle during inclement winter weather. Debtor's car payments are $475 per month and will continue for another three years if paid according to the contract. The trustee believes that the debtor could obtain necessary transportation at a lower cost. In deciding whether to object to the vehicle expense, what difference will it make to the trustee whether the debtor's income is above or below the applicable median income?

(a) The trustee objects to confirmation, arguing that debtor does not reasonably need the vehicle at all because, debtor could get to work and around town on the bus; a bus pass costs only $50 per month. This would increase debtor's disposable income by the $425 per month saved on payments plus the cost of insuring and maintaining the vehicle. Should the trustee prevail? Is the answer any different depending on whether the debtor has children?

(b) After the trustee loses this argument, he argues in the next case with similar facts that the debtor should be required to get a used vehicle, which would cost about half the amount that is still due on the Lexus, thereby increasing the debtor's disposable income by $250. Should the trustee prevail?

PROBLEM 10-5: IS THE COST OF FULL CABLE OR SATELLITE DISH TELEVISION SERVICE REASONABLY NECESSARY?

Debtor's monthly expenditures include $70 for cable television service, which includes the maximum number of stations, the premium movie channels and the extra sports broadcasts. The trustee objects, arguing that free local television service is available and nothing should be allowed for cable. Debtor responds by arguing that her budget includes only $50 for recreation for a family of four, that cable television is a major form of recreation for the family, and that if cable is disallowed her cost for entertainment and recreation will increase by more than $70. Should the trustee prevail? Would the trustee raise this objection if the debtor's household income were above the applicable median income?

PROBLEM 10-6: ARE THE EXPENSES OF CHILDREN WHO ARE COLLEGE STUDENTS REASONABLY NECESSARY?

Debtors have a 20-year-old daughter who is a junior in college.

(a) Daughter is attending State University and debtors contribute $4,000 per year toward her tuition, books and room and board. The trustee objects to this expense on the basis that debtors have above-median income and the expense formula of § 707(b)(2)(A)(ii)(IV) allows educational expenses only for children under age 18. Will the trustee prevail? Is the answer any different if the debtors have below-median income? The trustee argues that the expense is not a reasonable expense because, under applicable state law, the daughter became an adult when she turned 18. The trustee correctly points out that debtors have no legal obligation to support their daughter. Debtors argue that they have continuously supported their daughter, that $4,000 is a reasonable amount, and the fact that they are not legally obligated to support their daughter does not mean that she is not dependent on them for support.

(b) Would either answer differ if the daughter were at Ivy League University and debtors were contributing $15,000 per year toward her support?

———

3. *The Plan Must Provide that Creditors Receive At Least As Much As They Would Receive in a Chapter 7 Case (the Best Interests Test).*

Section 1325(a)(4)[16] requires that the debtor's plan result in a distribution to creditors of at least as much as they would receive in a Chapter 7 case. The calculation of the amount required includes both the net amount that could be realized if the trustee exercised her avoidance powers, *see* Unit 7.B.-F, plus the net amount that the trustee would realize from the liquidation of the debtor's assets that are not fully exempt. In calculating the net amount the Chapter 7 trustee would realize, keep in mind that the trustee may have to pay from the estate the cost of real estate brokers, auctioneers, attorneys, accountants and other professionals he hires to help him liquidate the estate. At a minimum, the trustee will be paid for his services. The maximum trustee compensation is established by § 326. All the probable Chapter 7 expenses are deducted before determining the amount, because costs of administration are paid before the creditors receive a distribution. These expenses can make a significant difference in how much the Chapter 13 debtor with non-exempt assets must pay.

Although the best interests test requires debtors to pay creditors not less than creditors would receive in Chapter 7, the payment terms are often more affordable in Chapter 13. The debtor pays the sum due over the life of the plan, which we have learned will be three to five years. In Chapter 7, if the debtor wants to buy a non-exempt asset from the trustee the trustee will want to be

---

[16] Section 1325(a)(4) provides:

(a) Except as provided in subsection (b), the court shall confirm a plan if—

> (4) the value, as of the effective date of the plan, of property to be distributed under the plan on account of each allowed unsecured claim is not less than the amount that would be paid on such claim if the estate of the debtor were liquidated under chapter 7 of this title on such date[.]

paid for the asset in a lump sum or over a very short period of time, because it is the Chapter 7 trustee's duty to liquidate the assets expeditiously and make distributions to creditors.

PROBLEM 10-7: HOW IS THE BEST INTERESTS TEST APPLIED?

Debtors have the following non-exempt assets that a Chapter 7 trustee would likely claim:

(1) $25,000 in equity in their $90,000 house, and
(2) $2,000 in tax refunds.

In addition, debtors made an $8,000 loan repayment to Mr. Debtor's parents which the Chapter 7 trustee is likely to claim was a preferential transfer. Debtors do not want to have Mr. Debtor's parents sued by a bankruptcy trustee or be required to return the $8,000. How much will debtors have to pay creditors under their Chapter 13 plan to satisfy the requirement that creditors be paid at least as much as they would be paid in a Chapter 7 case and to avoid having to recover the preference from Mr. Debtor's parents?

For purposes of your answer, you can assume that:

(i) a Chapter 7 trustee would incur $7,000 in costs for the realtor and closing costs to sell debtors' house, and

(ii) the trustee would be likely to incur at least $2,000 in legal fees to recover the $8,000 preference, and

(iii) the Chapter 7 trustee's compensation would be $7,250, based on the maximum compensation permitted by § 326(a).

D. Cars and Houses (How Much of the Plan Payment Goes to Pay for the Car and House?)

Most Chapter 13 debtors who have a house and one or more cars financed the purchase of those assets, and the creditor who advanced the money retains an interest in the house or car. In addition, the debtor often will have granted a second or third mortgage on her home as security for a debt consolidation loan, a home equity line of credit, or some other obligation. It is the debtor's inability to pay one or more of these obligations with the resulting foreclosure or threatened repossession that prompts the debtor to seek legal help. Chapter 13 provides the means by which the debtor can save her house and/or car, because it allows the debtor to cure defaults and, with respect to car loans, entirely restructure the payment obligation. Chapter 7 does not offer similar relief. Thus, many debtors trying to save their house or car use Chapter 13 rather than Chapter 7.

---

1. *Chapter 13 Provisions Regarding the Treatment of Claims Secured by Cars (and Other Assets Except Claims Secured Solely by the Debtor's Principal Residence).*

As we learned earlier in Unit 4, a claim is secured if the creditor has a lien on property of the estate and that property of the estate has economic value. § 506(a). The amount of the secured claim is limited to the economic value of the lien on property of the estate. Thus, a creditor who is owed $20,000 secured by a first lien on a debtor's car that is worth only $14,000 has a $14,000 secured claim and a $6,000 unsecured claim.

Section 1322(b) provides that the Chapter 13 plan may include one or more of the following provisions with respect to secured creditors.

11 U.S.C. § 1322(b)

> [T]he plan may– . . .
>
> (2) modify the rights of holders of secured claims, other than a claim secured only by a security interest in real property that is the debtor's principal residence, or of holders of unsecured claims, or leave unaffected the rights of holders of any class of claims;
>
> (3) provide for the curing or waiving of any default; . . . .
>
> (5) notwithstanding paragraph (2) of this subsection, provide for the curing of any default within a reasonable time and maintenance of payments while the case is pending on any unsecured claim or secured claim on which the last payment is due after the date on which the final payment under the plan is due[.]

Thus, the statute permits two approaches with respect to secured claims: (1) modify the claim or (2) cure defaults and reinstate the original payment terms. The debtor can cure the default and reinstate the original payment terms regardless of whether the creditor has accelerated the debt because of the debtor's default, *i.e.* declared the entire debt due and payable. If the original terms of the obligation extend beyond the duration of the Chapter 13 plan, which will usually be three to five years, the debtor may cure defaults during the Chapter 13 and then perform according to the original contract terms after the Chapter 13 case ends.

The seemingly endless possibilities that are presented by § 1322(b)(2), which permits modification of the secured claim (other than a claim secured solely by the debtor's principal residence), are limited by the requirements that must be met before the court can confirm the Chapter 13 plan. Section 1325(a)(5) provides that a plan cannot be confirmed unless:

> (A) the holder of such claim has accepted the plan;
>
> (B) (i) the plan provides that—

(I) the holder of such claim retain the lien securing such claim;

until the earlier of—

(aa) the payment of the underlying debt determined under nonbankruptcy law; or

(bb) discharge under section 1328; and

(II) if the case under this chapter is dismissed or converted without completion of the plan, such lien shall also be retained by such holder to the extent recognized by applicable nonbankruptcy law; and

(ii) the value, as of the effective date of the plan, of property to be distributed under the plan on account of such claim is not less than the allowed amount of such claim; and

(iii) if—

(I) property to be distributed pursuant to this subsection is in the form of periodic payments, such payments shall be in equal monthly amounts; and

(II) the holder of the claim is secured by personal property, the amount of such payments shall not be less than an amount sufficient to provide to the holder of such claim adequate protection during the period of the plan; or

(C) the debtor surrenders the property securing such claim to such holder[.]

Thus, unless the creditor holding the secured claim agrees to the proposed treatment or the debtor surrenders the collateral to the creditor holding the security interest, the creditor must retain its lien and must receive compensation the value of which equals the amount of the secured claim. The latter provision requires that a debtor who is going to pay the secured claim over time pay interest at a sufficient rate that the present value of the stream of payments equals the secured claim. This requirement is imposed so that the creditor is not in any worse position than it would have been if it had been allowed to foreclose on its collateral. Periodic payments must be equal monthly payments.

The following example may help explain the logic behind this requirement. A lender with a security interest in an automobile can often repossess and sell its collateral in a fairly short period of time, often as little as 30 days. Using our prior example, of the $20,000 obligation secured by the automobile worth $14,000, outside of bankruptcy if the debtor fails to make payments as agreed, the creditor repossesses the automobile and, after giving the debtor notice and a short period to pay the obligation in full, sells the automobile and realizes $14,000. The creditor then has $14,000 that it can either loan to another borrower who will pay the creditor interest, or otherwise invest. If Chapter 13 intervenes and the creditor is prohibited from foreclosing, and the debtor is going to pay the creditor over three to five years, the debtor must pay the creditor the $14,000 plus interest. Otherwise, the creditor will get less than the creditor would have gotten outside of bankruptcy.

In addition, the 2005 amendments to the Bankruptcy Code imposed a special rule that § 506, which limits a secured claim to the value of the debtor's interest in the property, does not apply to certain debts.

11 U.S.C. § 1325(a)

> (9). . . . For purposes of paragraph (5), section 506 shall not apply to a claim described in that paragraph if the creditor has a purchase money security interest securing the debt that is the subject of the claim, the debt was incurred within the 910-day preceding the date of the filing of the petition, and the collateral for that debt consists of a motor vehicle (as defined in section 30102 of title 49) acquired for the personal use of the debtor, or if collateral for that debt consists of any other

thing of value, if the debt was incurred during the 1-year period preceding that filing.

This amendment is commonly referred to as the "anti-cram down" provision. It prevents the Chapter 13 debtor who has purchased a vehicle within about 2 ½ years prior to bankruptcy for personal use or has incurred other secured debt within a year of bankruptcy from paying the secured creditor less than the full principal amount due on the debt if the debtor wants to retain the collateral. It should be noted that there is nothing in this provision that prevents the debtor from altering the interest rate, the amount of the monthly payments, or the other terms of the secured obligation if such alternation is permitted by the Bankruptcy Code.

Chapter 13 balances the rights of creditors and debtors. The debtor gets the benefit of more time to pay and the opportunity to keep the automobile; the creditor gets sufficient payments so that the creditor is no worse off than if bankruptcy had not intervened. The challenge in maintaining this balance is in the detail of determining the value of the creditor's collateral if the anti-cram down provision does not apply and the appropriate rate of interest. We learned about valuation of collateral in Unit 4, problem 4-14. The following case focuses on compensating creditors for the delay in payment.

SCS CREDIT CORP. V. TILL (*IN RE* TILL)

541 U.S. 465 (2004)

JUSTICE STEVENS announced the judgment of the Court and delivered an opinion, in which JUSTICE SOUTER, JUSTICE GINSBURG, and JUSTICE BREYER join.

To qualify for court approval under Chapter 13 of the Code, an individual debtor's proposed debt adjustment plan must accommodate each allowed, secured creditor in one of three ways: (1) by obtaining the creditor's acceptance of the plan; (2) by surrendering the property securing the claim; or

(3) by providing the creditor both a lien securing the claim and a promise of future property distributions (such as deferred cash payments) whose total "value, as of the effective date of the plan, ... is not less than the allowed amount of such claim." . . . The third alternative is commonly known as the "cram down option" because it may be enforced over a claim holder's objection. . . . Associates Commercial Corp. v. Rash, 520 U.S. 953, 957, 117 S.Ct. 1879, 138 L.Ed.2d 148 (1997).

Plans that invoke the cram down power often provide for installment payments over a period of years rather than a single payment. . . . In such circumstances, the amount of each installment must be calibrated to ensure that, over time, the creditor receives disbursements whose total present value[4] equals or exceeds that of the allowed claim. The proceedings in this case that led to our grant of certiorari identified four different methods of determining the appropriate method with which to perform that calibration. Indeed, the Bankruptcy Judge, the District Court, the Court of Appeals majority, and the dissenting Judge each endorsed a different approach. We detail the underlying facts and describe each of those approaches before setting forth our judgment as to which approach best meets the purposes of the Code.

I

On October 2, 1998, petitioners Lee and Amy Till, residents of Kokomo, Indiana, purchased a used truck from Instant Auto Finance for $6,395 plus $330.75 in fees and taxes. They made a $300 down payment and financed the balance of the purchase price by entering into a retail installment contract that Instant Auto immediately assigned to respondent, SCS Credit Corporation. Petitioners' initial indebtedness amounted to $8,285.24--the $6,425.75 balance of the truck purchase plus a finance charge of 21% per year for 136 weeks, or $1,859.49. Under the contract, petitioners agreed to make 68 biweekly payments to cover this debt; Instant Auto--and subsequently respondent--retained a purchase money security interest that gave it the right to repossess the truck if petitioners defaulted under the contract.

On October 25, 1999, petitioners, by then in default on their payments to respondent, filed a joint petition for relief under Chapter 13 of the Code. At the time of the filing, respondent's outstanding claim amounted to $4,894.89, but

---

[4]In the remainder of the opinion, we use the term "present value" to refer to the value as of the effective date of the bankruptcy plan.

the parties agreed that the truck securing the claim was worth only $4,000. . . . In accordance with the Code, therefore, respondent's secured claim was limited to $4,000, and the $894.89 balance was unsecured. . . .

The proposed plan . . . provided that petitioners would pay interest on the secured portion of respondent's claim at a rate of 9.5% per year. Petitioners arrived at this "prime-plus" or "formula rate" by augmenting the national prime rate of approximately 8% (applied by banks when making low-risk loans) to account for the risk of nonpayment posed by borrowers in their financial position. Respondent objected to the proposed rate, contending that the company was "entitled to interest at the rate of 21%, which is the rate ... it would obtain if it could foreclose on the vehicle and reinvest the proceeds in loans of equivalent duration and risk as the loan" originally made to petitioners. . . .

At the hearing on its objection, respondent presented expert testimony establishing that it uniformly charges 21% interest on so-called "subprime" loans, or loans to borrowers with poor credit ratings, and that other lenders in the subprime market also charge that rate. Petitioners countered with the testimony of an Indiana University-Purdue University Indianapolis economics professor, who acknowledged that he had only limited familiarity with the subprime auto lending market, but described the 9.5% formula rate as "very reasonable" given that Chapter 13 plans are "supposed to be financially feasible."[8] Moreover, the professor noted that respondent's exposure was "fairly limited because [petitioners] are under the supervision of the court." The bankruptcy trustee also filed comments supporting the formula rate as, among other things, easily ascertainable, closely tied to the "condition of the financial market," and independent of the financial circumstances of any particular lender. Accepting petitioners' evidence, the Bankruptcy Court overruled respondent's objection and confirmed the proposed plan.

The District Court reversed. It understood Seventh Circuit precedent to require that bankruptcy courts set cram down interest rates at the level the creditor could have obtained if it had foreclosed on the loan, sold the collateral, and reinvested the proceeds in loans of equivalent duration and risk. . . .

---

[8]The requirement of financial feasibility derives from 11 U.S.C. § 1325(a)(6), which provides that the bankruptcy court shall "confirm a plan if ... the debtor will be able to make all payments under the plan and to comply with the plan." See infra, at ----14.

On appeal, the Seventh Circuit endorsed a slightly modified version of the District Court's "coerced" or "forced loan" approach. . . . [T]he majority held that the original contract rate should "serve as a presumptive [cram down] rate," which either the creditor or the debtor could challenge with evidence that a higher or lower rate should apply. . . .

Dissenting, Judge Rovner . . . advocated either the Bankruptcy Court's formula approach or a "straightforward ... cost of funds" approach that would simply ask "what it would cost the creditor to obtain the cash equivalent of the collateral from an alternative source." . . .

II

The Code provides little guidance as to which of the rates of interest advocated by the four opinions in this case--the formula rate, the coerced loan rate, the presumptive contract rate, or the cost of funds rate-- Congress had in mind when it adopted the cram down provision. That provision, 11 U.S.C. § 1325(a)(5)(B), does not mention the term "discount rate" or the word "interest." Rather, it simply requires bankruptcy courts to ensure that the property to be distributed to a particular secured creditor over the life of a bankruptcy plan has a total "value, as of the effective date of the plan," that equals or exceeds the value of the creditor's allowed secured claim--in this case, $4,000. § 1325(a)(5)(B)(ii).

That command is easily satisfied when the plan provides for a lump-sum payment to the creditor. Matters are not so simple, however, when the debt is to be discharged by a series of payments over time. A debtor's promise of future payments is worth less than an immediate payment of the same total amount because the creditor cannot use the money right away, inflation may cause the value of the dollar to decline before the debtor pays, and there is always some risk of nonpayment. . . .

Three important considerations govern that choice. First, the Code includes numerous provisions that, like the cram down provision, require a court to "discoun[t] ... [a] stream of deferred payments back to the[ir] present dollar value," Rake v. Wade, 508 U.S. 464, 472, n. 8, 113 S.Ct. 2187, 124 L.Ed.2d 424 (1993), to ensure that a creditor receives at least the value of its claim.[10] We think it likely that Congress intended bankruptcy judges and trustees to follow essentially the same approach when choosing an appropriate interest rate under any of these provisions. Moreover, we think Congress would favor an approach that is familiar in the financial community and that minimizes the need for expensive evidentiary proceedings.

Second, Chapter 13 expressly authorizes a bankruptcy court to modify the rights of any creditor whose claim is secured by an interest in anything other than "real property that is the debtor's principal residence." 11 U.S.C. § 1322(b)(2). . . . Thus, in cases like this involving secured interests in personal property, the court's authority to modify the number, timing, or amount of the installment payments from those set forth in the debtor's original contract is perfectly clear. Further, the potential need to modify the loan terms to account for intervening changes in circumstances is also clear: On the one hand, the fact of the bankruptcy establishes that the debtor is overextended and thus poses a significant risk of default; on the other hand, the postbankruptcy obligor is no longer the individual debtor but the court-supervised estate, and the risk of default is thus somewhat reduced.[12]

Third, from the point of view of a creditor, the cram down provision mandates an objective rather than a subjective inquiry. . . . That is, although § 1325(a)(5)(B) entitles the creditor to property whose present value objectively equals or exceeds the value of the collateral, it does not require that the terms of the cram down loan match the terms to which the

---

[10]See 11 U.S.C. § 1129(a)(7)(A)(ii) (requiring payment of property whose "value, as of the effective date of the plan" equals or exceeds the value of the creditor's claim); §§ 1129(a)(7)(B), 1129(a)(9)(B)(I), 1129(a)(9)(C), 1129(b)(2)(A)(ii), 1129(b)(2)(B)(I), 1129(b)(2)(C)(I), 1173(a)(2), 1225(a)(4), 1225(a)(5)(B)(ii), 1228(b)(2), 1325(a)(4), 1228(b)(2) (same).

[12]Several factors contribute to this reduction in risk. First, as noted below, infra, at 1962, a court may only approve a cram down loan (and the debt adjustment plan of which the loan is a part) if it believes the debtor will be able to make all of the required payments. § 1325(a)(6). Thus, such loans will only be approved for debtors that the court deems creditworthy. Second, Chapter 13 plans must "provide for the submission" to the trustee "of all or such portion of [the debtor's] future ... income ... as is necessary for the execution of the plan," § 1322(a)(1), so the possibility of nonpayment is greatly reduced. Third, the Code's extensive disclosure requirements reduce the risk that the debtor has significant undisclosed obligations. Fourth, as a practical matter, the public nature of the bankruptcy proceeding is likely to reduce the debtor's opportunities to take on additional debt. Cf. 11 U.S.C. § 525 (prohibiting certain Government grant and loan programs from discriminating against applicants who are or have been bankrupt).

debtor and creditor agreed prebankruptcy, nor does it require that the cram down terms make the creditor subjectively indifferent between present foreclosure and future payment. Indeed, the very idea of a "cram down" loan precludes the latter result: By definition, a creditor forced to accept such a loan would prefer instead to foreclose.[14] Thus, a court choosing a cram down interest rate need not consider the creditor's individual circumstances, such as its prebankruptcy dealings with the debtor or the alternative loans it could make if permitted to foreclose. . . . Rather, the court should aim to treat similarly situated creditors similarly, . . . and to ensure that an objective economic analysis would suggest the debtor's interest payments will adequately compensate all such creditors for the time value of their money and the risk of default.

III

These considerations lead us to reject the coerced loan, presumptive contract rate, and cost of funds approaches. Each of these approaches is complicated, imposes significant evidentiary costs, and aims to make each individual creditor whole rather than to ensure the debtor's payments have the required present value. . . .

IV

The formula approach has none of these defects. Taking its cue from ordinary lending practices, the approach begins by looking to the national prime rate, reported daily in the press, which reflects the financial market's estimate of the amount a commercial bank should charge a creditworthy commercial borrower to compensate for the opportunity costs of the loan,

---

[14]This fact helps to explain why there is no readily apparent Chapter 13 "cram down market rate of interest": Because every cram down loan is imposed by a court over the objection of the secured creditor, there is no free market of willing cram down lenders. Interestingly, the same is not true in the Chapter 11 context, as numerous lenders advertise financing for Chapter 11 debtors in possession. See, e.g., Balmoral Financial Corporation, http://www.balmoral.com/bdip.htm (all Internet materials as visited Mar. 4, 2004, and available in Clerk of Court's case file) (advertising debtor in possession lending); Debtor in Possession Financing: 1st National Assistance Finance Association DIP Division, http://www.loanmallusa.com/dip.htm (offering "to tailor a financing program ... to your business' needs and ... to work closely with your bankruptcy counsel"). Thus, when picking a cram down rate in a Chapter 11 case, it might make sense to ask what rate an efficient market would produce. In the Chapter 13 context, by contrast, the absence of any such market obligates courts to look to first principles and ask only what rate will fairly compensate a creditor for its exposure.

the risk of inflation, and the relatively slight risk of default. [18] Because bankrupt debtors typically pose a greater risk of nonpayment than solvent commercial borrowers, the approach then requires a bankruptcy court to adjust the prime rate accordingly. The appropriate size of that risk adjustment depends, of course, on such factors as the circumstances of the estate, the nature of the security, and the duration and feasibility of the reorganization plan. The court must therefore hold a hearing at which the debtor and any creditors may present evidence about the appropriate risk adjustment. Some of this evidence will be included in the debtor's bankruptcy filings, however, so the debtor and creditors may not incur significant additional expense. Moreover, starting from a concededly low estimate and adjusting upward places the evidentiary burden squarely on the creditors, who are likely to have readier access to any information absent from the debtor's filing (such as evidence about the "liquidity of the collateral market," post, at 1973 (SCALIA, J., dissenting)). Finally, many of the factors relevant to the adjustment fall squarely within the bankruptcy court's area of expertise.

Thus, unlike the coerced loan, presumptive contract rate, and cost of funds approaches, the formula approach entails a straightforward, familiar, and objective inquiry, and minimizes the need for potentially costly additional evidentiary proceedings. Moreover, the resulting "prime-plus" rate of interest depends only on the state of financial markets, the circumstances of the bankruptcy estate, and the characteristics of the loan, not on the creditor's circumstances or its prior interactions with the debtor. For these reasons, the prime-plus or formula rate best comports with the purposes of the Code. . . .

We do not decide the proper scale for the risk adjustment, as the issue is not before us. The Bankruptcy Court in this case approved a risk adjustment of 1.5%, and other courts have generally approved adjustments of 1% to 3%. Respondent's core argument is that a risk adjustment in this range is entirely inadequate to compensate a creditor for the real risk that the plan will fail. There is some dispute about the true scale of that risk--respondent claims that more than 60% of Chapter 13 plans fail, Brief for Respondent 25, but petitioners argue that the failure rate for approved Chapter 13 plans is much lower. We need not resolve that dispute. It is

---

[18] We note that, if the court could somehow be certain a debtor would complete his plan, the prime rate would be adequate to compensate any secured creditors forced to accept cram down loans.

sufficient for our purposes to note that, under 11 U.S.C. § 1325(a)(6), a court may not approve a plan unless, after considering all creditors' objections and receiving the advice of the trustee, the judge is persuaded that "the debtor will be able to make all payments under the plan and to comply with the plan." Ibid. Together with the cram down provision, this requirement obligates the court to select a rate high enough to compensate the creditor for its risk but not so high as to doom the plan. If the court determines that the likelihood of default is so high as to necessitate an "eye-popping" interest rate, the plan probably should not be confirmed.

V

The dissent's endorsement of the presumptive contract rate approach rests on two assumptions: (1) "subprime lending markets are competitive and therefore largely efficient"; and (2) the risk of default in Chapter 13 is normally no less than the risk of default at the time of the original loan. Although the Code provides little guidance on the question, we think it highly unlikely that Congress would endorse either premise.

. . .

Even more important, if all relevant information about the debtor's circumstances, the creditor's circumstances, the nature of the collateral, and the market for comparable loans were equally available to both debtor and creditor, then in theory the formula and presumptive contract rate approaches would yield the same final interest rate. Thus, we principally differ with the dissent not over what final rate courts should adopt but over which party (creditor or debtor) should bear the burden of rebutting the presumptive rate (prime or contract, respectively).

Justice Scalia identifies four "relevant factors bearing on risk premium[:] (1) the probability of plan failure; (2) the rate of collateral depreciation; (3) the liquidity of the collateral market; and (4) the administrative expenses of enforcement." Post, at 1973. In our view, any information debtors have about any of these factors is likely to be included in their bankruptcy filings, while the remaining information will be far more accessible to creditors (who must collect information about their lending markets to remain competitive) than to individual debtors (whose only experience with those markets might be the single loan at issue in the case). Thus, the formula approach, which begins with a concededly low estimate of the appropriate interest rate and requires the creditor to present evidence supporting a higher rate, places the evidentiary burden on the more knowledgeable party, thereby facilitating more accurate calculation of the appropriate interest rate.

If the rather sketchy data uncovered by the dissent support an argument that Chapter 13 of the Code should mandate application of the presumptive contract rate approach (rather than merely an argument that bankruptcy judges should exercise greater caution before approving debt adjustment plans), those data should be forwarded to Congress. We are not persuaded, however, that the data undermine our interpretation of the statutory scheme Congress has enacted.

The judgment of the Court of Appeals is reversed, and the case is remanded with instructions to remand the case to the Bankruptcy Court for further proceedings consistent with this opinion.

It is so ordered.

Justice Thomas, concurring in the judgment.

This case presents the issue of what the proper method is for discounting deferred payments to present value and what compensation the creditor is entitled to in calculating the appropriate discount rate of interest. Both the plurality and the dissent agree that "[a] debtor's promise of future payments is worth less than an immediate payment of the same total amount because the creditor cannot use the money right away, inflation may cause the value of the dollar to decline before the debtor pays, and there is always some risk of nonpayment." Ante, at 1958; post, at 1968. Thus, the plurality and the dissent agree that the proper method for discounting deferred payments to present value should take into account each of these factors, but disagree over the proper starting point for calculating the risk of nonpayment.

I agree that a "promise of future payments is worth less than an immediate payment" of the same amount, in part because of the risk of nonpayment. But this fact is irrelevant. The statute does not require that the value of the promise to distribute property under the plan be no less than the allowed amount of the secured creditor's claim. It requires only that "the value ... of property to be distributed under the plan," at the time of the effective date of the plan, be no less than the amount of the secured creditor's claim. 11 U.S.C. § 1325(a)(5)(B)(ii) (emphasis added). Both the plurality and the dissent ignore the clear text of the statute in an apparent rush to ensure that secured creditors are not undercompensated in bankruptcy proceedings. But the statute that Congress enacted does not require a debtor-specific risk adjustment that would put secured creditors in the same position as if they had made another loan. It is for this reason that I write separately. . . .

II

The allowed amount of the secured claim is $4,000. . . . The statute then requires a bankruptcy court to identify the "property to be distributed" under the plan. Petitioners' Amended Chapter 13 Plan (Plan) provided:

> "The future earnings of DEBTOR(S) are submitted to the supervision and control of this Court, and DEBTOR(S) shall pay to the TRUSTEE a sum of $740 per month in weekly installments by voluntary wage assignment by separate ORDER of the Court in an estimated amount of $170.77 and continuing for a total plan term of 36 months unless this Court approves an extension of the term not beyond 60 months from the date of filing the Petition herein." App. to Pet. for Cert. 77a.

From the payments received, the trustee would then make disbursements to petitioners' creditors, pro rata among each class of creditors. The Plan listed one priority claim and four secured claims. For respondent's secured claim, petitioner proposed an interest rate of 9.5%. . . . Thus, petitioners proposed to distribute to respondent a stream of cash payments equaling respondent's pro rata share of $740 per month for a period of up to 36 months. . . .

Although the Plan does not specifically state that "the property to be distributed" under the Plan is cash payments, the cash payments are the only "property" specifically listed for distribution under the Plan. Thus, although the plurality and the dissent imply that the "property to be distributed" under the Plan is the mere promise to make cash payments, the plain language of the Plan indicates that the "property to be distributed" to respondent is up to 36 monthly cash payments, consisting of a pro rata share of $740 per month.

The final task, then, is to determine whether petitioners' proposed 9.5% interest rate will sufficiently compensate respondent for the fact that instead of receiving $4,000 today, it will receive $4,000 plus 9.5% interest over a period of up to 36 months. Because the 9.5% rate is higher than the risk-free rate, I conclude that it will. I would therefore reverse the judgment of the Court of Appeals.

Justice Scalia, with whom THE CHIEF JUSTICE, Justice O'Connor, and Justice Kennedy join, dissenting.

My areas of agreement with the plurality are substantial. We agree that, although all confirmed Chapter 13 plans have been deemed feasible by a bankruptcy judge, some nevertheless fail. . . . We agree that any deferred payments to a secured creditor must fully compensate it for the risk that such a failure will occur. . . . Finally, we agree that adequate compensation may sometimes require an " 'eye-popping' " interest rate, and that, if the rate is too high for the plan to succeed, the appropriate course is not to reduce it to a more palatable level, but to refuse to confirm the plan.

Our only disagreement is over what procedure will more often produce accurate estimates of the appropriate interest rate. The plurality would use the prime lending rate--a rate we know is too low--and require the judge in every case to determine an amount by which to increase it. I believe that, in practice, this approach will systematically undercompensate secured creditors for the true risks of default. I would instead adopt the contract rate--i.e., the rate at which the creditor actually loaned funds to the debtor--as a presumption that the bankruptcy judge could revise on motion of either party. Since that rate is generally a good indicator of actual risk, disputes should be infrequent, and it will provide a quick and reasonably accurate standard.

. . .

QUESTIONS ABOUT *TILL*:

1. The Supreme Court approved the Tills using Chapter 13 to reduce the interest rate on their automobile loan from the contract rate of 21% to 9.5% (prime plus 1.5% for risk of nonpayment). Who gets the benefit of the money that will be saved by the reduced interest rate?

2. After *Till* does the debtor or the creditor have the burden of proving how much the risk adjustment should be? Is this appropriate? Why?

3. What factors may be relevant to determining the size of the risk adjustment?

4. Will the *Till* decision impact the determination of the appropriate interest rate in bankruptcy cases other than cases under Chapter 13? Compare footnotes 10 and 14 of the opinion.

PROBLEM 10-8: WHAT INTEREST RATE DOES DEBTOR HAVE TO PAY THE CAR LENDER?

Debtor owns a five-year-old car worth $6,500. Debtor owes EZ Finance $6,500 secured by the car. Debtor proposes the following payments for EZ in her plan: $6,500 amortized over the remaining 5 years of her plan with interest at 8%. Prime rate is currently 6.5%. EZ objects to the interest rate proposed and the five year payout arguing that they are not adequate to compensate it for the risk of default. The car already has been driven 90,000 miles and EZ argues that it is not realistic that the car will last another five years. EZ complains that it currently charges 22% interest to borrowers with credit histories similar to debtor, which is similar to the rate established in the loan agreement between debtor and EZ. Debtor had a prior Chapter 13 case, which was dismissed a year ago because debtor failed to make required plan payments. Should EZ prevail? Is your answer any different if debtor's attorney provides evidence that the earlier Chapter 13 was dismissed because debtor missed work because of illness, but debtor is fully recovered, and debtor agrees to an order that will direct her employer to send the plan payment directly to the trustee (commonly known as "a wage order"), which increases the probability that the plan will be successfully completed? Is your answer any different if EZ had originally provided debtor with 0% financing?

PROBLEM 10-9: HOW SHOULD THE CAR LENDER'S COLLATERAL BE VALUED?

Debtor purchased an old pick-up truck to use in her business three months before bankruptcy for $7,000. The dealer included a 30-day warranty as part of the purchase. Debtor paid $500 down and dealer financed the remaining $6,500 balance. Debtor filed Chapter 13 before she made her first payment. Her plan values the truck and proposes to pay dealer $4,500 to satisfy the secured debt. Debtor argues that she overpaid because she was desperate and the truck is not worth any more than $4,500. The plan will pay off the obligation in the same three years as originally agreed between the parties. The wholesale value of the truck is $3,000, the private-party value of the truck is $4,500, and its retail value is $6,000. You represent the dealer, who objects to the proposed valuation and only being paid $4,500 on account of its secured claim. What arguments do you make? How would your arguments change if the debtor purchased the truck for personal use rather than business use? Remember the Supreme Court's decision in *Rash* on page 70 of the text, particularly footnote 6, § 506(b)(2) and the provision immediately following § 1325(a)(9), both of which were added by the 2005 amendments to the Bankruptcy Code.

---

2. *Special Rule for Claims Secured Solely by the Debtor's Principal Residence.*

The plan cannot modify the claim of a creditor secured only by an interest in the debtor's principal residence. § 1322(b)(2). Thus, the debtor generally cannot bifurcate a partially secured mortgage claim into a secured claim and an unsecured claim and cannot modify the interest rate, the required postpetition payments (except a balloon payment as discussed below), or other monetary or nonmonetary obligations imposed by the security agreement.

That does not mean that the debtor cannot use Chapter 13 creatively to solve her home mortgage problem. As long as the debtor can maintain current payments, the debtor may choose to sell or refinance the home during the Chapter 13. In the process the debtor may be able to raise money to cure a default or to pay other creditors.

One question that had led much litigation was the question of when was it too late for the debtor to cure defaults in her home mortgage. The question was legislatively answered in 1994 through adoption of § 1322(c)(1), which provides:

> (c) Notwithstanding subsection (b)(2) and applicable nonbankruptcy law –
>
> (1) a default with respect to, or that gave rise to, a lien on the debtor's principal residence may be cured under paragraph (3) or (5) of subsection (b) until such residence is sold at a foreclosure sale that is conducted in accordance with applicable nonbankruptcy law; [.]

In most states, real property lien foreclosures take several months. At any time before the foreclosure sale occurs, the debtor can file Chapter 13 and cure the default and reinstate the loan.

Another frequent area of litigation is with respect to § 1322(b)(2) which provides that a plan may:

> (2) modify the rights of holders of secured claims, other than a claim secured only by a security interest in real property that is the debtor's principal residence, or of holders of unsecured claims, or leave unaffected the rights of holders of such claims.

This provision contains what is commonly referred to as an "anti-modification rule with respect to debtor's principal residence." The litigated issue is whether a creditor who has a security interest in the residence, but whose claim is wholly unsecured under the Code because the residence has insufficient value to secure any part of the obligation, is protected by this anti-modification rule. The majority of the courts that have considered the question, including all six federal courts of appeals that have considered the issue, focus on the requirement that the creditor hold a secured claim. Under § 506(a), a creditor has a secured claim only if it has a security interest in the debtor's property and that security has actual value. If the security interest does not have actual value, the anti-modification rule does not apply. The minority view interprets § 1322(b)(2) to prohibit modification of the claim of any creditor whose debt is secured solely by the debtor's residence, regardless of whether the security interest has actual value. To understand the point, consider the following factual scenario:

> Debtor has a residence worth $150,000.
>
> Debtor owes Bank $155,000 secured by a first mortgage on her residence.
>
> Debtor owes Finance Co. $25,000 secured by a second mortgage on her residence.

Under the majority view, debtor's plan can treat Finance Co. as an unsecured creditor. Under the minority view, debtor must pay Finance Co. in full because of the anti-modification provision of § 1322(b)(2), although debtor may cure any default over the life of the plan.

---

3. *Can the Debtor Cure the Home Mortgage Balloon Payment over Time?*

Some home loans have a balloon payment rather than having affordable monthly payments for the duration of the loan. For instance, a loan may have payments established based on what it would take to pay the loan over 30 years, but the entire balance is due five years after the date the loan is made. Such a required payoff is commonly referred to as a balloon payment (or, in darker circles, a "bullet" payment).

Section 1322(c)(2) allows debtors to use Chapter 13 for relief if they cannot pay the balloon payment in full when due, notwithstanding the general anti-modification rule. Section 1322(c)(2) provides:

> (c) Notwithstanding subsection (b)(2) and applicable nonbankruptcy law – . . .
>
> > (2) in a case in which the last payment on the original payment schedule for a claim secured only by a security interest in real property that is the debtor's principal residence is due before the date on which the final payment under the plan is due, the plan may provide for the payment of the claim as modified pursuant to section 1325(a)(5) of this title.

This section allows the debtor to pay the balloon through the plan. Because no regular monthly payment is due if the entire debt has come due, the debtor may not be required to make monthly payments or to make payments as large as originally required by the contract prior to the balloon, if the creditor is otherwise adequately protected. The debtor may be able to use Chapter 13 to obtain time to refinance or sell the property with a balloon payment.

PROBLEM 10-10: HOUSE PROBLEMS

1. Debtor owes Friendly Bank $70,000 secured by a mortgage on debtor's principal residence, which is worth $100,000. Debtor is $6,000 behind on her payments to Friendly. Although debtor's plan will cure the arrearage, the plan does not provide for any payments on the arrearage for years. Interest on the $6,000 arrearage will be paid at a rate that meets the legal requirements of Chapter 13. At

the end of two years the Debtor's plan provides that Friendly's arrearage plus interest will be paid in a single payment through the refinance or sale of the debtor's residence. Debtor wants to use her plan payments to pay her high-interest-rate car loan before paying Friendly. Friendly objects, arguing that secured creditors should be treated equally and it is not fair to make it wait two years for its payment. The judge overrules Friendly's objection. What rationale justifies the judge's decision?

2. Debtor, facing foreclosure on her mortgage a little more than two years ago, refinanced the loan through EZ Finance. Unfortunately, EZ's terms were onerous. Debtor's interest rate increased from 7% to 12%, she paid $5,000 in loan and closing costs, which she borrowed from EZ, and she agreed to repay the entire balance in two years. The house is worth $100,000 and debtor owes EZ $75,000. In order to make the monthly payments to EZ, debtor moved in with relatives and rented out her home. Using the rents and her other income, debtor made the monthly payments due to EZ. She has no ability to pay the balloon. She could sell her house, but she cannot complete a sale before EZ completes its foreclosure. Debtor consults you regarding whether she should accept EZ's offer to refinance again at a cost of another $5,000. How do you advise debtor? What do you tell debtor about bankruptcy?

E. Differences in the Treatment of Leased Houses and Cars v. Mortgaged Houses and Cars

Debtors often are parties to leases at the time they file Chapter 13. Many debtors rent the premises where they live. Some debtors lease rather than purchase automobiles.

As we learned in greater detail in Unit 8 on the treatment of leases and executory contracts, Section 365 of the Code forces the trustee who wants to be assured of retaining the benefits of a lease to assume the lease and, upon assumption, promptly cure any defaults. Such defaults may be cured through the plan. Section 1322(b)(7) gives the Chapter 13 debtor the power to assume or reject leases and executory contracts in the debtor's plan.

A debtor who does not want to retain the leased property will "reject" the lease. As long as the debtor rejects the lease without assuming it, the lessor will have a prepetition claim for any lease amounts due at the time of filing and any damages arising from the breach of the lease. The lessor will also have the right to recover the leased property. The lessor's rejection claim will be an unsecured claim, unless the lessor has a security interest in assets of the debtor securing performance of the lease. The consequences of assumption and rejection are discussed in greater detail in Unit 8.

Chapter 13 debtors who want to keep leased property usually assume the lease and cure the defaults. This option is potentially far less flexible than the treatment of secured claims. Recall, with respect to secured claims, the debtor does not have to pay more than the value of the collateral (except with respect to the claims secured solely by the debtor's principal residence, personal vehicle purchase-money debts incurred within 910 days of bankruptcy and certain other secured debt incurred within one year of bankruptcy). In addition, under certain circumstances, the debtor may be able to repay the secured debt at an interest rate that is lower than the contract rate. If the debtor has a leased vehicle and wants to keep it, she cannot "cram down" the debt to the value of the collateral and cannot alter the charge for the use of the money effectively imbedded in the lease payment. Finally, with respect to secured claims, there is no requirement that the debtor promptly cure defaults. Thus, the debtor who has leased her house and automobile will have to cure any defaults more quickly than if she had purchased them and was behind in performing her mortgage and automobile purchase payment obligations.

PROBLEM 10-11: DIFFERENCES IN LEASING AND LENDING IN CHAPTER 13

1. You are interviewing a debtor in your office about her financial and legal problems. She tells you that she makes $250 per month payments on her car. What questions do you ask debtor so that you can properly advise her?

2. You represent a debtor who has leased a two-year-old car worth $15,000, with a monthly lease payment of $400. Debtor is three payments behind. When the lease matures in one year, the debtor has the choice of returning the car or purchasing it for $17,000. Debtor needs a car to get to work and would like to keep her leased car. She can afford to pay the current lease payments, but she wants to pay the minimum she can toward curing the lease arrears because of her tight family budget. What terms will you propose that you think will allow debtor to retain her leased car? If the debtor assumes the lease through the plan, what rights and obligations will she have when the lease matures in one year?

   What could the debtor do differently in her plan if she had purchased the same car instead of leasing it, and her monthly payments under the purchase contract were the same amount as the lease payments?

F. CLASSIFICATION OF UNSECURED CLAIMS (CAN THE DEBTOR PAY SOME UNSECURED CLAIMS MORE THAN OTHERS?)

Chapter 13 debtors often want to pay certain unsecured claims in full. The following are a few of the reasons that a debtor might want to make sure that certain creditors are paid in full. First, some debts are excepted from the Chapter 13 discharge. § 1328(a). Student loans are the most common example of debts that fall in this category. The debtor will want to pay the nondischargeable debt during the Chapter 13; otherwise the debtor will be forced to repay whatever remains of the nondischargeable debt, including postpetition interest, after completing the Chapter 13 case. The debtor wants a complete, not a partial, fresh start after making Chapter 13 payments for three to five years. Second, in order to get a loan or other credit, many debtors had to have someone who was more creditworthy guarantee payment of the obligation. If the debtor does not pay that obligation, the co-signer, who is often a parent or other relative, will have to pay the debt. In order to maintain family harmony, the debtor does not want this to happen. Third, some debtors who have committed crimes are on probation or parole and have obligations under a criminal sentence to pay restitution for the benefit of the crime victim as a condition of avoiding imprisonment. If the debtor fails to make the restitution payments as ordered, the criminal court may require the debtor to go to jail.

A debtor who wants to make sure that one or more of her creditors are paid in full will often not have enough money to pay all the unsecured creditors in full. Chapter 13 provides two primary plan mechanisms through which the debtor can potentially accomplish the goal of paying some unsecured creditors in full even if that is better treatment than provided to the rest of the unsecured creditors.

First, section 1322(b)(1) provides that the plan may:

> designate a class or classes of unsecured claims, as provided in section 1122 of this title, but may not discriminate unfairly against any class so designated; however, such plan may treat claims for a consumer debt of the debtor if an individual is liable on such consumer debt with the debtor differently than other unsecured claims[.]

Examination of § 1122, which is referenced in § 1322(b)(1), tells us that the "plan may place a claim or an interest in a particular class only if such claim or interest is substantially similar to the other claims or interests of such class." § 1122(a). If a plan classifies claims, the plan must "provide the same treatment for each claim within a particular class." § 1322(a)(3). Using these provisions, the debtor may confirm a Chapter 13 plan that divides the unsecured creditors into more than one class and treats the classes differently, provided that, if more than one claim is included within a particular class, the claims are "substantially similar" and the separate classification does not discriminate unfairly.

Second, if the debtor were to pay obligation(s) that the debtor wants to treat preferentially according to the established contractual payment schedule and the final payment would not be made until after completion of the Chapter 13 plan payments, the debtor has an alternative approach available. Section 1322(b)(5) provides that a plan may:

> provide for the curing of any default within a reasonable time and maintenance of payments while the case is pending on any unsecured claim or secured claim on which the last payment is due after the date on which the final payment under the plan is due[.]

This allows the debtor to cure any default and pay the balance according to the contractual terms. If the debtor chooses this approach, the debtor will not be done paying the debt upon completion of the Chapter 13 plan because, by definition in the statute, the debt must have payments due after completion of the plan.

The opportunity to classify separately unsecured claims does not alter any of the other requirements for confirmation of a Chapter 13 plan. The debtor's plan still must meet the "best interests" test of § 1325(a)(4). In other words, each creditor, including those in the class receiving poorer treatment, must receive at least what the creditor would have received in a Chapter 7 case. In Chapter 7 cases, all nonpriority unsecured creditors are generally treated the same. § 726(a)(2) - (3). Thus, if the debtor had a Chapter 7 case in which the Chapter 7 trustee would have distributed $5,000 to the unsecured creditors and that distribution would have resulted in unsecured creditors receiving payment of 25% of their claims, the debtor cannot confirm a Chapter 13 plan that distributes $5,000 to unsecured creditors by paying the entire $5,000 to the class of unsecured creditor(s) the debtor wants to pay and nothing to the other class of unsecured creditors. That plan will not satisfy the "best interests" test imposed by § 1325(a)(4).

The propriety of such separate classification can be determined either before confirmation on motion after notice and hearing, Bankr. R. 3013, or as part of the hearing on confirmation at which the court must decide whether the plan complies with the legal requirements.

IN RE WILLIAMS

253 B.R. 220 (Bankr. W.D. Tenn. 2000)

JENNIE D. LATTA, Bankruptcy Judge.

The court scheduled status conferences in each of the referenced Chapter 13 cases which propose to separately classify and preferentially treat student loan claims. No objections to the proposed classifications were raised by any creditor or the standing Chapter 13 trustee. Nevertheless, the bankruptcy judge has an independent obligation to determine whether a plan fulfills the requirements for confirmation under Chapter 13.

The issue before the court is whether a plan that proposes to separately classify and fully repay nondischargeable student loan debt unfairly discriminates against other unsecured creditors who will receive only partial repayment of their dischargeable claims. For the reasons set forth below, the court determines that the proposed plans are not capable of confirmation because they discriminate unfairly against general unsecured creditors. . . .

I. BACKGROUND FACTS

In each of these cases, the debtor proposes to pay 100% of his or her student loan claim over the life of the plan. Each of the plans is expected to terminate after 60 months. Two of the plans specify no distribution to the other unsecured creditors, but leave that percentage to be determined by the Chapter 13 trustee after the bar date for filing proofs of claim has passed. The other three plans propose paying a specified percentage to the general unsecured creditors: the Kings propose to pay 15%, Mr. Williams to pay 20%, and the Hunters to pay 25%. . . .

II. ANALYSIS

Section 1322(b)(1) provides in pertinent part that a debtor's plan may "designate a class or classes of unsecured claims, as provided in section 1122 of [title 11], but may not discriminate unfairly against any class so designated." Section 1122 requires that a claim or interest be placed in a particular class only if the claim or interest is substantially similar to other claims or interests of that class, but permits dissimilar claims to be classified together for administrative convenience. See 11 U.S.C. § 1122(a) and (b). Implicit in section 1122 is the requirement that claims be sufficiently dissimilar to warrant separate classification. . . . In Chapter 11 cases where confirmation of the plan requires the acceptance of the plan by at least one class of impaired claims, a reasonable limitation upon a debtor's ability to separately classify claims prevents inappropriate "gerrymandering" to obtain an accepting class. Chapter 13 does not provide for acceptance of the plan by the vote of creditors, thus the only purpose served by a separate designation of unsecured claims in Chapter 13 is discrimination in treatment. Discrimination between classes of unsecured claims generally takes the form of a difference in the percentage of payment or the order of distribution. Discrimination is said to be unfair when there is no valid reason to prefer one group of unsecured claims over another. . . . If there is no valid reason for discrimination, there is also no valid reason for separate classification in Chapter 13. . . .

George Stevenson, the standing Chapter 13 trustee, . . . argues that section 1322(b)(1) requires that a specially designated class of unsecured creditors not be treated worse than general unsecured creditors, but does not prohibit better treatment of the designated class. Mr. Stevenson is correct in one sense--section 1322(b)(1) does not prohibit better treatment of a designated class. Mr. Stevenson is incorrect in another sense because designation of one class necessarily involves designation of a second class. As was shown, in Chapter 13 the only purpose for such designation is discrimination in treatment. After secured claims and administrative expenses are provided for, the balance of payments under a Chapter 13 plan are divided among the unsecured claims. To discriminate in favor of one class of unsecured claims necessarily results in discrimination against another class of unsecured claims. What is required is that the discrimination not be unfair.

In these cases, the debtors propose to separately classify their student loan claims from other unsecured claims, and to pay their student loan claims "100%." Ms. Haten, Mr. and Mrs. King, and Mr. and Mrs. Hunter propose to pay interest on the student loan claims as well. The debtors, as proponents of the plans, bear the burden of proving that the proposed classification does not discriminate unfairly. . . . This court has previously quoted with approval the comments of Bankruptcy Judge Barbara Sellers concerning separate classification of claims in Chapter 13 cases:

> Any classification of unsecured claims must pass a test of fairness unless that classification involves consumer debts for which co-signers were obtained. Unlike Chapter 11, unsecured creditors in Chapter 13 are not afforded an opportunity to vote. Further, unless their claims are unusually large, such creditors generally lack economic incentive to object to confirmation of a low dividend plan. Therefore, the primary burden for scrutinizing the differing treatment of separately classified unsecured claims in Chapter 13 falls, first on the Chapter 13 trustee, and then on the court.

In re Riggel, 142 B.R. 199, 202 (Bankr.S.D.Ohio 1992).

Four factors must be considered in determining whether a proposed classification scheme is proper:

1. Whether the discrimination has a reasonable basis;

2. Whether the debtor can carry out the plan without such discrimination;

3. Whether the classification has been proposed in good faith; and

4. The nature of the treatment of the class discriminated against.[1]

. . .

The debtors have put forth a number of justifications for the separate classification of their student loan debts. The primary reason offered for the separate classification is that the student loan claims, unlike the general unsecured claims, are not dischargeable in bankruptcy. See 11 U.S.C. § 523(a)(8).[2] Related to this is the argument that the debtors will not receive the benefit of a fresh start if they are not allowed to fully repay their student loans during the pendency of their plans. The debtors argue that the remedies available to student loan creditors, such as wage garnishment and set off of income tax refunds distinguishes these claims from other general unsecured claims. The trustee argues that the fact that Congress has rendered student loans nondischargeable except in cases of undue hardship demonstrates a strong public policy in favor of full repayment of student loans. Another distinction between student loans and other unsecured loans is the length of the period for repayment of most student loans. Pursuant to section 1322(b)(5), if the last payment on the student loan is due after the final payment under the plan is due, the plan may provide for the curing of any default and the maintenance of ongoing payments. This treatment can only be accomplished through separate classification of the student loan claim.

---

[1]This is the test most commonly used by courts to determine whether proposed discrimination is unfair. . . .

[2]Section 1322(a)(2) provides:

(a) The plan shall--

(2) provide for the full payment, in deferred cash payments, of all claims entitled to priority under section 507 of this title, unless the holder of a particular claim agrees to a different treatment of such claim.

11 U.S.C. § 1322(a)(2).

The court agrees that there are a number of reasonable bases for separately classifying student loan claims from other general unsecured claims. The more important and difficult question is what degree of discrimination in the treatment of student loan claims is necessary and appropriate. The determination of unfair discrimination lies within the discretion of the bankruptcy judge and is to be made on a case by case basis. . . .

A. Interest Payments

The first type of discrimination proposed by three of the debtors is the payment of interest on their student loan claims, but not on other unsecured claims. Creditors are not entitled to include unmatured (or "post-petition") interest as part of their claims in bankruptcy proceedings. See 11 U.S.C. § 502(b)(2); . . . In order to be confirmed, a Chapter 13 plan . . . is not required to provide for the payment of interest on priority claims (including administrative claims) or general unsecured claims. . . . 11 U.S.C. §§ 1322(a)(2),[34] . . . The student loan creditor cannot compel the payment of post-petition interest on its claim from the bankruptcy estate, but may compel the payment of interest from the debtor after completion of the Chapter 13 plan because interest on nondischargeable debts is nondischargeable. . . .

The debtors in these cases argue that their interest in a fresh start justifies the payment of interest on their student loan claims, but not on other unsecured claims. The debtors want to emerge from their Chapter 13 cases with a full discharge of all their debts, including their student loan debts. . . . The court does not believe that the debtors' interest in a fresh start should override the requirement of fairness in distribution.[6] After completion of their Chapter 13 plans, these debtors should be left with very little ongoing debt, and should be able to structure an appropriate agreement for the repayment of interest accrued on their student loans during the pendency of their Chapter 13 plans.

---

[3]Section 1322(a)(2) provides:

(a) The plan shall–

(2) provide for the full payment, in deferred cash payments, of all claims entitled to priority under section 507 of this title, unless the holder of a particular claim agrees to a different treatment of such claim [.]

[6]A debtor cannot expect an unfettered fresh start when one of the debtor's debts is nondischargeable. . . .

In the alternative, the Bankruptcy Code itself provides one approved method of preferring student loan claims over other unsecured claims. Section 1322(b)(5) . . . provides for the curing of any default within a reasonable time and maintenance of payments on unsecured claims on which the last payment is due after the final payment under the plan is due. Many student loan claims will have remaining terms that extend beyond a three- to five-year plan. The maintenance of ongoing payments necessarily involves the payment of post-petition interest. Pre-petition interest will be included in the creditor's proof of claim consisting of the arrearage to be paid (cured) within a reasonable time. Through this method, a debtor should be able to fully repay student loan arrearages during the plan, and reestablish the original loan repayment schedule. This type of discrimination is specifically contemplated and sanctioned by the Bankruptcy Code. . . . Because the Bankruptcy Code contemplates the curing of any default within a reasonable time, a debtor may pay 100% of a student loan arrearage while paying less than 100% of other unsecured claims, so long as the degree of discrimination is necessary to the debtor's success under the plan. . . .

B. Acceleration of Student Loans

1. The Hunters

The Hunters' proposed plan contemplates full repayment of their student loan even though under its original terms the loan would not be repaid until at least 2007. The Hunters borrowed funds under the PLUS program . . . to enable their son to attend Alabama State University. The son did not complete his studies and has not been able or has not offered to assist his parents in repaying the loan. The Hunters propose to pay 100% of their PLUS loan during their five year plan, but only 25% of their other unsecured debt. In effect, the Hunters propose that their unsecured creditors subsidize their son's educational efforts. The Hunters do not wish to file a Chapter 7 case because they have equity in their home. Mr. Hunter receives military disability income of $1,476 per month. Mrs. Hunter plans to retire from teaching school and expects to receive a retirement income of $1,695 per month. The ongoing payments on the PLUS loan would be $121.30 per month. Mr. Hunter testified that Mrs. Hunter is retiring upon the advice of her doctor, . . . but the Hunters have not sought a hardship discharge[10] with respect to their PLUS loan nor apparently have they sought disability relief from their lender.

Absent the establishment of a hardship under section 523(a)(8), the court does not find it reasonable that the debtors expect to receive a fresh start after five years through this Chapter 13 plan, when they originally agreed to and expected a ten-year repayment term for their PLUS loan.

. . . The Hunters argue that leaving a student loan unpaid after the completion of a Chapter 13 case is an "unnecessary impairment of the Debtors' right to a 'fresh start' after bankruptcy," citing In re Whittaker, 113 B.R. 531 (Bankr.D.Minn.1990); In re Boggan, 125 B.R. 533 (Bankr.N.D.Ill.1991); and In re Tucker, 159 B.R. 325 (Bankr.D.Mont.1993). The court in In re Whittaker permitted the payment of a child support arrearage in full before the payment of general unsecured claims. Boggan and Tucker provide that the nondischargeability of student loan claims provides a reasonable basis for a debtor to prefer student loan claims through his Chapter 13 plan so long as the general unsecured creditors receive at least what they would have received in Chapter 7. This court agrees with the conclusion of Whittaker, and would permit the Hunters to cure the arrearage on their PLUS loan in full through their plan, even if that would result in a greater percentage being paid on the student loan arrearage than that being paid to general unsecured creditors. What the Hunters propose however, is more akin to prepayment of an ongoing child support obligation rather than the curing of an arrearage. The Whittaker opinion does not support such treatment. The court has reviewed the Boggan and Tucker opinions. Unfortunately, neither of them provides information concerning the remaining term of the student loans at issue. Thus the court cannot determine whether payment in full of the student loans in those cases resulted in an acceleration of the repayment of those loans such as is proposed by the Hunters. This court does not believe that acceleration of the Hunters' PLUS loan is necessary to the success of their plan, or that such treatment is fair to the general unsecured creditors. . . .

2. Annette Haywood Burton

. . . Ms. Burton proposes to pay 100% of this loan and a percentage to be determined after all proofs of claim are filed

---

[10]Section 523(a)(8) provides that a student loan may be discharged if the debtor can prove that repayment of the loan would cause an undue hardship on the debtor or his dependents. . . .

to other general unsecured creditors. Assuming a repayment period of ten years, it would appear that this loan, which was obtained in 1998, would qualify as a long term obligation for treatment under section 1322(b)(5). For the reasons stated earlier, the court does not believe that it is fair to permit the acceleration of student loans through a Chapter 13 plan at the expense of other unsecured creditors. . . .

C. Greater Percentage

Assuming that the remaining debtors have student loans for which the last payment is due before the last payment under their proposed plans (i.e., that section 1325(b)(5) does not apply), the third type of discrimination proposed for student loans in these cases is the payment of 100% of these claims while other unsecured claims are paid a much lower percentage. Neither Ms. Haten nor the Kings have articulated a need for such discriminatory treatment other than their desire to emerge from their Chapter 13 plans debt free. In the clear majority of reported cases, the courts have concluded that the nondischargeability of a student loan by itself is not enough to permit debtors to pay student loans in full while the other general unsecured creditors receive less than 100% of their claims. . . . Clearly plans could be proposed by Ms. Haten and the Kings that would provide the same percentage repayment to all unsecured creditors, with the balance of the student loan claims surviving the completion of the Chapter 13 plans. Neither Ms. Haten nor the Kings introduced proof of any special circumstances that would prevent them from completing payment of their student loans after the conclusion of their Chapter 13 plans.

Both Ms. Haten and the Kings, through their attorney, assert that in a Chapter 7 liquidation, there would be no assets available for distribution to unsecured creditors. These debtors have left open the percentage to be paid to general unsecured creditors pending the bar date for filing proofs of claim, but they assert that payment of any amount to these creditors will satisfy the best interest of creditors test. Mr. Fox asserts that so long as the Chapter 13 plan proposes to pay more to general unsecured creditors than they would have received under Chapter 7, discrimination in favor of student loan creditors is fair. The court does not agree.

Chapter 13 is a strictly voluntary provision for the repayment of debts. The court must assume that the debtors in these cases chose Chapter 13 over Chapter 7 because of some perceived advantage to themselves. The debtors cannot, therefore, ignore the requirements for confirmation of a Chapter 13 plan, including the requirement that the plan not discriminate unfairly among classes of unsecured creditors.

Both of the student loans in these cases are relatively small. TSAC filed a proof of claim in the amount of $1,586.10 in Ms. Haten's case. USAF filed a proof of claim in the amount of $2,151.67 in the Kings' case. On the one hand, this means that an amendment to the plan to provide for the same percentage to be paid to the student loan creditor as to other creditors would result in a rather small increase in the percentage to be paid to other unsecured creditors. On the other hand, the size of these claims also means that it would be relatively easy for the debtors to complete the repayment of their student loans after completion of their plans. Again the court cannot determine the remaining length of the original loan terms in these cases. If these are long term debts the court would permit the debtors to maintain ongoing payments and cure any arrearage over the life of the plan. If these loans are now short term obligations, the court will permit the debtors to discriminate in favor of the student loan creditors so long as the percentage to be paid on the student loan claims is no more than 30 percentage points in excess of the percentage to be paid to general unsecured claims. That is, if the debtor proposes to pay 100% of his student loan claim, he must propose to pay at least 70% of his general unsecured claims. Such discrimination will be considered fair by the court. The debtors bear the burden of showing unique circumstances to support a greater degree of discrimination.

D. Preferential Payment

A final type of discrimination proposed for student loans in these cases is the full repayment of the student loan claims before the payment of general unsecured claims. In an unrelated case, Mr. Stevenson, the standing Chapter 13 trustee, has testified that in this district those claims classified as "Class I, unsecured," are paid in full before general unsecured creditors receive any distribution. . . . The court is aware from personal experience that a substantial number of Chapter 13 cases fail within the first 18 months. Unlike claims for child and spousal support, student loan claims do not enjoy a statutory priority for distribution. It was in the 1990 amendments to the Bankruptcy Code that student loans were made nondischargeable in Chapter 13. . . . In 1994, child and spousal support obligations were given seventh priority in distribution. . . . Had Congress intended that student loans also enjoy priority of distribution, it could have specifically provided for it. . . . The effect of classifying student loan claims as Class I unsecured is to give such claims priority of distribution. Even if a debtor were to propose 100% repayment to general unsecured creditors, if those creditors are not paid concurrently with student loans, they may in fact receive no distribution at all. There is nothing to prevent the debtors from making enough plan payments to pay their student loans in full and then voluntarily dismissing their cases with no distribution to general unsecured creditors. This imposes an unfair risk on the general unsecured creditors and will not be permitted. . . . None of the debtors in these cases, except perhaps the Hunters, have articulated any reason for paying their student loan debts before their other unsecured debts.[14]

III. CONCLUSION

Section 1322(b)(1) is a creditor protection device. . . . It was not intended as a means for debtors to focus solely upon their interests and does not justify unfair discriminatory treatment. . . . The court is aware that there are substantial protections available to student loan debtors outside the bankruptcy process. . . . The filing of a Chapter 13 case should be a last resort, and indeed provides little relief when the debtor's primary problem is a nondischargeable student loan. . . .

To ensure equity of distribution the court provides the guidelines contained in this opinion. Of course, the determination of whether a particular plan discriminates unfairly is to be made on a case by case basis, and the court invites debtors with unique circumstances to seek a hearing. This judge will not confirm Chapter 13 plans that provide for the payment of interest to student loan creditors, but not to other unsecured creditors; that accelerate the repayment of student loans at the expense of general unsecured creditors; that provide for repayment of 100% of student loan claims when other unsecured claims are not paid at least 70%; or that provide for the repayment of student loans before other unsecured claims are paid. This judge will permit arrearages on student loans to be paid in full, even though other unsecured claims will not be paid in full, if the student loan is treated as a long term debt pursuant to section 1325(b)(5).

[14]For example, this court routinely permits debtors to preferentially repay traffic court tickets and costs to enable the debtors to reestablish their driver's licenses. The court believes that this treatment furthers the purposes of Chapter 13 by permitting debtors to drive to and from work in order to support themselves and make payments called for by their plans.

Finally, the court encourages debtors to seek discharge of their student loans under section 523(a)(8) in appropriate circumstances. . . .

PROBLEM 10-12: SHOULD SEPARATE CLASSIFICATION OF THE DEBT DUE THE FAMILY DOCTOR BE APPROVED?

Debtor has $25,000 in unsecured nonpriority debt, which includes $2,500 owed to the family doctor. Debtor wants to pay the long-time family doctor in full, because she is concerned that, if she does not, the doctor might not continue to provide the same excellent care, which has included after-hours house calls, in the future. If debtor is allowed to classify the doctor's claim separately and pay it 100%, debtor can afford to pay other creditors only 10% of their claims during the three-year Chapter 13 plan debtor will propose. If the classification is not allowed, the unsecured creditors will received payment of 20% of their claims.

(a) Should the court approve the separate classification?

(b) If the answer is no, would the answer differ if debtor's child has a serious medical problem and needs continuing care from the doctor?

(c) If the answer is no, should the classification be permitted if debtor proposes to extend the duration of the plan by one year and to pay the doctor 100% and the other unsecured nonpriority creditors 20%?

PROBLEM 10-13: SHOULD THE COURT ALLOW THE DEBTOR TO CURE A DEFAULT ON THE LONG- TERM CAR LOAN AND PAY THE AUTO LENDER IN FULL, EVEN THOUGH THE AUTO LENDER IS UNDERSECURED?

Debtor obtained a car loan more than 910 days before bankruptcy. She is $4,000 in arrears on the obligation. The auto lender is undersecured. Debtor owes $20,000 to the auto lender, but the car is worth only $15,000. Debtor proposes a three-year plan that will allow the debtor to cure the $4,000 arrearage during the first year of the plan and pay the auto lender the remaining balance according to the contract terms. The remaining unsecured creditors will receive 25% payment on their claims. The trustee objects on the basis that the plan unfairly discriminates in favor of the auto lender. Debtor responds by arguing that his budget is tight and he wants to get current on his auto loan in case he is unable to complete his plan. He must have a car to retain his job. Should the court approve the separate classification?

PROBLEM 10-14: SHOULD THE COURT APPROVE SEPARATE CLASSIFICATION OF CRIMINAL RESTITUTION OR TRAFFIC FINES?

A year before filing Chapter 13, debtor was convicted of criminal manslaughter because he ran over and killed a pedestrian while driving under the influence of alcohol. The incident prompted debtor to come to terms with his alcoholism. He has joined Alcoholics Anonymous and has been sober for one year. Part of his criminal sentence was the requirement that he pay $75,000 in restitution for the benefit of the victim's family. If he fails to pay the restitution, his probation can be terminated and he may have to report to prison. Debtor owes $50,000 in other unsecured debt. Debtor proposes a five-year Chapter 13 plan that will pay his restitution in full and nothing to his other unsecured creditors. One of the unsecured creditors objects to the proposed classification and disparate treatment, arguing that the creditors should not bear the burden of debtor's criminal sentence. Debtor responds by arguing that, unless the separate classification and treatment is permitted, he will go to prison and none of his creditors will receive anything. Should the court approve the separate classification?

G. USE OF CHAPTER 13 TO DEAL WITH A DEMANDING TAX COLLECTOR.

As we learned in Unit 9, certain debts are excepted from discharge in an individual Chapter 7 case. The most common tax debts excepted from the individual debtor's Chapter 7 discharge are certain income tax liabilities. § 523(a)(1).

Chapter 13 takes a different approach than Chapter 7. Rather than except the pertinent tax obligation from discharge, as required by the following three Bankruptcy Code sections, Chapter 13 requires the debtor to pay these common tax debts, which are priority debts, in full.

Section 1322(a)(2) provides:

> The plan shall– . . .
>
> > (2) provide for the full payment, in deferred cash payments, of all claims entitled to priority under section 507 of this title, unless the holder of a particular claim agrees to a different treatment of such claim; ....

Section 507(a) provides:

> The following expenses and claims have priority in the following order: . . . .
>
> > (8) Eighth, allowed unsecured claims of governmental units, only to the extent that such claims are for–
> >
> > > (A) a tax on or measured by income or gross receipts--

> (i) for a taxable year ending on or before the date of the filing of the petition for which a return, if required, is last due, including extensions, after three years before the date of the filing of the petition;
>
> (ii) assessed within 240 days, plus any time plus 30 days during which an offer in compromise with respect to such tax that was made within 240 days after such assessment was pending, before the date of the filing of the petition; or
>
> (iii) other than a tax of a kind specified in section 523(a)(1)(B) or 523(a)(1)(C) of this title, not assessed before, but assessable, under applicable law or by agreement, after, the commencement of the case; . . .
>
> (D) an employment tax on a wage, salary, or commission of a kind specified in paragraph (3) of this subsection earned from the debtor before the date of the filing of the petition, whether or not actually paid before such date, for which a return is last due, under applicable law or under any extension, after three years before the date of the filing of the petition; . . .

The tax debts are not excepted from discharge.[15] Consequently, they are discharged in a Chapter 13 case even though they are not discharged in other types of bankruptcy cases.

As illustrated by the following problem, Chapter 13 can often be used by an individual debtor to deal effectively with unpaid tax debts.

---

[15] The statute that applies to the discharge granted to a Chapter 13 debtor who completes her plan, § 1328(a), is quoted in footnote 5 on page 338. The income tax debts are included in § 523(a)(1)(A) which is not included in the exceptions to the Chapter 13 discharge if the debtor completes her plan.

PROBLEM 10-15: HOW MUCH WILL A CHAPTER 13 DEBTOR HAVE TO PAY THE TAX COLLECTOR AND OVER HOW LONG A PERIOD CAN THE DEBTOR STRETCH OUT THE PAYMENTS?

Before bankruptcy, debtor, as a sole-proprietor, operated a store selling low-carbohydrate foods. After a couple of good years, the business started losing money rapidly when regular grocery stores started offering low-carbohydrate foods in every department. Debtor had spent the money earned during the good years rather than saving, it because debtor thought the good times would continue. Debtor owes the Internal Revenue Service $12,000 for two-year-old income taxes. The IRS has told debtor that any payment plan it will work out informally must be completed within one year and she must pay interest at 8% per annum. Debtor is now working as a clerk in a retail store and she can afford to pay the IRS only $250 per month after paying her family living expenses. If debtor files Chapter 13, how much will she have to pay the IRS? Will she have to pay interest on the IRS debt? How long will debtor have to complete her payments to the IRS? [Hint regarding whether interest is required. Compare the language of § 1322(a)(2) above with § 1325(a)(5)(B)(ii) discussed in the *Till* case at page 366 above which provides:

> (5) with respect to each allowed secured claim provided for by the plan--
>
> > (B) ...(ii) [the plan provides that] the value, as of the effective date of the plan, of property to be distributed under the plan on account of such claim is not less than the allowed amount of such claim[.]]

H. USE OF CHAPTER 13 BY DEBTORS WHO OPERATE A BUSINESS.

Chapter 13 can be used by self-employed debtors. Often the source of the financial distress for such individuals is business debts. Chapter 13 provides a relatively prompt and inexpensive way to deal with business debts. Let's look at how filing Chapter 13 affects the ability of the debtor to operate her business and how some of the common types of business debts are dealt with by Chapter 13 debtors.

Section 1304 contains special provisions applicable to only Chapter 13 debtors who are engaged in business. It provides, in part:

> (a) A debtor that is self-employed and incurs trade credit in the production of income from such employment is engaged in business.
>
> (b) Unless the court orders otherwise, a debtor engaged in business may operate the business of the debtor and, subject to any limitations on a trustee under sections 363(c) and 364 of this title and to such limitations or conditions as the court prescribes, shall have, exclusive of the trustee, the rights and powers of the trustee under such sections.

The business Chapter 13 debtor may use property of the estate in the ordinary course of business. § 363(c)(1). The debtor may incur ordinary unsecured debt postpetition in the ordinary course of business. § 364(a). These Bankruptcy Code sections allow many business debtors who file Chapter 13 to continue operating their businesses with no disruption and with no court or trustee permission or orders. Note that the ability to continue operating is limited; the debtor cannot engage in transactions outside the ordinary course of business and cannot incur postpetition debt that is either secured or outside the ordinary course of business, without complying with the applicable subsection of § 363 or § 364.

In analyzing whether an individual business debtor with financial problems can effectively use Chapter 13, the first step is to figure out whether the debtor's business produces enough income after payment of all current business expenses to pay the debtor's living expenses and Chapter 13 plan payments. To aid in this analysis, the business Chapter 13 debtor must complete and file a Schedule D-2, which sets forth the projected business gross receipts and expenses. On the following page is an example of a Schedule D-2 from an actual case.

UNITED STATES BANKRUPTCY COURT
DISTRICT OF OREGON

In re

SINDELAR, Sally Loujean,

Debtor(s)

) Case No. 302-36662-elp13
) EX. D-2
) FINANCIAL REVIEW OF DEBTOR'S
) *NONFARMING* BUSINESS
) [File With the Statement of Affairs in Chapter 12
) and 13 Cases If Debtor Earns Any Income
) From Operation of a NONFARMING Sole
) Proprietorship Business or Debtor or an Insider
) Owns 20% or More of a NONFARMING Corporation]

(NOTE: ONLY INCLUDE information directly related to the NONfarming business operation. This information is to be from the corporate books where necessary. If an item of Income or Expense does not apply indicate with "N/A.")

ATTACH COPY OF SCHEDULE C FROM PRIOR YEAR'S TAX RETURN (OR EXPLAIN ABSENCE).

INDICATE ACCOUNTING METHOD USED: XX Cash Basis ____ Accrual Basis

BUSINESS NAME, ADDRESS AND PHONE NUMBER: Sindelar Foster Care, PO Box 17478, Portland, OR 97217

NATURE AND STARTING DATE OF BUSINESS AND PERCENTAGE OF OWNERSHIP: Adult Foster Care - 1986 - 100%

PROJECTED ANNUAL BUSINESS INCOME:		
1. Gross Sales or Receipts	$ 807,147.00	
2. Returns and Allowances	( )	
3. Less Cost of Goods Sold	( )	
4. Other Income		
5. Gross Income		$ 807,147.00
PROJECTED ANNUAL BUSINESS EXPENSES (DO NOT Include Payments Paid Through Plan):		
6. Advertising		
7. Car and Truck Expenses	2,100.00	
8. Commissions and Fees		
9. Secured Debt Including Interest (attach list)		
10. Employee Benefits (other than on line 14) **HEALTH INS.**	48,000.00	
11. Insurance (other than health)	1,020.00	
12. Legal and Professional Services	12,000.00	
13. Office Expenses	2,208.00	
14. Pension/Profit-Sharing Plans		
15. Rent or Leases		
a. Vehicles, Machinery, Equipment (attach list)		
b. Other Business Property (attach list) **3 HOMES**	48,192.00	
16. Repairs and Maintenance	14,200.00	
17. Supplies (if not included in line 3) **INCLUDES FOOD**	30,780.00	
18. Taxes and Licenses		
a. Payroll Taxes	142,116.00	
b. Income/Self-Employment Tax	15,996.00	
c. Other Taxes/Licenses	1,200.00	
19. Travel	300.00	
20. Meals and Entertainment		
21. Utilities	20,348.00	
22. Wages	408,000.00	
23. Other expenses (list separately):		
24. Total Expenses		$ 746,460.00
PROJECTED ANNUAL NET INCOME (line 5 less line 24)		$ 60,687.00
ESTIMATED AVERAGE NET MONTHLY INCOME		$ 5,057.25

(Attach explanation if not same as amount listed on Schedule I for the question "Regular income from operation of business ...")

Exhibit D-2 (8/1/99)

(21)

The debtor's living expenses are calculated on Schedule J, an example of which was included on page 351.

Business debt will fall into three primary categories. The first category is secured debt and lease obligations. We already learned on pages 362 - 381 what can be done with respect to secured debt and on pages 383 - 384 what the plan can and must provide with respect to leases. The second category is unsecured debt. We know from pages 360 - 361 that the debtor must pay creditors not less than they would receive in a Chapter 7 case. In addition, unless the debtor is paying creditors in full, the plan must provide that all the debtor's projected disposable income for 36 months or 60 months, depending upon whether the debtor's income is below the median income, be paid to the unsecured creditors if the trustee or an unsecured creditor objects. Sometimes the debtor will chose to pay unsecured creditors more than the minimum required. The third primary category of business debt is tax debt.

If the debtor's business is not generating sufficient net income to pay the debtor's living expenses and required plan payments, the debtor will have to do one or more of the following (a) make changes to the business operations that increase the receipts and income, (b) cut the business expenses, and/or (c) reduce the debtor's living expenses. All that can be done through the Chapter 13 plan is financial restructuring. All the financial restructuring in the world will not do the debtor any good if the business is not any good. Put another way, some businesses do not make money even if you take away all the debt. A debtor who owns such a business cannot use Chapter 13 to save the business unless she can make changes in the business that make the business sufficiently profitable to allow it to pay its restructured debt and the debtor's living expenses.

Thus, Chapter 13 will not provide effective relief to all eligible Chapter 13 debtors with financial problems. It is part of the attorney's role as counselor to help the business debtor figure out whether Chapter 13 will help.

PROBLEM 10-16: CHAPTER 13 BUSINESS DEBTOR

Sally Sindelar operates two foster homes that care for elderly disabled people. At the time of bankruptcy, she has three employees who work in the foster homes. When she filed her case she had $225,000 in secured claims, consisting of a $120,000 mortgage on one of the foster homes, a $100,000 mortgage on the other foster home and a $5,000 debt secured by equipment worth $8,000 that is used in the two homes. The equipment has a remaining useful life of 5 years. Sally has $15,000 in mortgage arrearages and $102,000 in unsecured debt. Sally has lost money each of the last two years operating the foster homes. She has developed a business plan to turn her finances around by converting one of the homes to a day care facility for people with Alzheimer's. Although the new day care operation will need $3,000 worth of furniture and equipment, Sally expects that can raise the $3,000 by selling furniture from the foster care home she is going to close. Because it will take some time to build the day care business, she projects that for the first year she can pay $600 per month in plan payments, thereafter she can pay $1,000 per month. Can Sally keep operating her foster care business after filing? Will filing Chapter 13 prevent Sally from selling the furniture? From buying new furniture and equipment? From opening the new day care business? Can Sally pay lower monthly payments at the beginning of her plan? If Sally tells her lawyer that she needs to skip her plan payment each January because she has extraordinary expenses that month for licensing fees, what would the lawyer advise Sally?

I. What Does the Requirement that the Case be Filed in Good Faith and the Plan be Proposed in "Good Faith" Mean?

Section 1325(a) requires that the debtor both file the petition in good faith and propose the plan in good faith. The term "good faith" is vague. Courts have not developed a consistent approach, let alone one that produces predictable outcomes, as to how to determine good faith. Because of the vagueness and breath of "good faith," creditors frequently assert that the debtor does not satisfy the "good faith" requirements.

Some courts use a general standard, such as good faith which is determined by the "totality of the circumstances" or "requires "honesty of intention." Other courts either supplement the general standard with, or, rely instead on, a list of factors. One frequently cited list of the factors is:

1. The amount of the proposed payments and the amount of the debtor's surplus;
2. The debtor's employment history, ability to earn and likelihood of future increases in income;
3. The probable or expected duration of the plan;
4. The accuracy of the plan's statements of debts, expenses and percentage repayment of unsecured debt and whether any inaccuracies are an attempt to mislead the court;
5. The extent of preferential treatment between classes of creditors;
6. The extent to which secured claims are modified;
7. The type of debt sought to be discharged and whether any such debt is nondischargeable in Chapter 7;

8. The existence of special circumstances such as inordinate medical expenses;

9. The frequency with which the debtor has sought relief under the Bankruptcy Reform Act;

10. The motivation and sincerity of the debtor in seeking Chapter 13 relief; and

11. The burden which the plan's administration would place upon the trustee.

In re Estus, 695 F.2d 311, 317 (8th Cir. 1982).

PROBLEM 10-17: DO THE FOLLOWING CHAPTER 13 CASES MEET THE GOOD FAITH REQUIREMENTS?

1. This is debtor's third Chapter 13 case in eighteen months. Her first case was dismissed after she failed to appear at her § 341(a) meeting of creditors because her car broke down. Her second case was dismissed because she fell behind in her plan payments because she was temporarily unemployed. Debtor proposes a plan that is similar to the plan in her second case. Has debtor proposed the plan in good faith? Is your answer any different if each of the three cases was filed on the eve of the foreclosure on debtor's home mortgage?

2. The recent dissolution of Debtor's marriage resulted in Debtor being ordered to pay his ex-spouse $50,000 to equalize the division of property. Debtor's lawyer explains to debtor that debts arising from property division in a dissolution are

not dischargeable in a Chapter 7 case, but they are dischargeable in a Chapter 13 case. Debtor does not want to pay the $50,000 because he is mad at his ex-spouse and he considered the award unfair. Debtor files Chapter 13 and proposes a 60-month plan. The plan payments are only enough to pay for debtor's car, priority taxes, mortgage arrears and his legal fees. Debtor's ex-spouse objects on the basis that the debtor has neither filed the case in good faith nor proposed the plan in good faith. Will the ex-spouse prevail? Would the outcome be any different if Debtor agreed to the terms of the dissolution decree rather than having the $50,000 obligation created by a judge's decision?

J. WHAT OTHER REQUIREMENTS MUST THE DEBTOR SATISFY TO CONFIRM A PLAN?

Section 1308, which was added by the 2005 amendments to the Bankruptcy Code, requires that the debtor file all tax returns due for the four years preceding the bankruptcy. The court cannot confirm the debtor's plan unless the debtor has filed the required tax returns. § 1325(a)(9). This is a helpful requirement because without the tax returns it is difficult to determine the amount of debtor's priority tax debt which must be paid before the plan can be completed.

In addition, a debtor who has an obligation to pay a domestic support obligation must have paid all support due postpetition before the court can confirm the debtor's plan. § 1325(a)(8). This prevents debtors from paying their Chapter 13 plan payments while falling behind in their support obligations.

K. How Do Chapter 13 Cases End?

The objective of most debtors who file Chapter 13 is to obtain a discharge from the unsecured debts that the debtor did not pay through the plan. Before a Chapter 13 debtor can receive a discharge, the debtor must satisfy three requirements. First, the debtor must perform the plan or satisfy the requirements for a hardship discharge discussed below. Second, the debtor must complete a personal financial management course. § 1328(g). Third, if the debtor is required to pay a domestic support obligation, the debtor must certify that the debtor has paid in full the domestic support obligations due postpetition and the full amount of the prepetition domestic support obligations due under the Chapter 13 plan. § 1328(a).

The debtor will not receive a discharge if the debtor received a discharge in a Chapter 7, 11 or 12 case filed within four years preceding the filing of the Chapter 13, or in a earlier Chapter 13 case filed within two years preceding the filing of the current case. § 1328(f).

If the debtor satisfies the prerequisites and has not received a discharge in an earlier bankruptcy within the pertinent period, the Chapter 13 debtor can receive a discharge of any debts not paid through the plan, except those that are nondischargeable under § 1328, in one of two ways. First, a Chapter 13 debtor can complete payments under his plan and be granted a discharge under § 1328(a). Second, if the debtor is unable to complete her plan payments for reasons beyond her control, but has paid creditors at least what they would receive in a Chapter 7 case, the debtor may be granted a "hardship" discharge under § 1328(b).

Approximately two-thirds of Chapter 13 debtors never receive a discharge. Their cases are either dismissed or converted, usually to Chapter 7.

Many of the debtors who fail to complete their plans do so because of unanticipated adverse financial circumstances such as loss of a job, reduction in employment income, or unexpected medical or other expenses. For some debtors, the failure to complete the plan is the result of happier circumstances, such as an increase in income that allows them to pay creditors in full without a Chapter 13 case, or bringing their house, car, or other secured debt payments current, thereby eliminating the financial problem that brought them to Chapter 13 in the first instance.

L. Chapter 13 v. Chapter 7 (What Difference Will it Make If a Debtor Uses Chapter 13 Rather than Chapter 7?)

Some debtors use Chapter 13 because they want to repay their creditors. In such cases, the creditors often receive far more than if the debtor had filed Chapter 7. Sometimes the Chapter 13 debtor is able to repay her creditors in full. The Chapter 13 debtor, particularly one who repays a substantial portion of her debt, often feels good about the repayment and may feel that there is less stigma in using Chapter 13 than in using Chapter 7.

Notwithstanding the potentially disparate treatment of creditors under the two chapters, the law does not require credit reporting agencies to distinguish between Chapter 7 and Chapter 13 on the debtor's credit reports. Both types of cases remain on the debtor's credit record for 10 years from the time the case is filed.

Chapter Choice.

The following hypothetical illustrates why a debtor might be better served by filing a Chapter 13 case than a Chapter 7 case, and reviews the difference in outcome between the two chapters.

It involves Joe, the warehouseman who we met in Problem 10-3 on page 355. In Problem 10-3 we learned about Joe's income and expenses and calculated his disposable income.

Joe's assets and liabilities are as follows:

Assets:

	Value	
House	$	96,000.00
Ford Pickup - debt incurred 3 years ago	$	9,000.00
Household Goods	$	2,000.00
Clothes & Personal Items	$	1,000.00
401(k) Account	$	10,000.00
Cash and Bank Accounts	$	175.00

Liabilities:

	Amount	
Bank (1st Lien on House) (Includes $3,600 Arrearage)	$	70,000.00
Bank (Secured by Truck)	$	12,000.00
IRS (Income Taxes from Prior Year)	$	600.00
Credit Card Debt (Unsecured)	$	25,000.00

Former Spouse (Child Support-Unsecured)	$	4,000.00
Former Spouse (Property Division-Unsecured)	$	9,000.00

Exemptions

Joe has the following exemptions available:

Home Equity	$	10,000.00
Vehicle	$	1,500.00
Household Goods	$	3,000.00
Clothes and Personal Items	$	1,750.00
Retirement Benefits, Including 401(k)		Unlimited

PROBLEM 10-18: IF JOE FILES CHAPTER 13, WHAT TREATMENT WILL HE PROPOSE FOR HIS CREDITORS?

Assume that Joe wants to keep his house and his truck. To answer the question, work through the following analysis:

1. Calculate how much Joe can afford to pay in plan payments. In Problem 10-3 you calculated Joe's disposable income in two different ways: (a) if Joe's income is below the applicable median income, and, (b) if Joe is an above-median income debtor. Is the amount that Joe can afford in plan payments different than either of the disposable income calculations?

2. Calculate how much Joe will pay his secured creditors monthly during his Chapter 13. In doing the calculations, consider the following information:

   a. No interest is payable on Joe's mortgage arrearage.

   b. With respect to the truck payments, the prime rate is 9% and the rate charged to borrowers with a credit history like Joe's is 22%. The following chart gives you the monthly payment, depending on the length of the payout and the interest rate.

$9,000 Balance	Monthly Payment 9% per annum	Monthly Payment 10.5% Per annum	Monthly Payment 12% per annum	Monthly Payment 22% per annum
5 year payout	$187	$193	$200	$244
4 year payout	$224	$230	$237	$279
3 year payout	$286	$293	$299	$339

3. Calculate the minimum Joe will have to pay the unsecured creditors.

   a. What is the disposable income Joe must commit to the plan? For purposes of this problem assume that Joe waited four months after he first consulted with you to file his Chapter 13 case.

   b. If Joe has no disposable income, but actually has cash available that he could pay creditors, because of the use of historic rather than current income and the artificial way the means test [§ 707(b)(2)(A) and (B)] calculates expenses, does Joe have to pay any of that cash to the creditors? Why?

c. How much must Joe pay unsecured creditors to satisfy the "best interests" test of §1325(a)(4)?

4. What is the total amount of the priority claims that Joe must pay in full through his plan? You should assume that you have charged Joe $1,000 in attorney fees and he paid you in full before you filed the case.

5. You are now in a position to figure out what treatment Joe will propose for his creditors. What will you propose? Disregard Chapter 13 trustee charges for purposes of your calculation.

PROBLEM 10-19: WHAT BENEFITS DID JOE GET FROM FILING CHAPTER 13 RATHER THAN CHAPTER 7?

1. With respect to his house.

2. With respect to his truck.

3. With respect to his past-due income tax obligation and his past-due child support obligation.

4. With respect to his obligation to his former spouse for property division.

Unit 11

Legal and Other Issues to Watch for in Chapter 11

> A corporate reorganization is a combination of a municipal election, an historical pageant, an anti-vice crusade, a graduate school seminar, a judicial proceeding, and a series of horse trades, all rolled into one—thoroughly buttered with learning and frosted with distinguished names. Here the union of law and economics is celebrated by one of the wildest ideological orgies in intellectual history. Men work all night preparing endless documents in answer to other endless documents, which other men read in order to make solemn arguments.

THURMAN W. ARNOLD, THE FOLKLORE OF CAPITALISM 230 (1937).

A. BACK TO THE FUTURE: HOW SHOULD CHAPTER 11 CASES END?

Up to now, this book's focus has been on the fresh start for and rehabilitation of individuals. While we don't abandon individuals in this unit, we turn our focus to the intersection of bankruptcy and business. Let's start with the basic, obvious, yet important notion that some businesses have more economic value if kept together rather than taken apart. Not only are there cases in which the sum of the parts is worth "more" than the parts individually, there is also a human component in keeping a business together, in the form of jobs for individuals and communities.

As we have seen, creditors have the ability to effectively dismantle their debtors, either through state court collection procedures or chapter 7 bankruptcy. And recall that chapter 7 doesn't much help the business that is not an "individual," that is, a flesh-and-blood human. Section 727(a)(1) is pretty clear: "The court shall grant the debtor a discharge, *unless*—(1) the debtor is not an individual . . . ."

So what is to be done with a business that is worth more together than apart? Can these values to be preserved? Yes. The Code preserves going concern values in what typically is referred to as "reorganization." As stated by the Supreme Court in *United States v. Whiting Pools, Inc.*, 462 U.S. 198, 203 (1983), "[b]y permitting reorganization, Congress anticipated that the business would continue to provide jobs, to satisfy creditors' claims, and to produce a return for its owners. . . . Congress presumed that the assets of the debtor would be more valuable if used in a rehabilitated business than if 'sold for scrap.'"

But how do businesses "reorganize" in bankruptcy? Typically, they do it through a chapter 11 bankruptcy, the centerpiece of which is confirmation of something called a plan of reorganization. What is a plan? We'll explore this in some detail, but keep in mind that the Code does not specify the form or content of a form plan; it leaves the details to the plan proponent. Thus, the contents of a plan are limited only by a proponent's imagination (and some Code sections we'll look at later).

But as written, the statutory goal of Chapter 11 is confirmation of a plan. To facilitate confirmation, the Code allows a Chapter 11 plan to do things that can not be done under state law or under Chapter 7.

Under state law, non-assenting creditors are not in any way bound to a plan of restructuring. If D has 100 creditors and all of the creditors except N agree to a plan of restructuring, N is not bound by its provisions. N can still act unilaterally to collect its claim. And N's unilateral collection actions often prevent D from making the distributions to the other 99 creditors as provided in the plan of restructuring,

While all creditors are bound by the distribution scheme in Chapter 7, so is the debtor. The provisions of Chapter 7, and not the debtor, determine who gets what. Recall section 726(a) and (b).

In Chapter 11, unlike Chapter 7, the provisions of the plan determine who gets what. And, in Chapter 11, unlike state law, the provisions of the plan will be binding on nonassenting creditors if the plan is approved by the requisite majorities of creditors and the bankruptcy court. *Cf.* 11 U.S.C. § 1141(a)("provisions of a confirmed plan bind . . . any creditor . . . whether or not . . . such creditor . . . has accepted the plan.")

While confirmation of a Chapter 11 plan is the statutory goal of a Chapter 11 case, most Chapter 11 cases do not end in confirmation. One fairly recent study reports that (i) less than 30% of all Chapter 11 cases end in a confirmed plan, (ii) approximately 35% of the Chapter 11 cases are dismissed, and (iii) approximately 35% of the Chapter 11 cases are converted to Chapter 7 cases. *See* Steven H. Ancel & Bruce A. Markell, *Hope in the Heartland: Chapter 11 Dispositions in Indiana and Southern Illinois, 1990-1996*, 50 S.C.L. REV. 343 (1999).

Questions

1. Why do you think so many chapter 11 cases do not end with a confirmed plan?

2. Is a Chapter 11 case, a "failure" if no plan is confirmed? Is a Chapter 11 case a "success" if a plan is confirmed?

We have been talking about the most important document in a Chapter 11 case – the plan. Now let's look at the people who are involved in a Chapter 11 case.

———

B. PEOPLE INVOLVED IN A CHAPTER 11 CASE

1. Debtor

11 U.S.C. § 101(13)

"debtor" means person or municipality concerning which a case under this title has been commenced;

11 U.S.C. § 109(b), (d)

(b) A person may be a debtor under chapter 7 of this title only if such person is not--

(1) a railroad;

(2) a domestic insurance company, bank, savings bank, cooperative bank, savings and loan association, building and loan association . . .

(d) Only a railroad, a person that may be a debtor under chapter 7 of this title . . . may be a debtor under chapter 11 of this title.

———

2. Debtor in Possession

Who is responsible for a business that files? We have seen in the typical chapter 7 case, an independent trustee is appointed. And in other common law countries such as Canada and England, a trustee or other independent agent is almost always appointed; no sense in having those responsible for the financial mess continue on, is there?

Read on.

11 U.S.C. § 1101(1)

"debtor in possession" means debtor except when a person that has qualified under section 322 of this title is serving as trustee in the case; . . . .

---

a. Debtor in Possession as a New Legal Entity

There is considerable language in case law and commentary stating that the debtor in possession is a new entity, separate and legally distinct from the debtor. It is not clear exactly what this statement means. It is not even clear that the statement that the debtor in possession is a separate legal person is even accurate. In *NLRB v. Bildisco & Bildisco*, 465 U.S. 513 (1984), a case involving a rejection of collective bargaining agreement by the debtor in possession, the Court summarily dismissed the notion that the debtor in possession was a separate legal entity from the debtor:

> Obviously, if the debtor-in-possession were a wholly 'new entity', it would be unnecessary for the Bankruptcy Code to allow it to reject executory contracts, since it would not be bound by such contracts in the first place. For our purposes, it is sensible to view the debtor-in-possession as the same 'entity' which existed before the bankruptcy petition, but empowered by virtue of the Bankruptcy Code to deal with its contracts and property in a manner it could not have done absent the bankruptcy filing.

---

11 U.S.C. § 1107(a)

[Debtor in Possession as "Trustee"]

(a). . . a debtor in possession shall have all of the rights . . . and shall perform . . . the functions and duties . . . of a trustee serving in a case under this chapter.

11 U.S.C. § 1108

[Operating the Business as a Debtor in Possession]

Unless the court, on request of a party in interest and after notice and a hearing, orders otherwise, the trustee may operate the debtor's business.

Reading section 1108 together with section 1107, it is clear that a debtor in possession operates the business in most Chapter 11 cases. What is less clear is who operates the debtor in possession.

---

b. Questions: Who Operates the Debtor in Possession?

1. ***Should*** the officers and directors of a corporation in bankruptcy be responsive to the needs and wishes of the shareholders or the needs and wishes of the creditors?

2. ***Should*** the shareholders of a corporation in Chapter 11 be able to remove directors and elect new directors?

---

3. Trustee

a. Comparison of Pre-1978 Bankruptcy Act and Present Bankruptcy Code

The Code was preceded by the Bankruptcy Act of 1898.[16] That act contained four separate chapters for the reorganization of businesses. Chapter VIII (the Act used Roman numbers; the Code uses Arabic) dealt with railroad reorganizations. Chapter X covered

---

[16]During most of the Nineteenth Century, there was no federal bankruptcy law. Before 1898, there was a federal bankruptcy law in effect only from 1800 to 1801, 1841 to 1843, and from 1867 to 1878.

reorganizations of corporations' secured debt, unsecured debt, and equity. Chapter XI was intended to govern arrangements of **unsecured** debts of individuals, partnerships, and corporations. Chapter XII was available only to noncorporate debtors with encumbered real estate.

Under the Bankruptcy Act of 1898, the issue of displacement of the debtor's management – who was to run the business – was determined in large part by the form of bankruptcy. The appointment of a trustee was mandatory under Chapter VIII in all cases, and under Chapter X when the debtor's liability exceeded $250,000. In most Chapter XI and Chapter XII cases, however, the debtor remained in control of the business as a debtor in possession unless the court for "cause shown" appointed a receiver.

There is no provision for the appointment of a receiver in Chapter 11 of the Code; indeed, it is prohibited. 11 U.S.C. § 105(b). In Chapter 11, the debtor in possession will usually continue to operate the business after the filing.

The House Report accompanying a draft of the Code provides the following justification for this approach:

> [V]ery often the creditors will be benefitted by continuation of the debtor in possession, both because the expense of a trustee will not be required, and the debtor, who is familiar with his business, will be better able to operate it during the reorganization case. A trustee frequently has to take time to familiarize himself with the business before the reorganization can get under way. Thus, a debtor continued in possession may lead to a greater likelihood of success in the reorganization. Moreover, the need for reorganization of a public company today often results from simple business reverses, not from any fraud, dishonesty, or gross mismanagement on the part of the debtor's management. Even if the cause is fraud or dishonesty, very frequently the fraudulent management will have been ousted shortly before the filing of the reorganization case, and the new management, very capable of running the business, should not

> be ousted by a trustee because of the sins of former management.
>
> . . . [F]acilitation of the reorganization to the benefit of the debtor and the creditors, militates against the appointment of a trustee. . . . Debtors' lawyers that participated in the development of a standard for the appointment of a trustee were adamant that a standard that led to too frequent appointment would prevent debtors from seeking relief under the reorganization chapter, and would leave the chapter largely unused except in extreme cases. One of the problems that the Bankruptcy Commission recognized in current bankruptcy and reorganization practice is that debtors too often wait too long to seek bankruptcy relief. Too frequent appointment of a trustee would exacerbate that problem, to the detriment of both debtors and their creditors.

H. REP. 595, 95TH CONG., 1ST SESS. 232-34 (1977).

---

b. Grounds for the Appointment of a Trustee or an Examiner

11 U.S.C. § 1104(a)

> (a) At any time after the commencement of the case but before confirmation of a plan, on request of a party in interest or the United States trustee, and after notice and a hearing, the court shall order the appointment of a trustee--
>
> > (1) for cause, including fraud, dishonesty, incompetence, or gross mismanagement of the affairs of the debtor by current management, either before or after the commencement of the case, or similar cause, ...
> >
> > (2) if such appointment is in the interests of creditors, any equity security holders, and other interests of the estate, ...; or
> >
> > (3) if grounds exist to convert or dismiss the case under section 1112, but the court determines that the appointment of a trustee or an examiner is in the best interests of creditors and the estate.

---

c. Duties of a Trustee or Examiner

11 U.S.C. § 1106

(a) A trustee shall--

(1) perform the duties of a trustee specified in sections 704(2) [account for all property], 704(5) [examine proofs of claim and object to improper claims], 704(7) [provide information to parties in interest], 704(8) [file reports of operations], and 704(9) [file a final report] of this title; . . .

(3) except to the extent that the court orders otherwise, investigate [and as provided in paragraph (4) below, report] the acts, conduct, assets, liabilities, and financial condition of the debtor, the operation of the debtor's business and the desirability of the continuance of such business, and any other matter relevant to the case or to the formulation of a plan; . . .

(5) as soon as practicable, file a plan under section 1121 . . . , or recommend conversion of the case to a case under chapter 7, 12, or 13 of this title or dismissal of the case; . . .

(b) An examiner appointed under section 1104(d) of this title shall perform the duties specified in paragraphs (3) and (4) of subsection (a) of this section, and, except to the extent that the court orders otherwise, any other duties of the trustee that the court orders the debtor in possession not to perform.

PROBLEM 11-1: APPOINTMENT OF TRUSTEE OR EXAMINER

1. If you had represented a major creditor in the Enron bankruptcy, would you have filed a motion seeking the appointment of a trustee? Or an examiner?

2. In the WorldCom bankruptcy, the debtor agreed to the appointment of an examiner. If you had represented the debtor, would you have agreed to the appointment of an examiner?

---

4. *Office of the United States Trustee*

28 U.S.C. § 581

(a) The Attorney General shall appoint one United States trustee for each of the . . . Federal judicial districts [a later statute exempts Alabama and the Northern District of North Carolina] . . .

28 U.S.C. § 586

(a) Each United States trustee, within the region for which such United States trustee is appointed, shall—

. . .

(3) supervise the administration of cases and trustees in cases under chapter 7, 11, 12, or 13 of title 11 by, whenever the United States trustee considers it to be appropriate—

. . .

(B) monitoring plans and disclosure statements filed in cases under chapter 11 of title 11 and filing with the court, in connection with hearings under sections 1125 and 1128 of such title, comments with respect to such plans and disclosure statements;

. . .

(E) monitoring creditors' committees appointed under title 11;

(F) notifying the appropriate United States attorney of matters which relate to the occurrence of any action which may constitute a crime under the laws of the United States and, on the request of the United States attorney, assisting the United States attorney in carrying out prosecutions based on such action;

> (G) monitoring the progress of cases under title 11 and taking such actions as the United States trustee deems to be appropriate to prevent undue delay in such progress; . . . .

> (8) in any case in which the United States trustee finds material grounds for any relief under section 1112 of title 11, the United States trustee shall apply promptly after making that finding to the court for relief.

"SELF-DESCRIPTION"

Statement of John E. Logan, Director, Executive Office for the United States Trustees before the Economic and Commercial Law Subcommittee on the Judiciary, House of Representatives, Concerning Oversight of the United States Trustee System, November 1, 1991:

> The creation of the United States Trustee Program reflects the fact that a bankruptcy case is not like a two-party lawsuit, where adversaries actively litigate the issues before the court in furtherance of their own self interests. A chapter 11 case can involve extensive restructuring of business activities and negotiations of a wide variety of claims. Many of these matters do not directly involve particular creditors, even though the matters may eventually have an adverse impact on all creditors. Moreover, it is the unusual case where there is a significant creditor interest.

> The court's role as adjudicator and catalyst for moving cases forward remains essential to the administration and supervision of chapter 11 cases, as are the efforts of the private interests involved. The United States Trustee Program adds an important new element: The presence of an independent office having the responsibility to encourage simultaneously greater participation of creditors and other interested parties as well as monitoring and maintaining the efficiency, effectiveness and integrity of how a particular case is moving through the system.

> The extent of the Program's participation in a chapter 11 case is often determined by the amount and quality of creditor

participation. This approach is premised on both the law's intent, as well as the wise use of resources. The United States Trustee seeks to encourage greater participation in chapter 11 cases through the formation of official committees and by conducting meetings of creditors under section 341 of the Bankruptcy Code. In most cases, creditors committees are appointed from among those creditors with an active interest in serving on a committee. The process seeks to ensure representation of the range of creditor interest present in a case, as well as maintaining communications among creditors and other interested parties. . . .

The Program is also active in overseeing the protection of estate assets and monies in chapter 11 cases by establishing procedures to ensure the debtor's fiduciary responsibilities are met. Such procedures typically address such matters as insurance, the payment of taxes during the case, and the filing of monthly operating reports disclosing a debtor's financial status. . . .

---

5. Committees

a. Who Are on Committees?

11 U.S.C. § 1102

(a)(1) . . . [A]s soon as practicable after the order for relief under chapter 11 of this title, the United States trustee shall appoint a committee of creditors holding unsecured claims and may appoint additional committees of creditors or of equity security holders as the United States trustee deems appropriate. . . .

(b)(1) A committee of creditors appointed under subsection (a) of this section shall ordinarily consist of the persons, willing to serve, that hold the seven largest claims against the debtor of the kinds represented on such committee . . . .

---

b. What Do Committees Do?

11 U.S.C. §§ 1102(a)(3); 1103(c)

(a)(3) A committee . . . shall—

(A) provide access to information for creditors who–
(i) hold claims of the kind represented by that committee; and
(iii) are not appointed to the committee; [and]

(B) solicit and receive comments from the creditors described in subparagraph (A). . . .

(c) A committee appointed under section 1102 of this title may—

(1) consult with the trustee or debtor in possession concerning the administration of the case;

(2) investigate the acts, conduct, assets, liabilities, and financial condition of the debtor, the operation of the debtor's business and the desirability of the continuance of such business, and any other matter relevant to the case or to the formulation of a plan;

(3) participate in the formulation of a plan, advise those represented by such committee of such committee's determinations as to any plan formulated, and collect and file with the court acceptances or rejections of a plan;

(4) request the appointment of a trustee or examiner under section 1104 of this title; and

(5) perform such other services as are in the interest of those represented.

PROBLEM 11-2: COMMITTEE MEMBERSHIP: BENEFITS AND BURDENS

1. Your client C holds one of the seven largest claims against the debtor, D Corp. C wants your advice as to whether it should serve on the committee. What are the benefits of committee membership? The burdens? Does it affect your answer to know that the Bankruptcy Review Commission found that from January 1993 to January 1996, creditors'

committees were appointed in only 15.3% of the then-pending chapter 11 cases? BANKRUPTCY: THE NEXT TWENTY YEARS—NATIONAL BANKRUPTCY REVIEW COMMISSION FINAL REPORT, OCTOBER 20, 1997, at 642 & n. 1629 (1997).

2. Is C eligible to serve on the committee if its claim is secured?

3. In D Corp.'s bankruptcy case, a group of shareholders has asked the bankruptcy judge to appoint a committee of equity security holders under 11 U.S.C. § 1102(b)(2). The creditors' committee has a filed motion in opposition, arguing that D Corp. is insolvent. What should the court do?

C. BEGINNING A CHAPTER 11 CASE

1. Before You File

a. Who Do You Tell about Plans for a Chapter 11 Plan?

Federal securities law deals with questions relating to what a public company can tell "favored" shareholders such as Martha Stewart about financial problems and plans for solving those problems. Bankruptcy law does not directly deal with questions relating to what a business should tell its "favored" creditors about possible plans to file for Chapter 11 relief. Nonetheless, such questions are real and really important.

Consider the following hypothetical. Bubba N' Bubbi's, Inc, (B) a chain of restaurants selling bagels with grits has decided to file a Chapter 11 petition. B buys all of its bagels on 20 days credit from St. Viateur's Bagels (S). And, B has obtained most of its funding from a group of banks led by First Bank (F). F is B's principal commercial bank: B's payroll account and most of its other significant bank accounts are at F. B's business plan is based on continued bagel shipments from S and continued funding from F. Should B tell S about its pending Chapter 11 filing? Should B tell F about its pending Chapter 11 filing?

Remember that the automatic stay of section 362 does not arise until a bankruptcy petition is actually filed. A business that tells its creditors about its plans to file for bankruptcy is vulnerable to collection actions by such creditors until it actually files.

---

b. Who Do You Pay Before You File for Bankruptcy?

Recall some more bankruptcy law. Payments to creditors within 90 days before a bankruptcy filing are vulnerable to "avoidance actions" under sections 547 and 550. And, such avoidance actions will be unsuccessful if the payments meet the "ordinary course" requirements of section 547.

In most instances, the limitations on paying creditors before filing for bankruptcy are practical problems, not preference problems.

First, the problem of finding the money to pay creditors. Most debtors look to Chapter 11 because they do not have the money to pay creditors – or at least do not have the money to pay all their creditors all that is owed.

Second, the problem of deciding which creditors to pay and how much to pay them. Given that a debtor contemplating Chapter 11 does not have the money to pay all its creditors all that they are owed, how does a business decide who to pay and how much to pay them? Most businesses owe for goods and services that they have been provided but not yet billed. And often these unbilled amounts are owed to the most "critical vendors."

---

2. Starting the Case

a. Filing the Papers

Look at Official Forms 1, 6 and 7 to see the papers that a chapter 11 debtor is required to file to start a case. That's all that's necessary. But in the WorldCom case, the debtor in possession lawyers filed no less than 26 different pleadings concurrently with its petition. Most had to do with corporate governance (the resolutions of WorldCom's board authorizing the filing), and some with housekeeping (the debtor in possession's lawyers needed authority to be employed on behalf of the estate). But some filings had to do with creditors.

---

b. Paying "Critical Vendors" and Employees in WorldCom.

At the first day of hearings, the bankruptcy court entered most of the 26 orders requested by WorldCom, including an order authorizing payments to *pre-petition* employees and *pre-petition* creditors who were deemed to be "critical vendors." No paper filed cited any Code provision which specifically authorized payments to employees. Judge Gonzalez's "critical vendors" order provided in part:

> ORDERED that, pursuant to section 105(a) of the Bankruptcy Code, the Debtors' are authorized, but not directed, to pay prepetition amounts owed to Critical Vendors, in the Debtors sole discretion and in accordance with the terms of such obligations; *provided, however,* that as a condition to payment hereunder, such Critical Vendors agree to supply goods and services to the Debtors during the pendency of these cases on customary trade terms; and provided further, that the

> aggregate of such payments pursuant to this Order shall not exceed $70 million; . . .

In re WorldCom., Inc., 2002 WL 1732647 (Bankr. S.D.N.Y. July 22, 2002).

QUESTIONS ABOUT *WORLDCOM* FIRST DAY ORDERS

1. In *WorldCom*, the bankruptcy petition was filed on Sunday. The next day, Judge Gonzalez held a hearing on the 26 motions, and entered orders on all of them, including the critical vendor order set forth above. Do you think all people affected by these orders were represented at the hearing?

2. As a result of the critical vendor order, certain prepetition claims were paid in full immediately. At the time of the hearing, when do you think the parties believed the "non-critical" vendors would be paid? Do you think they believed the "non-critical" vendors would be paid in full as well? *Cf.* XL/Datacomp, Inc.. v Wilson (*In re* Omegas Group, Inc.), 16 F.3d 1443, 1445 (6th Cir. 1994) ("Understandably, creditors of bankrupt debtors often feel like restaurant patrons who not only hate the food but think the portions are too small [Footnote: Attributed to Woody Allen in *Annie Hall* in 1977, but possibly dating from the Mesozoic Era.]. To press the analogy, they also don't like having to wait in line for a table, possibly being seated to find out the kitchen has just closed. The bankruptcy court is a little like a soup kitchen, ladling out whatever is available in ratable portions to those standing in line; nonetheless, scarcity begets innovation in the hungry creditor's quest to get a little more than the next fellow.").

3. What language in Section 105(a), reprinted below, supports Judge Gonzalez's critical vendor order?

---

11 U.S.C. § 105(a)

> The court may issue any order, process, or judgment that is necessary or appropriate to carry out the provisions of this title. No provision of this title providing for the raising of an issue by a party in interest shall be construed to preclude the court from, sua sponte, taking any action or making any determination necessary or appropriate to enforce or implement court orders or rules, or to prevent an abuse of process.

4. WorldCom filed before the 2005 bankruptcy legislation was passed. Part of that legislation was the addition of Section 503(a)(9) to the Code. That section grants a priority for:

   > (9) the value of any goods received by the debtor within 20 days before the date of commencement of a case under this title in which the goods have been sold to the debtor in the ordinary course of such debtor's business.

   If Section 503(b)(9) was part of the Code when WorldCom was filed, do you think it would have made a difference? What if the primary providers of things a debtor needs provide services, and not goods? (Think of a professional firm as a debtor, and FedEx as the creditor).

---

c. Paying Critical Vendors

IN RE KMART CORP.

359 F.3d 866 (7th Cir. 2004)

Before EASTERBROOK, MANION, and ROVNER, Circuit Judges.

EASTERBROOK, Circuit Judge.

On the first day of its bankruptcy, Kmart sought permission to pay immediately, and in full, the pre-petition claims of all "critical vendors." (Technically there are 38 debtors: Kmart Corporation plus 37 of its affiliates and subsidiaries. We call them all Kmart.) The theory behind the request is that some suppliers may be unwilling to do business with a customer that is behind in payment, and, if it cannot obtain the merchandise that its own customers have come to expect, a firm such as Kmart may be unable to carry on, injuring all of its creditors. Full payment to critical vendors thus could in principle make even the disfavored creditors better off: they may not be paid in full, but they will receive a greater portion of their claims than they would if the critical vendors cut off supplies and the business shut down. Putting the proposition in this way implies, however, that the debtor must *prove,* and not just allege, two things: that, but for immediate full payment, vendors *would* cease dealing; and that the business will gain enough from continued transactions with the favored vendors to provide some residual benefit to the remaining, disfavored creditors, or at least leave them no worse off.

Bankruptcy Judge Sonderby entered a critical-vendors order just as Kmart proposed it, without notifying any disfavored creditors, without receiving any pertinent evidence (the record contains only some sketchy representations by counsel plus unhelpful testimony by Kmart's CEO, who could not speak for the vendors), and without making any finding of fact that the disfavored creditors would gain or come out even. The bankruptcy court's order declared that the relief Kmart requested--open-ended permission to pay any debt to any vendor it deemed "critical" in the exercise of unilateral discretion, provided that the vendor agreed to furnish goods on "customary trade terms" for the next two years--was "in the best interests of the Debtors, their estates and their creditors". The order did not explain why, nor did it contain any legal analysis, though it did cite 11 U.S.C. § 105(a). . . .

Kmart used its authority to pay in full the pre-petition debts to 2,330 suppliers, which collectively received about $300 million. This came from the $2 billion in new credit (debtor-in-possession or DIP financing) that the bankruptcy judge authorized, granting the lenders super-priority in post-petition assets and revenues. See *In re Qualitech Steel Corp.,* 276 F.3d 245 (7th Cir.2001). Another 2,000 or so vendors were not deemed "critical" and were not paid. They and 43,000 additional unsecured creditors eventually received about 10¢ on the dollar, mostly in stock of the reorganized Kmart. Capital Factors, Inc., appealed the critical-vendors order immediately after its entry on January 25, 2002. A little more than 14 months later, after all of the critical vendors had been paid and as Kmart's plan of reorganization was on the verge of approval, District Judge Grady reversed the order authorizing payment. 291 B.R. 818 (N.D.Ill.2003). He concluded that neither § 105(a) nor a "doctrine of necessity" supports the orders. . . .

Section 105(a) allows a bankruptcy court to "issue any order, process, or judgment that is necessary or appropriate to carry out the provisions of" the Code. This does not create discretion to set aside the Code's rules about priority and distribution; the power conferred by § 105(a) is one to implement rather than override. . . . Every circuit that has considered the question has held that this statute does not allow a bankruptcy judge to authorize full payment of any unsecured debt, unless all unsecured creditors in the class are paid in full. . . . We agree with this view of § 105. "The fact that a [bankruptcy] proceeding is equitable does not give the judge a free-floating discretion to redistribute rights in accordance with his personal views of justice and fairness, however enlightened those views may be." . . .

A "doctrine of necessity" is just a fancy name for a power to depart from the Code. Although courts in the days before bankruptcy law was codified wielded power to reorder priorities and pay particular creditors in the name of "necessity"—see *Miltenberger v. Logansport Ry.,* 106 U.S. 286, 1 S.Ct. 140, 27 L.Ed. 117 (1882); *Fosdick v. Schall,* 99 U.S. 235, 25 L.Ed. 339 (1878)—today it is the Code rather than the norms of nineteenth century railroad reorganizations that must prevail. *Miltenberger* and *Fosdick* predate the first general effort at codification, the Bankruptcy Act of 1898. Today the Bankruptcy Code of 1978 supplies the rules. Congress did not in terms scuttle old common-law doctrines, because it did not need to; the Act curtailed, and then the Code replaced, the entire apparatus. Answers to contemporary issues must be found within the Code (or legislative halls). Older doctrines may survive as glosses on ambiguous language enacted in

1978 or later, but not as freestanding entitlements to trump the text. . . .

So does the Code contain any grant of authority for debtors to prefer some vendors over others? Many sections require equal treatment or specify the details of priority when assets are insufficient to satisfy all claims. E.g., 11 U.S.C. §§ 507, 1122(a), 1123(a)(4). Appellants rely on 11 U.S.C. §§ 363(b), 364(b), and 503 as sources of authority for unequal treatment. Section 364(b) reads: "The court, after notice and a hearing, may authorize the trustee to obtain unsecured credit or to incur unsecured debt other than under subsection (a) of this section, allowable under section 503(b)(1) of this title as an administrative expense." This authorizes the debtor to obtain credit (as Kmart did) but has nothing to say about how the money will be disbursed or about priorities among creditors. . . . . Section 503, which deals with administrative expenses, likewise is irrelevant. Pre-filing debts are not administrative expenses; they are the antithesis of administrative expenses. Filing a petition for bankruptcy effectively creates two firms: the debts of the pre-filing entity may be written down so that the post-filing entity may reorganize and continue in business if it has a positive cash flow. . . . Treating pre-filing debts as "administrative" claims against the post-filing entity would impair the ability of bankruptcy law to prevent old debts from sinking a viable firm.

That leaves § 363(b)(1): "The trustee [or debtor in possession], after notice and a hearing, may use, sell, or lease, other than in the ordinary course of business, property of the estate." This is more promising, for satisfaction of a pre-petition debt in order to keep "critical" supplies flowing is a use of property other than in the ordinary course of administering an estate in bankruptcy. Capital Factors insists that § 363(b)(1) should be limited to the commencement of capital projects, such as building a new plant, rather than payment of old debts--as paying vendors would be "in the ordinary course" but for the intervening bankruptcy petition. To read § 363(b)(1) broadly, Capital Factors observes, would be to allow a judge to rearrange priorities among creditors (which is what a critical-vendors order effectively does), even though the Supreme Court has cautioned against such a step. . . . Yet what these decisions principally say is that priorities do not change unless a statute supports that step; and if § 363(b)(1) is such a statute, then there is no insuperable problem. If the language is too open-ended, that is a problem for the legislature. Nonetheless, it is prudent to read, and use, § 363(b)(1) to do the least damage possible to priorities established by contract and by other parts of the Bankruptcy

Code. We need not decide whether § 363(b)(1) could support payment of some pre-petition debts, because *this* order was unsound no matter how one reads § 363(b)(1).

The foundation of a critical-vendors order is the belief that vendors not paid for prior deliveries will refuse to make new ones. Without merchandise to sell, a retailer such as Kmart will fold. If paying the critical vendors would enable a successful reorganization and make even the disfavored creditors better off, then all creditors favor payment whether or not they are designated as "critical." This suggests a use of § 363(b)(1) similar to the theory underlying a plan crammed down the throats of an impaired class of creditors: if the impaired class does at least as well as it would have under a Chapter 7 liquidation, then it has no legitimate objection and cannot block the reorganization. . . . For the premise to hold true, however, it is necessary to show not only that the disfavored creditors *will* be as well off with reorganization as with liquidation--a demonstration never attempted in this proceeding--but also that the supposedly critical vendors would have ceased deliveries if old debts were left unpaid while the litigation continued. If vendors will deliver against a promise of current payment, then a reorganization can be achieved, and all unsecured creditors will obtain its benefit, without preferring any of the unsecured creditors. . . .

Doubtless many suppliers fear the prospect of throwing good money after bad. It therefore may be vital to assure them that a debtor will pay for new deliveries on a current basis. Providing that assurance need not, however, entail payment for pre-petition transactions. Kmart could have paid cash or its equivalent. (Kmart's CEO told the bankruptcy judge that COD arrangements were not part of Kmart's business plan, as if a litigant's druthers could override the rights of third parties.) Cash on the barrelhead was not the most convenient way, however. Kmart secured a $2 billion line of credit when it entered bankruptcy. Some of that credit could have been used to assure vendors that payment would be forthcoming for all post-petition transactions. The easiest way to do that would have been to put some of the $2 billion behind a standby letter of credit on which the bankruptcy judge could authorize unpaid vendors to draw. That would not have changed the terms on which Kmart and any of its vendors did business; it just would have demonstrated the certainty of payment. If lenders are unwilling to issue such a letter of credit (or if they insist on a letter's short duration), that would be a compelling market signal that reorganization is a poor prospect and that the debtor should be liquidated post haste.

Yet the bankruptcy court did not explore the possibility of using a letter of credit to assure vendors of payment. The court did not find that any firm would have ceased doing business with Kmart if not paid for pre-petition deliveries, and the scant record would not have supported such a finding had one been made. The court did not find that discrimination among unsecured creditors was the only way to facilitate a reorganization. It did not find that the disfavored creditors were at least as well off as they would have been had the critical-vendors order not been entered. For all the millions at stake, this proceeding looks much like the Chapter 13 reorganization that produced *In re Crawford,* 324 F.3d 539 (7th Cir.2003). Crawford had wanted to classify his creditors in a way that would enable him to pay off those debts that would not be discharged, while stiffing the creditors whose debts were dischargeable. We replied that even though classification (and thus unequal treatment) is possible for Chapter 13 proceedings, see 11 U.S.C. § 1322(b), the step would be proper only when the record shows that the classification would produce some benefit for the disfavored creditors. Just so here. Even if § 362(b)(1) [*sic*] allows critical-vendors orders in principle, preferential payments to a class of creditors are proper only if the record shows the prospect of benefit to the other creditors. This record does not, so the critical-vendors order cannot stand.

AFFIRMED.

---

d. Questions about *KMart* and *WorldCom*

1. Would Judge Easterbrook have entered a first day order authorizing payments to critical vendors for goods delivered prepetition to WorldCom?

2. Would Judge Easterbrook have entered a first day order authorizing payments to WorldCom employees for days worked for WorldCom prepetition? How about for those vendors who had delivered goods within 20 days of filing? *See* 11 U.S.C. § 503(b)(9); 546(c).

D. Operating the Business in Chapter 11: An Overview

Realization of a Chapter 11 debtor's "going concern" value generally requires that the debtor *be* a going concern—that the debtor continue to operate after filing its Chapter 11 petition, Chapter 11 authorizes such continued business operations.

---

1. *Authority to Operate*

Recall that Section 1108 states that "[T]he trustee may operate the debtor's business," and that Section 1107 states that "a debtor in possession shall have all the rights . . . of a trustee serving in a case under this chapter."

As should be clear from re-reading (reading?) these excerpts from the Code, authority to operate the business is not a problem for a Chapter 11 debtor. And, as should be obvious without reading anything, money to operate the business is the problem for most Chapter 11 debtors.

---

2. *Money to Operate: A First View*

If a business files its Chapter 11 petition because it does not have enough money to operate, why will it have enough money to operate after it files for Chapter 11?

a. Savings from Not Paying Pre-Bankruptcy Claims until Confirmation of a Plan[17]

No provision in Chapter 11 expressly states that a Chapter 11 debtor does not pay pre-bankruptcy claims until confirmation of a plan. *Cf.* 11 U.S.C. § 549. Nonetheless, lawyers, their clients, and bankruptcy judges know that is how Chapter 11 works. Now you do too.

---

b. Earnings from Business Operations

Similarly, lawyers, their clients and bankruptcy judges know that a business in Chapter 11 can use earnings from business operations to pay the costs of continued operations. Law students need to know the legal basis for this – and they need to know why most such earnings are generally "cash collateral" and why creditors generally agree to a Chapter 11 debtor's use of their cash collateral.

---

[17]A Chapter 11 debtor's "savings" from not paying prepetition claims of creditors during the course of the case are somewhat reduced by the Chapter 11 debtor's paying postpetition bills from lawyers and other professionals during the course of the case.

E. Operating the Business in Chapter 11: Use of Property of the Estate, Including Cash Collateral

1. *Use of Property of the Estate That Is Not Cash Collateral and Sections 363(c)(1), 363(e) and 541(a)(6)*

a. Section 363(c)(1) and a Debtor's Use of Property of the Estate

Section 363(c)(1) provides that a Chapter 11 debtor[18] "may use property of the estate in the ordinary course of business without notice or hearing."[19] Accordingly, after filing for Chapter 11, Kmart can continue to use its cash registers and its blue lights and sell its clothes and toys —all property of the estate.

Note that there is no exception for encumbered property. Accordingly, it would seem from reading section 363(c)(1) that a Chapter 11 debtor can use and sell property that is encumbered by liens. But then read section 363(e).

---

b. Section 363(e) and Adequate Protection of Lien Holder

Section 363(e) provides an "adequate protection" limits on a debtor's use or sale or encumbered property. Section 363 provides in part:

> [O]n request of an entity that has an interest in property used, sold or leased . . . by the trustee, the court . . . shall condition such use, sale or lease as is

---

[18]Actually, section 363(c) refers to a "trustee", not a debtor in possession. But we know from section 1108 that a chapter 11 debtor in possession has the same rights as a trustee.

[19]Section 363(c)(1) should be read together with section 363(e).

necessary to provide adequate protection of such interest.

---

c. Section 541(a)(6) and Earnings as Property of the Estate

And, a Chapter 11 debtor's postpetition earnings will usually be property of the estate. *See* 11 U.S.C. § 541(a)(6)("Proceeds product, offspring, rents or profit from property of the estate").[20] To illustrate, when Kmart filed for bankruptcy on January 22d and, that afternoon, Epstein bought a Windjammer Super Duper Tank Top at the local Kmart, the $7.99 he paid was "property of the estate." Similarly, the millions that United Airlines received for tickets sold after its December 2002 bankruptcy filing are property of the estate.

Accordingly, it would seem from reading section 363(c)(1) that a Chapter 11 debtor can use earnings from its business operations without asking anybody for approval. But then read section 363(c)(2).[21]

---

2. *Use of Property of the Estate That Is Cash Collateral*

a. Definition of Cash Collateral

11 U.S.C. § 363(a)

In this section, "cash collateral" means cash, negotiable instruments, documents of title, securities, deposit accounts, or other cash equivalents whenever acquired in which the

---

[20]The 2005 Act added Section 1115 to the Code which makes post-petition earnings from individual chapter 11 debtors property of the estate, much like Section 1306 makes such earning property of the chapter 13 estate.

[21]We know that section 363(c)(1) does not "tell" you to read section 363(c)(2) – we are telling you to read section 363(c)(2).

estate and an entity other than the estate have an interest and includes the proceeds, products, offspring, rents, or profits of property and the fees, charges, accounts or other payments for the use or occupancy of rooms and other public facilities in hotels, motels, or other lodging properties subject to a security interest as provided in section 552(b) of this title, whether existing before or after the commencement of a case under this title.

PROBLEM 11-3: WHAT IS CASH COLLATERAL?

1. S makes a loan to D Department Stores (D). D grants S a security interest in its inventory to secure repayment of the loan. D files for bankruptcy. Is the inventory "cash collateral?"[22]

2. Same facts as #1. After filing for bankruptcy, D sells some of the inventory for cash. Is that cash "cash collateral"?

3. Same facts as #1. After filing for bankruptcy, D sells some of the inventory on credit. Are the accounts receivable from the sale of inventory "cash collateral"?

4. Same facts as #3. The customers to whom D sold the inventory pay D. Are the payments "cash collateral"?

5. Same facts as #1. D receives cash from the sale of its parking lot. Is that cash "cash collateral"?

6. Before filing for bankruptcy, D sold $6,000,000 of accounts receivable to F for $4,500,000. After D's bankruptcy, are the payments that F receives on these accounts receivable D's "cash collateral"?

---

[22]The first five questions are so easy – we can answer them: no, yes, no, yes, no. A variation of the sixth question was too hard for a bankruptcy judge to answer without an evidentiary hearing.

b. Rules for Use of Cash Collateral

11 U.S.C. § 363(c)(2)

The trustee [or debtor in possession] may not use, sell, or lease cash collateral under paragraph (1) of this subsection unless—(A) each entity that has an interest in such cash collateral consents; or (B) the court, after notice and a hearing, authorizes such use, sale, or lease in accordance with the provisions of this section.

---

11 U.S.C. § 363(e)

(e) Notwithstanding any other provision of this section, at any time, on request of an entity that has an interest in property used, sold, or leased, or proposed to be used, sold, or leased, by the trustee, the court, with or without a hearing, shall prohibit or condition such use, sale, or lease as is necessary to provide adequate protection of such interest.

---

11 U.S.C. § 552(a)

Except as provided in subsection (b) of this section, property acquired by the estate or by the debtor after the commencement of the case is not subject to any lien resulting from any security agreement entered into by the debtor before the commencement of the case.

Problem 11-4: Cash Collateral Deals

1. D is a Chapter 11 debtor. Before bankruptcy, D borrowed from C and granted C a security interest in all of its present and future accounts receivable. After bankruptcy, D wants to use the cash it receives from the collection of its accounts receivable to operate the business. Does D need to obtain C's approval? The court's approval?

2. Same facts as #1. How can D obtain the needed approval? Can D satisfy sections 363(c)(2)(B) and 363(e) by granting C a replacement lien in accounts receivable from post-bankruptcy operations?

F. OPERATING A BUSINESS IN CHAPTER 11: OBTAINING NEW CREDIT AFTER THE BANKRUPTCY FILING

At most, section 363 enables a Chapter 11 debtor to use the cash that its business generates. Generally, a Chapter 11 debtor needs more; it needs additional credit and funding. To counter the understandable reluctance of vendors and lenders to extend credit to Chapter 11 debtors, section 364 of the Bankruptcy Code provides incentives. Please read section 364.

---

1. *Postpetition Credit and Section 364*

11 U.S.C. § 364

(a) . . . the trustee may obtain unsecured credit and incur unsecured debt in the ordinary course of business allowable under section 503(b)(1) of this title as an administrative expense.

(b) The court, after notice and a hearing, may authorize the trustee to obtain unsecured credit or to incur unsecured debt other than under subsection (a) of this section, allowable under section 503(b)(1) of this title as an administrative expense.

(c) If the trustee is unable to obtain unsecured credit allowable under section 503(b)(1) of this title as an administrative expense, the court, after notice and a hearing, may authorize the obtaining of credit or the incurring of debt—

(1) with priority over any or all administrative expenses of the kind specified in section 503(b) or 507(b) of this title;

(2) secured by a lien on property of the estate that is not otherwise subject to a lien; or

(3) secured by a junior lien on property of the estate that is subject to a lien

(d)(1) The court, after notice and a hearing, may authorize the obtaining of credit or the incurring of debt secured by a senior or equal lien on property of the estate that is subject to a lien only if--(A) the trustee is unable to obtain such credit otherwise; and (B) there is adequate protection of the interest of the holder of the lien on the property of the estate on which such senior or equal lien is proposed to be granted.

(2) In any hearing under this subsection, the trustee has the burden of proof on the issue of adequate protection.

PROBLEM 11-5: APPLYING SECTION 364 TO VENDORS

Your client, C, sells dairy products to a group of supermarkets, D. C bills D monthly. D files a Chapter 11 petition. Should C continue to sell dairy products to D on credit? Should C obtain court approval? See paragraphs (a), (b) and (c) of section 364. *See also* 11 U.S.C. §§ 1129(a)(9)(A), 726(b).

Agree to diff treatment?

PROBLEM 11-6: APPLYING SECTION 364 TO NEW LENDERS

Before filing for bankruptcy, United Airlines approached a consortium of creditors, C, about obtaining

$300,000,000 of new financing. C declined. Should C be any more willing to provide United Airlines with $300,000,000 in debtor in possession financing under section 364?

———

2. Section 364 and Existing Lenders

Your client X is the primary lender to D, a chain of furniture stores. X has a lien on all of the assets of D, including after-acquired inventory, accounts receivable and the proceeds therefrom. The amount owed to X far exceeds the value of X's collateral. D files a Chapter 11 petition. D needs additional financing. What inducements can D offer X to extend postpetition financing? See sections 11 U.S.C. §§ 364 and 552(a) and the *Saybrook* case set out below.

———

a. "Cross-Collateralization"

SHAPIRO V. SAYBROOK MFG. CO. (*IN RE* SAYBROOK MFG. CO.)
963 F.2d 1490 (11th Cir. 1992)

COX, Circuit Judge:

Seymour and Jeffrey Shapiro, unsecured creditors, objected to the bankruptcy court's authorization for the Chapter 11 debtors to "cross-collateralize" their pre-petition debt with unencumbered property from the bankruptcy estate. The bankruptcy court overruled the objection and also refused under the Bankruptcy Code to grant a stay of its order pending appeal. The Shapiros appealed to the district court which dismissed the case as moot under section 364(e) because the Shapiros had failed to obtain a stay. We conclude that this appeal is not moot and that cross collateralization is not authorized under the Bankruptcy Code. Accordingly, we reverse and remand.

I. Facts and Procedural History

Saybrook Manufacturing Co., Inc., and related companies (the "debtors"), initiated proceedings seeking relief under Chapter 11 of the Bankruptcy Code on December 22, 1988. On December 23, 1988, the debtors filed a motion for the use of cash collateral and for authorization to incur secured debt. The bankruptcy court entered an emergency financing order that same day. At the time the bankruptcy petition was filed, the debtors owed Manufacturers Hanover approximately $34 million. The value of the collateral for this debt, however, was less than $10 million. Pursuant to the order, Manufacturers Hanover agreed to lend the debtors an additional $3 million to facilitate their reorganization. In exchange, Manufacturers Hanover received a security interest in all of the debtors' property--both property owned prior to filing the bankruptcy petition and that which was acquired subsequently. This security interest not only protected the $3 million of post-petition credit but also secured Manufacturers Hanover's $34 million pre-petition debt.

This arrangement enhanced Manufacturers Hanover's position vis-a-vis other unsecured creditors, such as the Shapiros, in the event of liquidation. Because Manufacturers Hanover's pre-petition debt was undersecured by approximately $24 million, it originally would have shared in a pro rata distribution of the debtors' unencumbered assets along with the other unsecured creditors. Under the financing order, however, Manufacturers Hanover's pre-petition debt became fully secured by all of the debtors' assets. If the bankruptcy estate were liquidated, Manufacturers Hanover's entire debt—-$34 million pre-petition and $3 million post-petition—would have to be paid in full before any funds could be distributed to the remaining unsecured creditors.

Securing pre-petition debt with pre- and post-petition collateral as part of a post-petition financing arrangement is known as cross-collateralization. The Second Circuit aptly defined cross-collateralization as follows:

> [I]n return for making new loans to a debtor in possession under Chapter XI, a financing institution obtains a security interest on all assets of the debtor, both those existing at the date of the order and those created in the course of the Chapter XI proceeding, not only for the new loans, the propriety of which is not contested, but [also] for existing indebtedness to it.

Otte v. Manufacturers Hanover Commercial Corp. (In re Texlon Corp.), 596 F.2d 1092, 1094 (2d Cir.1979).

Because the Second Circuit was the first appellate court to describe this practice in In re Texlon, it is sometimes referred to as Texlon-type cross-collateralization. Another form of cross-collateralization involves securing post-petition debt with pre-petition collateral. This form of non-Texlon-type cross-collateralization is not at issue in this appeal. The Shapiros challenge only the cross-collateralization of the lenders' pre-petition debt, not the propriety of collateralizing the post-petition debt.

The Shapiros filed a number of objections to the bankruptcy court's order on January 13, 1989. After a hearing, the bankruptcy court overruled the objections. The Shapiros then filed a notice of appeal and a request for the bankruptcy court to stay its financing order pending appeal. The bankruptcy court denied the request for a stay on February 23, 1989.

The Shapiros subsequently moved the district court to stay the bankruptcy court's financing order pending appeal; the court denied the motion on March 7, 1989. On May 20, 1989, the district court dismissed the Shapiros' appeal as moot under 11 U.S.C. §364(e) because the Shapiros had failed to obtain a stay of the financing order pending appeal, rejecting the argument that cross-collateralization is contrary to the Code. The Shapiros then appealed to this court.

II. Issues on Appeal

1. Whether the appeal to the district court and the appeal to this court are moot under section 364(e) of the Bankruptcy Code because the Shapiros failed to obtain a stay of the bankruptcy court's financing order.

2. Whether cross-collateralization is authorized under the Bankruptcy Code.

III. Contentions of the Parties

The lenders argue that this appeal is moot under section 364(e) of the Bankruptcy Code. That section provides that a lien or priority granted under section 364 may not be overturned unless it is stayed pending appeal. Even if this appeal were not moot, the Shapiros are not entitled to relief. Cross-collateralization is a legitimate means for debtors to obtain necessary financing and is not prohibited by the Bankruptcy Code.

The Shapiros contend that their appeal is not moot. Because cross-collateralization is not authorized under bankruptcy law, section 364(e) is inapplicable. Permitting cross-collateralization would undermine the entire structure of the Bankruptcy Code by allowing one unsecured creditor to gain priority over all other unsecured creditors simply by extending additional credit to a debtor. . . .

V. Discussion

A. Mootness

We begin by addressing the lenders' claim that this appeal is moot under section 364(e) of the Bankruptcy Code. Section 364(e) provides that:

> The reversal or modification on appeal of an authorization under this section to obtain credit or incur debt, or of a grant under this section of a priority or a lien, does not affect the validity of any debt so incurred, or any priority or lien so granted, to an entity that extended such credit in good faith, whether or not such entity knew of the pendency of the appeal, unless such authorization and the incurring of such debt, or the granting of such priority or lien, were stayed pending appeal.

The purpose of this provision is to encourage the extension of credit to debtors in bankruptcy by eliminating the risk that any lien securing the loan will be modified on appeal.

. . .

By its own terms, section 364(e) is only applicable if the challenged lien or priority was authorized under section 364. . . . We can not decide if this appeal is moot under section 364(e) until we decide the central issue in this appeal – whether cross collateralization is authorized under section 364. Accordingly, we now turn to that question.

B. Cross-Collateralization and Section 364

Cross-collateralization is an extremely controversial form of Chapter 11 financing. Nevertheless, the practice has been approved by several bankruptcy courts. . . .

The issue of whether the Bankruptcy Code authorizes cross-collateralization is a question of first impression in this court. Indeed, it is essentially a question of first impression before any court of appeals. Neither the lenders' brief nor our own research has produced a single appellate decision which either authorizes or prohibits the practice.

. . .

The Second Circuit expressed criticism of cross-collateralization in In re Texlon. The court, however, stopped short of prohibiting the practice altogether. At issue was the bankruptcy court's ex parte financing order granting the lender a security interest in the debtor's property to secure both pre-petition and post-petition debt. The court, in an exercise of judicial restraint, concluded that:

> In order to decide this case we are not obliged, however, to say that under no conceivable circumstances could "cross-collateralization" be authorized. Here it suffices to hold that ... a financing scheme so contrary to the spirit of the Bankruptcy Act should not have been granted by an ex parte order, where the bankruptcy court relies solely on representations by a debtor in possession that credit essential to the maintenance of operations is not otherwise obtainable.

In re Texlon, 596 F.2d at 1098. Although In re Texlon was decided under the earlier Bankruptcy Act, the court also considered whether cross-collateralization was authorized under the Bankruptcy Code. "To such limited extent as it is proper to consider the new Bankruptcy Act, which takes effect on October 1, 1979, in considering the validity of an order made in 1974, we see nothing in §364(c) or in other provisions of that section that advances the case in favor of 'cross-collateralization.' " In re Texlon, 596 F.2d at 1098 (citations omitted).

Cross-collateralization is not specifically mentioned in the Bankruptcy Code. We conclude that cross-collateralization is inconsistent with bankruptcy law for two reasons. First, cross-collateralization is not authorized as a method of post-petition financing under section 364. Second, cross-collateralization is beyond the scope of the bankruptcy court's inherent equitable power because it is directly contrary to the fundamental priority scheme of the Bankruptcy Code.

Section 364 authorizes Chapter 11 debtors to obtain secured credit and incur secured debt as part of their reorganization. . . .

By their express terms, sections 364(c) & (d) apply only to future—i.e., post-petition—extensions of credit. They do not authorize the granting of liens to secure pre-petition loans. 

. . .

Given that cross-collateralization is not authorized by section 364, we now turn to the lenders' argument that bankruptcy courts may permit the practice under their general equitable power. Bankruptcy courts are indeed courts of equity, 11 U.S.C. §105(a), and they have the power to adjust claims to avoid injustice or unfairness. Pepper v. Litton, 308 U.S. 295, 60 S.Ct. 238, 84 L.Ed. 281 (1939). This equitable power, however, is not unlimited.

. . .

Section 507 of the Bankruptcy Code fixes the priority order of claims and expenses against the bankruptcy estate. 11 U.S.C. §507. Creditors within a given class are to be treated equally, and bankruptcy courts may not create their own rules of superpriority within a single class. Cross-collateralization, however, does exactly that. As a result of this practice, post-petition lenders' unsecured pre-petition claims are given priority over all other unsecured pre-petition claims. . . .

. . . We disagree with the district court's conclusion that, while cross—collateralization may violate some policies of bankruptcy law, it is consistent with the general purpose of Chapter 11 to help businesses reorganize and become profitable. Rehabilitation is certainly the primary purpose of Chapter 11. This end, however, does not justify the use of any means. Cross- collateralization is directly inconsistent with the priority scheme of the Bankruptcy Code. Accordingly, the practice may not be approved by the bankruptcy court under its equitable authority.

VI. Conclusion

Cross-collateralization is not authorized by section 364. Section 364(e), therefore, is not applicable and this appeal is not moot. Because Texlon-type cross-collateralization is not explicitly authorized by the Bankruptcy Code and is contrary to the basic priority structure of the Code, we hold that it is an impermissible means of obtaining post-petition financing. The judgment of the district court is REVERSED and the case is REMANDED for proceedings not inconsistent with this opinion.

REVERSED and REMANDED.

---

b. Questions about *Saybrook*

1. *Facts of the case*

   1.1. When did the bankruptcy court enter its order approving cross collateralization? When did the Fifth Circuit reverse and remand? Anything "interesting" happen between 1988 and 1992?

   1.2. Who objected? Why did the debtor agree to the cross-collateralization? Why didn't the creditors' committee object? Asleep

2. *Vocabulary*. What is "Texlon-type cross collateralization"? S has a security interest in all of D's personal property. D files for bankruptcy. S agrees to provide post-petition financing for D under section 364 if all of its post-petition advances are secured by both D's post-petition assets and D's pre-petition assets. Is that cross-collateralization? Is that Texlon-type cross-collateralization?

PROBLEM 11-7: COMPARISON OF CASH COLLATERAL FINANCING UNDER SECTION 363 AND DEBTOR IN POSSESSION FINANCING UNDER SECTION 364

D owes your client S $7,000,000 and has a security interest in all of D's assets. D files a Chapter 11 petition. S is willing to lend D an additional $1,000,000. Should you try to structure the deal so that (i) S loans D $8,000,000 and (ii) D uses $7,000,000 of the $8,000,000 of debtor in possession financing to repay the $7,000,000 prepetition loan?

---

c. 11 U.S.C. § 364(d) Superpriority

IN RE QUALITECH STEEL CORP.
276 F.3d 245 (7th Cir. 2001)

EASTERBROOK, Circuit Judge.

Qualitech Steel Corporation had a short, unhappy, and expensive life. Formed in 1996 to exploit new technologies for producing specialty steels, Qualitech spent more than $400 million building two plants. Both took longer to build than expected, were more costly to construct and operate than expected, and generally performed below expectations. By March 1999, when it entered bankruptcy, Qualitech had not reached full scale and was losing about $10 million a month trying to get there. It owed secured lenders about $265 million; the security included almost all of the firm's assets. Management deemed Qualitech's facilities worth about $225 million when the bankruptcy proceeding began, so the unsecured creditors had little to hope for—little, but not nothing. Qualitech has sought to recover about $4 million from creditors in preference-avoidance actions under the Bankruptcy Code, and these recoveries would be shared among all unsecured creditors (including the secured lenders, to the extent their loans exceeded the value of the security).

Everyone recognized from the outset that the plants should be sold, either to an established producer or to someone willing to take considerable risk in an effort to get the plants working to original hopes. Some investment in keeping the operations going pending sale might be justified as the purchase of an option in obtaining the benefits of any upturn in the business's prospects. Efforts to obtain new financing were unsuccessful, however, as all available assets were encumbered. Some (but not all) of the original secured lenders offered to put a total of $30 million in new capital into the venture, if they received a super-priority interest. Such a transaction required demoting the other secured lenders' position and substituting new security under 11 U.S.C. § 364(d)(1). The only other assets in sight were the proceeds of preference-recovery actions (also known as avoidance actions). After notice and a hearing, the bankruptcy court approved debtor-in-possession (DIP) financing of $30 million, with super-security and an award of replacement security to the senior lenders, to the extent that this was necessary to maintain their financial position. No one appealed or sought a stay. In August 1999 all of Qualitech's operating assets were sold for consideration that the bankruptcy court deemed equivalent to $180 million. (The bid was complex and subject to potential adjustments that could raise or lower its effective value. The unsecured creditors contended that the bid should be valued at $227 million, but the bankruptcy judge chose the lower value. No one doubts that this bid, whatever its worth, was the best deal that could be obtained.)

The first $30 million of the proceeds went to the DIP financers, leaving $150 million for the old secured creditors. They accordingly invoked the provision giving them extra security—first dibs in the preference-recovery kitty, which would make up some but far from all of the loss. The unsecured creditors contended, however, that the secured lenders could not have lost anything; after all, if the $30 million investment were prudent, it should have improved these creditors' position. But the bankruptcy judge concluded that good money had been thrown after bad, that the secured lenders' position had been eroded by at least the value of the anticipated preference recoveries, and that they therefore were entitled to a substitute security interest in that collateral. The district court affirmed, and the unsecured creditors have appealed to us. As a practical matter, the decision is final for the purpose of 28 U.S.C. § 158(d), because the plan for the distribution of the sale proceeds is the effective plan of reorganization. All of Qualitech's operating assets have been sold; the secured lenders' claim reaches all actual and potential assets of the estate, and the unsecured lenders have been wiped out. Particular avoidance actions remain to be decided, but each is a separate adversary action, independently appealable later. What we have now winds up the main proceedings, and the existence of these collateral avoidance disputes does not make the order less final.

Even if the sale should be valued at $227 million rather than $180 million, the secured creditors suffered a loss as a result of the DIP financing. They had security worth $225 million going in and $197 million (maximum) coming out. The difference is substantially more than the highest estimate of any sums that could be recovered in avoidance actions, so § 364(d)(1) entitles the secured lenders to those sums. This assumes that the assets really were worth $225 million in March 1999. Maybe they weren't; if whoever owned them had to pony up $10 million per month to keep them viable, the discounted value of that expenditure stream had to be subtracted from the anticipated sale price in order to determine the assets' present value. If Qualitech had turned over the keys and deeds to the secured lenders in March, they would have had to bear these costs themselves. Yet the $225 million value is the original estimate of Qualitech's management; it is not some hokey number that the secured creditors cooked up to disguise the fact that maintenance outlays had to be subtracted from any eventual sale price. The unsecured creditors might have argued in the bankruptcy court that $225 million was just a seat-of-the-pants figure that should be reevaluated to determine how much the secured lenders really lost. But no such argument was made in either the bankruptcy court or the district court, and hints along these lines in the appellate brief are far too late. We must take it as established that (a) in March 1999 the secured creditors had interests worth $225 million, yet (b) in August 1999 these interests were worth, at most, $197 million after paying off the DIP lenders. These two figures compel affirmance of the judgment.

Instead of tackling this calculation head on, the unsecured creditors beat about the bush. They contend, for example, that courts do not favor using § 364 to give pre-petition lenders security interests in the proceeds of avoidance actions. That's an accurate assessment. Section 364(d) is supposed to be a last resort.

Perhaps the authorization of DIP financing and the associated use of preference-recovery proceeds for "adequate security" was imprudent; that some of the secured lenders refused to advance any more funds, even with super- security, suggests as much. (Though the fact that others of their number put up extra money, knowing that they were undersecured, implies a belief that keeping Qualitech alive had a positive option value.) But the time to make this point is long past. The bankruptcy judge did authorize financing with additional security to the original lenders. The unsecured creditors did not seek a stay, and it is too late to tell those among the secured lenders that opposed this DIP financing that they, rather than the unsecured creditors, must swallow the loss from the decision even though § 364(d) requires their protection.

The unsecured creditors' remaining arguments fare no better. It makes no difference who bears the burden of persuasion on valuation issues under § 364(d), because the secured lenders lost more than the value of the avoidance actions on any calculation. And the argument that we should reverse the judgment so that the bankruptcy judge can receive additional evidence from the secured creditors' files overlooks the fact that the unsecured creditors did not seek this information until the day before the evidentiary hearing (too late, the bankruptcy judge held) and did not raise the discovery issue on appeal to the district court until filing their reply brief. The point has been forfeited.

AFFIRMED.

G. PLAN PREPARATION

1. Overview

In Chapter 7 cases, the Code expressly answers the question: "who gets what?" Section 726(a) provides for the distribution of "property of the estate" and, in numbered paragraphs, sets out the order of distribution; section 726(b) then mandates that if there is not sufficient property of the estate to pay all of the claims in one of the section 726(a) kinds of clams, then "payment . . . shall be made pro rata among claims of the kind specified in each such particular paragraph of section 726(a)". Section 704 backs this up by requiring distributions to creditors to be made "as expeditiously as is compatible with the best interests of the parties in interest."

The only way to vary the baseline set by Section 726 is the Chapter 11 plan. In Chapter 11 cases, it is the plan that answers the question "who gets what." And, the answer provided by a Chapter 11 plan can be much more "creative" than section 726's answer.

First, distributions in a Chapter 11 plan are not limited to "property of the estate." Second, the "classes" of claims in a Chapter 11 plan can be very different from the kinds of claims in section 726. Third, "expeditiously" does not appear in Chapter 11 or in most descriptions of most Chapter 11 plans.

---

2. *Who and When?*

Section 1121 answers the question of who can file a plan. In reading section 1121 notice that:

- the debtor at any time in any chapter 11 case can file a plan [section 1121(a)];
- ***only*** the debtor can file a plan unless either a trustee has been appointed [section 1121(c)(1)] or statutory time deadlines have expired [section 1121(c)(2),(3), 1121(d)].

And, in reading section 1121 and the following problems, think about what "exclusivity" is and why it is important.

SECTION 1121 AND PLAN EXCLUSIVITY

11 U.S.C. § 1121

(a) The debtor may file a plan with a petition commencing a voluntary case, or at any time in a voluntary case or an involuntary case.

(b) Except as otherwise provided in this section, only the debtor may file a plan until after 120 days after the date of the order for relief under this chapter.

(c) Any party in interest, including the debtor, the trustee, a creditors' committee, an equity security holders' committee, a creditor, an equity security holder, or any indenture trustee, may file a plan if and only if—

(1) a trustee has been appointed under this chapter;

(2) the debtor has not filed a plan before 120 days after the date of the order for relief under this chapter; or

(3) the debtor has not filed a plan that has been accepted, before 180 days after the date of the order for relief under this chapter, by each class the claims or interests of which are impaired under the plan.

(d)(1) Subject to paragraph (e) on request of a party in interest and after notice and a hearing, the court may for cause reduce or increase the 120-day period or the 180-day period referred to in this section. . . .

(2)(A) The 120-day period specified in paragraph (1) may not be extended beyond a date that is 18 months after the date of the order for relief under this chapter.

(B) The 180-day period specified in paragraph (1) may not be extended beyond a date that is 20 months after the date of the order for relief under this chapter.

PROBLEM 11-8: PLAN EXCLUSIVITY

1. D Corp. files a Chapter 11 petition on April 5. The debtor files its Chapter 11 plan thirty days later. What is the first date that another party in interest can file a competing plan (without seeking an order under section 1121(d) shortening time)?

2. D Co files a Chapter 11 petition on December 7. A Chapter 11 trustee is appointed on January 15. Can the trustee file a Chapter 11 plan? Can D Co. still file a Chapter 11 plan? Can a creditor of D Co. file a Chapter 11 plan? Can there be more than one plan filed?

3. Did the debtor file a Chapter 11 plan "before 120 days after the date of the order for relief under this chapter" in the Enron case? In WorldCom? In Kmart? In United Airlines? What happens in a Chapter 11 case if no plan is filed within this

statutory period? *See* 11 U.S.C. §§ 1121(c), (d); 1112(b)(4).

4. Megacorp files its chapter 11 case on January 1, 2006. On June 1, 2007, it files its fifth request to extend the exclusive periods found in Section 1121 so that Megacorp will be the only entity that can file a plan up to and including October 1, 2007. The evidence, such as it is, before the court indicates that such an extension would be in the best interests of creditors and the estate. May the court grant the motion?

---

3. What is in the Chapter 11 Plan?

Section 1123 is entitled "contents of the plan." Section 1123 is, however, only one of the sections that governs what is in the plan. While compliance with section 1123 is essential, it is also essential to remember that a Chapter 11 plan will be effective only if it is approved by the requisite number of creditors and by the court. Accordingly, in the "real world", the answer to "what is in the Chapter 11 plan" is controlled not only by section 1123 but also by what the requisite number of creditors will accept (section 1126) and what the court will confirm (section 1129).

a. Importance of Concept of Class of Claims

The concept of classification of claims is the best example of the relationship of sections 1123 and 1126 and 1129. First, section 1123(a)(1) requires that a Chapter 11 plan designate classes of creditor claims. These different classes may be treated differently (although section 1123(a)(4) requires the same treatment for all claims within the same class). Accordingly, it would seem from section 1123 that Congress believed that a debtor might want to create different classes of claims for economic reasons. It might, for example, pay vendors who are not in the business of making long-term loans (such as trade creditors) more quickly than lenders who are in the business of extending credit (such as banks).

Second, while Section 1129(a) requires that all classes consent to the plan,[23] class consent doesn't require unanimity. Rather, section 1126 establishes the test for determining whether a class accepts a plan: acceptance occurs when creditors holding more than one-half of the total *number* of claims voting accept the plan, and the number so accepting also hold claims worth at least two-thirds of the *amount* of claims voting (11 U.S.C. § 1126(c)). This test applies separately to each class of claims. Accordingly, it would seem from section 1126 and 1129 that a debtor might want to create different classes of claims for voting reasons—for example, placing a dissenting creditor with a large claim in a separate class.

---

b. Definition of Class of Claims

We did not leave out the Code's definition of "class" or "class of claims" No Code section provides these definitions.

---

11 U.S.C. § 1122

(a) Except as provided in subsection (b) of this section, a plan may place a claim or an interest in a particular class only if such claim or interest is substantially similar to the other claims or interests of such class.

(b) A plan may designate a separate class of claims consisting only of every unsecured claim that is less

---

[23]There is an important exception to this called "cramdown," but we will get to that later. In any event, even in cramdown, section 1129(a)(10) requires at least one consenting impaired class. Accepts Plan

than or reduced to an amount that the court approves as reasonable and necessary for administrative convenience.

PROBLEM 11-9: CLASSIFICATION OF SECURED CLAIMS

1. D Co.'s creditors include F who has a first mortgage on Blackacre, S who has a second mortgage on Blackacre. D Co. also has many unsecured lenders and vendors. Can D Co.'s plan place all its creditors in the same class? Can D Co.'s plan put both F's claim and S's claim in the same class? What statutory language controls the answers to these questions?

2. All of D Inc.'s creditors are unsecured except for S. S is owed $2,000,000 and has a lien on D Inc.'s assets that have a value of no more than $1,500,000. Can D Inc.'s Chapter 11 plan put S in one class all of its other creditors in another class?

---

c. Classification of Secured Claims

IN RE KECK, MAHIN & CATE
241 B.R. 583 (Bankr. N.D. Ill. 1999)

RONALD BARLIANT, Bankruptcy Judge.

Keck, Mahin & Cate ("Keck" or "the Debtor") was once a leading Chicago law firm with as many as 350 attorneys and 10 offices. In the 1990s, however, the firm's fortunes began to decline and it was never able to recapture its past glory. . . . In 1997, more than a century after the firm began in the practice of law, Keck ceased the representation of clients and continued only in a wind-up capacity. Apparently Keck was unable to wind-up its affairs to the satisfaction of all its creditors, however, because five trade creditors filed an involuntary bankruptcy petition against the firm under chapter 7 of the United States Bankruptcy Code on December 16, 1997. On December 31, 1997, upon Keck's request, the case was converted to chapter 11. Presently before the Court is the confirmation of the Third Amended Joint Chapter 11 Plan ("the

Plan"), proposed jointly by Keck and the Official Committee of Unsecured Creditors.

The Plan enjoys broad support by creditors and former partners, but is opposed by . . . a former partner, who (in common with other partners) holds a secured claim . . .

Class III consists of the secured claims of partners who lent the Debtor approximately $4,625,000 to pay a portion of the Bank Group's secured loan ("the Sub-Debt Holders"). The loans are secured by security interests, subordinated only to the Bank Group's security interests, in virtually all of the Debtor's assets. The only such asset of any importance is accounts receivable. Since the Bank Group has been satisfied, the Sub-Debt Holders' lien is now senior. Based on alleged inequitable conduct of the Debtor and its partners, the Creditor's Committee and a major creditor have contended that the Sub-Debt claims should be equitably subordinated. . . .

Mr. Dennis O'Dea is a Non-Participating Partner of the Debtor and the lone rejecting member of Class III . . ., Mr. O'Dea also argues that his Sub-Debt claim should be separately classified. "[A] plan may place a claim ... in a particular class only if [it] is substantially similar to the other claims of such class." § 1122(a). Commonly, each secured claim is placed in a separate class. But that is because usually each such claim is secured by distinct rights to property of yhe estate. Secured creditors typically have either liens on different assets, or, if their liens are on the same asset, one has a higher priority than the other. In this case, however, each Sub-Debt claim is secured by a common interest in the same collateral, and each Sub-Debt Holder has the same right to pro rata payment from that collateral. Hence, each Sub-Debt Holder is in the same relationship to the Debtor and its assets as all other Sub-Debt Holders. Therefore, these claims are substantially similar, and, accordingly, Mr. O'Dea's objection to their classification in a single class is overruled. . . .

PROBLEM 11-10: REASONS FOR CLASSIFICATION OF UNSECURED CLAIMS

1. X Corp.'s chapter 11 plan provides for two classes of unsecured claims: (1) claims under $3,000; and (2) claims above $3,000. Under this plan, each class (1) claim will be paid in full in cash on the

effective date of the plan and each class (2) claim will be paid 90% of its amount owed over a nine-year period. What is the probable reason for classification? Hint: see 11 U.S.C. § 1122(b).

2. Z's Chapter 11 plan provides for two classes of unsecured claims: (1) vendor claims; and (2) lender claims. Under the plan, each class (1) claim will be paid 50% of its amount over a one-year period, and each class (2) claim will be paid 70% of its amount over a five-year period. What is the probable reason for the classification?

3. Same facts as #2 except that the plan provides to treat claims in each class the same: 60% of the amount owed over a three-year period. What is the probable reason for the classification?

---

d. Classification of Unsecured Claims for Economic Reasons

In re Dow Corning Corp.

280 F.3d 648 (6th Cir.), *cert. denied*, 537 U.S. 816 (2002)

BOYCE F. MARTIN, JR., Chief Circuit Judge.

Years after Dow Corning Corporation filed a petition for reorganization under Chapter 11 of the Bankruptcy Code, and following extensive and vigorous negotiations, the third proposed plan of reorganization for Dow was submitted to the bankruptcy court. The bankruptcy court confirmed the Amended Joint Plan of Reorganization for Dow and the district court affirmed the bankruptcy court's Confirmation Order. Certain claimants who voted against the Plan appealed. The second issue presented is whether the Plan's classification of foreign claimants complies with the Bankruptcy Code's classification requirements. For the following reasons we AFFIRM the bankruptcy court's determination regarding the Plan's classification.

I.

For nearly thirty years, Dow was the predominant producer of silicone gel breast implants, accounting for almost fifty percent of the entire market. In addition, Dow supplied silicone raw materials to other manufacturers of silicone gel breast implants.

In the 1980s, certain medical studies suggested that silicone gel may cause auto-immune tissue diseases such as lupus, Scleroderma and rheumatoid arthritis. In 1992, the Food and Drug Administration ordered that silicone gel implants be taken off the market and Dow ceased manufacturing and marketing its silicone implants. Soon thereafter, tens of thousands of implant recipients sued Dow and its two shareholders, the Dow Chemical Company and Corning, Incorporated, claiming to have been injured by auto-immune reactions to the silicone in their implants. . . .

Dow filed a petition for reorganization under Chapter 11 of the Bankruptcy Code. . . .

Under the Plan, a $2.35 billion fund is established for the payment of claims asserted by (1) personal injury claimants, (2) government health care payers, and (3) other creditors asserting claims related to silicone-implant products liability claims. The $2.35 billion fund is established with funds contributed by Dow's products liability insurers, Dow's shareholders and Dow's operating cash reserves. . . .

Under the Plan, claimants who choose to settle are channeled to the Settlement Facility, a legal entity created by the Plan and authorized to negotiate payments out of funds set aside for that purpose. Claimants who choose to litigate are channeled to the Litigation Facility, a legal entity created by the Plan that is essentially substituted for Dow as a defendant in the claimant's lawsuit.

The Plan divides claims and interests into thirty-three classes and subclasses. Classes 6.1 and 6.2 are composed of foreign breast-implant claimants who are given the opportunity to either settle or litigate their claims. Settlement payments to foreign breast implant claimants are between 35% and 60% of the amounts to be paid to domestic breast-implant claimants. . . .

For the following reasons we hold that the Plan's classification of foreign claimants meets the Code's requirements.

Under the Plan, a foreign claimant is defined as someone who (1) is not a United States citizen, (2) is not a resident alien, or (3) did not have his or her medical procedure performed in the United States. Plan §§ 1.67. The Plan creates two classes for foreign claimants. Class 6.1 consists of claimants who are from a country that either (1) belongs to the European Union, (2) has a common law tort system, or (3) has a per capita Gross Domestic Product of greater than 60% of the United States's per capita Gross Domestic Product. Class 6.2 consists of claimants from all other countries. Class 5 generally consists of domestic breast- implant claimants. Class 6.1 claimants receive settlement offers of 60% of analogous domestic claimants' settlements, and Class 6.2 receive settlements of 35% of the domestic claimants' settlements. Members of both classes retain the option to litigate against the Litigation Facility for the full value of the claim should they deem the settlement offer inadequate.

The various groups of foreign claimants argue that their claims are not worth less than those of the domestic tort claimants and, therefore, should not be classified separately from domestic claims. The issue is whether the Plan improperly classifies the foreign claimants separately from domestic claimants. For the following reasons we hold that the separate classification is not improper.

The Bankruptcy Code provides that "a plan may place a claim or an interest in a particular class only if such claim or interest is substantially similar to the other claims or interests of such class." 11 U.S.C. § 1122(a). This circuit has recognized that section 1122(a), "by its express language, only addresses the problem of dissimilar claims being included in the same class." In re U. S. Truck Co., 800 F. 2d 581, 585 (6th Cir. 1986). Section 1122(a) does not demand that all similar claims be in the same class. To the contrary, the bankruptcy court has substantial discretion to place similar claims in different classes. We have observed that "Congress incorporated into section 1122 .... broad discretion to determine proper classification according to the factual circumstances of each individual case."

In this case, the bankruptcy court determined that the evidence supported the factual assumptions upon which the classifications are based, and that given those facts, the Plan's classifications are proper. For example, the bankruptcy court found the testimony of three widely recognized expert witnesses helpful. . . . Id. They offered quantitative evidence demonstrating that the highest tort awards in various other countries were significantly lower than in the United States. For example, one expert witness testified that the highest non-pecuniary award in injury cases in Australia is approximately

$230,000. The bankruptcy court found these witnesses credible, in contrast to the foreign claimants' witnesses, who the court found to be "unhelpful."

Based on such evidence, the bankruptcy court found that "without question, the evidence on the record shows that tort recoveries in the United States tend to be significantly higher than those in foreign jurisdictions." Though the foreign claimants point to countervailing considerations, their arguments, at best, show that there was conflicting evidence on the factual assumptions underlying the classification scheme. The foreign claimants have not shown that the facts used to support the separate classifications for foreign and domestic claimants were clearly erroneous.

Second, the various groups of foreign claimants contend that their claims are more valuable than claims originating from other countries in their respective classes. They argue that the various claims in their class are not "substantially similar" as required by section 1122(a). They further argue that by giving identical consideration to class members whose claims are of different value, they are not being treated the same as other members of their class in violation of the Code's requirement that claimants within a class be treated equally. 11 U.S.C § 1123(a)(4).

This issue, therefore, turns on whether the Plan improperly places foreign claims that are not "substantially similar" in the same class. For the following reasons we find that the bankruptcy court's determination that the claims within a given class are "substantially similar" is not clearly erroneous.

The bankruptcy court relied on the testimony of a leading expert in comparative law methodology, Basil Markenisis, who pointed to legal, economic, and cultural factors supporting the bankruptcy court's conclusion that the claims within each class are "substantially similar." Markenisis discussed (1) the availability of social safety nets in other countries, (2) other countries' reliance on judges as opposed to juries, (3) limitations on punitive damages, (4) unavailability of contingency fees, (5) limitations on strict liability doctrines, (6) cultural factors, (7) reluctance to use lawyers, especially in the Far East, and (8) reliance upon semi-official medical reports in Europe. The bankruptcy court concluded, based on such evidence, that the claims are "substantially similar." Though the foreign claimants offer countervailing considerations, they have offered no evidence to indicate that the facts relied upon by the bankruptcy court were clearly erroneous. Moreover, we note that all foreign claimants retain the right to pursue full payment of their claims in the Litigation Facility. The fact that foreign claimants maintain the litigation option further supports the finding that the Plan does not treat claims that are in the same class unequally.

IV.

For the reasons set forth above, we AFFIRM the bankruptcy court's determination that the Plan's classification of foreign claimants meets the Bankruptcy Code's requirements. In addition, we AFFIRM the district court's determination that, when there are "unusual circumstances," the bankruptcy court may enjoin non-consenting creditors' claims against a non-debtor to facilitate a Chapter 11 plan of reorganization. However, we REMAND this case to the district court for those matters needing additional findings.

QUESTIONS ABOUT *DOW CORNING* AND CLASSIFICATION OF CLAIMS

1. Note that the Plan divides claims into "thirty-three classes and subclasses." What is the legal difference between a "class" of claims and a "subclass" of claims?

2. Did the bankruptcy court find that all of the foreign breast implant claims are substantially similar?

3. Did the bankruptcy court find that foreign breast implant claims are not substantially similar to the domestic breast implant claims?

---

e. Review of What We Have Done with Classifications of Claims and Preview of What We Will Do Later with Classification of Claims

Dow Corning applied sections 1123(a)(1) and 1122 to a plan that created multiple classes of unsecured claims for financial reasons – to distribute less to foreign tort claimants. Later, we will again apply sections 1123(a)(1) and 1122 to a plan that created multiple classes of unsecured claims for plan confirmation reasons – to satisfy the requirements of section 1129(a)(10) that at least one "impaired" class accepted the plan.

H. PREPARING FOR CONFIRMATION: THE CREDITOR VOTING PROCESS

The late Professor MacLachlan described a business reorganization under the bankruptcy laws as a "composition in bankruptcy." JAMES MACLACHLAN, BANKRUPTCY 371 (1956). More recently (but not recently) a (then) prominent Los Angeles bankruptcy lawyer, J. Ronald Trost,[24] wrote that "Reorganization plans are essentially contracts between the debtor and its creditors." J. Ronald Trost, *Business Reorganizations Under Chapter 11 of the New Bankruptcy Code*, 34 BUS. LAW. 1309, 1327 (1979).

You need to question what you read. Particularly if it was written either by a guy who changes the spelling of his last name[25] or someone who uses his first initial and middle name.[26]

---

[24]Mr. Trost later smelled the coffee and moved to New York; one of us (Markell) learned from Trost when he was in Los Angeles and declined (politely) the invitation to follow him to New York. And for the record (since Trost is still *very* much alive), one of us (Markell) disagrees with the slur buried in the footnote that follows the next footnote. We (or at least Markell) think it is more significant that Trost goes by "Ron" or "J. Ronald" but never "Jay" or whatever the "J." stands for; when our minds are not otherwise occupied, we wonder what the "J." hides.

[25]Professor MacLachlan changed the spelling of his name from "McLaughlin" when he was older even than your senior author, "correcting an error made in Scotland about 1835." J. HANNA & J. MACLACHLAN, CASES AND MATERIALS ON CREDITORS' RIGHTS, at viii n.1 (4th ed. 1951). To be crystal clear, the "senior" author is Epstein. The rest of us are, comparatively speaking, spring chickens.

[26]Remember G. Gordon Liddy and H. Howard Hunt and L. Ron Hubbard and P. Diddy Combs and...

Although don't be too hasty about dismissing Mr. Trost's saying. *See* Miller v. United States, 363 F.3d 999 (9th Cir. 2004), in which the Ninth Circuit not only held a plan of reorganization was a contract, but used California common law

A Chapter 11 plan is similar to a composition, similar to a contract, in that it will be necessary to obtain consent from at least some creditors. A Chapter 11 plan is different from a composition or any other form of contract in that it binds not only the creditors who agree to it but other creditors as well. The binding nature of the plan requires extra steps to ensure that its fairness – to provide an index of fairness other than consent. The first such step is regulation of the manner in which consent is obtained.

---

1. Disclosure of Adequate Information Before Creditors Vote

In Chapter 11, creditors assent to a plan by voting to accept the plan. While Chapter 11 does not require that all creditors consent to the plan, it contemplates that creditors will receive "adequate information" about the plan and have the opportunity to vote on the plan.

Note section 1125's phrase: "adequate information." According to legislative history, "The premise underlying . . . Chapter 11 . . . is the same as the premise of the securities laws. If adequate disclosure is provided to all creditors and stockholders whose rights are to be affected, then they should be able to make an informed judgment of their own, rather than having the court or the Securities and Exchange Commission inform them in advance whether the proposed plan is a good plan." H. REP. 595, 93D CONG., 1ST SESS. 226 (1977). Accordingly, a bankruptcy court does not review a plan before it is submitted to creditors and stockholders for vote. Instead, the bankruptcy court reviews the inadequacy of the information about the plan provided to creditors and stockholders.

---

principles of contract interpretation to determine what it required.

Section 1125(b) requires the creditors and stockholders be provided with "a written disclosure statement approved after notice and hearing by the court as containing adequate information." "Adequate information" is defined in section 1125(a). Although courts acknowledge that what constitutes "adequate information" varies from case to case, several courts have developed checklists.

---

a. Requirement of Adequate Information

11 U.S.C. § 1125(b)

(b) An acceptance or rejection of a plan may not be solicited after the commencement of the case under this title from a holder of a claim or interest with respect to such claim or interest, unless, at the time of or before such solicitation, there is transmitted to such holder the plan or a summary of the plan, and a written disclosure statement approved, after notice and a hearing, by the court as containing adequate information. . . .

---

b. Definition of Adequate Information and 11 U.S.C. § 1125(a)

(a) In this section–

(1) "adequate information" means information of a kind, and in sufficient detail, as far as is reasonably practicable in light of the nature and history of the debtor and the condition of the debtor's books and records, including a discussion of the potential material Federal tax consequences of the plan to the debtor any successor to the debtor, and a hypothetical investor typical of the holders of claims or interests in the case, that would enable a hypothetical reasonable investor typical of holders of claims or interests such a hypothetical investor of the relevant class to make an informed judgment about the plan, but adequate information need not include such information about any other possible or proposed plan and in determining whether a disclosure statement provides adequate information, the court shall consider the complexity of

the case, the benefit of additional information to creditors and other parties in interest, and the cost of providing additional information;

---

c. Judicial Checklists for Adequate Information

Numerous courts have prescribed a list of disclosures which typically should be included in a disclosure statement. For example, in *In re* Scioto Valley Mortgage Co., 88 B.R. 168 (Bankr. S.D. Ohio 1988) the court adopted a 19-point nonexhaustive list of types of information that may be required in a disclosure statement:

1. The circumstances that gave rise to the filing of the bankruptcy petition;

2. A complete description of the available assets and their value;

3. The anticipated future of the debtor;

4. The source of the information provided in the disclosure statement;

5. A disclaimer, which typically indicates that no statements or information concerning the debtor or its assets or securities are authorized, other than those set forth in the disclosure statement;

6. The condition and performance of the debtor while in Chapter 11;

7. Information regarding claims against the estate;

8. A liquidation analysis setting forth the estimated return that creditors would receive under Chapter 7;

9. The accounting and valuation methods used to produce the financial information in the disclosure statement;

10. Information regarding the future management of the debtor, including the amount of compensation to be

paid to any insiders, directors, and/or officers of the debtor;

11. A summary of the plan of reorganization;

12. An estimate of all administrative expenses, including attorneys' fees and accountants fees;

13. The collectibility of any accounts receivable;

14. Any financial information, valuations or pro forma projections that would be relevant to creditors' determinations of whether to accept or reject the plan;

15. Information relevant to the risks being taken by the creditors and interest holders;

16. The actual or projected value that can be obtained from avoidable transfers;

17. The existence, likelihood and possible success of non-bankruptcy litigation;

18. The tax consequences of the plan; and

19. The relationship of the debtor with affiliates.

Several reported decisions have used this checklist.

Another bankruptcy judge prepared a different list – a list of the causes of delay and expense in Chapter 11. He included disclosure statements on the list, stating:

> The process of preparing a disclosure statement and then dealing with the objections and the hearing is an expensive and time consuming process. It is especially troubling in those circumstances in which the creditor objects to the disclosure statement in a strategic effort to improve its treatment under the plan. Regardless, the process can adversely impact the debtor in two ways. First, it can result in substantial fees for attorneys and accountants. Second, it can result in a substantial diversion of the management time from the debtor's business and the reorganization process.... The suspicion is that in the average small to medium size chapter 11 case, the time and money spent on this process is largely wasted because creditors are not interested in all of the

disclosures that are presently required and thus they do not read the disclosure statement.

See Honorable Steven Rhodes, *Eight Statutory Causes of Delay and Expense in Chapter 11 Bankruptcy Cases*, 67 AM. BANKR. L.J. 287, 316-17 (1993).

PROBLEM 11-11: WHAT IS DISCLOSED?

1. Epstein Airlines, Inc. has filed its Chapter 11 plan and disclosure statement. C, a creditor, objects to the disclosure statement because it fails to mention articles in Business Week, Forbes and the Wall Street Journal that are critical of Epstein Airlines, Inc.'s business plan and management team. What should be the result?

2. Epstein Discount Stores has filed its Chapter 11 plan and disclosure statement. The creditors' committee objects to the disclosure statement because it fails to mention that (i) WalMart has expressed an interest in buying Epstein Discount Stores, Inc. and (ii) the creditors' committee would prefer that WalMart own Epstein Discount Stores, Inc. What should be the result?

PROBLEM 11-12: WHO DISCLOSES?

1. If in the Epstein Discount Stores case exclusivity has ended, and the creditors committee files its own plan, providing for the sale of Epstein Discount Stores to WalMart, will the creditors' committee have to file a disclosure statement?

2. D files a plan and disclosure statement in its Chapter 11 case, and the court approves the disclosure statement. The creditors' committee is opposed to the plan and wants to send material to

creditors urging them to vote against the plan. Does section 1125 require that the creditors' committee submit its solicitation material to the bankruptcy court for approval? Is section 1121 relevant to your answering this question about section 1125?

---

2. *Prepackaged Plans*

a. **When and Why?**

In some cases, parties have been negotiating long and hard before the bankruptcy case is even filed. A majority of creditors may have agreed to a sensible workout plan, but some creditors may be "holding out," trying to use their leverage as holdouts to extract special deals for their particular consent. In such cases, if all the work and disclosure is done before the filing, it would be economic waste for the parties to ignore what has gone on.

The Bankruptcy Code recognizes this. It allows the solicitation and voting to occur pre-petition. Once the case is filed, the plan proponent usually immediately files the plan and all disclosure materials, and asks for a joint hearing on the plan and disclosure statement. Section 1126(b) then permits the votes so solicited to count if "the solicitation of such acceptance or rejection was in compliance with any applicable nonbankruptcy law, rule, or regulation governing the adequacy of disclosure in connection with such solicitation; or . . . if there is not any such law, rule, or regulation, such acceptance or rejection was solicited after disclosure to such holder of adequate information, as defined in section 1125(a) of this title." *In re* Pioneer Finance Corp., 246 B.R. 626, 630 (Bankr. D. Nev. 2000) (describing the difference between a prepackaged plan and a prenegotiated plan). *See also* 11 U.S.C. § 1125(g).

Prepackaged plans are typically used when the debtor has relatively constant amounts of debt, such as the bonds or debentures of publicly-traded companies. It does not work well when the debt is trade debt, widely disbursed and constantly changing.

b. What Are The Possible Problems?

What can go wrong with a "pre-pack"? A fair amount. As we have seen, one of the great benefits for debtors in bankruptcy is the automatic stay of Section 362. It stops unilateral collection efforts by creditors while the debtor regroups. But by definition, the negotiation of a pre-pack occurs before the filing, and hence before the effectiveness of the automatic stay. This skews negotiating leverage somewhat.

PROBLEM 11-13: PROBLEMS WITH A PRE-PACK

Jonas, Inc. sells garments on a wholesale basis to retailers such as K-Mart, Wal-Mart and the like. Due to an ill-advised leveraged buyout several years ago, it is currently in a precarious financial situation. It believes that it can survive if it gathers together its creditors (consisting of trade creditors who shipped goods to Jonas on unsecured credit, and the bondholders who received their bonds in the leveraged buyout).

At the meeting, things don't go well. Jonas is proposing to pay trade creditors in full, and to issue new bonds in exchange for the old bonds – but the new bonds will be only 80% of face amount of the old bonds, will carry a lower (but market) interest rate, and will be repayable over a 15-year period. As it now stands, the bonds are due in three years.

Several bondholders balk at the package. They leave the meeting, and the next Jonas hears of them they have sued on their bonds, and have sought a pre-judgment attachment of all of Jonas' inventory.

1. What can Jonas do? Does it matter if the bondholders who sued hold only 2% of the outstanding bond issue?

2. Would it matter if instead of the bondholders, the dissident creditors were trade creditors (who would otherwise stand to be paid in full if the pre-pack goes through)? If they were disgruntled insiders suing over their severance package?

3. If Jonas just pays the dissident bondholders, what do you think the reaction will be from the other bondholders? The trade creditors?

Another risk of a prepackaged plan is that the bankruptcy court will not approve of the pre-filing solicitation. "A proponent of a prepackaged plan takes a substantial risk that, at the confirmation stage of the case, the Court may determine that the proposed disclosure statement or process of solicitation are inadequate." *In re* Colorado Springs Spring Creek Gen. Imp. Dist., 177 B.R. 684, 691 (Bankr. D. Colo. 1995). There is some guidance here, in that most prepackaged plans, to the extent that ask for changes in securities, are subject to federal and state securities laws. Again, *see* 11 U.S.C. § 1125(g).

---

c. Acceptance Before Filing

11 U.S.C. § 1126(b)

(b) For the purposes of subsection (c) and (d) of this section, a holder of a claim or interest that has accepted or rejected the plan before the commencement of the case under this title is deemed to have accepted or rejected such plan, as the case may be, if—

(1) the solicitation of such acceptance or rejection was in compliance with any applicable nonbankruptcy law, rule, or regulation governing the adequacy of disclosure in connection with such solicitation; or

(2) if there is not any such law, rule, or regulation, such acceptance or rejection was solicited after disclosure to such holder of adequate information, as defined in section 1125(a) of this title.

BANKR. R. 3018(b)

Acceptances or Rejections Obtained before Petition

. . . .A holder of a claim or interest who has accepted or rejected a plan before the commencement of the case under the Code shall not be deemed to have accepted or rejected the plan if the court finds after notice and hearing that the plan was not transmitted to substantially all creditors and equity security holders of the same class, that an unreasonably short time was prescribed for such creditors and equity security holders to accept or reject the plan, or that the solicitation was not in compliance with § 1126(b) of the Code.

---

11 U.S.C. § 341(e)

(e) Notwithstanding subsections (a) and (b), the court, on the request of a party in interest and after notice and a hearing, for cause may order that the United States trustee not convene a meeting of creditors or equity security holders if the debtor has filed a plan as to which the debtor solicited acceptances prior to the commencement of the case.

PROBLEM 11-14: "UNPACKING" A PREPACK

D Corp., a retailer, is negotiating a pre-packaged plan. D Corp. is concerned about the impact of bankruptcy on its business operations and is willing to file for Chapter 11 only on "quick-track, pre-pack."

Your client C, a creditor, is opposed to the pre-packaged plan that D Corp. is proposing. It now seems likely that the requisite majorities will accept the plan. What can C do to block ("unpack") the prepackaged plan process?

I. Consensual Confirmation

1. *Overview*

Chapter 11 contemplates not only a vote on the plan by the debtor's creditors and stockholders, but also a review of the plan by the bankruptcy court. A bankruptcy judge has the statutory power to confirm a Chapter 11 plan that has not received the necessary majorities; a bankruptcy judge has the power not to confirm a plan that has been accepted by all holders of claims and interests.

Section 1128 requires the bankruptcy court to hold a hearing on confirmation and give the parties in interest notice of the hearing so that they might raise objections to confirmation. Section 1129 contains the confirmation standards.

Subject to the limited exceptions of section 1129(c) and (d), a plan that has been accepted by every class of claims and interests must be confirmed by the bankruptcy court if the enumerated requirements of paragraph (a) are satisfied.

Absent opposition to the plan, the bankruptcy court's application of section 1129(a) tends to be perfunctory. A common practice is for the plan proponent merely to proffer the testimony of a representative of the debtor affirming compliance with each of the 13 enumerated requirements of section 1129(a). Commonly there are no confirmation problems under section 1129(a). Nonetheless, since we aspire to prepare uncommon lawyers . . .

---

2. *The Basic Consent Requirement: Voting*

11 U.S.C. § 1129(a)(8)

(a) The court shall confirm a plan only if all of the following requirements are met:

. . .

(8) With respect to each class of claims or interests—

(A) such class has accepted the plan; or

(B) such class is not impaired under the plan.

Section 1129(a)(8) is one of the thirteen mandatory confirmation requirements, and in some respects it is the most important. It requires that, to confirm a plan consensually, each class of creditors must accept the plan.

---

a. The Standard for Voting: The Math of Counting Votes

Section 1126(c) and section 1126(d) deal with the questions of how many creditors and how many shareholders must accept the plan. Please read these provisions. Note that section 1126 focuses on classes of claims and classes of interests. Section 1126 does *not* require that each and every member of a class of claims or interests accept a Chapter 11 plan. Under section 1126(c), a class of claims has accepted a plan when more than one-half in number and at least two-thirds in amount of those actually voting on the plan accept the plan. Under section 1126(d), a class of interests (think equity securities) has accepted a plan when two-thirds in amount of those actually voting on the plan accept the plan.

"One-half." "Two-thirds." If you can still do fractions (½, ⅔), you can do the math of counting acceptances under section 1126.

---

11 U.S.C. § 1126(c), (d)

(c) A class of claims has accepted a plan if such plan has been accepted by creditors, other than any entity designated under subsection (e) of this section, that hold at least two-thirds in amount and more than one-half in number of the allowed claims of such class held by creditors, other than any entity designated under subsection (e) of this section, that have accepted or rejected such plan.

(d) A class of interests has accepted a plan if such plan has been accepted by holders of such interests, other than any entity designated under subsection (e) of this section, that hold at least two-thirds in amount of the allowed interests of such class held by holders of such interests, other than any entity designated under subsection (e) of this section, that have accepted or rejected such plan.

PROBLEM 11-15: MEANS AND METHODS OF VOTING

1. Flintco has ten unsecured creditors, each of which is owed $10 (for a total debt of $100). They are all classified together for purposes of Flintco's plan. Does the class accept or reject the plan under the following scenarios:

   (a) Five creditors turn in ballots. Three vote in favor of the plan, and two reject it.

(b) Six creditors turn in ballots. Four vote in favor of the plan, and two reject it.

(c) Only one creditor turns in a ballot, and votes in favor of the plan.

(d) No creditor turns in a ballot.

2. Assume the facts in Problem 1, above except now the ten creditors are owed money as follows: Two creditors are owed $30 each, and the remaining eight creditors are owed $5 each (again for a total of $100 in debt). Does the class accept or reject the plan under the following scenarios:

   (a) All creditors turn in ballots. The two creditors holding $30 claims each vote in favor of the plan; all other creditors reject it.

   (b) All creditors turn in ballots. The two creditors holding $30 claims each vote in favor of the plan, as do two creditors holding $5 claims. All other creditors reject it.

   (c) All creditors turn in ballots. All eight creditors owed $5 vote in favor of the plan; the two other creditors reject it.

   (d) All creditors turn in ballots. Seven of the eight creditors owed $5 and one of the creditors owed $30 vote in favor of the plan; the remaining two creditors (one with a $30 claim and one with a $5 claim) vote to reject.

   (e) The following are the only votes cast: One creditor holding a $30 claim votes to accept; one creditor holding a $5 claim votes to reject.

---

b. Approved Claims, Contingent Claims and Voting

11 U.S.C. § 1126(a)

(a) The holder of a claim or interest allowed under section 502 of this title may accept or reject a plan. . . .

STONE HEDGE PROP. V. PHOENIX CAPITAL CORP. (*IN RE* STONE HEDGE PROP.)

191 B.R. 59 (Bankr. M.D. Pa. 1995)

Opinion

Confronting the court are legal issues concerning valuation under Federal Rule of Bankruptcy Procedure 3012 and temporary allowance under Federal Rule of Bankruptcy Procedure 3018. Motions to value the claim and to temporarily allow a claim have been filed by Phoenix Capital Corporation, ("Phoenix"), in conjunction with the presentation of separate plans of reorganization filed by the Debtor as well as Phoenix.

Significantly, Phoenix is the principal secured creditor of the Debtor having filed a proof of claim in the amount of Two Million Five Hundred Ninety-Two Thousand Seven Hundred Eighty-Nine and 36/100 Dollars ($2,592,789.36). The Debtor not only disputes the validity of the claim by way of a separate adversary filed against Phoenix, it vehemently opposes the temporary allowance of Phoenix's claim and a determination that Phoenix's claim is secured to any extent. . . .

A review of the history of the Debtor's relationship with Phoenix would be helpful.

Stone Hedge Properties is a Pennsylvania general partnership organized in 1988 and situate in Wyoming County, Pennsylvania. The principals of Stone Hedge Properties are members of the Kenia family who decided that the best way to maximize the value of their family farm was to convert it into an eighteen-hole golf course. Financing for that endeavor was secured through PNC Bank. Prior to the bankruptcy, the Debtor and PNC Bank agreed that the debt should be restructured but, unfortunately, the restructuring resulted in creating an obligation that the Debtor could not afford to meet on a regular basis.

On June 7, 1993, the Debtor filed for relief under Chapter Eleven of the United States Bankruptcy Code. On June 23, 1993, PNC Bank sold its paper, then representing approximately Two Million Three Hundred Fifty Thousand Dollars ($2,350,000.00) in debt, to Phoenix for a negotiated consideration of One Million Three Hundred Fifteen Thousand Dollars ($1,315,000.00). Principals of Phoenix were former employees of a PNC Bank subsidiary that was servicing the PNC mortgage. Phoenix was formed for the purpose of acquiring distressed assets for investment.

Phoenix maintains that its debt, for plan purposes, should now be valued at the face amount of the mortgage together with accrued interest, attorney's fees and costs. They further maintain that the collateral securing this debt, i.e. the golf course and its equipment, as well as the housing development which abuts Stone Hedge, should be valued at no more than Two Million Eighty Thousand Dollars ($2,080,000.00) in accordance with the testimony of their expert, John Carl Shultz, Jr. This would make Phoenix significantly undersecured. This obviously would have a significant impact on the ability of the Debtor to confirm their plan pursuant to the criteria suggested in the case of *In Re John Hancock Mutual Life Insurance Co., 987 F.2d 154 (3rd Cir. 1993).*

The Debtor argues just as strenuously that the Phoenix claim should not be allowed to any extent because of the inequities apparent from the restructuring of the loan and the subsequent assignment of that loan to an entity composed of former employees of the bank. They further argue that should this court allow the claim to any extent, it should be limited to the consideration paid by Phoenix for the mortgage, i.e. One Million Three Hundred Fifteen Thousand Dollars ($1,315,000.00), and not the actual balance due the mortgage of Two Million Three Hundred Fifty Thousand Dollars ($2,350,000.00).

The Debtor further argues that, regardless of the amount to which Phoenix is allowed, the value of the collateral at issue; the golf course, the land development and the equipment, is Four Million Five Hundred Thousand Dollars to Five Million Dollars ($4,500,000.00 - $5,000,000.00) and, therefore, Phoenix is fully collateralized. . . .

Phoenix has asked that we value their collateral under Federal Rule of Bankruptcy Procedure 3012 and temporarily allow their claim under Federal Rule of Bankruptcy Procedure 3018. The interplay of Code Sections 1126 and 502 typically require adjudication of the Motion for Temporary Allowance in order to afford the creditor some substantive input in the plan adjudication. 11 U.S.C. § 1126(a) indicates that a holder of a claim allowed under Section 502 may accept or reject a plan. Section 502(a) indicates that a claim is deemed allowed unless a debtor objects. A creditor whose claim is objected to is therefore disenfranchised from voting on the plan unless the objection is adjudicated prior to plan voting or a mechanism, such as temporary allowance, is provided for. Since claims litigation is often drawn out, thereby defeating one of the essential purposes of the Code, i.e. expedited and efficient administration of the bankruptcy estate, the bankruptcy rules provide that, for voting purposes only, the court can temporarily allow a claim in such an amount as the "court deems proper".

At the outset, we wish the parties to make no mistake that we are not, at this juncture, dealing with an estimation issue under 11 U.S.C. § 502(c), which appears to confine itself to "contingent or unliquidated" claims for distribution purposes.

In essence, the Phoenix claim is a liquidated claim specific in dollar amount but apparently subject to a contingent and unliquidated counterclaim that may offset Phoenix's claim or, in fact, exceed it. . . .

In conjunction with this dispute between the parties, Phoenix contemporaneously with its Motion for Temporary Allowance, requested that the court value its claim. . . .

Federal Rule of Bankruptcy Procedure 3001(f) indicates that an executed and filed proof of claim constitutes prima facie evidence of the validity and amount of the claim. Nevertheless, the Debtor need only present evidence supporting its objection to shift the burden of proving the claim to the claimant, who bears the ultimate burden of proving the claim. *In Re Rasbury, 141 Bankr. 752, 757 (N.D.Ala. 1992)*. . . .

We view the following factors as critical in considering whether we shall temporarily allow the Phoenix claim and, if allowed, the degree to which we make such allowance: (1) the manner in which the claim was initially scheduled by the Debtor; (2) the proof of claim filed by the creditor; and (3) the objection (adversary counterclaim) of the Debtor.

Since our principal consideration must be an accommodation of the underlying purpose of the Code, we first must identify what that purpose is. "The fundamental purpose of reorganization is to prevent a debtor from going into liquidation, with an attendant loss of jobs and possible misuse of economic resources." *National Labor Relations Board v. Bildisco & Bildisco, 465 U.S. 513, 528, 104 S. Ct. 1188, 1197, 79 L. Ed. 2d 482 (1984)* citing H.R.Rep. No. 95-595, p. 220 (1977).

The statutory scheme advancing the reorganization contemplates that both secured and unsecured creditors will have a "weighted" influence in the eventual program by which a debtor solves its financial dilemma.

Since both the Debtor's plan and the Phoenix plan recognize the possibility that the Phoenix claim would eventually be allowed, we recognize no fundamental concern in temporarily allowing the Phoenix claim to some degree. Additionally, the Debtor recognizes the PNC claim (now held by Phoenix) as undisputed, liquidated and non-contingent in its original schedules. No one, including the Debtor, has argued that there was a lack of consideration for the PNC-Stone Hedge loan. Rather, the Debtor argues that Phoenix should not be allowed to reap an exorbitant profit from its One Million Three Hundred Fifteen Thousand Dollar ($1,315,000.00) investment when it may have benefitted from "insider" information. To a limited degree, and in a context that only permits this court to cursorily examine that issue, the Debtor's point is well-made and there is a possibility that some part of the Phoenix claim will be disallowed.

The courts have long considered that bankruptcy courts were essentially courts of equity and the proceedings in those courts were inherently proceedings in equity. *Pepper v. Litton, 308 U.S. 295, 304, 60 S. Ct. 238, 244, 84 L. Ed. 281 (1939).* Since we sit as a court of equity in passing on the allowance of claims *(Id. at p. 307 and 245),* then necessarily we sit as same in passing on the temporary allowance of claims. While it violates no elemental principal to award a claimant the profits attendant to its good investment, we cannot help but be mindful of the allegations of surreptitious conduct suggested by the Debtor. While such allegations alone are insufficient to deny temporary allowance of the entire claim, it does cause this court to hesitate allowing this claim in a manner never originally contemplated by the parties, i.e. as unsecured. When this bankruptcy was filed, the Debtor posited in its schedules that Phoenix was totally secured. When it filed its chapter eleven plan, it adopted the same premise. When Phoenix proposed its chapter eleven plan, it considered itself fully secured. Presumably, when the prepetition creditors of the Debtor dealt with Stone Hedge, they considered PNC Bank, predecessor of Phoenix, to be fully secured. Although we have yet to consider the valuation of this collateral, we herein conclude that the claim of Phoenix should be temporarily allowed up to the value of its collateral or its debt, whichever is the lesser, and denied for any amount in excess thereof. This would allow Phoenix to vote as a secured creditor, which was their historical posture, but not as an unsecured creditor, a position never anticipated by any party prior to the case. Of course, all parties recognize that the impact of this decision affects only the voting on the plan and is not any indication of the eventual disposition of the pending adversary action between the parties.

Next, we must address the valuation of the collateral. [After reviewing the testimony of various appraisers, the court concluded as follows:]

This discussion allows us to find that the value of the Phoenix collateral, pursuant to its Motion to value same, totals Two Million Five Hundred Sixty-Seven Thousand Dollars ($2,567,000.00). Having already determined to temporarily allow Phoenix's claim as secured up to the value of its collateral or the amount of its debt, whichever is less, and having concluded that insufficient cause has been demonstrated at this juncture to reject the Phoenix proof of claim of Two Million Five Hundred Ninety-Two Thousand Seven Hundred Eighty-Nine and 36/100 Dollars ($2,592,789.36), we conclude that the claim of Phoenix should be temporarily allowed as a secured claim in the total amount of Two Million Five Hundred Sixty-Seven Thousand Dollars ($2,567,000.00). To the extent that this renders the balance of their claim, i.e. Twenty-Five Thousand Seven Hundred Eighty-Nine and 36/100 Dollars ($25,789.36), unsecured, the court will deny the Motion to temporarily allow any part of Phoenix's claim as unsecured for the reasons enunciated earlier in this opinion. . . .

Furthermore, since we temporarily conclude that Phoenix is not over-collateralized, they have shown no entitlement to accruing interest on their claim at this juncture. We accordingly issue the preliminary injunction without any requirement by Stone Hedge to make regular payments to Phoenix. . . .

---

c. Presumptive Consent: Nonimpairment

11 U.S.C. § 1126(f)

(f) Notwithstanding any other provision of this section, a class that is not impaired under a plan, and such holder of a claim or interest of such class, are conclusively presumed to have accepted the plan, and solicitation of acceptances with respect to such class from the holders of claims or interests of such class is not required.

PROBLEM 11-16: VOTES FROM NON-IMPAIRED CLASSES

Many prepacked plans leave the claims of trade creditors unimpaired; that is, they do not seek to alter the legal, equitable or contractual rights of such creditors. Given Section 1126(f), what is the advantage of that tactic?

This, however, raises the question as to what "impairment" is. Read on . . .

---

d. The Alternate Consent Requirement: "Nonimpairment"

11 U.S.C. § 1124

[A] class of claims or interests is impaired under a plan unless, with respect to each claim or interest of such class, the plan—

(1) leaves unaltered the legal, equitable, and contractual rights to which such claim or interest entitles the holder of such claim or interest; or

(2) notwithstanding any contractual provision or applicable law that entitles the holder of such

claim or interest to demand or receive accelerated payment of such claim or interest after the occurrence of a default—

(A) cures any such default that occurred before or after the commencement of the case under this title, other than a default of a kind specified in section 365(b)(2) of this title;

(B) reinstates the maturity of such claim or interest as such maturity existed before such default;

(C) compensates the holder of such claim or interest for any damages incurred as a result of any reasonable reliance by such holder on such contractual provision or such applicable law; and

(D) does not otherwise alter the legal, equitable, or contractual rights to which such claim or interest entitles the holder of such claim or interest.

PROBLEM 11-17: APPLYING IMPAIRMENT

1. All of the claims in Class 3 of X Co.'s plan are based on notes, payable over 10 years at 6% interest. The plan proposes to pay Class 3 claims over 3 years at 6.5% interest. Are Class 3 claims impaired under section 1124?

2. The claim in Class 2 is a 20-year note, secured by Blackacre. Prior to filing for Chapter 11 relief, the debtor defaulted on this mortgage note. That default triggered an acceleration so that the entire debt is now due and payable and triggered a default interest rate of 11%. What does the plan have to provide in order for Class 2 to be not impaired under section 1124?

3. The claims in Class 4 are unsecured claims by vendors If the plan provides for payment in full of Class 4 within 30 days of the effective date, is Class 4 impaired? Is it relevant that Chapter 11 debtor could have paid Class 4 on the effective date — that any impairment is "artificial"?

---

e. Presumptive Dissent: Elimination of Interest

Insolvency for a corporate debtor generally means that, if the debtor's assets were all sold, there would not be sufficient proceeds to pay all creditors, let alone any equity holders. In short, the equity interests are 'out of the money.' But if a plan recognizes the consequences of insolvency, and eliminates all equity interests, should those equity interests be allowed to vote on the plan? See below.

---

11 U.S.C. § 1126(g)

(g) Not withstanding any other provision of this section, a class is deemed not to have accepted a plan if such plan provides that the claims or interests of such class do not entitle the holders of such claims or interests to receive or retain any property under the plan on account of such claims or interests.

---

f. Voting in Good Faith

Creditors usually vote according to their economic self-interest, and that assumption is built into section 1126(c)'s test for whether a class has accepted. But what if they don't? What if the creditor irrationally hates the debtor's management? What if the creditor is a competitor who would love nothing less than the economic death of the debtor?

---

11 U.S.C. § 1126(e)

(e) On request of a party in interest, and after notice and a hearing, the court may designate any entity whose acceptance or rejection of such plan was not in good faith, or was not solicited or procured in good faith or in accordance with the provisions of this title.

FIGTER LTD. V. TEACHERS INS. & ANNUITY ASS'N (*IN RE* FIGTER LTD.)

118 F.3d 635 (9th Cir. 1997)

FERNANDEZ, Circuit Judge:

Figter Limited, a Chapter 11 debtor and owner of Skyline Terrace, an apartment complex, appeals from the district court's affirmance of the bankruptcy court's decision that Teachers Insurance and Annuity Association of America (Teachers), the holder of a $15,600,000 promissory note secured by a first deed of trust on Skyline Terrace, bought twenty-one unsecured claims in good faith and that it could vote each one separately. We affirm.

BACKGROUND

Figter filed a voluntary petition under Chapter 11 of the Bankruptcy Code. It owns Skyline Terrace, a 198-unit residential apartment complex located in Los Angeles. Teachers is a creditor. It holds a $15,600,000 promissory note executed by Figter. The note is secured by a first deed of trust on Skyline Terrace and by $1,400,000 of cash on hand. In fact, Teachers is Figter's only secured creditor and is the only member of Class 2 in a reorganization plan proposed by Figter. The plan contemplates full payment of Teachers' secured claim, but at a disputed rate of interest. Thus, under Figter's plan, Teachers' claim is not impaired. The plan calls for the impairment of Class 3 unsecured claims by payment at only 80% of their face value.

Teachers has opposed Figter's reorganization plan from its inception because, among other things, that plan contemplates the conversion of Skyline Terrace Apartments into condominiums, with payment to and partial releases by Teachers as the units sell. That could easily result in a property that was part condominium and part rentals, if the plan ultimately fails in operation.

[After the court found that Teachers' claim was fully secured,] Teachers purchased twenty-one of the thirty-four unsecured claims in Class 3 at one hundred cents on the dollar, for a total purchase price of $14,588.62. Teachers had made the same offer to all of the Class 3 claim holders, but not all accepted it. The offer remained open. . . . As a result, Figter's plan is unconfirmable because it is unable to meet the requirements of 11 U.S.C. § 1129(a)(10); there will not be an impaired, consenting class of claims. That will preclude a "cram down" of Teachers' secured claim under 11 U.S.C. § 1129(b). Figter has appealed in an attempt to avoid that result. . . .

DISCUSSION

Figter asserts that Teachers should be precluded from voting its purchased Class 3 claims because it did not buy them in good faith. Figter also asserts that even if the claims were purchased in good faith, Teachers cannot vote them separately, but is limited to one total vote as a Class 3 creditor. If Figter were correct in either of its assertions, it could obtain Class 3 approval of its plan and enhance its chances of cramming down Teachers' Class 2 claims. But Figter is not correct.

A. *Good Faith.*

The Bankruptcy Code provides that "on request of a party in interest, and after notice and a hearing, the court may designate any entity whose acceptance or rejection of [a] plan was not in good faith, or was not solicited or procured in good faith or in accordance with the provisions of this title." 11 U.S.C. § 1126(e). In this context, designate means disqualify from voting. The Bankruptcy Code does not further define the rather murky term "good faith." That job has been left to the courts.

The Supreme Court brought some clarity to this area when it decided *Young v. Higbee Co.*, 324 U.S. 204, 65 S. Ct. 594, 89 L. Ed. 890 (1945). In *Young,* the Court was discussing the predecessor to § 1126(e) when it declared that if certain persons "had declined to accept [the] plan in bad faith, the court, under section 203 could have denied them the right to vote on the plan at all." *Id.* at 210-11, 65 S. Ct. at 598 (footnote omitted). It went on to explain that the provision was intended to apply to those "whose selfish purpose was to obstruct a fair and feasible reorganization in the hope that someone would pay them more than the ratable equivalent of their proportionate part of the bankrupt assets." *Id.* at 211, 65 S. Ct. at 598. In other words, the section was intended to apply to those who were not attempting to protect their own proper interests, but who were, instead, attempting to obtain some benefit to which they were not entitled. *See also Insinger Machine Co. v. Federal Support Co. (In re Federal Support Co.),* 859 F.2d 17, 19 (4th Cir. 1988). While helpful, those reflections by the Court do not fully answer the question before us. Other courts have further illuminated the area.

If a person seeks to secure some untoward advantage over other creditors for some ulterior motive, that will indicate bad faith. *See In re Marin Town Ctr.,* 142 B.R. 374, 378-79 (N.D. Cal. 1992). But that does not mean that creditors are expected to approach reorganization plan votes with a high degree of altruism and with the desire to help the debtor and their fellow creditors. Far from it.

> If a selfish motive were sufficient to condemn reorganization policies of interested parties, very few, if any, would pass muster. On the other hand, pure malice, "strikes" and blackmail, and the purpose to destroy an enterprise in order to advance the interests of a competing business, all plainly constituting bad faith, are motives which may be accurately described as ulterior.

In re Pine Hill Collieries Co., 46 F. Supp. 669, 671 (E.D. Pa. 1942). That is to say, we do not condemn mere enlightened self interest, even if it appears selfish to those who do not benefit from it. *See id.*

Thus, if Teachers acted out of enlightened self interest, it is not to be condemned simply because it frustrated Figter's desires. That is true, even if Teachers purchased Class 3 claims for the very purpose of blocking confirmation of Figter's proposed plan. See 255 Park Plaza Assocs. Ltd. Partnership v. Connecticut General Life Ins. Co. (In re 255 Park Plaza Assocs. Ltd. Partnership), 100 F.3d 1214, 1218-19 (6th Cir. 1996). That self interest can extend even further without being an ulterior motive. It has been held that a creditor commits no wrong when he votes against a plan of a debtor who has a lawsuit pending against the creditor, for that will not, by itself, show bad faith. *See Federal Support Co.,* 859 F.2d at 20; *see also In re A.D.W., Inc.,* 90 B.R. 645, 651 (Bankr. D. N.J. 1988); *In re Landau Boat Co.,* 8 B.R. 432, 436 (Bankr. W.D. Mo. 1981). It has also been held that no bad faith is shown when a creditor chooses to benefit his interest as a creditor as opposed to some unrelated interest. *See In re Landing*

Assocs., Ltd., 157 B.R. 791, 803 (Bankr. W.D. Tex. 1993); *In re Peter Thompson Assocs., Inc.,* 155 B.R. 20, 22 (Bankr. D. N.H. 1993). And the mere fact that a creditor has purchased additional claims for the purpose of protecting his own existing claim does not demonstrate bad faith or an ulterior motive. "As long as a creditor acts to preserve what he reasonably perceives as his fair share of the debtor's estate, bad faith will not be attributed to his purchase of claims to control a class vote." *In re Gilbert,* 104 B.R. 206, 217 (Bankr. W.D. Mo. 1989).

Courts, on the other hand, have been sensitive to situations where a company, which was not a preexisting creditor, has purchased a claim for the purpose of blocking an action against it. They have seen that as an indication of bad faith. *See In re Keyworth,* 47 B.R. 966, 971-72 (Bankr. D. Colo. 1985). The same has been true where creditors were associated with a competing business and desired to destroy the debtor's business in order to further their own. *See In re MacLeod Co., Inc.,* 63 B.R. 654, 655 (Bankr. S.D. Ohio 1986); *see also In re Allegheny Int'l, Inc.,* 118 B.R. 282, 289 (Bankr. W.D. Pa. 1990). And when the debtor had claims against itself purchased by an insider or affiliate for the purpose of blocking a plan, or fostering one, that was seen as a badge of bad faith. *See In re Holly Knoll Partnership,* 167 B.R. 381, 389 (Bankr. E.D. Pa. 1994) (fostering); *In re Applegate Property, Ltd.,* 133 B.R. 827, 834-35 (Bankr. W.D. Tex. 1991) (blocking). Figter would have us add that in a single asset bankruptcy, claim purchasing activities, like those of Teachers, are in bad faith. It cites no authority for that, and we see no basis for establishing *that* as a per se rule.

In short, the concept of good faith is a fluid one, and no single factor can be said to inexorably demand an ultimate result, nor must a single set of factors be considered. It is always necessary to keep in mind the difference between a creditor's self interest as a creditor and a motive which is ulterior to the purpose of protecting a creditor's interest. Prior cases can offer guidance, but, when all is said and done, the bankruptcy court must simply approach each good faith determination with a perspicacity derived from the data of its informed practical experience in dealing with bankrupts and their creditors.

Here, the bankruptcy court did exactly that. It decided that Teachers was not, for practical purposes, the proponent of an alternate plan when it sought to purchase the Class 3 claims. Nor, it found, did Teachers seek to purchase a small number of claims for the purpose of blocking Figter's plan, while injuring other creditors, even if it could do that in some circumstances. Rather, Teachers offered to purchase all Class 3 claims, and only some of those claimants' refusals to sell precluded it from doing so. Moreover, Teachers was a lender, not a competing apartment owner. It acted to protect its interests as Figter's major creditor. It reasonably feared that it could be left with a very complex lien situation, if Figter went forward with its plan. Instead of holding a lien covering the whole of the property, it could have wound up with separate fractured liens on various parts of the property, while other parts were owned by others. That could create a very undesirable mix of owners and renters and of debtors and nondebtors. Added to that was the actual use of cash, which was collateral for the debt owed to Teachers. It cannot be said that Teachers' concerns were irrational.

Based on all that was before it, the bankruptcy court decided that in this case Teachers was a creditor which acted in a good faith attempt to protect its interests and not with some ulterior motive. We cannot say that it erred in making that ultimate determination.

B. *Voting.*

Figter's fallback position is that even if Teachers did act in good faith, it must be limited to one vote for its twenty-one claims. That assertion is answered by the language of the Bankruptcy Code, which provides that:

> A class of claims has accepted a plan if such plan has been accepted by creditors . . . . that hold at least two-thirds in amount and *more than one-half in number of the allowed claims* of such class held by creditors . . . that have accepted or rejected such plan.

11 U.S.C. § 1126(c) (emphasis added). That language was interpreted in *Gilbert,* 104 B.R. at 211, where the court reasoned:

> The formula contained in Section 1126(c) speaks in terms of the *number of claims,* not the number of creditors, that actually vote for or against the plan. . . . Each claim arose out of a separate transaction, evidencing separate obligations for which separate proofs of claim were filed. Votes of acceptance . . . are to be computed only on the basis of filed and allowed proofs of claim. . . . [The creditor] is entitled to one vote for each of his unsecured Class X claims.

That same view was iterated in *Concord Square Apartments of Wood Cty, Ltd. v. Ottawa Properties, Inc. (In re Concord Square Apartments of Wood Cty., Ltd.),* 174 B.R. 71, 74 (Bankr. S.D. Ohio 1994), where the court held that a creditor with "multiple claims, has a voting right for each claim it holds." We agree. It would not make much sense to require a vote by creditors who held "more than one-half in number of the allowed claims" while at the same time limiting a creditor who held two or more of those claims to only one vote. If allowed claims are to be counted, they must be counted regardless of whose hands they happen to be in. . . .

Of course, that is not to say that a creditor can get away with splitting one claim into many, but that is not what happened here. Teachers purchased a number of separately incurred and separately approved claims (each of which carried one vote) from different creditors. There simply is no reason to hold that those separate votes suddenly became one vote, a result which would be exactly the opposite of claim splitting.

Therefore, the bankruptcy court did not err.

CONCLUSION

Figter hoped to obtain approval of a reorganization plan, which would require Teachers to thole what it saw as a diminution of its creditor's rights. Those hopes were dashed when Teachers bought up most of the Class 3 claims in an effort to protect its own Class 2 claim. Because the bankruptcy court determined that Teachers acted to protect its valid creditor's interest, rather than for ulterior motives, it held that Teachers had acted in good faith. That precluded designation of Teachers' purchased claims. The bankruptcy court also determined that Teachers could vote each of its twenty-one claims separately; it was not limited to a single vote. The district court affirmed those decisions. Because the bankruptcy court did not err in either its factual or its legal determinations, we agree with the district court and affirm the decision.

AFFIRMED.

QUESTIONS ABOUT *FIGTER*

1. What facts were important to the bankruptcy court's decision? Was it important that "Teachers did not pursue its plan"? That Teachers offered to purchase all Class 3 claims?

2. The leading case disallowing the vote of purchased claims is *In re* Allegheny International, Inc., 118 B.R. 282 (Bankr W.D. Pa. 1990). In *Allegheny*, Japonica Partners, a coalition of investment bankers who were not prepetition creditors of the debtor, purchased enough claims to block the debtor's plan and thereby open the way for confirmation of its own competing plan. Japonica's plan contemplated converting its purchased debt into a controlling stock interest in the debtor. The bankruptcy court held that Japonica's votes rejecting the debtor's plan were cast in bad faith. Is *Figter* distinguishable from *Allegheny*? *See generally* Lawrence B. Gutcho & David A. Fidler, *Purchasing Claims to Block Bankruptcy Cramdown Plans: A New Weapon For Creditors*, 115 BANKING L.J. 4 (1998).

---

3. *The Other Primary Confirmation Requirements*

a. Good Faith

11 U.S.C. § 1129(a)(3)

(a) The court shall confirm a plan only if all of the following requirements are met: . . . .

> (3) The plan has been proposed in good faith and not by any means forbidden by law.

IN RE DOW CORNING CORP.
244 B.R. 673 (Bankr. E.D. Mich. 1999)

AMENDED OPINION ON GOOD FAITH

ARTHUR J. SPECTOR, Chief Judge.

The Debtor and the Official Committee of Tort Claimants negotiated and on November 9, 1998 filed a Joint Plan of Reorganization. . . . [On July 30, 1999], the Court issued its Findings of Fact and Conclusions of Law on the matter of the confirmation of the Plan. This opinion is one of several which will serve to supplement and explicate some of the findings and conclusions. . . .

A number of parties objected to confirmation of the Plan on the ground that the Proponents failed to satisfy the requirements of § 1129(a)(3). For the reasons which follow, the Court finds that the Plan was filed in good faith and not by any means forbidden by law.

The Bankruptcy Code does not define the term "good faith." Courts have taken a variety of approaches when applying it. *See Tenn-Fla Partners v. First Union National Bank of Florida,* 229 B.R. 720, 734 (W.D.Tenn.1999) (explaining three different approaches). This is not surprising, however, for it is difficult to place precise boundaries around such a fuzzy concept. *Laguna Assoc. Ltd. Partnership v. Aetna Cas. & Surety Co.* (*In re Laguna Assoc. Ltd. Partnership*), 30 F.3d 734, 738 (6th Cir.1994)("[G]ood faith is an amorphous notion, largely defined by factual inquiry." (quoting *In re Okoreeh-Baah,* 836 F.2d 1030, 1033 (6th Cir.1988)).

Several courts borrow the concept of good faith from jurisprudence under §§ 362(d)(1) and 1112(b) of the Bankruptcy Code. Those sections focus primarily on the debtor's pre-petition conduct. By the time a case reaches the plan confirmation stage, pre-petition behavior is largely irrelevant. Instead, when considering whether a plan satisfies the § 1129(a)(3) requirement, the focus of the court must be on the plan itself. *In re Madison Hotel Assoc.,* 749 F.2d 410, 425 (7th Cir.1984). This issue is whether the plan "will fairly achieve a result consistent with the objectives and purposes of the Bankruptcy Code." *Id.* . . .

One court explained the rationale for this standard this way:

> [§ 1129(a)(3)] reads as follows: "The court shall confirm a plan only if all of the following requirements are met: (3) The plan has been *proposed* in good faith and not by any means forbidden by law." 11 U.S.C. § 1129(a)(3) (emphasis added). Thus, it is the plan's *proposal* which must be (a) in good faith and (b) not by a means forbidden by law.
>
> T]he purpose of 1129(a)(3) was to insure that the *proposal* of a plan of reorganization was to be done in good faith and not in a way that was forbidden by law. Indeed one commentator, in comparing Section 1129(a)(3) with its predecessor sections under the Bankruptcy Act, has indicated that the focus of 1129(a)(3) is upon the conduct manifested in obtaining the confirmation votes of a plan of reorganization and not necessarily on the substantive nature of the plan.

In re Sovereign Group, 1984-21 Ltd., 88 B.R. 325, 328 (Bankr.D.Colo.1988) (citing 5 *Collier on Bankruptcy* ¶ 1129.02 (15th ed.1984)). . . .

Moreover, in our view, placing the amorphous concept of good faith outside the confines of all of the other elements for confirmation of the plan, even outside § 1129(b)'s cramdown requirements, is intended to allow courts to utilize their gut feeling about a plan's effects:

> We have always been reluctant to seize upon "good faith" as an easy way out of confirming a difficult or questionable plan. We believe that a finding of lack of good faith in proposing a plan ought to be extraordinary and should not substitute for careful analysis of other elements necessary for confirmation. Haines, *Good Faith: An Idea Whose Time Has Come and Gone,* Norton Bankruptcy Law Adviser (April 1988). However, we also believe that a court of equity must use all of its senses to determine whether a proposed course is fair and equitable. A bankruptcy judge is more than a pair of ears to hear the argument and a pair of eyes to read the law. Furthermore, the mind, which may tell us intellectually that there is nothing technically "illegal" in a particular course of action, is not always the final arbiter. Sometimes a bankruptcy judge's nose tells him/her that something doesn't smell right and further inquiry is warranted. (Others may call this "common

> sense.") As a human being, a bankruptcy judge may allow the heart to influence a decision even though, as a judge, he/she should beware not to let emotions stand in the way of justice. Sometimes, a bankruptcy judge's stomach may turn, when he/she is preparing to sign a particular judgment or order. This queasiness is reflective of the judge's sense that for some, perhaps inarticulable, reason, it just isn't right to grant the relief requested. In the context of plan confirmation in bankruptcy cases, when this is the way the judge feels, it may be because the plan has not "been proposed in good faith." In short, the reading of the law should be tempered by the judge's sense of equity--what is *just* in the circumstances of the case. If there are objective facts to support this feeling, perhaps the plan should not be confirmed.

In re John P. Timko et al., No. 87-09318 (unpublished) (Bankr.E.D.Mich. July 22, 1988). For a plan where this test is put to use *see In re Barr,* 38 B.R. 323, 325 (Bankr.E.D.Mich.1984) (Bernstein, J.) ("At this stage the maxim 'be just before being generous' is called to mind. Mr. E. Barr's generosity to his family members would, if approved by this Court, result in a discharge of close to one million dollars of unsecured debts. That is simply unacceptable when for all practical purposes the Debtors continue to manage their same business. No amount of refined (or strained) analysis can still the moral outrage that the Debtors' plan triggers. At some point, a court of equity has to say, no, this cannot be....If 'good faith' is to have any moral significance, the Debtors' plan cannot be found to be deserving of that appellation."). Thus, courts frequently do and ought to reject sloppy reliance on good faith to cover all sorts of more specific objections covered by specific confirmation standards.

Applying this standard to facts of the instant case after carefully reviewing the Plan and the entire record, the Court finds that the Proponents of the Plan have met their burden of showing that the Plan was proposed and formulated in "good faith" under § 1129(a)(3). The Plan was proposed in a legitimate effort to rehabilitate a solvent but financially-distressed corporation, besieged by massive pending and potential future product liability litigation against it--an articulated policy objective of chapter 11. A plan proposed as a means to resolve tort liability claims does not violate the § 1129(a)(3) "good faith" confirmation requirement. *See, e.g., In re Johns-Manville Corp.,* 68 B.R. 618, 632 (Bankr.S.D.N.Y.1986). The evidence is clear that the legal costs and logistics of defending the worldwide product liability lawsuits against the Debtor threatened its vitality by depleting its financial resources and preventing its management from focusing on core business matters. *See In re Dow Corning Corp.,* 211 B.R. 545, 552-553 (Bankr.E.D.Mich.1997). The Debtor "is a real company with real debt, real creditors and a compelling need to reorganize in order to meet these obligations" and is therefore, exactly the type of debtor for which chapter 11 was enacted. *See In re Johns-Manville Corp.,* 36 B.R. 727, 730 (Bankr.S.D.N.Y.1984). As testified by Tommy Jacks, Arthur B. Newman, Scott Gilbert and Ralph Knowles, the Plan was the result of intense arm's-length negotiations between parties represented by competent counsel who were guided by an experienced Court-appointed mediator and the findings and recommendations of highly qualified experts. The Plan incorporates procedures to effectively resolve the multitude of tort claims that drove the Debtor into bankruptcy and will allow the Debtor to emerge from bankruptcy as a viable corporation with the ability to pay its creditors the full amount to which they are entitled, to continue providing a return for its stockholders, to pay taxes to the federal government and to innumerable state and local governments, and to provide jobs for its employees. This is exactly the result envisioned by the drafters of chapter 11.

The Official Committee of Unsecured Creditors ("U/S CC") was among the parties who objected on good-faith grounds. Its arguments are basically no more than attempts to revisit and reargue objections it made to the Plan under other provisions. Its claim that the Plan unjustly enriches the Debtor's shareholders at the expense of the unsecured commercial creditors by not paying them according to their legal entitlements is just another way of arguing that the commercial creditors are entitled to postpetition interest at their contract rate. This issue has already been disposed of in two other opinions by this Court.

Similarly, the U/S CC's § 1129(a)(3) objection, based on the allegedly improper so-called "third-party releases" is and will be more appropriately addressed and disposed of in another separate opinion of the Court.

Likewise, the U/S CC's § 1129(a)(3) objection based on the Plan's payment of allegedly invalid and unenforceable claims merely reiterated the arguments it made under its § 502(b) objection. That objection was overruled in yet another separate opinion.

Like the other objections, the U/S CC's fourth and fifth objections, arguing that the process by which the Plan was formulated and proposed was "inequitable, unconscionable and impermissible" and that the Plan "contains inequitable, unconscionable and impermissible terms and conditions" rely on arguments made in support of objections under §§ 1129(a)(1), (2), and (7), as well as other arguments that were separately decided by the Court, and will be discussed in greater detail in an opinion to be released in the future. In essence, the U/S CC argues that the Plan as formulated and proposed is inequitable because it treats the unsecured commercial creditors less favorably than a previous plan by not paying them postpetition interest at their contract rate. This objection was sustained in this Court's opinion on cramdown of Class 4 and is rendered moot by the Plan's self-correcting mechanism. Moreover, the "good-faith" determination under § 1129(a)(3) is to be made with regard only to the plan proposed to be confirmed and without regard to any prior plans. *See In re Sound Radio, Inc.,* 93 B.R. 849, 854 (Bankr.D.N.J.1988), *aff'd in part and remanded in part on other grounds,* 103 B.R. 521 (D.N.J.1989), *aff'd* 908 F.2d 964 (3rd Cir.1990) ("The plain meaning of § 1129(a)(3) has nothing to do with prior plans, but rather with the plan which is presently before the court.").

Therefore, because the Court has disposed of all the U/S CC's objections on which its § 1129(a)(3) objection is based, and because the Plan advances the policy objectives of chapter 11, § 1129(a)(3) is satisfied.

McCormick v. Banc One Leasing Corp. (*In re McCormick*)

49 F.3d 1524 (11th Cir. 1995)

Before Anderson and Carnes, Circuit Judges, and Roney, Senior Circuit Judge.

PER CURIAM:

The debtor appeals the denial of his Chapter 11 reorganization plan for lack of good faith in an order which simply stated that "The Debtor's invocation of his Fifth Amendment privilege in connection with this case demonstrates that the Plan of Reorganization was not filed in good faith." The debtor had invoked the Fifth Amendment and refused to testify in a related adversary proceeding. The district court affirmed without opinion. This appeal comes without the benefit of a brief from the appellee.

On the simple issue presented by this appeal, we hold that the debtor's assertion of the Fifth Amendment in a related adversary proceeding, standing alone, when all other aspects of his Chapter 11 Plan of Reorganization are consistent with the goals of the Bankruptcy Code, is not sufficient evidence of bad faith to merit the denial of his plan.

In order to be confirmed, a Chapter 11 reorganization plan must be submitted in good faith and not by any means forbidden by law. 11 U.S.C. § 1129(a)(3). While the Bankruptcy Code does not define the term, courts have interpreted "good faith" as requiring that there is a reasonable likelihood that the plan will achieve a result consistent with the objectives and purposes of the Code. *In re Block Shim Development Company-Irving,* 939 F.2d 289, 292 (5th Cir.1991); *In re Madison Hotel Associates,* 749 F.2d 410, 425 (7th Cir.1984); *In re Coastal Cable T.V., Inc.,* 709 F.2d 762, 764-65 (1st Cir.1983) (in corporate reorganization, plan must bear some relation to statutory objective of resuscitating a financially troubled company).

Where the plan is proposed with the legitimate and honest purpose to reorganize and has a reasonable hope of success, the good faith requirements of section 1129(a)(3) are satisfied. *Kane v. Johns-Manville Corp.,* 843 F.2d 636, 649 (2nd Cir.1988); *In re Sun Country Development, Inc.,* 764 F.2d 406, 408 (5th Cir.1985); *In re Mulberry Phosphates, Inc.,* 149 B.R. 702, 707 (Bankr.M.D.Fla.1993).

The focus of a court's inquiry is the plan itself, and courts must look to the totality of the circumstances surrounding the plan, *Block Shim,* 939 F.2d at 292; *Madison Hotel,* 749 F.2d at 425, keeping in mind the purpose of the Bankruptcy Code is to give debtors a reasonable opportunity to make a fresh start. *Sun Country,* 764 F.2d at 408.

Other than the debtor's refusal to testify in a related adversary proceeding, the totality of the circumstances surrounding Timothy McCormick's proposed reorganization plan would seem to negate any specific showing of bad faith. McCormick, who filed an individual, voluntary petition for relief under Chapter 11 of the Bankruptcy Code, complied with all necessary financial and other disclosure requirements. McCormick timely filed the required schedules and statement of financial affairs, and he testified at the meeting of creditors. The bankruptcy court approved the disclosure statement. The debtor secured the necessary number of the ballots by creditors in favor of the plan.

McCormick proposed to distribute approximately $23,000 to his creditors along with another $200 per month for 36 months. Apparently, McCormick could have filed a Chapter 7 petition, liquidating all his assets and obtaining a discharge, leaving his creditors in worse condition than under the Chapter 11 plan.

There is no doubt that the Fifth Amendment privilege extends to bankruptcy proceedings. *McCarthy v. Arndstein,* 266 U.S. 34, 45 S.Ct. 16, 69 L.Ed. 158 (1924). In Chapter 7 liquidation cases, the Bankruptcy Code provides that absent a grant of immunity, the debtor is free to invoke his Fifth Amendment privilege and still receive a discharge from his debts. 11 U.S.C. § 727(a)(6)(B); *In re Martin-Trigona,* 732 F.2d 170 (2nd Cir.), *cert. denied,* 469 U.S. 859, 105 S.Ct. 191, 83 L.Ed.2d 124 (1984).

The Bankruptcy Code does not dictate nor have we found any other court to have held that a bankruptcy court may deny confirmation of a reorganization plan solely because the debtor refused to testify on the basis of the privilege against self-incrimination in a related proceeding during the pendency of a Chapter 11 case.

While his case was proceeding, one of McCormick's creditors, First Interstate Credit Alliance, Inc., filed a separate adversary proceeding against McCormick seeking to declare a debt non-dischargeable under section 523 of the Code. During a related deposition, McCormick asserted his Fifth Amendment privilege against self-incrimination and refused to testify. Notably, McCormick and First Interstate later agreed to a compromise on the dispute. The bankruptcy court entered an order approving the compromise. Prior to the final confirmation hearing, after McCormick filed the necessary disclosure statement and proposed reorganization plan, three creditors, Advanta Leasing Corporation, Banc One Leasing Corporation, and First Interstate, filed objections to the confirmation claiming McCormick's plan was not proposed in good faith, as required by section 1129(a)(3) of the Bankruptcy Code. Only Advanta cited as its reason for objecting to the plan McCormick's assertion of the Fifth Amendment during the course of the proceedings. The bankruptcy court concluded that McCormick's failure to testify in some of the proceedings was contrary to the goals of the Bankruptcy Code and was evidence he did not propose the plan in good faith.

As long as McCormick's failure to testify at the First Interstate deposition did not impede the basic bankruptcy administration of his case, however, assertion of his Fifth

Amendment privilege alone cannot be the basis for denying confirmation of his plan. *E.g., In re Connelly,* 59 B.R. 421 (Bankr.N.D.Ill.1986).

It may well be that the bankruptcy court may have denied McCormick's confirmation for reasons additional to his refusal to testify in the First Interstate deposition, or that his refusal impeded the administration of the Chapter 11 plan in a way not disclosed by this record. If so, that issue may be addressed on remand. Being unable to find support in this record for the bankruptcy court's finding of bad faith under section 1129(a)(3) of the Bankruptcy Code on the refusal to testify alone, however, we must vacate the decision of the district court and remand for further proceedings consistent with this opinion . . . .

VACATED AND REMANDED.

PROBLEM 11-18: GOOD FAITH AND CONFLICTING ALLEGIANCES

Before it filed for chapter 11 bankruptcy, Perris Air, Inc. agreed to its lenders' demands that it bring in a 'workout' specialist to run the company. Frank Bestwin was chosen by the management of Perris Air from a short list of three acceptable persons provided by the lender.

Frank has a deal with Perris Air for compensation that is fair and consistent with other similar air carriers. He also has a deal with the lenders to pay him a $1 million "success fee" upon confirmation of any plan in which the lenders are paid in full.

Frank develops such a plan. The unsecured creditors' committee does not care for it. Do they have a valid objection under 11 U.S.C. § 1129(a)(3)?

---

b. The Chapter 7 Test: aka, the "Best Interests of Creditors"

11 U.S.C. § 1129(a)(7)

(a) The court shall confirm a plan only if all of the following requirements are met: . . . .

(7) With respect to each impaired class of claims or interests—

(A) each holder of a claim or interest of such class—

(i) has accepted the plan; or

(ii) will receive or retain under the plan on account, of such claim or interest property of a value, as of the effective date of the plan, that is not less than the amount that such holder would so receive or retain if the debtor were liquidated under chapter 7 of this title on such date; . . . .

IN RE SIERRA-CAL

210 B.R. 168 (Bankr. E.D. Cal. 1997)

OPINION

CHRISTOPHER M. KLEIN, Bankruptcy Judge:

The issue, which appears to be a question of first impression, is whether in plan confirmation proceedings the mandatory disallowance of certain claims pursuant to 11 U.S.C. § 502(d) should be imposed when calculating the hypothetical chapter 7 liquidation required by the "best interests" test.

This court concludes that § 502(d), which mandatorily disallows claims of creditors who received avoidable transfers or who owe the estate, does apply in the "best interests" test analysis under 11 U.S.C. § 1129(a)(7)(A)(ii). A plan of reorganization fails the "best interests" test when it purports to give any value to a creditor who has a claim disallowable under § 502(d) at the expense of creditors and interest holders who are not under a § 502(d) disability and who would receive a distribution in a hypothetical chapter 7 liquidation in which § 502(d) is enforced.

This court further concludes that a plan proponent has an affirmative duty under 11 U.S.C. § 1125 to disclose all known § 502(d) disabilities, even if that means that the plan proponent must confess or inform against affiliates, insiders, and friends.

The confirmation of such a plan, assuming adequate disclosure, could occur only if either: (1) the § 502(d) disability is removed by reversing all avoidable transfers and disgorging all funds owed to the trustee; or (2) all affected creditors and interest holders actually accept the plan.

FACTS

Sierra-Cal is a debtor in possession that operated a hotel ("lodge") in South Lake Tahoe, California, until it was sold for $2,750,000 in a combination of cash and secured notes.

The estate now consists of about $440,000 on deposit in the registry of the court plus the stream of income on $325,000 in secured notes that are payable over ten years.

The first deed of trust, all outstanding taxes, and expenses of sale were previously extinguished by payment through escrow. The plan of reorganization provides for liquidating the remaining debt.

The remaining secured debt is owed to insiders, all of whom have relationships that center about Carl R. Corzan, who is the debtor corporation's president. Corzan, directly and through affiliates and relatives, owns or controls about 91.2 percent of the debtor corporation's shares.

CRC Trust, an affiliate that owns 25.5 percent of the debtor corporation, holds a deed of trust securing a debt of about $293,000. The plan proposes to pay CRC Trust in full from the sale proceeds on deposit in the registry of the court.

SCF, Inc. ("SCF"), another Corzan entity that owns 18.5 percent of the debtor, has two secured claims. One is a junior deed of trust securing a debt of about $223,000 that would be paid $90,000 on the effective date of the plan, with the balance paid over ten years. The other is a personal property security interest on furnishings and equipment securing a debt listed as

$66,000, the outstanding balance of which would be paid on the effective date of the plan.

SCF's personal property security interest is not supported by a financing statement that has been recorded in accordance with Article 9 of the Uniform Commercial Code and, hence, is avoidable under the bankruptcy trustee's "strongarm" power. This debt has also been reduced by more than $28,000 during the course of this chapter 11 case, at least $10,000 of which was paid by the debtor without court authorization and, accordingly, is also avoidable by a bankruptcy trustee as an unauthorized postpetition transfer.

The plan was modified to treat the personal property claim as unsecured after the pertinent facts were disclosed for the first time during Corzan's testimony at the confirmation hearing. The debtor conceded that the security interest could not withstand a trustee's "strongarm" avoiding power and that there had been avoidable postpetition transfers.

Unsecured claims that are not disputed are approximately $7,500. The objecting creditor, a lessee of the debtor whose lease was rejected early in the case, has a disputed unsecured claim in excess of $175,000. The unsecured claims will be paid from a percentage of net revenues in annual payments over a period of seven years with interest at 8 percent.

The various Corzan entities will retain their ownership interests.

DISCUSSION

I.

The initial focus is on § 1129(a)(7), which is an essential element for confirmation of a plan of reorganization that cannot be finessed by a "cram down" under § 1129(b).

The primary method of satisfying § 1129(a)(7) is the "best interests" test prescribed by § 1129(a)(7)(A)(ii) that contrasts the plan distributions with distributions in a hypothetical chapter 7 liquidation. The key issue presented here is the application of the § 502(d) disability in the context of the "best interests" test.

The alternative method of satisfying § 1129(a)(7) with respect to an impaired class is actual acceptance by each creditor who would do better in a chapter 7 liquidation than under a chapter 11 plan.[6]

A

The "best interests" test permits a plan to be confirmed without actual acceptance by each holder of a claim or interest that would be impaired by the plan if each holder "will receive or retain under the plan on account of such claim or interest property of a value, as of the effective date of the plan, that is not less than the amount that such holder would so receive or retain if the debtor were liquidated under chapter 7 of this title on such date." 11 U.S.C. § 1129(a)(7)(A)(ii).

The "best interests" concept is a cornerstone of the theoretical underpinnings of chapter 11. It stands as an "individual guaranty to each creditor or interest holder that it will receive at least as much in reorganization as it would in liquidation." 7 COLLIER ON BANKRUPTCY ¶ 1129.03[7] (Lawrence P. King et al. eds., 15th. ed. rev. 1997) ("COLLIER"); *In re Best Prods. Co.,* 168 B.R. 35, 71-72 (Bankr.S.D.N.Y.1994).

The "best interests" test must be satisfied even with respect to claims that are not eligible to vote because they are contingent or disputed. *Bell Rd. Inv. Co. v. M. Long Arabians (In re M. Long Arabians),* 103 B.R. 211, 216 (9th Cir.BAP 1989).

If a prompt chapter 7 liquidation would provide a better return to particular creditors or interest holders than a chapter 11 reorganization, then a reorganization is inappropriate and a chapter 11 plan should not be confirmed.

Applying the "best interests" test requires the court to conjure up a hypothetical chapter 7 liquidation that would be conducted on the effective date of the plan.

The hypothetical liquidation entails a considerable degree of speculation about a situation that will not occur unless the case is actually converted to chapter 7. It contemplates valuation according to the depressed prices that one typically receives in distress sales. 7 COLLIER ¶ 1129.03[7] [b][iii]. It requires estimation of disputed and contingent claims and of chapter 7 administrative expenses. *Id.* And it requires

[6]Since § 1129(a)(7) applies only to impaired classes, it can be bypassed entirely by leaving the pertinent class unimpaired.

application of the chapter 7 distribution scheme, taking into account such matters as subordinations (11 U.S.C. § 510) and recoveries from general partners (11 U.S.C. § 723) that would be applied in a chapter 7 liquidation. *M. Long Arabians,* 103 B.R. at 216-17. One such matter, as this court now holds, is mandatory disallowance of claims. *See* 7 COLLIER ¶ 1129.03[7][c].

Liquidation value and expenses of administration are less speculative in this instance than in most because the estate has been reduced to $715,000 in notes and cash: two secured notes have a present value of $275,000; $440,000 is on deposit in the registry of the court. After deducting remaining expenses of administration of $40,000, about $675,000 would be available to be distributed to creditors and interest holders.

The total nominal claims are about $768,000, of which the unsecured claims are $182,500, including the $175,000 disputed claim of the objecting creditor that, the court estimates, has a value of $87,500.[11] Thus, for purposes of the hypothetical liquidation, unsecured claims are $95,000 and total nominal secured claims are about $675,000.

The question becomes the order in which claims would be paid in a hypothetical chapter 7 liquidation.

B

Mandatory claim disallowance under § 502(d) is one Bankruptcy Code provision that applies in chapter 7 liquidations. It requires that the court disallow "any claim" of any entity from which property is recoverable by a trustee, or that is the transferee of an avoidable transfer, unless and until the property is turned over and the transfer is paid.

The § 502(d) disallowance is in the nature of an affirmative defense to a proof of claim and does not provide independent authority for affirmative relief against the creditor. *Parker N. Am. Corp. v. Resolution Trust Corp. (In re Parker N. Am. Corp.),* 24 F.3d 1145, 1155 (9th Cir.1994). As an affirmative defense, § 502(d) can even be asserted when an affirmative

---

[11]Estimating the disputed claim for the limited purpose of the "best interests" test's hypothetical liquidation calls for application of straightforward expected value analysis, based on the court's analysis of the record of the case, reflecting a "50-50" likelihood of success on the merits. Specifically, the probability of success is .5. Accordingly, the expected value (Expected Value = Probability x Claim) is .5 x $175,000 = $87,500 . . . .

recovery from the creditor under the pertinent avoiding statute would be time- barred.

Formally, § 502(d) operates as a temporary disability. It is temporary in the sense that the disallowance ceases when the creditor disgorges the property in question. Nevertheless, it can be crippling in at least three respects.

First, the disability is mandatory. The statutory language "the court shall disallow" leaves no latitude for the court once the predicate rights are determined.

Second, while actual adjudication of the avoidance status of the creditor ultimately is necessary, the mere assertion of a prima facie § 502(d) defense is sufficient to place the claim in a status in which it is neither allowed nor disallowed. *See Katchen v. Landy,* 382 U.S. 323, 330, 86 S.Ct. 467, 473, 15 L.Ed.2d 391 (1966) (Bankruptcy Act § 59g).

Third, because the focus is on the creditor and not on the specific claim, a small avoidable transfer may require disallowance of all the creditor's claims, even a large secured claim, until the avoidable transfer is disgorged. *See id.* at 330 n. 5, 86 S.Ct. at 473 n. 5. Thus, in this instance, the two avoidance issues involving the $66,000 personal property interest (defeat of secured status under "strongarm" power and unauthorized postpetition transfers) would also prevent payment on the $323,000 deed of trust.

1

No reported decision appears to focus upon the question whether § 502(d) must be applied when calculating the hypothetical liquidation under the "best interests" test for chapter 11 plan confirmation. Nevertheless, the straightforward language of the Bankruptcy Code makes § 502(d) a provision that affects the distribution scheme in a chapter 7 liquidation.

The description of the hypothetical liquidation in legislative history of § 1129(a)(7)(A)(ii) does not directly mention § 502(d). The legislative history does, however, cite subordinations under § 510 as an example of how the hypothetical liquidation sweeps in the complexities of the chapter 7 liquidation scheme, including the specialized rules regarding partnership and community property distributions. The leading treatises and commentators similarly omit mention of § 502(d). 7 COLLIER ON BANKRUPTCY ¶ 1129.03[7][C]; 4 NORTON BANKRUPTCY LAW & PRACTICE 2D § 92.14

(William L. Norton, Jr. et al. eds.1996); Richard M. Cieri et al., *"The Long and Winding Road": The Standards to Confirm a Plan of Reorganization Under Chapter 11 of the Bankruptcy Code (Part I),* 3 J. BANKR. L. & PRAC. 3, 54 (1993).

But it is generally agreed that all provisions applicable in a chapter 7 liquidation are to be taken into account when the court determines what sums would be paid to whom in a hypothetical liquidation.

If an actual chapter 7 liquidation were to occur on the date of the hypothetical liquidation, it is beyond cavil that a creditor who is under a § 502(d) disability would receive nothing.

Since the central focus of the "best interests" test for plan confirmation is on what would occur in an actual chapter 7 liquidation, this court holds that any applicable § 502(d) disability must be taken into account in the test's hypothetical liquidation.

2

The "best interests" analysis in plan confirmation being hypothetical, it is not necessary (as would be required in an actual liquidation) to adjudicate the creditor's § 502(d) status before imposing the § 502(d) disability.

In computing the hypothetical chapter 7 liquidation, the court is entitled to view the entire record of the case and to engage in rational speculation about what would occur in a chapter 7 liquidation. Among other things, the court can hypothesize that certain claims would evoke the objection of a chapter 7 trustee and can speculate about the likely fate of such objections, bearing in mind the protective purpose of the "best interests" test.

3

The § 502(d) disability applies to SCF on two counts, based upon this court's assessment of the record, for purposes of a hypothetical liquidation.

The testimony of the debtor's principal at the confirmation hearing established that at least $10,000 of estate funds had been used postpetition without authority in partial payment of SCF's $66,000 prepetition claim, which warrants an inference of transfers avoidable under § 549. And the testimony established that SCF's personal property security interest securing the $66,000 claim is unrecorded, which warrants an inference of avoidability pursuant to the trustee's § 544 "strongarm" power.

In a hypothetical liquidation, a competent chapter 7 trustee would be able to recover against SCF under § 544 and § 549. Hence, SCF is subject to the § 502(d) disability for two, independent reasons.

If SCF were not subject to the § 502(d) disability, the unsecured claims would be paid about 56 percent of their total in a chapter 7 liquidation.[18] Since the present value of the payments promised to unsecured creditors would provide payment of between 90 and 100 percent of the unsecured claims, the "best interests" test would have been satisfied in the hypothetical scenario.

SCF, however, is under a § 502(d) disability, which requires that all of its claims be disallowed in the hypothetical chapter 7 liquidation. In consequence, the unsecured claims would be paid in full and would, pursuant to § 726(a)(5), receive interest at the legal rate from the date of the filing of the petition, after which funds would be returned to owners pursuant to § 726(a)(6).

Since the plan does not propose to pay sums that have a present value that reflects interest at the legal rate from the date of the filing of the petition, the "best interests" test is not satisfied when the § 502(d) disability is imposed.

4

The debtor orally modified the plan at the close of the confirmation hearing in an attempt to cure the defect by providing that SCF would be paid the balance on its personal property security interest as an unsecured claim. This modification does not, however, surmount the hurdle.

a

Merely treating the unpaid balance of the personal property security interest as an unsecured claim does not cure the § 502(d) disability for two reasons. First, the avoidable

---

[18] Present value of funds available on liquidation $675,000-- $40,000 expenses of administration--$293,000 CRC secured claim--$223,000 SCF secured real estate claim--$66,000 SCF secured personal property claim = $53,000 available to pay on unsecured claims of $95,000 (55.8%).

underlying security agreement must have been actually revoked in order to comply with § 502(d). Second, the modification does not reverse the unauthorized postpetition transfers that are avoidable under § 549 and that form an independent basis for the § 502(d) disability.

b

Nor does the oral modification enable the plan to pass the "best interests" test under § 1129(a)(7)(A)(ii).

Treating the $66,000 personal property claim as an unsecured claim would mean that $119,000 would be available to pay unsecured claims of $161,000. A dividend of 74 percent is less than the full payment plus interest that unsecured creditors would otherwise receive in the hypothetical liquidation.

The same result would apply if the plan were further modified to treat SCF's real property claim as unsecured. In that event $342,000 would be available to pay claims of $384,000. An 89 percent dividend is still less than full payment plus interest.

Hence, the modification that occurred orally on the record at the confirmation hearing is inadequate.

C

[The court then denied approval of the disclosure statement for failure to provide a liquidation analysis that complied with the above analysis.]

PROBLEM 11-19: THE HOLDOUT

Airtime, Inc. has proposed a chapter 11 plan which pays its unsecured creditors 50¢ on the dollar. 95% of its unsecured creditors, in number and amount, have voted in favor of the plan. The sole negative vote is Delay, Inc., which comes to you for advice. Delay's management shows you a spreadsheet that indicates that if Airtime were liquidated in chapter 7, creditors would receive 55¢

on the dollar. Does Delay have a valid objection to plan confirmation?

What if the 55¢ calculation did not take into account the chapter 7 trustee's 3% fee, which would bring the proposed distribution down to 49%? What if the difference between Delay's calculations and Airtime's calculations is in the present value each places on patent technology owned by Airtime, a technology all agree is at least three years away from producing profits?

---

c. Feasibility

11 U.S.C. § 1129(a)(11)

(a) The court shall confirm a plan only if all of the following requirements are met: . . . .

> (11) Confirmation of the plan is not likely to be followed by the liquidation, or the need for further financial reorganization of the debtor or any successor to the debtor under the plan, unless such liquidation or reorganization is proposed in the plan.

DANNY THOMAS PROP. II LTD PTSHP. V. BEAL BANK, S.S.B. (*IN RE* DANNY THOMAS PROP. II LTD PTSHP.)

241 F.3d 959 (8th Cir. 2001)

Before BEAM and MORRIS SHEPPARD ARNOLD, Circuit Judges, and DOTY, District Judge.

MORRIS SHEPPARD ARNOLD, Circuit Judge.

Danny Thomas Properties II Limited Partnership (DT/II) and Danny Thomas Properties III Limited Partnership (DT/III; collectively, the debtors) each own a portion of the Le Marquis apartment complex in North Little Rock, Arkansas. When the debtors filed separate petitions for relief under the federal bankruptcy laws, *see* 11 U.S.C. §§ 101-1330, Beal Bank, the debtors' primary creditor, objected to their plans of reorganization, *see* §§ 1101-1174.

The bankruptcy court refused to "cram down" the plans, that is, to confirm them over Beal's objections, because the court found that the plans did not establish that future liquidation or further reorganization was unlikely, *see* § 1129(a)(11). *See In re Danny Thomas Properties III Limited Partnership,* 231 B.R. 298, 303-04 (Bankr.E.D.Ark.1999). The district court affirmed the decision of the bankruptcy court, the debtors appealed, and we affirm.

I.

During the late 1980s and early 1990s, the debtors experienced numerous financial difficulties that required them to restructure their loan agreements with the United States Department of Housing and Urban Development (HUD), their primary lender at the time. In 1995, Beal purchased the debtors' mortgage loans from HUD. Later that year, the debtors became financially unable to meet their obligations to Beal, and in response to foreclosure proceedings brought by Beal, they petitioned for protection pending reorganization under the federal bankruptcy laws. *See* § 1121(a). The debtors have continued to operate Le Marquis since that time as debtors-in-possession. *See* § 1107(a), § 1108.

The debtors filed reorganization plans that proposed to pay off Beal's claim, currently valued at approximately $2,220,000, based on a 30-year amortization schedule but requiring installment payments for the first 10 years and then a balloon payment for the balance. The plans also described the debtors' strategy for ensuring successful reorganization. As part of that strategy, the debtors proposed to establish maintenance reserve accounts into which each debtor would place $50,000 per year for five years to cover future maintenance costs for Le Marquis.

The debtors also included, however, so-called "drop dead" provisions in their reorganization plans as a secondary guarantor of the plans' success. In these provisions, the debtors consented to the initiation of immediate foreclosure proceedings against Le Marquis should the debtors fail to cure a default within 45 days of receiving notice from Beal of the default. In the event of an ongoing bankruptcy proceeding, moreover, the plans gave Beal the right to obtain an *ex parte* order, *see* § 362(f), granting relief from the automatic stay provisions, *see* § 362(a), of the bankruptcy statutes.

II.

Before a bankruptcy court may "cram down" a reorganization plan over the objections of a creditor, the court must determine that the plan is "fair and equitable," *see* § 1129(b)(1). With respect to a secured creditor, such as Beal, this requirement means that the creditor must receive payments with a present value that equals the value of the secured claim. *See* § 1129(b)(2)(A)(i)(II).

The provision allowing a "cramdown" also requires that the bankruptcy court find that the plan meets various requirements specified in § 1129(a). One of these requirements is a finding by the court that "[c]onfirmation of the plan is not likely to be followed by the liquidation, or the need for further financial reorganization, of the debtor or any successor to the debtor under the plan, unless such liquidation or reorganization is proposed in the plan," *see* § 1129(a)(11). This statutory provision establishes what is commonly known as the "feasibility" requirement, and as a practical matter it requires the court to find that the plan is "workable" before it may be confirmed. *See In re Monnier Brothers,* 755 F.2d 1336, 1341 (8th Cir.1985).

The debtors contend that the "drop dead" provisions make the reorganization plans feasible as a matter of law. They maintain that the "drop dead" provisions amount to liquidations and that because these liquidations are contemplated within the plans, the requirements of § 1129(a)(11) are automatically met. Beal contends that the provisions do not provide for liquidations, as that term is used in the bankruptcy laws, but are merely agreements by the debtors to consent to foreclosure proceedings.

We agree with Beal that the "drop dead" provisions do not amount to liquidations for purposes of § 1129(a)(11). "Liquidation in or out of bankruptcy means the end of a [debtor's] existence," *Maytag Corp. v. Navistar International Transportation Corp.,* 219 F.3d 587, 591 (7th Cir.2000). The "drop dead" provisions here do not contemplate the end of the debtors' existence, but merely allow Beal to foreclose on their primary asset. It is true that foreclosure by Beal would leave the debtors as nearly-empty shells, but the debtors would nonetheless continue to exist and would be free to pursue new opportunities. The "drop dead" provisions are, therefore, more closely akin to clauses that permit a sale of assets, an action that is contemplated by the bankruptcy laws as a proper part of a reorganization plan. *See* § 1123(a)(5)(D); *see also* 7 *Collier on Bankruptcy* ¶ 1123.02[4] (Lawrence P. King ed., 15th ed. rev.2000). Because the provisions offered by the debtors do not provide for liquidations, the language is entitled to no special significance under § 1129(a)(11), and thus the provisions certainly cannot make the reorganization plans feasible as a matter of law.

Even if the "drop dead" provisions amounted to liquidations, we could not accept the debtors' contention that providing for liquidation in the event of a default in a reorganization plan renders a plan feasible as a matter of law. Were we to do so, a bankruptcy court would be required to find that even the most implausible of reorganization plans is feasible so long as the plan provided that the debtor would liquidate if the plan failed. To require the court to confirm a reorganization plan merely because it allows future liquidation would eliminate the courts' duty under § 1129(a)(11) to protect creditors against " 'visionary schemes,' " *In the Matter of Pizza of Hawaii, Inc.,* 761 F.2d 1374, 1382 (9th Cir.1985), quoting what is now 7 *Collier on Bankruptcy* ¶ 1129.03[11] (Lawrence P. King ed., 15th ed. rev.2000). We therefore reject the debtors' contention that their plans are feasible as a matter of law.

We recognize that in certain situations a plan may be rendered feasible by the inclusion of a provision similar to the "drop dead" provisions involved in this case. *See, e.g., In the Matter of 203 North LaSalle Street Partnership,* 126 F.3d 955, 962 (7th Cir.1997), *rev'd on other grounds, Bank of America National Trust and Savings Association v. 203 North LaSalle Street Partnership,* 526 U.S. 434, 437, 458, 119 S.Ct. 1411, 143 L.Ed.2d 607 (1999); *In the Matter of T-H New Orleans Limited Partnership,* 116 F.3d 790, 803-04 (5th Cir.1997); and *In re Nite Lite Inns,* 17 B.R. 367, 370 (Bankr.S.D.Cal.1982). Each of these cases involved a reorganization plan proposing that in the event of a default a particular asset would be sold to cover the creditor's secured claim. Rather than declaring the plans feasible as a matter of law, however, the court in each of these cases examined the facts supporting the plans and found them to be feasible because the liquidation alternative guaranteed payment of the secured claim. These cases thus fail to support the debtors' contention that the inclusion of the "drop dead" provisions makes their plans feasible as a matter of law. The debtors show merely that such provisions are entitled to be considered by a bankruptcy court when evaluating a plan's prospects for success.

III.

Having rejected the argument that the debtors' plans are feasible as a matter of law, we turn to a review of the bankruptcy court's determination that they were in fact not feasible. While a reorganization plan's "[s]uccess need not be guaranteed," *In re Monnier Brothers,* 755 F.2d at 1341, the bankruptcy court cannot approve a plan unless it has at least a reasonable prospect for success. *See id.* With respect to Beal, a secured creditor, the debtors must show, as we have said, that it is reasonably likely that the plan will result in full payment of Beal's secured claim. The debtors bear the burden of establishing the feasibility of their plans by a preponderance of the evidence. *See In re Euerle Farms, Inc.,* 861 F.2d 1089, 1091-92 (8th Cir.1988).

We first address the reorganization plan that DT/III proposed. The bankruptcy court found that in year 1 of the plan DT/III will be responsible for an interest payment to Beal of approximately $169,700, a payment on a claim for past-due management company fees of approximately $4,900, and other miscellaneous claims totaling approximately $24,600, for a total of approximately $199,200. Combining this total with the $50,000 payment, noted earlier, that DT/III promises to make to its maintenance reserve account, the court found that DT/III will need approximately $249,200, at a minimum, in net operating income to meet its obligations. DT/III does not seriously dispute these numbers other than to contend that the plan proposes to make no payments to the management company unless there is sufficient cash flow to do so. While the bankruptcy court questioned whether any management company would work for free, we give DT/III the benefit of the doubt and assume that it would require an approximate total of only $244,300 in net operating income to meet its year 1 obligations.

During the confirmation hearing, DT/III's own expert witness testified that DT/III's net operating income during year 1 would be approximately $196,700 if management fees resulting from year 1 operations were paid, and approximately $221,300 without payment of the fees. Even if we assume that no management fees will be paid, DT/III's projected net operating income is approximately $23,000 less than needed to fund DT/III's plan during the first year. DT/III fails to address this testimony on appeal, but instead cites other projections showing an increase in revenue based upon its belief that both rental and occupancy rates will increase.

Feasibility determinations must be "firmly rooted in predictions based on objective fact," *In re Clarkson,* 767 F.2d 417, 420 (8th Cir.1985). After carefully reviewing the record, however, we believe that DT/III's projections have little basis in anything other than sheer speculation. At the very least, they do not convince us that the bankruptcy court clearly erred in accepting the testimony of DT/III's expert and concluding on the basis of that testimony that DT/III will operate at a deficit during the first year of its reorganization plan.

We also find no error in the bankruptcy court's determination that DT/III will operate at a significant loss throughout the life of its proposed plan. DT/III's initial deficit will prevent it from being able to fund its maintenance reserve account fully, thus limiting its ability to perform the maintenance required to keep the property at its current value. The bankruptcy court concluded that Le Marquis is an aging property that will continue to deteriorate without regular maintenance, a conclusion that the record amply supports. Common sense dictates that the deterioration of the property is likely to have two important effects on the success of DT/III's reorganization plan: First, the property will probably be less attractive to potential tenants, with a resulting decrease in either rental prices or occupancy rates, and, second, as the property deteriorates it will continue to become less valuable as collateral for Beal's claim. These difficulties are likely to be exacerbated in the later years of the plan, for which a finding of feasibility is already much more difficult for a court to make because of the hazards involved in estimating future income. *See* 7 *Collier on Bankruptcy* ¶ 1129.03 [11]. The failure to fund the maintenance reserve accounts fully therefore makes it highly unlikely that DT/III's reorganization plan will succeed.

We do not believe that the "drop dead" provisions of the reorganization plan can save this otherwise infeasible plan, unlike the similar provisions in *203 North LaSalle Street, T-H New Orleans,* and *Nite Lite Inns,* because nothing in the record indicates that Le Marquis will remain more valuable than Beal's secured claim during the life of the plan. While the bankruptcy court did not make a specific finding as to the value of Le Marquis, DT/III's reorganization plan does note that, at this time, a foreclosure sale would not bring an amount greater than the amount of Beal's secured claim. Combining this admission with the bankruptcy court's finding that the property will deteriorate, DT/III becomes unable to show that the execution of the "drop dead" provisions will fully satisfy Beal's claim. We thus detect no error in the bankruptcy court's determination that the plan was not feasible.

DT/II's reorganization plan is virtually identical to DT/III's plan. Since DT/II's plan suffers from the same infirmities as the DT/III plan does, we conclude that the bankruptcy court did not err by finding that DT/II's plan was not feasible.

IV.

For the foregoing reasons, we affirm the judgments of the district court.

Problem 11-20: Factors Affecting Feasibility

1. Dingus Marketing is a real estate development company currently in chapter 11. It has filed a plan and disclosure statement which show that for the 18 months following plan confirmation, reorganized Dingus will lose money. The same projections, however, assume that real estate prices are rising (which seems to be the case), and that they will be able to refinance or sell properties at the 18-month mark to pay any shortfalls. Is the plan feasible? Would it help if the plan gave the secured lenders the absolute right to foreclose in 18-months?

2. Take the facts in #1 above, but now add that the lenders have produced expert testimony that the real estate market will be flat over the next 18 months. Dingus' expert disagrees, and sees at least a 8% annual increase. If both experts are equally credible, has Dingus met its obligation to show feasibility? Just how much better does Dingus' expert have to be?

---

d. Paying Administrative Claims in Full

11 U.S.C. § 1129(a)(9)

(a) The court shall confirm a plan only if all of the following requirements are met: . . . .

(9) Except to the extent that the holder of a particular claim has agreed to a different treatment of such claim, the plan provides that—

(A) with respect to a claim of a kind specified in section 507(a)(1) or 507(a)(2) of this title, on the effective date of the plan, the holder of such claim will receive on account of such claim cash equal to the allowed amount of such claim; . . . , and

(C) with respect to a claim of a kind specified in section 507(a)(8) of this title, the holder of such claim will receive on account of such claim regular installment payments in cash—

(i) of a total value, as of the effective date of the plan, equal to the allowed amount of such claim; and

(ii) over a period ending not later than 5 years after the date of the order for relief under section 301, 302, or 303; and

(iii) in a manner not less favorable than the most favored nonpriority unsecured claim provided for by the plan (other than cash payments made to a class of creditors under section 1122(b)); and

(D) with respect to a secured claim which would otherwise meet the description of an unsecured claim of a governmental unit under section 507(a)(8), but for the secured status of that claim, the holder of that claim will receive on account of that claim, cash payments, in the same manner and over the same period, as prescribed in subparagraph (C).

PROBLEM 11-21: QUESTIONS ABOUT ADMINISTRATIVE PRIORITY

1. Which of the following kinds of claims are covered by Section 507(a)(1), such that Section 1129(a)(9) requires them to be paid in full on the plan's effective date?

   (a) Post-petition trade credit (goods or services bought on credit after the filing)?

   (b) Debtor-in-Possession financing under Section 364?

   (c) Claims of the attorneys for the official committee of creditors holding unsecured claims?

   (d) Claims of the debtor in possession's attorneys?

   (e) Damages payable to third-parties due to an uninsured post-petition fire that destroyed an adjoining building to the debtor in possession's headquarters?

2. Debtor has significant unpaid and unsecured tax claims. May it pay such claims:

   (a) Over a ten-year period?

   (b) Over a three-year period, if it also is paying its general unsecured creditors (by way of a separate class) over five years?

(c) What result in (b) if the plan provides that the unsecured creditor class were to be paid in three years, and the class of tax claims were to be paid in five years?

(d) Does it matter if the tax claim is secured?

(e) May the interest rate on the payout be the general market rate used for all other classes of creditors? *See* 11 U.S.C. § 511.

---

4. *The "Other" Confirmation Requirements*

There are, to be sure, sixteen separate confirmation requirements. Above, we looked at only five — voting, 11 U.S.C. § 1129(a)(8), good faith, 11 U.S.C. § 1129(a)(3), the "best interests" test, 11 U.S.C. § 1129(a)(7), feasibility, 11 U.S.C. § 1129(a)(11), and payment of administrative and tax claims, 11 U.S.C. § 1129(a)(9).

That leaves eleven others. Some of these are specialized, such as Section 1129(a)(6), which requires approval of any regulatory agency with jurisdiction over the debtor. Some are the product of political wrangling for special interests, such as Section 1129(a)(12), which requires the estate to be current in its United States Trustee payments, and Section 1129(a)(13), which requires estates to be current in benefits covered by Section 1114. Others apply only to individuals (paragraphs (14) and (15) and will be discussed later).

Of the remaining seven, four speak directly to public policy concerns. Section 1129(a)(10) requires the consent of at least one impaired, non-insider class.[11] Sections 1129(a)(4) and 1129(a)(5) require disclosure and approval

---

[11]This requirement would seem to be superfluous given Section 1129(a)(8)'s requirement that each class consent, but we will see that paragraph (8)'s requirement can be relaxed in "cramdown," which is explored in the next section.

of compensation paid to plan proponents and those proposed to be post-confirmation management. Section 1129(a)(16) provides that debtors who are non-profit entities may not override nonbankruptcy law restrictions on such entities.

That leaves two – Sections 1129(a)(1) and 1129(a)(2), which require, respectively, that the plan and the plan proponent comply with chapter 11 and title 11. That seems redundant, doesn't it? Doesn't everyone and every plan have to comply with the Code? Well, many hot battles are waged under these sections. How so? Read on.

IN RE DOW CORNING CORP.

280 F.3d 648 (6th Cir.), *cert. denied*, 537 U.S. 816 (2002)

BOYCE F. MARTIN, JR., Chief Circuit Judge.

Years after Dow Corning Corporation filed a petition for reorganization under Chapter 11 of the Bankruptcy Code, and following extensive and vigorous negotiations, the third proposed plan of reorganization for Dow was submitted to the bankruptcy court. The bankruptcy court confirmed the Amended Joint Plan of Reorganization for Dow and the district court affirmed the bankruptcy court's Confirmation Order. Certain claimants who voted against the Plan appealed. The first principal issue presented here is whether a bankruptcy court may enjoin a non-consenting creditor's claims against a non-debtor to facilitate a reorganization plan under Chapter 11 of the Bankruptcy Code. For the following reasons, we AFFIRM the district court's conclusion that, under certain circumstances, a bankruptcy court may enjoin a non-consenting creditor's claim against a non-debtor to facilitate a Chapter 11 plan of reorganization. However, the factual findings of the bankruptcy court do not demonstrate that such an injunction is appropriate in this case. Therefore, we REMAND to the district court.

For nearly thirty years, Dow was the predominant producer of silicone gel breast implants, accounting for almost fifty percent of the entire market. In addition, Dow supplied silicone raw materials to other manufacturers of silicone gel breast implants.

In the 1980s, certain medical studies suggested that silicone gel may cause auto-immune tissue diseases such as lupus, Scleroderma and rheumatoid arthritis. . . . Soon thereafter, tens of thousands of implant recipients sued Dow and its two shareholders, the Dow Chemical Company and Corning, Incorporated, claiming to have been injured by auto-immune reactions to the silicone in their implants. . . . Dow filed a petition for reorganization under Chapter 11 of the Bankruptcy Code. . . .

Under the Plan, a $2.35 billion fund is established for the payment of claims asserted by (1) personal injury claimants, (2) government health care payers, and (3) other creditors asserting claims related to silicone-implant products liability claims. The $2.35 billion fund is established withfunds contributed by Dow's products liability insurers, Dow's shareholders and Dow's operating cash reserves. As a quid pro quo for making proceeds available for the $2.35 billion fund, section 8.3 of the Plan releases Dow's insurers and shareholders from all further liability on claims arising out of settled personal injury claims, and section 8.4 permanently enjoins any party holding a claim released against Dow from bringing an action related to that claim against Dow's insurers or shareholders. Plan §§ 8.3, 8.4. . . .

The bankruptcy court confirmed the Plan, but construed the non-debtor release and injunction provisions to apply only to consenting creditors. Although the bankruptcy court determined that it has authority under the Bankruptcy Code to enjoin a non-consenting creditor's claims against non-debtors, it decided, based on non-bankruptcy law, that such injunctions are inappropriate as applied to non-consenting creditors, and construed the Plan accordingly. The district court affirmed the bankruptcy court's Confirmation Order but reversed the bankruptcy court's interpretation of the release and injunction provisions of the Plan. The district court interpreted the non-debtor release and injunction provisions of the Plan to apply to all creditors, consenting and non-consenting. . . .

The first issue we are asked to decide is whether a bankruptcy court has the authority to enjoin a non-consenting creditor's claims against a non-debtor to facilitate a reorganization plan under Chapter 11 of the Bankruptcy Code. This is a question of first impression in this Circuit.

The Bankruptcy Code does not explicitly prohibit or authorize a bankruptcy court to enjoin a non-consenting creditor's claims against a non-debtor to facilitate a reorganization plan. However, bankruptcy courts, "as courts of equity, have broad authority to modify creditor-debtor relationships." United States v. Energy Resources Co., 495 U.S. 545, 549, 110 S.Ct. 2139, 109 L.Ed.2d 580 (1990). For example, section 105(a) of the Bankruptcy Code grants a bankruptcy court the broad authority to issue "any order, process, or judgment that is necessary or appropriate to carry out the provisions of this title." 11 U.S.C. § 105(a). This section grants the bankruptcy court the power to take appropriate equitable measures needed to implement other sections of the Code.

Consistent with section 105(a)'s broad grant of authority, the Code allows bankruptcy courts considerable discretion to approve plans of reorganization. Energy Resources Co., 495 U.S. at 549, 110 S.Ct. 2139. Section 1123(b)(6) permits a reorganization plan to "include any ... appropriate provision not inconsistent with the applicable provisions of this title." 11 U.S.C. § 1123(b)(6). Thus, the bankruptcy court, as a forum for resolving large and complex mass litigations, has substantial power to reorder creditor-debtor relations needed to achieve a successful reorganization. For example, under the doctrine of marshaling of assets, "[t]he bankruptcy court has the power to order a creditor who has two funds to satisfy his debt to resort to the fund that will not defeat other creditors." In re A.H. Robins Co., 880 F.2d 694, 701 (4th Cir.1989). Moreover, it is an "ancient but very much alive doctrine ... [that] ... a creditor has no right to choose which of two funds will pay his claim." Id. Likewise, when a plan provides for the full payment of all claims, enjoining claims against a non-debtor so as not to defeat reorganization is. consistent with the bankruptcy court's primary function.

For the foregoing reasons, such an injunction is "not inconsistent" with the Code, and is authorized by section 1123(b)(6).

Nevertheless, some courts have found that the Bankruptcy Code does not permit enjoining a non-consenting creditor's claims against a non-debtor. . . . These courts primarily rely on section 524(e) of the Code, which provides that "the discharge of the debt of the debtor does not affect the liability of any other entity on, or the property of any other entity for, such debt." 11 U.S.C. § 524(e). However, this language explains the effect of a debtor's discharge. It does not prohibit the release of a non-debtor.

The bankruptcy court concluded that non-debtor releases were authorized by section 1123(b)(6), but were precluded by a non-bankruptcy law limitation on the bankruptcy court's equity power. In re Dow Corning Corp., 244 B.R. at 744. We disagree. The bankruptcy court cited Grupo Mexicano de Desarrollo v. Alliance Bond Fund, Inc., 527 U.S. 308, 322, 119 S.Ct.. 1961, 144 L.Ed.2d 319 (1999), for the proposition that a court's use of its general equity powers "is confined within the broad boundaries of traditional equitable relief." The Grupo Mexicano Court explained that, "the equity jurisdiction of the federal courts is the jurisdiction in equity exercised by the High Court of Chancery in England at the time of the adoption of the Constitution and the enactment of the original Judiciary Act, 1789." Based upon this principle, the Grupo Mexicano Court vacated an injunction preventing a toll road operator from dissipating, transferring, or encumbering its only assets to the prejudice of an unsecured note holder because traditional equity jurisprudence did not allow such remedies until a debt had been established. The bankruptcy court, applying the Grupo Mexicano analysis, concluded that non-consensual, non- debtor releases were also unprecedented in traditional equity jurisprudence, and therefore exceeded the bankruptcy court's equitable powers.

The district court rejected this argument on the grounds that the releases were authorized by "sufficient statutory authority under the Bankruptcy Code." For the following reasons, we agree with the district court. In Grupo Mexicano, the Supreme Court distinguished its own holding from that in United States v. First National City Bank, 379 U.S. 378, 85 S.Ct. 528, 13 L.Ed.2d 365 (1965). 527 U.S. at 326, 119 S.Ct. 1961. First National approved an injunction preventing a third-party bank from transferring any of a taxpayer's assets. The Grupo Mexicano Court distinguished that holding on the grounds that the First National case "involved not the Court's general equitable powers under the Judiciary Act of 1789, but its powers under the statute authorizing tax injunctions." Thus, because the district court had a statutory basis for issuing such an injunction, it was not confined to traditional equity jurisprudence available at the enactment of the Judiciary Act of 1789. The statute in First National gave courts the power to grant injunctions "necessary or appropriate for the enforcement of the internal revenue laws." 26 U.S.C. § 7402(a) (1964). Similarly, the Bankruptcy Code gives bankruptcy courts the power to grant injunctions "necessary or appropriate to carry out the provisions of [the Bankruptcy Code]." 11 U.S.C. § 105(a). We conclude that due to this statutory grant of power, the bankruptcy court is not confined to traditional equity jurisprudence and therefore, the bankruptcy court's Grupo Mexicano analysis was misplaced.

Because we determine that enjoining a non-consenting creditor's claim against a non-debtor is "not inconsistent" with the Code and that Grupo Mexicano does not preclude such an injunction, we turn to when such an injunction is an "appropriate provision" of a reorganization plan pursuant to section 1123(b)(6). Because such an injunction is a dramatic measure to be used cautiously, we follow those circuits that have held that enjoining a non- consenting creditor's claim is only appropriate in "unusual circumstances.". In determining whether there are "unusual circumstances," our sister circuits have considered a number of factors, which are summarized in our holding below. We hold that when the following seven factors are present, the bankruptcy court may enjoin a non-consenting creditor's claims against a non-debtor: (1) There is an identity of interests between the debtor and the third party, usually an indemnity relationship, such that a suit against the non-debtor is, in essence, a suit against the debtor or will deplete the assets of the estate; (2) The non-debtor has contributed substantial assets to the reorganization; (3) The injunction is essential to reorganization, namely, the reorganization hinges on the debtor being free from indirect suits against parties who would have indemnity or contribution claims against the debtor; (4) The impacted class, or classes, has overwhelmingly voted to accept the plan; (5) The plan provides a mechanism to pay for all, or substantially all, of the class or classes affected by the injunction; (6) The plan provides an opportunity for those claimants who choose not to settle to recover in full and; (7) The bankruptcy court made a record of specific factual findings that support its conclusions.

For several reasons, the record produced by the bankruptcy court in this case does not support a finding of "unusual circumstances" such that we can endorse enjoining non-consenting creditors' claims against a non-debtor.

QUESTIONS ON *DOW CORNING*

1. Just where in the Code is the term "unusual circumstances"?

2. Sections 1129(a)(1) and (a)(2) require compliance with title 11 and chapter 11. What about Dow's

plan arguably did not comply with either of these two statutes?

3. Can you use *Dow Corning* to confirm a plan for the corner drugstore that has a provision enjoining banks from pursuing the officers and directors of the drugstore post-confirmation for the unpaid portion of any pre-petition debt? Would it matter if the officer and directors had each given the banks a personal guaranty?

J. NON-CONSENSUAL CONFIRMATION: "CRAMDOWN"

Sometimes not all classes will consent. For example, a single secured creditor may comprise a single class, see *Keck Mahin* above at page 464, and may have interests significantly different than the remaining creditors. Or a sufficient minority of creditors may have ulterior motives to shut down the debtor (think of a class of unsecured creditors containing a significant minority of creditors who hold antitrust claims against the debtor, or who are competitors of the debtor).

What's a debtor in possession, or creditor who wants the debtor to continue, to do? The answer is found in Section 1129(b)(1). It reads "if all of the applicable requirements of subsection (a) of this section ***other than paragraph (8)*** are met with respect to a plan . . .the court . . . shall confirm the plan . . . if . . . ."

As a consequence, there are two plan confirmation alternatives:

- by the court's finding that ***all*** of the requirements of section 1129(a), *including* section 1129(a)(8) have been satisfied; ***or***

- by the court's finding that *all* of the requirements of section 1129(a) ***except*** section 1129(a)(8), **and**

that all of the other requirements of section 1129(b) have been satisfied.[12]

Looking to section 1129(b) to confirm notwithstanding a non-asseting class is commonly called a "cram down" Or a "cramdown." But you will look in vain in the Code for that term; it does not appear in the Code. Neither does the phrase "cram down."[13]

Seemingly everyone else knows what a cram down is. The Sixth Circuit in the *U.S. Truck* case below. The Supreme Court in the *Rash* case. Even the novelist Richard Dooling.

RICHARD DOOLING, WHITE MAN'S GRAVE 4, 7-9 (1995)

Randall lived and breathed the Bankruptcy Code, and intimidated anybody who crossed him by quoting it chapter, section, and verse. The famous biologist James Watson lived and breathed the problem of DNA until the structure of the double helix was revealed to him in a dream. Descartes nodded off and discovered the order of all the sciences in a dream. The nineteenth-century chemist Friedrich August Kekulé von Stradonitz dreamed of a serpent swallowing its tail, and woke up to discover the closed carbon ring structure of the benzene molecule. When Randall Killigan slept, he dreamed sections of the U.S. Bankruptcy Code, and woke up to discover money—lots of it—eagerly paid by clients who had insatiable appetites for his special insights into the Code. . . .

The attorneys representing all the major creditors in the WestCo Manufacturing case had arrayed themselves around a conference table, with their associates sitting demurely behind them, notepads and pens at the ready. The table was

---

[12]Remember, one of the requirements of section 1129(a) is section 1129(a)(10)'s requirement that "at least one class of claims that is impaired under the plan has accepted the plan." Accordingly, the court can use this second, 1129(b) alternative to plan confirmation only if there is at least one class that has accepted the plan. We referred to this confirmation requirement above in note 11.

[13]"Cramdown" and "cram down" and "cram-down" are used interchangeably. Indeed, the Supreme Court has used both the "cramdown" and "cram-down" in the same sentence. Blanchette v. Connecticut General Ins. Corp., 419 U.S. 102, 167 (1974) (Douglas, J., dissenting).

studded with notebook computers, briefcases, pitchers of ice water, notepads, cellular phones, and glasses fogging in the sunlight pouring in from the bay windows. Randall took his place at the head of the table and prepared to divide the spoils of WestCo Manufacturing among the lawyers for the various classes of creditors.

In primitive societies, the dominant male of the tribe apportioned the kill according to the skill and valor of the members of the hunting party. As far as Killigan was concerned, nothing much had changed for twentieth-century man, except that the weapons had become rules—complex and abstract rules—and the warriors were now lawyers. The kill was relatively bloodless (except for the occasional unhinged, atavistic client who showed up now and again on the six o'clock news dragging a lawyer around in a noose of piano wire attached to a shotgun). In Randall's hands, the U.S. Bankruptcy Code was a weapon, anything from a blazing scimitar to a neutron bomb, depending upon how much destruction he was being paid to inflict on his client's adversaries. International corporate behemoths—like WestCo—were weakened strays bleeding money, suffocated by debt, and falling behind the pack, where they could be picked off, dropped in the crosshairs of Randall's scope rifle, and plundered like carcasses rotting in the sun.

But bankruptcy law went far beyond the hunt, for the kill was always followed by brutal, expensive combat among the contending classes of creditors. Sure, passions ran high at Troy when Agamemnon took Achilles' beautiful sex slave for himself, but a bondholder who's being asked to take out-of-the-money warrants instead of principal plus interest at 14 percent is something else. Blood and gore. Section 1129 of the Code coyly referred to it as "plan confirmation," but when things went awry every bankruptcy lawyer in the country called the process "cram down," and for a good reason. After months or years of acrimonious, adversarial proceedings, one supreme warrior eventually emerged with a plan of reorganization, which he crammed down the throats of the vanquished creditors, so the spoils could be distributed to the victorious. . . .

We will look at the cram down requirements of section 1129(b) later. For now, please remember, we look at section 1129(b) *only* if all of section 1129(a) requirements ***other than section 1129(a)(8)*** have been satisfied.

One more time—section 1129(b) applies *only* if there is at least one impaired class that did not accept the plan. But at least one impaired class *must* accept; that is, you can't use the cramdown power if no class consents to the plan. That didn't used to be the case in Chapter XII cases under the Act, *In re* Marietta Cobb Apts. Co., 3 Bankr. Ct. Dec. (CRR) 720 (Bankr. S.D.N.Y. 1977), and for a short while under the Code. But in 1984, Congress amended the Code to add Section 1129(a)(10), which requires that at least one class of impaired claims accept the plan. This amendment has caused pressures on how plan proponents create their classes.

---

1. *Initial Skirmishes: Classifying and Gerrymandering*

11 U.S.C. § 1122(a)

[A] plan may place a claim or an interest in a particular class only if such claim or interest is substantially similar to the other claims or interests of such class.

---

11 U.S.C. § 1129(a)(10)

(a) The court shall confirm a plan only if all of the following requirements are met: . . . .

(10) If a class of claims is impaired under the plan, at least one class of claims that is impaired under the plan has accepted the plan, determined without including any acceptance of the plan by any insider.

IN RE U.S. TRUCK CO., INC.

800 F.2d 581 (6th Cir. 1986)

CORNELIA G. KENNEDY, Circuit Judge.

The Teamsters National Freight Industry Negotiating Committee (the Teamsters Committee), a creditor of U.S. Truck Company, Inc. (U.S. Truck) – the debtor-in-possession in this Chapter 11 bankruptcy proceeding – appeals the District Court's order confirming U.S. Truck's Fifth Amended Plan of Reorganization. The Teamsters Committee complains that the plan does not satisfy three of the requirements of 11 U.S.C. § 1129. . . .

Section 1129 contains two means by which a reorganization plan can be confirmed. The first way is to meet all eleven of the requirements of subsection (a), including (a)(8) which requires all impaired classes of claims or interests to accept the plan. The other way is to meet the requirements of subsection (b), which, first, incorporates all of the requirements of subsection (a), except for that contained in subsection (a)(8), and, second, imposes two additional requirements. Confirmation under subsection (b) is commonly referred to as a "cram down" because it permits a reorganization plan to go into effect over the objections of one or more impaired classes of creditors. In this case, U.S. Truck sought approval of its plan under this "cram down" provision. . . .

The Teamsters Committee's first objection is that the plan does not meet the requirement that at least one class of impaired claims accept the plan, see 11 U.S.C. § 1129(a)(10), because U.S. Truck impermissibly gerrymandered the classes in order to neutralize the Teamsters Committee's dissenting vote.

In this case, U.S. Truck is using its classification powers to segregate dissenting (impaired) creditors from assenting (impaired) creditors (by putting the dissenters into a class or classes by themselves) and, thus, it is assured that at least one class of impaired creditors will vote for the plan and make it eligible for cram down consideration by the court. We agree with the Teamsters Committee that there must be some limit on a debtor's power to classify creditors in such a manner. The potential for abuse would be significant otherwise. Unless there is some requirement of keeping similar claims together, nothing would stand in the way of a debtor seeking out a few impaired creditors (or even one such creditor) who will vote for the plan and placing them in their own class.[8] . . .

The District Court noted three important ways in which the interests of the Teamsters Committee differ substantially from those of the other impaired creditors. Because of these

---

[8]We need not speculate in this case whether the purpose of separate classification was to line up the votes in favor of the plan. The debtor admitted that to the District Court. . . .

differences, the Teamsters Committee has a different stake in the future viability of the reorganized company and has alternative means at its disposal for protecting its claim. The Teamsters Committee's claim is connected with the collective bargaining process. In the words of the Committee's counsel, the union employees have a "virtually unique interest." These differences put the Teamsters Committee's claim in a different posture than the Class XI claims. The Teamsters Committee may choose to reject the plan not because the plan is less than optimal to it as a creditor, but because the Teamsters Committee has a noncreditor interest--e.g., rejection will benefit its members in the ongoing employment relationship. Although the Teamsters Committee certainly is not intimately connected with the debtor, to allow the Committee to vote with the other impaired creditors would be to allow it to prevent a court from considering confirmation of a plan that a significant group of creditors with similar interests have accepted. Permitting separate classification of the Teamsters Committee's claim does not automatically result in adoption of the plan. The Teamsters Committee is still protected by the provisions of subsections (a) and (b), particularly the requirements of subsection (b) that the plan not discriminate unfairly and that it be fair and equitable with respect to the Teamsters Committee's claim. In fact, the Teamsters Committee invokes those requirements, but as we note in the following sections, the plan does not violate them.

QUESTIONS AND NOTES RELATING TO *U.S. TRUCK*

1. In *U.S. Truck*, the Sixth Circuit states that "there must be some limit on a debtor's power to classify creditors in such a manner." Why? What is the Sixth Circuit's "limit"? Is the Sixth Circuit's limit on classifying claims to satisfy section 1129(a)(10) different from the limit suggested by the National Bankruptcy Review Commission in 1997: "Section 1122 should be amended to provide that a plan proponent may classify legally similar claims separately, if, upon objection, the proponent can demonstrate that the classification is supported by a 'rational business justification.'" NAT'L BANKRUPTCY REV. COMM'N, BANKRUPTCY: THE NEXT TWENTY YEARS, THE NATIONAL BANKRUPTCY

REVIEW COMMISSION FINAL REPORT, RECOMMENDATION 2.4.16, at 567 (1997).

2. In *U.S. Truck*, the Sixth Circuit upheld the confirmation of a *U.S. Truck* Chapter 11 plan that classified the union's unsecured claim for the debtor's breach of its collective bargaining agreement separate from other unsecured claims. If *U.S. Truck's* Chapter 11 plan had included the union's claim in the same class as other unsecured claims, would the Sixth Circuit have upheld a bankruptcy court's confirmation of that plan over the objection of some other unsecured creditor?

3. Most of the reported cases on classifying as gerrymandering involve single asset real estate cases in which:

   - the debtor owns a building or land;
   - the building or land is subject to a mortgage;
   - the amount secured by the mortgage is much greater than the value of the building or land;
   - the deficiency claim of the mortgage holder is much greater than all of the other unsecured claims combined;
   - the holder of the mortgagor is voting both its secured claim and its unsecured claim *against* confirmation of the plan.

In these cases, the debtor can meet the requirement of section 1129(a)(10) only by classifying the deficiency claim separate from other unsecured claims. In these cases, court commonly consider the "1111(b) election" and the "new value corollary/exception" and section 1129(b)(1) "unfairly discriminates" and other stuff we are fixing to cover.

---

2. *Cram Down and "Not Discriminate Unfairly"*

11 U.S.C. § 1129(b)(1)

[I]f all of the applicable requirements of subsection (a) of this section other than paragraph (8) are met with respect to a plan, the court, on request of the proponent of the plan, shall confirm the plan notwithstanding the requirements of such paragraph if the plan does not discriminate unfairly, . . ., with respect to each class of claims or interests that is impaired under, and has not accepted, the plan.

PROBLEM 11-22: "NOT DISCRIMINATE UNFAIRLY"

1. D's Chapter 11 plan has two classes of unsecured claims: Class V, which includes the unsecured claims of "critical vendors" and Class O which includes all other unsecured claims. The plan proposes to pay Class V claims in full within three months of the effective date of the plan and pay Class O claims 10% of the amount owed, over a three year period. If Class V accepts the plan and Class O does not, can the court still confirm the plan?

2. Same facts as #1 except that 75% of the claims (in number and amount) in Class O accept the plan. Can the court confirm the plan?

IN RE SENTRY OPERATING CO. OF TEXAS, INC.

64 B.R. 850 (Bankr. S.D. Tex. 2001)

WESLEY W. STEEN, Bankruptcy Judge.

In this contested matter, the Court must decide whether to confirm a chapter 11 plan over the objection of a class of unsecured creditors that has rejected the plan. These creditors argue . . .) that a chapter 11 plan cannot be confirmed over their rejection and objection if it proposes to pay them a lesser percentage than it proposes to pay other creditors of equal rank. The Court concludes that . . . the plan proponents have not met their burden to prove that the class definitions are drawn sufficiently narrowly and have not met their burden to prove that the plan does not discriminate unfairly

. . .

The SCI-L debt is secured by a lien and security interest in all assets involved in these cases.

. . .

Summary of Classification of Claims, Plan Treatment, and Acceptance/Rejection

	Accept/ Reject	Number – % Voting for	Claims – % Voting for	Amount to be paid	Percent of claim to be paid
Class 1, SCI-L	Impaired, Insider, Accepts			Approx. $21 million (Note 1)	61%
Class 2, Priority	Unimpaired			Approx. $4,440	100%
Class 3, Unsecured Trade Creditors	Impaired, Accepts	100%	100%	Approx. $400,000	100%
Class 4, Other Unsecured Creditors	Impaired	20% (See Note 2)	11% (See Note 2)	Approx. $100,000	1% (Note 3)
Class 5, Ford Motor Credit	Unimpaired			Approx. $66,443	100%
Class 6, Stillwater National Bank	Unimpaired			Approx. $66,443	100%
Class 7, Equity	Deemed to reject			Nothing	

Note 1: SCI-L will receive all of the value of the company ($23 million) less approximately $1.5 million to be used to fund other payments under the plan.

Note 2: For reasons set forth below, the Court concludes that the votes of the Stumpff group should not be counted but the Subordinated Investor votes should be counted. Debtors counted and recounted the Class 4 votes, but even after the recount the report was admittedly incorrect. The percentages related in the table are reasonably close to the correct count based on the Court's determination that the votes of Subordinated Investors should be counted, but not the votes of the Stumpff group.

Note 3: $100,000 divided among total claims of $10,469,737.51 listed for class 4 in Debtor's revised vote tally.

. . .

Bankruptcy Code Section 1129(b) does not define "discriminate unfairly." In this case, the issue is whether the Plan discriminates unfairly by proposing to pay a greater percentage distribution to Class 3 creditors than it pays to Class 4 creditors, even though both have equal rank under state law and under the distribution priorities of the Bankruptcy Code. It is clear that the Plan discriminates between the two groups of creditors since it proposes to pay one set 1% of their claims and it proposes to pay the other group 100%. The Plan proponents argue that SCI-L has a lien on all assets and therefore the Plan does not discriminate unfairly because Class 4 has no legal right to a distribution. They argue that SCI-L is merely giving up part of its entitlement, and that Class 4 has no legal right to complain. . . .

In general, the Bankruptcy Code is premised on the rule of equality of treatment. Creditors with claims of equal rank are entitled to equal distribution. But § 1129(b) obviously permits some discrimination, since it only prohibits unfair discrimination. The task is to determine what constitutes "fair" discrimination.

A very persuasive historical analysis and proposed test is presented by Bruce A. Markell, entitled *A New Perspective on Unfair Discrimination in Chapter 11* (hereafter "Markell"). In that article, Markell observes that:

> ... [U]nfair discrimination is best viewed as a horizontal limit on nonconsensual confirmation ... Just as the fair and equitable requirement regulates priority among classes of creditors having higher and lower priorities, creating inter-priority fairness, so the unfair discrimination provision promotes intra-priority fairness, assuring equitable treatment among creditors who have the same level of priority.

Markell proposes the following test:

> In particular, I propose that a Chapter 11 plan is presumptively subject to denial of confirmation on the basis of unfair discrimination, even though it provides fair and equitable treatment for all classes, when there is (1) a dissenting class; (2) another class of the same

> priority; and (3) a difference in the plan's treatment of the two classes that results in either (a) a materially lower percentage recovery for the dissenting class (measured in terms of the net present value of all payments), or (b) regardless of percentage recovery, an allocation under the plan of materially greater risk to the dissenting class in connection with its proposed distribution.

Under this test, the Plan is "presumptively subject to denial of confirmation." However, Markell suggests that the presumption can be overcome by proof of one of two exceptions.

The plan proponent may overcome the presumption based on different percentage recoveries by showing that a lower recovery for the dissenting class is consistent with the results that would obtain outside of bankruptcy, or that a greater recovery for the other class is offset by contributions from that class to the reorganization.

At first blush, the first exception might seem to cover this Plan: "a lower recovery for the dissenting class is consistent with the results that would obtain outside of bankruptcy." But nowhere in the article does Markell suggest that a secured lender may simply purchase the assent of an unsecured class by giving up part of its claim. Markell seems to suggest that the "results that would obtain outside of bankruptcy" has to do with pre-petition status of creditors and their legitimate expectations about relative rights and likelihood of payment. His example of appropriate discrimination between trade claims in one class and deficiency claims of a non-recourse secured creditor in another class. The discrimination is justified in this example because outside of bankruptcy the non-recourse creditor has no expectations of recovery on its deficiency claim. Since any recovery in bankruptcy is more than the creditor would get outside of bankruptcy, discriminatory treatment may not be unfair.

In the Plan, there is no such justification for gross discrimination between the percentage payouts to Classes 3 and 4. Class 3 contains some small creditors whose continued work with the funeral homes would probably provide some value. However, Class 3 contains many more national creditors (some of them very large) who appear to be paid for reasons other than preservation of value. Thus there does not appear to be sufficient "contribution to preservation of value through the plan" that justifies a payout differential. Although there are equity investors in Class 4 who might be paid differently based on expectations and inside information, there are also ex-proprietors of small funeral homes in Class 4 who sold businesses to the Debtor and did not share control or insider information. While a deferred payout and possibly risk differential among the different kinds of creditors in this case might be justified, a 99% payout differential is not justified. Adopting the Markell proposal, the Court concludes that the plan discriminates unfairly.

Even more persuasive is the interrelationship of creditor protections evidenced in the statutory confirmation requirements. Bankruptcy Code § 1129(a)(7) protects all creditors in all classes against receiving less than what they would receive in liquidation, even if their class were to accept the plan. The "fair and equitable" requirement of 1129(b) protects each class of creditors against involuntary loss of their priority status, vis a vis other classes of different rank. The "does not discriminate unfairly" requirement in § 1129(b) protects each class of creditors against involuntary loss of their equal distribution rights vis a vis other creditors of equal rank.

To accept SCI-L's argument that a secured lender can, without any reference to fairness, decide which creditors get paid and how much those creditors get paid, is to . . . read section 1129(b) requirements out of the Code. If the argument were accepted with respect to § 1129(b) "unfair discrimination requirement," there is no logical reason not to apply it to the § 1129(b) "fair and equitable" requirement, or to the § 1129(a)(10) requirement that at least one class has accepted the plan. To accept that argument is simply to start down a slippery slope that does great violence to history and to positive law. There are devices at law, such as foreclosure, in which the secured lender is not required to negotiate with unsecured creditors, to obtain consent of at least one class of impaired creditors, or to be fair. But the advantage of an equity receivership, and its descendant the chapter 11 reorganization, is (among others) (i) that going concern value is preserved or enhanced, (ii) that the debtor (in this case in league with the secured lender) is left in possession and control of the business to decide how to restructure it, (iii) that executory contracts can be assumed or rejected, (iv) that preferences and fraudulent conveyances can be recovered, and (v) that all other creditors are held at bay under an automatic stay while the plan is formulated and implemented. The Bankruptcy Code establishes the price of these powerful equitable tools (when any class of creditors is impaired) as negotiation to win over the acceptance of an impaired class and treatment of all non-accepting classes fairly, equitably, and without unfair discrimination. SCI-L proposes to obtain the benefits of equitable tools without paying the price. The statute has no provision for that, and the Court is unwilling to read these requirements out of the Code.

The Court, at this point, is not required (or able) to define the limits of "unfair discrimination" in this case. The plan, as indicated above, fails to meet other confirmation requirements. The fact that Class 4 creditors would receive nothing in a liquidation might or might not be influential under the right circumstances. All that the Court need determine at this stage is that the dire financial consequences of foreclosure is not sufficient to sustain a finding that the proposed discriminatory Plan treatment of Class 4 is fair and equitable.

CONCLUSION

The plan does not meet all of the confirmation requirements of Bankruptcy Code Section 1129. Therefore, by separate order issued this date, plan confirmation is denied. To consider additional orders for the expedient and economical prosecution of this case, the Court will conduct a status conference under Bankruptcy Code § 105(d).

NOTES ON *SENTRY*

1. Under the rationale of *Sentry*, could a plan separately classify tort and trade creditors into different unsecured classes, and then pay each 100% on the dollar, albeit with the trade creditor class being paid off in six months and the tort class being paid off in six years? Is that unfair discrimination? What if the plan not only proposes differences in the timing of the payout, but also different payouts, such as 100% to the "necessary" trade creditors, but only 10% to the tort claimants.

2. The so-called "Markell test" has been challenged as too soft and too uncertain. *See* The Committee on Bankruptcy and Corporate Reorganization of the Association of the Bar of the City of New York, *Making the Test for Unfair Discrimination More "Fair": A Proposal*, 58 BUS. LAWYER 83 (2002); Markell has replied. Bruce A. Markell, *Slouching*

Towards Fairness: A Reply to the ABCNY's Proposal on Unfair Discrimination, 58 BUS. LAWYER 109 (2002).

---

3. *Cram Down and "Fair and Equitable"*

While section 1129(b) does not use the phrase "cram down," it does use other phrases, and one of the most important phrases is "fair and equitable."[9] In order for a plan to be cram downed on a class, that plan must be fair and equitable as to that class. To determine whether a plan is "fair and equitable" to a non-assenting class, it is helpful to look to section 1129(b)(2), which contains a series of non-exclusive examples of fair and equitable treatment.[10] And to apply these examples in section 1129(b)(2), it is necessary to know whether the non-assenting class is a class of secured claims or a class of unsecured claims or interests.

---

4. *Cram Down of Secured Claims*

Let's do cram down of secured claims first. Assume that there was a secured claim class that did not accept the plan. In determining whether to confirm the plan notwithstanding the non-assenting secured class, the court will look to section 1129(b)(2)(A).

---

[9]The phrase "fair and equitable" is taken from railroad reorganization cases in the first part of the 20th century. It will be helpful to you at some point to gain some understanding of these cases and you can gain that understanding by reading Bruce A. Markell, *Owners, Auctions and Absolute Priority in Bankruptcy Reorganizations*, 44 STAN. L. REV. 69 (1991). For now, it will be more helpful to you to read 1129(b)(2) and the material below applying 1129(b)(2).

[10]We look at applications of the fair and equitable rule that aren't covered by the examples below at page 571.

11 U.S.C. § 1129(b)(2)(A)

(2) For the purpose of this subsection, the condition that a plan be fair and equitable with respect to a class includes the following requirements:

(A) With respect to a class of secured claims, the plan provides—

(i) (I) that the holders of such claims retain the liens securing such claims, whether the property subject to such liens is retained by the debtor or transferred to another entity, to the extent of the allowed amount of such claims; and

(II) that each holder of a claim of such class receive on account of such claim deferred cash payments totaling at least the allowed amount of such claim, of a value, as of the effective date of the plan, of at least the value of such holder's interest in the estate's interest in such property;

(ii) for the sale, subject to section 363(k) of this title, of any property that is subject to the liens securing such claims, free and clear of such liens, with such liens to attach to the proceeds of such sale, and the treatment of such liens on proceeds under clause (i) or (iii) of this subparagraph; or

(iii) for the realization by such holders of the indubitable equivalent of such claims.

---

a. Secured Creditor Cramdown 101A: Payment in Full with Non-Cash Property

_IN RE_ SEATCO, INC. (_SEATCO_ I)
257 B.R. 469 (Bankr. N.D. Tex. 2001)

[The debtor manufactured custom van and truck seating and related accessories for the van and truck conversion industry. As a result of a combination of factors – including borrowing costs with its principal lender, CIT Group/Business Credit, Inc. ("CIT"), loss of business due to putatively substandard materials provided by a third party vendor, and market shrinkage, Debtor filed for chapter 11 protection. Before it filed, however, the debtor had diverted its receivables away from a lock-box arrangement CIT had set up, and had intentionally misrepresented its financial condition to CIT. The debtor's plan of reorganization, which is at issue in the case below, proposed to issue a term note to CIT in replacement of CIT's pre-petition revolving loan. The disputed terms of this new note are discussed below. As you will CIT did not consent to the proposed treatment, and fought against having that treatment involuntarily imposed upon them (or in the lingo of the trade, "crammed down" their throats.)]

BARBARA J. HOUSER, Bankruptcy Judge

. . .

3. The Interest Rate, Retention of Liens, and Financial Covenants

While CIT agrees that "as a general matter, the Plan appears to make an attempt to comply with Sec. [*sic*] 1129(b)(2)(A)(i)," it contends that its treatment is insufficient to satisfy the requirements for confirmation under section 1129(b)(2)(A)(i). In particular, CIT contends that it does not retain sufficient lien rights under the Plan, that the Plan does not provide sufficient detail as to the terms of its treatment (*i.e.*, covenants and events of default), and that the interest rate proposed in the Plan is insufficient to cause CIT to receive deferred cash payments having a present value, as of the effective date of the Plan, equal to its allowed secured claim.

. . .

The Plan and the proposed plan implementation documents . . . provide that CIT retains its prepetition liens and that those liens extend to assets "now owned or hereafter acquired," . . . and now provide CIT with sufficient covenants to protect its interests in its collateral. . . . CIT's objections are moot.

Finally, CIT contends that it is not receiving deferred cash payments under the Plan that have a present value equal to its allowed secured claim. CIT contends that it must receive interest at the contract rate provided in the Prepetition Loan Agreement – rather than the lesser interest rate provided in the Plan – in order for it to receive deferred cash payments with a proper present value. Under the Class 2A Note and the Class 2B Note, CIT receives a variable rate of interest equal to the Prime Rate (as defined) plus 2%, adjusted annually and capped at 13.5% per annum. Under the Prepetition Loan

Agreement, the pre-default rate of interest was prime plus 3.75% per annum.

The present value analysis associated with the deferred cash payment requirement of section 1129(b)(2)(A)(i) is controversial. This present value requirement, which compensates the secured creditor for the delay in receiving payments in respect of its allowed secured claim, includes, by definition, an interest component. The Bankruptcy Code is silent, however, as to the rate of interest necessary to permit a secured creditor to obtain the present value of its allowed secured claim.

In *Heartland Federal Sav. & Loan Assoc. v. Briscoe Enter., Ltd., II (In re Briscoe Enter., Ltd., II)*, 994 F.2d 1160, 1169 (5th Cir. 1993), the Fifth Circuit noted that "courts have used a wide variety of different rates as benchmarks in computing the appropriate interest rate (or discount rate as it is frequently termed) for the specific risk level in their cases." *See id.* In *In re T-H New Orleans Ltd. Partnership*, 116 F.3d 790, 800 (5th Cir. 1997), the Fifth Circuit was "asked to establish a particular formula for determining an appropriate cramdown interest rate" and declined to do so. After quoting the above language from its earlier decision in *Briscoe II*, the Court stated:

> We will not tie the hands of the lower courts as they make the factual determination involved in establishing an appropriate interest rate; they have the job of weighing the witness' testimony, demeanor and credibility. Thus, absent clear error, we will not disturb the bankruptcy court's determination.

Id. After repeating its earlier comments in *Briscoe II* that "often the contract rate will be an appropriate rate" and that "numerous courts have chosen the contract rate if it seemed to be a good estimate as to the appropriate discount rate," *id.* at 801, the Court upheld the bankruptcy court's determination that the contract rate was the appropriate interest rate in that case.

Here, both the Debtor and CIT offered testimony with respect to the appropriate interest rate to be provided to CIT under the Plan. The Debtor's expert, Jeff Fritts ("Fritts"), testified that after considering all of the circumstances, the terms of the Class 2A Note, the Class 2B Note, and the Class

2 Loan Agreement were commercially reasonable.[8] Fritts further testified that CIT should be able to sell the Class 2A Note and the Class 2B Note for enough to pay off its loan balance (*i.e.*, its allowed secured claim). Finally, Fritts testified that CIT was receiving a stream of payments under the Plan that had a present value equal to the amount of CIT's secured claim.

CIT's loan officer, Steven Siar ("Siar"), testified that he believed the Debtor is a worse credit risk now than it was at the time the original loans were made; that the Plan's proposed interest rate is insufficient to compensate CIT for its increased risk; and that CIT would not make the loan proposed under the Plan. Siar testified further that the increased "riskiness" of the loan is a function of the Debtor's bankruptcy filing, its conduct immediately prior to and immediately after the filing, a decline in the Debtor's business and in its market, and a perceived increase in the risk of non-collection.

After considering both witnesses' testimony, demeanor and credibility, the Court finds that the Plan provides deferred cash payments having a present value, as of the effective date of the Plan, equal to CIT's allowed secured claim. On a going concern basis, CIT is significantly oversecured. The interest rate proposed in the Plan (prime plus 2%, adjusted annually and capped at 13.5%) includes a risk premium sufficient to account for the fact that CIT is not receiving its money today. CIT's loan under the Plan is not riskier than its prepetition loan. The evidence is undisputed that the Debtor's financial projections take market and market share declines into account. Moreover, CIT's continuing concerns over the problems that arose early in this case, now expressed as increased riskiness, have been addressed previously. The Plan interest rate is reasonable and adequately compensates CIT for risk. Thus, the Plan satisfies section 1129(b)(2)(A)(i) of the Code and CIT's objection to confirmation is overruled. . . .

---

[8]On cross-examination, Fritts admitted that the absence of covenants in the Class 2A Loan Agreement would be of concern to him as a lender, that it would be "reasonable" to expect the Debtor to agree to those kinds of covenants, and that in the absence of covenants, he would not make the loan. The Debtor agreed to modify the loan agreement to include the covenants stating that "I think Mr. Hesse is making a good point on these covenants. We did not focus on the terms of these covenants in drafting this note. I admit that we should have done that . . . so I apologize to Mr. Hesse and to the Court for having to go through this, but I . . . just didn't want to interrupt him earlier."

CIT was apparently unhappy with the above decision. They asked Judge Houser to reconsider. Her response follows.

IN RE SEATCO, INC. (*SEATCO* II)
259 B.R. 279 (Bankr. N.D. Tex. 2001)

BARBARA J. HOUSER, Bankruptcy Judge

Before the Court is the Motion for Approval of Third Modification of Plan and for Reconsideration of Order Denying Confirmation and Request for Expedited Hearing (the "Second Motion to Modify and Reconsider"). . . .

II. CIT'S OBJECTIONS

. . .

B. Cramdown

CIT objects to confirmation of the Further Modified Plan by cramdown (*i.e.*, over its objections). CIT contends that the Further Modified Plan does not provide it with "anything vaguely resembling the indubitable equivalent of its rights as required by 11 U.S.C. § 1129(b)(2)." . . . Specifically, CIT contends that its rights as a revolving lender cannot be modified in a plan of reorganization without its consent or a finding that it is receiving the indubitable equivalent of its rights under § 1129(b)(2)(A)(iii). The Court disagrees.

A plan of reorganization may be confirmed over the objection of a secured creditor if it does not discriminate unfairly against, and is fair and equitable to, that secured creditor. *See* 11 U.S.C. § 1129(b)(1). Section 1129(b)(2)(A) provides three alternative ways in which a plan may be found to be fair and equitable – (i) that the creditor retain its liens and receive deferred cash payments, of a value, as of the effective date of the plan, of its allowed secured claim; (ii) that the property securing the claim be sold, with the creditor's lien attaching to the sale proceeds, and the lien on proceeds being treated consistent with (i) or (iii) ***or*** (iii) that the creditor receive the indubitable equivalent of its claims. *See* 11 U.S.C. § 1129(b)(2)(A). While a finding of indubitable equivalence would allow the Court to confirm the Further Modified Plan over CIT's objection under § 1129(b)(2)(A)(iii), so too would a finding under § 1129(b)(2)(A)(i) that CIT was retaining its liens and receiving deferred cash payments having a value, as of the effective date of the Plan, equal to CIT's allowed secured claim. *See Wade v. Bradford*, 39 F.3d 1126, 1130 (10th Cir.

1994) ("Because the debtors' plan satisfied the requirements of § 1129(b)(2) (A)(i), creditor was not entitled to the 'indubitable equivalent' of his claims as described in § 1129(b)(2)(A)(iii). These requirements are written in the disjunctive, requiring the plan to satisfy only one before it could be confirmed over creditor's objection."); *Heartland Federal Sav. & Loan Ass'n. v. Briscoe Enters., LTD., II (In re Briscoe Enterprises, LTD., II)*, 994 F.2d 1160, 1168 (5th Cir. 1993), *cert. denied*, 510 U.S. 992, 126 L. Ed. 2d 451, 114 S. Ct. 550 (1993) ("While this Court has held that simple technical compliance with one of the three options in 1129(b)(2)(A) may not necessarily satisfy the fair and equitable requirement, it has not transformed the 'or' in 1129(b)(2)(A) into an 'and.' As we hold that the plan satisfies 1129(b)(2)(A)(i), we need not attempt to decipher the meaning of 'indubitable equivalent.'").

As CIT well knows, this Court did not find in the Original Memorandum Opinion that the Plan provided CIT with the indubitable equivalent of its rights under § 1129(b)(2)(A)(iii), nor was the Court required to so find to overrule CIT's objection to confirmation. Rather, the Court found that CIT was retaining its liens under the Plan and receiving deferred cash payments having a present value, as of the effective date of the Plan, equal to CIT's allowed secured claim. . . . Based upon this finding the Court concluded that the Plan satisfied § 1129(b)(2)(A)(i) of the Bankruptcy Code. . . .

CIT reurges its earlier contention that a secured creditor who lends under a prepetition revolving line of credit is entitled to special protections in a bankruptcy case. Specifically, CIT contends that such a secured creditor enjoys unique, prepetition collateral protections (*i.e.*, pursuant to its loan agreement, the borrower's receivables are collected (usually in a lock box account at the lender's bank), those collections are used to pay down the existing loan, and then new monies are advanced to the borrower based upon a formulaic calculation derived from eligible receivables and inventory), and that such a lender cannot have these collateral protections[10] modified over its objection pursuant to a plan of reorganization unless the Court finds that the lender is receiving the indubitable equivalent of its prepetition rights in accordance with § 1129(b)(2)(A)(iii). CIT contends that such a lender is entitled to these special protections, notwithstanding the fact that the lender cannot be forced to

---

[10]Under this type of lending facility, the amount of the loan outstanding at any time is directly tied to the amount of available collateral (*i.e.* receivables and inventory).

continue to lend to its borrower, now a chapter 11 debtor-in-possession.

CIT cites no authority to support its contentions. This absence of authority is not surprising because the plain meaning of various provisions of the Bankruptcy Code compels the opposite conclusion.

To analyze CIT's contention, the Court must first decide whether a secured creditor who advances monies pursuant to a prepetition revolving line of credit can have its prepetition loan agreement modified by a chapter 11 plan of reorganization. The Bankruptcy Code clearly provides such a right to modify. Section 1123(b)(1) specifically provides that "*a plan may impair*[11] or leave unimpaired *any class of claims, secured* or unsecured, or of interests," (*see* 11 U.S.C. § 1123(b)(1) (emphasis added)) and § 1123(b)(5) specifically provides that "*a plan may modify the rights of holders of secured claims, other than a claim secured only by a security interest in real property that is the debtor's principal residence*, or of holders of unsecured claims, or leave unaffected the rights of holders of any class of claims." *See* 11 U.S.C. § 1123(b)(5) (emphasis added). While § 1123 does except a secured creditor whose claim is secured by the debtor's principal residence from its terms, there is no exception for secured creditors who advanced monies pursuant to a prepetition revolving line of credit. For CIT's position to be correct, § 1123(b)(5) would have to be modified to exclude that class of secured creditor from its terms.

Since the Bankruptcy Code clearly permits a modification of the prepetition loan agreement of a secured creditor who advanced monies under a prepetition revolving line of credit, the next question is what protections are available to such a creditor before the Court can confirm a plan of reorganization over its objection. The Bankruptcy Code answers that question as well. First, the plan must satisfy all of the requirements of § 1129(a)(1)-(13) that are applicable to the debtor. *See* 11 U.S.C. § 1129(a). Second, the plan cannot "discriminate unfairly" against the objecting secured creditor and the plan must be "fair and equitable" to that creditor. *See* 11 U.S.C. § 1129(b)(1). As noted previously, § 1129(b)(2)(A) is written in the disjunctive and the fair and equitable test is satisfied if either § 1129(b)(2)(A)(i) or (iii) is met. . . .

---

[11]Impairment is defined in § 1124 of the Bankruptcy Code. Generally, a claim is impaired unless the plan leaves the legal, equitable, and contractual rights of the claimant unaltered. 11 U.S.C. § 1124(1).

The Court found previously that CIT is retaining its liens under the Plan – CIT retains security interests in all of the assets (*i.e.*, real property) or types of assets (*i.e.*, inventory, receivables, proceeds, etc.) in which it held security interests under the Prepetition Loan Agreement – and that the Plan provides that CIT receive deferred cash payments under the Plan that have a present value, as of the effective date of the Plan, equal to CIT's allowed secured claim. . . . Again, for CIT's position to be correct, § 1129(b)(2)(A)(i) would have to be modified to exclude a secured creditor who lent monies pursuant to a prepetition revolving line of credit from its terms.

But a secured creditor like CIT is entitled to more than just literal compliance with § 1129(b)(2)(A)(i) – it is entitled to assurance that the debtor will be able to perform the plan and thus, the secured creditor will receive the payments provided for under the plan. In the Bankruptcy Code's parlance, the creditor is entitled to have the Court find that "confirmation of the plan is not likely to be followed by the liquidation, or the need for further financial reorganization, of the debtor." *See* 11 U.S.C. § 1129(a)(11). In other words, the creditor is entitled to a finding that the plan is feasible -- the reorganized debtor can perform the plan and make those payments promised to it under the plan.

CIT did not object to feasibility of the Plan. The undisputed evidence is that the Debtor's financial projections are reasonable, take current market conditions into account, and that the Debtor will be able to perform the Plan in accordance with its terms. Based upon this evidence, the Court found the Plan to be feasible.

In sum, CIT is retaining all of its liens and will receive deferred cash payments having a present value, as of the effective date of the Plan, equal to its allowed secured claim. The Plan is feasible and the Debtor should be able to make all of the payments the Plan requires to be made to CIT. If, however, the Debtor defaults on its payments to CIT under the Plan, CIT is entitled to foreclose all of its security interests without further Order of the Court.

Finally, CIT contends that this Court, as a court of equity, should deny confirmation of the Further Modified Plan because to confirm it would reward fraud and conversion. The Court disagrees. What confirmation of the Further Modified Plan does is give other creditors the opportunity to recover on their claims against the Debtor. CIT is fully secured and is being paid in full under the Further Modified Plan. CIT will, in all likelihood, be paid in full if the Debtor does not successfully reorganize and is liquidated. Of significance, however, if the Further Modified Plan is confirmed, thereby enabling the Debtor to successfully reorganize, unsecured priority claims (Classes 4 and 5) will be paid in full with interest and general unsecured claims (Class 6) will receive a 35% distribution on their allowed claims paid over 6 years without interest. These unsecured creditors get nothing if the Debtor does not successfully reorganize.

There is no question that the Debtor breached the Prepetition Loan Agreement when it diverted receivables from CIT's lock box and then requested additional advances under the prepetition Revolver. However, virtually every debtor is in default of its prepetition loan agreements with its secured lender when it files bankruptcy. If CIT has independent claims for fraud and conversion against Kester, individually, for these actions, CIT is free to pursue him notwithstanding confirmation of the Further Modified Plan. Confirmation of the Further Modified Plan will not reward Kester for fraud and conversion if CIT can, in fact, prove its claims against him; but confirmation of the Further Modified Plan will give other creditors the opportunity to receive distributions on account of their allowed claims against the Debtor. For these reasons and the reasons set forth in the Original Memorandum Opinion, the Court concludes that the Further Modified Plan satisfies all of the Bankruptcy Code's requirements for confirmation over CIT's objection. As the Court found in the Original Memorandum Opinion, all other requirements for confirmation of the Further Modified Plan under § 1129(a) of the Bankruptcy Code that are applicable to the Debtor are satisfied.

PROBLEM 11-23: KEY COMPONENTS OF CRAMDOWN

1. Seatco focuses on two aspects of determining whether the value of the stream of payments (that is, the scheduled payments under the note) is equal to the secured claim: the interest rate to be paid, and the value of the collateral. Where have we seen these issues before? *See Rash v. Commercial Associates*, *supra* at page 66; *Till v. SCS Credit Corp.*, *supra* at page 366.

2. How do you go about establishing the applicable interest rate? Do you bring into court recent copies of the *Wall Street Journal*? Economists who read the *Wall Street Journal*? Investment bankers who say they read the *Wall Street Journal*? What if a tax claim is involved? *See* 11 U.S.C. § 511.

---

b. Determining Secured Claims: The "Dreaded" Section 1111(b) Election

Section 1129(b)(2)(A) uses the phrase "secured claims" and then refers to "secured claims" repeatedly as "such claims or "such claim." We have repeatedly cited to section 506 when referring to "secured claims." But section 1111(b) also is relevant, and thus we must look at the election given certain secured creditors in section 1111(b).

Section 506(a) determines what is a "secured claim" for most purposes under the Bankruptcy Code. If, for example, D has filed a Chapter 7 case and it owes S $1,000 and the debt is secured by property with a value of $700, then under section 506(a) S has a secured claim of $700. S would also have an unsecured claim of $300, unless the loan was non-recourse.

Section 1111(b), applicable only in Chapter 11 cases, changes section 506(a) in two ways that can be important in applying section 1129(b)(2)(A) to a nonassenting secured class whose collateral is not sold during the case or under the plan. In particular:

- Section 1111(b)(1)(A) gives even the secured creditor with a nonrecourse claim the same rights as a secured creditor with a recourse claim.

- Section 1111(b)(2) enables any nonassenting secured class whose collateral is not sold during the case to elect to have its claim allowed and treated as a secured claim for the full amount of the debt rather than a lower amount measured by its collateral's value (as section 506 generally requires.)

Look again at the above example (D owed S $1,000 and the debt is secured by property with a value of $700). Under section 1111(b)(2), S could elect to have its full $1,000 debt simply treated as a secured claim.

After reading this example, the benefits of making a section 1111(b) election should seem obvious. After carefully reading section 1129(b)(2)(A) and remembering what you have learned about the plan approval process, the costs of a section 1111(b) election should be equally obvious.

PROBLEM 11-24: UNDERSTANDING SECTION 1129(b)(2)(A)(i)(I) WITH NO SECTION 1111(b) ELECTION

1. D Co. a Chapter 11 debtor, owes S $1,000,000. The debt is based on a note which provides for interest at 10% and 20 equal monthly payments of interest and principal. D Co.'s payment of the note is secured by a first mortgage on Blackacre. Assume the following facts:

   - Blackacre has a value of $700,000; and
   - D Co. intends to retain Blackacre; and
   - S has not made a section 1111(b); and
   - every class of claims other than the S secured claim class has accepted the plan.

   Will the court cram down a plan that pays S $700,000 on the confirmation date?

2. Same assumed facts as #1. Will the court cram down a plan that pays S $350,000 six months after the effective date of the plan and $350,000 more six months later? Why not?

3. Same assumed facts as #1. Will the court cram down a plan that pays S $350,00 six months after the effective date of the plan and $350,000 more six months ***with interest***?

4. Would your answers to #1 and #3 change if S made a section 1111(b) election?

---

c. Markell's Explanation of Section 1129(b)(2)(A) and the Section 1111(b) Election

Examine sub-clause (II) of section 1129(b)(2)(A) with the following example in mind: an overall debt of $1,000, and collateral worth $750. If the holder of this secured claim does not elect under Section 1111(b)(2), then it will have a secured claim of $750, and an unsecured deficiency claim of $250, even if the claim was non-recourse under non-bankruptcy law. If it elects under Section 1111(b)(2), then it loses any deficiency, but it gets a $1,000 secured claim.

Will it get a Chapter 11 plan distribution worth $1,000 as of confirmation? No. Sub-clause (II) only requires that it get "deferred cash payments" totaling $1,000. So the undiscounted stream of payments only has to add up to $1,000. The value of such "deferred cash payments," however, have to have a "value, as of the effective date of the plan," not of the allowed amount of the claim — $1,000 — but "the value of the such holder's interest in the estate's interest in such property," or $750.

How can this work? This can be done by giving the creditor a note in the full amount of the allowed claim that bears a below market interest rate. Thus, it will not have a present value equal to its face amount (it would have to have a market rate of interest to have a value equal to its face), but something lesser.

---

d. Gerry Munitz's[12] Explanation of Section of 1129(b)(2)(A) If No Section 1111(b) Election

With attribution to Shakespeare, the rub to the cramdown power is that it requires the plan to be "fair and equitable." Fair and equitable is a term of legal art and includes, but is not limited to, the absolute priority rule. The absolute priority rule provides that no junior class may receive or retain property under a plan unless rejecting senior classes receive or retain property, as of the effective date of the plan, equal to the allowed amount of their claims. As applied to a secured creditor with a lien on Blackacre, no value derived from Blackacre can be diverted to other creditors unless the lienholder's claim receives full compensation. Full compensation, however, does not require immediate payment in cash. Conversely, the absolute priority rule bars a premium being paid to a class.

Section 1129(b)(2)(A) contains three alternative tests, any one of which satisfies absolute priority as to a secured claim. The first test (§ 1129(b)(2)(A)(i)) contains two conditions. The first condition [of section 1129(b)(2)(A)(i)] requires that the lien on the collateral, whether retained by the debtor or transferred to another entity, remains in place. § 1129(b)(2)(A)(i)(I). The second condition [of section 1129(b)(2)(A)()i)] is that deferred payments have a present value, as of the effective date of the plan, equal to the allowed amount of the secured claim. If the secured creditor's allowed claim is $1 million, the present value of the deferred payments on the effective date of the plan must be $1 million. § 1129(b)(2)(A)(i)(II). The issues that arise with respect to the determination of present value include the term of the new obligation, the rate of interest and the inclusion of provisions necessary to provide the secured creditor with full compensation. This process is an art and not a science.

---

[12]Gerry Munitz is a Chicago bankruptcy lawyer— a great "senior" (even older than Epstein) lawyer.

The second alternative for cramming down a secured claim is that the property (collateral) be offered for sale free and clear of liens with the liens to attach to the proceeds of sale. § 1129(b)(2)(A)(ii). The sale process must recognize the right of the secured creditor to credit bid its lien under § 363(k). If the proceeds of sale are not immediately paid to the secured creditor, the deferred cash payments must meet the present value test of subsection 1129(b)(2)(A)(i)(II) or the indubitable equivalent test discussed below. While § 363(k) permits the court to deny the right to credit bid, the only basis for doing so would be that the validity or amount of the lien is in legitimate dispute. In that event, a secured creditor desiring to become the owner of its collateral would have to pay its bid in cash and then recover the cash upon later sustaining the validity and amount of its lien position.

The third method of satisfying the cramdown power as to a secured creditor is to provide it with the "indubitable equivalent" of its allowed claim. § 1129(b)(2)(A)(iii). This is a catchall provision comparable to that contained in § 361(3) involving the grant of adequate protection. Turnover of all of the collateral to the secured creditor is an indubitable equivalent."

Gerald F. Munitz, *Treatment of Secured Claims In Chapter 11 Cases*, PRACTICING LAW INSTITUTE, *24th Annual Current Developments in Bankruptcy and Reorganization*, 838 PLI/Comm 747 (April 11, 2002).

PROBLEM 11-25: ELECTING AND CRAMMING

1. C has a $1 million nonrecourse note from D. The note is secured by D's plant. The bankruptcy court acting pursuant to Bankruptcy Rule 3012 has valued the plant at $700,000. D's Chapter 11 plan provides that C will receive a $1 million note, secured by the plan. The note will mature in four years and, until maturity, will bear an annual interest rate of 3.5%. D makes a section 1111(b) election and votes against the plan. Can the court confirm the plan?

2. Same facts as #1 except that the court confirms the plan and one year after confirmation, D sells the plant for $900,000. Who gets the proceeds? How much of the sale proceeds would C have received if it had not made the section 1111(b) election?

3. Trick question: Same facts as #1 except that:

   - the debt was a recourse debt; and
   - the plan proposes to sell the property for $700,000 and pay the proceeds of the sale to S in full satisfaction of S's secured claim.

   Can S make the section 1111(b) election and block plan confirmation because it is not receiving the full amount of its secured claim?

4. Harder question. D owns an apartment building. D owes $300,000 to your client S; the debt is secured by the apartment complex. S believes that the apartment complex has a value of $200,000. D owes other, unsecured creditors a total of $40,000. D has filed for Chapter 11 relief. Do you advise S to make a section 1111(b) election? What, if any, additional information, do you need to advise S? *Cf.* Bankr. R. 3014.

PROBLEM 11-26: REPLACEMENT COLLATERAL AND SECTION 1129(b)(2)(A)(i)(III)

D Co., a Chapter 11 debtor, owes S $5,000,000. S has a first mortgage on Blackacre. Advise D Co. as to whether the court will cram down a plan that sells Blackacre to T free and clear of S's mortgage and grants S a first mortgage on Redacre.

PROBLEM 11-27: STOCK PLANS AND SECTION 1129(b)(2)(A)

D Co., a Chapter 11 debtor, owes S $20,000,000. The debt is secured by all of D Co.'s buildings and equipment. D Co. wants to use its stock to satisfy S's secured debt. S is unwilling to agree to any Chapter 11 plan that replaces its secured debt with stock. Advise D Co. as to how to determine the amount of its stock that it will have to issue to S so that a court will cram down a plan that replaces S's secured debt with stock.

---

5. *Cram Down of Unsecured Claims*

a. Cram Down of Unsecured Claims and the Fair and Equitable Requirement

11 U.S.C. § 1129(b)(2)(B)(ii)

(2) [T]he condition that a plan be fair and equitable with respect to a class includes the following requirements:

(B) With respect to a class of unsecured creditors-

. . .

(ii) the holder of any claim or interest that is junior to the claims of such class will not receive or retain under the plan on account of such junior claim or interest any property.

---

b. 11 U.S.C. § 1129(b)(2)(B)(ii) as the "Absolute Priority Rule"

As Judge Hyman, a bankruptcy judge in Florida explains "if unsecured creditors do not receive payment in full on their allowed claims, then no holder of a claim or interest junior to those of the unsecured creditors may retain any property under the plan. This provision [1129(b)(2)(B)(ii)] is commonly referred to as the "absolute priority rule." *In re* Gosman, 282 B.R. 45, 47

(Bankr. S.D. Fla. 2002). *See generally* CHARLES JORDAN TABB, THE LAW OF BANKRUPTCY 868-71 (1997).

PROBLEM 11-28: APPLYING SECTION 1129(b)(2)(B)(i) TO PLANS THAT DISTRIBUTE CASH TO THE NON-ASSENTING CLASS

D Co.'s Chapter 11 plan provides that each holder of a class 7 unsecured claim will receive a note for the full amount of its claim. The note is payable in 7 years with 4.3% interest. D Co.'s shareholders will receive all of the stock of the reorganized D Co. If class 7 is a non-assenting class, will the court confirm the plan under section 1129(b)(2)(B)(i)? What, if any, additional information do you need to answer this question?

PROBLEM 11-29: APPLYING SECTION 1129(b)(2)(B)(i) TO PLANS THAT DISTRIBUTE STOCK TO THE NON-ASSENTING CLASS

D Co.'s Chapter 11 plan provides that 49% of the stock of the reorganized D Co. will be distributed to holders of unsecured class 7 claims and that the other 51 % of the stock will be distributed to D Co.'s existing shareholders. If class 7 is a non-assenting class, will the court confirm the plan under section 1129(b)(2)(B)? Again, what, if any, additional information do you need to answer this question?

---

6. *Cram Down of Unsecured Claims and "New Value"*

a. Sarah Borders[13] Explanation of "New Value"

Briefly, the new value doctrine is either an exception or a corollary (depending on one's point of view) to the absolute priority rule of Section 1129(b)(2) of the Bankruptcy Code. A strict application of the absolute priority rule prohibits junior classes of claims or interests from receiving or retaining any property under a reorganization plan unless senior classes are paid in full. See 11 U.S.C. § 1129(b)(2)(B)-(C). Where the new value doctrine is recognized, however, the former owners of the debtor may retain ownership if they contribute capital to the debtor that is "new, substantial, necessary for the success of the plan, reasonably equivalent to the value retained, and in the form of money or money's worth." In re 203 N. LaSalle St. Partnership, 126 F.3d 955, 963 (7th Cir. 1997). The new value doctrine is most commonly associated with Case v. Los Angeles Lumber Products Co., 308 U.S. 106 (1939), in which the Supreme Court discussed the doctrine in dicta.

Sarah Robinson Borders, *Hot Topics With Respect to Real Estate Bankruptcy Issues*, PLI, Doing Deals 2003, 1357 PLI/Corp. 461, 465, (2003).

BANK OF AM. N.T. & S.A.V. 203 N. LASALLE ST. P'SHIP

526 U.S. 434 (1999)

Justice SOUTER delivered the opinion of the Court.

The issue in this Chapter 11 reorganization case is whether a debtor's prebankruptcy equity holders may, over the objection of a senior class of impaired creditors, contribute new capital and receive ownership interests in the reorganized entity, when that opportunity is given exclusively to the old equity holders under a plan adopted without consideration of alternatives. We hold that old equity holders are disqualified from participating in such a "new value" transaction by the

[13] Sarah Borders is a bankruptcy lawyer in Atlanta - a great young (significantly younger than Epstein) lawyer.

teiins of 11 U.S.C. § 1129(b)(2)(B)(ii), which in such circumstances bars a junior interest holder's receipt of any property on account of his prior interest.

I

Petitioner, Bank of America National Trust and Savings Association (Bank), is the major creditor of respondent, 203 North LaSalle Street Partnership (Debtor or Partnership), an Illinois real estate limited partnership. The Bank lent the Debtor some $93 million, secured by a nonrecourse first mortgage on the Debtor's principal asset, 15 floors of an office building in downtown Chicago. In January 1995, the Debtor defaulted, and the Bank began foreclosure in a state court.

In March, the Debtor responded with a voluntary petition for relief under Chapter 11 of the Bankruptcy Code, 11 U.S.C. § 1101 *et seq.,* which automatically stayed the foreclosure proceedings, see § 362(a).. The Debtor's principal objective was to ensure that its partners retained title to the property so as to avoid roughly $20 million in personal tax liabilities, which would fall due if the Bank foreclosed. The Debtor proceeded to propose a reorganization plan during the 120-day period when it alone had the right to do so, see 11 U.S.C. § 1121(b); see also § 1121(c) (exclusivity period extends to 180 days if the debtor files plan within the initial 120 days). The Bankruptcy Court rejected the Bank's motion to terminate the period of exclusivity to make way for a plan of its own to liquidate the property, and instead extended the exclusivity period for cause shown, under § 1121(d).

The value of the mortgaged property was less than the balance due the Bank, which elected to divide its undersecured claim into secured and unsecured deficiency claims under § 506(a) and § 1111(b). Under the plan, the Debtor separately classified the Bank's secured claim, its unsecured deficiency claim, and unsecured trade debt owed to other creditors. See § 1122(a). The Bankruptcy Court found that the Debtor's available assets were prepetition rents in a cash account of $3.1 million and the 15 floors of rental property worth $54.5 million. The secured claim was valued at the latter figure, leaving the Bank with an unsecured deficiency of $38.5 million.

So far as we need be concerned here, the Debtor's plan had these further features:

(1) The Bank's $54.5 million secured claim would be paid in full between 7 and 10 years after the original 1995 repayment date.

(2) The Bank's $38.5 million unsecured deficiency claim would be discharged for an estimated 16% of its present value.

(3) The remaining unsecured claims of $90,000, held by the outside trade creditors, would be paid in full, without interest, on the effective date of the plan.

(4) Certain former partners of the Debtor would contribute $6.125 million in new capital over the course of five years (the contribution being worth some $4.1 million in present value), in exchange for the Partnership's entire ownership of the reorganized debtor.

The last condition was an exclusive eligibility provision: the old equity holders were the only ones who could contribute new capital.

The Bank objected and, being the sole member of an impaired class of creditors, thereby blocked confirmation of the plan on a consensual basis. The Debtor, however, took the alternate route to confirmation of a reorganization plan, forthrightly known as the judicial "cramdown" process for imposing a plan on a dissenting class.

There are two conditions for a cramdown. First, all requirements of § 1129(a) must be met (save for the plan's acceptance by each impaired class of claims or interests, see § 1129(a)(8)). Critical among them are the conditions that the plan be accepted by at least one class of impaired creditors, see § 1129(a)(10), and satisfy the "best-interest-of-creditors" test, see § 1129(a)(7). Here, the class of trade creditors with impaired unsecured claims voted for the plan, 126 F.3d, at 959, and there was no issue of best interest. Second, the objection of an impaired creditor class may be overridden only if "the plan does not discriminate unfairly, and is fair and equitable, with respect to each class of claims or interests that is impaired under, and has not accepted, the plan." § 1129(b)(1). As to a dissenting class of impaired unsecured creditors, such a plan may be found to be "fair and equitable" only if the allowed value of the claim is to be paid in full, § 1129(b)(2)(B)(i), or, in the alternative, if "the holder of any claim or interest that is junior to the claims of such [impaired unsecured] class will not receive or retain under the plan on account of such junior claim or interest any property," § 1129(b)(2)(B)(ii). That latter condition is the core of what is known as the "absolute priority rule.

The absolute priority rule was the basis for the Bank's position that the plan could not be confiuned as a cramdown. As the Bank read the rule, the plan was open to objection simply because certain old equity holders in the Debtor Partnership would receive property even though the Bank's unsecured deficiency claim would not be paid in full. The Bankruptcy Court approved the plan nonetheless, and accordingly denied the Bank's pending motion to convert the case to Chapter 7 liquidation, or to dismiss the case. The District Court affirmed, as did the Court of Appeals.

The majority of the Seventh Circuit's divided panel found ambiguity in the language of the statutory absolute priority rule, and looked beyond the text to interpret the phrase "on account of " as permitting recognition of a "new value corollary" to the rule.

We granted certiorari to resolve a Circuit split on the issue. The Seventh Circuit in this case joined the Ninth in relying on a new value corollary to the absolute priority rule to support confiunation of such plans. . . . The Second and Fourth Circuits, by contrast, without explicitly rejecting the corollary, have disapproved plans similar to this one.). We do not decide whether the statute includes a new value corollary or exception, but hold that on any reading respondent's proposed plan fails to satisfy the statute, and accordingly reverse.

II

The terms "absolute priority rule" and "new value corollary" (or "exception") are creatures of law antedating the current Bankruptcy Code, and to understand both those terms and the related but inexact language of the Code some history is helpful. The Bankruptcy Act preceding the Code contained no such provision as subsection (b)(2)(B)(ii), its subject having been addressed by two interpretive rules. The first was a specific gloss on the requirement of § 77B (and its successor, Chapter X) of the old Act, that any reorganization plan be "fair and equitable." The reason for such a limitation was the danger inherent in any reorganization plan proposed by a, debtor, then and now, that the plan will simply turn out to be too good a deal for the debtor's owners. . . . Hence the pre-Code judicial response known as the absolute priority rule, that fairness and equity required that "the creditors ... be paid before the stockholders could retain [equity interests] for any purpose whatever." *Northern Pacific R. Co. v. Boyd,* 228 U.S. 482, 508, 33 S.Ct. *554, 57* L.Ed. 931 (1913). . . .

The second interpretive rule addressed the first. Its classic formulation occurred in *Case v. Los Angeles Lumber Products Co.,* in which the Court spoke through Justice Douglas in this dictum:

"It is, of course, clear that there are circumstances under which stockholders may participate in a plan of reorganization of an insolvent debtor.... Where th[e] necessity [for new capital] exists and the old stockholders make a fresh contribution and receive in return a participation reasonably equivalent to their contribution, no objection can be made....

"[W]e believe that to accord 'the creditor his full right of priority against the corporate assets' where the debtor is insolvent, the stockholder's participation must be based on a contribution in money or in money's worth, reasonably equivalent in view of all the circumstances to the participation of the stockholder." 308 U.S., at 121-122, 60 S.Ct. 1.

. . . [T]he *Case* observation . . . never rose above the technical level of dictum in any opinion of this Court. . .. Hence the controversy over how weighty the *Case* dictum had become, as reflected in the alternative labels for the new value notion: some writers and courts (including this one) have spoken of it as an exception to the absolute priority rule . . . while others have characterized it as a simple corollary to the rule. . . .

Which of these positions is ultimately entitled to prevail is not to be decided here, . . . [Even if the Court recognized a new value corollary, the] Bank's objection would require rejection of the plan at issue in this case. It is doomed, we can say without necessarily exhausting its flaws, by its provision for vesting equity in the reorganized business in the Debtor's partners without extending an opportunity to anyone else either to compete for that equity or to propose a competing reorganization plan. Although the Debtor's exclusive opportunity to propose a plan under § 1121(b) is not itself "property" within the meaning of subsection (b)(2)(B)(ii), the respondent partnership in this case has taken advantage of this opportunity by proposing a plan under which the benefit of equity ownership may be obtained by no one but old equity partners. Upon the court's approval of that plan, the partners were in the same position that they would have enjoyed had they exercised an exclusive option under the plan to buy the equity in the reorganized entity, or contracted to purchase it from a seller who had first agreed to deal with no one else. It is quite true that the escrow of the partners' proposed investment eliminated any formal need to set out an express option or exclusive dealing provision in the plan itself, since the court's approval that created the opportunity and the partners' action to obtain its advantage were simultaneous. But before the Debtor's plan was accepted no one else could propose an alternative one, and after its acceptance no one else could obtain equity in the reorganized entity. At the moment of the plan's approval the Debtor's partners necessarily enjoyed an exclusive opportunity that was in no economic sense distinguishable from the advantage of the exclusively entitled offeror or option holder. This opportunity should, first of all, be treated as an item of property in its own right. . . . While it may be argued that the opportunity has no market value, being significant only to old equity holders owing to their potential tax liability, such an argument avails the Debtor nothing, for several reasons. It is to avoid just such arguments that the law is settled that any otherwise cognizable property interest must be treated as sufficiently valuable to be recognized under the Bankruptcy Code. Even aside from that rule, the assumption that no one but the Debtor's partners might pay for such an opportunity would obviously support no inference that it is valueless, let alone that it should not be treated as property. And, finally, the source in the tax law of the opportunity's value to the partners implies in no way that it lacks value to others. It might, indeed, be valuable to another precisely as a way to keep the Debtor from implementing a plan that would avoid a Chapter 7 liquidation.

Given that the opportunity is property of some value, the question arises why old equity alone should obtain it, not to mention at no cost whatever. The closest thing to an answer favorable to the Debtor is that the old equity partners would be given the opportunity in the expectation that in taking advantage of it they would add the stated purchase price to the estate. But this just begs the question why the opportunity should be exclusive to the old equity holders. If the price to be paid for the equity interest is the best obtainable, old equity does not need the protection of exclusiveness (unless to trump an equal offer from someone else); if it is not the best, there is no apparent reason for giving old equity a bargain. There is no reason, that is, unless the very purpose of the whole transaction is, at least in part, to do old equity a favor. And that, of course, is to say that old equity would obtain its opportunity, and the resulting benefit, because of old equity's prior interest within the meaning of subsection (b)(2)(B)(ii). Hence it is that the exclusiveness of the opportunity, with its protection against the market's scrutiny of the purchase price by means of competing bids or even competing plan proposals, renders the partners' right a property interest extended "on account of " the old equity position and therefore subject to an unpaid senior creditor class's objection.

It is no answer to this to say that the exclusive opportunity should be treated merely as a detail of the broader transaction that would follow its exercise, and that in this wider perspective no favoritism may be inferred, since the old equity partners would pay something, whereas no one else would pay anything. If this argument were to carry the day, of course, old equity could obtain a new property interest for a dime without being seen to receive anything on account of its old position. But even if we assume that old equity's plan would not be confirmed without satisfying the judge that the purchase price was top dollar, there is a further reason here not to treat property consisting of an exclusive opportunity as subsumed within the total transaction proposed. On the interpretation assumed here, it would, of course, be a fatal flaw if old equity acquired or retained the property interest without paying full value. It would thus be necessary for old equity to demonstrate its payment of top dollar, but this it could not satisfactorily do when it would receive or retain its property under a plan giving it exclusive rights and in the absence of a competing plan of any sort. Under a plan granting an exclusive right, making no provision for competing bids or competing plans, any determination that the price was top dollar would necessarily be made by a judge in bankruptcy court, whereas the best way to determine value is exposure to a market. This is a point of some significance, since it was, after all, one of the Code's innovations to narrow the occasions for courts to make valuation judgments, as shown by its preference for the supramajoritarian class creditor voting scheme in § 1126(c). In the interest of statutory coherence, a like disfavor for decisions untested by competitive choice ought to extend to valuations in administering subsection (b)(2)(B)(ii) when some form of market valuation may be available to test. the adequacy of an old equity holder's proposed contribution.

Whether a market test would require an opportunity to offer competing plans or would be satisfied by a right to bid for the same interest sought by old equity is a question we do not decide here. It is enough to say, assuming a new value corollary, that plans providing junior interest holders with exclusive opportunities free from competition and without benefit of market valuation fall within the prohibition of § 1129(b)(2)(B)(ii).

The judgment of the Court of Appeals, accordingly, is reversed, and the case is remanded for further proceedings consistent with this opinion.

It is so ordered.

---

b. Sarah Borders' Explanation of *LaSalle*

The Supreme Court did not determine whether the Los Angeles Lumber dicta regarding new value survived the enactment of the Bankruptcy Code in 1978. Instead, the Court said, the debtor's plan was "doomed ... by its provision for vesting equity in the reorganized business in the Debtor's partners without extending an opportunity for anyone else either to compete for that equity or to propose a competing reorganization plan." 119 S. Ct. at 1422. Because no party other than old equity had an opportunity to obtain the reorganized debtor's partnership interests, the Court concluded that old equity had received the partnership interests "on account of their "junior ... interest [s], in violation of Section 1129(b)(2)(B)(ii) of the Bankruptcy Code. The Court suggested, but did not hold, that the termination of exclusivity, market valuations of the reorganized debtor's equity, or perhaps both will be required before a new value plan is confirmable.

Sarah Robinson Borders, *Hot Topics With Respect To Real Estate Bankruptcy Issues,* PLI, Doing Deals 2003, 1357 PLI/Corp. 461, 467 (2003).

---

7. *Other "Fair and Equitable" Concepts*

The history of section 1129(b) is not linear. In its earliest versions during the legislative process, it simply recited what today is section 1129(b)(1) — that a plan be fair and equitable. Later amendments to the bill that became the 1978 code attempted to codify various components of that phrase, but always with the self-awareness that the bill did not include everything.

Ultimately, Congress settled for the current structure of section 1129(b)(1); a recitation of the general "fair and equitable" standard in section 1129(b)(1), coupled with possible examples of various treatments in section 1129(b)(2).

This codification process carried over the old statutory language, with noted changes. One key uncodified component is the "no premium" rule which does not permit any class to be paid more than in full.

Other possible components, however, have not been fully tested under the Code. These include the rule regarding step-ups to compensate for loss of priority, *In re* Imperial '400' Nat'l, Inc., 374 F. Supp. 949, 958 (D.N.J. 1974); and the possible rule regarding the inclusion of postpetition interest. In addition, cases under the Code have construed its terms to achieve new wrinkles, such as a prohibition against plans which create undue or unfair risk for pre-petition creditors, Aetna Realty Inv., Inc. v. Monarch Beach Venture, Ltd. (*In re* Monarch Beach Venture, Ltd.), 166 B.R. 428, 436 (C.D. Cal. 1993) (reverse mortage, although technically complying with absolute priority rule, did not pass under broader 'fair and equitable' rule. On these points generally, *see* 7 COLLIER ON BANKRUPTCY ¶ 1129.04[4][b] (15th Rev. ed. 2005).

PROBLEM 11-30: GREEDY BONDHOLDERS AND THE "FAIR AND EQUITABLE" RULE

Gotrocks, Inc. is in the gravel business. It issued $100,000,000 worth of unsecured bonds to the public three years ago. Due to some unfortunate accidents at the quarry, Gotrocks had to file chapter 11 last year. After a heated battle, the Official Bondholders' Committee prevailed in obtaining a termination of exclusivity, and has now proposed its own plan. The plan proposes to terminate old equity and the bonds, and issue common stock to pre-petition bondholders in amounts proportionate to such bondholders' pre-petition debt.

You represent the equity security holders committee. You have testimony from a semi-reputable investment banker that the value of Gotrocks, without any debt, is $110,000,000. Other than the bonds, there is only $5,000,000 of other unsecured debt, and no secured debt. Your review of the plan is that it meets all the requirements of Section 1129(a) except paragraph (8).

Do you have a legitimate objection to the bondholders' plan?

K. After Confirmation

A Chapter 11 case does not end with confirmation. After confirmation, the debtor continues operating its business (providing the plan does not call for liquidation) and makes the payments provided for in the plan.

Even though confirmation requires a finding that the plan is feasible, the debtor may encounter problems in paying or otherwise performing pursuant to the provisions of the plan. Postconfirmation problems raise questions about the effects of confirmation.

Section 1141 is entitled "Effect of Confirmation." Please read section 1141 and determine the effect of confirmation of the Chapter 11 plan in the following problems.

Effect of Confirmation and Section 1141

11 U.S.C. § 1141

(a) Except as provided in subsections (d)(2) and (d)(3) of this section, the provisions of a confirmed plan bind the debtor . . . and any creditor. . . whether or not . . . such creditor . . . has accepted the plan.

(b) Except as otherwise provided in the plan or the order confirming the plan, the confirmation of a plan vests all of the property of the estate in the debtor. . . .

(d) (1) Except as otherwise provided in this subsection, in the plan, or in the order confirming the plan, the confirmation of a plan-

(A) discharges the debtor from any debt that arose before the date of such confirmation, and any debt of a kind specified in section 502(g), 502(h), or 502(i) of this title, whether or not-

(i) a proof of the claim based on such debt is filed or deemed filed under section 501 of this title;

(ii) such claim is allowed under section 502 of this title; or

(iii) the holder of such claim has accepted the plan; and

. . .

(3) The confirmation of a plan does not discharge a debtor if-

(A) the plan provides for the liquidation of all or substantially all of the property of the estate;

(B) the debtor does not engage in business after consummation of the plan; and

(C) the debtor would be denied a discharge under section 727(a) of this title if the case were a case under chapter 7 of this title.

PROBLEM 11-31: IF THE DEBTOR DOES NOT MAKE PLAN PAYMENTS

1. D's Chapter 11 reorganization plan provides for the continuation of business operations and the issuance of notes to holders of unsecured claims. The notes are to be for 40% of the amount owed and are to be payable over five years. The plan is

confirmed. What are the rights of X, an unsecured creditor who voted against the plan? Of Y, an unsecured creditor who did not file a proof of claim? What if D is a corporation? *Cf.* 11 U.S.C. § 727(a)(1)

2. Same facts as #1. What are the rights of D's unsecured creditors if D defaults on its new payment obligations? Is D protected by the automatic stay? By the confirmation order?

3. D's Chapter 11 plan provides for the sale of all of its assets to Newco and the issuance of Newco notes to holders of unsecured claims. The notes are to be 40% of the amount owed and are to be payable over five years. The plan is confirmed. What are the rights *of* D's unsecured creditors against D? What if D is a corporation? *See* 11 U.S.C. §§ 1141(d)(3) and 727(a)(1).

4. D's Chapter 11 plan that provides for monthly payments to creditors for two years is confirmed. D is able to make the first three payments. Because of an unexpected deep drop in sales, D is not able to make the fourth payment. How can D modify its payment obligations under the confirmed plan? Section 1127(b) prohibits modification after "substantial consummation." *See* § 1101(c). If D can not modify its confirmed Chapter 11, can D file another Chapter 11 petition, *i.e.*, use "Chapter 22?" *Cf.* U.S.C. §§ 109(d), (g).

L. 363 SALES AS AN ALTERNATIVE/PRELUDE TO A CHAPTER 11 PLAN (AKA "CHAPTER 363")

11 U.S.C. § 363(b)

(b)(1) The trustee, after notice and hearing, may . . . sell . . ., other than in the ordinary course of business, property of the estate.

Notice that section 363(b) does not provide a limit on how much property of the estate may be sold. Nor does section 363(b) indicate what standard the bankruptcy judge should apply at the hearing.

WBQ P'SHIP V. VIRGINIA DEP'T OF MEDICAL ASSISTANCE SERVICES (*IN RE* WBQ P'SHIP)

189 B.R. 97 (Bankr. E.D. Va. 1995)

Memorandum Opinion

MARTIN V.B. BOSTETTER, Chief Judge.

The case at bar presents two questions for decision: whether the Chapter 11 debtor may sell nearly all its assets under 11 U.S.C. § 363(f) before filing a disclosure statement and liquidation plan, and if the sale is permissible under § 363(f), whether the Court can enjoin a creditor of the debtor from initiating a collection action against the third-party buyer. As to the first question, the debtor, WBQ Partnership, has moved to sell virtually all its assets, as part of its decision to liquidate under Chapter 11. The Internal Revenue Service ("IRS") and the Virginia Department of Medical Assistance Services ("DMAS"), have objected to the merits of the proposed sale. For the reasons that follow, we overrule these objections, and approve the sale proposed by the debtor.

As to the second question, DMAS contends that it can collect a portion of the gain realized from the sale pursuant to Va.Code Ann. § 32.1-329 (Michie 1992). Significantly, this Virginia statute authorizes DMAS to collect or "recapture" the gain either from the debtor, or if the debtor fails to pay DMAS, from the person buying the assets. By allowing DMAS to proceed against the buyer, we find that the Virginia statute conflicts with § 363(f) of the Bankruptcy Code, which authorizes a trustee to sell property free and clear of liens and other interests. Relying on the Supremacy Clause and § 105(a) of the Bankruptcy Code, we permanently enjoin DMAS from exercising its statutory rights against the buyer, as explained more fully below.

I.

The material facts are undisputed. For nearly 20 years, the debtor has operated a nursing home located in Stafford, Virginia, and has received Medicaid payments from DMAS, the state agency responsible for administering the federal Medicaid program in the Commonwealth of Virginia. The Medicaid program provides money to states which, in turn, enables them to fund medical treatment for the poor. *See* 42 U.S.C. § 1396. To receive Medicaid funding, a state must submit to the U.S. Secretary for Health and Human Services a "plan for medical assistance," *id.* § 1396a, which is "required to establish, among other things, a scheme for reimbursing health care providers [such as nursing homes] for the [costs of] the medical services provided to" Medicaid-qualified patients. *Wilder v. Virginia Hosp. Ass'n,* 496 U.S. 498, 502, 110 S.Ct. 2510, 2513, 110 L.Ed.2d 455 (1990).

Among the costs reimbursable under Virginia's plan is the depreciation of a nursing home's tangible assets. Similar to other states, Virginia "calculates depreciation according to a standard accounting method, dividing an asset's purchase price (say, $300,000) by its estimated useful life (say, 30 years), and reimbursing the facility for the resulting annual depreciation ($10,000 each year for 30 years)." *Hoodkroft Convalescent Ctr. v. New Hampshire Div. of Human Servs.,* 879 F.2d 968, 969 (1st Cir.1989) (interpreting an equivalent provision in New Hampshire), *cert. denied,* 493 U.S. 1020, 110 S.Ct. 720, 107 L.Ed.2d 740 (1990). Upon the sale of the asset, section 32.1-329 of the Virginia Code authorizes DMAS to "recapture" the depreciation it paid "to the extent that the sale price exceeds the depreciated original cost of the asset (*i.e.,* the original purchase price less all depreciation payments made before the sale)." *Id.* at 969-70 (citing Va.Code Ann. § 32.1-329 (Michie 1988)).

Returning to the illustration supplied in *Hoodkroft Convalescent Center, supra,* assume that over 15 years, DMAS pays a total reimbursement of $150,000 to the nursing home for the wear-and-tear of the asset. The asset's cost basis is thus reduced to $150,000 ($300,000 less $150,000). Assume further that the nursing home sells the asset to another nursing home for $500,000. Under the Virginia statute, DMAS may recover or "recapture" $150,000 as a depreciation overpayment, as indicated above. Va.Code § 32.1- 329(A). If the seller fails to reimburse DMAS for the recaptured depreciation, DMAS will deem the sale "ineffective" as to the Commonwealth of Virginia. At that point, DMAS may collect the recaptured depreciation using "any means available by law." *Id.* § 32.1-329(C). Such "means" include an action for attachment or levy, and most importantly, exercising a setoff against the Medicaid payments that would be owed to the buyer, as the new owner of the nursing home. *See id.* § 32.1-329(C) & (D).

The dispute at hand arises from the debtor's motion to sell its nursing home free and clear of DMAS's recapture rights. The nursing-home facility itself is situated on real property owned by Michael and Sherill Quigley, and William and Shirley Bagley. The debtor is a partnership comprised of Michael Quigley and William Bagley, and it owns the personal property connected with the nursing home. On February 11, 1993, the debtor filed for Chapter 11 relief under the Bankruptcy Code. According to the documents filed in this case, three deeds of trust encumber the real property. The first-priority trust secures a total indebtedness of $133,000, while two second-priority trusts secure a total indebtedness of $33,000. Additionally, the IRS asserts a claim totaling $426,834, a portion of which ($260,201) is secured by tax liens.

After filing its Chapter 11 petition, the debtor submitted a proposed disclosure statement and plan of reorganization. DMAS subsequently decreased the level of reimbursement it was paying the debtor, which in turn, reduced the amount of income that the debtor was receiving postpetition. According to the debtor, DMAS's action made the plan unconfirmable, and prompted the debtor to withdraw it. In an effort to resolve this Chapter 11 case, the debtor has decided to sell nearly all its assets, and divide the sale proceeds among its creditors pursuant to a liquidation plan that has not yet been filed. The debtor has thus entered into an asset-purchase agreement with Gilron, Inc. Under this agreement, which has not yet been approved by the Court, Gilron will buy the real property and the debtor's assets free and clear of liens and other interests, and the liens will attach to the proceeds resulting from the sale. The agreement, as amended, provides that Gilron will pay the purchase price entirely with cash. After the sale is completed, Gilron intends to continue operating the facility as a nursing home. The debtor has asked this Court to approve the proposed agreement under 11 U.S.C. § 363(f). [DMAS objected]

Turning to the purchase price, we note that a recent appraisal found the assets' "replacement-cost" value to be $785,000, their "going-concern" value to be $660,000, and their "as is" market value to be $515,000. The proposed agreement originally contemplated that Gilron would pay $700,000 for the assets, a price that exceeded their appraised going-concern value. DMAS subsequently determined, however, that the total amount of reimbursements it would pay to Gilron over time would be $515,000, which represents the "as is" market value of the assets, as mentioned above. DMAS's decision effectively reduced the purchase price to $515,000.

At this price, DMAS asserts that it is entitled to recapture a total of $196,000 in depreciation overpayments under Va.Code § 32.1-329. It is unlikely that DMAS will recover the entire $196,000 from the proceeds of sale, since DMAS concedes that its right of recapture is not a lien, and since a large portion of the assets already serve as collateral for the secured claims described above. Needless to say, the secured creditors must be paid in full before the unsecured creditors, such as DMAS, can receive their *pro rata* share of the remaining proceeds. DMAS thus contends that it has authority under Va.Code § 32.1-329 to satisfy any remaining deficiency by exercising its rights against Gilron.

Gilron asserts, and DMAS concedes, that should DMAS offset the "recaptured" depreciation against the Medicaid payments owed to Gilron, Gilron would lose the level of income necessary to operate the nursing home efficiently and economically. Accordingly, Gilron is not willing to complete the sale if DMAS is permitted to exercise its rights under Va.Code § 32.1- 329. The debtor contends that, if the sale is not consummated, there will be no hope of presenting a confirmable plan, and consequently, the debtor will be forced to either dismiss its case or liquidate under Chapter 7. It is undisputed that either outcome would compel the debtor to close its nursing home, dismiss all its employees, and release all its patients. The debtor asserts that closing the nursing home would impose a significant burden on the patients and their families, for the closest nursing home is twenty miles away, and it has no available beds to accommodate the patients released from the debtor's facility. In the debtor's view, the only available prospect for confirming a plan, and keeping the nursing home open, is to issue an injunction that forbids DMAS from exercising its rights against Gilron. The debtor has thus commenced this adversary proceeding, asking the Court to enjoin DMAS in conjunction with approving the proposed sale. In response, DMAS has moved for summary judgment, or in the alternative, for dismissal of the debtor's complaint on grounds that it fails to allege a colorable claim. *See* Fed.R.Civ.P. 12(b)(6).

II.

Before turning to the merits of the injunction and DMAS's motion, we must decide, as a threshold matter, whether the proposed sale satisfies the requirements of 11 U.S.C. § 363(f), since DMAS [has] challenged the validity of the sale itself. Section 363(f) provides as follows:

> The trustee may sell property *under subsection (b)* or (c) of this section *free and clear* of any interest in such property of an entity other than the estate, *only if*--(1) applicable nonbankruptcy law permits sale of such property free and clear of such interest; (2) such entity consents; (3) such interest is a lien and the price at which such property is to be sold is greater than the aggregate value of all liens on such property; (4) such interest is in bona fide dispute; *or* (5) such entity could be compelled, in a legal or equitable proceeding, to accept a money satisfaction of such interest.

11 U.S.C. § 363(f) (emphasis added). As the phrase "under subsection (b)" suggests, a sale must satisfy the requirements of § 363(b) before it can be approved under § 363(f). We accordingly turn to the language of § 363(b).

A.

In relevant part, § 363(b) provides that, following notice and an opportunity to be heard, a trustee or a debtor-in-possession "may use, sell, or lease, other than in the ordinary course of business, property of the estate." *Id.* § 363(b)(1). By its terms, § 363(b) does not require a Chapter 11 debtor to propose a plan of reorganization before it moves to sell its assets outside the ordinary course of business. Nevertheless, to prevent debtors from using § 363(b) as a vehicle for circumventing the creditor protections afforded under Chapter 11, the courts have imposed their own requirements for allowing liquidation sales before plan confirmation. At least one circuit has confined such sales "to emergencies where there is imminent danger that the assets of the ailing business will be lost if prompt action is not taken." *In re Solar Mfg. Corp.,* 176 F.2d 493, 494 (3d Cir.1949). More recent decisions have determined that pre- confirmation sales are permissible "when a sound business purpose dictates such action." *Stephens Indus., Inc. v. McClung,* 789 F.2d 386, 390 (6th

Cir.1986); *see also Committee of Equity Sec. Holders v. Lionel Corp. (In re Lionel Corp.),* 722 F.2d 1063, 1071 (2d Cir.1983). After reviewing the relevant authorities, we conclude that the "sound business purpose" test is the more sensible approach for providing creditors with a measure of protection outside the plan-confirmation process. We therefore adopt the line of decisions applying the sound business purpose test.

The sound business purpose test has four elements. A trustee or debtor-in-possession has the burden of proving that (1) a sound business reason or emergency justifies a pre-confirmation sale; (2) the sale has been proposed in good faith; (3) adequate and reasonable notice of the sale has been provided to interested parties; and (4) the purchase price is fair and reasonable. *In re Delaware & Hudson Rwy. Co.,* 124 B.R. 169, 176 (D.Del.1991); *see also In re Country Manor of Kenton, Inc.,* 172 B.R. 217, 220 (Bankr.N.D.Ohio 1994); *Titusville Country Club v. Pennbank (In re Titusville Country Club),* 128 B.R. 396, 399 (Bankr.W.D.Pa.1991).

As for the first element, which asks whether there is a sound business reason justifying a pre-confirmation sale, the debtor asserts that its business is suffering as a result of "minimal cash flow." The debtor also contends, without any contest or dispute, that it is unable to reorganize because it suffered a loss of income when DMAS decided to offset its claims against the postpetition Medicaid reimbursements that were owed to the debtor. The debtor therefore implies that a § 363 sale is necessary to prevent the value of its assets from deteriorating as a result of its financial problems. *Cf. In re Channel One Communications, Inc.,* 117 B.R. 493, 496 (Bankr.E.D.Mo.1990). Additionally, the debtor points out that a pre- confirmation sale would relieve the debtor's estate of "accruing interest, property taxes and insurance escrows," thereby benefiting creditors. We conclude that the debtor's undisputed assertions have presented a sound business reason for selling its property before plan confirmation, and accordingly, the debtor has satisfied the first element of the sound business purpose test.

We next consider whether the sale has been proposed in good faith. In this instance, a principal of Gilron, the proposed buyer, is the current manager of the debtor's facility, which raises the concern that the proposed sale might not be the product of an arm's length transaction. A negotiation conducted at arm's length helps to ensure that the agreed price ultimately will be fair and reasonable. Whether the purchase price here is fair and reasonable is the question we address below. For the moment, however, we consider the related question of whether the proposed sale involves disguised payments to insiders, perhaps in the form of consulting agreements and employment contracts that will benefit only the debtor's principals. *See* 1 David G. Epstein et al., *Bankruptcy* § 4-4, at 384-85 (1992). The IRS argues that the debtor's notice is defective inasmuch as it failed to divulge whether and to what extent the debtor's principals would be benefiting from the transaction. The IRS may be correct in this respect. But we find that the debtor cured this defect when its counsel assured us at a status hearing on September 19, 1995 that there are no collateral agreements benefiting the debtor's principals in connection with the proposed sale.

DMAS contends that the debtor is using the sale as a vehicle for nullifying its right of recapture. We are unpersuaded. After filing its Chapter 11 petition, the debtor submitted a proposed plan and disclosure statement, but later withdrew these documents because DMAS had reduced the level of Medicaid reimbursements paid to the debtor. In light of this circumstance, the debtor decided to attempt a "reorganization" in the form of inviting new equity to buy the business. To maximize the purchase price and enlarge the return to all creditors, the debtor has sought to enjoin DMAS from enforcing its recapture rights against the prospective buyer. Under these circumstances, we cannot find that the debtor has proposed this sale in bad faith.

The next issue we address is whether the debtor provided adequate and reasonable notice to interested parties. "Due process requires notice that is reasonably calculated, under the circumstances, to apprise an interested party of the pendency of an action." *Snug Enter., Inc. v. Sage (In re Snug Enter., Inc.),* 169 B.R. 31, 33 (Bankr.E.D.Va.1994) (citing *Mullane v. Central Hanover Bank & Trust Co.,* 339 U.S. 306, 314-15, 70 S.Ct. 652, 657, 94 L.Ed. 865 (1950)). In this context, "notice is sufficient if it includes the terms and conditions of the sale, if it states the time for filing objections, and if the estate is selling real estate, it generally describes the property." *In re Karpe,* 84 B.R. 926, 929 (Bankr.M.D.Pa.1988). Having reviewed the debtor's amended notice carefully, we conclude that all interested parties have received adequate and reasonable notice of the proposed sale. The amended notice generally describes the property to be sold, it discloses the purchase price and the manner of payment, and it fixes a time period for filing objections. Additionally, the amended notice identifies the proposed buyer, Gilron, Inc., and it properly divulges that a principal of Gilron, Ronald Bailey, is the current manager of the debtor's facility. The amended notice specifies that the assets will be sold free and clear of interests, and it explains that the debtor will seek to preclude DMAS from exercising its recapture rights under Va.Code § 32.1-329. Finally, we conclude that the detailed laundry list of "assets to be sold" reasonably notifies interested parties that the debtor is seeking to liquidate under 11 U.S.C. § 363. For these reasons, we find the amended notice to be reasonable and adequate.

The final question we address is whether the proposed price is fair and reasonable. Citing the decisions of *Chmil v. Rulisa Operating Company (In re Tudor Associates, Ltd., II)*, 20 F.3d 115, 119 (4th Cir.1994), and *Willemain v. Kivitz (In re Willemain)*, 764 F.2d 1019, 1023 (4th Cir.1985), the IRS contends that a proposed price is fair and reasonable if it constitutes at least 75% of the appraised value of the assets. The difficulty here is that neither *Tudor Associates* nor *Willemain* interpreted § 363(b). Rather, each of the cases involved an attack on a transfer that had already occurred, and the outcome of each case turned, in part, on whether the buyer was a bona fide or good-faith purchaser. Still, even if *Tudor Associates* and *Willemain* do supply the proper test for determining whether a price is fair and reasonable, we conclude that the price proposed here meets that test. In this instance, the proposed purchase price is $515,000, and as mentioned before, a recent appraisal found the replacement-cost value of the assets to be $785,000, the assets' going-concern value to be $660,000, and the assets' "as is" market value to be $515,000. Neither the IRS nor DMAS has challenged the numbers set forth in the appraisal. Relying on these numbers, we observe that the proposed price of $515,000 constitutes 78% of the assets' appraised going-concern value and 100% of their appraised "as is" market value. Under these circumstances, we conclude that the proposed price is fair and reasonable under the test set forth in *Tudor Associates* and *Willemain.*

The IRS indicates next that private sale agreements between a prospective buyer and a Chapter 11 debtor should be treated as suspect, and it implies further that a higher price for these assets could be gained at a public auction. *See In re Landscape Properties, Inc.*, 100 B.R. 445, 447-48 (Bankr.E.D.Ark.1988) (stating that an objection to a sale based simply on the fact that a higher offer exists must be sustained under certain circumstances); *In re Ohio Corrugating Co.*, 59 B.R. 11, 12 (Bankr.N.D.Ohio 1985) (holding that the method of sale providing the fullest measure of fairness is a public auction). By and large, we agree that a public auction can serve the interests of creditors more than a private deal reached between a Chapter 11 debtor and a prospective buyer. In the case at hand, however, we do not believe a public auction would command a higher price, given the unique situation presented here. Most significantly, DMAS has determined that the total amount of depreciation it will allow after the sale is $515,000. DMAS's decision has effectively imposed a ceiling on the value of the assets, since it is unlikely that any future nursing home would be willing to pay more than $515,000 for assets that will command a Medicaid reimbursement of only $515,000.

Even if the prospective buyer does not intend to treat Medicaid-qualified patients, it still must confront DMAS's right of recapture. As related above, if the sale produces a gain, the debtor must pay DMAS at least a portion of the gain, which will be designated as "recaptured depreciation." *See* Va.Code § 32.1-329(A). If the debtor fails to pay this sum, DMAS will deem the sale "ineffective" as to the Commonwealth of Virginia, and may then collect the recaptured depreciation, using "any means available by law," which includes an action for attachment or levy. *See id.* § 32.1-329(C) & (D). Of course, if the sale price is very low and there is no resulting gain, DMAS's right of recapture will not ensue. Accordingly, absent an injunction that forbids DMAS from exercising its statutory right of recapture, prospective buyers will have a tremendous incentive to bid a price so low that DMAS's right of recapture will not be invoked. For these reasons, we do not believe a public auction would produce a price appreciably higher than $515,000. We therefore find that the proposed price is fair and reasonable, and that the proposed sale satisfies the elements of the sound business purpose test under 11 U.S.C. § 363(b).

B.

Having found that the sale is permissible under § 363(b), we next consider whether the sale may be accomplished free and clear of "any interest," as provided by 11 U.S.C. § 363(f). Initially, we emphasize that the tax liens held by the IRS qualify as an "interest" under § 363(f), since the Bankruptcy Code defines the term "lien" as a "charge against or *interest* in property to secure payment of a debt or performance of an obligation." *Id.* § 101(37) (emphasis added). Perhaps the more significant question is whether the term "interest" extends beyond liens, encompassing DMAS's right of recapture. Since "lien" is a defined term under the Bankruptcy Code, it stands to reason that Congress would have used the term "lien" instead of "interest," had it intended to restrict the scope of § 363(f) to liens. Furthermore, § 363(f)(3) applies to situations in which "such interest is a lien," which suggests that liens constitute a subcategory of "any interest." Other courts have indicated that the term "interest" is broad, covering more than mere liens. *See, e.g., American Living Sys. v. Bonapfel (In re All American of Ashburn, Inc.),* 56 B.R. 186, 189-90 (Bankr.N.D.Ga.), *aff'd per curiam,* 805 F.2d 1515 (11th Cir.1986); *In re Manning,* 37 B.R. 755, 759 (Bankr.D.Colo.1984), *aff'd in part and remanded,* 831 F.2d 205 (10th Cir.1987). We likewise conclude, for the reasons stated above, that the term "interest" extends beyond liens.

Additionally, DMAS's right of recapture falls within the category of "any interest" that is subject to § 363(f). As mentioned before, if the purchase price exceeds the asset's depreciated basis, DMAS may "recapture" at least a portion of the realized gain. *See* Va.Code § 32.1-329. If the seller fails to reimburse DMAS for the recaptured depreciation, DMAS may proceed to collect the recaptured depreciation from the purchaser. *Id.* § 32.1-329(C). In essence, DMAS's right of recapture runs with the property, so it is more than a mere claim against the debtor. DMAS's right of recapture is an "interest in property" insofar as it grants DMAS the right to proceed against the transferee. DMAS emphasizes that it has a "contingent" interest since its right of recapture depends on whether a gain is realized from the sale, and whether the seller reimburses DMAS for the recaptured depreciation. Yet the plain terms of § 363(f) refer to "*any* interest." Accordingly, DMAS's "contingent interest" is not exempt from the reach of § 363(f).

Section 363(f) enumerates five conditions for allowing a sale free and clear of interests. The "or" that precedes subsection (f)(5) indicates that the five conditions are phrased in the disjunctive, meaning that property may be sold free of an interest if that interest falls into only one of the five conditions. *In re Collins,* 180 B.R. 447, 450 (Bankr.E.D.Va.1995). As for the tax liens held by the IRS, the proposed sale is permissible under subsection (f)(3), which authorizes a sale free and clear of an interest when "such interest is a lien and the price at which such property is to be sold is greater than the aggregate value of all liens on such property." 11 U.S.C. § 363(f)(3). There is a split of authority as to whether a price "greater than the aggregate value of all liens" means a price that exceeds the face amount of the liens encumbering the property, or alternatively, whether it means a price that exceeds the value of the liened property itself. One recent decision rendered in this district took the latter view, holding that a sale was permitted under § 363(f)(3) if the purchase price exceeded the value of the liened property. *Collins,* 180 B.R. at 451.

It could be argued, of course, that the situation at hand fails the *Collins* test since the purchase price merely equals the "as is" market value of the assets, and since the price is less than the going-concern value. But the court in *Collins* held that when the purchase price equals the value of the liened property, the sale is still permissible under § 363(f)(3) if the proposed price is the best obtainable under the circumstances, and if there are "special circumstances justifying a sale for less than the amount of the liens." *Id.* at 451. We have already determined that the price proposed in this instance is the best price obtainable under the circumstances. *See supra* part II.A. Additionally, it is unnecessary to decide whether "special circumstances" exist, since the proposed purchase price exceeds the face amount of the liens. Here, the proposed purchase price is $515,000, and the aggregate amount of the liens is $426,201. The IRS and trust holders are fully secured, and they will be adequately protected when their liens attach to the sale proceeds. *See Collins,* 180 B.R. at 452. Accordingly, with respect to the tax liens held by the IRS, the sale is permissible under § 363(f)(3).

As for DMAS's right of recapture, we observe that the proposed sale fails to satisfy the condition specified in subsection (f)(1), for applicable non-bankruptcy law, namely Va.Code § 32.1-329, does not permit a sale free and clear of DMAS's interest if the debtor fails to reimburse DMAS for the recaptured depreciation. The proposed sale also fails to satisfy subsections (f)(2) and (f)(3), since DMAS has not consented to the sale, and DMAS has asserted that its interest is not a lien. Additionally, DMAS's interest is not the subject of a bona fide dispute. In this instance, the debtor recognizes DMAS's interest, and is thus seeking an injunction to prevent its enforcement. Because there is no bona fide dispute concerning the extent or validity of DMAS's interest, subsection (f)(4) is unsatisfied.

The only remaining subsection is (f)(5), which permits a sale free and clear of any interest when "such entity [holding the interest] could be compelled, in a legal or equitable proceeding, to accept a money satisfaction of such interest." 11 U.S.C. § 363(f)(5). At the outset, it should be emphasized that § 363(f)(5) specifies a *money* satisfaction, which suggests that the interest must be reducible to a claim. The Bankruptcy Code defines "claim" as a "right to payment"--something that can be satisfied with money. *Id.* § 101(5); *see also In re Beker Indus. Corp.,* 63 B.R. 474, 478 (Bankr.S.D.N.Y.1986) (stating that "§ 363(f)(5) is to be interpreted ... as referring to those few interests in property that can, by operation of law, be reduced to dollars."). Accordingly, if a holder of an interest cannot be compelled to accept a cash award in lieu of equitable relief, the sale cannot proceed under § 363(f)(5).

To illustrate, suppose the interest in question is a restrictive covenant running with the land. Assume further that the debtor is violating the restrictive covenant, which prompts the adjacent landowners to seek a remedy, such as money damages. In this example, however, money damages would not be an adequate remedy because the debtor could conceivably pay the damages and continue violating the covenant, which would force the landowners to commence another lawsuit for subsequent violations. An adequate remedy available to the landowners would be prospective relief, namely an injunction that enforces the covenant as an equitable servitude. In this situation, there is nothing that can force the landowners to "forego equitable relief in favor of a cash award." *Gouveia v. Tazbir,* 37 F.3d 295, 299 (7th Cir.1994). For this reason, § 365(f)(5) would not permit a bankruptcy trustee to sell the land free of the restrictive covenant. *Cf. Gouveia,* 37 F.3d at 299-300 (concluding that the trustee could not sell the land free and clear of the covenant); *In re 523 E. Fifth Street Hous. Preserv. Dev't Fund Corp.,* 79 B.R. 568, 576 (Bankr.S.D.N.Y.1987) (holding that the property could not be sold free of the restrictive covenant).

We conclude, for the following reasons, that DMAS's right of recapture is not akin to the restrictive covenant set forth in the illustration above. Nor is it similar to the cleanup order addressed in *Torwico, supra.* Unlike the situations involving the restrictive covenant and the cleanup order, DMAS is not confronted with an ongoing violation of its interest. Nor is there the threat of an ongoing nuisance that confronted the court in *Torwico.* If the sale goes forward, DMAS's right of recapture will arise through a one-time transaction. In exercising this right, DMAS would collect a payment--either from the debtor or from the transferee, Gilron, Inc. The only threat confronting DMAS is the loss of money that would result from selling the assets free and clear of DMAS's interest. Accordingly, we conclude that DMAS's interest can be reduced to a claim, and is therefore subject to a hypothetical money satisfaction under 11 U.S.C. § 363(f)(5). . . .

We emphasize "hypothetical" satisfaction, since § 363(f)(5) authorizes a sale if the interest holder "*could be* compelled, in a legal or equitable proceeding, to accept a money satisfaction of such interest." *Id.* (emphasis added). The courts are divided, nevertheless, as to whether the statute requires a hypothetical payment that could fully satisfy the underlying debt. *Compare, e.g., In re Healthco Int'l, Inc.,* 174 B.R. 174, 176 (Bankr.D.Mass.1994) (holding that the terms "money satisfaction" mean "a payment constituting less than full payment of the underlying debt"), *with Richardson v. Pitt County (In re Stroud Wholesale, Inc.),* 47 B.R. 999, 1003 (E.D.N.C.1985) (holding that the terms "money satisfaction" mean "full satisfaction of creditors' interests" in liquidation sales), *aff'd per curiam,* 983 F.2d 1057 (4th Cir.1986) (unpublished disposition). However, the case at hand presents a situation that is different from both *Healthco* and *Stroud Wholesale,* since the interests involved in those cases were liens. Compared with unsecured claims, the Bankruptcy Code provides greater protection to claims secured by liens. For example, creditors are entitled to adequate protection and the indubitable equivalent of their secured claims. *See* 11 U.S.C. §§ 361, 1129(b)(2)(A)(iii). Accordingly, the debate concerning full payment is more relevant to liens. Because the right of recapture is neither a lien nor a right of setoff against the debtor, DMAS has at best an unsecured claim against the debtor. In a hypothetical equitable proceeding, such as a "cram down" of a Chapter 11 plan, DMAS could be compelled to accept less than full payment on its underlying unsecured claim. *See Healthco,* 174 B.R. at 176-77. Thus, with respect to DMAS's interest, the proposed sale satisfies § 363(f)(5). The objections of DMAS and the IRS are therefore overruled, and the sale proposed by the debtor is approved.

III.

[The court then held that Section 363 pre-empted the Virginia statute on recovering payments]

Based on the foregoing, IT IS

ORDERED that the Motion by the Virginia Department of Medical Assistance Services to Dismiss Complaint or in the Alternative, for Summary Judgment in its Favor be, and it hereby is, DENIED. It is further

ORDERED that the request of the debtor, WBQ Partnership, for injunctive relief be, and it hereby is, GRANTED insofar as the defendant, DMAS, is permanently enjoined from exercising its rights under Va.Code § 32.1-329 . . . .

PROBLEM 11-32: TO SELL OR NOT TO SELL?

Aviontrix is a short haul commuter airline. It has been pummeled by recent price cutting of airfares. It cannot continue in business. Fortunately, AirStrike, Inc., a prosperous company, has offered to buy the assets of Aviontrix for $25,000,000, but only if the sale is free and clear of any claims of Aviontrix's creditors. This is a fair price. Advise Aviontrix of whether it can sell its assets in bankruptcy as requested.

Would it make any difference if AirStrike's offer were still $25,000,000, but the consideration was not cash? Say, by a new issuance of AirStrike's publicly-traded bonds? By AirStrike common stock? If it were to be partially paid in scrip that would allow individual creditors of Aviontrix (disappointed passengers; pilots, mechanics) free travel on AirStrike?

Would it make any difference if AirStrike had given a security interest in all its assets to Rapacious Bank, and if:

- the sales price exceeded Rapacious' debt, and thus Rapacious consented? 11 U.S.C. § 363(f)(2).
- the sales price *didn't* cover the amount of the secured debt, and thus Rapacious refused to consent? 11 U.S.C. § 363(f)(3).
- Rapacious, at the last minute, refused to release its liens until AirStrike paid an undocumented "termination fee" that AirStrike believes (correctly) is bogus? 11 U.S.C. § 363(f)(4).

M. REMEDY FOR ABUSES: NON-CONSENSUAL DISMISSAL OR CONVERSION TO CHAPTER 7

11 U.S.C. § 1112(b)

(b)(1) Except as provided in paragraph (2) of this subsection, subsection (c) of this section, and section 1104(a)(3), on request of a party in interest, and after notice and a hearing, the court may absent unusual circumstances specifically identified by the court that establish that the requested conversion or dismissal is not in the best interests of creditors and the estate, the court shall convert a case under this chapter to a case under chapter 7 or dismiss a case under this chapter, whichever is in the best interests of creditors and the estate, if the movant establishes cause,

(2) The relief provided in paragraph (1) shall not be granted absent unusual circumstances specifically identified by the court that establish that such relief is not in the best interests of creditors and the estate, if the debtor or another party in interest objects and establishes that—

(A) there is a reasonable likelihood that a plan will be confirmed within the timeframes established in sections 1121(e) and 1129(e) of this title, or if such sections do not apply, within a reasonable period of time; and

(B) the grounds for granting such relief include an act or omission of the debtor other than under paragraph (4)(A)—

(i) for which there exists a reasonable justification for the act or omission; and

(ii) that will be cured within a reasonable period of time fixed by the court.

(3) The court shall commence the hearing on a motion under this subsection not later than 30 days after filing of the motion, and shall decide the motion not later than 15 days after commencement of such hearing, unless the movant expressly consents to a continuance for a specific period of time or compelling circumstances prevent the court from meeting the time limits established by this paragraph.

(4) For purposes of this subsection, the term "cause" includes—

(A) substantial or continuing loss to or diminution of the estate and the absence of a reasonable likelihood of rehabilitation;

(B) gross mismanagement of the estate;

(C) failure to maintain appropriate insurance that poses a risk to the estate or to the public;

(D) unauthorized use of cash collateral substantially harmful to 1 or more creditors;

(E) failure to comply with an order of the court;

(F) unexcused failure to satisfy timely any filing or reporting requirement established by this title or by any rule applicable to a case under this chapter;

(G) failure to attend the meeting of creditors convened under section 341(a) or an examination ordered under rule 2004 of the Federal Rules of Bankruptcy Procedure without good cause shown by the debtor;

(H) failure timely to provide information or attend meetings reasonably requested by the United States trustee (or the bankruptcy administrator, if any);

(I) failure timely to pay taxes owed after the date of the order for relief or to file tax returns due after the date of the order for relief;

(J) failure to file a disclosure statement, or to file or confirm a plan, within the time fixed by this title or by order of the court;

(K) failure to pay any fees or charges required under chapter 123 of title 28;

(L) revocation of an order of confirmation under section 1144 of this title, and denial of confirmation of another plan or a modified plan under section 1129 of this title;

(M) inability to effectuate substantial consummation of a confirmed plan;

(N) material default by the debtor with respect to a confirmed plan;

(O) termination of a confirmed plan by reason of the occurrence of a condition specified in the plan; and

(P) failure of the debtor to pay any domestic support obligation that first becomes payable after the date of the filing of the petition.

---

11 U.S.C. § 1104(a)(3)

(3) if grounds exist to convert or dismiss the case under section 1112, but the court determines that the appointment of a trustee or an examiner is in the best interests of creditors and the estate.

---

28 U.S.C. § 586(a)(8)

(8) in any case in which the United States trustee finds material grounds for any relief under section 1112 of title 11, the United States trustee shall apply promptly after making that finding to the court for relief.

N. Overview

One of the major changes brought about by the Bankruptcy Abuse Prevention and Consumer Protection Act of 2005 was a substantial revision of Section 1112(b). Before the amendment, courts had discretion to dismiss a case if in the best interest of creditors and the estate if cause was found, and the Code contained a list of ten non-exclusive examples of "cause."

The 2005 Act changed this structure. As a consequence of these changes, any analysis of revised Section 1112(b) involves looking at the grounds for cause, the test to be applied by the court when cause is alleged, and the procedure to be employed to determine whether the allegation of cause is true.

O. *Grounds of "Cause" for a Motion Under Section 1112(b)*

Before the 2005 Act, there were ten grounds for conversion or dismissal. There are now sixteen. Some of the new grounds are reasonably specific, such as the requirement in sub-paragraph (C), which relates to the "failure to maintain appropriate insurance that poses a risk to the estate or to the public." But others are broad and will present questions of interpretation. For example, sub-paragraph (E) states that cause exists if there is any "failure to comply with an order of the court," and sub-paragraph (F) covers any "unexcused failure to satisfy timely any filing or reporting requirement established by this title or by any rule applicable to a case under this chapter." Whether there is a materiality factor for (E), or an exception for delegated orders (such as subpoenas, orders regarding Rule 2004 exams and other ministerial matters) remains to be seen, and the scope of permissible excuses is also unknown.

P. *The New Test for Dismissal, Conversion or Appointment of a Trustee*

Under pre-2005 Act law, the court had discretion to convert or dismiss a case – the statute indicated that a court "may" convert or dismiss. The touchstone was the "best interest of creditors and the estate."

The new test would seem to be mandatory; that is, if one of the expanded grounds for "cause" exists, the court must – the statutory language is "shall" – convert, dismiss or appoint a trustee. But there is a thicket of language that qualifies this mandatory duty.

The first qualifier is in Section 1112(b)(1). The mandatory duty to convert, dismiss or appoint a trustee is excused if there are "unusual circumstances specifically identified by the court that establish that the requested conversion or dismissal is not in the best interests of creditors and the estate."

The second qualifier is found in paragraph (2). That paragraph also is an exception to the mandatory conversion, dismissal or appointment of a trustee. It applies if there are:

> [1] unusual circumstances specifically identified by the court that [2] establish that such relief is not in the best interests of creditors and the estate [3] if the debtor or another party in interest objects and [4] establishes that – [5] (A) there is a reasonable likelihood that a plan will be confirmed with the timeframes [established in chapter 11], [6] or if such sections do not apply, within a reasonable period of time; and [7] (B) the grounds for granting such relief include an act or omission of the debtor other than under paragraph (4)(A) [regarding substantial or continuing loss, and the absence of a reasonable likelihood of rehabilitation] [8] (i) for which there exists a reasonable justification for the act or omission; and [9] that will be cured within a reasonable period of time fixed by the court.

11 U.S.C. § 1112(b)(2) (all materials in brackets added and are not in the original).

So, conversion, dismissal or appointment of a trustee can be avoided if there is an objection, and a showing that: a confirmable plan is imminent, and that the omission or act that lead to the creation of cause was somehow justifiable, but is not likely to happen again.

Q. *THE NEW PROCEDURE WHEN A MOTION UNDER SECTION 1112 IS MADE*

Compounding this complicated approach to conversion or dismissal is the fact that the 2005 Act amended Section 1112 to require that motions under Section 1112 must be heard within 30 days of their filing, and must be determined with 15 days of the commencement of the hearing, unless the moving party consents to a continuance or "compelling circumstances prevent the court from meeting the time limits." 11 U.S.C. § 1112(b)(3). Thus, decisions regarding the life or death of the chapter 11 case will have to be made on an expedited basis.

PROBLEM 11-33: STRUGGLING TO STAY IN

1. Flapdoodle, Inc. is a chapter 11 debtor in possession. The Office of the United States Trustee has filed a motion under Section 1112(b) seeking to dismiss the case because Flapdoodle's management failed to show for two scheduled meetings with their office. Flapdoodle responds by saying that it just forgot; after all, it got into chapter 11 because it didn't manage its time well.

   What discretion does the judge have with respect to this motion?

2. Flapdoodle again. This time the motion is by a creditor who complains that Flapdoodle was a month late in filing its schedules and statement of affairs. Flapdoodle again concedes it was late and has no good excuse. It does point out, however, that the papers were filed, and that six months have passed since it complied with all filings.

   What discretion does the judge have with respect to this motion?

The list of "causes," however, is still non-exclusive. The following case is a good example of what else might found to be "cause."

In re SGL Carbon Corp.

200 F.3d 154 (3d Cir. 1999)

Opinion of the Court

Scirica, Circuit Judge.

The issue on appeal is whether, on the facts of this case, a Chapter 11 bankruptcy petition filed by a financially healthy company in the face of potentially significant civil antitrust liability complies with the requirements of the Bankruptcy Code. In this case, the Official Committee of Unsecured Creditors of SGL Carbon Corporation appeals the District Court's order denying its motion to dismiss SGL Carbon's Chapter 11 bankruptcy petition on bad faith grounds.

This case also presents the threshold issue whether we will adopt a "good faith" requirement for Chapter 11 petitions. We will. After undertaking the fact intensive analysis inherent in the good faith determination, we conclude that SGL Carbon's Chapter 11 petition lacks a valid reorganizational purpose and, therefore, lacks the requisite good faith. We will reverse.

I.

SGL Carbon is a Delaware corporation that manufactures and sells graphite electrodes used in steel production. In 1997, the United States Department of Justice commenced an investigation of alleged price-fixing by graphite electrode manufacturers, including the SGL Carbon Group.[2] Soon thereafter, various steel producers filed class action antitrust lawsuits in the United States District Court for the Eastern District of Pennsylvania against SGL Carbon and other graphite electrode manufacturers. The District Court consolidated the cases into a single class action and certified a class under Fed. R. Civ. P. 23(b)(3) consisting of all United States purchasers of graphite electrodes between 1992 and 1997. Many class members opted out of the class before the November 28, 1998 opt-out deadline and subsequently filed or threatened to file separate antitrust lawsuits. Since the class certification, six complaints have been filed in federal district court and one complaint has been filed in a Canadian court.

---

[2]In May 1999, SGL AG (SGL Carbon's parent) and its chairman Robert Koehler each pled guilty to several criminal antitrust charges and agreed to pay fines of $ 135 million and $ 10 million respectively. It is important to note that the guilty pleas and the payment of the criminal fines by the parent company occurred after the filing of the Chapter 11 petition and the District Court's denial of the motion to dismiss.

In June 1998, SGL Carbon's German parent SGL AG recorded a charge in Deutschmarks of approximately $ 240 million as its "best estimate" of the SGL Carbon Group's potential liability in the criminal and civil antitrust litigation.[4]

On December 16, 1998, at the direction of SGL AG, SGL Carbon filed a voluntary Chapter 11 bankruptcy petition in the United States District Court for Delaware. In SGL Carbon's Disclosure Statement, in a section addressing "Factors Leading to [the] Chapter 11 Filing," SGL Carbon only discussed the antitrust litigation. The bankruptcy filing contained a proposed reorganization plan under which only one type of creditor would be required to accept less than full cash payment for its account, namely the antitrust plaintiffs who obtained judgments against SGL Carbon. Under the plan, potential antitrust judgment creditors would receive credits against future purchases of SGL Carbon's product valid for 30 months following the plan's confirmation. The proposed plan also bars any claimant from bringing an action against SGL Carbon's affiliates, including its parent SGL AG, "based on, relating to, arising out of, or in any way connected with" their claims against SGL Carbon.

The next day, on December 17, in a press release, SGL Carbon explained it had filed for bankruptcy "to protect itself against excessive demands made by plaintiffs in civil antitrust litigation and in order to achieve an expeditious resolution of the claims against it." The press release also stated:

> SGL CARBON Corporation believes that in its case Chapter 11 protection provides the most effective and efficient means for resolving the civil antitrust claims.
>
> . . .
>
> "SGL CARBON Corporation is financially healthy," said Wayne T. Burgess, SGL CARBON Corporation's president. "If we did not face [antitrust] claims for such excessive amounts, we would not have had to file for Chapter 11. We expect to continue our normal business operations."
>
> . . . .
>
> However, because certain plaintiffs continue to make excessive and unreasonable demands, SGL CARBON Corporation believes the prospects of ever

---

[4]Although the record does not reflect the amount by which the $ 240 million reserve was increased by SGL AG subsequent to its guilty plea and accompanying fine, the parties have indicated that the reserve was increased. It is significant that, at the time of SGL Carbon's Chapter 11 petition, the $ 240 million reserve was in place and untouched.

> reaching a commercially practicable settlement with them are remote. After much consideration, SGL CARBON Corporation determined that the most appropriate course of action to address the situation without harming its business was to voluntarily file for chapter 11 protection. . . . .

Contemporaneous with the press release, SGL AG Chairman Robert Koehler conducted a telephone conference call with securities analysts, stating that SGL Carbon was "financially healthier" than before and denying the antitrust litigation was "starting to have a material impact on [SGL Carbon's] ongoing operations in the sense that . . . [it was] starting to lose market share." He also stated that SGL Carbon's Chapter 11 petition was "fairly innovative [and] creative" because "usually Chapter 11 is used as protection against serious insolvency or credit problems, which is not the case [with SGL Carbon's petition]."

Two weeks after SGL Carbon filed its petition and issued the press release, the United States Trustee formed a nine member Official Committee of Unsecured Creditors. Eight of the committee members are antitrust plaintiffs; two of the eight serve as class representatives and the other six have opted out of the class. In January 1999, the Committee filed a motion to dismiss SGL Carbon's bankruptcy petition on the grounds that it was a "litigation tactic designed to frustrate the prosecution of the civil antitrust claims pending against [SGL Carbon] and preserve[SGL Carbon's] equity from these claims." In re SGL Carbon Corp., 233 B.R. 285, 287 (D. Del. 1999).

The District Court held a hearing on the motion on February 17, 1999. Neither side presented witnesses. The evidence was entirely documentary or deposition testimony, including the deposition of SGL Carbon's Vice President Theodore Breyer, who directs the company's graphite electrode business in the United States. In his deposition, Breyer testified that SGL Carbon was financially healthy, having no overdue debts when it filed its Chapter 11 petition. Breyer stated that he recommended filing for bankruptcy because he believed SGL Carbon "could not expeditiously settle with the [antitrust] plaintiffs" absent Chapter 11 protection. Acknowledging that bankruptcy protection was the "sole reason" SGL AG's Executive Committee had authorized the Chapter 11 petition, Breyer testified that he believed filing for Chapter 11 would "change the negotiating platform" with plaintiffs and "increase the pressure on . . . plaintiffs to settle."

The District Court denied the Committee's motion to dismiss on April 23, 1999 assuming, without deciding, that 11 U.S.C. § 1112(b) imposes a duty of good faith upon bankruptcy petitioners. It further assumed this duty requires the proposed reorganization to further what it characterized as Chapter 11's purpose: " 'to restructure a business's finances so that it may continue to operate, provide its employees with jobs, pay its creditors and produce a return for its stockholders.' " SGL Carbon Corp., 233 B.R. at 288 (quoting H.R. Rep. No. 595 (1977) reprinted in 1978 U.S.C.C.A.N. 6179). The court made no findings that SGL Carbon filed for bankruptcy for reasons other than to improve its negotiating position with plaintiffs. But the court concluded the petition furthered the purpose of Chapter 11 because plaintiffs' litigation was imperiling SGL Carbon's operation by distracting its management, was potentially ruinous and could eventually force the company out of business. The court explained that

> the distractions of the litigation pose a serious threat to the continued successful operations of [SGL Carbon]. Further, the potential liability faced by [SGL Carbon] could very well force it out of business. Consistent with the policies and purposes of Chapter 11 which encourage early filing so as to increase the possibility of successful reorganization, the Court will not allow [SGL Carbon] to wait idly by for impending financial and operational ruin, when [SGL Carbon] can take action now to avoid such a consequence.

SGL Carbon Corp., 233 B.R. at 291.

The Committee has appealed.

II.

. . .

A.

The threshold issue is whether Chapter 11 petitions may be dismissed for "cause" under 11 U.S.C. § 1112(b) if not filed in good faith. Although we have not squarely addressed this issue, we implied in First Jersey Nat'l Bank v. Brown (In re Brown), 951 F.2d 564 (3d Cir. 1991), that Chapter 11 imposes a good-faith obligation. In Brown, we considered evidence of bad faith in reviewing the dismissal of a Chapter 11 petition, but concluded "the evidence . . . of bad faith . . . was not strong enough for us to say that it was established as a matter of law." Id. at 572. Because Brown focused on the adequacy of the record for making a good faith/bad faith determination, we did not expressly address whether "bad faith" constituted cause for dismissal. In this case, we make clear what we implied in Brown--Chapter 11 bankruptcy petitions are subject to dismissal under 11 U.S.C. § 1112(b) unless filed in good faith.

Four factors guide our adoption of a good faith standard -- the permissive language of § 1112(b), viewed in light of its legislative history; the decisions of our sister courts of appeals; the equitable nature of bankruptcy; and the purposes underpinning Chapter 11.

We begin with 11 U.S.C. § 1112(b), which allows the court to dismiss or convert a Chapter 11 petition for cause . . . . As many courts and commentators have noted, this language neither requires nor prohibits imposition of a "good faith" requirement on Chapter 11 petitions. But we have noted the provision that "cause" "includes" the ten enumerated factors strongly suggests those factors are not exhaustive and that a court may consider whether other facts and circumstances qualify as "cause." See Brown, 951 F.2d at 572; 7 Collier on Bankruptcy at 1112-20. That interpretation of § 1112(b) is strengthened by the statute's legislative history, which provides in part:

> [The] list [contained in § 1112(b)] is not exhaustive. The court will be able to consider other factors as they arise, and to use its equitable powers to reach an appropriate result in individual cases.

H.R.Rep. No. 595, at 405, reprinted in 1978 U.S.S.C.A.N. 5963, 6362. The Bankruptcy Code's rules of construction, which provide that "include" and "including" are not limiting terms, also support an expansive reading of § 1112(b). See 11 U.S.C. § 102(3). Section 1112(b), by its terms, therefore, does not preclude consideration of unenumerated factors in determining "cause." . . .

B.

Having determined that § 1112(b) imposes a good-faith requirement on Chapter 11 petitions, we consider whether SGL Carbon's Chapter 11 petition was filed in good faith.

The requisite fact intensive inquiry requires determining where SGL Carbon's petition falls along the spectrum ranging from the clearly acceptable to the patently abusive. We first review the District Court's findings of fact and then examine the totality of facts and circumstances to determine whether they support a finding of good faith. See In re Trident, 52 F.3d at 131; In re Marsch, 36 F.3d at 829; In re Laguna, 30 F.3d 734 at 738.

i.

As discussed in part I, the District Court found SGL Carbon's Chapter 11 petition was filed in good faith for two reasons: first, because the distractions caused by the antitrust litigation "posed a serious threat to [SGL Carbon's] continued successful operations," and second, because the litigation might result in a judgment that could cause the company "financial and operational ruin," SGL was required to file when it did. SGL Carbon, 233 B.R. at 291. Although mindful of the careful consideration given by the able District Court, we believe each of these findings of fact was clearly erroneous.

Although there is some evidence that defending against the antitrust litigation occupied some officers' time, there is no evidence this "distraction" posed a "serious threat" to the company's operational well being. At his deposition, Theodore Breyer testified the antitrust litigation consumed a significant portion of his time. But Breyer also noted the Carbon/Graphite Business Unit had met all of its financial targets during the nine months preceding filing. Additionally, Breyer testified that only his business unit was heavily involved in the antitrust litigation, recognizing that any management distraction effecting the rest of SGL Carbon resulted from the bankruptcy filing and not the antitrust litigation. As noted, SGL AG and SGL Carbon officers insisted the company was financially healthy despite the litigation. In addition, SGL AG's Chairman denied that the litigation was having a "material negative impact on [SGL Carbon's] operations." In light of all the evidence, we believe the District Court's finding to the contrary is mistaken. See United States v. U.S. Gypsum Co., 333 U.S. 364, 395, 92 L. Ed. 746, 68 S. Ct. 525 (1948).

We also find clearly erroneous that SGL Carbon's Chapter 11 petition was filed at the appropriate time to avoid the possibility of a significant judgment that "could very well force [SGL Carbon] out of business." There is no evidence that the possible antitrust judgments might force SGL Carbon out of business. To the contrary, the record is replete with evidence of SGL Carbon's economic strength. At the time of filing, SGL Carbon's assets had a stipulated book value of $ 400 million, only $ 100,000 of which was encumbered. On the date of the petition, SGL Carbon had $ 276 million in fixed and non-disputed liabilities. Of those liabilities, only $ 26 million were held by outsiders as the remaining liabilities were either owed to or guaranteed by SGL AG. Although SGL Carbon's parent,

SGL AG, recorded a $ 240 million charge on its books as "its best estimate of the potential liability and expenses of the SGL Carbon Group in connection with all civil and criminal antitrust matters," SGL Carbon is only one part of the SGL Carbon Group covered by the reserve. Furthermore, at the time SGL Carbon filed its petition, that is, before SGL AG paid its $ 135 million criminal fine, the $ 240 million reserve was untouched. In documents accompanying its petition, SGL Carbon estimated the liquidation value of the antitrust claims at $ 54 million. In contrast, no evidence was presented with respect to the amount sought by the antitrust plaintiffs beyond SGL Carbon's repeated characterization of their being "unreasonable."

Whether or not SGL Carbon faces a potentially crippling antitrust judgment, it is incorrect to conclude it had to file when it did. As noted, SGL Carbon faces no immediate financial difficulty. All the evidence shows that management repeatedly asserted the company was financially healthy at the time of the filing. Although the District Court believed the litigation might result in a judgment causing "financial and operational ruin" we believe that on the facts here, that assessment was premature. A Chapter 11 petition would impose an automatic stay on all efforts to collect the judgment and would allow the company the exclusive right to formulate a reorganization plan under which the amount of the judgment could be adjusted to allow the company to reorganize. SGL Carbon has offered no evidence it could not effectively use those protections as the prospect of such a judgment became imminent.[13] The District Court's finding that the petition had to be filed at that particular time to avoid financial ruin and therefore was made in good faith is clearly contradicted by the evidence.

The District Court was correct in noting that the Bankruptcy Code encourages early filing. See SGL Carbon, 233 B.R. at 291. It is well established that a debtor need not be insolvent before filing for bankruptcy protection. See, e.g., In re The Bible Speaks, 65 B.R. 415, 424 (Bankr. D. Mass. 1986); In re Talladega Steaks, Inc., 50 B.R. 42, 44 (Bankr. N.D. Ala. 1985). See also Daniel R. Cowans, Bankruptcy Law and Practice (7th ed. 1998) 232. It also is clear that the drafters of the Bankruptcy Code understood the need for early access to bankruptcy relief to allow a debtor to rehabilitate its business

---

[13]The Texaco Corporation's use of the bankruptcy protections is instructive. See In re Texaco, Inc., 84 B.R. 893 (Bank. S.D.N.Y. 1988). Texaco resorted to bankruptcy only after suffering an $ 11 billion judgment. Even saddled with such a large judgment, bankruptcy provided Texaco a means of reorganizing and continuing as a going concern.

before it is faced with a hopeless situation. Such encouragement, however, does not open the door to premature filing, nor does it allow for the filing of a bankruptcy petition that lacks a valid reorganizational purpose. See, e.g., In re Marsch, 36 F.3d at 828; In re Coastal Cable, 709 F.2d at 764; In re Ravick Corp., 106 B.R. 834, 843 (Bankr. D.N.J. 1989).

SGL Carbon, therefore, is correct that the Bankruptcy Code does not require specific evidence of insolvency for a voluntary Chapter 11 filing. But SGL Carbon cites no case holding that petitions filed by financially healthy companies cannot be subject to dismissal for cause. At any rate, as we explain more fully, SGL Carbon's ability to meet its debts is but one of many factors compelling the conclusion it did not enter Chapter 11 with a valid reorganizational purpose.

We do not hold that a company cannot file a valid Chapter 11 petition until after a massive judgment has been entered against it. Courts have allowed companies to seek the protections of bankruptcy when faced with pending litigation that posed a serious threat to the companies' long term viability. See, e.g., Baker v. Latham Sparrowbush Assocs. (In re Cohoes Indus. Terminal Inc.), 931 F.2d 222 (2d Cir. 1991); In re The Bible Speaks, 65 B.R. 415 (Bankr. D. Mass. 1986); In re Johns-Manville, 36 B.R. 727 (Bankr. S.D.N.Y. 1984). In those cases, however, debtors experienced serious financial and/or managerial difficulties at the time of filing. In Cohoes, the Court of Appeals for the Second Circuit found a good faith filing, in part, because "it [was] clear that Cohoes[the debtor] was encountering financial stress at the time it filed its petition . . . ." 931 F.2d at 228. In Bible Speaks, pending litigation had already had an adverse effect on the debtor's financial well being as it was experiencing "a cash flow problem which prevented it from meeting its current obligations," compounded by an inability to obtain financing. 65 B.R. at 426. In Johns-Manville, the debtor was facing significant financial difficulties. A growing wave of asbestos-related claims forced the debtor to either book a $ 1.9 billion reserve thereby triggering potential default on a $ 450 million debt which, in turn, could have forced partial liquidation, or file a Chapter 11 petition. See In re Johns-Manville, 36 B.R. at 730. Large judgments had already been entered against Johns-Manville and the prospect loomed of tens of thousands of asbestos health-related suits over the course of 20-30 years. See id. at 729. See also Sandrea Friedman, Note, Manville: Good Faith Reorganization or "Insulated" Bankruptcy, 12 Hofstra L. Rev. 121 (1983).

For these reasons, SGL Carbon's reliance on those cases is misplaced. The mere possibility of a future need to file, without more, does not establish that a petition was filed in "good faith." See, e.g., In re Cohoes Indus. Terminal Inc., 931 F.2d at 228 ("Although a debtor need not be in extremis in order to file [a Chapter 11] petition, it must, at least, face such financial difficulty that, if it did not file at that time, it could anticipate the need to file in the future."). SGL Carbon, by its own account, and by all objective indicia, experienced no financial difficulty at the time of filing nor any significant managerial distraction. Although SGL Carbon may have to file for bankruptcy in the future, such an attenuated possibility standing alone is not sufficient to establish the good faith of its present petition.

ii.

. . .

Despite those differing approaches, several cases hold that a Chapter 11 petition is not filed in good faith unless it serves a valid reorganizational purpose. . . . The In re Marsch Court articulated the relationship between the good faith determination and the dismissal of petitions filed merely for tactical advantage:

> The term "good faith" is somewhat misleading. Though it suggests that the debtor's subjective intent is determinative, this is not the case. Instead, the "good faith" filing requirement encompasses several, distinct equitable limitations that courts have placed on Chapter 11 filings. Courts have implied such limitations to deter filings that seek to achieve objectives outside the legitimate scope of the bankruptcy laws. Pursuant to 11 U.S.C. § 1112(b), courts have dismissed cases filed for a variety of tactical reasons unrelated to reorganization.

In re Marsch, 36 F.3d at 828 (citations omitted).

It is easy to see why courts have required Chapter 11 petitioners to act within the scope of the bankruptcy laws to further a valid reorganizational purpose. Chapter 11 vests petitioners with considerable powers--the automatic stay, the exclusive right to propose a reorganization plan, the discharge of debts, etc.--that can impose significant hardship on particular creditors. When financially troubled petitioners seek a chance to remain in business, the exercise of those powers is justified. But this is not so when a petitioner's aims lie outside those of the Bankruptcy Code. See United Sav. Ass'n

v. Timbers of Inwood Forest Assocs., Ltd. (In re Timbers of Inwood Forest Assocs., Ltd.), 808 F.2d 363, 373 (5th Cir. 1987) (en banc), aff'd, 484 U.S. 365, 98 L. Ed. 2d 740, 108 S. Ct. 626 (1988) (stating that if Chapter 11 plan does not have a rehabilitative purpose, the "statutory provisions designed to accomplish the reorganizational objectives become destructive of the legitimate rights and interests of creditors"); In re Little Creek, 779 F.2d at 1072 (explaining that Chapter 11 powers should be given only to debtors with "clean hands"); Furness, 35 B.R. at 1009 ("Chapter 11 was designed to give those teetering on the verge of a fatal financial plummet an opportunity to reorganize on solid ground and try again, not to give profitable enterprises an opportunity to evade contractual or other liabilities."); see also 7 Collier on Bankruptcy at 1112-22 (stating that dismissal is appropriate when costs of Chapter 11 are not justified).

Courts, therefore, have consistently dismissed Chapter 11 petitions filed by financially healthy companies with no need to reorganize under the protection of Chapter 11. See In re Marsch, 36 F.3d at 828-29; In re Argus Group 1700, 206 B.R. at 765-66; Furness, 35 B.R. at 1011-13; In re Talladega Steaks, Inc., 50 B.R. 42, 44 (Bankr. N.D. Ala. 1985). Those courts have recognized that if a petitioner has no need to rehabilitate or reorganize, its petition cannot serve the rehabilitative purpose for which Chapter 11 was designed. See In re Winshall Settlor's Trust, 758 F.2d 1136, 1137 (6th Cir. 1985) ("The purpose of Chapter 11 reorganization is to assist financially distressed business enterprises by providing them with breathing space in which to return to a viable state."); see also S. Rep. No. 95-989, at 9 reprinted in 1978 U.S.C.C.A.N. 5787, 5795 (noting that "Chapter 11 deals with the reorganization of a financially distressed enterprise . . . ").

The absence of a valid reorganizational purpose and the consequent lack of good faith by SGL Carbon is evident here. SGL Carbon's financial disclosure documents give no indication the company needed to reorganize under Chapter 11 protection. Prior to filing, SGL Carbon had assets of $ 400 million and liabilities of only $ 276 million, or a net worth of $ 124 million. In addition, there is no evidence that SGL Carbon had difficulty meeting its debts as they came due, that it had any overdue debts, or that it had defaulted on any debts. Nor is there any evidence that SGL had any difficulty raising or borrowing money, or otherwise had impaired access to the capital markets.

Statements by SGL Carbon and its officials confirm the company did not need to reorganize under Chapter 11. As discussed, in a press release issued when SGL Carbon filed its petition, the company's president insisted SGL Carbon was "financially healthy" and that its "normal business operations" would continue despite bankruptcy. In addition, SGL AG's Chairman Robert Koehler stated in a conference call with securities analysts that SGL Carbon was experiencing "healthy and growing success" and denied that the class action antitrust litigation was materially interfering with SGL Carbon's operations or its customer relationships. Koehler added that unlike most Chapter 11 cases, SGL Carbon's petition did not involve "serious insolvency or credit problems." SGL Carbon Vice President Theodore Breyer acknowledged in his deposition that SGL Carbon had no defaults nor any financial distress when it filed for Chapter 11.

An examination of the reorganization plan SGL Carbon filed simultaneously with its Chapter 11 petition also suggests the petition was not motivated by a desire to reorganize or rehabilitate SGL Carbon's business. Under the proposed plan, all creditors--including SGL Carbon's parent SGL AG--other than civil antitrust judgment creditors are to be paid in full in cash. Antitrust judgment creditors, by contrast, would be required to accept limited-time credits to purchase SGL Carbon's products. The plan's differing treatment of creditors suggests SGL Carbon's petition was not filed to reorganize the company but rather to put pressure on antitrust plaintiffs to accept the company's settlement terms. . . .

Based on the facts and circumstances of this case, we conclude SGL Carbon's Chapter 11 petition lacks a valid reorganizational purpose and consequently lacks good faith making it subject to dismissal "for cause" under 11 U.S.C. § 1112(b).

. . .

For the reasons stated, we will reverse the judgment of the District Court and remand to the District Court so that it may dismiss SGL Carbon's Chapter 11 petition.

QUESTIONS ON *SGL CARBON*

1. If SGL had not issued any press releases, or spoken to any securities analysts after its filing, would the result have been any different?

2. Hark back[14] to Section C.1 of this unit (page 432), where we spoke about who you would tell about a possible chapter 11 filing. Do you want to change your answer after reading *SGL Carbon*?

R. SPECIAL TYPES OF CHAPTER 11 CASES

The Bankruptcy Abuse Prevention and Consumer Protection Act of 2005 treats certain types of chapter 11 debtors differently. The changes are based mainly on status; that is, if you're a small business, then you have different rules. The following are descriptions of some of the new categories.

1. Small Business Cases

a. Overview

Small business debtors factor prominently in the Bankruptcy Abuse Prevention and Consumer Protection Act of 2005. It contains many changes for small businesses, as well as many changes for business debtors generally.

These changes affecting small business debtors had their origins in the 1997 report of the National Bankruptcy Review Commission. *See* H.R. REP. NO. 109-31, pt.1, at 19 (2005). The relevant provisions of the recommendations are found at NATIONAL BANKRUPTCY REVIEW COMM'N, BANKRUPTCY: THE NEXT TWENTY YEARS—NATIONAL BANKRUPTCY REVIEW COMMISSION FINAL REPORT, OCTOBER 20, 1997, at 609-60 (1997). That Commission started its work with the small business changes Congress had made in 1994. These 1994 changes gave chapter 11 debtors who had $2,000,000 or less in debt the option of dispensing with creditors'

---

[14]Unlike Markell and "old-timey" radio announcers on shows such as The Lone Ranger, Epstein, Nickles and Perris do not use the phrase "hark back."

committees, and opting for a fast-track to confirmation through the ability to combine a disclosure statement hearing with a hearing on plan confirmation.

The Review Commission thought these changes weren't enough, and were improperly aimed. *See* NATIONAL BANKRUPTCY REVIEW COMM'N, *supra*, at 611-15. They thought that there should be stricter adherence to fast timetables, and clear consequences for avoidable delay. Their recommendations reflected this viewpoint.

With few adjustments, the 2005 Act basically adopts the Commission's recommendations wholesale. Many think that these provisions escaped more intense review given the degree of attention centered on the consumer provisions of the 2005 Act.

The main amendments include: changes to the nature of small business bankruptcy through amendments to the applicable definitions and through making the small business provisions mandatory; changes to the scope of reporting and other duties; faster timelines for plan confirmation; severe penalties for failure to comply with the new rules; and provisions designed to ensure that small business debtors do not become serial filers.

b. Review of the Changes —Definitions

The Code has always defined small businesses with respect to outstanding debt, rather than by number of employees, assets, or income. While the $2 million level applicable before the 2005 Act remains, it has been altered somewhat in its application. For example, the old definition counted all debts; the new definition excludes from the debt limit any amounts owed to affiliates or insiders. 11 U.S.C. § 101(51D)(A). Also, if the debtor has less than $2 million in debt, but is part of a group of affiliated debtors that has more than $2 million in unaffiliated debt, that debtor is excluded from the definition, and is not eligible to be a small business debtor. 11 U.S.C. § 101(51D)(B).

How many debtors might be affected by this definition? The House Report with respect to the 2005 Act flatly states that "[m]ost chapter 11 cases are filed by small business debtors." H.R. REP. NO. 109-31, pt.1, at 19 (2005). This observation is backed by data the National Bankruptcy Review Commission used, which surveyed six districts (including Delaware), and noted that 72% of all chapter 11 debtors had liabilities of $2 million or less at filing. NATIONAL BANKRUPTCY REVIEW COMM'N, *supra*, at 631.[15] If an accurate extrapolation, the number picked up by the new definition will undoubtedly be higher, given the exclusion of insider and affiliate debt.

The new definition, however, does not rely on debt levels alone. There is one further, and troubling, gloss on the new definition. The 2005 Act adds the following language as a qualifying clause to the $2 million level; that is, if the following part of the definition found at 11 U.S.C. § 101(51)(D) is applicable, then the debtor is ***not*** a small business debtor:

> a case in which the United States trustee has not appointed under section 1102(a)(1) a committee of unsecured creditors ***or*** where the court has determined that the committee of unsecured creditors is not sufficiently active and representative to provide effective oversight of the debtor . . . .

The proposed interim rules attempt to ameliorate this uncertainty. They require the debtor to self-designate its status, and state that such designation will generally control unless a party objects or there is an affirmative finding that a committee is not "sufficiently active." Interim Rules 1020.

---

[15]If the threshold was set at $5 million, the Commission's original proposal, the average number jumped to 86%. *Id.*

Even so, the debtor might try to avoid this uncertainty by, prepetition, trying to form a committee of creditors (undoubtedly lead by a lawyer known to the debtor's lawyer), and then after filing have that committee confirmed as the official unsecured creditors' committee. If achieved, this would remove small business status. Indeed, Section 1102(b)(1) expressly anticipates such "carryover" representation "if such committee was fairly chosen and is representative of the different kinds of claims to be represented." *See* 11 U.S.C. § 1102(b)(1).

Thus, depending on whether the members were "fairly chosen," the strategy might work initially– but thereafter such committee will have to be active. If the court determines that "the committee of unsecured creditors is not sufficiently active and representative to provide effective oversight of the debtor," then the court may effectively change the case back to a small business case. See Interim Rule 1020.

c. Review of the Changes — Enhanced Duties and Disclosure

One theme of the small business amendments is that creditors deserve more and better information, presented in understandable and recognizable formats. Many sections of the small business amendments were framed with this goal in mind. In particular, there are four sections, two of which are uncodified, of the 2005 Act that require enhanced reporting in some way by small business debtors:

- *Section 433*, which directs the national Bankruptcy Rules Committee to prepare standard forms of disclosure statements and plans of reorganization for small business debtors;

- *Section 434*, which would add section 308 to the Bankruptcy Code regarding periodic reporting of financial operations by small business debtors;

- *Section 435*, which specifically directs the National Bankruptcy Rules Committee to develop forms to implement new section 308; and

- *Section 436*, which would add section 1116 to the Bankruptcy Code regarding enhanced filing and other duties of small business debtors.

Start first with new section 1116 of the Code. This section adds to the filing requirements of small business debtors, both at the time of filing and thereafter. In full, this section provides:

SEC. 1116. DUTIES OF TRUSTEE OR DEBTOR IN POSSESSION IN SMALL BUSINESS CASES

In a small business case, a trustee or the debtor in possession, in addition to the duties provided in this title and as otherwise required by law, shall—

(1) append to the voluntary petition or, in an involuntary case, file not later than 7 days after the date of the order for relief—

(A) its most recent balance sheet, statement of operations, cash-flow statement, and Federal income tax return; or

(B) a statement made under penalty of perjury that no balance sheet, statement of operations, or cash-flow statement has been prepared and no Federal tax return has been filed;

(2) attend, through its senior management personnel and counsel, meetings scheduled by the court or the United States trustee, including initial debtor interviews, scheduling conferences, and meetings of creditors convened under section 341 unless the court, after notice and a hearing, waives that requirement upon a finding of extraordinary and compelling circumstances;

(3) timely file all schedules and statements of financial affairs, unless the court, after notice and a hearing, grants an extension, which shall not extend such time period to a date later than 30 days after the date of the order for relief, absent extraordinary and compelling circumstances;

(4) file all postpetition financial and other reports required by the Federal Rules of

> Bankruptcy Procedure or by local rule of the district court;
>
> (5) subject to section 363(c)(2), maintain insurance customary and appropriate to the industry;
>
> (6) (A) timely file tax returns and other required government filings; and
>
> (B) subject to section 363(c)(2), timely pay all taxes entitled to administrative expense priority except those being contested by appropriate proceedings being diligently prosecuted; and
>
> (7) allow the United States trustee, or a designated representative of the United States trustee, to inspect the debtor's business premises, books, and records at reasonable times, after reasonable prior written notice, unless notice is waived by the debtor.

The scope of these requirements is broad, and generally tracks the recommendations of the Bankruptcy Review Commission. NATIONAL BANKRUPTCY REVIEW COMM'N, *supra*, at 641-43. But the effect of failing to adhere to them can be severe, as we will explore below.

d. Review of the Changes —Timelines and Fast Tracking

In addition to increasing the reporting burdens on small business debtors, the 2005 Act significantly steps up the timeframes under which small business debtors will operate. Initially, the exclusivity period for small business debtors is expanded from 120 days to 180 days. 11 U.S.C. § 1121(e)(1). But even in the absence of exclusivity, small business debtors must file their plan and disclosure statement (or the combined document) not later than 300 days after the order for relief. 11 U.S.C. § 1121(e)(2). Once the plan is filed, it must be confirmed within 45 days thereafter. 11 U.S.C. § 1129(e).

There is some possibility of extending these time frames, but the standard is rather strict. The court may extend them only if the debtor "(A) . . . demonstrates by a preponderance of the evidence that it is more likely than not that the court will confirm a plan within a reasonable period of time; [¶] (B) a new deadline is imposed at the time the extension is granted; and [¶] (C) the order extending time is signed before the existing deadline has expired." 11 U.S.C. § 1121(e)(3).

One might reasonably question whether these are realistic estimates of the maximum time frames in which a small business debtor can reorganize. The Bankruptcy Review Commission cited many studies regarding delay and low confirmation rates. The House Report accompanying S. 256, the bill that became the 2005 Act, states that "small business bankruptcy cases [are] often are the least likely to reorganize successfully." H.R. REP. NO. 109-31, pt.1, at 3 (2005).

One study they did not cite, however, found that with respect to approximately 2400 chapter 11 cases filed over a seven-year time frame, the average time to confirmation was just over 13 months (or about 390 days) — and the confirmation rate for these cases was approximately 40%. *See* Steven H. Ancel & Bruce A. Markell, *Hope in the Heartland: Chapter 11 Dispositions in Indiana and Southern Illinois, 1990-1996*, 50 S.C.L. REV. 343 (1999). If this study is at all representative, the deadlines and timelines imposed by the 2005 Act may be tough for small business debtors to live with.

e. So There Are More Duties and a Faster Timeline: So What?

The Bankruptcy Review Commission knew that its proposed substantive reforms would not work as intended unless backed by swift and sure sanctions. The 2005 Act follows the Commission's recommendations in this regard, substantially rewriting Section 1112(b) of the Code as explored above starting at page ?. This is part of an effort to "institut[e] a variety of time frames and enforcement mechanisms designed to weed out small business debtors who are not likely to reorganize." H.R. REP. NO. 109-31, pt.1, at 19 (2005).

As amended, Section 1112(b) includes the following as cause sufficient to dismiss or convert a chapter 11 case:

> (E) failure to comply with an order of the court;
> (F) unexcused failure to satisfy timely any filing or reporting requirement established by this title or by any rule applicable to a case under this chapter;
> (G) failure to attend the meeting of creditors convened under section 341(a) or an examination ordered under rule 2004 of the Federal Rules of Bankruptcy Procedure without good cause shown by the debtor;
> (H) failure timely to provide information or attend meetings reasonably requested by the United States trustee (or the bankruptcy administrator, if any);
> (I) failure timely to pay taxes owed after the date of the order for relief or to file tax returns due after the date of the order for relief;
> (J) failure to file a disclosure statement, or to file or confirm a plan, within the time fixed by this title or by order of the court;

As a consequence of these changes, any analysis of revised Section 1112(b) involves looking at the grounds for cause, the test to be applied by the court when cause is alleged, and the procedure to be employed to determine whether the allegation of cause is true.

PROBLEM 11-34: WELL MEANING BUT DISORGANIZED DEBTORS

1. Fumblerule, Inc. is a small business debtor in a small business case. You have told it the deadline to file schedules but the same disorganization that caused Fumblerule to file has caused it to miss the deadline. It comes into your office on the due date with a hopeless mass of papers and asks what it can do to get the deadline extended. What do you say?

2 Fumblerule again. It got away with late filing its schedules and now has filed its plan, some six months into the case. The plan has angered some of its creditors because it asks them to take bigger discounts than Fumblerule had previously indicated would be necessary. When you filed the plan, you immediately discovered that you'll have to amend it if you have any chance of obtaining a consenting class of creditors. Trouble is, it looks like you won't be able to meet with the creditors until next month. If you do meet with them 30 days after filing the plan, and want to amend the plan on file, what concerns might you have, especially if there are some creditors out there who still will object to the plan?

Experience indicates that a significant small business debtors will have their cases dismissed. *See* NATIONAL BANKRUPTCY REVIEW COMM'N, *supra*, at 645-46. The 2005 Act addresses this issue by depriving repeat filers the benefit of the automatic stay. In particular, the stay is denied to:

- Small business debtors who have a small business case pending at the time of the subsequent filing, 11 U.S.C. § 362(n)(1)(A);

- Small business debtors who had been a debtor in a small business case that had been dismissed at any time during the two years preceding the filing, 11 U.S.C. § 362(n)(1)(C);

- Small business debtors who had been a debtor in a small business case in which a plan had been confirmed at any time during the two years preceding filing, 11 U.S.C. § 362(n)(1)(C); or

- Any entity who had acquired substantially all of the assets or business of a small business debtor who had a case pending, or whose case was dismissed, or who had confirmed a plan, within the two years preceding the filing, 11 U.S.C. § 362(n)(1)(D).

There are some exceptions. The acquiring company has an exception if it can show that it acquired the assets or business of the small business debtor "in good faith and not for the purpose of evading" these rules. 11 U.S.C. § 362(n)(1)(D). They also do not apply to a non-collusive involuntary proceeding. 11 U.S.C. § 362(n)(2)(A). Finally, if the debtor can prove by a preponderance of the evidence that the new filing resulted "from circumstances beyond the control of the debtor [and which were] not foreseeable at the time the case then pending [presumably, the first case] was filed; and . . . it is more likely than not that the court will confirm a feasible plan, but not a liquidating plan, within a reasonable period of time." 11 U.S.C. § 362(n)(2)(B)(i)-(ii).

Note that the applicability of these provisions will be made in the second and newly filed case without any guaranty that there will be any findings in the first case that are helpful; there is no requirement upon dismissal of a small business case that the court make a finding as to what type of debtor the case involved.

There were other changes made in the small business subtitle. In a move to tighten the administration of small business cases, the United States trustee is given expanded powers to interview and assess the viability of small business debtors. 28 U.S.C. § 586(a)(3)(H) & (a)(7). As summarized in the House Report, these expanded duties include:

1. conduct an initial debtor interview before the meeting of creditors for the purpose of (a) investigating the debtor's viability, (b) inquiring about the debtor's business plan, (c) explaining

the debtor's obligation to file monthly operating reports, (d) attempting to obtain an agreed scheduling order setting various time frames (such as the date for filing a plan and effecting confirmation), and (e) informing the debtor of other obligations;

2. if determined to be appropriate and advisable, inspect the debtor's business premises for the purpose of reviewing the debtor's books and records and verifying that the debtor has filed its tax returns;

3. review and monitor diligently the debtor's activities to determine as promptly as possible whether the debtor will be unable to confirm a plan; and

4. promptly apply to the court for relief in any case in which the United States trustee finds material grounds for dismissal or conversion of the case.

H.R. REP. NO. 109-31, pt.1, at 93 (2005). As the House Report further estimates, these provisions will "require about 20 additional analysts to conduct over 2,300 site visits each year. CBO estimates that implementing this provision would cost about $15 million over the 2006–2010 period for the salaries, benefits, and travel expenses associated with those additional personnel." H.R. REP. NO. 109-31, pt.1, at 39 (2005).

PROBLEM 11-35: THE WHALE SWALLOWS THE MINNOW

GotBucks, Inc. is a multi-billion company listed on the New York Stock Exchange. It is interested in acquiring the technology of Pipsqueek, Inc. GotBucks is rebuffed by Pipsqueek, and GotBucks then plays hardball, essentially forcing Pipsqueek into a chapter 11 filing. Pipsqueek has $2.5 million in debt, which includes a

$750,000 loan from Pipsqueek's major owner, Harvey. No creditors' committee is ever formed in Pipsqueek's case, but it does indicate on its petition that it is a small business debtor.

GotBucks waits until Pipsqueek's period of exclusivity expires six months after the case is commenced, and then files its own plan. Under GotBuck's plan, all Pipsqueek's tangible and intangible assets will be transferred to GotBucks. Pipsqueek's creditors will receive the same amount as offered by Pipsqueek's plan, but GotBucks will pay it well in advance of the schedule Pipsqueek's plan calls for.

GotBucks' plan is confirmed. Eighteen months later, it comes to you having just been hit by a mammoth unfair competition judgment. Combined with other reversals, it believes it needs some time to reorganize its affairs before the judgment creditor levies upon GotBucks' assets. Can it file for chapter 11 and receive the benefit of the stay? Must it do anything other than filing? *See* 11 U.S.C. § 362(n)(1)(D).

---

2. Single Asset Debtors

Before the 2005 Act, the Code had special provisions regarding so-called "single asset real estate" debtors, also knows as SAREs. Added in 1994, these provisions consisted primarily of special grounds for relief from stay. Since 1994, however, the SARE provisions had little effect because the initial definition limited application of the SARE provisions to debtors with less than $4 million in debt.

The 2005 Act removed this limitation. 11 U.S.C. § 101(51B). This means that the SARE provisions may apply in large real estate cases; Rockefeller Center could be a SARE debtor. The definition will still exclude operating or "real" businesses, as it requires "a single property or project, other than residential real property with fewer than 4 residential units, which generates substantially all of the gross income of a debtor . . . and on which no substantial business is being conducted by a debtor other than the business of operating the real property and activities incidental" 11 U.S.C. § 101(51B).

The 2005 Act also changed Section 362(d)(3), which is the relief from stay provision that applies specifically to SARE debtors. In particular, the SARE debtor will have to pay its lenders for the privilege of staying in chapter 11; that is, Section 362(d)(3) requires to stay current on monthly payments to secured creditors. As an alternative to paying interest, the debtor can avoid termination of the stay and foreclosure by getting a confirmable plan on file within 90 days.

Before the 2005 Act a creditor whose claim was secured by single asset real estate could obtain relief from the automatic stay unless (1) the debtor filed a confirmable plan of reorganization, or (2) the debtor was making monthly payments "to each creditor whose claim is secured by such real estate . . . which payments are in an amount equal to interest at a current fair market rate on the value of the creditor's interest in the real estate." 11 U.S.C. § 362(d)(3). Court were divided as to whether a SARE debtor's rents could be used to make the required adequate protection payments. The Act resolves this split by amending section 362(d)(3)(B) to allow debtors to make payments to secured creditors from rents subject to a security interest or lien. As rents are usually the only source of funds for a SARE debtor, this makes life easier for such debtors.

PROBLEM 11-36: SAREs AND SMALL BUSINESS DEBTORS

1129 Partners owns a small apartment complex. It owes $1.75 million to First Bank, $25,000 to its management company, and $500,000 in notes to its partners. It is in default on the First Bank loan. If it files for chapter 11 relief, will it be governed by the SARE rules, the small business rules, both or neither?

---

3. Individuals (Flesh and Blood Humans) as Chapter 11 Debtors

Congress intended many of the 2005 Act's provisions require individual debtors to "pass" a means test as a condition of being able to obtain bankruptcy relief. Most of these provisions changes provisions found in chapter 7. But the drafters understood that these changes would cause many individuals to investigate the other available chapters. Since the Supreme Court has indicated that individuals not engaged in business may file chapter 11, Toibb v. Radloff 501 U.S. 157 (1991), chapter 11 is a possible option for such individuals.

To ensure individuals do not evade the reforms to chapter 7 by simply filing for chapter 11, Congress made many changes to chapter 11 with respect to individuals.

a. The Changes

1. Post-Petition Earnings From Services Are Property of the Estate

Section 1115 was added in 2005, and supplements the estate with property that would otherwise be excluded from the estate in an individual's chapter 7 case: post-petition earnings from services. It mirrors Section 1306, which accomplishes the same goal in chapter 13.

This expansion of property of the estate ensures that this additional property, which usually is necessary to fund or otherwise implement a plan of reorganization, is protected by the automatic stay. This is even the case with respect to entities which could pursue such property in a chapter 7 case, such as those holding postpetition claims.

This inclusion, however, does not change other provisions in chapter 11 which look to property of the estate as defined in section 541, such as the best interests of creditors test found in Section 1129(a)(7). There is also no requirement that property coming into the estate due only to the operation of section 1115(a) be listed in the debtor's schedules.

While Section 1115(a) adds this additional property into the estate, Section 1115(b) confirms the debtor's presumptive right to remain in possession of that property, as well as all other property of the estate. The right to remain in possession of this property of the estate is a major advantage for individual chapter 11 debtors, who would otherwise be required to turn over nonexempt property to the trustee in a chapter 7 case.

To ensure that this income is devoted to creditor claims, the new provisions provide that all earnings from personal service or other future income must be devoted to the plan, 11 U.S.C. § 1123(a)(8), although retention of such income as part of the plan will not give any class of creditors grounds to object on absolute priority grounds, 11 U.S.C. § 1129(b)(2)(B)(ii).

2. *Disposable Income Requirement Imported From Chapter 13*

Congress engrafted chapter 13's disposable income test as an additional chapter 11 confirmation requirement, found in new Section 1129(a)(15). This new requirement requires individual chapter 11 debtors to either pay all unsecured claims in full, or to devote an amount equal to five years' worth of the debtor's projected disposable income as property to be distributed under the plan. As with the best interest of creditors test found in Section 1129(a)(7), standing to object on this ground is given to any single unsecured creditor; it is irrelevant that the plan proponent obtained the consent of the class of unsecured creditors of which the objecting unsecured creditor is a member.

Central to the application of this paragraph is the concept of "disposable income," and the amounts of such disposable income that must be devoted to the implementation of the plan. "Disposable income" is a concept borrowed from chapter 13. Indeed, Section 1129(a)(15) itself refers to Section 1325(b)(2) for a definition of the concept.

3. Additional Confirmation Requirements

In addition to the new disposable income requirement found in Section 1129(a)(15), chapter 11 debtors will now have to ensure that their post-petition domestic support obligations (now a defined term — see 11 U.S.C. § 101(14A)) are current as of confirmation, 11 U.S.C. § 1129(a)(14), and that all tax information that was requested pre-confirmation has been provided. This latter requirement is found in an uncodified provision of the 2005 Act, Section 1228(b).

4. Delayed Entry of the Discharge Imported From Chapter 13

The last major change to chapter 11 for debtors is the delayed discharge. Under the 2005 Act, individual debtors in chapter 11 will not receive a discharge until after the completion of their plan payments. 11 U.S.C. § 1142(d)(5).

---

b. Comparison with Chapter 13

What are the major differences between chapter 13 and chapter 11 for individuals? Here's a short list:

- There is no co-debtor stay available as a matter of right in a chapter 13.
- The anti-cramdown provision added in 2005 to chapter 13, which does not allow bifurcation of a secured claim if the secured creditor is undersecured, does not apply in chapter 11
- The valuation standard contained in Section 506(a)(2), requiring retail valuation, does not apply in chapter 11.
- The chapter 11 disposable income test found in Section 1129(a)(15) may not incorporated the IRS expense limits applicable to some chapter 13 debtors – Section 1129(a)(15) only refers to Section 1325(b)(2), which calculates disposable income with reference to the debtor's actual expenses, and not to Section 1325(b)(3), which refers to the IRS collection standards for debtors whose income is above the applicable median income for their state.
- Disposable income under chapter 11 need only be devoted to the "property to be distributed under the plan," which presumably means it can be devoted to post-petition administrative claimants; in chapter 13, disposable income must be distributed for the benefit of unsecured creditors.
- Chapter 11 has a more expensive filing fee: $1000 versus $150.
- In some cases, chapter 13 plans can be less than five years; chapter 11 seems to require that the debtor devote at least five years' worth of disposable income to his or her plan.
- The maximum plan length in chapter 13 is five years; chapter 11 plans may extend longer than five years;.

- If the debtor could file under either chapter 11 or chapter 13, and is engaged in business, the small business provisions of chapter 11 will likely be applicable if a chapter 11 is filed.

- A chapter 13 debtor may discharge certain marital property settlements to the extent that they are covered in Section 523(a)(15), and chapter 13 debtors may discharge some forms of wilful and malicious injury that do not involve personal injury or death. Chapter 13 expressly permits separate classification of co-debtor claims; it is unclear whether a chapter 11 debtor has identical powers.

- If unable to complete a plan, a chapter 11 discharge for inability to complete a plan is somewhat easier to obtain than a chapter 13 hardship discharge. *Compare* 11 U.S.C. § 1328(b)(1) (discharge allowed without completion of plan payments only if the debtor's failure to complete payments is "due to circumstances for which the debtor should not be justly be held accountable") *with* 11 U.S.C. § 1141(d)(5)(B) (discharge allowed without completion of plan if modification of plan is not practicable)

- Debtors must solicit creditors for their votes after obtaining approval of a disclosure statement; there is no creditor voting in chapter 13.

- To obtain a discharge, a chapter 13 debtor must take financial education classes from an instructor approved by the Office of the United States Trustee. 11 U.S.C. § 1328(g). Chapter 11 has no such education requirement.

PROBLEM 11-37: HIGH INCOME INDIVIDUALS AND BIG CARS

Gary makes $100,000 per year as a software engineer. He has a new Ferrari 612 Scaglietti he bought three months ago for $250,000, paying $25,000 down and financing the remainder over 60 months at 12%, for a monthly payment of about $5,000. He has no other vices; he rents his apartment at a market rate, and has about $10,000 of personal effects, not counting his $5,000 home computer. He has about $1,000 in credit card balances.

Gary was laid off last month. He has maybe $3,000 in his checking account and his car payment is due next week. He was just hired at a new job, but at "only" $75,000 a year. He'll be taking home about $4,400 a month; his living expenses, not counting his car payment, are about $2,000 per month.

His "current monthly income" is higher than the applicable median for the state in which he lives. His personal effects are largely exempt, although the $3,000 in cash is not. The Ferrari is worth about $100,000 as is (Gary's put some dings in it). A $100,000 loan at 12% would require monthly payments, over five years, of about $2,200 per month.

What advice would you give Gary with respect to filing?

Part V

Courts and Jurisdiction

Unit 12

Where Does All of This Happen, and Who Makes It Happen?

In the main, the substantive law of bankruptcy is in title 11 of the United States Code. Questions of judicial power over bankruptcy-related matters are, in the main, answered in title 28 of the United States Code.

The question of which court has the power to adjudicate the litigation that arises in bankruptcy can be an important one. Many attorneys that represent parties with claims against the bankrupt or parties against whom the bankrupt has claims prefer to litigate in some forum other than the bankruptcy court. Some believe that the bankruptcy judge has a pro-debtor bias; others are simply more comfortable or more familiar with state court procedures; others prefer state court for reasons of delay — a state court generally has a larger backlog of cases than a bankruptcy court so that filing in state court delays any litigation.

In considering the question of which court has the power to adjudicate the litigation that arises in bankruptcy, it is helpful to consider the kinds of matters that can arise in bankruptcy.

Some matters will involve only bankruptcy law. For example, *D* files a Chapter 7 petition. The Chapter 7 trustee alleges that *B*'s payment of $40,000 to *C* a month before bankruptcy is recoverable by the estate under section 550 as a section 547 voidable preference. *C* contends that the $40,000 payment is protected from avoidance as a section 547(c)(2) ordinary course of business payment.

Other matters will involve both bankruptcy law and nonbankruptcy law. For example, *D* files a Chapter 7 petition. *C* files a secured claim that describes its Article 9 security interest. The bankruptcy trustee takes the position that *C*'s security interest is invalid because it was not properly perfected. If this is litigated, it will probably involve both the Bankruptcy Code's avoidance provisions and the Uniform Commercial Code's perfection provisions.

And, still other matters will not involve substantive bankruptcy law. For example, *D*, Inc., a Chapter 11 debtor, files a breach of contract claim against *X*.

A. History

The allocation of judicial power over bankruptcy matters has been, and still is, one of the most controversial bankruptcy issues. A general familiarity with prior statutory schemes and prior controversies is helpful to understanding the present situation.

1. 1898 Act

Under the Bankruptcy Act of 1898, bankruptcy courts had limited jurisdiction. This jurisdiction was commonly referred to as "summary" jurisdiction. (The phrase summary jurisdiction is somewhat misleading. First, it incorrectly implies that under the Bankruptcy Act of 1898, bankruptcy courts had a second, nonsummary form of jurisdiction. Bankruptcy courts had only summary jurisdiction; other courts had plenary jurisdiction. Second, it incorrectly implies that in resolving controversies, the bankruptcy judge always conducted summary proceedings.)

Summary jurisdiction extended to (1) *all* matters concerned with the administration of the bankruptcy estate and (2) *some* disputes between the bankruptcy trustee and third parties involving rights to money and other property in which the bankrupt estate claimed an interest. The tests for which disputes with third parties were within the bankruptcy judge's summary jurisdiction turned on issues such as whether (1) the property in question was in the actual possession of the bankrupt at the time of the commencement of the case, (2) the property in question was in the constructive possession of the bankrupt at the time of the commencement of the case, and (3) the third party actually or impliedly consented to bankruptcy court jurisdiction.

There was considerable uncertainty over which disputes were within the summary jurisdiction of the bankruptcy court. This uncertainty gave rise to considerable litigation.

2. 1978 Code

To eliminate this uncertainty, Congress in 1978 decided to create a bankruptcy court with pervasive jurisdiction. For apparently political reasons, Congress also decided that this bankruptcy court should *not* be an Article III court.

As you recall from your Constitutional Law course in law school or civics course in high school, Article III of the Constitution vests the judicial power of the United States in the United States Supreme Court and such inferior tribunals as Congress might create. To insure the independence of the judges appointed under Article III (the so-called constitutional courts), Article III provides them with certain protections. These include tenure for life, removal from office only by congressional impeachment, and assurance that their compensation will not be diminished. The constitutional courts created under Article III include the United States Supreme

Court, the United States Courts of Appeal, and the United States District Courts. The United States Customs Court (now the Court of International Trade) is also an Article III court; its judges may be, and often are, assigned to hear cases in the district courts and the courts of appeal.

Congress, in the exercise of its legislative powers enumerated in Article I of the Constitution, may create other inferior federal tribunals — the so-called legislative courts. Judges of these legislative courts need not be granted tenure for life. In addition, they can be removed by mechanisms other than congressional impeachment, and their salaries are subject to congressional reduction. Historically, these Article I legislative courts and their judges have been granted jurisdiction over limited and narrowly defined subject matters, like the Tax Court. In other instances, jurisdiction has been limited to narrowly defined geographical territories, such as the territorial courts, the District of Columbia courts, etc.

In amending title 28 in 1978, Congress gave bankruptcy judges none of the protections found in Article III of the Constitution. Nevertheless, the 1978 amendments to title 28 gave bankruptcy judges much of the power and responsibilities of an Article III judge. Since bankruptcy debtors can be just about any kind of individual or business entity, this meant that litigation in the bankruptcy courts could deal with almost every facet of business and personal activity.

3. *Marathon Pipeline Decision*

The 1978 grant of pervasive jurisdiction to a non-Article III bankruptcy court was successfully challenged in the *Marathon* case. Northern Pipeline Constr. Co. v. Marathon Pipeline Co., 458 U.S. 50 (1982).

In that case, Northern Pipeline, a Chapter 11 debtor, filed a breach of contract lawsuit against Marathon Pipeline in bankruptcy court. There was no question as to whether the bankruptcy court had jurisdiction over this lawsuit under the jurisdictional statute enacted in 1978, 28 U.S.C. § 1471(c). Marathon Pipeline did, however, question whether section 1471(c) conferred Article III judicial power on non-Article III courts in violation of the separation of powers doctrine and filed a motion to dismiss. A divided Supreme Court sustained Marathon's challenge.

The Court in *Marathon* was so divided that there was no majority opinion. Justice Brennan's opinion was joined by three other justices. Additionally, two justices concurred in the result. The holding of these six is perhaps best summarized in footnote 40 of Justice Brennan's plurality opinion which indicates that (1) the 1978 legislation does grant the bankruptcy court the power to hear Northern Pipeline's breach of contract claim, (2) the bankruptcy court, a non-Article III court, cannot constitutionally be vested with jurisdiction to decide such state law claims, and (3) this grant of authority to the bankruptcy court is not severable from the remaining grant of authority to the bankruptcy court.

After *Marathon*, Congress was urged to solve the constitutional dilemma by establishing bankruptcy courts as Article III courts. Congress rejected this solution. Instead, Congress in 1984[16] made the bankruptcy court a part of the federal district court, conferred jurisdiction in bankruptcy on the district court, and allocated judicial power in bankruptcy matters between the federal district judge and the bankruptcy judge.

---

[16]In the two-year gap between the 1982 *Marathon* decision and the 1984 legislation, the allocation of judicial power over bankruptcy was governed by an Emergency Rule adopted by all district courts.

It is easy for a law professor or law student to criticize the provisions allocating judicial power over bankruptcy matters. It is more difficult (but probably more important) for a lawyer or law student to understand how these provisions operate.

B. Provisions in Title 28 Allocating Judicial Power Over Bankruptcy

In understanding the present law allocating judicial powers over bankruptcy matters, it is necessary to understand three separate sections in title 28: (1) § 151, (2) § 1334, and (3) § 157. By understanding these three provisions you will understand that (1) bankruptcy courts are a part of the United States District Court but bankruptcy judges are different from district court judges, (2) bankruptcy cases are different from bankruptcy proceedings, (3) bankruptcy cases can be handled by either bankruptcy judges or federal district judges (depending on withdrawal of the reference), but not by state court judges and (4) bankruptcy proceedings can be tried by bankruptcy judges or federal judges (depending on withdrawal of the reference) or even state court judges (depending on where the lawsuit was filed and removal and abstention). To understand even more, please read the following descriptions of the three key sections in title 28:

1. Bankruptcy Court as Part of the District Court

28 U.S.C. § 151

In each judicial district, the bankruptcy judges in regular active service shall constitute a unit of the district court to be known as the bankruptcy court for that district. Each bankruptcy judge, as a judicial officer of the district court, may exercise the authority conferred under this chapter with respect to any action, suit, or proceeding and may preside alone and hold a regular or special session of the court, except as otherwise provided by law or by rule or order of the district court.

Section 151 refers to a bankruptcy judge and a bankruptcy court as a "unit" of the district court. It is important to keep this reference in mind when reading other sections in title 28 dealing with the allocation of judicial power in bankruptcy matters. When the term "district court" appears in section 1334 or section 157, it could be referring to the United States district judge and/or the bankruptcy judge. After all, the bankruptcy judge is a part of the district court — a "unit" of the district court.

---

2. *Grants of Jurisdiction to the District Court*[17]

28 U.S.C. § 1334(a), (b)

(a) Except as provided in subsection (b) of this section, the district courts shall have original and exclusive jurisdiction of all cases under title 11.

(b) Except as provided in subsection (e)(2), and notwithstanding any Act of Congress that confers exclusive jurisdiction on a court or courts other than the district courts, the district courts shall have original but not exclusive jurisdiction of all civil proceedings arising under title 11, or arising in or related to cases under title 11.

Section 1334(a) vests original and exclusive jurisdiction in the district court over all cases arising under the Bankruptcy Code. "Case" is a term of art used in both the Bankruptcy Code and the Bankruptcy Rules. "Case" refers to the entire Chapter 7, 9, 11, 12 or 13 —

---

[17]Section 1334(c) which deals with abstention will be separately considered later in this unit.

not just some controversy that arises in connection with it.

The term "case" is to be distinguished from the term "proceeding." A specific dispute that arises during the pendency of a case is referred to as a "proceeding." Section 1334(b) provides that the district courts have original but not exclusive jurisdiction over all civil proceedings, "arising under title 11, or arising in or related to cases under title 11."

"Proceedings" include "contested matters," motions brought in the main bankruptcy case and "adversary proceedings," lawsuits. Section 1334(b) grants the district court original but not exclusive jurisdiction over three types of "civil proceedings":

a. "Arising Under" Title 11

This involves adjudication of rights or obligations created by the Bankruptcy Code. For example, stay relief. A further example: preference litigation.

b. "Arising In" a Title 11 Case

This covers matters peculiar to bankruptcy but based on rights or obligations created by the Bankruptcy Code. For example, allowance or disallowance of claims. A further example: assumption or rejection of executory contracts.

c. "Related To" a Title 11 Case

This covers matters that impact on the bankruptcy case. While it is not a "catch-all," it certainly catches a lot. In *Celotex Corp. v. Edwards*, 514 U.S. 300 (1995), the Supreme Court held that entry of an injunction prohibiting a judgment creditor from executing on a supersedeas bond of a third party surety of the debtor was "related to." In so ruling, the Supreme Court stated:

The jurisdiction of the bankruptcy courts, like that of other federal courts, is grounded in, and limited by, statute. Title 28 U.S.C. § 1334(b) provides that "the district courts shall have original but not exclusive jurisdiction of all civil proceedings arising under title 11, or arising in or related to cases under title 11." The district courts may, in turn, refer "any or all proceedings arising under title 11 or arising in or related to a case under title 11 ... to the bankruptcy judges for the district." 28 U.S.C. § 157(a). Here, the Bankruptcy Court's jurisdiction to enjoin respondents' proceeding against Northbrook must be based on the "arising under," "arising in," or "related to" language of §§ 1334(b) and 157(a).

Respondents argue that the Bankruptcy Court had jurisdiction to issue the Section 105 Injunction only if their proceeding to execute on the bond was "related to" the Celotex bankruptcy. Petitioner argues the Bankruptcy Court indeed had such "related to" jurisdiction. Congress did not delineate the scope of "related to"[5] jurisdiction, but its choice of words suggests a grant of some breadth. The jurisdictional grant in § 1334(b) was a distinct departure from the jurisdiction conferred under previous Acts, which had been limited to either possession of property by the debtor or consent as a basis for jurisdiction. We agree with the views expressed by the Court of Appeals for the Third Circuit in Pacor, Inc. v. Higgins, 743 F.2d 984 (1984), that "Congress intended to grant comprehensive jurisdiction to the bankruptcy courts so that they might deal efficiently and expeditiously with all matters connected with the bankruptcy estate," id., at 994; see also H.R.Rep. No. 95-595, pp. 43-48 (1977), and that the "related to" language of § 1334(b) must be read to give district courts (and bankruptcy courts under § 157(a)) jurisdiction over more than simple proceedings involving the property of the debtor or the estate. We also agree with that court's observation that a bankruptcy court's "related to" jurisdiction cannot be limitless.[6]

---

[5]Proceedings "related to" the bankruptcy include (1) causes of action owned by the debtor which become property of the estate pursuant to 11 U.S.C. § 541, and (2) suits between third parties which have an effect on the bankruptcy estate. See 1 Collier on Bankruptcy P 3.01[1][c] [iv], p. 3-28 (15th ed. 1994). The first type of "related to" proceeding involves a claim like the state-law breach of contract action at issue in Northern Pipeline Constr. Co. v. Marathon Pipe Line Co., 458 U.S. 50, 102 S.Ct. 2858, 73 L.Ed.2d 598 (1982). The instant case involves the second type of "related to" proceeding.

[6]In attempting to strike an appropriate balance, the Third Circuit in Pacor, Inc. v. Higgins, 743 F.2d 984 (1984), devised the following test for determining the existence of "related to" jurisdiction:

> The usual articulation of the test for determining whether a civil proceeding is related to bankruptcy is whether the outcome of that proceeding could

We believe that the issue whether respondents are entitled to immediate execution on the bond against Northbrook is at least a question "related to" Celotex's bankruptcy. Admittedly, a proceeding by respondents against Northbrook on the supersedeas bond does not directly involve Celotex, except to satisfy the judgment against it secured by the bond. But to induce Northbrook to serve as surety on the bond, Celotex agreed to allow Northbrook to retain the proceeds of a settlement resolving insurance coverage disputes between Northbrook and Celotex. The Bankruptcy Court found that allowing respondents--and 227 other bonded judgment creditors--to execute immediately on the bonds would have a direct and substantial adverse effect on Celotex's ability to undergo a successful reorganization. It stated:

> [I]f the Section 105 stay were lifted to enable the judgment creditors to reach the sureties, the sureties in turn would seek to lift the Section 105 stay to reach Debtor's collateral, with corresponding actions by Debtor to preserve its rights under the settlement agreements. Such a scenario could completely destroy any chance of resolving the prolonged insurance coverage disputes currently being adjudicated in this Court. The settlement of the insurance coverage disputes with all of Debtor's insurers may well be the linchpin of Debtor's formulation of a feasible plan. Absent the confirmation of a feasible plan, Debtor may be liquidated or cease to exist after a carrion feast by the victors in a race to the courthouse.

In re Celotex, 140 B.R. 912, 915 (1992) (Celotex II).

In light of these findings by the Bankruptcy Court, it is relevant to note that we are dealing here with a reorganization under Chapter 11, rather than a liquidation under Chapter 7. The jurisdiction of bankruptcy courts may extend more broadly in the former case than in the latter.

---

conceivably have any effect on the estate being administered in bankruptcy.... Thus, the proceeding need not necessarily be against the debtor or against the debtor's property. An action is related to bankruptcy if the outcome could alter the debtor's rights, liabilities, options, or freedom of action (either positively or negatively) and which in any way impacts upon the handling and administration of the bankrupt estate." Id., at 994 (emphasis in original; citations omitted). The First, Fourth, Fifth, Sixth, Eighth, Ninth, Tenth, and Eleventh Circuits have adopted the Pacor test with little or no variation.

3. *Role and Power of the Bankruptcy Court*

28 U.S.C. § 157(a), (b)

(a) Each district court may provide that any or all cases under title 11 and any or all proceedings arising under title 11 or arising in or related to a case under title 11 shall be referred to the bankruptcy judges for the district.[7]

(b) (1) Bankruptcy judges may hear and determine all cases under title 11 and all core proceedings arising under title 11, or arising in a case under title 11, referred under subsection (a) of this section, and may enter appropriate orders and judgments, subject to review under section 158 of this title.

(2) Core proceedings include, but are not limited to—

(A) matters concerning the administration of the estate;

(B) allowance or disallowance of claims against the estate or exemptions from property of the estate, and estimation of claims or interests for the purposes of confirming a plan under chapter 11, 12, or 13 of title 11 but not the liquidation or estimation of contingent or unliquidated personal injury tort or wrongful death claims against the estate for purposes of distribution in a case under title 11;

(C) counterclaims by the estate against persons filing claims against the estate;

---

[7]Every district – yes, every district – has entered a local order referring bankruptcy matters to the bankruptcy court as anticipated by this provision. The provision in effect in New Mexico is typical: "IT IS ORDERED that all cases under Title 11 and all proceedings arising under Title 11 or arising in or related to a case under Title 11 are referred to the bankruptcy judges for the district to the extent permitted by law." Misc. Order No. 84-0324 (N.M., July 1, 1984). Just so you don't think it is only small states that have this short order, the general order of reference for the Southern District of New York has identical language. Gen. Order No. 61 (S.D.N.Y., July 10, 1984).

(D) orders in respect to obtaining credit;

(E) orders to turn over property of the estate;

(F) proceedings to determine, avoid, or recover preferences;

(G) motions to terminate, annul, or modify the automatic stay;

(H) proceedings to determine, avoid, or recover fraudulent conveyances;

(I) determinations as to the dischargeability of particular debts;

(J) objections to discharges;

(K) determinations of the validity, extent, or priority of liens;

(L) confirmations of plans;

(M) orders approving the use or lease of property, including the use of cash collateral;

(N) orders approving the sale of property other than property resulting from claims brought by the estate against persons who have not filed claims against the estate;

(O) other proceedings affecting the liquidation of the assets of the estate or the adjustment of the debtor-creditor or the equity security holder relationship, except personal injury tort or wrongful death claims; and

(P) recognition of foreign proceedings and other matters under chapter 15 of title 11.

Clearly, section 1334 confers jurisdiction over bankruptcy matters to the district court. It is equally clear that most federal district judges have neither the time nor the inclination to exercise this jurisdiction. Accordingly, section 157 empowers the district judge to refer bankruptcy matters to a bankruptcy judge.

The title of section 157 is "Procedures." As this title suggests, section 157 is not a jurisdictional provision. It does not confer jurisdiction on the bankruptcy judge. Rather, it deals with procedure — the role that the bankruptcy judge, a unit of the district court under section 151, is to play in exercising the jurisdiction conferred by section 1334 on the district court.

Section 157 differentiates between "core" and "noncore" proceedings. A nonexclusive list of core proceedings is set out in section 157(b)(2).

Obviously, if a matter is not a core proceeding, it is a "noncore proceeding." "Noncore proceeding" is neither defined nor illustrated in the statute. In noncore proceedings, the bankruptcy judge still can hold the trial or hearing, but generally[8] cannot issue a final judgment. She instead submits proposed findings of fact and law to the district court for review, section 157(c)(1).

The bankruptcy judge is empowered to determine whether a matter is a core proceeding or a noncore proceeding, section 157(b)(3). Remember that a determination that a proceeding is noncore does not mean that the matter is withdrawn from the bankruptcy judge. Remember that a bankruptcy judge can hear

---

[8]The bankruptcy judge can enter a final order or judgment in a noncore matter only if the parties consent, 28 U.S.C. § 157(c)(2). To help assist the parties in knowing when the bankruptcy judge may enter a final order, the Bankruptcy Rules require the parties' pleading to state that a matter is core or noncore, and to state affirmatively that they do not consent to entry of a final judgment by the bankrutpcy court. BANKR. R. 7008(a).

noncore proceedings and prepare proposed findings of facts and law.

---

4. *Centralizing Litigation (Or Not): Removal From and Remand Back to Other Courts*

28 U.S.C. § 1452

> (a) A party may remove any claim or cause of action in a civil action other than a proceeding before the United States Tax Court or a civil action by a governmental unit to enforce such governmental unit's police or regulatory power, to the district court for the district where such civil action is pending, if such district court has jurisdiction of such claim or cause of action under section 1334 of this title.
>
> (b) The court to which such claim or cause of action is removed may remand such claim or cause of action on any equitable ground. An order entered under this subsection remanding a claim or cause of action, or a decision to not remand, is not reviewable by appeal or otherwise . . . .

Occasionally, there may be litigation pending in state court that could be heard more quickly or more efficiently in bankruptcy court. If that is the case, *any* party (not just the debtor) can remove the action to bankruptcy court. Not only that, but unlike normal removal to federal court, a party need not remove the entire action; individual causes of action may be removed to federal bankruptcy court. All that is required is that the action be within the large scope of Section 1334.

This right of removal is not absolute. The rules require that in most cases removal occur within 90 days of the order for relief. BANKR. R. 9027(a)(2)(A). Even if timely, Section 1452(b) gives a broad right of remand on "any equitable ground." And if the bankruptcy court orders remand, that's the end of the story. The statute pretty clearly provides that "[a]n order entered . . .

remanding a claim or cause of action, or a decision to not remand, is not reviewable by appeal or otherwise."

In many mass tort cases, the debtor will remove pending tort cases pending against it in the various state courts. It also sometimes happens that pending non-bankruptcy cases that involve a non-dischargeable claim will be removed – a creditor suing an individual debtor being sued for fraud might, for example, remove the state court fraud case and then amend it to include a non-dischargeability count.

If you think that all of this – core, noncore, "related to" and removal – is a lot for a non-Article-III court to handle, you are not alone. Congress provided for a safeguard to ensure that, in proper cases, the Article III District Court can still hear the case.

---

5. *The Constitutional Escape Hatch — Withdrawal of the "Reference"*

As we saw above, every district has entered an order authorized by Section 157(a) that "refers" all bankruptcy matters within the scope of Section 1334 to the bankruptcy court for that district. But to preserve at least the pretense that district courts still are the residual keepers of Article III jurisdiction over bankruptcy, there has to be some way to get the case or parts of it "back" to the district court. In that way, the district judge can retain ultimate control over the role of the bankruptcy judge, and ensure that matters that require an Article III judge will get one.

---

28 U.S.C. § 157(d)

(d) The district court may withdraw, in whole or in part, any case or proceeding referred under this section, on its own motion or on timely motion of any party, for cause shown. The district court shall, on timely motion of a party, so withdraw a proceeding if the court determines that resolution of the proceeding requires consideration of both title 11 and other laws of the United States regulating organizations or activities affecting interstate commerce.

Section 157(d) authorizes the district judge to withdraw a case or proceeding from a bankruptcy judge. The first sentence of section 157(d) provides for permissive withdrawal "for cause shown." Under the second sentence of section 157(d), withdrawal of the reference is mandatory if "resolution of the proceeding requires consideration of both Title 11 and other laws of the United States regulating . . . interstate commerce."

In applying this provision, most courts disregard the "plain language" quoted above. The plain language of section 157(d) indicates that withdrawal of the reference is mandatory only if both the Bankruptcy Code and another federal statute must be construed to resolve the proceeding. Under the statute's "plain language," a district court would be required to withdraw the reference only in actions involving both bankruptcy and nonbankruptcy law — not in matters involving nonbankruptcy law alone. And, under the statute's plain language, the bankruptcy court would have to abstain on all matters that involve both bankruptcy law and a nonfederal statute regulating interstate commerce, regardless of how simple and straight forward the application of the other statute.

Because the "plain language" of section 157(d)'s second sentence plainly does not work, most courts have ignored the literal language of section 157(d) for mandatory withdrawal. Instead, these courts require that the reference be withdrawn if an action involves a "substantial and material" consideration of a nonbankruptcy federal statute regulating interstate commerce, regardless of whether the action also involves consideration of the Bankruptcy Code.

Withdrawal of the reference from the district court to the bankruptcy judge is also mandatory for (1) claims for wrongful death or other personal injuries, 28 U.S.C. § 157(b)(5), or (2) matters in which a party has a right to a jury trial unless the district court has authorized the bankruptcy judge to conduct the jury trial and the parties have consented, 28 U.S.C. § 157(c).

Remember that withdrawal under section 157(d) merely moves a matter from the bankruptcy judge to the federal district judge. Withdrawal under section 157(d) does not move a matter to a state court. That requires abstention.

---

6. *Abstention*

28 U.S.C. § 1334(c)

> (c) (1) Except with respect to a case under chapter 15 of title 11, Nothing in this section prevents a district court in the interest of justice, or in the interest of comity with State courts or respect for State law, from abstaining from hearing a particular proceeding arising under title 11 or arising in or related to a case under title 11.
>
> (2) Upon timely motion of a party in a proceeding based upon a State law claim or State law cause of action, related to a case under title 11 but not arising under title 11 or arising in a case under title 11, with respect to which an action could not have been commenced in a court of the United States absent jurisdiction under this section, the district court shall abstain from hearing such proceeding if an action is commenced, and can be timely adjudicated, in a State forum of appropriate jurisdiction.

Abstention under section 1334(c) moves litigation from bankruptcy court to a state court. In considering and applying the abstention provisions of section 1334(c), it is important to recall the jurisdictional provisions of section 1334(b). As you learned from your readings in constitutional law and/or federal courts, a federal court with jurisdiction over a matter or controversy must exercise that jurisdiction except under unusual circumstances. And, as you learned from reading this book, Congress provided for broad, pervasive bankruptcy jurisdiction in section 1334(b) to eliminate the costly litigation over jurisdiction that occurred under the Bankruptcy Act of 1898. As a result, some of the matters covered by the jurisdictional grant in section 1334(b) are not really bankruptcy matters, but are matters that would be better left to other courts. Section 1334(c) empowers the bankruptcy judge to leave such matters to other courts by abstaining.

Section 1334(c)(1) provides for permissive abstention. If the district court believes that abstention would be "in the interest of justice" or "in the interest of comity with State courts or respect for State law," it has the option of abstaining. Section 1334(c)(2) provides for mandatory abstention; if the following six requirements of section 1334(c)(2) are satisfied.

C. Operation of the Jurisdictional Provisions of the Present Law

In re Toledo
70 F.3d 1340 (11th Cir. 1999)

ANDERSON, Circuit Judge:

Carmen Sanchez filed the instant adversary proceeding against the trustee of the bankruptcy estate ("Estate") of Orlando and Maria Toledo, the debtors themselves, and the Continental National Bank of Miami ("Bank"). The bankruptcy court invalidated the Bank's mortgage on real estate owned by a partnership of which the debtors and Sanchez were the partners. The district court affirmed the bankruptcy court, applying the deferential standards of review applicable to "core" proceedings under the Bankruptcy Code. The Bank appeals. The issues presented for review are (i) whether the bankruptcy court had jurisdiction to hear this adversary proceeding, and (ii) if so, whether the district court was correct in treating it as a core proceeding rather than as a non-core proceeding requiring *de novo,* plenary review. For the reasons stated below, we hold that the bankruptcy court had jurisdiction, but that this was a non-core matter necessitating plenary review by the district court.

In 1988, Orlando and Maria Toledo, debtors in the underlying bankruptcy case, formed a partnership with Tomas and Carmen Sanchez called the Latin Quarter Center Partnership ("Partnership"). Each of the four partners held an equal one-fourth share. The purpose of the partnership was to hold, develop, and deal in certain contiguous parcels of real estate in downtown Miami ("Partnership Property"). No formal partnership agreement was ever entered into, but Orlando Toledo, acting alone, generally managed and acted on behalf of the partnership. Shortly after the Partnership came into being, Tomas Sanchez died, and his wife Carmen Sanchez (plaintiff in the instant adversary proceeding) succeeded to his 25% share, so that she then owned a total 50 interest in the Partnership. Orlando Toledo continued to act as managing partner and Carmen Sanchez was uninvolved in Partnership affairs.

In April of 1989, Orlando Toledo encountered personal financial difficulties. In order to assuage the Bank's concern about its position as one of his creditors and to induce it not to foreclose on a mortgage it held on his Key Biscayne personal residence, Toledo purported to convey a mortgage on the Partnership Property to the Bank to secure Toledo's personal indebtedness to the Bank in the approximate amount of $1,100,000. This was done without Sanchez' consent or knowledge. In taking this action, Toledo claimed to be acting in the capacity of a general partner as an agent for the Partnership. If the mortgage was valid, the Partnership Property thereby became a guarantee for Toledo's personal debt. Toledo also convinced McDonald's Corp., which had a $275,000 pre-existing purchase money mortgage on the Partnership Property, to subordinate its mortgage to the one newly granted to the Bank.

Orlando Toledo's financial outlook did not improve, and the Bank eventually obtained a judgment of foreclosure on both the Partnership Property and Toledo's Key Biscayne personal residence (which secured the same indebtedness) in Dade County circuit court in November 1992. . . . On January 11, 1993, the day before the scheduled foreclosure sale of the Key Biscayne residence, Orlando and Maria Toledo filed for Chapter 11 and thereby averted the sale.

Soon after the commencement of the bankruptcy case, a private sale of the Partnership Property to McDonald's Corp. was negotiated by Toledo, the Estate, and the Bank under supervision of the bankruptcy court. . . . The parties, apparently assuming that the bankruptcy court's stamp of approval was necessary in order to consummate the sale, applied to the court for approval even though the Partnership Property was not property of the Estate. Acting under purported authority of 11 U.S.C. § 363(f), Judge Weaver approved the sale in an order dated April 12, 1993.[3] . . .

Meanwhile, Sanchez filed the instant adversary complaint in the bankruptcy court against the trustee of the Estate, the debtors themselves, and the Bank (i) to determine entitlement to the proceeds of the sale of the Partnership Property to McDonald's Corp., and (ii) to contest the validity of the Bank's lien. The action was styled as a "Complaint to Determine Validity, Priority, and Extent of Lien and Ownership Interest." After four evidentiary hearings in which extensive testimony was taken from Orlando Toledo, employees of the Bank, and others, Judge Cristol of the bankruptcy court accepted Sanchez' argument and ordered that (i) the Bank had had no valid lien on the Partnership Property because it knew Toledo was conveying the mortgage for improper, non-partnership purposes, and (ii) the Bank must pay to Sanchez the $200,000 it had previously received from the sale of the Partnership Property. The bankruptcy court noted that it had jurisdiction under 28 U.S.C. § 1334, but never specifically confronted the question whether the adversary proceeding was core or non-core under 28 U.S.C. § 157. By issuing an order that purported to be final and binding, rather than submitting proposed findings of fact and conclusions of law to the district court, the bankruptcy court indicated that it viewed the proceeding as a core one of which it had full, plenary authority to dispose.

---

[3]Section 363(f) of the Bankruptcy Code provides that "[t]he trustee may sell property under subsections (b) and (c) of this section free and clear of any interest in such property of an entity other than the estate" upon certain conditions. It is questionable whether § 363(f) gives a bankruptcy court power to order or approve a sale of property that belongs only to an entity in which the estate holds an interest, and not to the estate itself. However, the validity of the sale order is not presently before this Court, and at any rate, it appears that the sale of the Partnership Property was a voluntary transaction, on favorable terms to the seller, to which all of the parties consented. Thus, we do not consider any issues relating to Judge Weaver's sale order.

Appealing to the district court, the Bank argued that (i) the bankruptcy court lacked subject matter jurisdiction to hear the adversary proceeding filed by Sanchez; (ii) the bankruptcy court erred in finding that the Bank knew Toledo lacked authority to mortgage the Partnership Property for personal purposes; . . . . The district court held that the bankruptcy court had subject matter jurisdiction and that the matter was a core matter. It then found, applying the "clearly erroneous" standard of review to the bankruptcy court's fact findings (the appropriate standard of review for bankruptcy court orders regarding core matters), that Toledo lacked authority to mortgage the Partnership Property for his personal purposes, and that the Bank was aware thereof. . . . Consequently, the district court affirmed the bankruptcy court's judgment.

On appeal to this court, the Bank argues first that the bankruptcy court lacked jurisdiction to entertain the adversary proceeding under 28 U.S.C. § 1334. Second, it argues that, even if the bankruptcy court had jurisdiction, such jurisdiction was in the nature of a non-core proceeding limiting the bankruptcy court's adjudicative powers. Third, the Bank reiterates its various substantive arguments as to why the bankruptcy court erred in its determination of the merits under Florida law; however, in light of our conclusion that this was a non-core proceeding, it is unnecessary for us to reach those issues.

The first question is whether the bankruptcy court had jurisdiction to entertain the instant adversary proceeding under 28 U.S.C. § 1334. Section 1334(b) provides that "the district courts shall have original but not exclusive jurisdiction of all civil proceedings arising under title 11, or arising in or related to cases under title 11." This provision creates jurisdiction in three categories of proceedings: those that "arise under title 11," those that "arise in cases under title 11," and those "related to cases under title 11." The bankruptcy court's jurisdiction is derivative of and dependent upon these three bases. The instant adversary proceeding did not "aris[e] under" or "aris[e] in" a case under the Bankruptcy Code. "Arising under" proceedings are matters invoking a substantive right created by the Bankruptcy Code. The "arising in a case under" category is generally thought to involve administrative-type matters. Hence, the only one of the three categories of proceedings over which the district court is granted jurisdiction in § 1334(b) that is potentially relevant to the instant case is proceedings "related to cases under title 11."

The Bank claims that the dispute between Sanchez and the Bank over entitlement to the proceeds of the Partnership

Property was not related to Toledo's underlying bankruptcy case and had no effect on Toledo or the Estate, and therefore the bankruptcy court had no jurisdiction to adjudicate that dispute. Blending the concepts of jurisdiction and the core versus non-core dichotomy, the district court held that the bankruptcy court had jurisdiction because the dispute was a "core proceeding" under 28 U.S.C. § 157(b)(2)(K).[6]

As both parties acknowledge, *Miller v. Kemira, Inc.* (*In re Lemco Gypsum, Inc.*), 910 F.2d 784 (11th Cir.1990), is the seminal case in this Circuit on the scope of the bankruptcy court's "related to" jurisdiction. In *Lemco Gypsum,* this Court adopted the following liberal test from *Pacor, Inc. v. Higgins,* 743 F.2d 984 (3d Cir.1984), for determining jurisdiction over an adversary proceeding:

> The usual articulation of the test for determining whether a civil proceeding is related to bankruptcy is whether the outcome of the proceeding could conceivably have an effect on the estate being administered in bankruptcy. The proceeding need not necessarily be against the debtor or the debtor's property. An action is related to bankruptcy if the outcome could alter the debtor's rights, liabilities, options, or freedom of action (either positively or negatively) and which in any way impacts upon the handling and administration of the bankrupt estate.

The key word in the *Lemco Gypsum/Pacor* test is "conceivable," which makes the jurisdictional grant extremely broad.

In the instant case, Sanchez was seeking a judicial determination of the extent and priority of liens and other interests in the Partnership Property so that the proceeds of the sale earlier approved by Judge Weaver's order could be distributed appropriately. . . . [I]f the Bank's mortgage was held invalid, as actually occurred, the Bank would have to look entirely to the Key Biscayne residence (or, more precisely, to what remained from the proceeds of the residence after satisfaction of BankAtlantic's first mortgage thereon) for satisfaction of its $1.8 million indebtedness. To the extent the

---

[6]Although whether something is a core proceeding is analytically separate from whether there is jurisdiction, by definition all core proceedings are within the bankruptcy court's jurisdiction. Core proceedings are defined in 28 U.S.C. § 157(b)(1) as "proceedings arising under title 11, or arising in a case under title 11," which is a subset of the cases over which jurisdiction is granted in § 1334(b).

value to which it was entitled from the residence was insufficient to satisfy this debt, the Bank would become an unsecured creditor causing the funds available for unsecured claims to be spread more thinly. A conceivable effect on the Estate thus exists in the possible partial satisfaction and consequent downward adjustment of the claim filed against the Estate by the Bank. . . .

Having found that the district court had jurisdiction over the adversary proceeding, we turn next to the question whether the district court correctly referred to it as a core proceeding under 28 U.S.C. § 157(b). If it was a core proceeding, the district court correctly applied normal, deferential standards of appellate review to the bankruptcy court's disposition of it. *See* 28 U.S.C. § 158(a); Fed. R. Bankr.P. 8013. If it was a non-core proceeding, the bankruptcy court could only submit proposed findings of fact and conclusions of law, not a final order or judgment, and the district court was obligated to conduct a *de novo* review of those matters to which the Bank objected. *See* 28 U.S.C. § 157(c)(1) ("In [a non-core] proceeding, the bankruptcy judge shall submit proposed findings of fact and conclusions of law to the district court, and any final order or judgment shall be entered by the district judge after considering the bankruptcy judge's proposed findings and conclusions and after reviewing de novo those matters to which any party has timely and specifically objected."); Fed. R. Bankr.P. 9033 (specifying the exact procedures to be followed by the district court in such cases).

Congress created the distinction between core and non-core proceedings in the Bankruptcy Amendments and Federal Judgeship Act of 1984 ("1984 Act"), in order to avoid the constitutional problems, identified in *Northern Pipeline Constr. Co. v. Marathon Pipe Line Co.,* 458 U.S. 50, 102 S.Ct. 2858, 73 L.Ed.2d 598 (1982), associated with the expansive bankruptcy court jurisdiction permitted under prior law.[9] 28 U.S.C. § 157(b)(2) lists fourteen specific types of actions that are considered core proceedings, *id.* § 157(b)(2)(A)-(N), and provides a fifteenth, catch-all category for "other proceedings affecting the liquidation of the assets of the estate or the adjustment of the debtor-creditor or the equity security holder relationship," *id.* § 157(b)(2)(*O*). The statutory list provides

---

[9]In *Northern Pipeline,* the Supreme Court held that allowing bankruptcy courts to hear a state-law breach-of-contract action was an impermissible delegation of the Article III powers reserved to the federal judiciary. The adjudication of state- created "private rights" was seen as too far removed from the "core" of the federal bankruptcy power, i.e., the restructuring of debtor-creditor relations.

that it is not intended to be exhaustive of the entire universe of core proceedings.

The district court held that the instant case was a core proceeding under 28 U.S.C. § 157(b)(2)(K), which applies to "determinations of the validity, extent, or priority of liens." This reliance on § 157(b)(2)(K) was misplaced. The district court apparently reasoned that since the purpose of the instant adversary proceeding was to obtain a judicial determination of the validity of the Bank's mortgage, which is a lien on real estate, it fit the language of subsection (b)(2)(K). However, the case law on (b)(2)(K) indicates that it encompasses only proceedings to determine the validity, extent, or priority of liens *on the estate's or the debtor's property.* Here, the real property on which the disputed mortgage existed belonged to the non-debtor Partnership, not to the Toledos or the Estate. The Estate owned a 50% interest in the Partnership, but no direct interest in the Partnership Property. Thus, § 157(b)(2)(K) is no basis for calling the instant proceeding a "core proceeding."

The distinction between property belonging to a partnership of which the debtor was partner, and property belonging to the debtor-partner, is well- established in bankruptcy law. . . . The only partnership property before the court during an individual's bankruptcy is the partner's personal property interest in the partnership, which consists of the individual's interest, if any, in the partnership assets after an accounting and payment of partnership debts out of the property belonging to the partnership."). The Partnership Property never entered the Estate in the instant case.

Nor do any of the other types of core proceedings appearing in § 157(b)'s list fit the instant adversary proceeding. To the extent that the literal wording of some of the types of proceedings might conceivably seem to apply, it should be remembered that engrafted upon all of them is an overarching requirement that property of the estate under § 541 be involved. Here, of course, the property in question was owned by the Partnership, not by Toledo himself.

Because the list in the statute is non-exhaustive, it is not the end of our inquiry whether the adversary proceeding was core. The most helpful explanation of what is a core proceeding, accepted almost universally by the courts, is found in the Fifth Circuit's decision in *Wood v. Wood* (*In re Wood*), 825 F.2d 90 (5th Cir.1987):

> If the proceeding involves a right created by the federal bankruptcy law, it is a core proceeding; for example, an action by the trustee to avoid a preference. If the proceeding is one that would arise only in bankruptcy, it is also a core proceeding; for example, the filing of a proof of claim or an objection to the discharge of a particular debt. If the proceeding does not invoke a substantive right created by the federal bankruptcy law and is one that could exist outside of bankruptcy it is not a core proceeding; it may be *related* to the bankruptcy because of its potential effect, but under section 157(c)(1) it is an "otherwise related" or non-core proceeding.

In *Wood,* the adversary proceeding in question was an action by a shareholder of a corporation of which the bankruptcy debtor was the only other shareholder, to obtain redress for allegedly improper stock issued to and dividends received by the debtor- shareholder or the estate. The Fifth Circuit held that under the above test this adversary proceeding was not a core proceeding because it was "simply a state contract action that, had there been no bankruptcy, could have proceeded in state court." Although the court had subject matter jurisdiction pursuant to the "related to" prong of § 1334(b), it was not a core proceeding.

Wood 's interpretation of § 157 rested heavily on the ostensible purpose of the 1984 Act, i.e., "to conform the bankruptcy statutes to the dictates of *Marathon* [v. *Northern Pipeline*]." The Fifth Circuit's test breathes life into the terms "core" and "non-core" by construing them in light of the constitutional concerns that prompted the enactment of the statute. In fact, it appears that the use of the word "core" was itself borrowed from Justice Brennan's reference in the plurality opinion to "the core of the federal bankruptcy power." What the Supreme Court, and by extension Congress, was concerned about was the plenary adjudication by bankruptcy courts of proceedings "related only peripherally to an adjudication of bankruptcy." Hence, the issue before us ultimately depends on whether the instant case was of the type with respect to which the *Northern Pipeline* Court rejected giving bankruptcy courts full adjudicative power.

. . . Sanchez' action to determine the validity, priority, and extent of liens on the Partnership Property did not invoke a substantive right created by bankruptcy law, and could clearly occur outside of bankruptcy.[11] Indeed, actions similar to the instant case are filed in state court all the time.

The linguistic structure of § 157 lends further support to this conclusion. Subsection (b)(1) equates core proceedings with those "arising under title 11, or arising in a case under title 11," whereas subsection (c)(1) makes "non-core" proceedings synonymous with "otherwise related to" proceedings. "The phrases 'arising under' and 'arising in' are helpful indicators of the meaning of core proceedings." "Arising under" means that a proceeding invokes a cause of action, or substantive right, created by a specific section of the Bankruptcy Code. "Arising in" describes administrative matters unique to the management of a bankruptcy estate. For example, as the *Wood* court explained, the filing of a claim against a bankruptcy estate triggers a core proceeding under § 157(b)(2)(B), but only because it "invoke[s] the peculiar powers of the bankruptcy court." However, the administrative act of filing such a claim must be distinguished from the state-law right underlying the claim, which "could be enforced in a state court proceeding absent the bankruptcy" and is non-core. In the instant case, the adversary proceeding sought to vindicate state-created common-law rights but did not utilize any process specially established by the Bankruptcy Code. Clearly, Sanchez' adversary proceeding neither "arose under" nor "arose in" the Bankruptcy Code as those terms of art have been understood, and therefore it must necessarily fall within the residual category of "otherwise related," i.e., non-core matters.

In conclusion, we hold that there was "related to" jurisdiction over the adversary proceeding under 28 U.S.C. § 1334, but that it was a non-core proceeding under 28 U.S.C. § 157. Because the district court mistook it for a core proceeding, it exercised only "clearly erroneous" review of the

---

[11]*Wood* is especially instructive because its facts are roughly analogous to those in the instant case. In *Wood,* the complaint filed in the bankruptcy court concerned the debtors' post-petition wrongful issuance of stock and payment of dividends (the debtors were controlling shareholders and directors of the corporation) to themselves, which violated the plaintiff's right as an equal shareholder. By comparison, the instant case concerns a debtor-partner's alleged manipulation of a partnership to exploit its property to secure personal debts, to the detriment of the other partner. In both cases, the right that the plaintiffs sought to vindicate involved a wrongful manipulation of the property of an entity other than the debtor (i.e., a corporation or partnership), and was essentially a state-law right based on principles of contract and/or fiduciary duty. Neither case is one involving a right created by bankruptcy law, or one which would arise only in bankruptcy. Rather, both cases invoke purely state-law rights and could exist outside bankruptcy.

bankruptcy court's findings of fact and "abuse of discretion" review of the bankruptcy court's application of waiver and estoppel, despite the Bank's specific objections to those findings and applications.[12] We remand with instructions to the district court to treat the bankruptcy court's findings of fact and conclusions of law entered at the October 13, 1994, hearing, and the accompanying February 23, 1995, and June 7, 1995 "judgments" granting Sanchez relief, as merely proposed findings of fact and conclusions of law, and to conduct the *de novo* review contemplated by § 157(c)(1) and Bankruptcy Rule 9033. The judgment of the district court is

VACATED AND REMANDED.

QUESTIONS AND NOTES ON *TOLEDO*

1. **"Related to" jurisdiction precedent**. In finding "related to" jurisdiction over an action to determine the validity of a lien on a nondebtor's property because the existence of that lien would affect the amount of the lienor's claim against the estate, the Eleventh Circuit relied on its earlier decision in *Lemco Gypsum* which relied on *Pacor* which had been relied on by the Supreme Court in *Celotex*. Why didn't the Eleventh Circuit in *Toledo* simply rely on the Supreme Court's decision in *Celotex*?

2. **Related to jurisdiction problem**: D's Chapter 11 plan provided for the sale of all of its assets to X, free and clear of liens and claims, including claims based on successor liability. The bankruptcy court confirmed the plan and entered an order expressly providing that the sale to X would not be subject to successor liability claims. The amount X paid D was distributed to D's creditors, D went out of business,

---

[12]It is evident from the tone of the district court's opinion that its review of certain issues was highly deferential to the bankruptcy court. For example, it stated that "there is a valid basis for the relief granted by the bankruptcy court to avoid an injustice to override the application of res judicata and collateral estoppel." District Court Order at 8. On remand, the district court should undertake a fresh, independent analysis of these issues.

and the Chapter 11 case was closed. A year later, P sued X, alleging successor liability. X asked the bankruptcy court to reopen D's bankruptcy case and enjoin P from proceeding with her successor liability suit. Does the bankruptcy court have jurisdiction?

3. **Core/non-core Statutory Language**: What statutory language supports the district court's core proceeding determination? What statutory language supports the Circuit Court's non-core ruling?

D. JURY TRIALS

Having a powerful, centralized court to handle all matters involving the debtor in a bankruptcy case may be a good idea, but might there be cases in which constitutional considerations require something different?

Jury trial is a cherished right enshrined in the Seventh Amendment to the Constitution. And the Supreme Court has held that when an estate representative seeks to obtain the liability of a party who has not participated in the bankruptcy, and a jury traditionally (or at least by 1791) established that liability, the defendant is entitled to a trial by jury. *See* Granfinanciera, S.A. v. Nordberg, 492 U.S. 33 (1989) (fraudulent transfer cause of action recognized at law at the time of the adoption of the constitution, and thus defendant in such an action entitled to a jury).

Does this mean that every time a trustee wants to sue on a preference or a fraudulent transfer, the court has to empanel a jury? Can bankruptcy courts even conduct jury trials?[13] Read on.

---

[13]We'll answer this question first. Yes. . . . Well, maybe. Congress has given bankruptcy courts the power to hold jury trials only if the local district court specifically permits such trials, and if the parties expressly consent. 28 U.S.C. § 157(e).

LANGENKAMP V. CULP
498 U.S. 42 (1990)

PER CURIAM.

This case presents the question whether creditors who submit a claim against a bankruptcy estate and are then sued by the trustee in bankruptcy to recover allegedly preferential monetary transfers are entitled to jury trial under the Seventh Amendment. This action was brought by petitioner Langenkamp, successor trustee to Republic Trust & Savings Company and Republic Financial Corporation (collectively debtors). Debtors were uninsured, nonbank financial institutions doing business in Oklahoma. Debtors filed Chapter 11 bankruptcy petitions on September 24, 1984. At the time of the bankruptcy filings, respondents held thrift and passbook savings certificates issued by debtors, which represented debtors' promise to repay moneys the respondents had invested.

Within the 90-day period immediately preceding debtors' Chapter 11 filing, respondents redeemed some, but not all, of debtors' certificates which they held. Thus, upon the bankruptcy filing, respondents became creditors of the now-bankrupt corporations. Respondents timely filed proofs of claim against the bankruptcy estates. Approximately one year after the bankruptcy filing, the trustee instituted adversary proceedings under 11 U.S.C. § 547(b) to recover, as avoidable preferences, the payments which respondents had received immediately prior to the September 24 filing. A bench trial was held, and the Bankruptcy Court found that the money received by respondents did in fact constitute avoidable preferences. . . . The United States District Court for the Northern District of Oklahoma affirmed. . . . On appeal, the United States Court of Appeals for the Tenth Circuit upheld the District Court's judgment on three grounds, but reversed on the issue of the holders' entitlement to a jury trial on the trustee's preference claims. *In re Republic Trust & Savings Co.,* 897 F.2d 1041 (1990). Relying on our decisions in *Granfinanciera, S.A. v. Nordberg,* 492 U.S. 33, 109 S.Ct. 2782, 106 L.Ed.2d 26 (1989), and *Katchen v. Landy,* 382 U.S. 323, 86 S.Ct. 467, 15 L.Ed.2d 391 (1966), the Tenth Circuit correctly held that "those appellants that did not have or file claims against the debtors' estates undoubtedly [were] entitled to a jury trial on the issue whether the payments they received from the debtors within ninety days of the latter's bankruptcy constitute[d] avoidable preferences." The Court of Appeals went further, however, concluding:

> "Although some of the appellants did file claims against the estates because they continued to have monies invested in the debtors at the time of bankruptcy, ... we believe they likewise are entitled to a jury trial under the rationale of *Granfinanciera* and *Katchen.* Despite these appellants' claims, the trustee's actions to avoid the transfers, consolidated by the bankruptcy court, were plenary rather than a part of the bankruptcy court's summary proceedings involving the 'process of allowance and disallowance of claims.'"

Petitioner contends that the Tenth Circuit erred in holding that those creditors of the debtors who had filed claims against the estate were entitled to a jury trial. We agree.

In *Granfinanciera* we recognized that by filing a claim against a bankruptcy estate the creditor triggers the process of "allowance and disallowance of claims," thereby subjecting himself to the bankruptcy court's equitable power. If the creditor is met, in turn, with a preference action from the trustee, that action becomes part of the claims-allowance process which is triable only in equity. *Ibid.* In other words, the creditor's claim and the ensuing preference action by the trustee become integral to the restructuring of the debtor-creditor relationship through the bankruptcy court's *equity jurisdiction.* As such, there is no Seventh Amendment right to a jury trial. If a party does *not* submit a claim against the bankruptcy estate, however, the trustee can recover allegedly preferential transfers only by filing what amounts to a legal action to recover a monetary transfer. In those circumstances the preference defendant is entitled to a jury trial.

Accordingly, "a creditor's right to a jury trial on a bankruptcy trustee's preference claim depends upon whether the creditor has submitted a claim against the estate." *Id.,* at 58, 109 S.Ct., at 2799. Respondents filed claims against the bankruptcy estate, thereby bringing themselves within the equitable jurisdiction of the Bankruptcy Court. Consequently, they were not entitled to a jury trial on the trustee's preference action. The decision by the Court of Appeals overlooked the clear distinction which our cases have drawn and in so doing created a conflict among the Circuits on this issue. For this reason we grant the petition for certiorari, reverse the judgment of the Court of Appeals for the Tenth Circuit, and remand for further proceedings consistent with this opinion.

It is so ordered.

QUESTIONS ON *LANGENKAMP*

1. What does *Langenkamp* say about the standard wisdom that a creditor should always file a proof of claim?

2. Now put the above question to practical use. What should a creditor do if it wants a jury trial and it is owed, say, $50,000, but believes that it likely received preferential payments during the reachback period of $100,000? Should it file a proof of claim? Is there any different result if the numbers are reversed; that is, if it is owed $100,000, but received preferences of $50,000? *See also* 11 U.S.C. § 502(d).

E. VENUE

So once you determine that a bankruptcy court has the power to hear and decide a matter, who (or what) decides where it is to be heard? It is a big country, after all, and, there are big bankruptcy cases.

---

28 U.S.C. § 1408

[A] case under title 11 may be commenced in the district court for the district—

> (1) in which the domicile, residence, principal place of business in the United States, or principal assets in the United States, of the person or entity that is the subject of such case have been located for the one hundred and eighty days immediately preceding such commencement, or for a longer portion of such one-hundred-and-eighty-day period than the domicile, residence, or principal place of business, in the United States, or principal assets in the United States, of such person were located in any other district; or

(2) in which there is pending a case under title 11 concerning such person's affiliate, general partner, or partnership.

PROBLEM 12-1: VENUE AND CHANGE OF VENUE IN BUSINESS CASES

G Inc. owns and operates a chain of grocery stores in Alabama, Arkansas, Louisiana and Mississippi. G Inc. also owns all of the stock of GS Inc., a small chain of health food stores in California, Nevada, Oregon and Washington. G Inc. is incorporated in Delaware. GS Inc. is incorporated in New York. The chief executive office of both G Inc. and GS Inc. is in Piggott, Arkansas.

On January 15, GS Inc. files a Chapter 11 petition in New York. Later that same day, G Inc. files a Chapter 11 petition in New York. On January 29, a group of creditors of G Inc.'s retain your firm to get G Inc.'s bankruptcy case moved from the Southern District of New York to Arkansas. Where are you going to file a change of venue motion? Should the court grant the motion? Will the court grant the motion?

Of course, the venue for a *case* can be different from the venue for a *proceeding*. The presumption in title 11 cases is that all proceedings and matters will be heard in the same court as the main case. 11 U.S.C. § 1409(a). This sometimes causes hardship — if a small vendor to WorldCom (say its janitorial service at its home office in Mississippi) was paid just before filing, does it have to hire New York lawyers to establish its ordinary course defense?

Section 1409(b), as amended in 2005, tries to take some of the sting out of this situation. It provides that efforts to collect consumer debts of less than $15,000 or any debts against non-insiders can be brought only where the defendant resides.

F. Appeals

Appeals from bankruptcy decisions are probably more complicated than they should be. Under the statute, the basic appeal right is to the district court of which the bankruptcy court is a unit. 28 U.S.C. § 158(a). Some circuits, notably the Ninth and the Tenth, have taken advantage of the congressional authorization to create "Bankruptcy Appellate Panels," which consist of three bankruptcy judges drawn from districts other than the district from which the appeal arises. 28 U.S.C. § 158(b). The jurisdiction of such "BAPs," as they are called, is wholly consensual; although the consent is usually assumed unless there is an affirmative election made to go to the district court. 28 U.S.C. § 158(c).

Once the district court or the BAP decides the appeal, there is a further level of appeal to the circuit court. And for that leg of the appeal (from the district court or BAP to the circuit), it is pretty much standard federal appellate process. 28 U.S.C. § 158(d).

G. Foreign Cases

As economic problems become more global, more international problems will crowd the docket of the United States bankruptcy courts.

In 2005, Congress took a large step towards establishing an international set of protocols for bankruptcies that touch more than one country. The 2005 Act added a new chapter to the Bankruptcy Code — chapter 15 — and in so doing radically changed the law regarding bankruptcies that affect the United States and other countries. This chapter is essentially an adoption of a model law on cross-border insolvencies promulgated in 1997 by the United Nations Commission on International Trade Law (UNCITRAL).[14]

In addition to the United States, the model law has been adopted by Eritrea, Japan, Mexico, Poland, Romania, South Africa, and within Serbia and Montenegro. It is expected that following the United States' adoption, other countries will adopt it as well. Europe has its own cross-border protocol, which came into effect on May 31, 2002. EC Regulation 1346/2000.

---

1. Chapter 15 Overview

In essence, a case under Chapter 15 is commenced by a petition filed by a foreign representative seeking "recognition" of a foreign insolvency proceeding. This description contains several defined terms; in short, something like a bankruptcy trustee in a foreign case will have standing to commence a proceeding in the United States to protect assets here for administration and distribution in the foreign insolvency proceeding. If the court recognizes the foreign proceeding under the principles set down in Chapter 15, the automatic stay and certain other protections of the Bankruptcy Code will apply. Chapter 15 is designed to encourage coordination among courts and estate representatives in different countries in the interest of avoiding inconsistent decisions that may hinder restructuring efforts.

Chapter 15 accomplishes these goals through four sets of provisions: (i) those related to the recognition of a foreign representative; (ii) those detailing the effects of

---

[14]These changes apply only to bankruptcy cases that are filed on or after October 17, 2005. A different and more limited provision, previously codified at Section 304 of the Bankruptcy Code, applied to cases before that date.

The discussion of Chapter 15 in the House Report, H.R. REP. 109-31, 109TH CONG., 1ST SESS. 105-119 (2005), is an adaption and expansion of the official UNCITRAL commentary. The full text of UNCITRAL's convention and commentary, together with a current list of adoptions, can be found at: http://www.uncitral.org/uncitral/en/uncitral_texts/insolvency/1997Model.html.

recognition of a foreign representative; (iii) those which attempt to foster inter-court cooperation; and (iv) those which have effect in all cases.

---

2. *Chapter 15 and Recognition of the "Foreign Representative"*

Chapter 15 is the vehicle by which foreign representatives can protect and obtain assets located in this country that relate to, or are owned by, a debtor with a case pending in another country. The 2005 Act amends the existing definition of "foreign representative" found in Section 101(24) to read as follows:

> (24) The term "foreign representative" means a person or body, including a person or body appointed on an interim basis, authorized in a foreign proceeding to administer the reorganization or the liquidation of the debtor's assets or affairs or to act as a representative of such foreign proceeding;

This definition in turn incorporates the revised definition of "foreign proceeding," found in Section 101(23), and which states:

> (23) The term "foreign proceeding" means a collective judicial or administrative proceeding in a foreign country, including an interim proceeding, under a law relating to insolvency or adjustment of debt in which proceeding the assets and affairs of the debtor are subject to control or supervision by a foreign court, for the purpose of reorganization or liquidation;

Foreign representatives have significant powers under Chapter 15. But to invoke them, the foreign representative must be "recognized." Indeed, a Chapter 15 case is commenced by the filing of a petition to be recognized by a foreign representative. 11 U.S.C. § 1504. Ultimate recognition, however, is governed by Section 1515, which provides:

§ 1515. Application for recognition

(a) A foreign representative applies to the court for recognition of a foreign proceeding in which the foreign representative has been appointed by filing a petition for recognition.

(b) A petition for recognition shall be accompanied by—

(1) a certified copy of the decision commencing such foreign proceeding and appointing te foreign representative;

(2) a certificate from the foreign court affirming the existence of such foreign proceeding and of the appointment of the foreign representative; or

(3) in the absence of evidence referred to in paragraphs (1) and (2), any other evidence acceptable to the court of the existence of such foreign proceeding and of the appointment of the foreign representative.

(c) A petition for recognition shall also be accompanied by a statement identifying all foreign proceedings with respect to the debtor that are known to the foreign representative.

(d) The documents referred to in paragraphs (1) and (2) of subsection (b) shall be translated into English. The court may require a translation into English of additional documents.

Basically, the foreign representative files documents issued by a foreign court or tribunal, that have been translated into English, and which establish that he or she is the authorized representative of a foreign insolvency proceeding. Once satisfactory documents have been produced, recognition is essentially automatic. 11 U.S.C. § 1517.

---

3. *The Effects of Recognition of a Foreign Representative*

Once a foreign representative is recognized, many substantive provisions of the Bankruptcy Code automatically apply. For example, with respect to any property in the United States,

- the automatic stay applies.
- the administrative provisions regarding sale of the property (including the ability to sell free and clear of liens and other interests) apply, as does Section 549 with respect to unauthorized post-petition transfers.
- the foreign representative may operate the debtor's business under Sections 363 and 552.

In addition, the foreign representative may apply for additional powers, which may include the taking of examinations (although not mentioned by name, this presumably covers examinations under Rule 2004) and any other power a trustee might have *except* for the commencement of avoidance powers actions (other than those under Section 549). 11 U.S.C. § 1521.

The foreign representative may, however, commence a separate case under any other applicable chapter, 11 U.S.C. § 1511, and once that case is commenced, the foreign representative has standing to pursue avoidance powers actions, such as preference actions under Section 547 and fraudulent transfer actions under Section 548, in that domestic case. 11 U.S.C. § 1523.

4. *Provisions Designed to Foster Inter-Court Cooperation*

Subchapters IV and V of Chapter 15 (11 U.S.C. § 1525 to 1532 contain a series of provisions designed to authorize and simply court-to-court communications with respect to bankruptcy cases pending in more than one country. The provisions authorize direct communication with a foreign court (11 U.S.C. § 1524(b)), and the entry of protocols or other agreed means of communication in a particular case (11 U.S.C. § 1527). Finally, there are provisions which attempt to coordinate a number of filings in affect countries, primarily by designation of one countries as a "foreign main proceeding" (which is to be where the debtor's "center of main interests" — something akin to a chief executive office, 11 U.S.C. § 1502(4), is located.)

As an example, if a United States debtor has property in Mexico, a United States trustee can commence a proceeding in Mexico to recover it (since Mexico has adopted the very same convention). The two courts – United States and Mexico – would then each be authorized to communicate with each other to make the process more efficient. Similarly, a Mexican *sindico* would then be able to commence a chapter 15 case in the United States if the debtor in his or her case had assets in the United States. The courts would still be able to communicate with one another.

---

5. *Provisions Which Affect All Cases*

Under new Section 103(k), some provisions of Chapter 15 affect all title 11 cases – that is, they apply in Chapter 7, 9, 11, 12 and 13 cases. They are:

- § 1505, which empowers the court to authorize a trustee or examiner under any other case to act in a foreign case in any manner permitted by foreign law;

- § 1513, which removes any and all disabilities of foreign creditors to appear in any pending case under title 11 to the extent that such disabilities are based upon their status as foreign creditors;

- § 1514, which applies to the claims of foreign creditors in domestic title 11 cases. Among other things, this provision requires notice to be given individually to creditors with foreign addresses if practical, and requires that notification of a domestic title 11 case contain certain notices regarding the time limits and the content of proofs of claim. Finally, the section requires additional time to file proofs of claim be given to creditors with foreign addresses, with such additional time being reasonable under the circumstances. 11 U.S.C. § 1514(d).

- § 1509, which applies even if a title 11 case is not pending, allows foreign representatives to commence Chapter 15 proceedings, and if they do, to then have the capacity to sue or be sued in any court in this country (including state courts). This includes a foreign representative's right, upon recognition, to apply to a non-bankruptcy court for such relief as is consistent with comity and cooperation.

Appendix: An Overview of Bankruptcy

Reprinted, with permission, from

Chapter 7
of
DAVID G. EPSTEIN,
BANKRUPTCY AND RELATED LAW IN A NUTSHELL
(7th ed. 2005)

The remainder of the nutshell will focus on bankruptcy. Initially, four basic differences between bankruptcy and state debtor-creditor law should be noted.

First, bankruptcy law is federal law.

Second, state law focuses on individual action by a particular creditor and puts a premium on prompt action by a creditor. The first creditor to attach the debtor's property, the first creditor to execute on the property, etc. is the one most likely to be paid. Bankruptcy, on the other hand, compels collective creditor collection action and emphasizes equality of treatment, rather than a race of diligence. While bankruptcy law does not require equal treatment for all creditors, all creditors within a single class are treated the same. After the commencement of a bankruptcy case, a creditor cannot improve its position vis-a-vis other creditors by seizing the assets of the debtor. Similarly, the debtor's ability to make preferential transfers to creditors before bankruptcy is considerably limited.

Third, the prospects for debtor relief are much greater in bankruptcy. For individual debtors, this bankruptcy relief may take the form of relief from further personal liability for debts because of a discharge. While no debtor is guaranteed a discharge, most individual debtors do receive a discharge. "One of the primary purposes of the bankruptcy act is to 'relieve the honest debtor from the weight of oppressive indebtedness and permit him to start afresh. . . .'" Local Loan Co. v. Hunt (1934). For business debtors, this bankruptcy relief may take the form of a restructuring of debts by reason of a confirmed Chapter 11 plan.

Fourth, the vocabulary of bankruptcy law is different from the vocabulary of state collection law. The Bankruptcy Code uses technical terms such as "automatic stay" and "impairment" that are not a part of state law. And, the Bankruptcy Code uses terms such as "debtor" and "redemption" that are a part of state law differently than state law. Accordingly, it is very important that you consistently and persistently check for the statutory definitions of terms used in the Bankruptcy Code.

A. BANKRUPTCY LAW

Article I of the Constitution empowers Congress to "establish uniform laws on the subject of Bankruptcies throughout the United States." For most of the 20th century, bankruptcy law was the Bankruptcy Act of 1898, commonly referred to as the "Bankruptcy Act." It was replaced in 1978 by a law commonly referred to as the "Bankruptcy Reform Act of 1978" or "Bankruptcy Code." The Bankruptcy Code has been regularly amended; the most comprehensive bankruptcy amendments were enacted in 1984.

This book will introduce you to bankruptcy one concept at a time: stays, then property of the estate, then exempt property, then . . . . That is the easiest way to gain an initial understanding of bankruptcy law. As one of the great bankruptcy teachers, Steve Riesenfeld, observed, "Bankruptcy law is a series of lumps. Do not make mashed potatoes out of it."

The book will also explore some of the connections or relationships of these various concepts. For example, a determination that a doctor's malpractice insurance is property of the estate when she files for bankruptcy can affect the application of the automatic stay to creditors' efforts to collect under that insurance. The various bankruptcy concepts are connected or related. To paraphrase the noted writer Erica Jong, the law of bankruptcy is a "zipless web."

Judge Grant expressed the same thought much more eloquently in In re Depew (1989): "The Bankruptcy Code is not a fragmented and disconnected collection of miscellaneous rules. It is a complex tapestry of ideas. The colors and patterns that are woven into its fabric combine to compliment and reinforce each other. In order to create a single unifying theme—the equitable treatment of creditors and financial relief for over-burdened debtors. In doing so, the tensions between these seemingly inconsistent objectives have been balanced and harmonized. Consequently, title 11's various provisions should not be viewed in isolation. Instead, the interpretation should reflect the interplay between all of its different parts, so that the Bankruptcy Code can operate as a coherent whole. The meaning given to any one portion must be consistent with the remaining provisions of the Bankruptcy Code."

The Bankruptcy Code divides the substantive law of bankruptcy into the following chapters:

Chapter 1, General Provisions, Definitions and Rules of Construction

Chapter 3, Case Administration

Chapter 5, Creditors, the Debtor, and the Estate

Chapter 7, Liquidation

Chapter 9, Adjustment of the Debts of a Municipality

Chapter 11, Reorganization

Chapter 12, Adjustment of the Debts of a Family Farmer With Regular Annual Income

Chapter 13, Adjustment of the Debts of an Individual With Regular Income

The provisions in Chapters 1, 3 and 5 apply in every bankruptcy case, unless otherwise specified. Accordingly, if you are working on a problem in a Chapter 11 case, it will be necessary to deal with the provisions of Chapters 1, 3, 5 and 11.

It is also necessary to deal with the Bankruptcy Rules. Pursuant to the authority of 28 USCA § 2075, the United States Supreme Court promulgated Bankruptcy Rules. These rules, not the Federal Rules of Civil Procedure, "govern procedure in United States Bankruptcy Courts," Rule 1001. The Bankruptcy Rules are divided into ten parts. Each part governs a different stage of the bankruptcy process. For example, Part 1 of the Rules, Rule 1002 through Rule 1019 deals with issues related to commencement of cases.

Bankruptcy law is also in large part state law. I am not here suggesting that there are state bankruptcy laws. Since Article I of the Constitution empowers Congress to enact uniform laws of bankruptcy and Congress has enacted such laws, principles of federal supremacy preclude state legislatures from enacting bankruptcy laws. Rather, bankruptcy law is in large part state law because courts applying the federal bankruptcy law look to state law to determine questions such as (1) what are the property rights of the debtor and (2) what are the claims of the creditors to that property. As the Supreme Court stated in Butner v. United States (1979):

Congress has generally left the determination of property rights in the assets of a bankrupt's estate to state law. Property interests are created and defined by state law. Unless some federal interest requires a different result, there is no reason why such interests should be analyzed differently simply because an interested party is involved in a bankruptcy proceeding.[15]

B. FORMS OF BANKRUPTCY RELIEF

There are two general forms of bankruptcy relief:

- liquidation; and
- rehabilitation or reorganization.

The Bankruptcy Code provides for these two forms of relief in five separate kinds of bankruptcy cases: (1) Chapter 7 cases, (2) Chapter 9 cases, (3) Chapter 11 cases, (4) Chapter 12 cases, and (5) Chapter 13 cases. This book does not deal with Chapters 9 and 12. Chapter 9 cases involve governmental entities as debtors, and it is infrequently used. Chapter 12 is limited to family farmer bankruptcy. This nutshell will deal with the three basic forms of bankruptcy relief: Chapter 7, Chapter 11 and Chapter 13.

---

[15] Increasingly, law professors and judges are questioning the extent to which judges should look to state law in applying provisions of the Bankruptcy Code. In law review articles, reported decisions and law school classrooms, questions are being asked about the relationship between bankruptcy law and state law, about the extent to which the Bankruptcy Code does and should change state law. For example, *D* enters into an employment contract with *C* Company that contains a covenant not to compete that completely complies with state law. Under state law, *D* cannot avoid her obligations under the covenant not to compete by breaching the contract; under state law, *C* Company can obtain injunctive relief to prevent *D* from competing. Should the result be different in bankruptcy? Should the Bankruptcy Code provisions on executory contracts and discharge and the bankruptcy policy of a fresh start enable *D* to avoid her obligations under the covenant not compete?

Chapter 7 is entitled "Liquidation." The title is descriptive. In a Chapter 7 case, the trustee collects the nonexempt property of the debtor, converts that property to cash, and distributes the cash to the creditors. The debtor gives up all of the nonexempt property she owns at the time of the filing of the bankruptcy petition in the hope of obtaining a discharge. A discharge releases the debtor from any further personal liability for her prebankruptcy debts.

Assume, for example, that *B* owes *C* $2,000. *B* files a Chapter 7 petition. *C* only receives $300 from the liquidation of *B*'s assets. If *B* receives a bankruptcy discharge, *C* will be precluded from pursuing *B* for the remaining $1,700.

As the preceding paragraph implies, every Chapter 7 case under the bankruptcy laws does not result in a discharge. Section 727(a) considered infra, lists a number of grounds for withholding a discharge. And, even if the debtor is able to obtain a discharge, she will not necessarily be freed from all creditors' claims. Section 523, considered infra, sets out exceptions to discharge.

The vast majority of bankruptcy cases are Chapter 7 cases. The term "bankruptcy" is often used to describe liquidation proceedings under the bankruptcy laws. References to "bankruptcy" in this nutshell should generally be regarded as references to liquidation cases.[16]

Chapters 11 and 13 generally deal with debtor rehabilitation or reorganization, not liquidation, of the debtor's assets. In a Chapter 11 or 13 case creditors usually look to future earnings of the debtor, not the property of the debtor at the time of the initiation of the bankruptcy proceeding, to satisfy their claims. The debtor retains its assets and makes payments to

---

[16]Older lawyers (like me) sometimes refer to Chapter 7 cases as "straight bankruptcy" cases and Chapters 11, 12 and 13 as "chapter proceedings."

creditors, usually from postpetition earnings, pursuant to a court approved plan.

Chapter 11, like Chapter 7, is available to all forms of debtors—individuals, partnerships and corporations. Chapter 13 can be used only by individuals with a "regular income" (as defined in section 101(27)) who have unsecured debts of less than $307,675 and secured debts of less than $922,975. These dollar amounts are adjusted periodically pursuant to section 104 to reflect changes in the Consumer Price Index.

C. BANKRUPTCY COURTS AND BANKRUPTCY JUDGES

1. *Under the Bankruptcy Act of 1898*

The Bankruptcy Act of 1898 provided for "bankruptcy referees." Originally, the judicial role of bankruptcy referees was relatively minor. The referee was primarily an administrator and supervisor of bankruptcy cases, not a judicial officer. Amendments to the Bankruptcy Act of 1898 made the bankruptcy referee more of a judicial officer. In 1973, the Bankruptcy Rules changed the title of the office from "bankruptcy referee" to "bankruptcy judge."

The 1898 Act used the term "courts of bankruptcy." A court of bankruptcy could be either the court of a federal district judge or the court of a bankruptcy judge. Any federal district court could be a "court of bankruptcy." Any judicial power conferred by the Bankruptcy Act of 1898 on the "court" could be exercised by either a federal district judge or a bankruptcy judge; any judicial power conferred by the Bankruptcy Act of 1898 on the "judge" could be exercised only by the federal district judge.

2. *Under the Present Law*

Congress deals with the bankruptcy court system separately from the substantive law of bankruptcy. The substantive law of bankruptcy is now in title 11 of the United States Code; the law relating to bankruptcy judges is in title 28.

Title 28 nowhere uses the term "bankruptcy referee." Section 152 of title 28 provides for "bankruptcy judges" to be appointed by the United States courts of appeals. Section 151 of title 28 states that these bankruptcy judges "shall constitute a unit of the district court to be known as the bankruptcy court." Under title 28, the bankruptcy court is not really a separate court; rather, it is a part of the district court.

Accordingly, the grant of jurisdiction over bankruptcy matters is to the district court, 28 USCA § 1334. The federal district judges then refer bankruptcy matters to the bankruptcy judges pursuant to 28 USCA § 157.

It is important to understand the differences between 28 USCA § 1334 and 28 USCA § 157. Section 1334 grants jurisdiction over bankruptcy cases and proceedings; all grants of jurisdiction are to the district court. Neither the phrase "bankruptcy court" nor the phrase "bankruptcy judge" appears in section 1334. Remember, however, that the bankruptcy judge is a unit of the district court under section 151. Thus, a grant of jurisdiction to the "district court" does not preclude the bankruptcy judge from playing a role in bankruptcy litigation.

Section 157 spells out the role that the bankruptcy judge is to play in bankruptcy litigation. Section 157 is entitled "Procedures" and deals with referral of matters from the "district court" to the bankruptcy judge. Section 157 is not a jurisdictional provision; it does not grant jurisdiction to the bankruptcy judges.

In summary, section 1334 speaks to what district courts can do and is jurisdictional. Section 157 deals with what the bankruptcy judges can do and is procedural.

The allocation of judicial power and responsibility over bankruptcy matters is one of the most controversial and complex areas of bankruptcy law and practice. I believe that you will find it easier to deal with the bankruptcy jurisdiction issues after you have gained a greater understanding of the substantive law of bankruptcy. Accordingly, bankruptcy jurisdiction issues will not be dealt with until later in this book.

D. Trustees

In every Chapter 7 case, every Chapter 12 case, every Chapter 13 case and some Chapter 11 cases,[17] there will be not only a bankruptcy judge but also a bankruptcy trustee. Generally, the bankruptcy trustee will be a private citizen, not an employee of the federal government.

A bankruptcy trustee is an active trustee. According to section 323 of the Bankruptcy Code, the bankruptcy trustee is "the representative of the estate." The filing of a bankruptcy petition is said to create an estate consisting generally of the property of the debtor as of the time of the bankruptcy filing. This estate is treated as a separate legal entity, distinct from the debtor. The bankruptcy trustee is the person who sues on behalf of or may be sued on behalf of the estate.

The powers and duties of a bankruptcy trustee vary from chapter to chapter. Recall that Chapter 7 bankruptcy is liquidation in nature. The duties of a bankruptcy trustee in a Chapter 7 case include:

---

[17]In Chapter 11, the bankruptcy court decides whether it is necessary to appoint a trustee, section 1104.

1. collecting the "property of the estate," i.e., debtor's property as of the time of the filing of the bankruptcy petition

2. challenging certain prebankruptcy and post-bankruptcy transfers of the property of the estate

3. selling the property of the estate

4. objecting to creditors' claims that are improper

5. in appropriate cases, objecting to the debtor's discharge, section 704.

Remember that there will be a bankruptcy trustee in every Chapter 7 case. And, in most Chapter 7 cases, most of the work is done by the Chapter 7 trustee.

There will also be a trustee in every Chapter 13 case, and in most Chapter 13 cases the trustee does most of the work. But, the person who works as a Chapter 13 trustee is different from the person who works as a Chapter 7 trustee, and the work that she does is different.

A Chapter 7 trustee is selected to serve as trustee in a particular Chapter 7 case. While a person often serves as trustee in more than one Chapter 7 case at a time, her work as a trustee is dependent on her being appointed or elected to serve as trustee in that case, sections 701 and 701. By contrast, one or more individuals is selected by the United States Trustee to serve as trustee for all of the Chapter 13 cases in his or her district—to be the "standing Chapter 13 trustee."

The duties of a Chapter 13 trustee also differ significantly from the duties of a Chapter 7 trustee. Section 1302 sets out the duties of a Chapter 13, and there seems to a considerable overlap between section

1302 and section 702 which sets out the duties of a Chapter 7 trustee.

The major differences between the work of a Chapter 13 trustee and the work of a Chapter 7 trustee mirror the major difference between Chapter 13 and Chapter 7: payments pursuant to a court approved plan as compared with payments pursuant to liquidation. Accordingly, a Chapter 13 trustee does not collect and liquidate the debtor's property. Instead, the Chapter 13 trustee reviews and, where appropriate, contests the debtor's plan of repayment, and, after court approval of the Chapter 13 plan of repayment, serves as disbursing agent for the payments to creditors under the plan.

While there is a bankruptcy trustee in every Chapter 7 case and every Chapter 13 case, there is rarely a bankruptcy trustee in a Chapter 11 case. In Chapter 11, a bankruptcy trustee will be appointed only if the bankruptcy judge decides, after notice and hearing, that there is "cause" or the "appointment is in the interest of creditors, any equity security holders, and other interests of the estate."

Remember also that Chapter 11, like Chapter 13, contemplates rehabilitation, not liquidation, and that Chapter 11, unlike Chapter 13, is available to corporations and partnerships as well as individuals. The typical Chapter 11 case involves a business that continues to operate after the bankruptcy petition is filed. If a bankruptcy trustee is named in such a case, he or she will take over the operation of the business. As noted above, generally there will not be a trustee in a Chapter 11 case. The debtor will usually remain in control of the business after the filing of a Chapter 11 petition; such a debtor is referred to as a "debtor in possession." Chapter XVII of this book will deal with Chapter 11 trustees and debtors in possession in more detail.

E. UNITED STATES TRUSTEES

There was no such thing as a United States trustee until the 1978 bankruptcy legislation. During the debate on bankruptcy legislation, considerable concern was expressed over the bankruptcy judges' involvement in the administration of bankruptcy cases. While both the House and the Senate seemed to agree that the bankruptcy judge should not perform administrative functions, there was disagreement over who should. The compromise was an experimental United States trustee program involving parts of 17 states and the District of Columbia. In 1986, Congress enacted amendments that made the United States trustee program virtually nationwide.

The United States trustee is a government official, appointed by the Attorney General. Essentially, the United States trustee performs appointing and other administrative tasks that the bankruptcy judge would otherwise have to perform.

To illustrate, the United States trustee, not the bankruptcy judge, selects and supervises the bankruptcy trustees. Although the United States trustee can act as trustee in a Chapter 7 case or a Chapter 13 case (but not a Chapter 11 case), he or she is not intended as a substitute for private bankruptcy trustees. The United States trustee is more of a substitute for the bankruptcy judge with respect to supervisory and administrative matters.

Index